The aim of the Oxford Classical Monographs series (which replaces the Oxford Classical and Philosophical Monographs) is to publish books based on the best theses on Greek and Latin literature, ancient history, and ancient philosophy examined by the Faculty Board of Literae Humaniores.

Pagan City
and Christian Capital

Rome in the Fourth Century

JOHN R. CURRAN

CLARENDON PRESS · OXFORD

*This book has been printed digitally and produced in a standard specification
in order to ensure its continuing availability*

OXFORD
UNIVERSITY PRESS

Great Clarendon Street, Oxford OX2 6DP

Oxford University Press is a department of the University of Oxford.
It furthers the University's objective of excellence in research, scholarship,
and education by publishing worldwide in

Oxford New York

Auckland Cape Town Dar es Salaam Hong Kong Karachi
Kuala Lumpur Madrid Melbourne Mexico City Nairobi
New Delhi Shanghai Taipei Toronto
With offices in
Argentina Austria Brazil Chile Czech Republic France Greece
Guatemala Hungary Italy Japan South Korea Poland Portugal
Singapore Switzerland Thailand Turkey Ukraine Vietnam

Oxford is a registered trade mark of Oxford University Press
in the UK and in certain other countries

Published in the United States
by Oxford University Press Inc., New York

ISBN 978-0-19-925420-0

Printed and bound by CPI Antony Rowe, Eastbourne

For M. T. D., my family
and my friends

Preface

Papers and books about Christianising the Roman Empire ought not to be encouraged . . . The concept is so big an aspect of Late Antiquity as to be all but beyond the control of the historian, and admits of so many layers of meaning and varieties of interpretation that it is in danger of becoming meaning*less*. If and when we have arrived at some understanding of the term, and of what factors may have led people to change to being Christians from having been something else, it is still hard to know what it would mean to any individual to shift religious allegiance in the generations after Constantine.[1]

Such well-judged circumspection has become more necessary than ever for students of late antiquity. The most innovative and important scholarship for a generation has recently subjected 'Christianity', 'paganism', 'religion', and 'conversion' to unprecedented historical scrutiny. Under rigorous examination, old certainties have subsided. The 'triumph of Christianity' has been unmasked as a deterministic model created by fifth-century churchmen; the vigour and complexity of ancient religious beliefs have been meticulously presented alongside the thoughts and activities of ancient people who called themselves Christian; and the 'desecularization' of ancient culture has been brilliantly charted, detailing how Christian ascetical thinking decamped from the wastes of the eastern Mediterranean to settle in the communities of early modern Europe.[2]

The spirit of this book is informed by these new perspectives and complexities of recent research, but its scope is more narrowly focused. The subject here is the nature of the change which shaped the topography and society of the city of Rome during the fourth century AD. My researches have been prompted and enlightened by three great scholars of the city. Charles Piétri's magisterial *Roma Christiana*,

[1] D. Hunt, 'Christianising the Roman Empire: The Evidence of the Code', in J. Harries and I. Wood (eds.), *The Theodosian Code* (London: Duckworth, 1993), 143–58. Here, 143.

[2] See P. Brown, *Authority and the Sacred: Aspects of the Christianisation of the Roman World* (Cambridge: Cambridge University Press, 1995); MacMullen, *Christianity and Paganism*; Markus, *End*.

published in 1976, remains the first point of reference for all aspects of the life of Christian Rome; Richard Krautheimer's many books and articles are an invaluable source for the architecture and landscape of the city; and Rodolfo Lanciani's admirably readable accounts of the rediscovery of ancient Rome are as learned as they are exciting. Where I have dissented from the opinions of these scholars, I have tried to do so with humility and respect.

At the time of writing a vast number of learned articles and monographs on aspects of the city of Rome are at the disposal of the student. The antiquities of the city are being catalogued and analysed to an unprecedented degree. But broad treatments of the fourth-century city of Rome which offer a synthetic account of politics, topography, and society are, however, virtually unknown. I have sought to meet the need for such a study by utilizing the expertise of a large number of scholars in diverse fields selecting what I believe to be some key themes in the history of the city at this time.

Like a number of others, I have sought to move away from seeing the history of the fourth century as a series of dramatic and significant conflicts between 'Christianity' and 'paganism' in various forms. Instead, I have chosen to concentrate on what I feel are hitherto neglected topographical and social themes in the history of the Roman community. What follows, then, is a substantial review of historical data, much of it long known, but some of it in my opinion frequently misunderstood.

In Part One, I examine the physical setting of the city of Rome as the necessary context within which to study the important social developments. The characterization of the third century as a period of chaos is challenged and with reference to Rome, some crucial political dynamics are established. These, it is argued, helped set the parameters which the Tetrarchs both reinforced and exceeded. This is the back-drop against which Maxentius is to be understood. It becomes possible to liberate him from his traditional historical backwater as an interlude in Constantine's rise to power and restore him to his position as an ambitious interpreter of *Romanitas* in the late empire. There follow implications for Constantine himself. In contrast to the pervasive orthodoxies of Constantine as a devoted but diffident Christian in Rome, an examination of his relationship with Maxentius' legacy permits a more complex but plausible analysis of his impact upon the city to be offered.

It is, I believe, unsatisfactory to consider the 'Christianization' of the topography solely or even chiefly through the study of the great imperial foundations. Students should not be left to think that no other building activity of significance took place and they have often been allowed to believe that the urban landscape of Rome was slowly and inexorably 'Christianized' at the expense of some monolithic 'pagan' topography. I have therefore provided a fuller picture by including for study the activities of the bishops of the city up until the later fourth century. These reveal that the extension of what we may call a 'sacred landscape' was anything but straightforward and by examining the topographical dimension to the growth of Roman Christianity we may come to appreciate the fragmented, violent, and destabilizingly territorial character of the Christian community. The little churches of Rome illustrate more clearly than the grand foundations of emperors the challenges which faced bishops of the city in the middle years of the century. In meeting these challenges, the scale and scope of episcopal ambitions for the Roman church began to burgeon, a development of lasting importance detectable first in the fourth century.

A thorough revision of our understanding of the transformations of fourth-century Roman topography prepares the way in Part Two for a new look at three crucial aspects of Roman society during the same period. First of all, in order to appreciate the social atmosphere within which change took place, I have considered it necessary to review the legal standing of the ancient *religio* of Rome. Though hardly complete, the retrievable archive of laws of the fourth century provides a coherent body of material which illuminates the attitudes of law-makers, the difficulties experienced in transforming these into law and the complexities of making law relevant to the ancient cults in a world where the Pontifex Maximus was Christian. What emerges, for almost the entire period under consideration, is a catalogue of compromise, inconsistency, and contradiction. The case-study of the entertainments at the Circus Maximus in Rome thus assumes considerable importance as an aspect of urban life which was both ancient and vigorously persistent under the Christian emperors. I argue below that the games of the Circus Maximus represent the clear obligations of the social élite to provide an important urban amenity but at the same time they traditionally offered an experience to racegoers that was intimately connected with Roman *religio*. The study undertaken here illustrates clearly the kind of techniques used by Christian emperors to exploit the ceremonial space and time of the Circus Maximus and its entertainments. Above all, by bringing into view the powerful integrative forces acting upon emperors, we can move decisively beyond seeing conflict as the model for interpreting fourth-century Roman society.

The alternative approach is nowhere of greater utility to the historian than in the case of Roman asceticism. Although extensively and continuously discussed in recent years, the study of Roman asceticism tends to be characterized by two perhaps understandable but unfortunate perspectives. First, many studies lift the ascetics from their social context and treat them as chapters in the history of western monasticism. Secondly, ascetics have too often been treated as a feature of the debate on the 'Christianization' of the Roman aristocracy, which has increasingly become a rather sterile prosopographical exercise aimed at assigning individuals to one camp or another. In my final chapter below, I restore these Christians to their urban world and by doing so it becomes possible to see where the real conflict of the fourth century is to be found: between Christians. It then becomes necessary to see many interested parties in the city drawing upon a common matrix of ideas and carrying these on into their own specific religious and social worlds.

This study thus invites the reader to view the familiar concepts of conflict, compromise, and continuity in rather unfamiliar contexts. If what emerges suggests confusion, contradiction, or even paradox then we may be a little closer to understanding the highly complex nature of the change which affected the physical and psychological world of Rome in the fourth century.

John Curran

Belfast
21 April 1999

Acknowledgements

This book began as a research project supervised by Professor Fergus Millar. Intuitively sensitive to the bewilderment of a Celt in Oxford, he has been generous over many years with advice and learning. Nicholas Purcell provided an introduction to the city of Rome and kindly took over the direction of the research for an exhilarating period. Most of the burden of overseeing this work, however, has fallen to Simon Price, under whose guidance I have been fortunate to enjoy the freedom to explore my own ideas and to learn from his acute thinking on religion. He has been unfailingly patient and sympathetic throughout the long months taken to complete this book.

Other friends in Oxford have helped to create the ideal environment for debate and research. Roger Batty, Danny Dawlish, Hugh Elton, Ruth Featherstone, David Jennings, Simon Loseby, Riccardo Rebonato, Rosamund Scott, and Lori-Ann Touchette have been stimulating and steadfast companions throughout. Julia and Sam Hamper have hosted innumerable trips to Oxford. John Matthews has kindly taken an interest in my work despite constantly being in demand himself. My original examiners, Bryan Ward-Perkins and Jill Harries, have helped save what follows from its grossest errors.

I am particularly indebted to the Provost and Fellows of Worcester College for welcoming me back in Michaelmas 1996 as a visiting scholar. Queen's University of Belfast granted the period of leave and also granted funding for fieldwork in Rome in 1997.

In Belfast, I have been doubly fortunate in having Brian Campbell as a colleague. Not only has he followed the progress of this work, reading the entire manuscript, but he has been for years a wise, urbane and most companionable friend. Professor Frederick Williams has proof-read the text with his customary care, good humour, and erudition. Gordon, Jill, and Emily Anthony have looked in sympathetically from the world of legal research and teaching. Art, Marie, Anna, Marie-Claire, and Oisín Hughes have exemplified the hospitality of the great city of Belfast over many evenings in the company of Mr Cohen. Martin McParland of Queen Street Studios, Belfast, has provided splendid drawings at short notice. Only Marie-Thérèse Davis knows what completing this book has really achieved, and cost. In dedicating it to her, to my parents William and Amy, and my brothers and sisters David, Ruth, Sarah, Rachael, Robert, and Julie, I would like to thank those closest to me in recent months for their love, without which nothing would have been possible.

Contents

List of Illustrations

(after p. 324)

List of Abbreviations

Barnes, *CE*	T. D. Barnes, *Constantine and Eusebius* (Cambridge, Mass.: Harvard University Press, 1981).
Barnes, *NE*	T. D. Barnes, *The New Empire of Diocletian and Constantine* (Cambridge, Mass.: Harvard University Press, 1982).
Bovini, *Edifici cristiani*	G. Bovini, *Edifici cristiani di culto d'età costantiniana a Roma* (Bologna: R. Pàtron, 1968).
Chastagnol, *Fastes*	A. Chastagnol, *Les Fastes de la Préfecture de Rome au bas-empire* (Paris: Nouvelles Éditions Latines, 1962).
Chastagnol, *La Préfecture*	A. Chastagnol, *La Préfecture urbaine à Rome sous le bas-empire* (Paris: Presses universitaires de France, 1960).
Coarelli, *Dintorni*	F. Coarelli, *Dintorni di Roma*, 2nd edn. (Rome: Laterza, 1993).
Coarelli, *Guida*	F. Coarelli, *Guida archeologica di Roma*, 3rd edn. (Rome: Laterza, 1993).
Cohen, *Description*	H. Cohen, *Description historique des monnaies frappées sous l'empire romain*, 2nd edn., 8 vols. (Paris: 1880–92).
Coleman-Norton	P. R. Coleman-Norton, *Roman State and Christian Church*, 3 vols. (London: SPCK, 1966).
Corcoran, *Empire*	S. Corcoran, *The Empire of the Tetrarchs* (Oxford: Clarendon Press, 1996).
Croke and Harries, *Conflict*	B. Croke and J. Harries (eds.), *Religious Conflict in Fourth-Century Rome* (Sydney: University of Sydney Press, 1982).
Ferrua, *Epigrammata*	A. Ferrua, *Epigrammata Damasiana*, Sussidi allo studio delle antichità cristiane, 2 (Vatican City: Pontificio Istituto di archeologia cristiana, 1942).

Frend, *Martyrdom*

Humphrey, *Roman Circuses*

Jones, *LRE*

Krautheimer, *Corpus*

Krautheimer, *Rome*

Lane Fox,
   Pagans and Christians
Lexicon

LP

MacMullen,
   Christianity and Paganism

Markus, *End*

Matthews, *Ammianus*

Matthews, *WA*

Millar, *ERW*

Momigliano, *Conflict*

W. H. C. Frend, *Martyrdom and Persecution in the Early Church* (Oxford: Blackwell, 1965).
J. Humphrey, *Roman Circuses: Arenas for Chariot Racing* (London: Batsford, 1986).
A. H. M. Jones, *The Later Roman Empire, 284–602*, 3 vols. (Oxford: Blackwell, 1964).
R. Krautheimer, *Corpus Basilicarum Christianarum Romanorum*, 5 vols. (Vatican City/New York: Pontificio Istituto di archeologia cristiana/Institute of Fine Arts, 1937–77).
R. Krautheimer, *Rome: Profile of a City, 312–1308* (Princeton: Princeton University Press, 1980).
R. Lane Fox, *Pagans and Christians* (Harmondsworth: Viking, 1986).
M. Steinby (ed.), *Lexicon Topographicum Urbis Romae*, 5 vols. (Rome: Quasar, 1993–).
L. Duchesne (vols 1 and 2) and C. Vogel (vol. 3) (eds.), *Le Liber Pontificalis, texte, introduction et commentaire*, 2nd edn. (Paris: de Boccard, 1955–7).
R. MacMullen, *Christianity and Paganism in the Fourth to Eighth Centuries* (New Haven: Yale University Press, 1997).
R. Markus, *The End of Ancient Christianity* (Cambridge: Cambridge University Press, 1990).
J. F. Matthews, *The Roman Empire of Ammianus* (London: Duckworth, 1989).
J. F. Matthews, *Western Aristocracies and Imperial Court, A.D. 364–425* (Oxford: Clarendon Press, 1975).
F. G. B. Millar, *The Emperor in the Roman World* (London: Duckworth, 1977).
A. Momigliano (ed.), *The Conflict between Paganism and Christianity in*

la *Rome chrétienne*, 2nd edn. (Rome: Storia e letteratura, 1959).

Whittaker, *Herodian*   C. R. Whittaker, *Herodian*, 2 vols. (Cambridge, Mass.: Heinemann, 1969).

Wissowa, *RK*   G. Wissowa, *Religion und Kultus der Römer*, 2nd edn. (Munich: Beck, 1912).

PART ONE

Topography

Emperors, Gods, and Violence in Third-Century Rome

INTRODUCTION

The third century is not a popular period of study for historians of the city of Rome. A host of problems with the available evidence make the reconstruction of a comprehensive history impossible. In the early years of the century, for example, the familiar and generally trustworthy guide Cassius Dio falters and then fades, leaving us less confidently in the company of Herodian, Aurelius Victor and, sometimes perilously, the *Historia Augusta* and Zosimus. Appeals to Christian authors lead into a frequently fragmentary collection of sectarian polemic, dense theological exegesis, and martyrological romances.

The archaeology of the city, rarely a satisfactory supplement to the written record, is particularly elusive. The regular rhythm of succeeding emperors and public building was clearly interrupted by circumstances which left the former unwilling or unable to express themselves through the kind of public architecture which is so important for understanding the early empire. The traditional structure and organization of public work, so obvious in the reliable series of *bolli* or brickstamps from the earlier period, seem to decline, leaving the historian to puzzle sometimes over crude, modest constructions of unknown builders. Even the catacombs, for all their size, remain astonishingly uncommunicative about the most fundamental details of the outside political world, or even the overwhelmingly anonymous multitude interred within them.

When the evidence permits a glimpse of affairs, it is often only to suggest that a fundamental shift of focus away from the city of Rome was taking place in the third century. Invasions and sustained foreign wars were drawing emperors to the geographical periphery of the empire. Usurpations were casting up individuals of markedly different ethnicity and psychology compared to the old families of the capital. And the collapse of the value of the old Roman coinage heralded a massive symbolic as well as an economic loss of credibility on the part of specifically Roman culture.

And yet, the emperors of Rome continued to have a relationship with the city, whether they resided in it or not. The most fundamental elements of Roman culture: *religio*, recreation, and technological skill continued to be deployed, however fitfully, in expressing that relationship. No study of the landscape of the Constantinian city can therefore afford to neglect the third century as the necessary background against which many of the most important features of the later period must be viewed. Only by considering the location and the medium of imperial self-presentation in the third century can we contextualize the aspirations and expectations of the emperors of Constantine's own time.

Within the general theme of the topographical development of the city, moreover, there is an important third-century confluence of religious innovation and experimentation. This, again, is the historical background to the religious choices of Diocletian and the Tetrarchs, Maxentius, and Constantine. As we shall see, even the fragmentary historical record of the third century reveals the striking self-confidence of some of Constantine's most prominent predecessors in making contact with new gods or deepening their relationships with the traditional deities of the state.

The relationship between emperors and *populus* on the other hand found expression above all in the former's patronage of mass popular recreation in the capital. The entertainments of Rome were a vital channel of communication between the ruling family and the citizens of the city. Prudent imperial sponsorship of the events and facilities was an obligation which permitted emperors sometimes to gauge the temper of citizens and instilled in citizens themselves a peculiarly Roman self-confidence. This complex interdependence of emperor and citizens was a marked feature of social relations in third-century Rome as it was to be for later emperors, and the chapter which follows traces the fundamental elements.

Particularly prominent in third-century society is the uneasy coexistence of civilian and soldier. A survey of the conflicts through the period reveals starkly the nature and extent of a problem which was to perplex the Tetrarchs, prompt the appearance of Maxentius, and attract a lasting and drastic solution from Constantine.

It is, finally, in his adoption of Christianity and the close sponsorship of the Roman Christians that Constantine has claimed a place in history. But the fourth-century historiographical record was of course decisively shaped by Constantine himself. It is a legitimate historical aim, therefore, to outline as far as possible, the condition and experience of the Christian community of Rome in the years before Constantine's appearance. By doing so, it becomes possible to lift the

Christian community out of the Constantinian historiographical tradition, and subject it more closely to examination on its own terms.

I. PUBLIC BUILDING AND THE TOPOGRAPHY OF ROME IN THE THIRD CENTURY

Tetrarchic, Maxentian, and Constantinian power manifested itself in the provision of monuments in the city centre. But the public space into which these symbols were inserted had been decisively shaped by Septimius Severus, himself a worthy model for later emperors, at the very beginning of the third century.

The Forum of Severus (fig. 1)

Severus' labours were designed to emphasize the legitimate culmination of an imperial career that had begun as usurpation.[1] The Forum area had been ravaged by fire near the end of Commodus' reign, perhaps in 191.[2] Severus, associating with himself other members of the imperial family, undertook the restoration of some of the most prominent sacred sites in the city centre.[3] Among Severus' new structures, the most significant was his arch.[4] Erected in 203 and standing at the edge of the ancient *Comitium*, the monument dominated the space between the Capitol and the central Forum. At 20.88 m high, 23.27 m wide, and 11.20 m deep, the brick and travertine arch was to be the most imposing imperial commission in this zone of the city for some eighty years.[5]

A group of figures stood on top of the structure: Severus was depicted in a six-horse chariot and his sons occupied lateral positions

[1] See J.-L. Desnier, '*Omnia et realia*: Naissance de *l'urbs sacra* sévérienne (193–204 ap. J.-C.)', *MEFRA*, 105 (1993), 547–620. Still important is H. W. Benario, 'Rome of the Severi', *Latomus*, 17 (1958), 712–22.

[2] Dio 73, 24; Herod. 1, 14, 4.

[3] With Julia Domna he repaired the *Atrium Vestae* which had its courtyard lengthened. The *Aedes Vestae* was also restored: *Lexicon*, i. 138–42, 'Atrium Vestae' (R. T. Scott); Coarelli, *Guida*, 100. Coin evidence: Cohen, *Description*, iv. 124, no. 232 ff. With Antoninus/Caracalla Severus repaired the Temple of Vespasian: *CIL* 6, 938 (preserved in the Einsiedeln Itinerary); Coarelli, *Guida*, 77. North-east of the Forum, Vespasian's Temple of Peace was restored and on the exterior north-eastern wall of the *Bibliotheca Pacis* Severus attached his new edition of the *Forma Urbis*: Coarelli, *Guida*, 143–5; Nash, *Pictorial*, i, 439. South-east of the Forum, restoration work was carried out on the *Porticus Margaritaria et Piperitaria*: Lugli, *MA*, suppl. I, 80.

[4] R. Brilliant, *The Arch of Septimius Severus in the Roman Forum*, MAAR, 29 (1967); *Lexicon*, i. 103–4 (Brilliant); Nash, *Pictorial*, i. 126–30; Coarelli, *Guida*, 71–3.

[5] *Lexicon*, i. 104 (Brilliant).

on individual mounts.[6] A grand inscription dominated both sides of the attic. As originally conceived, the text attributed to Severus and his two sons the restitution of the *Res Publica* and the extension of the *imperium* of the Roman People:

Imp. Caes. Lucio Septimio M. fil. Severo Pio Pertinaci Aug. Patri Patriae, Parthico Arabico et | Parthico Adiabenico, Pontific. Maximo, Tribunic. Potest. XI, Imp. XI, Cos. III, Procos., et | Imp. Caes. M. Aurelio L. fil. Antonino Aug. Pio Felici Tribunic. Potest. VI, Cos. Procos., ⟨P. P., | Optimis Fortissimisque Principibus⟩, | ob Rem Publicam restitutam imperiumque populi Romani propagatum | insignibus virtutibus eorum domi forisque, S. P. Q. R.[7]

The artistic programme enlarged upon the theme, combining scenes of military victory over Arabs and Parthians with references to appropriate deities. The keystones on either side of the main arch, for example, depicted Mars. In the spandrels over both sides of the main arch winged Victories holding trophies were represented, and at their feet *genii* of the four seasons. On the keystones of the flanking arches, four deities had been sculpted, two male and two female, although of the four, only Hercules is now identifiable. Fluvial gods adorned the flanking spandrels, among them personifications of Tigris and Euphrates. On the three visible sides of each of the column bases for the four columns on either side of the arch Roman soldiers were shown with Parthian prisoners.

Four large panels, two on either side of the arch, depicted scenes from Severus' two Parthian wars. Starting with the left-hand panel on the side facing the Forum, a number of episodes were juxtaposed in a single panel: the Roman army departing from its camp (at Carrhae or Zeugma); military engagement; a scene of *adlocutio* and the liberation of Nisibis, besieged by Parthians. The left-hand panel represented the Roman army attacking Edessa with siege engines and bringing about its surrender; the Osroenians and King Abgar submitting to Severus and the emperor discoursing with his men; Severus presiding over a council of war in a fortified encampment, and finally conducting the actual fighting.

The panels selected for the Capitol-facing side of the arch were less complex. One showed the attack on Seleucia on the Tigris, the flight of Parthians, the subsequent surrender of Seleucia and the submission of the Parthians to the emperor. The other portrayed an attack on

---

[6] See *BMC*, 5, 216, no. 320 = Nash, *Pictorial*, i. 127, fig. 134. Also Cohen, *Description*, iv. 'Severus', nos. 53, 104; 'Carac.', 14, 15.

[7] *CIL* 6, 1033, cf. 31230; *ILS* 425. The fourth line has been reworked, losing the phrase: 'P. Septimio L. fil. Getae nobilissimo Caesari'.

Ctesiphon using a siege engine and the subsequent fall of the city, then an *adlocutio* of the emperor in front of the same city.

Exactly how these images were selected and composed is unknown, but Severus certainly took pains to communicate depictions of his campaigns to the senate in Rome. There can be little doubt, however, about the impact of this impressive monument: its striking inscription and sculptural programme celebrated and commemorated the accession of Severus and his subsequent defeat of Julianus, Niger, and Albinus, and at the same time the Parthian victories of Severus, won only months prior to the dedication. It was a testament to the resounding military qualities of the emperor. As such, it echoed and complemented the arch of the most legitimate of emperors located in the same area: Augustus' own three-bayed monument to his Parthian successes, clearly in view diagonally across the Forum, between the temples of Castor and Pollux and Divus Julius.[8] But if Severus' arch evoked the triumphs of his illustrious predecessor, it also self-consciously pointed forward to the continuity of the dynasty by associating the emperor's sons in the achievements and strongly suggesting the eventual succession of Antoninus and Geta.

The construction of the arch required the substantial remodelling of the imperial Rostra. Squeezed in between it and the southern side of the great arch Severus located a distinctive new circular monument, 4.45 m in diameter. The *Umbilicus Urbis Romae* marked the conceptual centre of the Roman world, now radiating out from the foot of the most potent symbol of Severus' power.[9] The *Umbilicus* also complemented the *Milliarium Aureum* standing at the other end of the imperial Rostra, the milestone set up by Augustus in 20 BC to mark the precise point from which all distances from Rome should be measured.[10]

The new structures attracted a swarm of smaller monuments honouring the Severan dynasty directly: at the foot of the northern end of the Arch of Severus a mounted statue of the emperor was erected.[11] Between the Temple of Faustina and Antoninus and the 'Temple of Romulus' stood a statue of Julia Domna.[12] Fragments of marble tablets of varying sizes have been recovered from the central Forum area and Via Sacra recording dedications and honours offered

---

[8] See esp. Desnier, art. cit. (n. 1), 575, fig. 6.

[9] Coarelli, *Guida*, 73–4 with discussion of relationship to *mundus*.

[10] See *Lexicon*, iii. 250–1, s.v. 'Miliarium Aureum' (Z. Mari).

[11] See now *Lexicon*, ii. 231–2, 'Equus: Septimius Severus' (F. Coarelli). Herod. 2, 9, 6 reports that it occupied the spot where Severus in a pre-accession dream saw Pertinax being unseated by a great horse which then allowed him to mount. Cf. Dio (Xiph.) 75, 3, 3. The position was later occupied by the *Equus Constantini/Constantii: Lexicon*, ii. 226–7, s.v. 'Equus: Constantinus' (P. Verduchi); Platner and Ashby, 202.

[12] *CIL* 6, 36934.

on behalf of various groups, from the *kalatores* of the *pontifices* and *augures*, to the urban cohorts and *vigiles*.[13] Severus' efforts determined the layout of the Forum Romanum until almost the end of the third century. The emperor founded his legitimacy upon a sustained appeal to military success, the expression of dynastic ambitions and the self-conscious occupation of the central space of the Forum Romanum.[14]

New temples, gods, and emperors in the third century

Until the reign of Maxentius, most of the new temples built by emperors in the city of Rome during the third century were constructed in honour of deities originally worshipped in the eastern Mediterranean.[15] These buildings embodied the religious choices of emperors but it is important to emphasize that they were only the most conspicuous manifestation of the very public phenomenon of imperial tastes in *res sacra*.

Several of Severus' journeys are reported to have been the occasion of serious imperial enquiry into religious and astrological lore. The emperor's preferences were widely publicized at Rome by Dio whose relationship with the regime was close. When Severus visited the east in 199:

He enquired into everything, including things that were carefully hidden; for he was the kind of person to leave nothing, either human or divine, uninvestigated. Accordingly, he took away from practically all the sanctuaries all the books that he could find containing any secret lore, and he locked up the tomb of Alexander; this was in order that no one in future should either view Alexander's body or read what was written in the above-mentioned books.[16]

---

[13] *CIL* 6, 36932 (from area of Sant' Adriano, from the *kalatores* of the *pontifices* and *augures*, to Severus and Julia Domna); 36898 (from the Atrium Vestae, to Severus and Antoninus, set up by tribune of urban cohort?/vigiles?); 36929 (from Basilica Aemilia, to Severus and Antoninus, Roman tribes mentioned); 36933 (from Sacra Via in vicinity of 'Temple of Romulus', to Severus); 36931 (to Severus and Antoninus); 36930 (from Basilica Aemilia?, to Severus and Antoninus).

[14] Later third-century works in central Forum: minor improvements made under Severus Alexander to several 'Edicole compitali' and the augmentation of the 'umbilicus urbis': *CIL* 6, 30960–1; equestrian statues mentioned in the *Historia Augusta* in connection with the emperors Maximus and Balbinus; a golden statue depicting the 'genius populi Romani' set up by Aurelian on the Rostra: *Chron. 354* (*MGH* 1, 148).

[15] For a discussion of the problematic phrase 'oriental cults', see Turcan, *Cults*, 3–7.

[16] Dio (Xiph.) 76, 13, 2: καὶ ἐπολυπραγμόνησε πάντα καὶ τὰ πάνυ κεκρυμμένα. ἦν γὰρ οἷος μηδὲν μήτε ἀνθρώπινον μήτε θεῖον ἀδιερεύνητον καταλιπεῖν. κἀκ τούτου τά τε βιβλία πάντα τὰ ἀπόρρητόν τι ἔχοντα, ὅσα γε καὶ εὑρεῖν ἠδυνήθη, ἐκ πάντων ὡς εἰπεῖν τῶν ἀδύτων ἀνεῖλε καὶ τὸ τοῦ Ἀλεξάνδρου μνημεῖον συνέκλεισεν, ἵνα μηδεὶς ἔτι μήτε τὸ τούτου σῶμα ἴδῃ μήτε τὰ ἐν ἐκείνοις γεγραμμένα ἀναλέξηται. Cf. Dio 77, 13, 3 (Severus noting the variation in length of days in Scotland). Also *SHA, Sev.* 17, 4.

After a short visit to Africa at the end of 203, Severus became, for the first time in his reign, an emperor living in Rome. The cultural life of his resident court was marked by a pronounced interest in religious matters. The empress Julia Domna, chosen as wife by Severus because of her astrological profile, became the most powerful of Philostratus' patrons.[17] She was famous for her interest in philosophical and religious affairs.[18] She encouraged him to compose an influential biography of the great Apollonius of Tyana, perhaps supplying some of the source materials herself.[19] Severus himself received from Cassius Dio a work on dreams and omens which had foretold his ascent to the throne. The latter, encouraged by a favourable response from the emperor, composed a full history of the wars following the death of Commodus until the end of Severus' Parthian war. This work in turn was subsumed into the much larger project which survives in part today. Dio's writing about Severus both fostered and reflected the emperor's sense of destiny, a sense reflected time and again in Severus' own outlook.[20] It was common knowledge for example that the ceiling of the reception room of his Palatine residence had been painted with the constellations and his private apartment in the palace had a precise depiction of the alignment of the heavenly bodies at the moment of his own birth.[21] His intimate knowledge of his own horoscope convinced him in 208 as he set out for Britain that he would not return alive from the expedition. Thus when the *augures* noted that a statue of the emperor standing near one of the gates of Rome had been struck by lightning and the first three letters of his name destroyed, Severus was unsurprised to learn that the incident foretold his own death three years into the British campaign.[22]

Like his father, Caracalla had an appetite for divination and astrology.[23] The interest and indeed control of divination in others

---

[17] For her marriage to Severus: G. H. Halsberghe, 'Le culte de Dea Caelestis', *ANRW*, 2,17,4 (1984), 2203–23, at 2210. Patronage of Philostratus: G. Anderson, *Sage, Saint and Sophist: Holy Men and Their Associates in the Early Roman Empire* (London: Routledge, 1994), 36, 119. The Porta degli Argentari shows her sacrificing, an unusual depiction for an *augusta*: R. Lizzi and F. E. Consolino, 'Le religioni nell'impero tardoantico: persistenze e mutamenti', in A. Schiavone (ed.), *Storia di Roma 3*: L'Età tardoantica 1: Crisi e trasformazione* (Turin: Einaudi, 1993), 895–974, at 897.

[18] Philostratus, *Life of Apollonius* 1, 3. Cf. *SHA, Alex.*, 14, 7 where her niece is called 'mulier sancta'. For her contact with Origen, see below, 37.

[19] For her relationship with Philostratus, see G. Anderson, op. cit. (n. 17).

[20] See the honour paid to Hannibal's tomb: Dio 19, 65, 5 (Tzetzes *Chil.* 1, 798 ff.; Zonaras 9, 21). Cf. Dio 76, 13, 2.

[21] Dio 77, 11, 1.   [22] Ibid. 77, 11, 2.

[23] Dio 78 (79), 2 and 78 (79), 4, 5 (the prophecy of the Egyptian Serapio); Herod. 4, 12, 3 ff.. Cf. Dio 77 (78), 20, 4 for the death of Caecilius Aemilianus, governor of Baetica, allegedly for consulting an oracle of Hercules.

was a natural corollary. An African soothsayer who had foretold the succession of Caracalla's Praetorian Prefect Macrinus was dispatched by the governor to Rome where Flavius Maternianus, acting commander of troops in Rome in the emperor's absence, enquired into the case.[24] Another unknown seer was interrogated in Rome and prepared for dispatch to the emperor himself.[25]

When Caracalla showed his favour towards particular gods, his actions were communicated to the Roman populace or particular elements within the community. The dramatic execution of four *vestales*, probably in 214, coincided with an issue of coins with types depicting Caracalla sacrificing at the temple of Vesta.[26] And his preservation, apparently as a result of Aesculapius' intervention, prompted the appearance of coins in honour of that deity from Roman mints.[27]

But it seems that the cults of Egypt had the strongest attraction for the son of Severus. *Circa* AD 215, Caracalla constructed a new temple in honour of Isis and Serapis on the southern arm of the Quirinal in the Sixth Region of the city.[28] The remains of the structure were sketched in the Renaissance by several competent draughtsmen, including Giuliano da Sangallo and Andrea Palladio, and their drawings show a distinctive tripartite structure. A vast monumental stairway located on the western side of a walled temple precinct enclosed the actual temple building.[29] The grandiose layout of the complex may have deliberately recalled the Serapeum of Alexandria, which Caracalla had made his base during his visit to Egypt in the summer of 215.[30] Aurelius Victor

---

[24] Herod. 4, 12, 4 ff. See C. R. Whittaker, *Herodian* (Cambridge, Mass.: Loeb, 1969), i. 443 n. 3.

[25] Dio 78 (79), 7, 4–5.

[26] Dio 77 (78), 16, 2 (2); Herod. 4, 6, 4. Coins: *BMC*, 5, 450, no. 101; 458, no. 148; *RIC* 4. 1, 247, nos. 249–50; 251, nos. 271–2.

[27] Dio (Exc. Val.) 77 (78), 16, 7; Herod. 4, 8, 3; *SHA, Car.* 5, 8. Coins: *RIC* 4.1, 246, no. 238 (AD 214); 248, no. 251–3.

[28] *CIL* 6, 570 = *ILS* 4387 (from S. Silvestro al Quirinale); the so-called 'regionary catalogues' refer to a building called the 'Serapeum'. Cf. *SHA, Car.* 9, 10 noting the emperor's attachment to the cult but wrongly suggesting that he 'introduced' it to Rome.

[29] See R. Santangeli Valenziani, 'ΝΕΩΣ ΥΠΕΡΜΕΓΕΘΗΣ: Osservazioni sul tempio di piazza del Quirinale', *BC*, 94 (1991–2), 7–16 and Nash, *Pictorial*, s.v. 'Serapidis, templum' for useful reproductions of the drawings. Santangeli Valenziani's thesis that the temple was in fact Severus' in honour of Hercules and Dionysus cannot, to my mind, overcome Dio's failure (76 (77), 16, 3) to locate the latter at Rome. See Santangeli Valenziani, art. cit., 14, n. 42.

[30] Visit commemorated by coins: *RIC* 4.1, 249, no. 257; 303, no. 544. Cf. *NC* (6) 8 (1948), 33. For Serapeum as HQ: Dio (Xiph.) 77, 23, 2. For its evocation in Rome, see M. LeGlay, 'Sur l'implantation des sanctuaires orientaux à Rome', in *L'Urbs: Espace urbain et histoire: Ier siècle a. J.-C.–IIIᵉ siècle ap. J.-C.*, Collection de l'École française

reports that *Aegypti sacra* were removed from Egypt to Rome and many of these objects probably adorned the emperor's Roman temple.[31] Elagabalus' religious activities were memorably summarized by Dio:

he drifted into all the most shameful, lawless, and cruel practices, with the result that some of them, never before known in Rome, came to have the authority of tradition, while others that had been attempted by various men at different times, flourished merely for the 3 years 9 months and 4 days during which he ruled.[32]

Despite his co-option as a member of the college of Antoniniani and as 'sacerdos in aede Iovis Propugnatoris', even before he had entered the city after travelling from Antioch, Elagabalus had dispatched to Rome a portrait of himself dressed in priestly robes sacrificing to his god. The picture was to be placed in the senate house above the statue of Victory there.[33] The emperor had no problem in principle introducing his god to Rome. His mistake was to displace Roman Juppiter so insensitively. The decision was signalled by the early insistence upon inserting Elagabalus' name first in the prayers accompanying public sacrifices and supplementing his own title *pontifex maximus* with others showing his devotion to Elagabalus the god.[34]

The topographical impact of Elagabalus on Rome was determined by his service to the god whom he installed in the city (fig. 2). Herodian reports that a grand new temple with many altars was constructed.[35]

de Rome, 98 (Rome: École française de Rome, 1987), 551–2. For the mutual appreciation of Caracalla and Serapis, see *IGRR* 1, 1063 (Caracalla 'philoserapis') and A. Bernand, *Les Portes du désert* (Paris: Éditions du Centre national de la recherche scientifique, 1984), 245, no. 88 (Serapis 'philokaisar').

[31] Vict. *De Caes.* 21, 4.

[32] Dio 79 (80), 3, 3–4: ἐς δὲ δὴ τἆλλα πάντα καὶ αἰσχρουργότατα καὶ παρανομώτατα καὶ μιαιφονώτατα ἐξώκειλας, ὥστε τὰ μέν τινα αὐτῶν μηδ᾽ ἀρχὴν πώποτ᾽ ἐν τῇ Ῥώμῃ γενόμενα ὡς καὶ πάτρια ἀκμάσαι, τὰ δὲ καὶ τολμηθέντα ἄλλοτε ἄλλοις ὡς ἑκάστοις, ἔτεσι τρισὶ καὶ μησὶν ἐννέα ἡμέραις τε τέτταρσιν . . . See also Jer. *Chron.* a. 219 (Helm, 214): 'adeo impudice in imperio suo vixit, ut nullum genus obscentitatis omiserit.'

[33] Co-options: *CIL* 6, 2001; 2009. Picture: Herod. 5, 5, 6–7. For the cult generally, see F. G. B. Millar, *The Roman Near East* (Cambridge, Mass.: Harvard University Press, 1993), 306–8; R. Turcan, *Héliogabale et le sacre du Soleil* (Paris: Michel, 1985); id., *Cults*, 176 ff.

[34] Sacrifices: Herod. 5, 5, 7. Titles (including *sacerdos dei solis Elagabali, summus sacerdos Augustus* and *sacerdos amplissimus dei invicti solis Elagabali*): *BMC*, 5, 564–5, 569, no. 256; 571, no. 268; *ILS* 473, 475; *AE* (1908), 202; G. H. Halsberghe, 'Le culte de Deus Sol Invictus à Rome au III siècle après J. C.', *ANRW*, 2, 17, 4 (1984), 2186 n. 14.

[35] Herod. 5, 5, 8. Cf. *SHA Elag.* 1, 6: 'on the site of an earlier shrine to Orcus'; 3, 4: 'As soon as he entered the city . . . he established Elagabalus as a god on the Palatine hill close to the imperial palace and he built him a temple . . .'. Seemingly construction started in summer AD 219.

Recent excavations at the so-called 'vigna Barberini' have shed further
light on the huge temple podium first examined extensively in the
1930s.[36] The history and topographical development of this zone of the
Palatine have been variously interpreted.[37] But the dating of extensive
remodelling of the artificial platform to late second/early third century
combined with the literary evidence makes Elagabalus' *Heliogabalium*
the only convincing identification.[38] It was a highly unusual building,
seemingly modelled on the temple of the god at Emesa.[39] Standing on
the Palatine it was conveniently placed for the emperor's daily service
at the temple.[40]

A second temple was established in the suburbs of the city and was
the location of a festival held at the height of the summer. Nothing is
known of the form of the shrine but it would perhaps be surprising if it
was more traditional in design than that in the centre of Rome. Of its
location only a little more may be said. As the festivities included
spectacles and horse races, it is possible that the precise situation of the
temple was on the imperial estate 'ad spem veterem' in the south-east
suburbs of the city, a site which incorporated the only suitable venue
for horse racing in the so-called 'Varian Circus', named probably after
Elagabalus' family.[41]

Pursuing the cult of Elagabalus, the emperor's religious activities
were controversially public. He was known to have had himself
circumcised and he abstained from pork.[42] With his mother and
grandmother he presided over the ritual at Elagabalus' temple,
ceremonies which included dancing and, according to Dio, child

---

[36] See F. Chausson, '*Vel Iovi vel Soli*: Quatre études autour de la Vigna Barberini
(191–354)', *MEFRA*, 107 (1995), 661–795; M. Royo, 'Topographie ancienne et
fouilles sur la Vigna Barberini (XIXe siècle–début XXe siècle)', *MEFRA*, 98
(1986), 707–66.

[37] See *Lexicon*, iii. 10–11, s.v. 'Heliogabalus, Templum: Heliogabalium' (F. Coarelli);
i. 14–16, s.v. 'Adonaea' (M. Royo). For the suburban temple, see *Lexicon*, iii. 10, s.v.
'Heliogabalus, neos' (F. Coarelli).

[38] M. Royo, art. cit. (n. 37), 16 notes that the only datable brickstamps belong to
Faustina Iunior but concedes the possibility that the bricks were reused by a later
emperor. Perhaps more striking is the correlation between traces of the original flooring
and *SHA*, *Helio*. 24, 6 referring to 'plateas in Palatio'.

[39] *BMC*, 5, 615. See Turcan, *Cults*, 184, pl. 23; id., *Héliogabale*, fig. 21; *Annuaire de
Numismatique*, 14 (1890), 469–70.

[40] Halsberghe, art. cit. (n. 34), 2187.

[41] Site of temple: Herod. 5, 6, 6. For discussion of site: *Lexicon*, iii. 85, s.v. 'Horti
spei veteris' (F. Coarelli); C. Paterna, 'Il circo Variano a Roma', *MEFRA*, 108 (1996),
817–53. For a useful discussion of chronology and relevant coinage: H. R. Baldus, 'Zur
Aufnahme des Sol Elagabalus-Kultes in Rom, 219 n. Chr.', *Chiron*, 21 (1991), 175–8.
Also Harlsberge, art. cit. (n. 34), 2187. Circus: Coarelli, *Guida*, 239–40.

[42] Herod. 5, 6, 9 with Whittaker, *Herodian*, ii. 56 n. 1. See Halsberghe, art. cit. (n. 34),
2188 for what the worship of Elagabalus may have involved.

sacrifice.[43] He cut a bizarre figure in public, his dress and cosmetics earning him the nickname 'the Assyrian'.[44]

A series of highly irregular marriages involving both emperor and god further revealed the extraordinary character of the regime. The emperor's nuptials with the *vestalis* Julia Aquila Severa seem to show the coalescing of his own personality with that of Elagabalus the god, an impression strengthened by Elagabalus' explanation of the shocking union:[45] 'I did it in order that godlike children might spring from me, the high priest, and from her, the high priestess.'[46]

At the same time the god, too, sought a mate. The statue of Pallas was transferred to his temple as an indication that his favour had fallen upon her. But her martial associations are said to have upset the god, who summoned Urania/Dea Caelestis to the palace instead.[47] Julia Soaemias oversaw the minting of coins bearing the legend 'Venus Caelestis', neatly welcoming the African deity and associating her with the most respected of imperial patrons.[48] Dea Caelestis' statue and substantial wealth were brought from her home temple in Carthage to Rome to serve as a 'dowry'.[49] It is likely that Elagabalus constructed a temple for her on the Arx or Capitol, perhaps of oriental or African design.[50] The emperor also adopted a new matrimonial direction, rejecting his *vestalis* in favour of the more secular Annia Faustina.[51]

Elsewhere in the city, Elagabalus' god elicited strikingly idiosyncratic and public behaviour from the emperor of Rome. At the shrine to the god set up by Elagabalus in the suburbs of Rome, a festival was held at midsummer. Here, the populace and garrison attended spectacles and horse races at which some kind of imperial distributions took place. Those attending witnessed the emperor running backwards in front of a chariot containing his god's image.[52]

[43] Dance: Dio 79 (80), 14, 4. For the participation of senators and equites: Herod. 5, 5, 9. Child sacrifice: Dio 79 (80), 11.

[44] Ibid. Cf. Herod. 5, 5, 3–4.

[45] Date of first of two marriages: before Sept. 221: Herod. 5, 6, 2; *PIR* (2nd edn.) J 648. See Whittaker, *Herodian*, ii. 47 n. 3. For the celebrations, see Dio 79 (80), 9.

[46] Ibid. 3: ἵνα δὴ καὶ θεοπρεπεῖς παῖδες ἔκ τε ἐμοῦ τοῦ ἀρχιερέως ἔκ τε ταύτης τῆς ἀρχιερείας γεννῶνται, τοῦτ' ἐποίησα.

[47] Ibid. 12, 1–2; Herod. 5, 6, 3 ff.; *SHA, Elag.* 3, 4 and 6, 6–9. See Halsberghe, art. cit. (n. 17), 2213.

[48] *BMC*, 5, p. ccxxxiii.   [49] Herod. 5, 6, 5.

[50] *CIL* 6, 37170 = *ILS* 4438 (AD 259). See *AE* (1950), 51, 52. Also: *Lexicon*, i. 207 (L. Cordischi). Possible design of temple: Halsberghe, art. cit. (n. 17), 2220.

[51] Herod. 5, 6, 2. For her, see *PIR* 2 A 710 and Whittaker, *Herodian*, ii. 48 n. 1; Halsberghe, art. cit. (n. 17), 2213; id., art. cit. (n. 34), 2187–90.

[52] Herod. 5, 6, 6–9. See L. Robert, 'Deux concours grecs à Rome', *CRAI* (1970), 18–27.

Severus Alexander sought to distance himself from Elagabalus' excesses. Elagabalus the god was evicted from the Palatine and the statues of other deities which the emperor had placed in and around the structure were returned to their former locations.[53] The temple was turned over to a shrewdly selected Juppiter Ultor, the *dies natalis* of the temple coinciding exactly with the emperor's own.[54] The available documentary evidence supports the picture of Alexander as broader in his religious interests. The *Historia Augusta*, the faithful purveyor of a veritably hagiographical tradition, records Alexander as a respecter of Jewish and Christian privileges. The latter are reported to have received a favourable judgement in a dispute over a *locus publicus* adjacent to a Roman tavern.[55] At the same time, the emperor revered the ancient authority of the *pontifices* and *quindecemviri*.[56] The perceived contrast between Alexander and his predecessor made it possible for tendentious stories to circulate. The author of the *Historia Augusta* mischievously reported that the emperor's *lar* had included images of the holy men Apollonius, Christ, Abraham, and Orpheus.[57]

After Alexander and until Aurelian, the literary source material permits us only fleeting glimpses of emperors in religious contexts. Much of the fragmentary record concerns the traditional institutions of the state but there are references to innovation and the *public* dimension of this activity is significant. Although most of the information comes from the *Historia Augusta*, much is inherently plausible. Maximinus and Balbinus, for example, are reported by the usually reliable Dio to have divided the office of *pontifex maximus* for the first time.[58] The accession of Gordian III was marked by public sacrifices and the news of Maximinus' death was similarly celebrated.[59]

---

[53] Herod. 6, 1, 3.
[54] See F. Coarelli, 'La situazione edilizia di Roma sotto Severo Alessandro', in *L'Urbs: Espace urbain et histoire (1er siècle av. J.-C.-IIIe siècle ap. J. C.)*, Collection de l'École française de Rome, 98 (Rome: École française de Rome, 1987), 429–56, at 437–8, following Mommsen's emendation of 'Iovi Cultori' to 'Iovi Ultori' in the so-called 'Calendar of 354'. See Chausson, art. cit. (n. 36), 737 ff. Cf. Salzman, *On Roman Time*, 127. For an image: Turcan, *Cults*, 184, pl. 23. For coins honouring Juppiter generally: *BMC*, 6, 119–20, nos. 50–8 ('Iuno conservatrix' and 'Iovi conservatori' legends).
[55] Jews and Christians: *SHA, Alex.* 22, 4. Cf. 29, 2; 43, 6–7; 45, 7; 51, 7. Judgement: Jews and Christians: *SHA, Alex.* 49, 6.
[56] Priesthoods: *SHA, Alex.* 22, 5. Cf. 49, 2.
[57] *SHA, Alex.* 29, 2. For the story that he considered building a temple to Christ: 43, 6. For the publication of one of the key Christian precepts: 51, 8. Halsberghe, art. cit. (n. 34), 2193 argues that the tale arose from the emperor's known syncretism.
[58] Dio 53, 17, 8.
[59] Accession: *SHA, Max. et Balb.* 8, 4. Death: Herod. 8, 6, 7; *SHA, Max.* 24, 4; 7. *SHA, Max. et Balb.* 11, 4 with a reference to 'hecatombs'.

Maximinus and Balbinus presided over the *agon Capitolinus* at which they were fatally discordant.[60] Gordian's sole reign was disrupted by natural disasters which led to expiatory sacrifices and the consultation of the Sibylline books, one of several mid- and late-third-century references to the ancient collection.[61] In 242, the doors of the temple of Janus were opened prior to the emperor's departure for his final campaign in the east.[62] Philip too seems to have tapped into the city's traditions with impressive effectiveness in his short reign. Arriving in the city in the middle of 244, he may have had his own father as well as Gordian apotheosized.[63] After a series of campaigns in the north, on 21 April 248 he presided over magnificent 'secular' games to mark the city's one thousandth birthday.[64] As consul with his son a colleague, the games were particularly extravagant.[65]

The atmosphere at Valerian's court encouraged his friend Plotinus to hope that a Platonic experiment might be carried out in Campania.[66] Under Valerius' son Gallienus the closeness between an emperor and his favoured deity began to manifest itself in a striking new form as coins were produced which depicted the emperor's investiture by the god Sol.[67] The only indication that Gallienus' successor Claudius Gothicus exhibited any interest in religious affairs in Rome comes from Aurelius Victor who relates that he consulted the Sibylline Books prior to his campaign against the Goths. In what may admittedly be an embellished account, Victor records that the books demanded the dedication of the most prominent men to Victoria.[68] In judging

[60] Herod. 8, 8, 4. For the identification of the games, see Whittaker, *Herodian*, ii. 302 n. 2.　　　　　　　　　　　　　　　　　　　　　[61] *SHA, Gord.* 26, 1–2.
[62] Ibid. 3. 'Profectio Aug(usti)' coinage at Cohen, *Description*, v. 54, no. 294.
[63] Ibid. 180, 'Marinus' 1–2; *IGRR* 3, 1199–1200.
[64] Vict. *De Caes.* 28, 1 with the important statement: 'And since the name has reminded me, in my time, too, the eleven-hundredth anniversary passed in the consulship of a Philip but it was celebrated with none of the customary festivities, so drastically has the concern for the city of Rome diminished day-by-day.' See Zos. 2, 7; Claudian, *De sexto consulatu Honorii Augusti Panegyricus* ll. 388–91. Cf. (on Philip) Eutr. 9, 3; Oros. 7, 20, 2.
[65] *SHA, Gord.* 33, 3 alleges use of animals originally acquired by Gordian III. Certainly the coinage shows a diverse range of animals, many combined with '(ludi) saeculares Augg.': *RIC* 4.3, 62; 70–1. The 'saeculum novum' was also announced by coins: ibid., 71. Cf. 'miliarium saeculum': *RIC* 4. 3, 88; 93; 103. For *lupa* type: C. Dulière, *Lupa Romana. Recherches d'iconographie et essai d'interpretation* (Brussels–Rome: Institut historique Belge de Rome, 1979), 170.
[66] Porphyry *V. Plot.* 12.
[67] See P. A. Brunt's review of J. R. Fears, *Princeps a diis Electus*, Papers and monographs of the American Academy in Rome, 26 (Rome: American Academy in Rome, 1977) in *JRS*, 69 (1979), 173–4.
[68] Vict. *De Caes.* 34, 3–5. Cf. *Epit.* 34, 3 naming an identifiable individual

Claudius Gothicus to have 'revived the tradition of the Decii' Victor was undoubtedly reflecting a senatorial tradition which viewed Gallienus' more relaxed religious policies with suspicion.

The Sibylline Books were also reported to have been consulted by Aurelian seemingly around the time of Felicissimus' 'revolt' in Rome. They ordered the city to be 'purified' by the senate.[69]

In 274, following his impressive victories over Zenobia, Aurelian erected the Templum Solis. Himself the son of a priestess of a solar god at Sirmium, he attributed his success in the East to Sol Invictus Elagabalus of Emesa.[70] Giuliano Palladio sketched an unusual building lying just east of the the Corso in the sixteenth century, a structure widely held to be the remains of Aurelian's temple. It consisted of two adjacent colonnaded enclosures on a north–south orientation.[71] The smaller enclosure had apsidal ends and was some 90.5 m in length and 42.70 m wide. The larger enclosed a space 126 m long and 86.38 m wide and, as drawn by Palladio, had a rotunda structure at its centre. Nothing more can be said of the layout of the temple or the functions of its parts, although its swift integration into the life of the city may be indicated by a reference in the *Historia Augusta* to the stores of the *vina fiscalia* being housed in the *porticus* of the temple.[72] The sources are unanimous in describing the temple of Sol as being grandiose and magnificently decorated with objects including a silver statue of the emperor, depictions of his successes in the east and the spoils of Palmyra.[73] The location of the complex was highly significant: within metres, just across the Via Lata, were some of the most famous Augustan monuments in Rome: the Ara Pacis, and most importantly, the great *horologium* dominated by the obelisk of Psammetichus II brought by Augustus to Rome in 10 BC.[74]

The institution of both a new priesthood and annual games in the city (19–22 October) were a powerful demonstration of the emperor's attachment to his divine patron.[75] The *Epitome* records that Aurelian

(Pomponius Bassus, twice cos. and a *PUR* (Barbieri *Albo*, no. 1698)) who offered himself first. For the possible embellishment of the tale in the Constantinian period, see R. Syme, *Emperors and Biography* (Oxford: Clarendon Press, 1971), 204, 234.

[69] *SHA Aur.* 18, 5 ff. Cf. Vict. *De Caes.* 34, 3–5.

[70] Halsberghe, art. cit. (n. 34), 2195 ff. Zos. 1, 50–3. A vision of the emperor according to *SHA, Aur.* 25, 1–3. Cf. 22, 6.

[71] See *BC* (1894), plates xii–xiv; Coarelli, *Guida*, 2nd edn., 240.

[72] *Aur.* 35, 3; 48, 4.

[73] Vict. *De Caes.* 35, 7 'fanum . . . magnificum' Cf. Eutr. 9, 15; *SHA, Aur.* 39, 2; 39, 6; 10, 2; 25, 6; 28, 5; 35, 3; 48, 4; *SHA, Tac.* 9, 2; Zos. 1, 61. For spoils: Zos. 1, 61, 2; Platner and Ashby, 491 ff.

[74] See M. LeGlay, art. cit. (n. 30), 545–62, at 553–4.

[75] For an account of the presence of the cult of Sol at Rome prior to Aurelian, see

was the first of the emperors to don a diadem and splendidly bejewelled clothes.[76] There were signs of a radical new political theology.[77] With striking confidence, Aurelian told some mutinous soldiers that god, rather than the empire's soldiery, had installed him as emperor. Hercules was declared to be his 'consors' and Sol himself 'dominus imperii Romani' or 'conservator'.[78] Coins from 274, the year of Aurelian's triumph in Rome, termed the emperor 'restitutor orbis'.[79]

It is not really possible to speak of any consistent 'development' in the religious choices of third-century emperors. But the emperors who left the most pronounced impression on the source material were devotees of oriental gods. The real significance of the manifestations of these tastes is the degree to which they were public. Being an emperor left a man and his household free to experiment, although there existed the constant hazard of popular and military views.

The provision of public entertainment

As we have noted elsewhere, the Severans dominated the record of public building in the city of Rome. In the provision and maintenance of venues for mass entertainment, their contribution to the city in the third century overshadowed that of other emperors. But this fact should not obscure the importance which subsequent emperors attached to the entertainment of the city's inhabitants. It was above all in the provision of entertainment that the much attenuated imperial resources available for Rome were expended.

Bathing

The most significant of the civic amenities provided by Severus were his *thermae*, located in the southern First Region of the city and probably subsumed into the Baths of Caracalla.[80] The *Historia Augusta*

W. Quinn Schofield, 'Sol in the Circus Maximus', in *Hommages à Marcel Renard*, Collection Latomus, 102 (Brussels: Latomus, 1969), ii. 639–49; Halsberghe, art. cit. (n. 34), 2181 ff., esp. 2183 n. 8 for the details of the pre-Aurelianic priesthood at Rome. On Aurelian's adoption of Sol: ibid., 2195: 'la rénovation religieuse la plus importante du troisième siècle'.

[76] *Epit.* 35, 5. [77] Halsberghe, art. cit. (n. 34), 2200.
[78] Speech to soldiers: Petr. Patr. frg. 10, 6 = *FHG* 4, 198. Hercules: *ILS* 583 (from Pisaurum). Sol as 'dominus': Cohen, *Description*, vi. 177, no. 15 and 178, no. 17. Cf. *RIC* 5, 301, no. 319 and 321. See also F. Gnecchi, *I medaglioni Romani* (Bologna: Forni Editori, 1912), 2, 113 Aurelian, no. 2 and 3. As 'conservator': Cohen, *Description*, vi. 200, no. 228; *RIC* 5, 305, no. 353. Cf. *CIL* 3, 3020.
[79] *RIC* 5.1, 297–9; 304–5.
[80] *SHA, Sev.* 19, 5. See Inge Nielsen, *Thermae et Balneae: The Architecture and Cultural History of Roman Public Baths*, 2nd edn. (Aarhus: Aarhus University Press, 1993), 53.

alleges further 'Thermae Septimianae' in Region Fourteen, baths which fell into disuse soon after the aqueduct supplying the water collapsed, but there is no corroborating evidence and the reference may arise spuriously from the construction of a 'Porta Septimiana' in the same area.[81]

Caracalla's main contribution to the cityscape was the vast bathing complex located on a huge artificial terrace in the southern region of the city.[82] The building was a very early priority, begun as soon as he and Geta returned to Rome in 211; brickstamps bearing Geta's name show his involvement at the outset of the project.[83] The structure was modelled on the Baths of Trajan on the Oppian: a central building was enclosed by a perimeter wall with *exhedrae*.[84] The imposing central block measured 220 by 114 m, and it was dominated by a huge central *caldarium* measuring 58 by 24 m. This architectural marvel was covered by three enormous cross vaults supported by eight pilasters faced with granite columns. The *exhedrae* built into the walls of the great enclosure were among the grandest buildings in Roman architectural history.[85] On the longer side of the enclosure, artfully concealed behind a half stadium, were the huge water cisterns which fed the complex. They, in turn, were flanked by two large apsidal halls which were probably libraries.

The enormous labour occasioned by the construction of the baths necessitated other work in the same region. Access to the complex was gained by a grand new road, the so-called Via Nova, whch ran parallel to the Via Appia on the north-eastern side of the *thermae*.[86] The baths were ultimately supplied with water by the Aqua Marcia which was extensively cleaned, had a new spring added to its source and a new branch (the *Aqua Antoniniana/Antonia Iovia*) which fed into the cisterns at the rear of the structure.[87]

The new *Thermae Antoninianae* were a generous gift to the Roman people. They were the most extensive bathing accommodation ever provided for the city and were a massive indication of the emperor's public affection for the community.

---

[81] *SHA, Sev.* 19, 5. Porta Septimiana: ibid.

[82] Ibid. 21, 11; *Car.* 9, 4; Aur. Vict. *De Caes.* 21, 4; Eutrop. 8, 20, 1. See Nielsen, op. cit. (n. 80), 53–4; Coarelli, *Guida*, 372–5.

[83] *CIL* 15, 769; 4, 16, 17, 18, dating to the period Feb. 211–Feb. 212.

[84] The surrounding *peribolus* was the work of Elagabalus and Severus Alexander: Nash, *Pictorial*, ii. 434. See also Coarelli, *Guida*, 373.

[85] See *SHA, Car.* 9, 4 for the author's marvel at the ingenuity of the design of the 'cella soliaris' (*frigidarium*?).

[86] *SHA, Car.* 9, 9; Vict. *De Caes.* 21, 4; *Not. Reg.* XII; *CIL* 6, 103.

[87] Cleaning: *CIL* 6, 1245. The *Aqua Antoniniana/Antonia Iovia* passed over the so-called 'Arcus Drusi' just inside the Porta Appia.

Within a generation, however, another emperor was providing more bathing facilities. To Caracalla's bathing complex Severus Alexander added a famous portico. The Thermae Alexandrinae, seemingly an overhauling of the Thermae Neronianae, were constructed in the Campus Martius.[88] The Aqua Alexandriana, the last imperial aqueduct to be built, brought water for the new baths.[89]

After Alexander and well into the third century, the water supply and bathing establishments figured prominently in the much-diminished building activity of the emperors. Some public baths and fountains are attributed to Gordian III by perhaps an untrustworthy portion of the *Historia Augusta*.[90] Philip provided a reservoir for Trastevere which Victor acknowledges was notorious for water shortages.[91] And Decius constructed extensive baths whose central block measured 70 by 35 m on the Aventine.[92] These building projects, though barely recorded, reinforce the impression of a tenacious tradition of building on bathing establishments and the water supply by emperors in Rome during the third century.

The games

A substantial body of Severan evidence indicates that the *ludi* of the city of Rome continued to be the crucial point of contact between emperor and populace. When Severus wanted to demonstrate to the *populus* his affection for the dead Pertinax he ordered the dead emperor's golden image to be drawn around the racetrack of the Circus Maximus and three gilded thrones to be led in procession into the amphitheatres of the city.[93] But the mass gatherings of citizens at entertainments were also an opportunity for popular demonstrations. Dio witnessed one protest in the Circus Maximus against continued war shortly before the Saturnalia of 196 during which chants of 'How long are we to suffer such things?' and 'How long are we to be waging war?' were clearly heard.[94] Certainly as wars were

[88] See Nielsen, op. cit. (n. 80), 53 with n. 118. Depicted on coins of AD 226: Cohen, *Description*, iv. 431, no. 297; 449 f. nos. 479–80; 483 f. nos. 14 and 17. The provision of smaller baths (*balnea*) for each region alleged at *SHA, Alex.* 39, 3. For the (myth of the?) emperor's personal use of public baths: *SHA, Alex.* 42, 1.

[89] The aqueduct drew water from springs near Gabii, 17.7 km east of Rome and entered the city at the Porta Maggiore. No remains now stand in the city. They are, however, visible near Vigna Certosa.

[90] *SHA, Gor.* 32, 5 ff. including fanciful but uncorroborated plans.

[91] Vict. *De Caes.* 28, 1.

[92] Scant details known only from a sketch by Palladio: Nielsen, op. cit. (n. 80), 55 with n. 128; Coarelli, *Guida*, 400–1. See Vict. *De Caes.* 29, 1; *Chron. 354* (*MGH* 1, 147); Eutr. 9, 4.

[93] Dio (Xiph.) 75, 4, 1.   [94] Dio (Xiph.) 75 (76), 4, 2 ff.

successfully concluded, emperors marked the occasions with gifts of entertainments. The defeat of Albinus in 197 was followed by sumptuous spectacles, particularly *venationes*.[95] The emperor's *decennalia* celebrations in 202 were grander still. The entertainments were among the most elaborate ever staged in Rome. The Flavian amphitheatre played host to a series of spectacular *venationes* as Severus, punning on his own name, had one hundred animals put to the sword on each of the seven days of the celebration.[96] The same number was applied felicitously to the *ludi saeculares* held in 204.[97] Considered to be the seventh held in the history of the city, they coincided with the marriage of Severus' son Antoninus and the ending of the Parthian war in 203.

One of the reasons which made the entertainments so necessary but so hazardous was the degree to which the *populus* attending could be alert to the tides of court politics. When Severus heaped honours upon his ambitious prefect Plautianus, the latter was teased about his aspirations in the Circus Maximus: 'Why do you tremble? Why are you pale? You possess more than do the three [Severus, Caracalla, and Geta].' And when the prefect had been murdered, Dio recalled a particularly sycophantic chant made in Severus' presence: 'All do all things well, since you rule well.'[98]

Severus' sons, on the other hand, played out a rancorous and dangerous enmity before the Roman racegoing public. Taking an active interest in chariot racing, they supported different factions and Caracalla actually broke a leg in competition against his brother. Severus is reported to have become so concerned that he contemplated moving his sons to the country.[99] After the old emperor had died and the court returned to Rome from Britain, the hatred between the brothers expressed itself in terms designed to appeal to the mass spectators at the Circus Maximus. Caracalla, a supporter of the Blues, brought about the execution of a distinguished former

[95] Herod. 3, 8, 9. There was no triumph.

[96] Dio (Xiph.) 76 (77), 1, 5. Coins show one beast hunt held in the Circus Maximus whose barrier had been cunningly made up to resemble a ship out of which exotic and dangerous animals bounded into the track to face the *venatores*: see Humphrey, *Roman Circuses*, 116; A. Chastagnol, 'Aspects concrets et cadre topographique des fêtes décennales des empereurs à Rome', in *L'Urbs: Espace urbain et histoire*, Collection de l'École française de Rome, 98 (Rome: École française de Rome, 1987), 491–507, at 497–8 and fig. 5.

[97] See H. Pavis d'Esurac, 'Siècle et Jeux Séculaires', *Ktema*, 18 (1993), 79–89 for the calculation of the *saeculum*. Also G. B. Pighi, *De ludis saecularibus populi Romani Quiritium* (Milan: Società editrice 'Vita e pensiero', 1941). *AE* (1932), 70 for details of a woman who participated. Cf. P. Zanker, *The Power of Images in the Age of Augustus* (Ann Arbor: University of Michigan, 1988), 167 ff. for the Augustan celebrations.

[98] Dio (Xiph.) 76 (77), 2, 2; 6, 2.

[99] Racing: Dio (Xiph.) 76 (77), 7, 2–3. Threat to remove to country: Herod. 3, 13, 1.

champion charioteer, Euprepes, probably because he was associated with the team sponsored by Geta. After the latter's murder, Caracalla took particular care to express his enthusiasm for the city's entertainments. His *venationes* were noted for the seemingly endless supplies of exotic animals and the emperor exhibited a close involvement in the conduct of *munera*, forcing one gladiator to fight three men in succession.[100] The emperor's fiscal policies also attracted popular criticism at these entertainments. Requisitions and repeated payments of *aurum coronarium* angered Dio; the doubling of the *vicesima libertatis* and *hereditatium* harmed many more and the *Constitutio Antoniniana*, for all its cultural significance, was open to hostile interpretation as a means of gathering more revenue from the new citizens.[101] Aside from the general policies, Caracalla was notoriously generous to his favourites, a generosity which could be dismissed as fiscal recklessness. At one circus festival in Rome, beneath the Palatine itself, the freethinking *plebs* called out: 'We shall do the living to death, that we may bury the dead!'[102] And Caracalla's favourites were rudely jeered in the Circus.[103]

Consonant with Caracalla's attention to popular entertainment and to circus games in particular, he also carried out repairs and possibly an extension to the Circus Maximus itself. The *Chronicum Urbis Romae* mentions work on the 'ianuae circi' and indicates perhaps those on the eastern side of the structure.[104]

Appropriately, omens indicating the death of Caracalla are reported to have occurred at the circus races in Rome. On 9 April 217, when Caracalla was already dead, in celebrations to mark Severus' *dies natalis*, the statue of Mars carried in the *pompa circensis* fell over, and shortly afterwards, the Greens in the Circus Maximus were heard to hail 'Martialis', the name of the man subsequently found to have assassinated Caracalla.[105]

Under Elagabalus, some of the most important public decisions of the emperor were accompanied by mass entertainments. Thus *munera*

---

[100] Dio 77 (78), 6, 2. The gladiator ('Bato') was rewarded with a brilliant funeral.

[101] Dio 77 (78), 9, 2,ff. For a fuller bibliography on the *Constitutio*, see A. N. Sherwin-White, 'The *tabula* of Banasa and the *Constitutio Antoniniana*', *JRS*, 63 (1973), 86–98; id., *The Roman Citizenship* (Oxford: Clarendon Press, 1973), 380–94.

[102] Dio 77 (78), 10, 4: τοὺς ζῶντας ἀπολοῦμεν, ἵνα τοὺς τεθνεῶτας θάψωμεν.

[103] Herod. 4, 6, 4. Caracalla dispatched his bodyguard into the crowd.

[104] *MGH* 1, 147. Humphrey, op. cit. (n. 96), 117 thinks Caracalla may have repaired the *carceres*. Coarelli, *Guida*, 370–1 notes four substantial walls, 2.35 m thick: 'sembra probabile che si tratti di sostruzioni di un ampliamento del Circo'. See also *Lexicon*, i. 272–7, s.v. 'Circus Maximus' (P. Ciancio Rossetto).

[105] Dio 78 (79), 8, 1–2. See Whittaker, *Herodian*, i. 454 n. 1.

and *venationes* marked his marriage to Julia Cornelia Paula.[106] Like
Caracalla, Elagabalus demonstrated a love of charioteering, aligning
himself with the Greens and staging entertainments in the 'hippodrome' of the Palace.[107] The estate 'ad spem veterem' in the eastern
suburbs of the city was probably equipped for public or semi-public
entertainments under Elagabalus: a circus was constructed and linked
by a corridor to a small oval-shaped amphitheatre 88 m by 75.80.[108] In
the city, fire damage to the Flavian amphitheatre, sustained under
Macrinus, was repaired.[109]

In the most sustained programme of public building during the third
century, Alexander revitalized the workings of the major venues of
public entertainment at Rome. The *Historia Augusta* preserves details
of restorations carried out at the Circus Maximus, an unidentified
'stadium', and further repairs at the Amphitheatre of Vespasian.[110] The
latter re-opened in 222 and the occasion was commemorated by a series
of splendid coins, showing a two-order portico and the Meta Sudans
flanking the amphitheatre.[111]

Under Maximinus, Herodian notes that the emperor's financial
strictures jeopardized the city's food supply, *sportulae*, and the public
games. The response of the *populus* when temple decorations and
dedicated riches were melted down was a demonstration in defence
of *Romanitas*:

That was what the people particularly resented. The appearance of a siege,
when there was no fighting and no one armed, caused public concern. Some of
the lower classes turned to opposition and set a guard around the temples,
prepared to be slaughtered and killed in front of the altars rather than see their
country plundered.[112]

With Maximus, Balbinus, and Gordian III the same prominence was
afforded to the public entertainments. The *Historia Augusta* plausibly
records theatrical spectacles, circus *ludi*, and gladiatorial *munera* held
to mark the accession. And when Maximinus was reported dead in the

---

[106] Dio 79 (80), 9.   [107] Ibid. 14, 2.

[108] Circus: Paterna, art. cit. (n. 41), 839 and 845–6; Humphrey, op. cit. (n. 96), 552–7,
a Severan project completed by Elagabalus. Amphiteatre: *Lexicon*, i. 35–6, s.v.
'Amphitheatrum Castrense' (R. Volpe); iii, 85, s.v. 'Horti Spei Veteris' (F. Coarelli);
Coarelli, *Guida*, 239. At end of 'era severiana'.

[109] Dio 78 (79), 25, 2–3; *SHA, Helio.* 17, 8; *Lexicon*, i. 31 'Amphitheatrum' (R. Rea).

[110] *Alex.* 24, 3; 25, 3 ff.; 44, 8. Repair of the Theatre of Marcellus was also planned.
Cf. *Helio.* 17, 8 for the claim that Elagabalus also restored the Flavian Amphitheatre.

[111] *RIC* 4.2, 104 nn. 410–11; 73 n. 33 = *BMC*, 6 'Alex. Severus' 156 ff.

[112] Herod. 7, 3, 6: πένθος τε δημόσιον ἐνεποίει δίχα μάχης καὶ ἄνευ ὅπλων ὄψις πολιορκίας,
ὥς τινας τῶν δημοτῶν καὶ χεῖρας ἀντιθεῖναι καὶ τοὺς νεὼς φρουρεῖν, ἑτοίμως τε ἔχειν πρότερον
ἀναιρεθέντας πρὸ τῶν βωμῶν πεσεῖν ἢ σκῦλα τῶν πατρίδων ἰδεῖν.

city, a mass of citizens expressed their delight by gathering at the Circus Maximus, in Herodian's striking phrase: 'as though there were a public assembly there'.[113] Even among the meagre scraps of evidence for the middle years of the third century, popular entertainments are prominent. Gordian III's quinquennial games were praised and his collection of exotic beasts lent added brilliance to the magnificent games staged by his successor Philip to commemorate the city's one thousandth anniversary in 248.[114] The emperor also constructed an artificial lake which may have been used subsequently as a *naumachia*.[115] Decius restored the Flavian amphitheatre which had been damaged by fire again in 250.[116] It was doubtless one of the venues for Gallienus' decennial celebrations which took place in the city in 262 and were described with exotic unreliability by the *Historia Augusta*.[117]

The various elements comprising the elevation of Sol Invictus in the Roman pantheon show how Aurelian thought he could best be given the highest place among the city's gods. Besides a temple and a priesthood, the emperor naturally introduced games.[118] As late as the reign of Probus there seems to have been some kind of corporate senatorial sponsoring of games in the Circus Maximus, perhaps to mark an event connected with the emperor.[119]

Other building activities

Away from the Forum and excluding the venues of mass entertainment, imperial building activity concentrated on repair and restoration with the Severans again dominating the evidence. There were, nevertheless,

[113] Accession: *Max. et Balb.* 8, 4. Death of Maximinus: Herod. 8, 6, 8 with Whittaker, *Historia*, 13 (1964), 362. Cf. *SHA, Max.* 25, 3 ff. which says that games were actually being celebrated when news reached Rome. News was delivered to Balbinus and Gordian III as they were entering the theatre.

[114] Gordian: Vict. *De Caes.* 27, 7 (date unknown). Cf. Suet. *Nero* 12, 7. Coin types featuring the Colosseum: Cohen, *Description*, v. 37 nn. 165–6, similar to those of Severus Alexander. Philip: Vict. *De Caes.* 28, 1; Eutr. 9, 3; Oros. 7, 20, 2; *SHA, Gor.* 33, 3. For the use of the Circus Maximus: Humphrey, op. cit. (n. 96), 127.

[115] Vict. *De Caes.* 28, 1 perhaps the repair of an older structure.

[116] Hier., *Chron.* 218 (ed. Helm); Eutr. 9, 4. Cf. Vict. *De Caes.* 29, 1; Isid., *Chron.* (PL 83, 1046–7).

[117] Vict. *De Caes.* 33, 15; *SHA, Gall.* 8, 1–7. See also *RIC* 5.1, 138 nos. 92–6.

[118] Julian, *Or.* 4, 156 B–C. The games took place 19–22 October according to the Philocalian Calendar. 25 December celebrates 'dies natalis invicti', i.e. the rebirth of the Sun after winter and has no direct relationship with Aurelian's cult: Halsberghe, art. cit. (n. 34), 2198; Salzman, *On Roman Time*, 150.

[119] *Chron. 354* (*MGH* I, 148): 'hoc imp. senatores agitaverunt in circo maximo missos XIIII.' Cf. *SHA, Probus* 19, 2–4 where a 'forest' of trees is reported to have been placed in the arena and *venationes* staged.

some significant new structures and as with the temples of the third century it was Aurelian who was to make the most lasting and important contribution to the topography before the Tetrarchs.

At the south-eastern extremity of the Palatine, Severus erected a new and impressive monument: the Septizodium/Septizonium.[120] Although demolished by Sixtus V in 1588–9, the remains of the building were sketched by a number of antiquarians and artists, the most notable being Heemskerck, and from their work the main features can be discerned.[121] The structure was some 89 m in length. Described by Coarelli as a 'monumentale facciata-ninfeo', the building also resembled Roman theatrical *scaenae* of the period.[122] Three great niches constituted the core of the design. Seemingly, several tiers of masonry, supported by numerous columns, rose to an imposing height, making the structure one of the tallest in the Palatine zone. The architrave separating the first from subsequent storeys bore an inscription recording the dedication by Severus and Antoninus in 203.[123]

The purpose of the building is obscure. The *Historia Augusta* claims that Severus erected it to impress visitors to Rome arriving in the city along the Via Appia, and it was undoubtedly one of the most striking buildings in this region of the city. However, given Severus' astrological interests and his fondness for punning on his own name, the Septizonium is almost certain to have possessed some religious significance. If, as has been suggested, the building originally rose in seven storeys, it is possible that it reflected the astrological significance of the seven planets.[124] Certainly, some of the names associated with the monument through the medieval period suggest a planetary or zodiacal dimension.[125]

Elsewhere in Rome, Severus carried out repairs on a number of major monuments.[126] In 202 the Pantheon was restored in the names of Severus and Caracalla, and, making a rare concession to their predecessors, the emperors left Agrippa's original dedication on the building.[127] Nearby, the fire damage recently caused to the *templa* of Juppiter Stator and Juno Regina received attention, and the Porticus Octavia which enclosed the temples was seemingly completely restored

---

[120] *SHA, Sev.* 19, 5; 24, 3; *Geta* 7, 2; *Chron. 354*; *Notitia/Curiosum* Reg. X; Amm. 15, 7, 3. See Desnier, art. cit. (n. 1), 594 ff.

[121] See Nash, *Pictorial*, ii. 302–5.   [122] Coarelli, *Guida*, 175.

[123] *CIL* 6, 1032; 31229.   [124] Lugli, *RA*, 520.

[125] Septifolium; Septizonium; Sedem Solis; Septemsoliis: see Lugli, *RA*, 520.

[126] Note the repair of the Theatrum Pompeii by Q. Acilius Fuscus: *CIL* 8, 1439; 14, 154; and the Arcus Argentariorum, erected by silversmiths and merchants of the Forum Boarium in honour of the imperial family: *CIL* 6, 1035 (= *CIL* 6, 31232 = *ILS* 426) reworked three times to keep pace with court politics. See *Lexicon*, i. 105–6 (S. Diebner).

[127] *CIL* 6, 896; Coarelli, *Guida*, 328.

in the names of Severus and Antoninus, probably between 203 and
205.[128] Just beyond the old Porta Capena, the shrine of Honor and
Virtus was repaired after its collapse through age.[129]

In the south-east of the city, in the region of the Caelian, there were
significant arrangements following on from Severus' military reforms.
Imperial property was put to new use. T. Sextius Lateranus, the consul
of 197, received a *domus* from the emperor and close by, in the early
years of the reign, a huge new camp for the cavalry of the Severan
praetorians (*equites singulares*) was laid out on a grand north–south
axis.[130] The camp contributed to the notable military presence in this
part of Rome: the fifth cohort of *vigiles* was based a short distance to the
south-west; the Trajanic *castra priora* lay several hundred metres to the
north and the *castra peregrina* several hundred metres to the west, in
the vicinity of the later church of Santo Stefano Rotundo.[131] The
Caelian became a distinctive district of the city, combining rich
aristocratic houses and a concentration of military encampments.[132]

Only sketchy details are known of Caracalla's work in the city. The
Temple of Isis and Serapis in the Third Region of the city was built or
repaired.[133] A number of long-established sites were restored by
Severus Alexander. The Iseum on the Campus Martius was beautified
and the sanctuary of Dea Dia on the Via Campana with its links to the
Fratres Arvales was repaired grandly.[134] The *Fora* of Trajan and Nerva
are reported to have been beautified with colossal statues and a 'basilica
Alexandrina', perhaps part of his bathing complex, erected.[135] A series
of *horrea publica* are said to have been constructed to support the
resuscitation of the *cura annonae*.[136]

Under Aurelian, the city of Rome received more attention than at
any time since Severus Alexander. The porticus of Caracalla's baths
which had been damaged by fire was rebuilt, and the camp of the
urban cohorts on the Via Lata underwent a remodelling.[137] The mint
was closed, perhaps as a response to the disruption under its

---

[128] *CIL* 6, 1034, 31231. Coarelli, *Guida*, 309–11.   [129] *AE* 1946, 189.

[130] *Castra nova equitum singularium*: *Lexicon*, i. 246–8, s.v. 'castra equitum singularium, singulariorum' (C. Buzzetti).

[131] *Lexicon*, i. 249–50 'castra peregrina'.

[132] See *Lexicon*, i. 208–11 'Caelius Mons' (G. Gianelli); Coarelli, *Guida*, 246.

[133] *SHA*, *Car*. 9, 10; cf. *Trig. Tyr*. 25; *CIL* 6, 570; *IG* 14, 1024.

[134] Iseum: *SHA*, *Alex*. 26, 8; Dea Dia: Coarelli, art. cit. (n. 54), 433–4; id., *Dintorni*,
211–13.

[135] *Fora*: *SHA*, *Alex*. 26, 4 (Trajan); 28, 6 (Nerva). Statues of deified emperors
explicitly mentioned. Basilica: *SHA*, *Alex*. 26, 7.

[136] *SHA*, *Alex*. 39, 3. Impossible to verify but not inherently implausible given the
scale of other work.

[137] *Chron. 354* (*MGH* 1, 148). The same source claims that the *castra* was 'built' by
Aurelian but this is highly unlikely: see *Lexicon*, i. 255 (Coarelli).

procurator Felicissimus, but it is also worth remembering that coins were struck in Rome for Quintillus, Claudius Gothicus' brother and successor. The closure may even have precipitated the 'revolt' of the mint workers.[138] After a brief sojourn in the city in 270, Aurelian made his way north to confront the Vandals. He was defeated at Placentia by the Juthungi, a reverse which led to considerable anxiety that central Italy was about to be invaded.[139] The worst days of the 260s seemed about to return. In response to the threats of invasion, Aurelian decided to surround the city with a massive defensive wall. Work probably began in 271 and Aurelius Victor says explicitly that the project aimed to alleviate the vulnerability experienced by Rome under Gallienus.[140] It is difficult to exaggerate the physical and psychological impact of the wall of Aurelian which, constructed rapidly, came to enclose some 1,372 hectares and ran for a circuit of thirteen Roman miles. Even the emperor's own estate 'ad spem veterem' was crudely sliced in two and the so-called 'Amphitheatrum Castrense' ceased functioning.[141] The city of Rome which had not looked to its own defence on such a scale in over seven hundred years now took on the aspect of a frontier settlement, a vulnerable community in an insecure countryside.

2. SOLDIERS AND CIVILIANS

One of the most notable themes in social relations at Rome during the third century was the recurring problem between soldiers and civilians in the city. As usurper, Septimius Severus expressed strong dissatisfaction with the behaviour of the praetorian guard which he held responsible for the treacherous murder of Pertinax.[142] His first action upon reaching the city, even before Rome had been entered, was to cashier the units guarding the capital. In a dramatic meeting outside Rome,[143]

---

[138] Closure due to Felicissimus: *RIC* 5 (1), 256. Quintillus: *RIC* 5 (1), 239–47. Seemingly numerous. A sign of senatorial confidence? See Paschoud, *Zosime*, i. 162 n. 75. See below, 33–4.

[139] *Epit.* 35, 2; Continuator of Dio *FHG* IV, 197, fr. 10, 3. Cf. *SHA, Aur.* 21, 1.

[140] Vict. *De Caes.* 35, 7; cf. Eutr. 9, 15; *Epit.* 35, 6; *SHA, Aur.* 21, 9; 39, 2. For the arming of the population under Gallienus, see Zos. 1, 37, 2. Zos. 1, 49, 2 says the work was completed by Probus.

[141] *Lexicon*, i. 36.

[142] Herod. 2, 9, 8. One soldier singled out as responsible by Dio (Xiph.) 74, 10, 1. Named as 'Tausius' a Tungrian in *SHA, Pert.* 11, 9. For the possibility that the plot was centred on two or three hundred *equites singulares*, see Whittaker, *Herodian*, i. 169 n. 3.

[143] Dio (Xiph.) 75, 1, 1. Dio claims that those who came to the meeting were disarmed. Cf. Herod. 2, 13, 2: the men were to attend unarmed and in ceremonial dress.

he delivered a scathing harangue to the erstwhile defenders of the city: they had shamefully connived at the death of Pertinax and conducted a notorious auction.[144] Severus ordered them disarmed and divested of their uniforms before dismissing them from military service and the city of Rome.[145]

Those whom Severus appointed to replace the disgraced praetorian guard seem to have made an immediate and unfavourable impression upon educated opinion in the city. The emperor abolished the practice of recruiting the praetorians from Italy, Spain, Macedonia, and Noricum and opened the posts up to members of all the legions.[146] The size of the praetorian guard was doubled.[147] The result was that the garrison was now made up of men judged by Dio (Xiphilinus) to be: 'most savage in appearance, most terrifying in speech, and most boorish in conversation'.[148]

These soldiers received a number of *donativa*[149] and much more besides under Severus: they were permitted to form collegia; centurions and *principales* were enabled to wear equestrian rings; and ordinary ranks received the right of *conubium*. Their pay, in coin or in kind, was also increased.[150] And their substantial presence in the city necessitated major work in the south-east region of Rome where a huge new camp for the cavalry of the Severan praetorians (*equites singulares*) was constructed.[151]

The praetorians, their cavalry (*equites singulares*), and Severus' new legion II Parthica based at Albanum became the key to security and usurpation at Rome. When Caracalla finally achieved the assassination of his brother Geta in February 212 he made immediately for the *castra praetoria* where he put about the story that he himself had been the

---

[144] Herod. 2, 13, 5–9.

[145] Dio (Xiph.) 75, 1, 1; Herod. 2, 13, 10 ff. Severus' soldiers had occupied the Castra Praetoria to deny the praetorians access to their armouries: Herod. 2, 13, 12.

[146] Dio (Xiph.) 75, 2, 4. As my colleague Brian Campbell points out, most were from the Danubian provinces, as Severus rewarded those who had followed him. See also M. Durry, *Les Cohortes prétoriennes* (Paris: De Boccard, 1938), 247–9; A. Passerini, *Le coorti pretorie* (Rome: Signorelli, 1969), 171–82. For more sceptical views on the foreign troops: J. M. Carrie, 'Eserciti e strategie', in A. Schiavone (ed.), *Storia di Roma 3*: L'Età tardoantica 1: Crisi e trasformazione* (Turin: Einaudi, 1993), 83–154, at 88.

[147] See Carrie, art. cit. (n. 146), 87.

[148] Dio (Xiph.) 75, 2, 5–6: καὶ ἰδεῖν ἀγριωτάτων καὶ ἀκοῦσαι φοβερωτάτων ὁμιλῆσαί τε ἀγροικοτάτων ἐπλήρωσε.

[149] Including what Dio describes as the largest gift ever offered by an emperor to soldiers and commoners: ten gold pieces each. 200 million sesterces was expended: 76 (77), 1, 1.

[150] See J. B. Campbell, *The Emperor and the Roman Army 31 BC–AD 235* (Oxford: Clarendon Press, 1984), 170–1, 175–6, 401–2.

[151] See above, 25.

victim of a plot of Geta. Cash was offered to the soldiers, 2,500 Attic drachmae and a pay rise of fifty per cent, according to Herodian.[152] The *Historia Augusta* records a plausible story of a journey made to the camp of the Second Parthian Legion at Albanum with an account of the hostility of troops there until they were bought off.[153] It is certainly the case that soldiers of Rome's garrison were employed to destroy the new regime's enemies. Papinian was charged and seemingly executed by the guard and Cilo, the former Prefect of the City, was saved only when the populace and the *cohortes urbanae* forced Caracalla to have him released from Praetorian custody.[154]

Attitudes exhibited by Caracalla towards his personal protection alienated many at Rome. Educated opinion condemned Caracalla for looking only to his military forces for real support, and communications to the senate full of praise for distinguished bodyguards quietly scandalized the upper classes in the city.[155] In 213, in preparation for the forthcoming war with Parthia, Caracalla attempted to prove his destiny to govern the east by appealing to the legend of Alexander.[156] Likenesses of the Macedonian hero were set up in Rome and an élite force of bodyguards renamed 'Alexander's phalanx'.[157] One of the most contemptuous statements made publicly to senators by an emperor on the nature of imperial power dates to 215:

I know that my behaviour does not please you; but that is the very reason that I have arms and soldiers, so that I may disregard what is said about me.[158]

And the final interment of Caracalla's remains took place at the mausoleum of Hadrian at night because of the emperor's unpopularity with all but the soldiers. The same popularity precluded any *damnatio* on the part of Macrinus and guaranteed *consecratio*, organized, naturally, by the senate.[159]

Although Dio is fragmentary, it seems that Elagabalus also took care to contact both the praetorian guard and the Legio II Parthica prior to

---

[152] Herod. 4, 4, 7. The donative was less than half of the sum offered by Julianus and half that given by M. Aurelius but over ten times what Severus had given.

[153] *Car.* 2, 7–8. The legion did not receive the epithet 'Antoniniana': Whittaker, *Herodian*, i. 396 n. 1.

[154] Papinian: Dio 77 (78), 4, 1a; Herod. 4, 6, 1 ff. with Whittaker, *Herodian*, ii. 402 n. 2; Cilo: Dio 77 (78), 4, 2 ff. For others insulted by Caracalla, see 77 (78), 5, 3 ff.

[155] Ibid. 10, 4; Herod. 4, 7, 3 ff. For the lavish praise of Pandion, who distinguished himself against the Alamanni, see Dio 77 (78), 13, 6.

[156] See Whittaker, *Herodian*, i. 413 n. 2.

[157] Dio 77 (78), 7, 1–2; Herod. 4, 8, 1 ff.

[158] Dio (Xiph.) 77 (78), 20, 2: οἶδα μὲν ὅτι οὐκ ἀρέσκει τὰ ἐμὰ ὑμῖν. διὰ τοῦτο μέντοι καὶ ὅπλα καὶ στρατιώτας ἔχω, ἵνα μηδὲν τῶν λογοποιουμένων ἐπιστρέφωμαι.

[159] Dio 78 (79), 9, 1–3.

coming to Rome.[160] Comazon, Elagabalus' commander of the guard, tried a senior senator Seius Carus who was alleged to have intrigued with soldiers near Mount Albanus, almost certainly legionaries of the II Parthica.[161] Once he had entered the city, Elagabalus did what he could to attach the city's soldiers to himself. On the occasion of his marriage to Julia Cornelia Paula, they banqueted at a cost of 1,000 HS each, 400 HS more than had been spent on the *populus*.[162]

But as in his relations with the general urban community, Elagabalus soon began to fall foul of the garrison. It is reported that his extraordinary sexual identity became a source of disgust among populace and soldiers.[163] The association in the imperial power of Severus Alexander was clearly a means of bolstering support for the regime but the young emperor also became a focus for praetorian agitation. Seemingly late in 221, a rumour swept the city that Alexander had been the victim of a plot, news which precipitated a major outbreak of violence at the Castra Praetoria. Demands were issued that Alexander be produced and when Elagabalus complied, he was compelled to deliver over to the praetorians certain members of his household for summary justice.[164] When Elagabalus continued to intrigue against his colleague and refused to participate in the consular procession on 1 January 222, relations with the praetorians seem to have broken down altogether. By March 222, another rumour began to circulate that Alexander was dead and the praetorians shut themselves in camp refusing to provide a guard for Elagabalus until he presented himself with Alexander.[165] When the two appeared together, Elagabalus was detained in the Castra Praetoria and with his mother put to death.[166]

In a fundamental sense, then, Alexander owed his position to the praetorians. But this support was no guarantee of peace. Domitius Ulpianus, appointed commander, faced an unenviable task. The city was subjected to a three-day running battle between citizens and soldiers over some unknown quarrel early in Alexander's sole reign. The soldiers, threatened with defeat, set fire to parts of the city, forcing the citizens to come to terms.[167] The praetorians were also sensitive to

---

[160] Dio 79 (80), 2, 3. For widespread unrest in military units at the time, see Whittaker, *Herodian*, ii. 38 n. 2.

[161] For Comazon, see ibid. 64 n. 1. Trial: Dio 79 (80), 4, 6 where it is alleged that the real reason for the charge was the desire to seize Carus' property.

[162] Ibid. 9, 1–2.

[163] Ibid. 17, 1. Note the statement of the failure to secure praetorian guard support at 79 (80), 18, 4. See also Herod. 5, 7, 1; 8, 1.

[164] Dio 79 (80), 19, 2.   [165] Herod. 5, 8, 5.   [166] Dio 79 (80), 20, 1 ff.

[167] Dio (Xiph.) 80, 2, 2. Date: 223 or 224: *P. Oxy.* 2565. Whittaker, *Herodian*, ii. 87 n. 3 thought the cause was probably Ulpian's removal of the prefects Julius Flavianus and (Geminus?) Chrestus. See Zos. 1, 11.

the conduct of governors elsewhere in the empire. Ulpian received complaints against Dio Cassius who was governor of Pannonia and known to be particularly firm with the soldiery there.[168] And when Ulpian was murdered, in the very palace in the presence of Alexander and his mother, the praetorians' confidence was so high that Dio Cassius, then consul, found that not even the emperor could guarantee his safety in Rome.[169] Even when the two men met at Alexander's villa outside the city, the mood of the emperor's bodyguard was dangerous and unpredictable.[170] Not that the emperor himself could afford to be significantly more confident. Subversive support for his father-in-law gathered among elements of the praetorians before it could be suppressed.[171]

M. Antonius Gordianus Sempronianus, acclaimed as emperor in Africa, made carefully considered overtures to the garrison at Rome. The biggest donative in history was promised and the commander of the praetorians left in the city, P. Aelius Vitalianus (?), was assassinated as an adherent of Maximinus.[172] It is significant that when Gordian I had been replaced by Maximus and Balbinus, the chosen bodyguard of the senatorial emperors consisted of well born men of equestrian rank or military experience, not members of the praetorian guard.[173] Popular suspicion of the senatorial handling of the situation drew crowds to the Curia, especially after the election of Gordian III. At one of these meetings members of the praetorian guard were present.[174] Their colleagues remained with Maximinus at Aquileia, and although Herodian describes these men as being near their date of discharge, it is likely that they were seeking to ascertain details of the senate's plans. There can be no doubt, however, about the senate's hostility towards the praetorians. The latter may have crossed the *curiae limen* and were attacked by two senior members of the house. Herodian explicitly states that the times were dangerous and many citizens went about

---

[168] Dio (Xiph.) 80, 4, 2.

[169] Death of Ulpian: ibid. 2, 2. Threat to Dio: 80, 5, 1.

[170] Dio (Xiph.) 80, 5, 1. The consul ended up pleading some podiatric problem before retiring to Bithynia.

[171] Herod. 6, 1, 9. For identity, see Whittaker, *Herodian*, ii. 86 n. 2. Note *victoria* coin types from 225: *BMC*, 6, pp. 60, 61 and title 'invictus' from 229: *AE* (1899), 7.

[172] Herod. 7, 6, 4–9; *SHA, Gord.* 10, 5 ff. At 8 note letters and images of the Gordiani displayed 'in castris', a demonstration of praetorian loyalty? For Vitalianus see Whittaker, *Herodian*, ii. 193 n. 4.

[173] Noted ibid. 230 n. 1. For the reigns of Maximus, Balbinus, and Gordian III: M. Silvestrini, 'Il potere imperiale da Severo Alessandro ad Aureliano', in A. Schiavone (ed.), *Storia di Roma 3*: L'Età tardoantica 1: Crisi e trasformazione* (Turin: Einaudi, 1993), 155–91, at 161.

[174] For what follows: Herod. 7, 11, 1 ff.; *SHA, Max.* 20, 6; *Gor.* 22, 7–9 (misplaced chronologically); *Max. et Balb.* 9; 10, 4 ff. A hopeless confusion.

armed.[175] The remaining soldiers returned to the Castra Praetoria where they were attacked by a mob of citizens.[176] The attack was pressed home as far as the camp itself. Homemade weapons were supplemented by stores from the 'public armouries', probably located in the gladiatorial schools.[177] The most serious outbreak of violence since AD 69 now took place in the city of Rome. Bolstered by gladiators, the *populus* laid siege to the Castra Praetoria with the praetorians sallying out in damaging counter-attacks.[178] A halt to the fighting came when the military decision was taken to confront Maximinus at Aquileia and blockade the praetorians in Rome.[179] While his colleague Maximus assembled a force, Balbinus unsuccessfully tried to negotiate a truce between soldiers and civilians in Rome.[180] When the Aqua Julia-Tepula-Marcia on the *campus cohortium praetoriarum* was cut, depriving the camp of water, the praetorians resorted to desperate action. Herodian offers a vivid account of a praetorian attack which surged right down into the city, forcing the mob into the crowded houses overlooking the maze of narrow streets.[181] The soldiers after taking casualties from missiles hurled from the buildings set them on fire, killing many citizens and damaging the city extensively.[182]

These events at Rome seem to have played a role in undermining the morale of Maximinus' army encamped around Aquileia. Herodian states that members of the Legio II Parthica on service with the emperor enquired about the safety of their wives and children in the city and shortly afterwards Maximinus fell victim to a plot hatched by some soldiers with him at the city.[183]

The death of Maximinus left an imperial army for disposal. Maximus returned most elements to the provinces but the praetorians and Legio II Parthica accompanied him back to Rome.[184] The heads of Maximinus and his son were sent to the city where they were publicly displayed. The sources tell of rapturous scenes of joy and the offering of public sacrifices.[185] Herodian, in his striking phrase, says the citizens

---

[175] Herod. 7, 11, 4.
[176] Ibid. 5.   [177] Ibid. 6–8 with Whittaker, *Herodian*, ii. 236 n. 2.
[178] Herod. 7, 11, 9.   [179] Ibid. 12, 1–2.   [180] Ibid. 12, 2.
[181] Ibid. 12, 4 ff. For the water supply to the Castra Praetoria, see Ch. Bruun, *The Water Supply of Ancient Rome: A Study of Roman Imperial Administration*, Commentationes Humanarum Litterarum, 93 (Helsinki: Societas Scientiarum Fennica, 1991), 245 ff.
[182] Herod. 7, 12, 7: 'The section of Rome that burned down was wider in extent than the entire size of any of the largest cities elsewhere.'
[183] Herod. 8, 5, 8. Cf. *SHA, Max.* 23, 6–7.
[184] Herod. 8, 7, 7. Note manuscript error: Whittaker, *Herodian*, ii. 299 n. 3. *SHA, Max. et Balb.* 12, 7 wrongly says that the whole of Maximinus' army returned with Maximus.
[185] Herod. 8, 6, 7; *SHA, Max.* 24, 4.

gathered at the Circus Maximus 'as though there were a public assembly there'.[186] Balbinus offered hecatombs.[187] There was probably a feeling that the deaths of Maximinus and his son made the position of the praetorians in Rome untenable; many looked forward to the restoration of peace. But Maximus, returning to Rome with the remains of the garrison, decided to attach to himself a body of Germans which Herodian says he raised from provinces which remembered him fondly as a governor.[188] Their presence in the imperial entourage and ultimately in the city itself inflamed military jealousies among the ordinary soldiers of the traditional garrison. Though the Germans were quartered outside the city, their presence in the city was an obvious affront to the praetorians.[189] It was not difficult to imagine that something radical was being contemplated:

The example of how Severus disarmed the murderers of Pertinax served as a reminder to them.[190]

Thus, though the regime is reported to have been popular with the people in the city, many of the soldiers were seething with discontent.[191] Some at least harboured murderous aims. When relations between the emperors broke down over claims of precedence and mutual distrust, soldiers from the praetorian guard broke into the Palatine complex under cover of the *Agon Capitolinus* to seize the emperors.[192] Balbinus was slow to summon the Germans for fear that they might be turned upon him, a decisive hesitation which led to his own and Maximus' arrest.[193] It was apparently not the intention of the praetorians to kill the emperors in the palace. They wanted instead to take them back to the Castra Praetoria where their fate could be decided at leisure. Only when Maximus' German bodyguard appeared in the streets as the praetorians were hurrying home did the latter quickly murder the emperors.[194] The praetorians' favour had settled

---

[186] Herod. 8, 6, 8 with Whittaker, *Historia*, 13 (1964), 362. Cf. *SHA, Max.* 25, 3 ff. where games are reported to have been under way when news of the death of Maximinus was brought to Balbinus and Gordian III.

[187] Herod. 8, 6, 8. Cf. *SHA, Max.* 24, 7; *Max. et Balb.* 11, 4.

[188] Herod. 8, 7, 8. Cf. 8, 6, 6. Not dismissed as reported by *SHA, Max.* 24, 6.

[189] Herod. 8, 8, 1–2. *SHA, Max. et Balb.* 14, 8.

[190] Herod. 8, 8, 2: τό τε Σεβήρου ὑπόδειγμα, ὃς τοὺς Περτίνακα ἀποκτείναντας ἀπέζωσεν, εἰσῆει αὐτούς.

[191] *SHA, Max. et Balb.* 12, 8 is wholly plausible, referring to the praetorians in Rome (Magie's note notwithstanding). Cf. *SHA, Max. et Balb.* 13, 1–3 for rather fanciful details of how the military honours paid to the emperors humiliated the soldiers.

[192] For identification of the games, see Whittaker, *Herodian*, ii. 302 n. 2.

[193] Germans: Herod. 8, 8, 5; cf. *SHA, Max. et Balb.* 14, 3 ff. Arrest: Herod. 8, 8, 6.

[194] Herod. 8, 8, 7. *SHA, Max. et Balb.* 14, 7 says 'jeering at the senate and people, the soldiers took themselves off immediately to the camp'.

unenthusiastically upon Gordian III, a choice which resonated with the original desire of a sceptical *populus* to see Maximus and Balbinus joined by a member of Gordian I's family.[195] The Germans retired to their own quarters and are never heard of again.

Much of the material presented in the *Historia Augusta*'s *vita Gordiani* is fanciful, but it is clear that between August 241 and 242 the emperor married Furia Sabinia Tranquillina, the daughter of C. Furius Sabinius Aquila Timesitheus, the commander of the praetorian guard.[196] And it would seem to be significant that the only arch erected by an emperor between the reigns of Severus and Diocletian should have been that of Gordian III, apparently *within* the walls of the praetorians' camp.[197]

Sometime after July 244 Gordian's successor Philip received dedications from elements of both the praetorian guard and the Legio II Parthica.[198] But although their initial support for his regime may have been strong, a Roman tradition reports that when the emperor was killed at Verona on campaign against Decius, Philip's son M. Julius Severus Philippus was put to death in the praetorian camp at Rome where presumably he had been brought either for the purpose of elevating him emperor or of executing him and thus proving the loyalty of the guard to the new regime.[199]

Under Philip's successor Decius, in March 251 a revolt was raised by a certain Julius Valens. Victor's obvious emphasis 'at the urgent instance *of the common people*' may be an indication of hostility to the city's soldiery but in any event the rebellion was quickly suppressed.[200]

But violence resurfaced under Aurelian, when measures taken to control irregularities at the mint in Rome provoked another outbreak of violence in the city. Led by Felicissimus, *procurator summarum rerum*, and involving disgruntled mint workers, the unrest may have assumed the dimensions of a usurpation.[201] The rebels made a last stand on the

---

[195] Herod. 8, 8, 7. Cf. *SHA, Max. et Balb.* 15, 7. Both sources make it clear that Gordian III was selected by the praetorians without particular enthusiasm because there was no other suitable candidate. For chronology of the reign of Maximus and Balbinus: Whittaker, *Herodian*, ii. 309 n. 3. For the outbreak of peace between praetorians and populace, see *SHA, Gor.* 23, 1.

[196] Date: Paschoud on *Zos.*, 1. 17, 2. Marriage: *SHA, Gor.* 23, 6. Tranquillina: *ILS* 502–4; Timesitheus: *ILS* 1330. For a reference to the couple in the *Acta Arvalium*: *CIL* 6, 2114.

[197] See *Lexicon*, i. 95. The 'Arcus Gallieni' was a reworking of an earlier monument: ibid. 93–4. [198] *ILS* 505–6.

[199] Vict. *De Caes.* 28, 11. Supported by Dufraigne's commentary, 150 n. 9.

[200] Ibid. 29, 3; *Epit.* 29, 5; Cyprian *Ep.* 55, 9 'aemulus princeps'; *SHA, Tyr. Trig.* 20; Pol. Silv. 39–40 (*MGH* 1, 521): 'Priscus in Macedonia et Valens Romae tyranni fuerunt'.

[201] Vict. *De Caes.* 35, 6 says that Felicissimus had been inciting mint workers to file

Caelian where they were finally overwhelmed by the city's garrison but at a cost of some 7,000 soldiers killed.[202]

Victor's version of the rapid turnover of emperors following the death of Aurelian offers a valuable perspective on attitudes towards the army of the late third century. In the Latin tradition an *interregnum* intervened after the death of Aurelian, as the soldiers referred the choice of emperor to the senate. The latter responded by arguing that the task was properly that of the military but the legions persisted and the 75-year-old M. Claudius Tacitus became emperor in December 275.[203] The Greek tradition records that the transition was made swiftly and probably without reference to the *patres*.[204] In any case Tacitus seems to have been conveniently placed, living in Campania and travelling the short distance to Rome to be invested with the purple.[205] His successor Probus enjoyed a short but vigorous reign notable for a series of competent campaigns but also for a memorable sentiment attributed to him by Victor: that in due course soldiers would become unnecessary. The story might well reflect the sentiments of Victor's own day but it is not difficult to see that in the third century context of persistent tension between civilians and senators in Rome such a statement might constitute an appeal for civilian support.[206]

Subsequent events were not comfortably recalled by men like Aurelius Victor:

From this point on the power of the military increased and the right of appointing the emperor was snatched from the senate up to our own times.[207]

As during the period of the high empire, the praetorian guard played a prominent role in politics. The attitude of the guard towards emperors, candidates for imperial office, governors, and even other military units could have a vital bearing on public order. The reforms

off mint marks ('nummariam notam corrosissent'). An act of sacrilege?: R. Turcan, *Latomus*, 28 (1969), 948–59. See also Eutr. 9, 14, 1; *Epit.* 35, 4; *SHA, Aur.* 38, 2–4; 18, 4; 21, 5; 50, 5; Zos. 1, 49. A usurpation? Polemius Silvius calls Felicissimus 'tyrannus': (ed. Mommsen) I, 521–2.

[202] Vict. *De Caes.* 35, 6.

[203] Ibid. 35, 9. He calls the conduct of the legions at this period 'duly compliant': 37, 3. Cf. *SHA, Aur.* 40, 2–3; *Tac.* 1, 1; 2, 1 ff; 14, 5; *Epit.* 35, 10. For the possibility of an *interregnum* see *RIC* 5, 35, no. 361.

[204] Zon. 12, 28.

[205] *SHA, Tac.* 7, 5; Zon. 12, 28. Cf. Zos. 1, 63.

[206] Vict. *De Caes.* 37, 3. Cf. Eutr. 9, 17; *SHA, Prob.* 20, 4–5; 22, 4.

[207] Vict. *De Caes.* 37, 5: 'Abhinc militaris potentia convaluit ac senatui imperium creandique ius principis ereptum ad nostram memoriam.' The idea of senatorial election naturally a fiction.

of Severus were considered by élite contemporary observers to have created a new kind of military presence in the city and the enduring hostility of third- and fourth-century Latin sources referring to the guard reflects a dissatisfaction with the behaviour of this garrison. The degree to which critics were accurate in their accusations that the guard was made up of increasingly boorish soldiers is less important than the unambiguous perception of the city's élite that the praetorians were a malign presence in Rome. The ordinary citizens for their part are unlikely to have been more comfortable with the guardsmen as they were not infrequently on the receiving end of large-scale violence perpetrated by the soldiers. Thousands of Romans fell victim to the periodic actions of the guard, some imperially sanctioned, during the seventy-three years between Severus and Diocletian. And as we shall see, when the latter began a systematic reorganization of the empire, he took the opportunity to address the serious problem of the garrison of Rome, ostensibly on administrative grounds but in full awareness of the recent record of Praetorian soldiers in the city.

3. THE CHRISTIAN COMMUNITY IN ROME (FIGS. 3 AND 4)

The third century was a period of decisive importance in the history of the Christian church as it acquired the demographic, theological, and material base upon which its subsequent development was founded. The sources of the time shed light on the periodic collisions between the forces of the state and individual Christians or their church more generally, but we have no clear indication of the size of the Christian community either in the Mediterranean world or at Rome specifically.[208]

Tertullian claimed that Christians had been loyal to Severus' usurpation. The emperor for his part was well disposed towards them: he is reported to have been attended by the Christian healer Proculus, had Caracalla in the charge of a Christian nurse and was inclined to intervene personally to rescue Christians of high status endangered by their Christianity.[209] But the historical value of these statements for the church at Rome is unclear.[210] The *Historia Augusta*

[208] The historiographical problem well stated by L. Reekmans, 'L'implantation monumentale chrétienne dans le paysage urbain de Rome de 300 à 850', in *Actes du IXe Congrès internationale d'archéologie chrétienne*, Collection de l'École française de Rome, 123/Studi di Antichità cristiana, 41 (Rome: École française de Rome, 1989), 863: 'Les témoignages écrits, non plus, ne permettent pas de former une image suffisament fournie et concrète de l'établissement matériel du christianisme dans le capitale pendant les trois premiers siècles.' [209] *Ad Scap.* 2, 5; 4, 6–7. [210] See T. D. Barnes, *Tertullian: A Historical and Literary Study* (Oxford: Clarendon Press, 1971), 166–7 for the strongly apologetic nature of the *Ad Scap.*

on the other hand, claimed that Severus 'forbade conversion to Judaism under heavy penalties and enacted a similar law in regard to the Christians'.[211] But the suggestion is hardly trustworthy. The linking of Jews and Christians occurs elsewhere in the *Historia Augusta* in contexts which are demonstrably mischievous.[212] Eusebius' accounts of violence in Alexandria under Severus fail to mention any imperial directive and it would be safer to assume that where violence occurred, it did so as an expression of local enmities.

In Rome, Hippolytus' *In Danielem* may refer to an actual outbreak of violence at which citizens are alleged to have expressed a loathing for Christians and attacked their cemeteries, egged on enthusiastically by the city's Jews, but it is notoriously difficult to comprehend these fragmentary commentaries on Old Testament prophecies.[213] Their chief value lies in the reference to cemeteries in a Roman context as the setting for some kind of Christian activity. Tertullian's overriding impression of Severus' reign was that it had been a peaceful period for Christians.[214]

The absence of serious persecution allowed the Christians of Rome to extend property for the use of the church. Under bishop Zephyrinus (199–217) the Roman churchman Gaius drew the attention of the Montanist Proclus to two τρόπαια to Peter and Paul on the Mons Vaticanus and Ostian Way respectively. And during the same papacy, Hippolytus claimed that the deacon Callistus was placed in charge of what was to become the main Christian cemetery of Rome on the Via Appia.[215]

The *Historia Augusta* account of Elagabalus' desire to include Christian and Jewish items in his collection of sacred objects at the Heliogabalium is doubtless a fourth-century fiction but is probably based upon the peace enjoyed by the Christian community in Rome

[211] *Sev.* 17, 1: 'Iudaeos fieri sub gravi poena vetuit. Idem etiam de Christianis sanxit.'

[212] See T. D. Barnes, 'Legislation Against the Christians', *JRS*, 58 (1968), 32–50, at 40. Cf. Frend, *Martyrdom*, 320 ff. for the suggestion that there was a 'co-ordinated world-wide move against the Christians' which singled out the catechumenate. For Severus' hostility to magic, see A. Wypustek, 'Magic, Montanism, Perpetua and the Severan Persecution', *VC*, 51 (1997), 276–97.

[213] Hippolytus, 1, 20 (Bonwetch, 32). Cemeteries mentioned at 4, 51. Jews: *In Danielem et Susannam* 13 (Lagarde, 147). For highly sceptical view of passages: Barnes, art. cit. (n. 212), 42–3. Frend, *Martyrdom*, 322–3 thought Caecilia might have been a victim. For her *acta* (which actually date themselves to the reign of Severus Alexander) see H. Delehaye, *Étude sur le légendier romain, Subsidia Hagiographica*, 23 (1936), 77–96.

[214] *Ad Scap.* 4, 6–7.

[215] τρόπαια : Eus. *HE* 2, 25, 6. See J. M. C. Toynbee and J. B. Ward-Perkins, *The Shrine of Saint Peter* (London: Longmans, 1956), 128–9. Callistus: Hippolytus, *Elenchos* 9, 12, 14 (ed. Wendland, 248).

during his reign.[216] Indeed, in what may be an indication of the growing prominence of senior Roman clergy under the later Severans, Callistus (217–22) was the first bishop of Rome to be called 'pontifex maximus'.[217] Severus Alexander's efforts to reverse the worst excesses of Elagabalus' experiments made it possible for later writers to assert that he had been an enthusiastically syncretistic emperor.[218] Where contact between Christians and the court can be detected, it seems to have been cordial. Hippolytus dedicated his book *On Resurrection* to the emperor's mother, Julia Mammaea.[219] Eusebius described the latter as 'an uncommonly religious woman' who had even summoned Origen to Antioch for substantial discussions on Christian doctrine.[220]

The popularity of such prominent Christians at the court of Severus Alexander drew them to the attention of Maximinus Thrax. When he sought to rid himself of the old regime's less trustworthy elements, he singled out a number of senior churchmen. Bishop Pontianus (230–5) and Hippolytus the presbyter (and antipope) were sent into exile in Sardinia in 235.[221] The action may have been *ad hominem*. Within a month of Pontianus laying down his office a new bishop (Anteros) had taken his place.[222] No action was taken against him. His successor, Fabianus (236–50), is reported by the *Liber Pontificalis* to have embarked upon a major restructuring of the clerical hierarchy in Rome. The city was divided into seven regions, each served by a deacon, a subdeacon and a *notarius*, the latter being charged especially with the collecting of *gesta martyrum*. In addition, the bishop was able to have returned for Christian burial in Rome the remains of Pontianus and Hippolytus who had died in exile.[223] The truth of these claims is impossible to ascertain but they may indicate the unimpeded growth of the community in Rome in the years after Maximinus' early action.

This period of unbroken peace culminated in the active interest shown by Philip for Origen's theories. The emperor and his wife both corresponded with the bishop and gave rise to the famous statement

---

[216] *Elag.* 3, 5. See Barnes, art. cit. (n. 212), 42.

[217] Tertullian, *On Modesty* 1, admittedly an abusive reference in the context of an attack upon Callistus' recklessly liberal policy on adultery and fornication.

[218] *SHA, Alex.* 22; 29; 43; 45; 49. Barnes, art. cit. (n. 212), 42 considered them all to be inventions.

[219] Lost, save for 6 fragments in Syriac and 2 in Greek. See H. Achelis, *GCS* Hippolytus 1, 252 ff.

[220] *HE* 6, 21, 3. Cf. *SHA, Alex.* 14, 7 where she is called 'mulier sancta'.

[221] Eus. *HE* 6, 28; *LP*, i. 145 (ed. Duchesne).

[222] Liberian catalogue = *MGH* I, 75.

[223] Reorganization: *LP*, i. 64. Pontianus and Hippolytus: Liberian Catalogue = *MGH* I, 75.

first made by Eusebius in a famously unedited portion of his *Eccle-siastical History* that Philip had been a Christian.[224] When Cornelius, bishop of Rome AD 251–3, in an aside to Fabius of Antioch, stated that the church at Rome included 46 presbyters, 7 deacons, 7 subdeacons, 42 acolytes, 52 exorcists, readers, and doorkeepers and was sustaining through charitable work more than 1,500 widows and poor, he considered himself to be presiding over a major Christian community which had been allowed to burgeon without serious interference.[225]

This relative tranquillity was shattered by the persecution of Decius. In what was probably a partly political and partly religious policy, Decius implemented the first general persecution of Christians in the Roman empire.[226] Clearly, a number of initiatives were issued by the emperor, the first dating to the period shortly after his entrance into Rome in 249 and apparently attacking only the higher clergy.[227] More damagingly, however, a wide-ranging order followed compelling very large numbers of citizens to sacrifice to the ancestral gods.[228] At Rome, with the emperor actually present in the first months of the persecution, the Decian initiatives were applied vigorously. The emperor himself may have heard the case of Celerinus, an African Christian and friend of Cyprian.[229] Bishop Fabian and a number of presbyters were executed.[230] The emperor was reported by Cyprian to have claimed that he would rather have a rival for the imperial throne than tolerate another bishop of Rome.[231] The unreliable *Acta* of Trypho have a board of senior magistrates overseeing the implementa-tion of Decius' orders in Rome and it seems that one of the sites chosen for the sacrifice test in Rome was the Capitol itself. Celerinus reports that a Christian woman called Candida went as far as the Tria Fata before deciding not to sacrifce to Juppiter.[232]

Although there may have been few martyrdoms, the church at Rome

---

[224] *HE* 6, 34; 36, 1–4; 41, 9. Cf. Jer. *Chron.* 217 (ed. Helm); Oros. *Adv. Pag.* 7, 20. Eusebius (6, 34) alleges the emperor's attendance at a Paschal vigil and (6, 36, 1) letters of Origen to Philip and Otacilia Severa. See Barnes, *CE*, 351 n. 95.

[225] Eus. *HE* 6, 43, 11.

[226] For the significance of riots at Alexandria in 249, see Lane Fox, *Pagans and Christians*, 451–2. Frend, *Martyrdom*, 405 argues for traditionalism. See 'saeculum novum' coin types at *RIC* 4.3, 128; 147–8.

[227] See Eus. *HE* 6, 41, 10. Cf. Cyprian, *Ep.* 43, 3.

[228] See J. R. Knipfing, *HTR*, 16 (1923), 345. Lane Fox, *Pagans and Christians*, 455–6 doubts the universality.

[229] Cyprian, *Ep.* 22, 1. Cf. 39, 2. See Millar, *ERW*, 568.

[230] *LP*, i. 148 (ed. Duchesne). *Depositio martyrum = MGH* 1, 71.

[231] Cyprian, *Ep.* 55, 9.

[232] *Acta Tryph.* 4. See Lane Fox, *Pagans and Christians*, 459. Capitol: Cyprian, *Ep.* 21, 3 with G. W. Clarke, *The Letters of St. Cyprian of Carthage*, ACW, 43 (New York: Newman Press, 1984), 312–30.

was devastated by the impact of the persecution. Celerinus, whose own sister had apostatized, viewed the spiritual wreckage as a 'wasteland'.[233] Among the lapsed, the well-off came in for special criticism from the *confessores*.[234] And Cyprian was soon writing to his colleagues in the city of Rome on the subject of the *lapsi*, which was to cast up Novatianus as a serious problem for the Roman church.[235]

Gallus is reported to have renewed the persecution following Decius' death, but in Rome the bishop Cornelius was merely exiled to Centumcellae, not executed.[236] Thereafter, until the latter years of Valerian, peace settled upon the Christians of the city. Valerian took no action against the Christians during the earlier part of his reign. Dionysius of Alexandria went as far as to call his household 'a church of God'.[237] But in 257 the authorities suddenly demanded from almost all citizens of the empire a sacrifice to the ancestral gods.[238] For the first time the state targeted the property of the church. In a measure which shows that the highest levels in Roman goverment had grasped the significance of their burial places, the Christians were forbidden to assemble in their cemeteries.[239] In perhaps the summer of 258, the imperial policy was further defined in a *rescriptum* sent in response to a question which originated in the senate in Rome. The emperor ordered that bishops, presbyters, and deacons should be executed. Christian senators and *equites* should have their property confiscated at once and, if they persisted in their adherence, they too were to die. Christian *matronae* were to be exiled once their property had been seized. And in the emperor's own houshold Christian *liberti* were to be condemned to the fields as slaves.[240]

Cyprian claims that these orders were vigorously enforced in Rome

[233] Cyprian, *Ep.* 21, 2: 'in hac vastatione'.

[234] Ibid. 8, 2, 3, a veiled reference to the *fuga* of Cyprian in Carthage?: Clarke, op. cit. (n. 232), 203.

[235] Cyprian, *Ep.* 20, 2. For the situation in Africa, see Lane Fox, *Pagans and Christians*, 457 ff.

[236] Gallus: Eus. *HE* 7, 1. Cornelius: Cyprian, *Ep.* 61, 3 (to Lucius, Cornelius' successor). The *LP* 150–2 cobbled together a romantic martyrdom.

[237] Eus. *HE* 7, 10, 3 an exaggerated expression in the context of an approach to Gallienus. Duly noted by Frend, *Martyrdom*, 422.

[238] The terms gleaned from *Acta Cypriani* 1, 1 (Musurillo, no. 11). Cf. Eus. *HE* 7, 11, 7. See, however, K.-H. Schwarte, 'Die Christengesetze Valerians', in W. Eck (ed.), *Religion und Gesellschaft in der römischen Kaiserzeit* (Cologne: Böhlau, 1989), 103–63, esp. 111–16.

[239] *Acta Cypriani* 1, 1. Dionysius, struck by the effort to seize property, blamed Macrianus, Valerian's *curator summarum rationum*, for the initiative to persecute: Eus. *HE* 7, 10, 6. Cf. 7, 11, 8. See Millar, *ERW*, 566 ff.

[240] Cyprian, *Ep.* 80, 1. Cf. 59, 6. For the rescript, see Millar, *ERW*, 277, 570.

by a number of 'prefects', presumably the agents of the various units charged with the maintenance of public order in the city.[241] Certainly the more senior clerics suffered. Bishop Xystus and a number of his deacons were apprehended in a catacomb and executed on 6 August 258.[242] From less reliable sources we hear of the martyrdom of the archdeacon Laurentius and a number of female companions.[243]

When Gallienus called a halt to the persecution in 260 'by means of edicts', the restoration of the holy places to Christians was expressly ordered.[244] The restoration may have prompted another reorganization of church property. The *Liber Pontificalis* attributes to bishop Dionysius (259–68) the decision to assign priests for the urban churches and organize the cemeteries and parishes into dioceses.[245] Among the first to enjoy unimpeded access to Christian sites was the author of the first datable *graffito* (AD 260) from the Christian cult centre 'ad catecumbas' on the Via Appia.[246]

Gallienus' unprecedented guarantee of protection probably played a part in encouraging a significant growth in the Christian community at Rome. *Circa* 270 the great Porphyry claimed that disease was rife in the city of Rome because the worship of Jesus in the capital was so widespread that it had dissipated Aesculapius' healing powers.[247] Although Aurelian is reported by Eusebius to have contemplated persecution towards the end of his reign, no general action was ordered and the church remained unmolested. Beyond his walls, the Christian cemeteries of Rome were extended. As we saw, Dionysius was remembered for bringing about some significant reorganization of the parishes as cemeteries. *Arcosolia* or burial chambers are known to have been on sale during the papacy of Gaius (283–96) in the cemetery on the Via Appia which bore bishop Callistus' name.[248] And within the walls of Aurelian, the burgeoning community was served by a number of humble churches, at least some of which are likely to have been of ancient date.[249]

---

[241] Cyprian, *Ep.* 80, 1.

[242] Ibid. 1, 4; 81; *LP*, i. 155 (ed. Duchesne).

[243] Laurentius: *LP*, i. 155. Women: Ambrose, *De Off.* 1, 41; 2, 28.

[244] Reaffirmed in Gallienus' letter to the bishops of Egypt in 262: Eus. *HE* 7, 13. For dating, see Millar, *ERW*, 571 n. 28.   [245] *LP*, i, 157.

[246] Krautheimer, *Corpus*, iv. 115. The *Depositio martyrum* famously records a consular date of 258 in connection with the site but the significance of the entry is unclear. See Salzman, *On Roman Time*, 46–7; Toynbee and Ward-Perkins, op. cit. (n. 215), 169–70. The question should perhaps be asked of those who argue for a translation of relics to the Via Appia in 258: were the remains of the Apostles likely to be *safer* adjacent to the most important Christian cemetery in Rome at a time when the state had identified the cemeteries as locations of illegal assemblies?

[247] Theodoret of Cyrrhus, *De curatione Graec. affect.* 12 (*PG* 83, 1151).

[248] *ILCV* 2132.

[249] A famous debate over the situation and history of these churches. The classic

By the last quarter of the third century the Christians of Rome, whatever their number, had an organized and extensive network of cult buildings and cemeteries.[250] They were an unmistakable presence in the landscape of the city where the relative simplicity of their architecture should not be interpreted as an indication of self-consciousness.

CONCLUSION

Compared to the period of the so-called 'high' empire, the third century is rightly viewed as a time of considerable instability. The fragmentary and unsatisfactory nature of the source material reflects the difficulty which even contemporaries had in comprehending the pressures for change under which the empire and its institutions began to disintegrate. It is all the more significant, in these circumstances, that the themes considered in this chapter should have made such an impression on the surviving evidence.

Though the picture of the developing topography of the city of Rome is far from complete, it can safely be said that the urban space was subject to significant change prompted by a number of considerations. Severus sought to legitimize and promote his power by means of substantial projects in the city centre which derived its pre-tetrarchic layout from his efforts. His dynastic successors made significant contributions to the provision of venues for mass recreation in the city as grand expressions of patronage although, like all emperors of

early position was taken by J. P. Kirsch, *Die römischen Titelkirchen im Altertum* (Paderborn: 1918) and followed by Vielliard, *Recherches* who argued for continuity between primitive *domus ecclesiae* through to the *tituli* of fourth century and beyond. The feebleness of the archeological data was strongly stated by Ch. Piétri, 'Recherches sur les *domus ecclesiae*', *Révue des Études Augustiniennes*, 24 (1978), 3–21 but the importance of *domus* architecture in a number of cases has recently been reasserted by F. Guidobaldi, 'L'inserimento delle chiese titolari di Roma nel tessuto urbano preesistente: osservazioni ed implicazioni', *Quaeritur inventus colitur: Miscellanea in onore di Padre U. M. Fasola* (Vatican City: Pontificio Istituto di archeologia cristiana, 1989), 383–96; id., 'L'edilizia abitativa unifamiliare nella Roma tardoantica', in A. Giardina (ed.), *Società romana e impero tardoantico* 2 (Rome: Laterza, 1986), 165–237.

[250] For recent work on the catacombs, see L. De Santis and G. Biamonte, *Le catacombe di Roma* (Rome: Newton and Compton, 1997); U. M. Fasola, 'Le richerche di archeologia cristiana a Roma fuori le mura', in *Actes du XIe Congrès internationale d'archéologie chrétienne*, Collection de l'École française de Rome, 123 (Rome: École française de Rome, 1989), 2149–76; P. Pergola, 'Le catacombe romane: miti e realtà (a proposito del cimitero di Domitilla)', in A. Giardina (ed.), *Società romana e impero tardoantico* 2 (Rome: Laterza, 1986), 333–50; P. Testini, *Le catacombe e gli antichi cimeteri cristiani in Roma* (Bologna: Capelli, 1966).

Rome, they were periodically made aware of critical popular views at the entertainments. The scale of public building diminished steadily during the course of the century but it is notable that the three most important new temples in the city should have been such exotic, expensive, and impressive structures. Taken together with the construction of the walls of Aurelian, they constitute one of the clearest physical indications that the city was subject to change. But perhaps just as important, they indicate the degree to which imperial tastes in religious matters was public and likely to be mapped out on the landscape of Rome.

Also public and inclined to affect the urban space of Rome was the will of the praetorian garrison residing in the city. As emperors of the third century came to spend more time away from Rome, the direct influence of the guard on imperial succession naturally declined. It is important to realize, however, that the guard continued to exercise a periodically violent influence on life in the city during the third century. Writers of the period saw Severus as a decisive factor in the introduction of a new kind of praetorian soldier and regardless of the precise accuracy of such views, the truth is undeniable that the city became the setting for some of the most violent encounters between soldiers and civilians in Roman history. Acting sometimes upon imperial orders and sometimes on their own initiative, the praetorian cohorts put several thousands of Romans to death in the years which separated Severus and Diocletian. It is highly significant, as we shall see, that the latter should have sought to address directly the problem posed by the guard in Rome.

Diocletian was also to turn his attention to the Christians. The slender sources of the third century permit us to grasp some important developments within the Roman community during the period. The church seems to have acquired land steadily, located chiefly in the countryside around the city and devoted largely to the burial of the Christian dead. Inside Rome, relatively undistinguished churches were located in various regions, although there is no reason to think that such places were secret. The evidence we possess on persecution in the third century shows a slowly developing awareness on the part of the state with regard to the organization of the Christian community. Land and senior clerics were specifically targeted in the middle years of the century and easily seized because of the visibility of Roman Christianity. But although violent and disruptive, the persecutions rarely lasted long and toleration could be expected in due course.

2

Conservator Urbis: Maxentius in Rome

INTRODUCTION: ROME AND THE TETRARCHS

When Diocletian became emperor in November 284, Rome was still the greatest city of the empire. The density and grandeur of its monuments were unsurpassed; the size and self-confidence of the community were considerable. And yet, as Diocletian assumed power, there is evidence to suggest that Rome was actually a *damaged* city. In the first and most literal case, the final years of unrest before Diocletian's accession had been marked by a disastrous fire which had destroyed or damaged a number of significant buildings in the centre of the city. The Senate house, Forum of Caesar, Basilica Julia, and Graecostadium had all suffered.[1] The scale of work required to restore the city centre had not been seen in Rome since the Severans. Second, the third century had witnessed a series of disturbances involving soldiers of the city's garrison and the civilians of Rome. Serious unrest remained an unpredictable possibility. Third, the status of Rome within the empire itself had become less clear in the two generations before Diocletian. Emperors of the third century came less frequently to the empire's capital and some not at all. The senate was no longer the seedbed of the governing class. And Aurelian's great wall, though an undoubted comfort to citizens, was an ominous indication of the changed circumstances of the age.

The evidence shows that Diocletian recognized the prestige of the city. The 'genius populi Romani' was publicized on his coins and he lavished a huge new bathing complex on Rome. A panegyrical speaker claimed that the city was more fortunate under Diocletian and Maximian than it had been under Romulus and Remus.[2] But the haze of tetrarchic approval for the city's *symbolic* status merely exposed more starkly the fact that Rome had only a secondary place in Diocletian's new empire. Where Diocletian's predecessors had at least maintained the fiction, if not the fact, that the emperor's home was in Rome, he himself had no affection for the city and showed no

---

[1] *MGH* 1, 148.

[2] *Pan. Lat.* 10 (2), 13, 2. See M. Cullhed, *Conservator Urbis Suae: Studies in the Politics and Propaganda of the Emperor Maxentius* (Stockholm: P. Åström, 1994), 62.

inclination to establish his court there. Diocletian was to wait twenty years before he undertook even to visit the city of Rome.

The work of reconstruction in the city seems to have fallen upon Maximian. No comprehensive chronology is possible, but it is clear that a major effort was undertaken. For the first time since the Severans, *figlinae* can be documented, showing the overhauling of brick production.[3] The Chronographer of 354 records Maximian's work in Rome:

> Many public works were constructed by these emperors: the senate house, the Forum of Caesar, the Basilica Julia, the Theatre of Pompey, two porticoes, three *nymphaea*, two temples, Iseum and Serapeum, the New Arch, and Diocletian's Baths.[4]

The bare chronicle can be supplemented by archaeology. Like Severus before him, Maximian looked to the centre of the city as an appropriate platform upon which to place the architectural symbols of the dynasty. In addition to repairing the buildings damaged by fire under Carinus, Maximian oversaw a reshaping of the Forum area. The eastern end of the 'piazza' received a new *rostra* complementing the ancient structure beside Severus' arch. Like its predecessor, the *rostra* of Diocletian was surmounted by five ceremonial columns while a further seven were planted on the southern flank of the Forum, screening it from the Basilica Julia.[5] In the central area, a monumental column was erected which provided an optical focus for the whole layout.[6]

Carrying on the most vigorous trend of third-century imperial public building, Maximian also turned his attention to the provision of baths. Sited in the densely populated junction of the Quirinal and Viminal, the baths of the Tetrarchs were a huge and self-conscious act of patronage for the urban plebs. The enclosure measured a vast 380 by 370 m; the central bathing block 250 by 180 m. The huge cisterns were fed by a branch of the Aqua Marcia. The layout of the building

---

[3] F. Coarelli, 'L'Urbs e il suburbio', in A. Giardina (ed.), *Società romana e impero tardoantico 1: Istituzioni, ceti, economie* (Rome: Laterza, 1986), 2.

[4] *MGH* 1, 148: 'His imper. multae operae publicae fabricatae sunt: senatum, forum Caesaris, basilica Julia, scaena Pompei, porticos ii, nymfea iii, templa ii Iseum et Serapeum, arcum novum, thermas Diocletianas.'

[5] See *Lexicon*, ii. 342–3 'Forum Romanum (età tarda)' (C. F. Giuliani and P. Verduchi); H. Wrede, 'Der *genius populi Romani* und das Fünfsäulendenkmal der Tetrarchen', *Bonner Jahrbuch*, 181 (1981), 111–42. The columns can be seen behind the seated Constantine depicted on one of the Constantinian friezes of the Arch of Constantine: Nash, *Pictorial*, i. 198, fig. 223.

[6] Cf. the accession of Severus and Maximin Daia which took place on 1 May 305 at a column surmounted by a statue of Juppiter 5 kilometres outside of Nicomedia: Lact., *DMP* 19, 2.

combined the best elements of both the Baths of Caracalla and those of Trajan. The central structure housing the bathing pools and associated buildings modelled itself on Trajan's design standing on the Oppian. But in situating the central block in an unencumbered enclosure, Diocletian's baths recalled those of Caracalla in the south of the city. The great dedicatory inscription which appeared at several points on the exterior of the structure announced the *pietas* and patronage of the Tetrarchs in a particularly direct way. The project had been initiated by Maximian in 298–9 as he returned from campaigning in Africa, but it was dedicated to Diocletian, his senior co-emperor. The extraordinary effort made to secure the land for the baths was explicitly mentioned.[7] But the final consecration of the building for the Roman community was made in the names of all six emperors, two retired *augusti*, two reigning *augusti* and the two *caesares*.

Rome was also considered to be the only appropriate setting for Diocletian's *vicennalia* in November 303. More monuments accompanied the visit. *Vicennalia* bases were set up in the Forum and a triumphal arch, the so-called Arcus Novus, was sited on the Via Lata.[8] The arch joined at least two earlier arches over the Via Lata, in particular that of Claudius 150 m to the north, and seems to have incorporated earlier reliefs. Fragments in the Giardini di Boboli in Florence which may derive from Diocletian's arch depict the Dioscuri, Victories, and barbarian prisoners.[9]

The Tetrarchs, led by Maximianus, thus made a major architectural and topographical impact on the city of Rome. But Diocletian's *vicennalia* celebrations in the city were notoriously unhappy. Despite the impressive foundations of the bathing complex destined to bear his name, and despite the evidence that the triumph celebrated was particularly magnificent, featuring the spoils of his Persian war and exotic animals, Lactantius records that Diocletian was roundly abused by the populace.[10] It is likely that the incident took place in one of the major venues of popular entertainment at Rome and its impact was

---

[7] *CIL* 6, 1130 = *ILS* 646. Cf. Lact., *DMP* 7, 9 where Nicomedia is probably but not certainly meant: 'Diocletian had a limitless passion for building . . . Suddenly a great part of the city was destroyed and all the inhabitants started to migrate with their wives and children as if the city had been captured by an enemy.'

[8] The base surviving in the Forum is that of the *caesares*: A. Chastagnol, 'Aspects concrets et cadre topographique des fêtes décennales des empereurs à Rome', in *L'Urbs: Espace urbain et histoire (Ier siècle av. J.-C.-IIIe siècle ap. J. C.)*, Collection de l'École française de Rome, 98 (Rome: École française de Rome, 1987), 491–507, at 494. For the arch, see *Lexicon*, i. 101–2 (M. Torelli).

[9] See Nash, *Pictorial*, i. 120–5.

[10] Triumph: *MGH* 1, 148. Abuse: *DMP* 17, 1–3. *MGH* 1, 148 records the deaths of some 13,000 spectators at a circus event when part of the structure collapsed.

such that Diocletian, architect of a new empire, left the city in anger
before the year was out, enduring an unpleasant winter journey and
entering upon his ninth consulship at Ravenna on the first of January
304.[11] He was never to return and the final dedication of his great baths
in Rome took place in the absence of emperors.

The reasons for the hostility of the *populus* are not hard to find. For
all his energy and administrative skill, Diocletian had assigned an
unambiguously secondary rank to the city of Rome in his new
empire. The diminution of the formal status of Rome and Italy was
greatly accelerated by Diocletian's administrative reforms. Driven by
the requirements of a huge military establishment, Italy was divided
into eight districts in 297–8, henceforth to be governed by *correctores*.
These districts were themselves grouped into two regions: Italy north
of the Apennines (*regio annonaria*) and the rest of the peninsula, Sicily,
Sardinia, and Corsica (*regio suburbicaria*).[12] Diocletian made the *regio
annonaria* subject to taxation. Although Victor softens the blow by
suggesting that the impositions were modest enough, there is no
disguising the fact that the innovation was bitterly resented.[13]

In the new military structure, the praetorian garrison at Rome was
large and redundant. It is difficult to believe that Diocletian can have
been unaware of the recent role the guard had played in outbreaks of
violence at Rome. In fact, the knowledge is likely to have informed the
emperor's decison to reduce the number of praetorian cohorts and
'common citizens under arms'.[14] The decision may have been taken in
proximity to the *vicennalia* visit of 303 as Victor juxtaposes the
projected reform of the guard with the intriguing statement: 'and
very many people believe that it was indeed on this account that he
laid down the imperial power'.[15] At a cost of some serious inconvenience, then, the garrison was reduced but not eradicated.[16] The
process, however, would seem to have been controversial and was
probably so because it failed to satisfy anyone. Significantly, the
situation left by Diocletian was deemed unsatisfactory by his successor
Galerius less than ten years later. Lactantius reports that at the time
when the latter was conducting censuses in Italy, 'he [Galerius] had
abolished the camp of the praetorian guard'.[17] As we shall see, Galerius
determined upon the policy but did not carry it through, but it is clear

---

[11] Barnes, *NE* 93.   [12] Jones, *LRE* i. 45; 47; 1074 n. 16.
[13] Vict. *De Caes.* 39, 31: 'the immense evil of taxation was imposed upon part of
Italy'. Cf. Lact., *DMP* 7, 2 ff.; Jones, *LRE*, i. 61–6.
[14] Vict. *De Caes.* 39, 47.   [15] Ibid. 39, 47
[16] A *diploma* dated to January 306 seems to show ten cohorts still in existence: *AE* 24
(1961), 60, no. 240.
[17] Lact., *DMP* 26, 3.

that he, like Diocletian, detected a problem with the continued residence of the praetorians in Rome. In religious affairs, Diocletian has remained an enigmatic figure. He seems to have combined a conventional and conservative Roman piety with the creation of a radically new religious ideology which underpinned the tetrarchic sytem of government.[18] It was no great innovation to claim a close personal relationship with a god or gods; such relationships had been affirmed by many emperors from Augustus onwards. Diocletian, however, embodied the culmination of the marked tendency of third-century emperors to link their legitimacy to direct divine patronage. The concept was expressed in a characteristically extensive manner. The governmental hierarchy of the tetrarchy was fused to a perceived divine hierarchy which was evoked and reinforced by the use of the titles 'Jovius' and 'Herculius' for the senior *augusti* and their imperial assistants. Thus legitimacy and a sense of divine ordination were inextricably bound together.[19] Though never excluding the validity and influence of the state's other great gods, the pre-eminent role of Juppiter and Hercules came to dominate the iconography of empire.[20]

As with the religious choices of third-century emperors, the new alignment of Diocletian was highly public. Like Aurelian before him, Diocletian's court rituals attracted critical comment from educated opinion.[21] A powerful and distinctive ceremonial language became fashionable with panegyrists. The senior Tetrarchs could be 'diis geniti et deorum creatores'; imperial 'numina' hovered around the great cities of the empire and the concord of the Tetrarchs could be promoted as a form of 'aeternitas'.[22] But linking the fortunes of the tetrarchic system so publicly to the most venerable gods of the

[18] See F. Kolb, 'L'ideologia tetrarchica e la politica religiosa di Diocleziano', in G. Bonamente and A. Nestori (eds.), *I Cristiani e l'impero nel IV secolo* (Macerata: Università degli studi di Macerata, 1988), 17–44; Nixon and Rodgers, 43–54; S. Williams, *Diocletian and the Roman Recovery* (London: Batsford, 1985), 153 ff.

[19] See F. Kolb, *Diocletian und die Erste Tetrarchie: Improvisation oder Experiment in der Organization monarchischer Herrschaft?* (Berlin: De Gruyter, 1987), ch. 5, 'Iovius und Herculius: die Funktion der sakralen cognomina im tetrachischen System'.

[20] Note especially the depiction of Diocletian and Maximian *seated* being crowned by Juppiter and Hercules: I. Gnecchi, *I medaglioni romani* (Bologna: Forni Editori, 1912), i, pl. 5, no. 7. Cf. *RIC* 5.2, 167, no. 225 (Carus and son *standing* being crowned by Sol and Hercules). Honours for other gods: *ILS* 624; 625.

[21] Vict. *De Caes.*, 39, 4: 'Dominum palam dici passus et adorari se appellarique uti deum.' Cf. Jerome, *Chron.*, a. 296: 'Primus Diocletianus adorari se ut deum iussit et gemmas vestibus calciamentisque inseri, cum ante eum omnes imperatores in modum iudicum salutarentur et chlamydem tantum purpuream a privato habitu plus haberent.' See Nixon and Rodgers, 51–2.

[22] *ILS* 629. Cf. *Pan. Lat.* 11(3), 2, 3 where Maximian and Diocletian are referred to as 'vos dis esse genitos.' See B. Saylor Rodgers, 'Divine Insinuation in the *Panegyrici Latini*', *Historia*, 35 (1986), 69–99.

pantheon made the anomalous position of the empire's Christians and Jews more apparent. The latter had long been traditional beneficiaries of Roman tolerance on account of the great antiquity of their public ambivalence, but the number and confidence of the former was one of the phenomena of the age.[23]

The reasons for the so-called 'Great' persecution are controversial and have been extensively debated.[24] Some see Diocletian as a profoundly conservative man whose piety inspired a distinctive political theology and set him inevitably on a course which led to collision with the Christian church but whose many labours forestalled the actual persecution until some nineteen years after his accession.[25] His reactionary instincts are seen to climax in a series of apparently highly conservative imperial laws on marriage, prices, and the Manichees.[26] Others, however, doubt Diocletian's central role and suggest with Lactantius that the real force behind the decision to attack the Christian community was Galerius, summoned to join the imperial college in 293.[27]

Whatever the ultimate motivation of the persecution, it was certainly launched by emperors with a sense of occasion. The *Terminalia* of February 303 was considered to be the opportune moment for starting the attempt to terminate the Christian church in the empire.[28] The first action undertaken in the names of Diocletian and Maximian unambiguously attacked Christian property. First the most prominent church building in Nicomedia was assaulted, burned, and destroyed, and the following day an imperial edict was formally promulgated. The law ordered churches and their sacred books to be destroyed; Christians in imperial service were to lose their positions; *honestiores* were to lose the privileges of their rank. No Christian could act as a *delator* in

---

[23] Palestinian Talmud, *Aboda Zara* 5, 4: 'When the emperor Diocletian came here [Palestine] he decreed that sacrifices should be offered by all the people except the Jews.' The context a visit in the mid-280s? See Barnes, *NE*, 50 n. 25.

[24] Most recently, see A. Marcone, 'La politica religiosa: dall'ultima persecuzione alla tolleranza', in A. Schiavone, (ed.), *Storia di Roma 3*: L'Età tardoantica 1: Crisi e trasformazione* (Turin: Einaudi, 1993), 223–45.

[25] Vict. *De Caes.* 39, 45 for the emperor's respect for 'veterrimae religiones'. Kolb, art. cit. (n. 18) more sceptical.

[26] Marriage: *FIRA* 2, 558 f. (*Coll. legum mos. et rom.* 6, 4). See Corcoran, *Empire*, 173–4. Prices: T. Frank, *Economic Survey of Ancient Rome* (London: Oxford University Press, 1940), v. 310–421 with *AE* (1947), 52 ff. nn. 148–9. See Corcoran, *Empire*, 205–33. Manichees: *FIRA* 2, 580–1 (*Coll. legum mos. et rom.* 15, 3). See Corcoran, *Empire*, 135–6; Frend, *Martyrdom*, 477 ff.

[27] See esp. Barnes, *CE*, 15–27. Cf. H. A. Drake, 'Suggestions of Date in Constantine's *Oration to the Saints*', *AJPh*, 106 (1985), 335–49; Kolb, art. cit. (n. 18), 31 f.

[28] Lact., *DMP* 12, 1, though see the sceptical comments of Kolb, art. cit. (n. 18), 17 f.

cases of personal injury, adultery, or theft, and Christian *liberti* were to be re-enslaved.[29] The terms of the edict show in large part that the emperors chose as their points of attack the same areas of the Christian church as Valerian in the mid-third century: property and senior clerics.

Our information on the impact of this edict at Rome is extremely thin. The evidence is confined to the slenderest of sources: a note in Eusebius; some highly dubious *acta*; several polemical references, and the frequently tendentious *Liber Pontificalis*. Maximianus, officially in charge of Italy and Africa, probably had no difficulty seizing the holy places in Rome; the cemeteries were conspicuous and if the meeting places within the walls were not, their locations were easily ascertained. Similarly, the senior churchmen of the Roman community are also likely to have been known to the higher levels of administration. The fact remains, however, that the bishop of Rome at the time of the outbreak of persecution, Marcellinus, seems not to have been imprisoned at any stage, leading some to the conclusion that the order to arrest clergy was not enforced at Rome.

In fact, there may be a more complex reality behind the bishop's freedom. Marcellinus appeared in the fourth-century Roman church's own *depositio episcoporum* but not in its *feriale*, a document which included all his predecessors from the time of Fabian, martyred in 250.[30] The bishop's absence from the latter is glaring. Within two generations, although admittedly first from the mouths of Donatists, rumours were being circulated that bishop Marcellinus had been a *traditor* and, worse, had sacrificed to idols in Rome.[31] The spurious acts of the 'Council of Sinuessa', a fifth-century forgery, embroidered the tale and the *vita Marcellini* of the *Liber Pontificalis* recorded that the bishop had indeed apostatized but, mercifully given a second chance at martyrdom several days later, had met a more appropriate end.[32] The earlier documents suggest that there was something irregular about Marcellinus and despite the clear romanticism of the later texts, it seems that bishop Marcellinus may well have complied with the persecuting authorities. Certainly the Christian community at Rome was much disturbed in the years following Marcellinus' death. The see was vacant for some four years and the disputes which were to

---

[29] Lact., *DMP* 13; Eus. *HE* 8, 2, 4–5. See Corcoran, *Empire*, 179–81.

[30] *MGH* 1, 70; 71.

[31] Augustine, *Contra Litteras Petiliani Donatistae* 2, 202 (*PL* 43, 323) which also alleged the guilt of the presbyters Marcellus, Miltiades, and Silvester (all subsequent bishops of Rome?). Cf. id., *De Unico Baptismo* 27; *Breviculus Coll. cum Don.* 3, 18, 34 (*PL* 43, 645); *Gest. Collationis Carthaginiensis* 3, 489–514 (*PL* 11, 1255–6); the latter two documents also record the guilt of a certain 'Strato'.

[32] Sinuessa: Mansi, *Collectio Concil.* 1, 1250. Martyrdom: *LP*, i. 162.

erupt under Maxentius were violent and required vigorous policing
(see below 64–5).

As for martyrs, Roman Christians of the fourth and later centuries
tended to portray the 'Great' persecution of Diocletian as a bloodbath.
The *Liber Pontificalis* alleges some 17,000 martyrs all over the empire
within a thirty-day period.[33] Among the proliferation of *acta*, however,
very few accounts do not arouse suspicion. The list of those victims
who may be considered even remotely historical is thus short: Agnes,
Sebastian, Felix and Adauctus, Peter and Marcellinus.[34] It is thus more
accurate to see the last outbreak of persecution at Rome endangering
property more than life. But even as the Roman church dealt with the
attack on its properties and struggled with the impact of apostasy at
senior levels in the clergy, the man destined to bring freedom to the
Christians of the city was nursing his bruised imperial ambitions.

I. THE USURPATION OF MAXENTIUS[35]

On 21 April AD 289 the Gallic orator Mamertinus had delivered a
panegyric before the emperor Maximian, then residing at Trèves.[36]
The theological dimension to Diocletian's government had yet to
emerge and the tetrarchic meritocracy had not yet been designed.
Mamertinus accordingly felt no self-consciousness as he referred to
the son of Maximian as a future emperor:

That day will surely soon shine, when Rome will see you victors, your son happy
under your right hand, that son born with every good quality of nature for the
most glorious arts [of government]. The fortunate tutor who attends him will
need no labour to exhort to a love of glory this divine and immortal child.[37]

But Diocletian's appointment of two *caesares* in 293 was a setback to
Maxentius' dynastic ambitions. Henceforth the government of the
empire was to proceed on the basis of a judicious selection of the

---

[33] *LP*, i. 162.

[34] Agnes: *AASS* Jan. II, 714 ff. For the others, see J. Moreau, *La Persécution du
christianisme dans l'empire romain* (Paris: Presses universitaires de France, 1956), 120 ff.

[35] See now the important study of Cullhed, op. cit. (n. 2) a useful supplement to
E. Groag, 'Maxentius', *PW*, 14, 2417–84. The former reviewed by T. D. Barnes, *JRA* 9
(1996), 533–4. Also, W. Kuhoff, 'Ein Mythos in der römischen Geschichte: Der Sieg
Konstantins des Grossen über Maxentius vor den Toren Roms am 28. Oktober 312
n. Chr.', *Chiron*, 21 (1991), 127–74, at 121–37.

[36] *Pan. Lat.* 10 (2), ed. Galletier; Nixon and Rodgers, 41–75.

[37] *Pan. Lat.* 10 (2), 14, 1: 'Sed profecto mature ille inlucescet dies, cum vos videat
Roma victores et alacrem sub dextera filium, quem ad honestissimas artes omnibus
ingenii bonis natum felix aliquis praeceptor exspectat, cui nullo labore constabit
divinam immortalemque progeniem ad studium laudis hortari.'

ablest soldier-administrators available. This *Adoptivkaisertum* consigned the young Maxentius to the position of distinguished courtier
and a marriage was forged between him and Valeria Maximilla, the
daughter of the *caesar* Galerius by a redundant first wife.[38] Lactantius
records that Maxentius refused to offer obeisance to either his *Augustus*
father or father-in-law, a tale which may reflect his unhappiness at the
arrangements of 293.[39] Any hope of legitimate dynastic succession
disappeared finally with Maximian's abdication on 1 May 305. Lactantius, in a highly worked and hostile passage, reports that Maxentius
was considered for promotion by Diocletian but rejected by Galerius,
his father-in-law, as too boorish.[40] What may usefully be retained from
the account is the fleeting glimpse it provides of a frustrated and
disappointed man who felt that his own gifts had been summarily
overlooked.

Maximian, now in retirement, left the court and retired to his estates
in Lucania or Campania.[41] Maxentius, it seems, followed suit, and with
his family took up residence in Rome as a private citizen on an estate by
the Via Labicana in the south-eastern *campagna*.[42] A pair of inscriptions from the site record the *pietas* of Maxentius' son Valerius
Romulus towards his parents:

To Marcus Valerius Maxentius, lord and father, *clarissimus vir*. Valerius
Romulus, *clarissimus puer*, to his most kind father, on account of his love for
his father's affection.[43]

The matching inscription referred to Romulus' mother as *nobilissima
femina*, the daughter of an emperor, and suggests that the discrepancy
in the status of husband and wife was publicly known. Their recent
court connections doubtless made them significant figures in Roman

[38] See *PLRE* I, 576 'Valeria Maximilla 2' and *stemma* I. Cf. Barnes, *NE*, 38 who
argues that Valeria Maximilla could be the daughter of Galerius' second wife,
Diocletian's daughter of the same name.

[39] Lact., *DMP* 18, 9.

[40] Ibid. 11. Cf. *Epit. De Caes.* 40, 14. See Cullhed, op. cit. (n. 2), 17 ff.

[41] Lucania: Eutropius 9, 27, 2; 10, 2, 3. Campania: *DMP* 26, 7.

[42] Eutropius 10, 2, 3; *Epit. De Caes.* 40, 2. The distance of the estate from the city
is given by the latter as six miles (9.7 km), a figure revised to sixteen (25.7 km) by
E. Groag *PW* 14.2, 2421. Cullhed, op. cit. (n. 2), 32 n. 113 thinks the reference to a
'villa publica' as a residence is significant in indicating that Maxentius was more than
a *privatus*.

[43] *ILS* 666: 'Domino patri| M. Val. Maxentio | viro claris. | Val. Romulus c. p. |
pro amore | caritatis eius | patri benignissimo.' See *ILS* 667 for a parallel dedication to
Valeria Maximilla. The name Romulus might owe something to Maxentius' grandmother, Romula. Maxentius later made much of its evocative qualities but the name
itself was not uncommon. *PLRE* has seven entries under 'Romulus', almost all from the
fourth century.

society and Maxentius' imperial ambitions, so rudely curtailed at court, were quick to re-emerge in 306.

One of Diocletian's final and lasting reforms had been to reorganize the system of taxation in the empire. Northern Italy, which, like the rest of the peninsula, had long been immune from taxation, was henceforth subject to collections.[44] Rome and the rest of the Italy, however, had remained untouched. But in the autumn of AD 306, Galerius, now one of the senior emperors, decided to abolish the privileged status of Rome altogether.[45] Preparations were made for holding a census in Rome and Italy, and agents were dispatched from the court to oversee the procedure. The population of the city was extremely disturbed. It was certainly true that emperors were no longer habitually *resident* in Rome; they spent most of their time on campaign along the borders of the empire, but there lingered still a pride and sense of superiority among the inhabitants of the ancient city. The news that they were to be liable for taxation constituted a blow not only to their economic livelihoods but also to their self-esteem.

In addition to the civilian population, however, Galerius also managed to alienate the military presence. Diocletian had reduced the numbers of praetorian guardsmen in Rome and Galerius now proposed to disband the remaining units.[46] Since no emperor now lived in the city, there was of course no need for an imperial body-guard. But the guard had been, since the era of Augustus himself, a privileged group within the Roman army; their pay and conditions reflected their superior status compared to the ordinary legions. Understandably, the members of the guard living in Rome desired to retain their role in the city and had no intention of allowing themselves to be transferred to more dangerous and less well-paid duties elsewhere. The unrest cast the praetorians once again in the role of king-makers, the role they had had under the Julio-Claudian emperors and which had led to the unseemly auctions of the third century.

It was probably well known to the discontented elements in the city of Rome that the son of a former emperor was living close by. As we have seen, he himself may have harboured imperial ambitions, ambitions which had been rudely stifled by his father in 305. But it is likely that what galvanized all parties was news that Constantine, the son of

[44] See above, 46.

[45] Lact., *DMP* 23, 1 ff. for the general policy and 25, 5; 26, 2 for the inclusion of Rome.

[46] Lact., *DMP* 26, 3; Vict. *De Caes.* 39, 47.

[47] Explicitly suggested by Zos. 2, 9, 2: 'When his [Constantine's] image was exhibited at Rome as was customary, Maxentius, son of Maximianus Herculius, thought it intolerable that Constantine, the son of a harlot, should realize his ambition while he,

Constantius, had himself refused to accept the arrangements of 305.[47]
When Constantius died at York in Britain on 25 July 306, his soldiers
immediately acclaimed Constantine as *Augustus*.[48]

In Rome, soldiers also took the lead:

after Constantius died in Britain and his son Constantine succeeded him,
Maxentius, the son of Herculius, was suddenly hailed as emperor by the
praetorian soldiers in the city of Rome.[49]

Maxentius was formally approached and agreed to lead the discontented citizens and soldiers of Rome. Initially, however, he was less
sanguine than Constantine. Coins minted in Rome and Ostia in the
first months after his accession declared Maxentius to be not *Augustus*,
but *Princeps*, a title long defunct but one which recalled the emperors
of the first and second centuries who had actually resided in Rome.[50]
Maxentius may well have been avoiding the use of the title *Augustus*
until his legitimacy was formally acknowledged. On the other hand,
however, he was well aware that the title of *Princeps* evoked the great
emperors, notably Augustus himself (27 BC–AD 14), who had boasted
memorably that he found the city of Rome made of brick and left it
clothed in glittering marble.[51]

Whatever role was played by the title *Princeps*, it soon became clear
that the other emperors refused to recognize his claim.[52] Maxentius
decided that his own interests and those of Rome were better served by
the more familiar appellation. On 28 October 306, he was officially
declared *Augustus*.[53]

the son of a great emperor, should stand idly by and let others possess the power rightly
his by inheritance.'

[48] Full references in Barnes, *CE*, 298 n. 120.

[49] *Anon. Vales.* 3, 6; Vict. *De Caes.* 40, 5. Cf. Zos. 2, 9, 3 recording the support of
Lucianus, responsible for the free distribution of meat. Cullhed, op. cit. (n. 2), 41
wrongly thinks that the account shows that there was nothing spontaneous about the
revolt. See Vict. *De Caes.* 40, 5 who suggests that Maximianus Herculius had for a long
time restrained his son. For the praetorians, see M. P. Speidel, 'Les Prétoriens de
Maxence: Les Cohortes palatines romaines', *MEFRA*, 100 (1988), 183–6.

[50] Only gold and silver coinage, not bronze: C. E. King, 'The Maxentian Mints', *NC*,
19 (1959), 47–78, at 67. See also Cullhed, op. cit. (n. 2), 39–40; *RIC* 6, 367, nos. 135–7;
368, nos. 138, 140; 369, nos. 143–4, 147–8; 370, no. 153. For the striking appearance of
'sacrosanctus' as a Maxentian title, see C. Roncaioli Lamberti, 'L'appellativo *sacrosanctus* su un nuovo miliario massenziano della Valeria', *Epigraphica*, 52 (1990), 77–84.

[51] Barnes, *CE*, 30 is certainly right to suggest some political soft pedalling while
Maxentius waited for formal recognition from Galerius. Nevertheless, this title, when a
number of others (e.g. *caesar*, *imperator*) were available, seems significant. See also
Cullhed, op. cit. (n. 2), 33–4. Augustus: Suetonius, *Augustus* 28.

[52] Cf. Cullhed, op. cit. (n. 2), 41 ff. I cannot assign the same importance to Maximian.

[53] *Pan. Lat.* 12 (9), 16, 2; Lact., *DMP* 44, 3 ff. Cf. *CIL* I², 274.

2. BUILDING ACTIVITY IN ROME

Maxentius had been swept into power by a movement which was, however crudely, *Roman* in its outlook. The city of Rome which Maxentius took as his seat of power was, however, much changed from the world capital which Augustus had made it. The crises of the third century had drawn the emperors away from the city for long periods and Diocletian's system, designed to prevent the recurrence of those disastrous times, had designated the city of Rome as henceforth only the *symbolic* capital of the empire. It was still considered appropriate for emperors to shape the city centre for their ceremonial purposes, as Maximian had done, and it was politic to patronize the urban *plebs* by means of major venues for popular bathing which the Tetrarchs had duly provided. But nothing could conceal the senior *Augustus'* view of the city as of secondary importance.

Maxentius successfully deployed the same imposing monumentality as his tetrarchic forerunners and rivals, but the scope of his contribution to the topography of Rome was of an altogether broader type.[54]

The coins of the regime permit us to sample Maxentius' hostility towards the tetrarchic system and his own devotion to *Romanitas*. The mint at Rome produced a significant variation of coin-types. Late in 307, for example, Constantine, recently proclaimed *Augustus* and initially recognized by Maxentius, disappeared from Maxentius' issues.[55] Maximianus received the same treatment the following spring. The respective absences are explained by Maxentius' poor relations with both emperors. After 308, Maxentius himself dominated the *aes* issues.[56] Following the death of Maxentius' son, Romulus, in 309, a series of commemorative issues were struck in honour of 'Divus Romulus'.[57] By 310, when Maxentius' position had begun to deteriorate, a number of types appeared which recalled other emperors such as Constantius I, Maximianus (now safely dead), and Galerius.[58]

Thus the dynastic claims of Maxentius found a prominent place on the coins which circulated in Rome during his reign. These claims shared the coinage with elaborate and sustained appeals to the special relationship between Maxentius and Rome. Gold, silver, and bronze coins, from perhaps 308 onwards, carried the legend 'conservator urb. suae' and depicted Roma handing a globe to Maxentius, who was

---

[54] Thus *contra* Coarelli, art. cit. (n. 3), who advocates a Maximian-Maxentius continuum. Cf. Cullhed, 63: 'the most massive display of *romanitas* in the history of the empire, considering the brief period within which it was realized'.

[55] Early recognition of Constantine: *ILAlg.* 1, 3949 (between Theveste and Thala).

[56] *RIC* 6, 342.   [57] Ibid. 345–7.   [58] Ibid. 342.

dressed in consular robes.[59] Elsewhere, on gold issues, Maxentius was styled 'Princeps Imperii Romani' and the scene with Roma, mentioned above, recurred with the legend 'Romae Aeternae Auctrici Aug. N'.[60] On silver issues, a portrayal of the she-wolf with Romulus and Remus was paired with the legend 'Marti Propag. Imp. Aug. N.'.[61] Early *aes* types bore the legend 'Conservatores Urb. Suae' and referred to Maxentius himself, Herculius Maximianus, and Constantine Caesar.[62] By 309, however, the emphasis was more firmly on Maxentius alone and legends from this date may confidently be restored to read 'Conserv(ator) Urbis Suae'.[63] A desire to portray the immanence of this Maxentius, and his strong links to soldiers in the city, may be reflected in a rare *aes* type showing Maxentius on a platform accompanied by the legend 'Adlocutio Aug. N.'[64]

It is important to realize that the programme of construction in Rome was achieved in the face of repeated military emergencies in Italy. In the winter of 306–7 for example, Galerius ordered his *caesar* Severus to crush the usurpation. Maxentius' need for military authority led him to approach his father Maximian with an offer to come out of retirement and serve again as emperor.[65] The older man accepted with enthusiasm. He brought much-needed military credibility and experience to the camp of his son. After Severus had been defeated and captured, Galerius in 307 himself made plans to come to Rome.[66] This prompted Maxentius to open negotiations with Constantine to whom he offered his sister Fausta as bride. The wedding took place probably on 31 March 307 at Trèves in Gaul.[67] Although Maxentius' defences successfully repelled Galerius, some time later Maxentius' father Maximian began to intrigue against him.[68] Lactantius describes an ill-judged appeal which Maximian made to the soldiers and citizens of Rome during which he tore the imperial robe off his son's back. The outcome of the episode is significant: the

[59] Ibid. 345 (iii).

[60] Ibid. 340, 343. See R. A. G. Carson, 'Gold Medallions of the Reign of Maxentius', *Congresso internazionale di numismatica, Roma 11–16 settembre 1961, Atti*, 2 (1965), 347–52.

[61] *RIC* 6, 344.

[62] Ibid. 344.

[63] Ibid. 344–45, *aes* groups (ii) and (iii).

[64] Ibid. 345.

[65] Lact., *DMP* 26, 6–7. Apparently with the title of senior *augustus*: *RIC* 6, 367, no. 136 (gold); 370, nos. 156–7 (silver). All from Rome. The epithet disappears during 307.

[66] *Anon. Vales.* 7. Galerius asked Maxentius to petition for recognition. Cf. Groag, *PW*, 14, 2431 who is sceptical about negotiation.

[67] *Pan. Lat.* 6 (7). See Nixon and Rodgers, 178 ff. For Fausta, see J. W. Drijvers, 'Flavia Maxima Fausta', *Historia*, 41 (1992), 500–6. For Constantine's appearance with Maximinus on coins of Maxentius: *RIC* 6, 369, nos. 149–50; 431, no. 51 b–c (Carthage).

[68] April 308 according to Cullhed, op. cit. (n. 2), 44.

praetorians at once rallied to Maxentius and the old man was thrown out of the city.[69] Even as late as 309 a new *Augustus*, M. Licinianus Licinius, was appointed expressly for the destruction of Maxentius.[70] The fact that Maxentius was able, despite these military preoccupations, to devote energy and resources to major architectural projects in Rome is testimony to the value which he placed on the city and its history.

A proper chronology for Maxentius' buildings in Rome is not possible, so what follows is an interpretation of the significance of these buildings which takes account of chronological hints in the source material.[71]

It is not difficult to accept that an early priority for Maxentius was the physical defence of the city. Indeed, one of the strongest themes running through the sources concerns Maxentius' confidence in the walls of Rome when faced with threats. First Severus and then Galerius himself marched on Rome in 307 and it is probably to this year that we should date Maxentius' work on the walls. These were either repaired or heightened and particular attention was paid to the city gates.[72]

In the centre of the city, Maxentius can be said to have completed the work of renovation begun by the tetrarchs and Maximian in particular.[73] It is important to realize, however, that his own building activity constituted much more than mere continuation; it shows him to have possessed a more ambitious and a more *Roman* architectural vision of the city centre than any of predecessors since Septimius Severus.

[69] Lact., *DMP* 28, 1.   [70] *Anon. Vales.* 13.

[71] See J. J. Rasch, *Das Maxentius-Mausoleum an der Via Appia in Rom* (Mainz: Zabern, 1984), 70–1 for a list of buildings. Cf. T. L. Heres, *Paries: A Proposal for a Dating System of Late Antique Masonry: Structures in Rome and Ostia*, Studies in Classical Antiquity, 5 (Amsterdam: Rodopi, 1982), 101–6. Some evidence is simply too fragmentary to interpret coherently. *Notizie degli scavi*, 16 (1917), 22 = *BC* 45 (1917), 225, for example, seems to show a list of senators, perhaps dating to the reign of Maxentius, making contributions of 400,000 H S each towards the cost of some new construction. See Barnes, *NE*, 121–2.

[72] An early date suggested by Lact., *DMP* 27, 2. Heres, op. cit. (n. 71), 103–5 suggests repairs, but see I. A. Richmond, *The City Wall of Imperial Rome* (Oxford: Clarendon Press, 1930), 251–6 who thought heightening of wall and strengthening of gates.

[73] 'Secretarium senatus' repaired by *PUR* 'Flavianus' whom Platner and Ashby thought was Iunius Flavianus (*PLRE* 1, 344 'Flavianus 10'): *CIL* 6, 1718; Platner and Ashby *Topographical Dictionary*, 145 f. But see E. Nash, 'Secretarium Senatus', in L. Bonfante and H. von Heintze (eds.), *In Memoriam Otto J. Brendel* (Mainz: Zabern, 1976), 192–5 who argues for Nicomachus Flavianus (*PUR* 393–4). Basilica Aemilia 'presumably' also restored: Heres, op. cit. (n. 71), 222. She suggests also the *statio municipiorum*: ibid. 106, 352.

In keeping with his status as a resident emperor in Rome, Maxentius made improvements to his official residence in the Palatine complex. Bathing rooms of Maxentian date have been discovered in the south-eastern region of the Domus Augustana, overlooking the Circus Maximus. Severan substructures served as foundations but the Maxentian buildings were sophisticated and richly decorated in their own right.[74]

Maxentius' most extensive work was carried out just south-east of the Forum (fig. 5). Probably in 307, he turned his attention to the Temple of Venus and Roma dedicated by Hadrian in 135 but damaged by fire in 283 and again in 306.[75] The great Hadrianic terrace, measuring 145 by 100 m was retained and on it was constructed a new and imposing temple. The building had a distinctive layout, with two *cellae* being placed back-to-back. That occupied by Roma looked in towards the Forum while Venus, patroness of the imperial family, surveyed the Flavian amphitheatre. Porphyry columns framed the apses of each *cella* and the ceilings of each chamber were impressively coffered. The temple floor was covered with polychrome marble and the whole structure was surrounded by columns: twenty running along the long sides of the complex, ten on the shorter.[76]

Maxentius' structure was the largest and most impressive temple in Rome and the largest sanctuary associated with Roma in the Mediterranean world. A key religious site in Rome had been magnificently restored and amplified. Maxentius had taken the opportunity to demonstrate and celebrate the connection between the personified city and the ancient patroness of the imperial house. The building was no mere gesture of support to the traditions of the city, it was a self-consciously *Roman* contribution made by a resident Roman emperor.

Next to the temple of Venus and Roma, on the little ridge known as the Veleia, Maxentius erected another huge building, probably after

---

[74] See *Chron. of 354* (*MGH* I, 148): 'Thermas in palatio fecit'; Cullhed, op. cit. (n. 2), 56; Heres, op. cit. (n. 71), 238–41; S. Buranelli Le Pera, 'Terme "massenziane" ', *BC*, 91 (1986), 485 f.; J. J. Herrmann, 'Observations on the Baths of Maxentius on the Palatine', *MDAI*, Römische Abteilung, 83 (1976), 403–24; G. Carretoni, 'Terme di Severo e terme di Massenzio "in palatio" ', *Arch. Class.*, 24 (1972), 96–104.

[75] *Chron. of 354*: 'Hoc imperante templum Romae arsit et fabricatum est' (*MGH* I, 148). See Coarelli, art. cit. (n. 3), 3 ff., 21 ff.; A. Baratollo, 'Nuove richerche sull'architettura del tempio di Venere e Roma in età Adrianea', *Rheinisches Museum*, 80 (1973), 240–69, at 245 with n. 19. See also id., 'Il tempio di Venere e di Roma: un tempio "greco" nell'urbe', *RM*, 85 (1978), 397–410; Cullhed, op. cit. (n. 2), 52 ff.

[76] Coarelli, *Guida*, 115–16. The colonnades original? See Cullhed, op. cit. (n. 2), 50–2.

the same fire of 306 which had destroyed the old Templum Urbis.[77] A great basilica 100 m long by 65 wide, was laid out longitudinally, running south-east to north-west (figs. 6 and 7).[78] The north side of the structure was built up artificially in order to accommodate the basilica on this precise point of the Velia. The building was dominated by its central nave, 80 m long and 25 wide, rising to a height of 35 m. Eight huge columns of proconnesian marble flanked the nave and the terminating apse was lined with niches to hold statuary. There may have been a large statue of Maxentius in this apse.[79] The whole conception owed something to the great *thermae* halls of the baths of earlier emperors but the basilica of Maxentius adapted and advanced the techniques much further to enclose a vast and unencumbered space.

The reasons for the siting of the building here are, according to Coarelli 'molteplici e complesse, politiche, ideologiche e funzionali'.[80] The alignment of the basilica so carefully with the Temple of Venus and Roma suggests a connection between the buildings that was at the very least aesthetic. But the juxtaposition of the *cella* of Roma and Maxentius' basilica may have a special significance. Coarelli has argued that the curator of the work on the basilica was the Prefect of the City Attius Insteius Tertullus to whom the *corpus magnariorum* dedicated a statue whose base was recovered at the rear of the structure. The inscription thereon termed Tertullus 'praepositus fabricae', or 'fabricis'.[81] It was thus a prestigious architectural statement in support of the city's administration. It should not be forgotten that Maxentius was particularly anxious to associate the Prefects of the City closely with his own regime. He clearly aimed at a system whereby the Prefects of the City entered and left office on 28 October each year: the anniversary of his own acclamation as *Augustus*.[82]

The choice of the Veleia was no accident. According to Coarelli, Maxentius was tapping some of the most ancient traditions of the city. The most celebrated member of the *gens Valeria*, P. Valerius Publicola,

[77] See *Lexicon*, i. 170–3 (F. Coarelli); id., art. cit. (n. 3), 22 ff.; A. Minoprio, 'A Restoration of the Basilica of Constantine', *PBSR*, 12 (1932), 1–18; Coarelli, *Guida*, 111–13; Cullhed, op. cit. (n. 2), 50–2.

[78] The entrance onto the Sacra Via may have been part of the original conception of the building: *BC*, 91 (1986), 247–9, although the excavations cannot have been said to 'prove' this, *pace* Cullhed, op. cit. (n. 2), 51.

[79] Coarelli, art. cit. (n. 3), 32 (an unpublished opinion of Paul Zanker).

[80] *Lexicon*, i. 171. See also his discussion in art. cit. (n. 3), 4 ff.

[81] *Lexicon*, i. 171; Coarelli, art. cit. (n. 3), 22 ff. Tertullus: *PLRE* 1, 'Tertullus 6'. Statue base: *CIL* 6, 1696, found 'negli orti delle faniculle dette le Mendicanti i quali già furono del card. di Carpi in quella parte che riguarda il Colosseo' (Petrus Aloisius Galletti, 1776). See Lanciani, *FUR*, map 29.

[82] See Barnes, *NE*, 112.

had long been associated with the Veleia, near the Temple of the Penates: 'e cioè in un punto del colle che sembrerebbe corrispondere all'abside occidentale della basilica' where the huge statue of Maxentius stood.[83] The so-called 'Temple of Romulus' was not far away, at the foot of the Veleia, where literary sources locate the ancestral tomb of the Valerii.[84] With the Secretarium Tellurense in the same area, one can justifiably speak of a 'Forum of Maxentius'. Indeed, the conception may have been grander. In the early years of the twentieth century Boni systematically destroyed the late antique strata by lowering the ground level of the zone lying on the far side of the Via Sacra from the great basilica of Maxentius.

Moving away from the Velia, Maxentius also left his mark on the Sacra Via. A rotunda with flanking niches was constructed at the western corner of his great basilica.[85] This imposing 'tempietto' was constructed in brick and covered by a distinctive dome. On each side of the rotunda absidal chambers were added, linked to the main building by concave flanking walls into which were set four recesses suitable for statues. At least two and possibly four *cipollino* columns flanked the rotunda. Columns were also placed on each side of the door of the rotunda, supporting a cornice of richly carved white marble. Through the rear of the structure was a small door providing access to one of the rooms of Vespasian's Forum Pacis, possibly the Bibliotheca Pacis which was to become the church of SS. Cosma e Damiano.[86]

Several coins from the tetrarchic period depict rotundas.[87] One, from the mint at Ticinum in northern Italy, commemorated the memory of Constantius I, Constantine's father.[88] It showed a circular building surmounted by an eagle in flight and bore the legend: '[To] the memory of the deified Constantius'. Another, a *follis* from Thessalonika showed a rotunda with eagle above and bore the legend: '[To] the memory of the deified Galerius'.[89] Coarelli believes that the buildings shown on these coins were actually temples of the imperial cult, with the eagles representing the spirits of the deified emperors making their way heavenwards.[90]

In 309 Maxentius' elder son, Romulus, died and was deified. In true

---

[83] *Lexicon*, i. 171.

[84] Ibid.; and more extensively, Coarelli, art. cit. (n. 3).

[85] For what follows, see L. Luschi, 'L'iconografia dell'edificio rotondo nella monetazione massenziana e il "tempio del divo Romolo"', *BC*, 89.1 (1984), 41–54; Coarelli, art. cit. (n. 3), 11 ff.; Coarelli, *Guida*, 105–7; Nash, *Pictorial*, 268–71; Cullhed, op. cit. (n. 2), 52 ff.

[86] See P. B. Whitehead, 'The Church of SS. Cosma e Damiano in Rome', *AJA*, 31 (1927b), 18.

[87] See Luschi, art. cit. (n. 85).

[88] *RIC* 6, 294 nn. 96 ff. with pl. 4.

[89] See Luschi, art. cit. (n. 85), figs. 2 and 3.

[90] Coarelli, (n. 3), 13 f.

tetrarchic style, Maxentius issued commemorative coins. The icono-graphy is familiar: eagle in flight over a rotunda and an exhortation to honour the memory of the deceased. But is the rotunda shown on Maxentius' coins the building in the Forum? There are marked variations in the iconography of the rotunda structures depicted on Maxentius' coins. Some show a building made of unfaced brick, others a rotunda flanked by six columns.[91] These differences may be explained in a variety of ways: they may indeed be references to the rotunda of the Forum but they depict it in differing stages of construction; alternatively, they may be references to the rotunda in the Forum and a quite separate structure, that of the tomb of Romulus on the Via Appia. The difficulties of the coin evidence do not, however, constitute a strong case against ascribing the rotunda of the Forum to Maxentius. It is not difficult to imagine that Maxentius' coins should refer to *any* new building that was connected to the deceased Romulus; nor is it easy to dismiss the possibility that Maxentius would have established a cult centre in Rome in honour of the new *divus*.

On several coins, two figures are shown in niches flanking the building. The identity of the two figures is important. Frazer thought them to be Hercules and Victory, deities chosen to stress Maxentius' dynastic and tetrarchic credentials.[92] Coarelli, however, has argued that the figures represent the Dioscuri who were closely linked with the Dei Penates, the spirits who presided over the houses of citizens. The Dioscuri had decorated a temple of the Penates which stood from a very early date on the Velia.[93] As we have seen, it had been dramatically reshaped to make way for the huge basilica of the Prefect of the City. According to Coarelli's theory, this remodelling had in fact destroyed the old shrine of the Penates which was moved to a new site. Thus the rotunda which was shown on the coins of Maxentius was a building which housed the cult of the Penates *and* that of his own son, Romulus. What Maxentius had succeeded in doing, therefore, was fusing together one of the oldest cults in Rome to that of the Maxentian dynasty. The evocative name of his dead son made the process all the more poignant, and powerful.[94]

Right in the heart of the Forum, near the famous Lapis Niger, traditionally regarded as the tomb of Romulus the Founder of Rome, Maxentius' *curator aedium sacrarum*, Furius Octavianus, set up a

---

[91] See Nash, *Pictorial*, ii. figs. 1024 and 1025.

[92] Cited in Coarelli, art. cit. (n. 3), 16 ff.

[93] H. H. Scullard, *Festivals and Ceremonies of the Roman Republic* (London: Thames and Hudson, 1981), 65–6.

[94] For a full treatment of the temple of the *Penates* on the Veleia, see A. Dubourdieu, *Les Origines et le développement du culte des Pénates de Rome*, Collection de l'École française à Rome, 118 (Rome: École française à Rome, 1989), 399–419.

marble plinth. It has been suggested that the magnificent she-wolf now in the Palazzo dei Conservatori stood originally on top of this base.[95] A short but striking text accompanied the sculpture:

To unconquered Mars, Father, and to the founders of his eternal city. Our Lord Imperator Maxentius Pius Felix, unconquered Augustus [dedicated this].[96]

Two points are worth noting. First, there can be little surprise that Mars was singled out as a special deity watching over Rome and Maxentius. As we saw, the threat of war was never far away during Maxentius' time as emperor. The special relationship which he enjoyed with the praetorian guardsmen demanded a martial god as patron. Secondly, we can see even with this short inscription Maxentius' sense of occasion, because on the right hand side of the marble base, a date had been added, showing that the dedication had taken place on the ninth day before the kalends of May: 21 April, the Parilia and the anniversary of the founding of the city of Rome in 753 BC.[97]

A second inscription from the base of what was probably a statue of Maxentius was found between the Basilica Julia and the foot of the Capitol, indicating in all likelihood a sculpture standing in the central Forum area. The significance of the inscription is hard to determine:

censurae veteris pietatisque singularis domino nostro [M]axenti[o][98]

It is possible that Maxentius' overturning of Diocletian and Galerius' tax policies in Rome was commemorated but equally the suspension of some emergency measure might be indicated.

As was suggested earlier, Maxentius was not diffident about honouring his own son Romulus in the city founded by a demi-god of the same name. The profile of the deified child Romulus in the city centre was notable and may have been even more conspicuous. A fragmentary

---

[95] For the possibility that this famous sculpture may have been associated with the *domus Faustae* on the Lateran, see V. Santa Maria Scrinari, 'Per la storia e la topografia del Laterano', *BdA*, 50 (1965), 42 f.; V. Santa Maria Scrinari, *Il Laterano imperiale 1: Dalle "aedes Laterani" alla "domus Faustae"*, Monumenti di antichità cristiana, 11 (Vatican City: Pontificio Istituto di archeologia cristiana, 1991), 98–101, 118, fig. 64; C. Dulière, *Lupa Romana: Recherches d'iconographie et essai d'interprétation* (Brussels-Rome: Institut historique Belge de Rome, 1979), 23–4.

[96] *CIL* 6, 33856 = *ILS* 8935: 'Marti invicto patri | et aeternae urbis suae | conditoribus | dominus noster | imp. Maxent[iu]s P. F. | invictus Augu. | (*in latere dextro*): dedicata die xi kal. Maias | per Furium Octavianum v.c. | cur. Aed. Sacr.' Maxentius' name was subsequently erased.

[97] See H. Wrede, art. cit. (n. 5), 142.

[98] *CIL* 6, 33857 = 31394a; Cullhed, op. cit. (n. 2), 60.

inscription recovered from the top of the Arch of Constantine in recent
years shows what appears to be a dedication of a 'colossus' to Romulus
son of Maxentius by L. Cornelius Fortunatianus, a governor of Sardinia
under Maxentius.[99] It is tempting to identify the 'colossus' in question
with the huge bronze statue of Nero which stood to a height of 37 m
beside the amphitheatre of Vespasian to which it later gave its name.
This great statue had changed its identity a number of times in Roman
history. Beginning as Nero, it became the god Sol under Vespasian
towards the end of the first century. Commodus, at the end of the
second, had the statue remodelled to depict himself as Hercules but after
his death it reverted to being Sol.[100] It was therefore not unprecedented
for it to have one more change of identity. And for Maxentius, few
monuments could be more fitting memorials to his dead son.

Like all men of high social status, Maxentius divided his time
between business to be carried out in the city and a more leisurely
life in the countryside or *campagna* around Rome (fig. 8). A little over 3
kilometres along the Via Appia, where the road dips into a gentle valley
known in antiquity as 'in catecumbas', Maxentius intervened impressively to enhance an existing suburban villa[101] into one fit for an
emperor.[102] He knew well that Diocletian's system of government
had raised the status of cities like Milan, Trèves, Salonica, and
Nicomedia which now played host to emperors on a permanent or
semi-permanent basis. In each of these cities huge new palaces had
been built to house the emperor and his court. Frequently, the new
complexes modelled themselves on the *domus augustana* at Rome which
dominated the Palatine Hill and overlooked the Circus Maximus.[103]
Maxentius possessed the original complex of Palatine palace and
Circus Maximus, yet on the Via Appia he constructed a huge new
circus at the bottom of a slope on top of which rose a sumptuous

[99] See P. Peirce, 'The Arch of Constantine: Propaganda and Ideology in Late
Roman Art', *Art History*, 12 (1989), 404. Also A. Melucco Vaccaro, *Archeo*, 7.1 (1992),
101. Not mentioned in *Lexicon*, i. 86–91 s.v. 'Arcus Constantini' (A. Capodiferro).

[100] See *Lexicon*, i. 296–7 'Colossus' (C. Lega); Platner and Ashby, *Topographical
Dictionary*, 130–1.

[101] The original villa was apparently of second-century date, perhaps belonging to
Herodes Atticus. See Giuseppina Pisani-Sartorio and Raissa Calza, *La Villa di
Massenzio sulla Via Appia. Il palazzo—le opere d'arte*, I monumenti Romani, 6
(Rome: Istituto di studi romani, 1976), 113–21.

[102] *Chron. of 354*: 'fecit . . . circum . . . in catecumbas'. First identified by A. Nibby,
Roma nell'anno MDCCCXXXVIII: Parte 1: Antica (Rome, 1838), 632–44. For what
follows, see Rasch, op. cit. (n. 71); R. de Angelis Betolotti, G. Ioppolo, and G. Pisani-
Sartorio, *La Residenza imperiale di Massenzio. Villa, mausoleo e circo* (Rome: Fratelli
Palombi, 1988); Pisani-Sartorio and Calza, op. cit. (n. 101); Coarelli, art. cit. (n. 3),
41 ff.; Coarelli, *Dintorni*, 30–8; A. Frazer, 'The Iconography of the Emperor Maxentius'
Buildings in Via Appia', *Art Bulletin*, 48 (1966), 385–92. [103] See ibid.

suburban villa.[104] A corridor joined the villa to the *pulvinar* of the circus.[105] Just to the north of the great house stood a mausoleum consisting of a rotunda with pronaos in front enclosed by perimeter walls in *opus vittatum*. The main entrance opened onto the Via Appia and two minor doorways opened towards the circus and villa respectively. The latter were perhaps an indication of some kind of ceremonial connection between circus and mausoleum. An inscription from a statue base recovered from the complex clearly indicates the desire to commemorate Maxentius' son Romulus:

To the deified Romulus, man of most noble memory, consul ordinary for the second time, son of our lord Maxentius the unconquered and perpetual Augustus, grandson of the deified Maximianus senior and of the deified [Maximianus junior?][106]

Certainly the mausoleum and villa seem to be the earliest parts of the structure with the circus coming later.[107]

The reasons why Maxentius built the complex are obscure. As the builder of structures which had restored the centre of the city of Rome he was perhaps unimpressed by the hotch-potch of rooms which made up the traditional imperial palace on the Palatine; building on the Via Appia freed his hands and enabled him, in addition, to place close beside his residence the tomb of his son, since burial within the sacred confines of the city was forbidden by pontifical law. The mausoleum of Romulus was probably also destined to be Maxentius' own and that of his dynasty. In any event, Maxentius could be confident as the work neared completion that he had created an estate not only of outstanding beauty, but a home fit for a resident emperor whose presence in the city was the strongest statement that the position assigned to Rome by Diocletian was ultimately unacceptable.

3. MAXENTIUS AND THE CHRISTIANS[108]

For Maxentius' relations with the Christians of Rome we are reliant chiefly upon Eusebius and Lactantius. The latter's *De Mortibus*

---

[104] It could seat 10,000 spectators according to G. Ioppolo in Pisani-Sartorio and Calza, op. cit. (n. 101), 133–50. [105] Ibid. 121–9.

[106] *CIL* 6, 1138 = *ILS* 673: 'divo Romulo n(obilissimae) m(emoriae) v(iro) | co(n)-s(uli) or[d(inario) II] filio | d(omini) n(ostri) Maxenti[i] invict(i) | [ac perpet(ui)] aug(usto) nepoti | [di]vi [M]axim[i]ani sen(ioris) | [e]t divi [Maximiani iuni]oris ac.' Frazer, art. cit. (n. 102), 391 argues for a connection between the nearby Ara Maxima of Hercules and Maxentius' claims to represent the Herculian dynasty.

[107] For chronology of buildings: Rasch, op. cit. (n. 71), 40 f. Also Heres, op. cit. (n. 71), 105, 242–4, 312–14.

[108] See B. Kriegbaum, 'Die Religionspolitik des Kaisers Maxentius', *Archivum*

Persecutorum was written in Nicomedia between 313 and 315, after Lactantius had left Constantine's service and at a time when his admiration for the emperor was strong.[109] It is all the more significant, then, that he does not depict Maxentius as a persecutor.[110] Maxentius is undeniably pagan, in itself a serious fault, but his religiously inspired crime is merely a misplaced confidence in oracles which leads him to a fruitless consultation of the Sibylline books on the eve of his death.

With Eusebius, however, the portrayal of Maxentius is unrestrained. To tales of cruelty and lust are added details of witchcraft and human sacrifice.[111] But the record, so clear to Eusebius after the death of Constantine, when he penned the *Vita Constantini*, was more complex when the *Ecclesiastical History* was being revised sometime before 316.[112] There were facts that even Eusebius could not suppress:

at the beginning [Maxentius] counterfeited our faith in order to please and fawn upon the Roman populace; and for this reason ordered his subjects to give over the persecution against the Christians; for he was feigning piety and endeavouring to appear favourable and very mild above his predecessors.[113]

Soon after his accession, Maxentius decided not to enforce the persecutory legislation of Diocletian and Galerius. So favourable to the Christian community were Maxentius' policies that a hostile tradition was able to assert that he was a 'false' Christian, although no other evidence points to a personal devotion to Christianity.[114]

There may not have been a bishop in the city to whom the new policy could be announced. As we saw, internal divisions within the Christian community had left the episcopal office vacant for a number

---

Historiae Pontificae, 30 (1992), 7–54; Cullhed, op. cit. (n. 2), 72–3; D. DeDecker, 'La Politique religieuse de Maxence', *Byzantion*, 38 (1968), 472–562; S. Pezzella, 'Massenzio e la politica religiosa di Costantino', *Studi e materiali di storia delle religioni*, 38 (1967), 434–50; H. von Schoenebeck, *Beiträge zur Religionspolitik des Maxentius und Konstantin*, Klio Beiheft, 43, 2nd edn., (Aalen: Scientia Verlag, 1962); L. Duchesne, 'Constantin et Maxence', *Nuovo Bullettino di Archeologia cristiana*, 19 (1913), 29–35.

[109] See Barnes, *CE*, 13–14. At 14: 'He may be regarded, therefore, as an independent observer whose earlier reception at the court of Constantine need not impair the value of his testimony.'

[110] Lact., *DMP* 18, 9; 26; 44, 1 and 8. Note the remark at 43, 1: 'One of the adversaries of God still survived—Maximin [Daia]' and this while Maxentius still lived.

[111] *HE* 8, 14, 1 ff.; 9, 9, 2; *VC* 1, 33–7.

[112] For dates of editions of the *HE*, see Barnes, *CE*, 148–50.

[113] *HE* 8, 14, 1: ἀρχόμενος μὲν τὴν καθ᾽ ἡμᾶς πίστιν.

[114] *Pace* the ingenious but ultimately unconvincing ideas of DeDecker, art. cit. (n. 108). See also the inconclusive discussion of the appearance of a cruciform motif on coins minted during Maxentius' reign in Aquileia: von Schoenebeck, op. cit. (n. 108), 7; King, art. cit. (n. 50), 58.

of years following the death of Marcellinus late in 303.[115] Maxentius' decison may actually have encouraged the Christians of Rome to elect a new bishop in Marcellus.

The tensions within the Christian community did not take long to re-emerge. They were centred on the fate of the *lapsi*, those Christians who had complied with the persecutory legislation of Diocletian and Galerius. It is clear from *elogia* set up by Damasus (bishop of Rome 366–84) at the graves of Marcellus and his successor Eusebius, that violence broke out within the Christian church.[116] Damasus, presumably aware of the Constantinian version of Maxentius' reign, depicts the latter as a 'tyrant', but significantly makes no explicit suggestion that Maxentius was a persecutor. It is clear, in fact, that the exiles of Marcellus and Eusebius, ordered by Maxentius, were decreed with a view to preserving public order rather than attacking the Christian community.[117]

The actual conditions for government deteriorated as Maxentius' reign progressed. Security alerts were compounded by food shortages and fiscal emergencies. In these circumstances it seems strikingly significant that Maxentius should have decided formally in 311 to overturn the legislation hostile to the Christians.[118] Constantine's court propagandists brushed over the truth, but African Christians, more remote from the same court, remembered where responsibility lay for ending persecution formally at Rome:

The storm of persecution was over and finished; by God's command Maxentius sent a remission and liberty was restored to the Christians.[119]

[115] *LP*, i. 162. See Corcoran, *Empire*, 144, 185 discussing Optatus 1, 17 for Maxentius' possible involvement in disputes centring on Mensurius, bishop of Carthage, apparently before the restitution of property to the Christian church. *Pace* Corcoran, it is more likely that Maxentius really was tolerant than that the chronology is mistaken.

[116] See A. Ferrua, *Epigrammata Damasiana*, Sussidi allo studio delle antichità cristiane, 2 (Vatican City: Pontificio Istituto di archeologia cristiana, 1942), no. 40 (Marcellus): 'Veridicus rector labsos quia crimina flere | Praedixit, miseris fuit omnib. hostis amarus. | Hinc furor hinc odium sequitur, discordia, lites, | Seditio, caedes, solvuntur foedera pacis.| Crimen ob alterius Christum qui in pace negavit, | Finibus expulsis patriae est feritate tyranni.| Haec breviter Damasus voluit conperta referre,| Marcelli ut populus meritum cognoscere possit.' And no. 18 (Eusebius): 'Damasus episcopus fecit | Heraclius vetuit labsos peccata dolere | Eusebius miseros docuit sua crimina flere. | Scinditur in partes populus gliscente furore. | Seditio caedes bellum discordia lites | Extemplo pariter pulsi feritate tyranni | Integra cum rector servaret foedera pacis. | Pertulit exilium domino sub iudice laetus | Litore Trinacrio mundum vitamq. reliquit. | Eusebio episcopo et martyri.'

[117] The fanciful stories of persecution by Maxentius in the *vita Marcelli* (*LP*, i. 164) are without historical credibility.

[118] For Galerius' 'palinode': Lact., *DMP* 33, 11–35, 1; Eus., *HE* 8, 16, 1; 8, 17, 1–11. Corcoran, *Empire*, 186–7.

[119] Optatus Milevis I, 18: 'Tempestas persecutionis peracta et definita est. Jubente

4. THE END

At Rome, the security of Maxentius' position began to crumble. The main reason for his usurpation had been negative: the inhabitants of Rome had sought to resist the imposition of taxation on Rome. But the military successes won by Maxentius over Severus and Galerius had created a large army, since he had really defeated both by buying off their troops. This military establishment required maintenance. Additionally, the building programme through which Maxentius had resuscitated the centre of the city had cost a fortune. In these circumstances, Maxentius felt impelled to impose a tax in gold on the citizens of Rome. They paid up, but they did so with reluctance.[120]

The misgivings which these developments created were further strengthened by the effect of the secession of Africa from Maxentius' dominions in 308.[121] Africa was the main source of corn for Rome and the resultant food shortages precipitated riots in the city. Maxentius turned to the praetorian guard and we hear of 6,000 fatalities in the ensuing violence.[122] Although the corn supply was presently restored, relations between Maxentius and the population were undermined. Eusebian tales of Maxentius' behaviour towards senators and their wives may reflect his genuine unpopularity if not his actual crimes.[123]

In the summer of 311, Maxentius declared war on Constantine, vowing to avenge himself for the death of his father. The declaration of war was, of course, a pretext. Faced with a vacillating population at home he attempted to strike out and gain success against his nearest

Deo, indulgentiam mittente Maxentio, Christianis libertas est restituta.' See Corcoran, *Empire*, 144–5; Millar, *ERW*, 577–8. The relationship between Maxentius' decision and the toleration edict of Galerius is unknown. Cf. Aug., *Brevic. coll.* 3, 18, 34: 'illi [Donatistae] gesta alia recitarunt, in quibus legebatur Miltiades misisse diaconos cum litteris Maxenti imperatoris et litteris praefecti praetorio ad praefectum urbis, ut ea reciperent, quae tempore persecutionis ablata memoratus imperator Christianis iusserat reddi'; *c. part. Donati p. gest.* 13, 17: 'et [Donatistae] recitarunt etiam alia gesta, ubi legebatur Miltiadem misisse diaconos cum litteris Maxenti imperatoris et praefecti praetorio ad praefectum urbis, ut reciperent loca, quae fuerant a Christianis tempore persecutionis ablata.'

[120] Vict. *De Caes.* 40, 24. Cf. *Chron. of 354*: 'Romanis omnibus aurum indixit et dederunt'. Could *CIL* 6, 37118 be connected with the special tax? See Barnes, *NE*, 120–1. For Maxentius as 'spoliator templorum': *Pan. Lat.* 12 (9), 4, 4.

[121] See Barnes, *NE*, 14 for discussion of the date.

[122] *Chron. of 354* says citizens killed a Moesian soldier and sparked off the violence. Cf. Zos. 2, 13 who says the episode took place after fire damaged the temple of Fortune and a soldier uttered blasphemies. Maxentius credited with ending the violence.

[123] Eus., *HE* 8, 14, 2–5. See Barnes *NE*, 116 for possible connection with the resignation of Junius Flavianus (Feb. 312).

rival.[124] Maximian's memory enjoyed an unlikely renaissance for a short time. Coins minted by Maxentius made reference to his apotheosis and Constantine, who had concealed the real details of the death of Maximian, now tore down all images of him and erased all references in inscriptions.[125]

While Maxentius took up positions with his army near Verona, anticipating an attack from the north-east, Constantine suddenly attacked from the north-west.[126] Constantine's daring made a deep impression on those who followed him. Many believed that he had enjoyed some supernatural guarantee which had given him extraordinary confidence.[127] Because when he began to plan his attack, the soothsayers accompanying the army told him to hold off as unfavourable omens had been detected in the sacrifices.[128] Undeterred, Constantine pressed forward, winning skirmishes with Maxentian forces and turning the loyalty of towns in northern Italy. A crucial victory at Verona delivered the whole region to him and left the road to Rome wide open.

Maxentius retired to his capital. He had twice before resisted attempts to capture Rome. But the popular support which he had enjoyed at the time when Severus and then Galerius had been defeated had by now long gone. His hold on Rome may have become more repressive, affording Constantine's apologists the opportunity to tell dramatic tales. At games held on 27 October to commemorate his accession to power, the notoriously free-speaking populace of Rome declared that Constantine could not be beaten.[129] Maxentius, no longer confident that the city was solidly behind him, determined to engage Constantine outside Rome and led his forces northwards along the Via Flaminia on the morning of 28 October 312.[130] It was exactly six years since he had declared himself to be emperor. A story was later told by Lactantius that Maxentius consulted the Sibylline books.[131] The texts foretold the destruction of a great enemy of Rome. The literary motif is common enough, but the faith of Maxentius in the old cults of the city lends the account a distinct plausibility.

[124] Lact., *DMP* 43, 4. See Kuhoff, art. cit. (n. 35), 138 ff.

[125] Maximian's consecration: *CIL* 9, 4516 = *ILS* 647; *CIL* 10, 5805. Coins: *RIC* 6, 382, no. 243 f. and 250 f.; 404 nos. 24–6.

[126] For diplomatic and strategic implications: Maxentius expecting an attack from Licinius?, see Barnes, *CE*, 41.

[127] For a sane discussion, see T. D. Barnes, 'The Conversion of Constantine', *Classical Views*, *Échos du Monde classique*, 4 (1985), 371–91.

[128] *Pan. Lat.* 12 (9), 2, 5.

[129] Lact., *DMP* 44, 7. Kuhoff, art. cit. (n. 35), 150–1 more sceptical.

[130] See ibid. 138 ff.

[131] *DMP* 44, 8. Cf. Herodotus 1, 53, 3 (Croesus and Delphi).

When Maxentius arrived at the Saxa Rubra, he was confronted by an army whose soldiers are reported to have daubed a distinctive Christian symbol on their shields.

The battle itself was brief. Maxentius and his forces were swiftly pushed back towards Rome. At some point Maxentius summoned his mounted lifeguard, the *equites singulares*, and began a headlong retreat. The Milvian Bridge bearing the Via Flaminia into Rome had been cut as a defensive measure but a temporary escape route had been provided nearby in the form of a bridge of boats. As Maxentius and his horsemen crossed, the pontoons split apart, spilling men and horses into the water. Borne down by their armour, Maxentius and dozens of his companions were drowned in the Tiber.[132]

CONCLUSION

Maxentius, like Constantine, was a man who stood against some of the most powerful trends of his age. He rejected the tetrarchic system of government; he was an unenthusiastic persecutor of Christians; and he attempted to revive the city of Rome as the imperial capital.

The latter he achieved by means of an extensive programme of public building concentrated on the centre of the city and incorporating some of the most advanced and impressive building techniques ever employed at Rome. Maxentius' buildings resuscitated the Forum, augmented its grandeur considerably, and surpassed the scale of tetrarchic work in the city centre.

Maxentius' residence in the city for almost the whole duration of his reign was a presence of enormous significance, reversing as it did the developments of the third century which had compelled emperors to absent themselves from the city for long periods. His villa-circus-mausoleum complex on the Via Appia reveal his pretensions to be a great resident emperor and demonstrate also his commitment to the Roman community.

That community seems in the first instance at least to have been supportive of Maxentius' usurpation. It is probable, and hardly surprising, however, that the foundation of the emperor's power in the city was its military garrison, in particular the praetorian guard and the emperor's bodyguard, the *equites singulares*. When the population expressed its concern at Maxentius' goverment, the emperor seems to have fallen back naturally onto these military units for support. In

---

[132] *Pan. Lat.* 12 (9), 17, 1ff. Cf. 18, 1 for reference to Maxentius as a 'false Romulus' drowned by the Tiber. See also Lact., *DMP* 44, 9; Eus., *HE*, 9, 9, 4; Anonymus Valesianus, *Origo* 12.

these circumstances, it is highly significant that Maxentius chose not to enforce vigorously the legislation of Diocletian on the Christians. Indeed, Christians unaffected by Constantine's subsequent actions in the city credited Maxentius with liberating the community in the city.

These factors made Maxentius' short reign an impressive combination of military survival, architectural vision and flawed statecraft. They presented Constantine with awkward problems whose solutions formed the basis of the Constantinian achievement in the city of Rome.

3

Constantine and Rome:
The Context of Innovation

INTRODUCTION

Perhaps understandably, discussions of the date, nature, and implications of Constantine's 'conversion' have dominated the scholarship on the late empire.[1] The question, still open, is rightly regarded as one of the most important of the era. But it is important also to draw attention to the way in which Constantine's 'conversion' has tended to subordinate the subsequent events of the emperor's life. With regard to Constantine's relationship to the city of Rome, for example, the key activities of the emperor in the days, months, and years after the Milvian Bridge are very widely studied as evidence upon which to base assessments of Constantine's Christianity. Thus, from the problematic status of the temple of Juppiter Optimus Maximus, to the inscription on his famous arch beside the Colossus of Nero, the strength and character of the bond between Constantine and the Christian god is pursued. When it comes to the imperial church foundations, the Christianity of the emperor is again taken to be a most important factor, leading to the pervasive consensual view that Constantine avoided the 'pagan monumental centre' of the city and left it untouched as a conciliatory gesture to the pagan ruling élite.

In what follows, the actions of Constantine are restored more closely to their original context, a context where Constantine was not the liberator of the Christians but, like Severus before him, the avenging destroyer of an illegitimate regime. This is not, as we shall see, to deny him a genuine attachment, of whatever kind, to Christianity; it is to appreciate more fully the topographical impact of Christianity alongside the workings of imperial patronage and the dynamics of violent succession.

[1] Good sample bibliography in Th. Grünewald, *Constantinus Maximus Augustus* (Stuttgart: Franz Steiner, 1990), 283–97; Barnes, *CE*, 406–42. N. H. Baynes, *Constantine the Great and the Christian Church*, Proceedings of the British Academy, 15 (Oxford: Oxford University Press, 1929) is still outstanding on the earlier work.

I. CONSTANTINE AND THE CENTRE OF ROME:
OCTOBER 312

One of the commonest assessments of the impact of Constantine in the centre of the city is based not upon what he did do there but what he did not. An eminent scholarly tradition, stretching back from Richard Krautheimer to Charles Piétri, Andreas Alföldi, and the classic views of H. von Schoenebeck, maintains that Constantine decided not to erect Christian buildings in the centre of the city because he was anxious not to upset the pagan majority in Rome.[2] But this theory is clearly prescriptive; it has decided upon the nature of Constantine's Christianity a priori and assumes that a confident Christian emperor *should* have constructed a Christian church in the monumental centre. Ultimately, rather than puzzling over what modern scholars think Constantine ought to have done, it is more profitable to look at what he *did* do and attempt to appreciate him, as closely as possible, on his own terms.

Two features are outstanding in Constantine's relationship with the centre of Rome: his use of ceremony and his architectural impact. Both were designed to exhibit the imperial person publicly. These two elements were intertwined and for the purposes of the discussion which follows it will be necessary to prise apart for analysis themes whose impact can only be fully understood in combination.

On 29 October 312, the great procession of Constantine's army made its way from the north of the city via the Campus Martius to the Forum Romanum. A victorious army took possession of the city it had come to recover and the conquering general, as an emperor, staged an *adventus* that was to be remembered long after his death.[3] It is no accident that Constantine should have made his way to the heart of the city, since the Forum was both a natural topographical and a traditional ceremonial stage.[4] The victory parade itself was carefully managed to achieve the

[2] See e.g. L. Reekmans, 'L'implantation monumentale chrétienne dans le paysage urbain de Rome de 300 à 850', in *Actes du IXe Congrès internationale d'archéologie chrétienne*, Collection de l'École française de Rome, 123/Studi di Antichità cristiana, 41 (Rome: École française de Rome, 1989), 861–915, at 866; Krautheimer, *Rome*, ch. 1; Piétri, *RC*, i. 8; S. S. Alexander, 'Studies in Constantinian Church Architecture', *RAC*, 47 (1971), 261–330, at 283; R. Vielliard, *Recherches sur les origines de la Rome chrétienne*, 2nd edn. (Rome: Storia e letteratura, 1959), 59; A. Alföldi, *The Conversion of Constantine and Pagan Rome*, 2nd edn. (Oxford: Clarendon Press, 1969), 50; H. von Schoenebeck, *Beiträge zur Religionspolitik des Maxentius und Constantin*, Klio Beiheft, 43, 2nd edn. (Aalen: Scientia Verlag, 1962), 88.

[3] A. Degrassi (ed.), *Inscriptiones Italiae*, 13.2 (Rome: Istituto Poligrafico dello Stato, 1963), 257.

[4] See A. Chastagnol, 'Aspects concrets et cadre topographique des fêtes décennales des empereurs à Rome', in *L'Urbs: Espace urbain et histoire (1er siècle av. J.-C.–IIIe*

optimum visual impact. The body of Maxentius had been recovered from the banks of the Tiber and his severed head preceded the procession.[5] Constantine, seated in a chariot, followed behind his troops.[6] The senate and the people of Rome are reported to have flocked out to line his route.[7] Once in the centre of the city, Constantine hurried to take possession of the Palatine, where he stayed during his time at Rome.[8] The final acts associated with the emperor's arrival were all attempts on the part of Constantine to make himself known to different sections of the population of the city: he gave gladiatorial games and spectacles in the Circus Maximus; he made a formal speech to the Senate in the Curia; an *adlocutio* was delivered from the Rostra and, finally, *congiaria* were distributed.[9] It is obvious enough that Constantine was using the platform provided by the monumental centre in the most traditional of ways, but the absence of any reference in our sources to a visit to the Temple of Juppiter Optimus Maximus has been interpreted as proof that no such visit took place and that the emperor delivered an insult to the non-Christian community almost from the first moment of contact between the two.

Alföldi argued that Constantine would have delivered too great an insult to the pagan population of Rome in 312 if he had refused to visit the temple of Juppiter and for this reason believed that Constantine had sacrificed.[10] Straub disagreed, however, believing that Constantine had refused to offer sacrifice in 312 and instead had hurried off to the Palatine with an indiscreet haste which the panegyrist of 313 noted.[11] Paschoud offered a compromise: Constantine had 'assisted' in the celebrations of 312 but refused outright to mount the Capitol in 315

[5] *Pan. Lat.* 12 (9), 18, 3; cf. 4 (10), 31, 5 and Zosimus *NH* 2, 17, 1. The head was sent to Africa: *Pan. Lat.* 4 (10), 32, 6 'deforme prodigium'. For thanks offered to the Tiber: *Pan. Lat.* 12 (9), 18, 1. See A. Fraschetti, 'Costantino e l'abbandono del Campidoglio', in A. Giardina, (ed.), *Società romana e impero tardoantico 2. Roma: Politica, economia, paesaggio urbano* (Rome: Laterza, 1986), 59–98, at n. 5 for the abuse of corpses of emperors.

[6] *Pan. Lat.* 12 (9), 18, 3; cf. 4 (10), 31, 4; H. P. L'Orange and A. von Gerkan, *Der Spätantike Bildschmuck des Konstantinsbogens*, Studien zur Spätantiken Kunstgeschichte, 10 (Berlin: De Gruyter, 1939), 72–8; M. McCormick, *Eternal Victory* (Cambridge: Cambridge University Press, 1986), 86.

[7] *Pan. Lat.* 12 (9), 19, 1; 4 (10), 30, 4–5; 31, 1. Cf. Eusebius, *VC* 1, 39; *HE* 9, 9, 9.

[8] *Pan. Lat.* 12 (9), 19, 3.

[9] Games: *Pan. Lat.* 12 (9), 19, 6; speech in Curia: 12 (9), 20, 1; *adlocutio*: L'Orange and von Gerkan, op. cit. (n. 6), 80–9; *congiaria*: ibid. 89–102.

[10] Alföldi, op. cit. (n. 2), 61–2.

[11] *Pan. Lat.* 12 (9), 19, 3. See J. Straub, 'Konstantins Verzicht auf den Gang zum Kapitol', *Historia*, 4 (1955), 297 ff.

and 326.[12] Fraschetti has recently offered the ingenious theory that Constantine legitimized his seizure of the city in October 312 by ascending the Capitol but within a year the details of that episode had been buried in silence.[13]

If the procession which took place on 29 October 312 was part of a *triumphus*, then the climax to the ceremony ought to have been the depositing of the triumphing general's laurel wreath in the Temple of Juppiter Optimus Maximus on the Capitol.[14] The anonymous Gallic panegyrist of 313 makes no reference to any such act and nor do our other contemporary sources for this period: the Arch of Constantine, Lactantius, and Eusebius. It is worth considering, however, what kind of sources we actually possess for the entry of Constantine before going on to assess the significance of the absence of reference to a sacrifice on the Capitol. In the cases of the panegyrist at Trier and the Arch of Constantine in Rome we can say with certainty that the emperor himself was to be the most important listener and beholder. For their part, Lactantius and Eusebius were upholders of an uncompromising Christianity. Lactantius was violently hostile to the old cults and Eusebius was quite capable of glossing or passing over inconvenient details. None of these sources was therefore designed to record all that Constantine did, only to record what their respective creators thought should be remembered. This kind of source is unable therefore to prove that Constantine did not sacrifice to Juppiter on the Capitol.

On the question of whether the procession of 312 was a triumph or not, the evidence of the panegyrics is inconclusive. Sabina MacCormack has demonstrated that by this date, connotations of triumph and victory had become an integral part of the *adventus* ceremony.[15] The indications that Constantine's entry in 312 was a triumph are confined to vague references in the panegyrics of 313 and 321: 'ioci triumphales' or 'nulli tam laeti triumphi . . . Quis triumphus illustrior?'[16] The language used to describe the *adventus* was subject to the same trends as the ceremony itself and we therefore cannot confidently accept the use of triumphal terminology as evidence that an actual triumph took place.

[12] F. Paschoud, 'Zosime 2, 29 et la version païenne de la conversion de Constantin', in id., *Cinq études sur Zosime* (Paris: Belles lettres, 1975), 24–62.

[13] Fraschetti, art. cit. (n. 5).

[14] See E. Künzl, *Der römische Triumph* (Munich: C. H. Beck, 1988), ch. 6, 'Triumphator und Gott'. Also, W. Kuhoff, 'Ein Mythos in der römischen Geschichte: Der Sieg Konstantins des Grossen über Maxentius vor den Toren Roms am 28. Oktober 312 n. Chr.', *Chiron*, 21 (1991), 127–74, at 165 n. 101.

[15] S. MacCormack, *Art and Ceremony in Late Antiquity* (Berkeley: University of California Press, 1981), 34 ff.

[16] *Pan. Lat.* 12 (9), 18, 3; 4 (10), 30, 5. Cf. 4 (10), 32, 1. See Nixon and Rodgers, 322 n. 116.

The Arch of Constantine, since its selection was of visual material, merits special treatment. L'Orange has pointed out that the frieze on the eastern end of the Arch of Constantine shows an *adventus*, not a triumph. The elements of the triumph are well known, the *triumphator* stood in the *currus triumphalis* (Constantine sits in an ordinary *currus*), the procession was preceded by lictors and senators (both are absent), animals for sacrifice, and spoils are also usual (but not evident here).[17] The Calendar of Philocalus, dating from the middle of the century, recorded the day of 29 October as an *adventus*.[18]

Quite apart from the absence of firm evidence in the source material, it is worth asking whether it would have been possible for Constantine to hold a triumph in 312. The essential element in organizing a triumph was surely time. On 29 October 312 Constantine had won a major battle only forty-eight hours earlier. Even after he had entered the city, time was short. He entered Rome at the end of October and by mid-January he was in Milan for a summit with Licinius.[19] He had therefore spent only two months in the city. In that brief period he was expected to cancel Maxentius' acts, oversee the transfer of Maxentius' property to his own family, and ensure the smooth transition of power.[20]

The procession of 29 October 312 was not, therefore, a triumph but a military victory parade coupled with an imperial *adventus*.[21] The Arch of Constantine commemorated a triumph held in 315 which itself celebrated a victory achieved in 312. The victorious *adventus* of Constantine was recorded on the friezes sculpted around that date. The creators of these friezes and the makers of the arch knew, however, that a visit by Constantine to the Capitol was not to be depicted, either because it had not taken place or because it had become clear that Constantine did not want it displayed. But we need not think that the builders of the arch were troubled by either possibility. As we shall see, they did portray the emperor and his father sacrificing normally elsewhere on the structure.

Constantine may or may not have visited the Capitol and sacrificed there. If he did sacrifice, he did so in some other capacity than that of *triumphator*.[22] It is to be remembered that Constantine was still

---

[17] L'Orange and von Gerkan, op. cit. (n. 6), 77 n. 2; see Künzle, op. cit. (n. 14), ch. 5, 'Organisation'.

[18] See n. 3.   [19] Seeck, *Regesten*, 160.

[20] Cancellation of Maxentius' acts: *CT* 15, 14, 3; 4. Seeck, *Regesten*, 160 dates these laws to January 313. Death penalty for informers: *CT* 10, 10, 2 (1 Dec. 312 according to Seeck, *Regesten*, 160, an indication that informing was a problem as opportunists sought to benefit under the new regime?). See Corcoran, *Empire*, 153–4, 188–9.

[21] Cf. the Arch of Galerius at Salonica: K. F. Kinch, *L'Arc de triomphe de Salonique* (1890), pl. 6.

[22] Sacrifice at the Capitol upon entering the city was a powerful tradition, but there

Pontifex Maximus; that he did not object to being associated on coins and on his arch with non-Christian deities and he did not conceive a campaign of destruction against paganism.[23] If a sacrifice on the Capitol did take place, the Christian sources omitted to mention it for reasons which can hardly surprise us. On the other hand, it is difficult to accept MacCormack's suggestion that the Gallic panegyrist of 313 was badly informed on Constantine's actions in Rome.[24] Not only had Constantine spent a great deal of time in Gaul but Augustine's later testimony shows that panegyrists could have access to a number of informed sources, whether private citizens or members of the imperial court.[25] Fraschetti's suggestion that the sources, especially the panegyrist of 313, had exercised some kind of 'censura o autocensura' thus explains much.[26] It is a very different matter, however, to proceed from the editorial processes of the Gallic panegyrist to suggest that Constantine himself was embarrassed or otherwise uncomfortable about the circumstances of his entrance in 312. For this there is no compelling evidence in support and powerful arguments against.

However unsatisfactory the conclusion to the question of Constantine and the Capitol in 312, this particular controversy must not be allowed to obscure the significance which the centre of the city as Constantine found it had for his official entry into Rome. When the Palatine had been occupied and the important speeches made, the problem of the traces of the former master of the city could be addressed.

---

were examples of exceptions. Vespasian preferred to sacrifice to the *lares* in the Palatine: Josephus, *BJ* 7, 4, 1 (68–74). *SHA, Heliog.* 15, 7 reports the refusal of Elagabalus to ascend the Capitol though admittedly the tale may be a veiled late fourth-century attack on Constantine himself. See L. Cracco-Ruggini, 'Elagabalo, Costantino e i culti "Siriaci" nella *Historia Augusta*', in G. Bonamente and N. Duval (eds), *Historiae Augustae Colloquium MCMXC* (1991), 123–46. It may be worth noting that the oft-quoted passage *Pan. Lat.* 7 (6), 8, 7 of 307 (which Constantine may have heard) can be read chiefly as a reference to Maximian's 'triumphant' character and achievements rather than to any actual visit to the Capitol. It is worth reflecting how differently this latter passage might be interpreted if it had referred to Constantine!

[23] For the continuing importance of the function of the Pontifex Maximus, see below 187–8. Coins: M. R. Alföldi, 'Die Sol-Comes Münze vom Jahre 325: Neues zur Bekehrung Constantins', *Mullus: Festschrift Th. Klauser* (Münster: Aschendorff, 1964), 10–16; P. Bruun, 'Una permanenza del "Sol Invictus" di Costantino nell'arte cristiana', in G. Bonamente and F. Fusco (eds.), *Costantino il grande* (Macerata: Pubblicazioni della Facoltà di lettere e filosofia, 1992), i. 219–30; G. H. Halsberghe, *The Cult of Sol Invictus* (Leiden: Brill, 1972), 167–70. Paganism: J. Curran, 'Constantine and the Ancient Cults of Rome: The Legal Evidence', *Greece and Rome*, 43 (1996), 68–80.

[24] MacCormack, op. cit. (n. 15), 34.

[25] *Confessions* 6, 6.

[26] Fraschetti, art. cit. (n. 5), 63–9.

2. CONSTANTINE AND THE DESTRUCTION OF THE MEMORY OF MAXENTIUS IN THE CENTRE OF ROME

As with Severus, Constantine's victory heralded the advent of a new ruling dynasty. The memory of Maxentius, however, remained an embarrassment to the new regime. Constantine had links with Maxentius about which he could do little; prior to their final war he had reached a diplomatic and political arrangement with the dead emperor which had been sealed by marriage to Fausta, Maxentius' sister.[27] But since at least 310, Constantine had been establishing his independence from the tetrarchic scheme by asserting his descent from the obscure Claudius Gothicus.[28] He had also had Maximianus killed after the latter's treachery in 309. The monumental traces of Maxentius in Rome remained as a memorial to the six years which he had spent as emperor, an illegitimate position which Constantine could no longer concede. With the destruction of the traces of Maxentius in Rome, Constantine realized the extinction of the Herculian line. The apparent breadth of the attempts which Maxentius had made in manufacturing his special relationship with Rome were systematically replaced by new elements in the same idiom.

Constantine projected the liquidation of his rival's memory in a number of ways. After the military victory had been won at the Milvian Bridge, the remaining elements of Maxentius' military forces, apparently the strongest base of his power, were destroyed.[29] Constantine disbanded the praetorian guard and razed the camp of the *equites singulares* which had stood on the Caelian since the days of the Severans.[30] In addressing the problem, Constantine joined some distinguished predecessors and though his decisive and final solution was a calculated political gesture aimed at Maxentius' regime, there can be little doubt that he was aware that the disbanding of the guard also closed a troubled chapter in the history of social relations at Rome.

A comprehensive propaganda campaign then undermined the claims of Maxentius to be a legitimate *Augustus* and branded his reign as a period of unparalleled brutality. Traces of this assault upon the reputation of Maxentius can be seen in the contemporary source material which survives. The Trier panegyric and the *Origo Constantini* both questioned Maxentius' relationship with Maximianus Augustus. According to the latter source, on the day after the Battle of the

---

[27] *PLRE*, i. 325–6. Also, J. W. Drijvers, 'Flavia Maxima Fausta', *Historia*, 41 (1992), 500–6.

[28] See R. Syme, 'The Ancestry of Constantine', *Bonner-Historia-Augusta-Colloquium 1971*, Antiquitas Reihe 4. Beiträge zur Historia Augusta Forschung, 11 (1974), 237–53.

[29] Vict. *De Caes.*, 40, 25.   [30] See below, 96.

Milvian Bridge, Maxentius' mother (Eutropia) was questioned about her son's parentage and admitted that he was the son of a Syrian.[31] Maxentius became the *tyrannus* who had oppressed Rome and Constantine became the city's *liberator*.[32] In the panegyric delivered at Trier in 313, Maxentius was referred to as a 'falsum Romulum', an accusation which neatly embraced his promotion of an idealized Rome and his thwarted dynastic plans.[33] Fully a generation later, the perception of Maxentius as a tyrant had become enshrined in the state's official record of events. In the calendar of 354, 28 October was marked by the words 'evictio tyranni'.[34]

Constantine himself therefore became the *liberator* of the city. And although waiting more than twenty years before officially declaring Maxentius to have been a persecutor of Christians, Constantine became the saviour of the Christian community of Rome.[35] Eusebius' *Vita Constantini* was the most enthusiastic purveyor of the Constantinian version of events:

The whole body of the senate, and others of rank and distinction in the city, freed as it were, from the restraint of a prison, along with the whole Roman population . . . received him.[36]

In both the *Vita* and the *Ecclesiastical History*, Eusebius gave the episode a new interpretation when Constantine was compared to Moses, leading the People of Israel to safety while their enemies perished in the waters of the Red Sea.[37]

Eusebius further claims in both the *Vita* and the *Ecclesiastical History* that a statue was set up by Constantine in the most public place in Rome:

He, as one possessed of natural piety towards God, was by no means stirred by their shouts nor uplifted by their praises, for well he knew that his help was from God; and straightaway he gave orders that a memorial of the Saviour's Passion should be set up in the hand of his own statue; and indeed . . . they set

---

[31] Anonymus Valesianus, *Origo Constantini* 4, 12. Cf. *Pan. Lat.* 12 (9), 4, 4.

[32] Vict. *De Caes.*, 40, 24; Eusebius, *VC* 1, 39 cf. 41. See Grünewald, op. cit. (n. 1), 63 ff.

[33] *Pan. Lat.* 12 (9), 18, 1. Cf. the reference to the 'tyrant's generals' in Anonymus Valesianus, *Origo Constantini* 4, 12; Vict. *De Caes.*, 40, 23: 'in transgressu Tiberis interceptio est, tyrannidis anno sexto'. See the discussion of the Arch of Constantine below, 86 ff.

[34] Degrassi, op. cit. (n. 3), 257. 28 October was also Maxentius' *dies natalis*: *Pan. Lat.* 12 (9), 16, 2.

[35] J. Moreau, *De la mort des persécuteurs*, Sources chrétiennes, 39 (Éditions du Cerf, 1954), 19–20.

[36] *VC* I, 41. Cf. Constantius II's visit to Rome. See below, 192.

[37] *HE* 9, 9, 10–11; *VC* 1, 39. See MacCormack, op. cit. (n. 15), 37–8.

him in the most public place in Rome holding the Saviour's sign in his right hand.[38]

The statue held τὸ σωτήριον σημεῖον in its right hand. Henri Grégoire, in an article published in 1932, argued that the statue to which Eusebius referred had in its hand not a Christian cross, but a *vexillum*, a form of military standard made from a spear with a cross-bar on which regimental colours were suspended.[39] Grégoire demonstrated that earlier Christian sources had referred to the similarity between this symbol and the Christian cross.[40] The Christian monogram appeared late in the iconography of Constantine whereas the military element was explicit from 312 onwards. Thus the depiction of Constantine holding this military symbol was an unambiguous promotion of military power and political legitimacy.

A colossal statue of Constantine has been known in Rome since at least the fifteenth century and the depiction was certainly military in character. It originally stood in the Basilica of Maxentius and will be discussed below.[41] More important at this point is the existence of a much less well-known colossal right hand, almost the same size as the more famous hand (1.61 m compared with 1.66 m).[42] This hand was recovered near the Capitol and although it lacks an attachment for a sceptre, its similarity to the fragments of the statue of Constantine suggest that it was a slightly smaller version of the same sculpture.[43] This fact would corroborate the later fourth-century ecclesiastical historian Rufinus, writing for the Latin west in the 390s:

indeed straightaway when the senate as an honour erected *images* to him triumphing, it ordered the *vexillum* of the holy cross to be painted in his right hand.[44]

---

[38] *HE* 9, 9, 10–11. Cf. *VC* 1, 40 where the object is described as 'a lofty spear in the shape of a cross': . . . ὑψηλὸν δόρυ σταυροῦ σχήματι. See also Vict. *De Caes.* 40, 28: 'statuae locis quam celeberrimis, quarum plures ex auro aut argenteae sunt'. See Kuhoff, art. cit. (n. 14), 170–1.

[39] H. Grégoire, 'La statue de Constantin et la signe de la croix', *L'Antiquité classique*, 1 (1932), 135–43, at 138 ff.

[40] Among the sources cited: Justin Martyr, *Apologia* 1, 55; Minucius Felix, *Octavius* 29; Tertullian, *Apologia* 16, 6 and *Ad Nationes* 1, 12.

[41] See below, 82.

[42] H. Stuart-Jones, *Catalogue of the Palazzo dei Conservatori* (1912), 12; K. Fittschen and P. Zanker, *Katalog der römischen Porträts in den Capitolischen Museen und den anderen kommunalen Sammlungen der Stadt Rom* 1 (Mainz: von Zabern, 1985), 148.

[43] Ibid.

[44] *HE* 9, 9, 10–11: 'statim denique ubi imagines sibi ob honorem triumphanti senatus erexit, vexillum dominicae crucis in dextra sua iubet depingi.'

Rufinus, who had certainly visited Rome, states that more than one image was set up. Unsurprisingly, the destruction of Maxentius was followed by a *programmatic* promotion of Constantine through images. One symbol at least was peculiarly prominent in the composition of these images. Although we cannot be certain about the meaning of *vexillum* in Rufinus, we may recall the inscription accompanying the most prominent statue of Constantine in Rome, as recorded by Eusebius:

By this salutary sign, the true proof of bravery, I saved and delivered your city from the yoke of the tyrant; and moreover I freed and restored to their ancient fame and splendour both the Senate and the People of the Romans.[45]

If the Eusebian version is accepted as it stands, that the statue of Constantine held a cross, then it is clear that the emperor had placed a prominent expression of his Christianity in the centre of the city where, as the traditional view states, Constantine was hesitant about asserting his new religious disposition.[46] But Rufinus, who had probably *seen* the statue in Rome, made an important emendation to Eusebius' version of the inscription which accompanied the statue:

Under this singular banner which is the badge of true virtue, I restored the city of Rome, the senate and the Roman people, snatched away by the yoke of tyrannical despotism, to pristine liberty and nobility.[47]

The *signum* was not 'saving' but 'singular', a tribute to the remarkable soldierly qualities of the new emperor. But it may not be unreasonable to see as well a brutal military pun. Constantine's *signum singulare* had been hoisted high as a consequence of victory over a tyrant whose *singulares* had failed to save him.

Like his third-century and tetrarchic predecessors, Constantine looked to the monumental centre of the city as the appropriate area in which to concentrate the symbols of his political legitimacy. The Constantinian themes of military victory, deliverance, and deference to the Senate and People were certainly repeated on other monuments and were quickly absorbed into the honorific vocabulary of loyal senators.[48]

In the account of Constantine's relationship with Rome given by

[45] Ibid. 11.

[46] As argued, e.g. by F. Heim, *La Théologie de la victoire de Constantin à Théodose*, Théologie historique, 89 (Paris: Beauchesne, 1992), 41 ff. Also, Barnes, *CE*, 46; 308 n. 18.

[47] *HE* 9, 9, 10–11: 'in hoc singulari signo quod est verae virtutis insigne, urbem Romam senatumque et populum Romanum, iugo tyrannicae dominationis ereptam pristinae libertati nobilitatique restitui'. See Grünewald, op. cit. (n. 1), 70–1.

[48] *CIL* 6, 1140–6. See Grünewald, op. cit. (n. 1), 63 ff.

Aurelius Victor, a clear order of events is outlined: the victory of Constantine and the death of Maxentius are followed by the *adventus* of the victor, the dissolution of the praetorian guard, the rededication of the buildings of Maxentius, and then the state of affairs in the east where Licinius confronted Maximin Daia.[49] On this chronology, it is certain that the problem of monuments which still bore the tyrant's name was addressed very early in Constantine's reign and, on the strength of Aurelius Victor, one can believe that action was taken in the autumn and winter of 312–13.

Nazarius, who delivered his panegyric in 321, praised the work of Constantine in providing the city with new buildings: 'all the most celebrated things in the city gleam with new work'.[50] It is unclear whether Nazarius had in mind among the genuine buildings of Constantine the structures in the Forum area which came to bear his own name but were not built by him. What took place there was more than a *damnatio memoriae*. As discussed above, the buildings of Maxentius were undeniably grand. They were clearly the work of an emperor who had a strong sense of the city's past as well as a desire once again to make Rome a genuine imperial capital around the person of a resident emperor by reviving its monumental centre. It would have been quite unprecedented for a new emperor to tear down the buildings of his predecessor as a political gesture. Such an action might, in any case, have rebounded on Constantine leaving his actions open to interpretation as a punishment inflicted on the city for supporting Maxentius. Thus the best course of action was to use the grandeur of what remained standing as a testament to the clemency, power, and *romanitas* of the new emperor. Once Constantine's wishes became clear, the Senate obliged, dedicating first a golden statue in Constantine's honour to some unknown god and overseeing the dedication of a golden shield on behalf of Italy:[51]

In addition, all the monuments which Maxentius had constructed in magnificent manner, the temple of the city and the basilica, were dedicated by the senate to the meritorious services of Flavius.[52]

As Coarelli has pointed out, Aurelius Victor is the only source which stands in the way of the complete success of the Constantinian

[49] Vict., *De Caes.*, 40, 23 ff.

[50] *Pan. Lat.* 4 (10), 35, 4: 'Celeberrima quaeque urbis novis operibus enitescunt.'

[51] Ibid. 12 (9), 5, 4 with Nixon and Rodgers, 331 n. 157 for an inconclusive discussion of the identity of this god. For statues of gold and silver, see also Vict. *De Caes.*, 40, 28.

[52] Ibid. 26: 'Adhuc cuncta opera, quae [Maxentius] magnifice construxerat, Vrbis fanum atque basilicam, Flavii meritis patres sacravere' (trans. Bird).

propaganda. If it were not for Aurelius Victor, we might yet be identifying the Basilica of Maxentius as that of Constantine.[53] Already in the middle of the fourth century, the regionary catalogues were referring to the building as the 'Basilica Constantiniana'.[54]

The changes made to the layout of the great Basilica of Maxentius were carried out in the first quarter of the fourth century and may be assigned with some confidence to Constantine (figs. 6 and 7).[55] It is difficult, however, to determine the reason why all the revisions were made. Into the long side facing south-west and parallel to the Sacra Via, Constantine opened a second entrance.[56] The area above the new entrance may have given Constantine the opportunity to place a prominent inscription on the most visible side of the basilica declaring it to have been built or completed by him.[57] The modification may also have given the building a more impressive entrance since the Maxentian narthex on the south-east side was faced immediately by the bulk of the Temple of Venus and Roma. It might even be that the purpose in opening the second entrance was to allow easier access from the Palatine, but this is entirely speculative.

We can be more confident about the construction of a second apse in the north-east side of the *basilica* immediately opposite the new entrance on the Sacra Via. Some reconstructions of the building place a large statue of Constantine in a niche in this apse, but this is by no means certain.[58] Certainly, there is evidence of a functional role for this part of the building which was screened off from the rest by some kind of balustrade.[59] A platform which may well have been for the seats of *iudices* was placed around the apse.[60] The original floor decoration, which was still largely in place and recorded in 1830, showed a different layout in the floor panels in this apse, but it is possible that this layout dates to the time of Maxentius.[61]

In what has been taken to be the original apse of the building, located

[53] F. Coarelli, 'L'Urbs e il suburbio', in A. Giardina (ed.), *Società romana e impero tardoantico 1: Istituzioni, ceti, economie* (Rome: Laterza, 1986), 1–58, at 3.

[54] A. Nordh, *Libellus de Regionibus Vrbis Romae* (Lundae: Gleerup, 1949), 78, 100.

[55] *Pace* T. L. Heres, *Paries: A Proposal for a Dating Dystem of Late Antique Masonry: Structures in Rome and Ostia*, Studies in Classical Antiquity, 5 (Amsterdam: Rodopi, 1982), 111–12 who points out that there is little direct evidence; the circumstantial is powerful. Here I follow closely *Lexicon*, i. 170–3 (F. Coarelli); Coarelli, art. cit. (n. 53); A. Minoprio, 'A Restoration of the Basilica of Constantine', *PBSR*, 12 (1932), 1–18. Cf. H. Kähler, 'Konstantin 313', *JDAI*, 67 (1952), 1–30.

[56] Recently challenged, but far from conclusively, by *BC*, 91 (1986), 247–9. See above, 57–9.

[57] Minoprio, art. cit. (n. 55), 3–4 with the excellent pl. iii. Cf. the case of the 'temple of Romulus' below, 83.

[58] Minoprio, art. cit. (n. 55), pl. viii.

[59] See above, 58.

[60] Minoprio, art. cit. (n. 55), 14–16.

[61] Ibid. pl vii.

in the north-west side, Constantine placed a very large statue of himself. This statue was not a reworking of some older sculpture and H. Stuart-Jones said of it:

In no other statue which has come down to us did the art of the time reach the same grandeur . . . [it] was clearly a work by a fine and original artist who knew how to produce a colossal work not unworthy to stand in so magnificent a building as the *basilica*.[62]

It is probable that the original Basilica of Maxentius had had a large statue of that emperor as well. This was now replaced as Constantine located a colossal symbol of his own presence in this building and the centre of Rome. Coarelli has suggested that the Basilica of Maxentius was used for judicial purposes by the Urban Prefect and if we accept this theory then the presence both of the statue of Constantine and, originally, of his predecessor here is particularly significant.[63] The statue which Constantine put up was acrolithic, as suggested by the seven fragments found in the Basilica of Maxentius in 1486.[64] He was depicted seated, wreathed, and probably wearing a cuirass and *paludamentum*. A patina was applied to the flesh parts of the sculpture to give them the appearance of ivory, and the bronze of garments and armour was probably gilded. The right hand was extended and held a staff, and is widely regarded as being the statue which Eusebius of Caesarea described.[65] Given what we have seen of the themes which Constantine exploited from the first moment of contact with Rome, it is not at all surprising that this statue should have had such a martial appearance.

A short distance from the Basilica of Maxentius, Constantine's appropriation of the monuments of Maxentius continued with his intervention at the so-called 'Temple of Romulus'. According to Coarelli, who investigated the figures flanking the rotunda on contemporary coins, Maxentius had attempted to fuse the cult of the Penates with the memory of his own son.[66] He postulated two phases to the building of this rotunda.[67] The second involved a refacing of the

---

[62] Stuart-Jones, op. cit. (n. 42), 5–6; Coarelli, art. cit. (n. 53), 32 considers the possibility that the statue was a reworked image of Maxentius. This unlikely according to Fittschen and Zanker, op. cit. (n. 42), 149. For the possibility of a Hadrianic prototype, see C. Evers, 'Remarques sur l'iconographie de Constantin: à propos du remploi de portraits des "bons empereurs"', *MEFRA*, 103 (1991), 785–806.

[63] See above, 58.

[64] H. Buddensieg, 'Die Konstantinbasilika in einer Zeichnung Francescos di Giorgio und der Marmorkoloss Konstantins des Grossen', *Münchner Jahrb. d. bild. Kunst*, 13 (1962), 37–48.

[65] For two early plans of the building showing the base of the statue *in situ*, see Minoprio, art. cit. (n. 55), 12, fig. 10. For Eusebius, see 77–8 above.

[66] Coarelli, art. cit. (n. 53). See above, 58–9.

outside upon which an inscription was placed which was seen by at least two sixteenth-century antiquarians. The *Corpus Inscriptionum Latinarum* gives the conservative reading of Panvinio:

ab altera parte: *ab altera*:
CONSTANTIN   MAXIMO . . . ME . . .[68]

The recording of a dedication *to* Constantine on the walls of this 'temple' is problematic. In contrast, Ligorio's reading was more complete and was accompanied by a sketch of the inscription.[69] It reads:

Imp Caes Constantinus Maximus Triumph (*ab alio latere*)

Pius Felix Augustus.[70]

Thus, on this version of the inscription, Constantine restored or rededicated the building. Coarelli argues that the 'temple' was dedicated to Juppiter Stator, which appeared in both the *Curiosum* and the *Notitia* whereas the temple of Romulus did not.[71] It is not necessary to accept Coarelli *in toto* and in particular, Ligorio's reading is by no means as clear as Coarelli would like. But the parallel with Severus Alexander and Elagabalus demonstrates clearly that such a rededication was possible, and precedented. Regardless of the actual identity of the building, Constantine's intervention at the site is certain as was his desire to destroy the dynastic significance of the building for Maxentius.

Constantine did not confine his interest solely to the monuments of Maxentius; he also attempted to overshadow the impact of his successor by providing grand buildings of his own. Strictly speaking, Constantine's intervention at the Circus Maximus did not constitute a new undertaking. According to Aurelius Victor, the Circus Maximus was 'excultus mirifice' and Nazarius described the improvements in 321.[72] Humphrey has suggested that Constantine may have increased the seating capacity by adding a further tier of seats around the existing circus (fig. 9). Traces of pillars and buttresses of late Roman date have been understood to support this view.[73] Constantine thus took his place alongside the great builder-emperors of Rome and, like his tetrarchic

---

[67] Ibid. 10–12. See above, 59–60.   [68] *CIL* VI, 1147.
[69] For Ligorio's sketch, see G. B. deRossi in *BAC*, 5 (1867), 66, fig. 1.
[70] Cited in Coarelli, art. cit. (n. 53), 11.   [71] Ibid.
[72] Vict. *De Caes.*, 40, 27; cf. *Pan. Lat.* 4 (10), 35, 5.
[73] J. Humphrey, *Roman Circuses* (London: Batsford, 1981), 129 with fig. 44;
P. Ciancio Rossetto, 'Circo massimo', in *Roma archeologia nel centro 1: L'area archeologica centrale*, Lavori e studi di archeologia, 6 (Rome: De Luca, 1986), 213–23.

predecessors, he concentrated his attention on the major venues of public entertainment and recreation.

One of the most impressive of the Maxentian structures was the complex on the Via Appia which incorporated a villa, mausoleum, and circus. Frazer has demonstrated that the circus and its entertainments here were not part of a funerary cult but rather are to be seen as a conscious evocation of the tetrarchic *palatium* and circus based upon the relationship between the Palatine Hill and the Circus Maximus.[74] According to Ioppolo, the capacity of this circus was a good deal smaller, at ten thousand, than the Circus Maximus which approached a quarter of a million.[75] Humphrey maintains that the circus on the Via Appia had not been designed to compete with the Circus Maximus, but there can be little doubt that the prestige of the older circus suffered under Maxentius.[76] This was the first circus to be built in Rome since the so-called Circus Varianus in the Horti Variani under the Severans.[77] For the emperor to appear to require a circus, ostensibly for the populace but placed outside the the city which already contained an apparently adequate venue, was a situation unlike that in a tetrarchic capital on the frontier where the emperor clearly needed such a structure. Rome was well supplied with both the Circus Maximus and the Circus Flaminius.[78]

Though this site passed into Constantine's hands, and a statue recovered from the villa has been identified as a head of Claudius Gothicus or Constantius Chlorus, it is clear from his decision to improve the facilities at the Circus Maximus that the new emperor was making a deliberate gesture to the racegoing populace. Maxentius could be depicted as a remote and self-indulgent presence outside the walls. It ought not to be forgotten that the proximity of the mausoleum of the Maxentian dynasty to the Via Appia circus may also have played a role in Constantine's decision to suspend the use of this venue, but it is also significant that the mausoleum structure apparently remained unmolested.[79]

The work carried out by Constantine on the Circus Maximus was

[74] A. Frazer, 'The Iconography of the Emperor Maxentius' Buildings in Via Appia', *Art Bulletin*, 48 (1966), 385–92. Not a private circus: Humphrey, *Roman Circuses*, 586. See above 62–3.

[75] Ibid. 591–2.   [76] Ibid. 601.   [77] For the Circus Varianus, see above, 12.

[78] For the Circus Flaminius in the earlier period, see T. P. Wiseman, 'The Circus Flaminius', *PBSR*, 42 (1974), 3–26.

[79] G. Pisani Sartorio and R. Calza, *La villa di Massenzio sulla Via Appia: Il palazzo, le opere d'arte*, I Monumenti romani, 6 (Rome: Istituto di studi romani, 1976), 184–6 with pl. xvii for the bust recovered from the circus on the Via Appia and identified variously as Claudius Gothicus, Constantius Chlorus, and Maxentius himself. Coarelli in *Dintorni*, 36 argues that the circus was never used; *contra*, see the discussion of Humphrey, op. cit. (n. 73), 582–602.

not a genuinely original project but was certainly carried out with one eye on what Maxentius had done elsewhere. The same may be the case with the Baths of Constantine which were started very early in his reign, sometime before 315.[80] Maxentius too had built baths, but they were much smaller in scale and were located on the Palatine, suitable for the first emperor in a generation living permanently at Rome.[81] Maxentius did not, therefore, emulate the spirit which had prompted Maximianus and Diocletian to give the city the largest of all its bathing establishments in 305 or 306 on the junction between the Quirinal and Viminal Hills. To this spirit Constantine now returned. The new baths were considerably smaller than those of Diocletian and were located on a large artificially created terrace approximately one-fifth of the way between the Forum of Trajan and the Baths of Diocletian. A number of private dwellings were covered over by the platform upon which the new baths came to stand. The building was squeezed into the space between the Vicus Longus, Alta Semita, Clivus Salutis, and the Vicus Laci Fundani. There was no space for a large *peribolus* so a semicircular enclosure bounded the north side of the complex. The baths were oriented north–south and the main entrance was through the perimeter to the north. An impressive flight of steps on the western side, however, led down into the Campus Martius.[82] The closeness of one of the Campus Martius' more imposing monuments, the Temple of Serapis, is notable and the controversial Porticus Constantini has been placed along the street onto which the Temple of Serapis opened.[83] The attempt to divine the motivation behind the siting of the baths here is not made easier by the fact that almost nothing of them remains. The argument that this was the only space available should not be overstated. There were many other suitable sites which could be supplied with water.[84] Though little is known of the demographic

---

[80] Inge Nielsen, *Thermae et Balnea: The Architecture and Cultural History of Roman Public Baths*, 2nd edn. (Aarhus: Aarhus University Press, 1993), 56; S. Vilucchi, 'Terme di Costantino', in *Roma archeologia nel centro 1: L'area archeologica centrale*, Lavori e studi di archeologia, 6 (Rome: De Luca, 1986), 357–9; Nash, *Pictorial*, ii. 448–53.

[81] See above, 57.

[82] Vilucchi, art. cit. (n. 80); Platner and Ashby *Topographical Dictionary*, 525–6. For the appearance of Maxentian brickstamps, see M. Steinby, 'L'industria laterizia di Roma nel tardo impero', in A. Giardina (ed.), *Società romana e impero tardoantico 2. Roma: Politica, economia, paesaggio urbano* (Rome: Laterza, 1986), 99–164, at 142.

[83] G. Lugli, *I monumenti antichi di Roma e suburbio III: A traverso le regioni* (Rome: Bardi, 1938), 311; M. Santangelo, 'Il Quirinale nell'antichità classica', *APARA*, Serie 3, Memorie, 5 (1941), 203–10, esp. 206.

[84] Constantine was apparently involved in repairing the baths of Caracalla: see *AE* (1946), no. 82. See also his repair of the Aqua Virgo: *CIL* 6, 31564. For the Baths of Helena, see J. F. Merriman, 'The Empress Helena and the Aqua Augusta', *Archeologia*

patterns in this area of the city, it may be said that the complex was ideally suited to serve both the hills of the east and north-east of the city and the Campus Martius. It is interesting that Aurelius Victor should comment that these baths were 'opus ceteris haud multo dispar'.[85] Their functional compactness may have been designed to compare favourably with the Baths of Diocletian quite close by.

The most famous monumental statement of Constantine's personality and his systematic recasting of the character of Maxentius is the triumphal arch which rises close to the eastern end of the Forum (figs. 10 and 11).[86] Constantine made his second short visit to Rome in the summer of 315 and stayed in the city from 18 July until sometime in September.[87] His purpose in coming was to mark his *decennalia* and combine these celebrations with a triumph, which marked his defeat of Maxentius. The arch, which had probably been begun shortly after the *adventus* of 312, was finished in time for Constantine's second arrival and depicted scenes from his recent campaign in 312 as well as selected imperial virtues. It took its place confidently alongside the amphitheatre of Vespasian, the Meta Sudans, and the Colossus. Visitors coming into the city along the Via Appia saw Constantine's monument loom up against the background of Maxentius' temple to Venus and Roma and his great Basilica.

The arch was constructed almost completely from pieces taken from the monuments of earlier emperors and the only portions which are genuinely Constantinian are long friezes over the side arches and at the ends of the arch, the reliefs at the base of the columns, the two medallions of the arch ends and the spandrel reliefs.[88] Traditionally, rather much has been made of the provenance of the materials.[89] It is

---

Classica, 29 (1977), 436–46; S. Palladio, 'Le terme elenianae a Roma', *MEFRA*, 108 (1996), 855–74.

[85] Vict., *De Caes.*, 40, 27.

[86] See *Lexicon*, i. 86–91 s.v. 'Arcus Constantini' (A. Capodiferro), with full bibliography; L'Orange and von Gerkan, op. cit. (n. 6). Also the much underrated article by J. Ruysschaert, 'Essai d'interprétation synthétique de l'Arc de Constantin', *APARA*, Rendiconti, 35 (1962–3), 79–105.

[87] Degrassi, op. cit. (n. 3), 485. Cf. Eusebius, *VC* 1, 48.

[88] Nash, *Pictorial*, i. 104 still has the best photographs.

[89] For example P. Peirce, 'The Arch of Constantine: Propaganda and Ideology in Late Roman Art', *Art History*, 12 (1989), 387–418; see B. Brenk, 'Spolia from Constantine to Charlemagne', *DOP*, 41 (1987), 102–9. For two recent views of provenance, see P. Barceló, 'Una nuova interpretazione dell'arco di Costantino', in G. Bonamente, F. Fusco, (eds.), *Costantino il Grande* (Macerata: Pubblicazioni della Facoltà di lettere e filosofia, 1992), 105–14, who argues that materials from the Lateran camp of the *equites singulares* were used. Also R. Turcan, 'Les Tondi d'Hadrien sur l'arc de Constantin', *CRAI*, (1991), 53–80 who argues for the temple of Hercules at Hadrian's villa at Tibur.

doubtful that the architects deliberately sought out pieces from the monuments of emperors known to be 'good'. It is even more difficult to believe that the two most important viewers of the monument, Constantine himself and the populace of Rome, would have understood the significance of such a subtle composition. But one may confidently note that, like all monuments of the type, the Arch of Constantine was designed to complement the other arches of the centre, ranging its honorand alongside the greatest of emperors.

No other single building with which Constantine was involved encapsulates so completely the essence of his public personality and policy in the centre of Rome. Facing north and south on the front and back of the structure, an inscription dominated the attic of the arch:

To the Emperor Caesar Flavius Constantine, Maximus, Pius, Augustus, the Roman Senate and people dedicated this arch, decorated with his victories, because, at the prompting of the divinity, by the greatness of his mind, he with his army at one moment by a just victory avenged the state both on the tyrant and on all his faction. To the liberator of the city. To the establisher of peace.[90]

The scholarly anxiety to quantify the Christianity of Constantine by reading this inscription with some ideal Christian emperor in mind, has led to the minutest exegesis of the reference to the *divinitas* in the text. But like the language of the panegyrics from which it comes, this short text has defied modern interpretation. The phrase either refers to the Christian God, or it does not. First of all, there is the view that the dedicating party (the Senate and People of Rome) made no reference to the Christian God to whom Constantine attributed his victory. This was either because they were unaware of the precise identity of this god, or because they refused to use any other form of address for him.[91] Secondly, however, it has been suggested that what is being alluded to in this inscription is the special relationship which Constantine enjoyed with Sol in the early years of his reign and for which the coins of the period provide ample evidence.[92] What has often been overlooked is the fact that the inscription is but one element in a complex matrix of symbols.

---

[90] *CIL* VI, 1139 = *ILS* 694: 'Imp Caes Fl Constantino Maximo | P F Augusto S P Q R | Quod instinctu divinitatis mentis | Magnitudine cum exercitu suo | Tam de tyranno quam de omni eius | Factione uno tempore iustis | Rempublicam ultus est armis | Arcum triumphis insignem dicavit. (On sides of interior arch): liberatori urbis | fundatori quietis.' For what follows, Grünewald, op. cit. (n. 1), 63–92 is fundamental.

[91] See J. H. W. G. Liebeschuetz, *Continuity and Change in Roman Religion* (Oxford: Clarendon Press, 1979), 277–91, esp. 288.

[92] See Grünewald, op. cit. (n. 1), 46–61; M. R. Alföldi, art. cit. (n. 23); A. Alföldi, op. cit. (n. 2), ch. 5; Liebeschuetz, op. cit. (n. 91), 288 ff.; Lane Fox, *Pagans and Christians* 657–8.

The arch itself, for example, is located firmly in the symbolism and ceremonial of the third-century *decennalia*. On the north-facing side, the short phrases 'votis x/votis xx' are to be found over the side arches. In his article on the Arcus Novus of Diocletian, Chastagnol convincingly restored similar phrases as: 'vota [soluta] X vota [suscepta] XX'.[93] Thus the Constantinian Arch would appear to be referring to 'votis [solutis] X/votis [susceptis] XX'. These words were complemented by the phrases 'sic X/sic XX' on the same position on the south side of the arch.

The contrast between Constantine as liberator and Maxentius as tyrant, preserved in the literary accounts of 312, was carefully drawn here as well. Like Augustus and Severus, Constantine's usurpation culminated in ringing denunciations of a *factio* and the restitution of the *res publica*.[94] Two short inscriptions on the insides of the central arch proclaim Constantine as 'Liberator' and 'Fundator quietis'. Both inscriptions are placed over fragments of a Trajanic frieze which depict a battle scene and the victorious *imperator*, flanked by Victory and Mars.[95]

The six long friezes which are of Constantinian date show scenes from the events which led up to the entry into Rome as well as the emperor's actions afterwards. They are not, apparently, in chronological order. On the north side of the monument, facing the city, Constantine's civil virtues are depicted.[96] One frieze shows the emperor delivering an *adlocutio* from the Rostra and the other his *liberalitas* towards the populace; he is shown, seated, distributing coin to men filing past his throne. On the attic of the arch on the same side, four panels of Marcus Aurelius' reign show, from east to west, scenes of *adventus*, *profectio*, *liberalitas*, and the emperor dispensing justice.

In between the Constantinian friezes and the panels on the north side from the reign of Marcus Aurelius are four tondi of Hadrianic date. Originally these showed Hadrian himself and various attendants, but in each of the four tondi as used in the Arch of Constantine the heads have been recut by later craftsmen so that they resemble Constantine himself or his father, Constantius Chlorus.[97] Two of the

[93] Chastagnol, art. cit. (n. 4), 504.

[94] See Grünewald, op. cit. (n. 1), 63–77; B. Saylor Rodgers, 'The Metamorphosis of Constantine', *CQ*, 39 (1989), 233–46; Ch. Wirszubski, *Libertas as a Political Idea at Rome During the Late Republic and Early Principate* (Cambridge: Cambridge University Press, 1950), 103–6.   [95] *CIL* 6, 1139.

[96] MacCormack, op. cit. (n. 15), 37 f.

[97] L'Orange and von Gerkan, op. cit. (n. 6), 34–102 originally thought that the heads were those of Licinius. This is no longer widely believed. See R. Calza, 'Un problema di iconografia imperiale sull'arco di Costantino', *APARA*, Rendiconti, 32 (1960), 131–61; Ruysschaert, art. cit. (n. 86).

four tondi have the emperor (Constantine?) participating in hunting scenes (about to thrust his spear into a boar, standing over the carcass of a dead lion). The other two show sacrifice scenes, with Chlorus sacrificing first to Apollo and then to Hercules. All the imperial heads are nimbate.

The south side of the arch is altogether more military in theme.[98] The Constantinian friezes portray the siege of Verona and the battle of the Milvian Bridge, where Maxentius and his army are shown floundering in the waters of the Tiber. The Aurelianic panels show, from west to east, scenes which depict martial virtues: the selection of a king for an allied state (*rex datus*), the emperor's military *clementia*, *adlocutio* to the troops, and a *lustratio* of the army and its standards. As before, two of the Hadrianic tondi depict sacrifice scenes. Constantine sacrifices to Diana and possibly also to Silvanus (the head of the sacrificant cannot be restored). One of the other Hadrianic medallions shows Chlorus leading his horse through a city gate while the last of the four has him on horseback about to strike a running bear. The imperial heads on this side of the arch have been more damaged than those on the north side but von Gerkan and L'Orange understood them to have been recut like the others and there is no reason to doubt this.[99] None of the heads on the Hadrianic tondi on this side are nimbate.

On the ends of the arch, with much less space available, the chief adornments are a Constantinian frieze and a Constantinian medallion. These medallions are the only depictions of deities alone. Facing west is Luna in a *biga* declining into the sea. Immediately below this scene is a frieze showing the *profectio* of Constantine from Milan.[100] On the eastern end of the arch a medallion has Sol in a *quadriga*, rising from the sea, and below it the frieze shows the *adventus* of Constantine in 312.[101] Clearly a special significance attached itself to the two Constantinian medallions and the scenes on the friezes with which they were associated. MacCormack argues that they demonstrate Constantine's decision to break with the tetrarchic pantheon and align himself instead with the solar deities.[102]

The Arch of Constantine was a particularly complex and balanced piece of late antique propaganda. The most important message which it conveyed was that it commemorated Constantine as the conqueror of Maxentius, defined as a tyrant. Constantine was consequently the

---

[98] See n. 96.

[99] L'Orange and von Gerkan, op. cit. (n. 6).

[100] Ibid. 51–9. [101] Ibid. 72–8.

[102] MacCormack, op. cit. (n. 15), 36: 'a fundamental theme of the Tetrarchy—the association of the emperors with Hercules and Juppiter, with all that could result from this, in the interpretation, for instance, of victory—was dismissed . . . the juxtaposition with Sol transforms Constantine's entry into a cosmic event.'

liberator of Rome. Only one element in the whole structure was duplicated exactly: the inscription which announced these facts.

A very full picture was given of the successor to Maxentius through references to his military virtues: he was shown to be slow to go to war but wholehearted when he did so and, above all, successful. His peacetime qualities also found a place on the arch. He was pious, as the depictions of him sacrificing to a number of gods showed, but he was particularly close to Sol and Luna who had watched over his final campaign and his entry into the city. His clemency was promoted and his generosity specifically praised in a frieze of Constantinian date. The prominent presence of Constantine's father on the arch added the legitimacy of succession and emphasized Maxentius as a usurper.

After a careful analysis of the activities of Constantine in the centre of the city, it seems that the 'problem' of the missing Christian building in the centre of the city can be solved only with reference to the traditional role played by the city centre in imperial propaganda and ceremonial. The single-mindedness of Constantine in the monumental centre is apparent in the considerable trouble which he incurred in promoting his own person there. There is no reason to think that what was carried out here was in any way a second choice or compromise. Alongside the imposing monuments of previous emperors Constantine placed his own. In a sense, however, the expectations of Rome had been greatly raised by Maxentius. Constantine's military victory cost Maxentius his monumental legacy as well as his life. The latter's *romanitas* may or may not have been popular with the *populus* and it was certainly an anachronistic fantasy. But it was achieved with considerable impressiveness and Constantine was determined not to be upstaged.

3. CONSTANTINE'S CHRISTIAN BUILDINGS IN ROME

A vast scholarly literature has been written on the church buildings founded by Constantine in Rome and elsewhere.[103] The dimensions,

---

[103] See e.g. H. Brandenburg, 'Die konstantinischen Kirchen in Rom. Staatsragender Kult und Herrscherkult zwischen Tradition und Neuerung', in O. Brehm and K. Sascha (eds.), Μουσικὸς ἀνήρ: *Festschrift für Max Wegner zum 90. Geburtstag, Antiquitas*, R. 3, No. 32 (Bonn: Habelt, 1992), 27–58; id., *Roms frühchristliche Basiliken des 4. Jhs* (Munich: Heyne, 1979); P. Corby Finney, 'Early Christian Architecture: The Beginnings' (a review article), *HTR*, 81 (1988), 319–39; R. Krautheimer, *Early Christian and Byzantine Architecture*, 4th edn. (Harmondsworth: Penguin, 1986), 39–67; S. S. Alexander, 'Studies in Constantinian Church Architecture', *RAC*, 47 (1971), 281–330 and *RAC*, 49 (1973), 33–44; R. Krautheimer, 'The Constantinian Basilica', *DOP*, 21 (1967), 115–40; J. B. Ward-Perkins, 'Memoria, Martyr's Tomb and

stylistic elements, and architectural forerunners of Constantine's great churches have been extensively debated. But the study of Constantinian church architecture has tended to overshadow consideration of certain broader topographical questions. Here, two related themes will be treated: first, why Constantine built what he did build in Rome and second, how he came to choose the sites for his buildings. As we saw, in the monumental centre of the city, Constantine's public image revealed itself to the Roman public in a number of different ways. The same complex self-revelation was evident in the case of the Christian churches of Rome, with monuments of significant scale and impact being exploited to express Constantine's public relationship with the Christian community of the city.

The organization of building

We have very little information about how the great Constantinian Christian building projects were organized in Rome. We may attempt to infer some conclusions from what we know of practice in the Holy Land under him but a certain caution is necessary because the basilicas built there were of a very special nature and arrangements for them need not have been exactly paralleled in the west. The *Liber Pontificalis* alleges that in several cases Constantine constructed churches 'ex suggestu' of the successive bishops of Rome, Sylvester and Mark.[104] It is not difficult to imagine that when Constantine took the decision to erect Christian buildings he liaised with the bishop, since the latter would certainly have been aware of the significant points in the Christian topography of the city as well as the size of the congregations which would be served by the new basilicas. This was certainly the pattern in the east. In the case of the great basilica built in Tyre, which was finished under Licinius in 316 or 317, Eusebius makes it clear that the bishop of the city, Paulinus, was closely involved in the work.[105] After the eastern empire came into Constantine's hands in 324, he initiated a building programme which envisaged the monumentalization of various holy sites in and around Palestine. In 325 or 326 the basilica at Golgotha was begun.[106] Constantine wrote a letter on the necessary preparations to Makarios, then

Martyr's Church', *JTS*, 17 (1966), 20–38; R. Krautheimer, 'Constantine's Church Foundations', in *Atti VII congresso internazionale di archeologia cristiana* (Vatican City: Pontificio Istituto di archeologia cristiana, 1965), 237–55; id., 'Mensa-Coemeterium-Martyrium', *Cahiers Archéologiques*, 11 (1960), 15–40; J. B. Ward-Perkins, 'Constantine and the Christian Basilica', *PBSR*, 22 (1954), 69–90.

[104] Saint Peter's: *LP*, i. 176 n. ad loc. Cf. basilica at Ostia in same *vita*. Resources for basilica on Via Ardeatina in response to suggestion of bishop Marcus: *LP*, i. 202 (see below, 119). Later basilica in honour of Saint Agnes reported built at the request of 'Constantia': ibid., 207 and see 128–9 below. [105] *HE* 10, 4, 1.
[106] Krautheimer, op. cit. (n. 103), 60.

bishop of Jerusalem.[107] He informed the bishop that the deputy of the
Praetorian Prefect of the Orient and the governor of the province
(Palaestina) had been told to expect requests for building materials
from Makarios. As for columns and marbles, Makarios was to write to
Constantine himself for what he needed. The emperor even asked
Makarios whether he thought that a panelled ceiling would suit the
new structure. For labour and materials, the bishop should see the
aforementioned magistrates. Plans were mentioned in this letter but it
is not known who drew them up. The emperor's thoughts on the whole
subject are general and he seems not to have been intimately acquainted
with any plans or designs. At Golgotha, we know from later fourth-
century sources of the names of two individuals (Zenobius and the
presbyter Eustathius) who were closely connected with the work.[108]
They may have been architects but we cannot be certain.

As for the extent of the work undertaken by Constantine at Rome,
little evidence survives apart from the buildings themselves. The
confusion of brickstamps bearing the names of his predecessors used
in Constantine's buildings is probably an indication of the scale and
pace of construction in the city.[109]

In addition to the admittedly inconclusive evidence of brickstamps, a
pair of laws from the 330s relating to African craftsmen shows at least
that Constantine was anxious to encourage the study of architecture. In
the first, the emperor offered trainees a salary and they and their
parents were to be exempt from compulsory civic services.[110] The
second law released a long list of specified trades from certain forms of
taxation.[111] These professions included architects, makers of panelled
ceilings, carpenters, and mosaicists. Although these laws come from
Africa and there is no direct evidence that they related to the work at
Rome, it is nevertheless significant that the emperor should personally
foster the study of architecture in this way and that he should protect
the kind of artisans particularly involved with the building and
decoration of public monuments. It is even possible that labour was
imported into the city to carry out some of the work.

The available evidence shows, therefore, that Constantine took the
building of churches extremely seriously and offered every encouragement to the builders once an appropriate site had been chosen. As with
his non-Christian public architecture in the city, however, the actions

[107] Eusebius, *VC* 3, 30 ff.

[108] See discussion in Krautheimer, 'Constantine's Church Foundations', 237–55, at
240–41. See S. Gibson and J. E. Taylor, *Beneath the Church of the Holy Sepulchre,
Jerusalem: The Archaeology and Early History of Traditional Golgotha* (London:
Committee of the Palestine Exploration Fund, 1994).

[109] M. Steinby, art. cit. (n. 82), 142; Coarelli, art. cit. (n. 53), 2–3.

[110] *CT* 13, 4, 1.   [111] Ibid. 2 with Pharr's n. 9 on p. 390.

of Maxentius encouraged Constantine to demonstrate his superior patronage of the Christian cult.

The Lateran (fig. 12)

With the death of Maxentius, a vast amount of imperial property which had belonged to the defeated emperor passed to Constantine. In addition to the property which had belonged to Maxentius himself or his followers, Constantine found himself in possession of two major military camps which were now redundant, as the corps to which they had belonged had been shattered by the defeat at the Milvian Bridge.[112] Taking a decision which resolved finally the troubled relationship between these soldiers and the population of Rome, Constantine now dissolved the remaining elements of the units. Henceforth the city was to be policed only by the *cohortes urbanae*.[113] As we saw, Maxentius had enjoyed a particularly close relationship with the *equites singulares*, his lifeguard at the Milvian Bridge and thus a major prop to his political position in the years up to 312.[114] The camp of the *equites* lay on the Caelian Hill, close to the walls of Aurelian on the south side of the city.[115] Though the surviving units of horse guards, on grounds of their political unreliability, had been disbanded, the empty camp remained a potent symbol of one of the bases of Maxentian power.

In the same area of the city, certain other properties came into Constantine's hands: what remained of the old *Domus Lateranorum* which had been confiscated by the imperial *fiscus* as far back as the first century and the *Domus Faustae*, of which we hear in 313, may have been a property which was originally Fausta's in the days before her marriage to Constantine.[116] This imperial demesne was surrounded by a 'green belt' of aristocratic *domus*.[117]

[112] See above, 76.

[113] Vict. *De Caes.*, 40, 25: 'Quorum odio, praetoriae legiones ac subsidia factionibus aptiora quam urbi Romae sublata penitus, simul arma atque usu indumenti militaris.' See Chastagnol, *La Préfecture*, 64–66.

[114] See above, 52–3.

[115] Identified by E. Josi, 'Scoperte nella basilica costantiniana al Laterano', *RAC*, 11 (1934), 335–58. The latest firmly dated inscription belongs to AD 241 but see A. Ferrua, 'Nuove iscrizioni degli Equites Singulares', *Epigraphica*, 13 (1951), 96–141 nos 119 and 120 with pl. on p. 115. These two appear to be dedicated to Diocletian and Maximianus. For acceptance of the theory that the *equites* were in occupation up until Constantine, see M. P. Speidel, 'Maxentius and his *equites singulares* in the Battle of the Milvian Bridge', *Classical Antiquity*, 5 (1986), 253–62.

[116] Optatus Milevitanus, *De Donatistarum* 1, 23. For the Domus Faustae, see *Lexicon*, ii. 97–9 s.v. 'domus Faustae' (P. Liverani); E. Nash, 'Convenerunt in domum Faustae in Laterano. S. Optatus Milevitani 1, 23', *Römische Quartalschrift*, 71 (1976), 1–21.

[117] See *Lexicon*, i. 208–11 s.v. 'Caelius Mons' (G. Gianelli); V. Santa Maria Scrinari, *Il Laterano imperiale 1. Dalle aedes Laterani alla domus Faustae*, Monumenti di antichità

In the first few years of his reign and probably during the years 312–13, Constantine decided to build a Christian church on the Caelian Hill. It is now generally agreed that the basilica on the Caelian Hill was the first of Constantine's Christian buildings. The *Liber Pontificalis* lists the Lateran basilica (Basilica Constantiniana) first among the foundations of Constantine in its *vita Sylvestri*.[118] This may or may not be treated as an indication of when the structure rose. The author of the *Liber Pontificalis* was quite capable of tampering with evidence relating to Constantinian foundations to create an historical precedent for the Christian topography of Rome at a later date. The Lateran basilica was firmly understood to be the episcopal seat by the sixth century and its primacy at that later date could be well served by tracing it back to the time of Constantine. The evidence of the African Christian Optatus, on the other hand, has often often been presented as proof that the site on the Caelian was in Christian hands at an early date. Optatus recorded that the first papal synod to deal with the Donatists was held 'in domum Faustae, in Laterano' and was conducted by bishop Miltiades who died in January 314.[119] There is, however, no indication that Constantine had given this *domus* to the Christian community, or that it constituted the bishop's official residence at this time and it could well be that the estate was chosen only for its convenience. More reliable, as a means of dating the foundation of the basilica, is the list of endowments made by Constantine to the Caelian basilica for its upkeep.[120] All were in Italy and the western empire, controlled by Constantine after 312 and not supplemented by those in the east until after the defeat of Licinius in 324. Foundations after this date usually received at least some properties in the east. This evidence may stand therefore, as a *terminus ante quem*. Perhaps the most interesting of all the isolated scraps of relevant material is Cesare Barovio's sixteenth-century *Martyrologium Romanum* which probably derives from a twelfth-century *Descriptio Ecclesiae Lateranensis*.[121] The tradition preserved in the latter document was almost certainly ancient by that time. Barovio recorded:

Quinto idus Nov. Romae dedicatio basilicae Salvatoris.[122]

Church dedications in the fourth century took place on Sundays and the only days which suit are in November 312 and again in 318.

cristiana, 11 (Vatican City: Pontificio Istituto di archeologia cristiana, 1991); Krautheimer, *Corpus*, v. 24 ff.; Piétri, *RC*, i. 6 ff.; A. M. Colini, 'Storia e topografia del Celio nell'antichità', *APARA*, Serie 3, Memorie, 7 (1944), 319–78, at 344–59.

[118] *LP*, i. 172.   [119] See n. 116.

[120] See the judicious remarks of R. P. Davis, *The Book of Pontiffs (Liber Pontificalis)* (Liverpool: Liverpool University Press, 1989), pp. xix ff.

[121] Krautheimer, *Corpus* v. 10.   [122] Ibid.

Krautheimer has suggested that the earlier date might be a dedication of the church and the later the consecration.[123] He also points out that if the word *dedicatio* is to be understood in its strictest legal sense, it can refer only to the formal act of ceding land for the purposes of building the church.[124] Thus, the earlier date would seem the most likely. On this theory, the decision to build the church was taken on 9 November 312, barely a fortnight after the Battle of the Milvian Bridge and was intended as some kind of *ex-voto* foundation for Constantine's success there.

All that can be said with absolute confidence is that the Lateran basilica belongs in the early part of Constantine's reign. Piétri suggested the first ten or fifteen years and Bruun was rather more specific in proposing a date around 320 for the inception of the plan and building of the church.[125]

It was a building that was to serve the liturgical meetings of the Roman Christian community but at the same time it was to be a building that accorded with the new status of the Christians. The *persona* of Constantine was also to be projected by this work. As Piétri points out, the Lateran was 'un édifice pour la piété palatine'.[126] This church, one of Constantine's earliest undertakings in the city, must announce him as a serious builder on the scale of his tetrarchic predecessors. In the idiom of Roman public building, these requirements could only mean that the building should be very large. Thus, like Aurelian or Elagabalus, the resources of *Staatsarchitektur* were mobilized in the service of a deeply personal and public attachment to an oriental deity.[127]

Naturally a suitable site would need to be found. The Caelian was the best of the available areas because it, uniquely, allowed Constantine to make three crucial statements through the building. First, as imperial property, the site was ideal for Constantine to demonstrate his personal fostering of the project and thus his personal piety to the Christian God. Secondly, as the basilica was to be the episcopal seat, it was particularly appropriate that the Christian bishop would now find himself housed in one of the most respectable and wealthy districts in

---

[123] Ibid. 90; P. Testini, G. Cantino Wataghin, and L. Pani Ermini, 'La cattedrale in Italia', in *Actes du XIe Congrès international d'archéologie chrétienne 1986*, Collection de l'École Française de Rome 123/Studi di Antichità cristiana, 61) (Vatican City: Pontificio Istituto di archeologia cristiana, 1989), 5–17, at 16, where the dedication date is suggested as 9 Nov. 318.

[124] Krautheimer, *Corpus*, v. 90.

[125] Piétri, *RC*, i. 5; P. Bruun, 'The Church Triumphant *Intra Muros*', *Rivista ticinese di numismatica e antichità classiche*, 10 (1981), 353–74, at 372. Note his possible completion date is the Vicennalia of 326.

[126] Piétri, *RC*, i. 3.　　　　　　[127] See Brandenburg, art. cit. (n. 103), 34.

the city. Barely 600 metres north-west of the new basilica lay a major imperial property *intra muros*: the Sessorian Palace. The prestige given to the area by the residence of Helena Augusta should not be under-estimated. The strength of her affection for this palace was indicated by her conversion of one of its vast halls into a church designed to house the True Cross.[128] Finally, but no less important, given what we have seen in the centre of the city, this new structure was to obliterate the traces of Maxentius' horse guards. The desire to dispel the spectre of Maxentius necessitated that the building rise quickly and the sub-structures of the barrack blocks provided convenient foundations for the church. There is nothing to indicate that any previously venerated Christian shrine occupied the site or stood nearby. Monumentalizing a Christian *memoria* was not a factor in the construction of the basilica.

Constantine built the great church which has been known as the Basilica Constantiniana, Basilica Salvatoris, and finally as San Giovanni in Laterano.[129] From the inner façade to the apex of the apse, the structure measured 99.76 m. The interior of the basilica was divided longitudinally into four aisles and a nave. The inner aisles were 90.55 m long, the outer, 74.88. It had a central nave 18.73 m wide.[130] Almost the whole bulk of the building rose directly on top of the Praetorium and a number of the barrack blocks of the camp of the *equites singulares*. Though in ground plan the church appears to have been cross-shaped, it had no transept like that later developed at Saint Peter's basilica. This was because no martyr shrine was preserved in this portion of the church.[131]

The Lateran was probably the earliest Christian church which Constantine built *ex novo*. Though it combined architectural elements which were entirely traditional in public architecture, it was unpre-cedentedly large and was the first building in Rome to be specifically designed for the needs of the Christian community. It is absurd to think of this grand structure cowering in fear of the temples of the centre among the palaces of the wealthiest citizens of Rome. Its creation was in fact a grandiose gesture of the emperor's personal debt to the Christian God, his favour for the Christians of Rome and his ruthless obliteration of the hated *equites singulares*.

[128] For the Sessorianum, see D. Colli, 'Il Palazzo Sessoriano nell'area archeologica di S. Croce in Gerusalemme: Ultima sede imperiale a Roma?', *MEFRA*, 108 (1996), 771–815; Colini, art. cit. (n. 117); Coarelli, *Guida*, 238–42; Davis, op. cit. (n. 120), p. xxiii suggests a later date. For the mausoleum of Helena, see 102 below.

[129] Krautheimer, *Corpus*, v. 1–97; Piétri, *RC*, i. 4–11; Bruun, art. cit. (n. 125).

[130] Measurements from Krautheimer, *Corpus*, v. 72 ff.

[131] J. B. Ward-Perkins, 'Constantine and the Christian Basilica', *PBSR*, 22 (1954), 69–90, at 82–5.

The Via Appia (fig. 13)

Of Constantine's intervention at the Via Appia the *Liber Pontificalis* says nothing.[132] Indeed, until the major excavations which began at San Sebastiano in 1915, bishop Damasus of Rome (366–84) was believed to be the builder of the ancient basilica on the site, on the strength of a notice in his *vita* later in the *Liber Pontificalis*.[133]

At the beginning of the fourth century, the site which was later to be occupied by the basilica was crowded with remains of a villa and a street of mausolea housing the remains of tombs built by imperial freedmen of Trajanic date.[134] Within the complex a Christian *memoria* had been constructed, dedicated to the memories of the apostles Peter and Paul. The *memoria* consisted of a trapezoidal courtyard 23 m × 18 m at its broadest points. Two *loggie* flanked the courtyard which had a flight of steps leading down to a spring. In the western corner of the complex was a small niche, built into one of the walls, which seems to have contained some object of veneration.[135] Christians had been gathering at the site since the middle of the third century, when one of them scribbled a *graffito* with a consular date on the stucco of one of the walls of the enclosure.[136]

This courtyard was engulfed by a U-shaped basilica constructed at the site some time in the fourth century. The basilica was 73.4 m long from entrance to the back of the apse, and 30.5 m wide.[137] The many corpses discovered neatly laid into its floors reveal it to have been a large covered cemetery and therefore like a number of other fourth-century Christian basilicas in the city (Via Tiburtina, Labicana, Vatican, and Nomentana).[138] Unusually, the main bulk of the *memoria* of the apostles lay inside the nave. Though the obvious interpretation that the *memoria* was preserved suggests itself, it is in fact impossible to ascertain whether access to the third-century courtyard of the venerated shrine was still possible after the basilica was built. Krautheimer has even suggested a split-level arrangement because the problems of

[132] See Krautheimer, *Corpus*, iv. 99–147; Coarelli, *Dintorni*, 24–30; Piétri, *RC*, i. 40–6. [133] *LP*, i. 211.

[134] See L. de Santis and G. Biamonte, *Le catacombe di Roma* (Rome: Newton & Compton, 1997), 44 ff.; A. Ferrua, *La basilica e la catacomba di S. Sebastiano* (Vatican City: Pontificia commissione di archeologia sacra, 1990); E. Jastrzebowska, *Untersuchungen zum christ. Totenmahl aufgrund der Monumente des 3. und 4. Jhs unter der Basilika des Hl. Sebastian in Rom* (Frankfurt: P. D. Lang, 1981), 42 ff. with fig. 2.

[135] Krautheimer, *Corpus*, iv. 112 ff. [136] Ibid. 103. See above, 40.

[137] Ibid. 119; 140.

[138] Ibid. 133 with figures 117a, 117b, and 118 which give an excellent idea of how such basilicas were paved with tombs. For these basilicas, see W. N. Schumacher, 'Die konstantinischen Exedra-Basiliken', in J. G. Deckers, H. R. Seeliger, and G. Mietke (eds.), *Die Katakombe "Santi Marcellino e Pietro": Repertorium der Malereien* (Vatican

preserving the *memoria* within what can be known of the ancient building and its floor were so difficult.[139]

To the southern side of the lateral wall a grand mausoleum was attached. An apsed, rectangular structure, it was designed for an occupant of high status but seemingly never occupied by that person, since before the end of the fourth century two other mausolea had been placed within it.[140]

The site was certainly important because of its association with several prominent Christian martyrs. The *Feriale Ecclesiae Romanae* records that Sebastianus and the Apostle Peter were both commemorated 'in Catacumbas', though not on the same day.[141] Sebastian's crypt was probably on the site before the basilica was constructed.[142] The later fashion for *basilicae ad corpus* probably ensured that this Basilica Apostolorum lost its original name in favour of the one it now bears: San Sebastiano. Saint Sebastian's remains appear never to have left the site. Whether or not it was recognized at the time it was built, therefore, the Basilica Apostolorum was always a basilica *ad corpus*.

From comparison with other buildings, the layout of the basilica looks familiarly Constantinian. The history of the building is, however, most difficult to reconstruct and is fraught with controversy. In the opinion of Krautheimer, the basilica itself was a uniform construction and was set up in a comparatively short building period.[143] Among the many burial slabs used to cover the corpses of those interred in the basilica, a few are dated. The earliest datable inscription (349) comes from one of the small mausolea buildings abutting the basilica (the mausoleum of the Uranii).[144] Piétri, in the absence of more convincing evidence, took this inscription to be evidence for a construction date sometime in the second quarter of the fourth century. The strength of such evidence can easily be overestimated, however, as so few datable inscriptions survive. A threshold with a Constantinian monogram on it is no further help as it can be read as referring to Constantine, Constantine II, or Constantius II.[145]

City: Pontificio Istituto di archeologia cristiana, 1987), 132–86; F. Tolotti, 'Le basiliche cimeteriali con deambulatorio del suburbio romano: Questione ancora aperta', *RM*, 89 (1982), 153–211.

[139] Krautheimer, *Corpus*, iv. 142.

[140] Brandenburg, art. cit. (n. 103), 44 thought the intended occupant might have been Fausta. F. Tolotti, art. cit. (n. 138), 192 thought Helena.

[141] *MGH* 1, 71: 'III Kal. Iul. Petri in Catacumbas et Pauli Ostiense, Tusco et Basso coss.' [AD 258]. Sebastianus was remembered on the 13th day before the kalends of February. The translation theory most recently put by Brandenburg, art. cit. (n. 103), 43. See Salzman, *On Roman Time*, 46 and below, 130–1.

[142] Krautheimer, *Corpus*, iv. 142.   [143] Ibid. 145.

[144] *ICUR* (NS) 5, 13296.   [145] Krautheimer, *Corpus*, iv. 136.

The structural analysis of the building reveals its mysterious nature more clearly. Krautheimer originally thought that the details of the masonry were inconclusive.[146] A more recent and specialized study of imperial building techniques has suggested that the masonry used here shares the same characteristics as that used barely 100 metres from the church at the villa, mausoleum, and circus of Maxentius: the brickwork was in *opus vittatum* with wide mortar beds, pale mortar with large red granules, and heterogeneous particles.[147] Krautheimer himself drew attention to the unusual elliptical window arches which can still be seen in parts of the original walls remaining as part of the present church. The same elliptical plan was evident in the layout of the ambulatory arcade and seemed to him to be attributable to the idiosyncracies of the architect. Precisely the same characteristics were to be found only in the ornamental niches of the central pier of the tomb of Romulus just along the Via Appia: 'it seems probable that the architect who designed Romulus' tomb was also responsible for the Basilica Apostolorum'.[148] But Rasch's dedicated study of the mausoleum complex has suggested that Krautheimer's 'similarities' are in fact too superficial.[149] Nevertheless, doubts remain. It is possible that the basilica is a genuine Constantinian building but was achieved by the same architect who constructed the tomb of Romulus which remained intact very close by. Alternatively, it is possible that Maxentius himself began work on a Christian basilica employing the architect who had served him so well previously. This latter explanation would thus explain the failure of the *Liber Pontificalis* to attribute the foundation to Constantine.

The unambiguous links between Constantine and a number of other Christian basilicas of the design found on the Via Appia (Via Labicana, Via Tiburtina) may be deceptive. There was nothing to stop Constantine taking over the work of his predecessor in the city centre. The question of the construction of the Basilica Apostolorum is thus one of the most important issues presently facing the students of the Constantinian era.

The Via Labicana (figs. 14 and 15)

The history and layout of the site on the Via Labicana before and after Constantine is still a much disputed question.[150] The remains are to be

---

[146] Id., 'Mensa-Coemeterium-Martyrium' (n. 103), 22.

[147] Heres, op. cit. (n. 55), 105–6.

[148] Krautheimer, *Corpus*, iv. 145.

[149] J. J. Rasch, *Das Maxentius-Mausoleum an der Via Appia in Rom* (Mainz: Zabern, 1984), 48 n. 425.

[150] The most important bibliography: Deckers, Seeliger, Mietke, op. cit. (n. 138); J. Guyon, *Le cimetière aux deux lauriers*, BEFAR, 264 (1987); id., 'Dal praedium

found 3.3 km from the Porta Maggiore along the Via Casilina (Via Labicana). The only standing portion is part of a large rotunda mausoleum (Tor Pignattara).

Immediately before Constantine's intervention, the site contained a Christian catacomb, there at least from the second century.[151] An extensive imperial house also stood here, identified originally by Ashby.[152] Finally, a non-Christian necropolis was nearby and it included a special plot for the members of the imperial life guard, the *equites singulares*, around which Maxentius had provided an enclosure.[153]

Guyon's excavations have established that the Constantinian complex here comprised a U-shaped basilica, a large rotunda-mausoleum attached to the basilica and the pre-existing enclosure on the north and south sides of the basilica.[154] The basilica was 65 m long and 29 m wide.[155] A central nave was flanked by two others which were separated from it by columns. The aisles formed an ambulatory around the apse end. Into the floor of this basilica, as at a number of other Constantinian *basilicae*, had been lowered the remains of thousands of Christian dead. It was a special covered enclosure for the purpose.

A large wedge of imperial property in the south-east of the city taken either from Maxentius himself, his followers, or some combination of the two, is reported by the *Liber Pontificalis* to have become the *possessio* of the empress Helena. Some of this land was given to the new church to provide funds for its upkeep:

The farm Laurentum close to the aqueduct, with a bath and all the land from the Porta Sessoriana as far as the Via Praenestina, by the route of the Via

imperiale al santuario dei martiri. Il territorio "ad duas lauros" ', in A. Giardina, op. cit. (n. 53), 299 ff.; J. Guyon, L. Strüber, and D. Manacorda, 'Recherches autour de la basilique constantinienne des saints Pierre et Marcellin sur la via Labicana à Rome: Le Mausolée et l'enclos au nord de la basilique', *MEFRA*, 93 (1981), 991–1056; Krautheimer, *Corpus*, ii. 191–204; F. W. Deichman and A. Tschira, 'Das Mausoleum der Kaiserin Helena und die Basilika der Heiligen Marcellinus und Petrus an der Via Labicana vor Rom', *JDAI*, 72 (1957), 44–110; Th. Ashby and G. Lugli, 'La villa dei Flavi cristiani "ad duas lauros" e il suburbano imperiale ad oriente di Roma', *APARA*, Memorie, 2 (1928), 157–92; R. Giordani, 'Postille in margine al complesso dei Santi Marcellino e Pietro al III miglio della via Labicana', *Latomus*, 55 (1996), 127–47. More generally, see de Santis and G. Biamonte, op. cit. (n. 134), 252 ff.

[151] Krautheimer, *Corpus*, ii. 203.

[152] Ashby and Lugli, art. cit. (n. 150), 158 ff.; Krautheimer, *Corpus*, ii. 203; Deichmann and Tschira, art. cit. (n. 150), 50 f.

[153] Guyon, op. cit. (n. 150), 30–3. Enclosure: Guyon, Strüber, and Manacorda, art. cit. (n. 150), 1019 f.

[154] The area enclosed was 8,000 square metres: Guyon, op. cit. (n. 150), 229.

[155] Krautheimer, *Corpus*, ii. 199.

Latina as far as Mons Gabus, the property of the empress Helena, revenue 1120 solidi.[156]

The fact that no properties given to the church came from the eastern empire, which came into Constantine's control in 324, can be interpreted as indicating that the basilica was founded before that date.

No Christian martyr is known to have been associated with the site. The mid-fourth-century *Feriale Ecclesiae Romanae* mentions only the obscure Gorgonius in connection with the Via Labicana.[157] Guyon concluded that the basilica had created the martyrs as later Christians would not accept any other reason for the basilica's existence.[158]

What is notable, however, is the association of the region with the bodyguard of Constantine's predecessor. Deichmann pointed out that fragments of *stelae* referring to *equites singulares* had been found all along the Via Labicana and it is clear that in the construction of the building which Constantine placed 'ad duas lauros' a large number of such *stelae* were used. Most were placed in the foundations of the basilica walls where a solid mass of concrete rests on top of trenches cut into the *cappellaccio*. Krautheimer noted: 'The top layers of this mass consist, almost exclusively, of fragments of tombstones of the *Equites Singulares*'.[159] Guyon's recent monograph on the site has demonstrated that the graveyard of the *equites* was still in use up until tetrarchic times and probably also up until the death of Maxentius.[160] The selection of these *stelae* does not look haphazard. Such tombs, like all in the *suburbium*, were protected by ancient laws from despoliation.[161] These laws were set aside or ignored in the interests of completing the basilica. Clearly, the realization of the basilica enabled Constantine to desecrate the necropolis of the *equites singulares* as part of his *damnatio memoriae* of Maxentius. Guyon was convinced that this had happened although he admitted the difficulty of discovering precisely where the burial ground was.[162] At the Lateran, Constantine had erased the traces of the camp of the *equites*;

---

[156] *LP*, i. 183: 'Fundum Laurentum iuxta formam cum balneum et omnem agrum a porta Sessoriana usque ad Via Penestrina [*sic*] a via itineris Latinae usque ad montem Gabaum, possessio Augustae Helenae, praest. sol. I CXX.' See Duchesne's note at 199 n. 91. Coarelli, art. cit. (n. 53) has recently argued that the area was not a single estate but a patchwork of *fundi*.

[157] *MGH* I, 72; Piétri, *RC*, i. 30. For the emergence of Saints Marcellinus and Peter at the site, see 147 below.

[158] Guyon, op. cit. (n. 150), 262.

[159] Krautheimer, *Corpus*, ii. 197; see Deichmann and Tschira, art. cit. (n. 150), pl. 10, 11, 14; Guyon, op. cit. (n. 150), figs. 116, 128, 139.

[160] Ibid. 30–3.

[161] See the case of Saint Peter's below, 111.

[162] Guyon, op. cit. (n. 150), 238.

now he destroyed the other symbol of their close relationship to the reigning emperor: a graveyard close to one of the emperor's suburban villas.

The villa was still a very important site after the basilica had been built. Sometime before 324–6 a rotunda mausoleum 27.74 m in diameter and 25.42 m high was attached to the western end of the basilica, a dramatic illustration of the desire of the imperial family to associate themselves directly with those who used and were buried in the church.[163] This was an imperial mausoleum. Constantine himself was over forty when he entered the city in 312 and his mother, Helena, was more than sixty years old. It is therefore not surprising that dynastic mausolea should make an early appearance in his building projects. After her death *c.*330, Helena's remains were deposited in the mausoleum, though the military themes on the sarcophagus have given rise to a popular theory that Constantine himself had intended to be buried here.[164] It is important, however, to realize that villa-mausoleum complexes were not at all unusual in this area of the *campagna* and along with the Via Appia and Via Labicana sites, another fourth-century example stood beside the Via Praenestina.[165] Constantine and his family transformed the gesture of linking the emperor's favoured dead (the most recent case being the *equites singulares*) with himself by providing funerary basilicas for the *milites Christi*.

San Lorenzo fuori le mura (fig. 16)

The present basilica lies about one kilometre east of Porta San Lorenzo and is in fact the modified remains of two medieval basilicas, constructed by the bishops Pelagius II (579–90) and Honorius (1216–27)

---

[163] Deichmann and Tschira, art. cit. (n. 150), 178 reported finding a coin embedded in the mortar of the mausoleum. It might have been deposited either during the construction (suggesting a *terminus post quem* of 324–6) or in the addition of marble revetments which adorned the exterior of the building (making 324–6 a *terminus ante quem*). I accept the latter here. See Coarelli, *Dintorni*, 176–7.

[164] Death of Helena (Augusta since 325: *PLRE* I, 410–11): Eusebius, *VC* 3, 47. Her remains were moved in the twelfth century to Santa Maria in Ara Coeli: Deichmann and Tschira, art. cit. (n. 150), 65, 80. Mausoleum intended for Constantine suggested early by P. Franchi De' Cavalieri, 'I funerali ed il sepolcro di Costantino Magno', *Mélanges d'archeologie et d'histoire*, 36 (1916–17), 205–61, at 245 ff.; Guyon, op. cit. (n. 150), 256–8.

[165] Considered Constantinian until the authoritative publication of J. J. Rasch, *Das Mausoleum bei Tor de'Schiavi in Rom* (Mainz: Zabern, 1993), who dates the rotunda to the period 305/6 and 307/9 whereas the basilica belongs to a building period some forty-two years later: 78, 80. For earlier views, see Ashby and Lugli, art. cit. (n. 150); Coarelli, *Dintorni*, 162–6; Piétri, *RC*, i. 33 ff.; L. Luschi and A. Ceccherelli, 'Mausoleo "dei Gordiani" e adiacente basilica', *BC*, 92 (1987–8), 421–7.

respectively.[166] This church was situated in a carefully constructed site which had been created by the removal of a large portion of a hill which overlooked the *Ager Veranus* (9.7 m above the height of the nave of the basilica).[167] From the Renaissance until the excavations of the late forties and early fifties of this century, this double basilica was generally believed to stand on the site formerly occupied by Constantine's basilica.[168]

The *Liber Pontificalis* is the only early source to attest the intervention of Constantine at the site:

Then the emperor built a basilica to the martyr Saint Laurence on the Via Tiburtina at the Ager Veranus, above the *arenarium* of the crypt; to reach the body of the martyr Saint Laurence he built steps for going up and down. In that place he built an apse and decorated it with purple marble, and above the burial place he sealed it with silver, and decorated it with railings of the finest silver.[169]

The excavations carried out by the Pontifical Academy and the Institute of Fine Arts of New York University unearthed a large U-shaped basilica a short distance to the south of the present church of San Lorenzo. Only the foundations remained but they were in *opus listatum*, the masonry favoured by Constantine.[170] The basilica itself had a distinctive plan. It was laid out on a longitudinal axis. A central nave (16.2 m wide) was separated on either side from two aisles by a colonnade and the two aisles linked together to form an ambulatory at the apse end of the structure (diameter of 32.85 m). The apse end of the church had seven arches opening into it though the proper entrance was at the façade end which pointed east. The building was 97.6 m long

---

[166] Krautheimer, *Corpus*, ii. 1–144, at 35 ff. particularly important. Also, de Santis and Biamonte, op. cit. (n. 134), 219 ff.; H. Geertman, 'The Builders of the Basilica Maior in Rome', in *Festen aan A. N. Zadoks-Josephus Jitta bij haar zeventigste verjaardag* (Groningen-Bussum: Tjeent Willink, 1976), 277–99. Geertman argues unconvincingly for a later construction date for the Basilica Maior (under Sixtus III: 432–40). He attaches too much significance to the presence of an architrave and seven arches in the apse. I prefer to see them as artistic variations within the broader Constantinian theme. See Coarelli, *Dintorni*, 179–80.

[167] Krautheimer, *Corpus*, ii. 24; 113 ff.

[168] Older views summarized by G. Bovini, *Edifici cristiani di culto d'età costantiniana a Roma* (Bologna: R. Pàtron, 1968), 198–205; Krautheimer, *Corpus*, ii. 18–23.

[169] *LP*, i. 181: 'eodem tempore [the papacy of Sylvester (314–35)] fecit basilicam beato Laurentio Martyri Via Tiburtina in agrum Veranum supra arenario cryptae et usque ad corpus Sancti Laurenti martyris fecit grados ascensionis et descensionis. in quo loco construxit absidam et exornavit marmoribus porphyreticis et desuper loci conclusit de argento et cancellos de argento purissimo ornavit.'

[170] Bovini, *Edifici cristiani*, 210.

and 34.2 m wide, making it the largest of all the so-called 'ambulatory' basilicas in Rome.

A very large number of Christian graves were found within the building and it is clear that it was what Krautheimer has called a 'cemeterium subteglatum'. The entire inner space of the church seems to have been given over to Christian burials which were often several layers deep in the nave and aisles.[171] Two funerary inscriptions were found at the site and they show that in the late antique period, this building was known as the Basilica Maior.[172] It might be suggested that the epithet 'maior' indicates that another basilica stood on the site at the time of these inscriptions and thus that Constantine or someone shortly before or after him built a smaller basilica directly over the tomb of Saint Laurence. The passage from the *Liber Pontificalis* quoted above claims, however, that Constantine built an 'apse' at the site of the martyr's tomb. Though it is now impossible to verify this statement, it is not out of the question that Constantine's intervention at the martyr's grave included making the gallery in which he was buried into a small underground *basilica*.[173]

The endowments made by Constantine to the church for its upkeep included properties in the east of the empire and it has been plausibly argued that this indicates that the foundation took place sometime after the eastern empire came into Constantine's hands in 324.[174]

The Basilica Maior was not a basilica *ad corpus*, that is, it did not lie directly on top of the tomb of any martyr. As we have seen, the tomb of Saint Laurence lay in the catacomb in the hillside to the north of the Constantinian foundation. Nevertheless, the proximity of the basilica to the known site of the tomb of Laurentius seems to have been deliberate.[175] If the *Liber Pontificalis* can be accepted, then Constantine improved access to the tomb of the martyr as well as building the great funerary basilica. It was not necessary for the tomb of Laurentius to be the focus of the Basilica Maior.

The choice of site may have been determined in part by the fact that this area of the *campagna* appears to have been imperial property. One of the estates in Italy which the *Liber Pontificalis* claims was given to the site was:

---

[171] Krautheimer, 'Mensa-Coemeterium-Martyrium', 15–40, at 18 ff. repr. in R. Krautheimer and C. L. Striker, *Architectural Studies in Memory of Richard Krautheimer* (Mainz: von Zabern, 1996).

[172] Diehl, *ILCV*, 2129, 2129 n.

[173] See the discussion of the problem of S. Paolo fuori le mura below, 104 ff.

[174] *LP*, i. 181 ff.; Piétri, *RC*, I, 39. For Constantinian brickstamps, see Steinby, art. cit. (n. 82), 144.

[175] Krautheimer, *Corpus*, ii. 67; id., art. cit. [1960] (n. 103), 15. At some stage an altar was placed at the tomb: Piétri, *RC*, i. 38; Bovini, *Edifici cristiani*, 192.

the property of one Cyriaces, a religious woman, of which the fisc had taken possession in the time of the persecution, the farm Veranus.[176]

It has been suggested too that the name of this zone of the *campagna*, the 'Ager Veranus', derived from lands which belonged to the emperor Lucius Verus (161–9). The Via Tiburtina certainly appears to have been lined with large numbers of tombs belonging to imperial servants.[177]

Significantly, the basilica was extremely close to the Via Tiburtina, a major road leading into the eastern portion of the city. The site was therefore easily accessible to funeral processions coming from the eastern quarters of the city. At the same time, it constituted the grandest mausoleum in that area of the *campagna* and its impressive size was obvious to all who travelled on that road.

The basilica which Constantine built beside the Via Tiburtina was different in both design and function to that constructed on the Lateran site. Where the Lateran was a solitary experiment, the layout of the Basilica Maior was used at least twice by Constantine.[178] Despite the obvious differences, however, the same desire to emphasize the emperor's personal piety and patronage on a grand scale was evident in the choice of imperial land for the large church. Similar sites in the *campagna* to the east and south-east of the city illustrate the same themes.

San Paolo fuori le mura (fig. 17)

The present basilica of Saint Paul stands approximately two kilometres distant from the walls of Aurelian on the right-hand side of the road to Ostia. In the seventh century, the author or compiler of the *Liber Pontificalis* included a passage in his work stating that Constantine had founded a basilica in honour of Saint Paul on the Via Ostiensis.[179] This is the only literary reference up until that time to make this claim. Unfortunately, this is one of the more dubious sections in the *Liber Pontificalis*. Constantine is, for example, called 'Augustus Constantinus' instead of the more usual 'Constantinus Augustus'. A variant manuscript reading states that 'Constantinus Augustus et dominus Constantius Augustus', that is, the sons of Constantine, were responsible for

[176] *LP*, i. 182: 'Veranum fundum, possessio cuiusdam Cyriacae religiosae feminae, quod fiscus occupaverat tempore persecutionis.'

[177] Platner and Ashby, *Topographical Dictionary*, 3; Th. Ashby, 'The Classical Topography of the Roman Campagna II', *PBSR*, 3 (1906), 89 ff.; Krautheimer, *Corpus*, ii. 28.

[178] This pattern repeated at sites on the Via Appia, Via Ardeatina, Via Labicana, Via Praenestina, and Via Nomentana.

[179] *LP*, i. 178.

building the basilica.[180] The donation list of properties provided by Constantine for the upkeep of the site bears a very close resemblance to that connected with the basilica dedicated by the same emperor to Saint Peter. All, for example, are reported to have been in the east and a list of gifts given by the emperor includes a great golden cross 150 Roman pounds in weight; exactly the same gift is alleged to have been made to Saint Peter's. As we shall see, if a Constantinian basilica was ever built at this site, it was certainly much smaller than Saint Peter's. Krautheimer has concluded from looking at the evidence of the *Liber Pontificalis* that it or its sources had deliberately concocted a parity between the two great churches of the medieval city:

The entire passage is intended to make S. Paolo appear as important as old Saint Peter's and, although Constantine or his sons may have built a (small) church on the site, we consider this reference an interpolation of later date.[181]

The archaeological evidence is very slight and extremely controversial. It derives from observations made beneath the modern basilica after it was destroyed by fire in July 1823. Some sketches of the area beneath the altar were made by Virginio Vespignani in 1838 and then in 1850, when a new *baldacchino* was being placed over the high altar, Belloni discovered some earlier substructures.[182]

Whatever had lain beneath the modern basilica in antiquity, it had stood among a large number of mausolea which were in use right up until the fourth century.[183] The altar of the basilica which was built towards the end of the fourth century by Theodosius I, Valentinianus II, and Honorius stood directly over a tomb. This mausoleum was of ancient construction, being in *opus reticulatum* and was dated by Belvederi to the second half of the first century AD.[184] On one of the walls was the inscription 'salus populi'. Directly above this tomb, and laid into the floor of the late fourth-century basilica, were four fragments of a marble slab which had been pieced together to form a single cover. The two larger sections of this slab bore respectively the inscriptions 'Paulo' and 'apostolo mart.'.[185] An unresolved argument has focused on the date of these inscriptions to Paul and opinions are divided between a Constantinian date (De Rossi/Silvagni) and a period contemporary with the erection of the Theodosian basilica.[186] It should

---

[180] Krautheimer, *Corpus*, v. 97.

[181] Ibid. v. 97. Cf. Davis, op. cit. (n. 120), p. xxii.

[182] Bovini, *Edifici cristiani*, 392.   [183] Krautheimer, *Corpus*, v. 112.

[184] G. Belvederi, 'L'origine della basilica ostiense', *RAC*, 22 (1946), 103–38, at 132.

[185] Krautheimer, *Corpus*, v. 88 says it is not earlier than 400.

[186] Ibid. 117. See B. M. Apollonj-Ghetti, 'Le basiliche cimiteriali degli apostoli a Roma', in *Saecularia Petri et Pauli*, Studi di antichità, 28 (Vatican City: Pontificio Istituto di archeologia cristiana, 1969), 9–34, at 30 f.

be pointed out that the datives used in the inscription make it seem less like a sepulchral text and more like a dedication. Additionally, the slabs may well not have lain originally where they now do. At some later date holes were cut into the plates to allow the lowering of *brandea* into a space beneath which was believed to be the burial chamber of the apostle.[187]

Belloni's excavations in the middle of the nineteenth century revealed an elliptical apse close to and under the high altar. It pointed due east, indicating that the orientation of the building to which it belonged was exactly opposite to that of the Theodosian basilica which was entered from the west. The inner radius of the apse was 3.8 m.[188] The tomb of Saint Paul lay barely 1.5 m from the back of this apse. From these humble data, Belloni deduced a plan for a 'basilica' which had stood on the site prior to the Theodosian building and which had been engulfed by it when the latter was built.[189] Belloni's details included a *quadriporticus* and three naves; both features were well known from other fourth-century basilicas.[190] In fact, neither could be demonstrated here. Belvederi remarks:

Che questa cella fosse una basilica a tre navate e avesse un atrio, come il Belloni ha disegnato, è una fantasia la quale non è stata suffragata da alcuna testimonianza monumentale.[191]

So apart from the suspect references in the *Liber Pontificalis*, there was nothing to link Constantine directly with the site. Even if the literary account could be accepted, two serious archaeological difficulties remain. First, the 'basilica' which Belloni claimed to have found would certainly be the least impressive of all Constantine's known works in Rome. This does not accord with the apparent richness of the endowment recorded in the *Liber Pontificalis*. Secondly, if Constantine did construct a small basilica here because he was honouring the grave of a martyr and apostle, the remains of the apse-tomb arrangement show that access to the tomb was more difficult than in any other Constantinan church.

Apollonj-Ghetti has suggested that the hill which overlooked the site presented particular technical difficulties which were more serious than at the Vatican.[192] Thus, he argues, the construction of a church on the same scale was out of the question. This may well be the case, though it is surprising that Constantine should have overlooked the simple

---

[187] Belvederi, art. cit. (n. 184), 107 ff. For *brandea* see ibid. 117 ff. and Bovini, *Edifici cristiani*, 395.   [188] Krautheimer, *Corpus*, v. 118.

[189] An infamous sketch. See Bovini, *Edifici cristiani*, 393, fig. 49.

[190] For example San Clemente. See Piétri, *RC*, i. 470–3.

[191] Belvederi, art. cit. (n. 184), 121.   [192] Apollonj-Ghetti, art. cit. (n. 186), 22.

solution adopted later in the century by the three emperors. The fact that the entrance to the basilica would have to be from the west and away from the main road would not have worried him since he used a similar orientation at the Basilica Maior.

The problems associated with attributing the foundation of a basilica here to Constantine are, in fact, too serious to believe that he intervened at the site. The remains of a building which Belloni discovered must have been a *memoria* to Paul which had originally been the apostle's mausoleum and which preserved it as the core of the shrine. As we saw earlier, Eusebius mentions a *tropaion* to Paul on the Via Ostiensis which was pointed out by the presbyter Gaius around the year 200.[193] At some stage before the Constantinian era, an apse was added to the *memoria*. When, in 386, the three emperors Theodosius I, Valentinianus II, and Arcadius wrote to Sallustius, the Prefect of the City, to ask him to supervise the building of a massive new church, they noted that there was already an ancient basilica-shaped building on the site:

To us, upon consideration of the veneration already sacred from ancient times, desiring to adorn the *basilica* of Paul the Apostle. . . .[194]

This ancient structure was the *memoria* of Paul. By the time that the trio of Christian emperors were writing, the commonest specialized Christian building in Rome was the basilica. The emperors knew that the *memoria* had an apse and they therefore considered it to be a basilica.

It is impossible to conclude with any certainty why Constantine did not build a basilica at the site. Three possibilities may be considered. First, that he possessed no will to do so because the apostle Paul was not as important to him as Peter. It is difficult to believe, however, that Constantine could have been blind to the strong significance which attached to Paul even at this date; the festival calendar of the Roman church specifically linked the two great apostles in a liturgy held three days before the kalends of July.[195] Secondly, there is the possibility that Paul's body was not to be found at the site any longer in Constantine's day. Belvederi has suggested that it was in fact at the *memoria* on the Via Appia where Constantine did build a basilica.[196] Unfortunately, this theory rests upon an unconvincing reading of the letter to Sallustius in which the basilica already on the site was referred to as 'sacrata' and not

[193] *HE* 2, 25, 7. See above, 36.
[194] *CSEL* 35, 46–7 = Coleman-Norton, 2, no. 211: 'antiquitus iam sacratam basilicam Pauli Apostoli.'
[195] *MGH* 1, 71.
[196] Belvederi, art. cit. (n. 184), 132.

'sacra'. There seems to be no reason for believing that 'sacrata' means 'consecrated to an apostle whose remains once lay here'. Belvederi's thesis must therefore be rejected. Thirdly, it may be suggested that Constantine did envisage the building of a basilica in honour of Paul, but was unable for various reasons to realize it. As we shall see, the basilica in honour of the prince of the apostles, Saint Peter, was not an early Constantinian project. The provision of cemetery-basilicas on imperial estates as well as the building of the Lateran appear to have occupied the city's builders before and during the construction of the apostolic basilica. Naturally, Constantine's builders could not be everywhere at once. It is striking, also, that a number of the Constantinian buildings required large-scale engineering work to prepare the sites chosen. Saint Peter's and the baths on the Quirinal are obvious examples, but the Basilica Apostolorum was also raised up, at its apse end, on a similar platform. When the late fourth-century emperors decided to erect their great basilica to Saint Paul, it was necessary for them to destroy a branch road (*diverticulum*) of the Via Ostiensis and to reorientate their building 180 degrees from the original alignment of the *memoria*. It seems quite possible therefore that the death of Constantine intervened before a decision to start work at Saint Paul's tomb was taken.

Saint Peter's *Basilica*: Old Saint Peter's (figs. 18, 19, and 20)

Whatever else may be said about the basilica erected by Constantine in honour of Saint Peter, it should be pointed out at once that no monument in Rome paid greater tribute to his Christian piety.[197] In Rome, it was the only cross-shaped basilica to be built by him and it was the only one which definitely and deliberately included an existing *martyrium*.[198] Constantine was certainly aware of the status of Saint Peter and his shrine when he decided to build the church. Saint Peter's basilica was, accordingly, the largest of all the buildings of Constantine in Rome. Like the Lateran, it was laid out longitudinally as a large hall with an apse in the middle of one of the short sides. According to Alfarano, whose Renaissance measurements were in *palmi* and have

[197] A long bibliography: here, I have relied chiefly upon Krautheimer, *Corpus*, v. 165–286; J. M. C. Toynbee and J. B. Ward-Perkins, *The Shrine of Saint Peter and the Vatican Excavations* (London: Longmans, 1956); J. H. Jongkees, *Studies on Old St. Peter's*, Archeologica Traiectina, 8 (Groningen: J. B. Wolters, 1966). See also A. Arbeiter, *Alt-St. Peter in Geschichte und Wissenschaft: Abfolge der Bauten, Rekonstruktion, Architekturprogramm* (Berlin: Mann, 1988); F. Castagnoli, *Il Vaticano nell'antichità classica*, Studi e documenti per la storia del Palazzo apostolico vaticano, 6 (Vatican City: Biblioteca Apostolica Vaticana, 1992).

[198] Krautheimer, op. cit. [1986] (n. 103), 59.

been converted into metres, the central nave was 90.54 m long, 23.64 m
wide and 37.91 m high. The total width of the nave and four aisles was
63.56 m. Unlike the Lateran, the Vatican basilica was preceded by a
narthex and an atrium, measuring, on the longitudinal axis of the
church, 11.82 m and 57.09 m.[199] The basilica had an innovative feature
in a specially designed transept, inserted between the top of the nave
and the apse. The distance from the end of the nave to the beginning of
the apse measured 17.39 m. The apse itself was 9.81 m deep. Thus
from the atrium (which was preceded by a flight of steps) to the back of
the apse was a distance of approximately 186 m. The Lateran, which
had no atrium, measured from narthex to apse only 98.50 m in
comparison.[200] According to Krautheimer, the new church could
hold a congregation fully twenty-five per cent larger than the basilica
on the Caelian Hill.[201]

Enormous efforts were made to build the basilica on precisely this
spot on the Vatican Hill in such a way that the shrine of Saint Peter
could be included in the transept. A functioning necropolis was
partially destroyed by a vast artificial terrace, stretching from near
the crown of the hill back down eastwards, towards the city.

Saint Peter's was the most significant basilica which Constantine
gave the Christian city. Its special design of atrium, basilica, and
transept met the requirements for a large congregation, the preservation of a sacred point in the Christian topography, and the provision of
a very large cemetery for the Christian dead.

It is clear, however, that for all the grandeur and careful design, the
construction of this basilica was not the first of Constantine's building
projects. An urn, containing the ashes of Trebellena Flaccilla and a
coin minted in Arles between 317 and 320, was found by the Vatican
excavators in the middle of this century deposited in one of the
mausolea underlying the nave of the Constantinian church.[202] This
mausoleum was thus still accessible and in use at that date. On the basis
of some archaeological indications that access to one of the other
mausolea was possible, Prandi has gone further and suggested that
non-Christian burials were taking place while the building work on the
church was under way.[203] The donation lists referring to Saint Peter's

[199] Krautheimer, *Corpus*, v. fig. 195. For the difficulties in dealing with Alfarano's
figures, see Jongkees, op. cit. (n. 197), 3 ff. The information is usefully tabulated at
25–8.

[200] Piétri, *RC*, i. 9.   [201] Krautheimer, op. cit. [1986] (n. 103), 56.

[202] See R. Giordani, 'Note sulla cronologia della costruzione della basilica vaticana',
Studi Romani, 35 (1987), 346–58, at 349 ff.

[203] A. Prandi, 'Il sepolcro di S. Pietro in Vaticano durante la costruzione della
basilica', in *Atti del II Congresso Nazionale di Archeologia cristiana 1969* (1971), 377–80;
Piétri, *RC*, i. 58 with n. 4.

which were recorded by the *Liber Pontificalis* show that the donation was made after the victory over Licinius in September 324, since all the properties are in the eastern portion of the empire.[204] Furthermore, as Alföldi and Piétri agree, the title of *victor*, which was used by Constantine in a dedicatory inscription in the basilica, was not used by him before the period 323–4.[205] A theory first advocated by Seston attempts to establish a firm date by an examination of a law preserved in the *Codex Theodosianus*.[206] In 349 Constans promulgated a law punishing the crime of *violatio sepulchri*. The measure was made retrospective by some sixteen years, to 333. Seston thought that 333 was therefore the date when Constantine formally enacted an exemption from punishment for the workers at the Vatican site. He believed that work on demolishing the cemetery began in this year. But Jongkees has pointed out convincingly that 333 must actually mark the *end* of the work on the necropolis.[207] Piétri concludes that the work began in the second half of Constantine's reign and was not finished until after his death, when the apse inscription was set up.[208]

At this point mention should be made of a further theory which has been used to provide an approximate date for the construction of the basilica. It concerns a group of inscriptions relating to the cult of Magna Mater and Attis which appear to have come from the Vatican where an oriental shrine, the *Phrygianum*, was known to be situated. More specifically, the inscriptions refer to the cult act of the *taurobolium*, a ritual cleansing effected by the sacrificing of a bull directly over the cult member who stood below in a specially constructed pit. One of the inscriptions was recovered in 1919 and was clearly of fourth-century date.[209] It records the 'scattering' of twenty-eight years of darkness when the dedicant underwent the the *tauro-* and *criobolium*. This text has been taken in conjunction with the absence of datable inscriptions relating to the cult on the Vatican between April 319 and

[204] *LP*, i. 177 ff.; Krautheimer, *Corpus*, v. 171; Piétri, *RC*, i. 53.

[205] See Alföldi, op. cit. (n. 2), 59; Piétri, *RC*, i. 51; Grünewald, op. cit. (n. 1), 134 ff.

[206] W. Seston, 'Hypothèse sur la date de la basilique constantinienne de Saint Pierre de Rome', *Cahiers archéologiques*, 2 (1947), 153–9 with *CT* 9, 17, 2 (28.3.349). See Toynbee and Ward-Perkins, op. cit. (n. 197), 197.

[207] Jongkees, op. cit. (n. 197), 33.

[208] Piétri, *RC*, i. 54–5. Piétri, *RC*, i. 64 says that the site was not ready until after 354, when the *depositio martyrum* shows a continuing festival of Saint Peter being commemorated on the Via Appia. See J. F. Baldovin, *The Urban Character of Christian Worship: The Origins, Development and Meaning of Stational Liturgy*, Orientalia Christiana Analecta, 228 (Rome: Pontificium Institutum Studiorum Orientalium, 1987), 110 n. 20 argues that the building could be complete but not in full liturgical use. See Krautheimer, *Corpus*, v. 272.

[209] M. J. Vermaseren, *CCCA* 3 (1977), 56 ff., no.239. See Giordani, art. cit. (n. 202). For the so-called 'Phrygianum', see Castagnoli, op. cit. (n. 197), 71–80.

350. *Ex silentio* it is argued that the above inscription refers to a ceasing of the cult for a period of twenty-eight years sometime between these two dates while the basilica of Peter was being built. There is in fact only a superficial case to be made for this theory. The crucial text need not refer to the cult but to the *personal* 'darkness' of the dedicant, the kind of individual impurity which other dedicants in the fourth century claimed had been washed away for periods of twenty years.[210]

It is worth recalling the advice which Constantine gave bishop Makarios of Jerusalem prior to the building of the great basilica at Golgotha. That church was to be constructed in such a way that:

not only the church itself as a whole may surpass all others whatsoever in beauty, but that the details of the building may be of such a kind that the fairest structures in any city of the empire may be excelled by this.[211]

The Christian churches of Constantine were constructed within the framework of the public architecture of the late empire, where particular importance was attached to size, grandeur, and richness. Ultimately, the imperial qualities of the emperor himself were expected to be revealed by what he built.

Among other things, the basilica dedicated to Saint Peter was an example of Constantine's self-promotion through a monumental Christian medium.[212] The layout of Old Saint Peter's shows that a definite progression through atrium–narthex–nave–transept (*memoria*) was intended. On the triumphal arch which divided the transept from the nave of the basilica was an inscription, battered but readable in 1506:

Because under Your leadership the world rose up triumphant to the skies, Constantine, himself victorious, has founded this hall in Your honour.[213]

The inscription was accompanied, perhaps later, by a mosaic which depicted Constantine giving a model of the church to Christ and Saint Peter.[214] While the mosaic showed Constantine as a Christian builder, the inscription celebrated his military victories under the tutelage of Christ.[215] Constantine is 'victor' and the 'leadership' of the Christian God is redolent here of the 'instinctu divinitatis' of the Arch of Constantine in the city centre, set up some years earlier.[216] There is also, possibly, an attempt to portray Constantine as the natural leader

[210] See below, 266–7.   [211] Eusebius, *VC* 3, 31.

[212] Krautheimer, art. cit. [1965] (n. 103), 242: '[the churches were to be] worthy of his generosity and piety, his philotimia, and of the Catholic and Apostolic Church.'

[213] *ICUR* I, 4092: 'Quod duce te mundus surrexit in astra triumphans Hanc Constantinus Victor tibi condidit aula(m).'

[214] Constantine seems to have placed an aniconic mosaic in the original church: *LP*, i. 176; Krautheimer, *Corpus*, v. 171, 172.

[215] Jongkees, op. cit. (n. 197), 39–40.   [216] See above, 87.

of some kind of spontaneous popular movement ('mundus . . . triumphans'), a theme which he is known to have encouraged after the defeat of Maxentius in 312.

Moving on beneath the triumphal arch in the basilica of Constantine, Maffeo Veggio was able to read, in the apse, around 1450, the mutilated inscription:

Constantini . . . expiata . . . hostili incursione.[217]

Krautheimer originally thought that this fragmentary text made reference to the war against Licinius.[218] It has also been linked to a victory by the same emperor over the Sarmatians in 322–3 and to a victory of Constans in 342.[219]

A second inscription in the apse was recorded by the ninth-century Einsiedeln Sylloge and read:

This [basilica] which you see and which every *pietas* inhabits, is the Seat of Justice, the House of Faith, the Hall of Chastity, which delights resplendent in the virtues of father and son and with praises of the *genitor* makes equal its donor.[220]

Though Krautheimer conceded that this text 'may but need not be contemporary' with the sylloge itself, he actually thought that there was no need to date it later than 337.[221] Ruysschaert argued that the father and son mentioned are members of the Holy Trinity and not Constantine or his sons.[222] On this interpretation, the second half of the inscription can only be understood as the physical building (*aula*) rejoicing at the *virtutes* of God and Christ. But if this is supposed to be a theological reading, then it sounds somewhat bizarre. As Piétri comments: 'le vocabulaire théologique de la dédicace heurterait décidément'.[223] In the context of the other original inscriptions, however, it must be a reference to the completion of a stage or the whole of the work by one of the sons of Constantine. This son was anxious to present himself as joint founder with his father and chose the most

---

[217] *ICUR* I, 4095.

[218] Krautheimer, *Corpus*, v. 171.

[219] R. Krautheimer, 'A Note on the Inscription in the Apse of Old St. Peter's', *DOP*, 41 (1987), 317–20, at 318.

[220] *ICUR* I, 4094: 'Iustitiae sedis fidei domus aula pudoris haec est | Quam cernis pietas quam | possidet omnis quae patris | Et fili virtutibus inclyta gaudet auctoremque suum | Genitoris laudibus aequat.'

[221] Krautheimer, *Corpus*, v. 172.

[222] J. Ruysschaert, 'L'inscription absidale primitive de S.-Pierre: Texte et contexte', *APARA*, Rendiconti, 40 (1967–8), 171 ff.

[223] Piétri, *RC*, i. 56, cf. n. 5 where he usefully refers to a Damasian epigram where the *una virtus* is stressed.

prominent point in the building at which to make his statement.
Krautheimer, who originally followed Ruysschaert, changed his posi-
tion in 1987 and thinks now that the inscription was composed for
Constantius II who was in control of Rome from 352 to 361.[224]

Other arrangements stressed the dynastic idea. Constantine associated himself with the Augusta Helena in presenting a particularly
ostentatious gift to Saint Peter's. If the *Liber Pontificalis* can be trusted,
sometime before the death of Constantine's mother Helena around
330, a golden cross was placed in the most significant area in the
building, on top of the shrine of Peter in the transept:

Constantine Augustus and Helena Augusta. He surrounds this house with a
royal hall gleaming with equal splendour.[225]

There is even a slight ambiguity in the reference to a 'domus regalis'
which has been built by an Augustus and an Augusta.

The great basilica which Constantine constructed in honour of Saint
Peter was a later project of the emperor. It is difficult to imagine that he
was deterred by the difficulty of the task which was completed with
such ingenuity and determination. The building itself was a lasting
testament to the enthusiasm which Constantine came to feel for the cult
of Peter. Alongside the Christian piety of Constantine, however, many
of the traditional propagandist aims of imperial public building may be
observed. In particular, the monument paid tribute to Constantine's
military successes and was also used to promote the dynastic ideal.
Constantius II, after his father, gladly announced himself to the
Christian congregation in exactly the same way.

CONCLUSION

The temptation to identify the extraordinary personality of Constantine with a new beginning in Roman history is strong and understandable. But the disconcerting remains of his monumental presence
in Rome prevent such a sweeping view.

Constantine's piety was tempered by a formidable political instinct.
Maxentius had been the most Roman of recent emperors and Constantine's revelation of himself to the populace of the newly captured
city began where Maxentius had emphasized his own *Romanitas* most
strongly. The earliest of his churches swallowed up the camp of
Maxentius' disbanded horse guards and was under construction
within months of his arrival in the city. The site intended for his

---

[224] Krautheimer, art. cit. (n. 219).
[225] *LP*, i. 176: 'Constantinus Augustus et Helena Augusta hanc domum Regalem
simili fulgore coruscans aula circumdat.'

own burial probably obliterated a special funerary enclosure for the same unit, close to an imperial property.

The employment of imperial property at the Lateran and to the south and east of the city emphasized Constantine's personal patronage of the Christian cult. The vast basilicas erected here performed the dual function of providing much needed burial space and showing Constantine to be the equal of recent imperial builders. Some important details permit us to assess the essential character of Constantine's Christianity. He showed little or no interest in the traces of Paul in Rome. And in honouring Peter with an enormous building project late in his reign he saw no embarrassment in using the great church as a platform upon which to honour, simultaneously, Christ as Saviour, Peter as Apostle, and himself as the bearer of worldly responsibility and the agent of Christian victory.

4

The Christianization of the
Topography of Rome, AD 337–384

INTRODUCTION

The post-Constantinian status of Christianity made the founding of
churches and buildings for Christian use much simpler. There was no
longer any necessity to avoid drawing attention to Christian places of
worship and appropriate architectural forms could now be developed.[1]
That Rome had come to possess a distinctive and comprehensive
Christian topography by the end of the fifth century or beginning of
the sixth is beyond question. But to describe the process by which
Christianity *came* to dominate the landscape simply as 'Christianization', without precise definition, can lead to misunderstanding.
Richard Krautheimer in his chronicle of the city of Rome states:

> The Church, though backed by the imperial court and by the urban masses
> inside the city, had a hard time asserting her position. The struggle, at times
> bitter, ended early in the fifth century with the triumph of the Church, no
> longer contested. Only from then on does the map of Rome increasingly reflect
> the city's Christian character, and this remains so until 1870.[2]

Krautheimer, as his subsequent discussion shows, was clearly aware
that the 'Christianization' of the city did not affect all areas equally.
Nevertheless, there are three problems in this understanding of
'Christianization'. First, 'Christianization' as understood by Krautheimer and others, tends to lend to the 'Christians' such a homogeneity as

---

[1] See ·90 n. 103 above. For what follows, note especially H. O. Maier, 'The
Topography of Heresy and Dissent in Late Fourth-Century Rome', *Historia* 44
(1995), 232–49; L. Reekmans, 'L'Implantation monumentale chrétienne dans la zone
suburbaine de Rome du iv au ix siècle', *RAC*, 44 (1968), 173–207, with a very useful
map; and id. 'L'implantation monumentale chrétienne dans le paysage urbain de Rome
de 300 à 850', in *Actes du XIe Congrès international d'archéologie chrétienne 1986*,
Collection de l'École française de Rome, 123/Studi di Antichità cristiana, 41 (Rome:
École Française de Rome, 1989), 861–915; F. Guidobaldi, 'Ricerche di archeologia
cristiana a Roma (dentro le mura)', in op. cit., 2127–48; U. M. Fasola, 'Le ricerche di
archeologia cristiana a Roma fuori le mura', in op. cit., 2149–76; H. Geertman, 'Forze
centrifughi e centripete nella Roma cristiana: Il Laterano, la basilica Iulia e la basilica
Liberiana', *Rendiconti della pontificia accademia Romana di archeologia*, 59 (1986–7),
63–91. [2] Krautheimer, *Rome*, 33.

to suggest that the 'non-Christians' were what stood between them and the realization of their Christian capital.[3] This, as will become clear, is not completely accurate. Second, 'Christianization' can suggest a systematic and inexorable transformation of the landscape of the city. In fact, the circumstances of change in the fourth century did not permit any such process.[4] Third, and most important, the use of the term 'Christianization' in this unguarded way can imply that the identity and definition of Rome remained unchanged, that the city merely changed hands at the end of some kind of 'struggle'.[5] In fact, the extension of Christianity into the public space of Rome was to bring with it the last redefinition of the city in antiquity.

I. BISHOP JULIUS AND HIS PREDECESSORS

Constantine, with the exception of the Lateran complex and modifications to the Sessorianum, had not built any Christian meeting places in the interior of the city. But it was not to the emperor alone that the Christian community looked for the provision of buildings for community use. Long before Constantine's accession, the Christians of Rome had possessed buildings for meetings. These had probably been provided by wealthy individuals or by means of some kind of subscription among the faithful. From these *domus ecclesiae*, whatever their location, the transmission of Christian ideas had been carried out.[6] They became the focus of neighbourhood liturgies and almsgiving. Where Constantine's great buildings dedicated themselves for the most part to the care of the Christian dead, the unassuming and functional churches of the interior serviced the living. In Rome, the Christian emperors of the fourth century never took to themselves the responsibility for providing churches in the heart of the city; that duty was left to the bishops.

During Constantine's reign, the Roman bishops had continued their ancient obligation to provide places of worship. Two general points may be noted: first, there is no indication that they duplicated the architectural scale or style of Constantine and second, there is no

---

[3] J. F. Baldovin, *The Urban Character of Christian Worship: The Origins, Development and Meaning of Stational Liturgy*, Orientalia Christiana Analecta, 228 (Rome: Pontificium Institutum Studiorum Orientalium, 1987). Piétri is also too general with his concept of 'une géographie nouvelle', *RC*, i. 3 and 574.

[4] Noted well by J. Guyon, 'Roma: Emerge la città cristiana', in A. Schiavone (ed.), *Storia di Roma 3**. *L'Età tardoantica 2: I luoghi e le culture* (Turin: Einaudi, 1993), 53–68, at 60.

[5] *Contra* Reekmans, art. cit. (n. 1), 861: 'Rome est un example de continuité entre l'Antiquité et le Moyen Age.'   [6] See above, 40–1.

evidence that the bishops, in the building of Christian monuments, felt their choice of sites to be limited to those of the emperor. There is therefore good reason for distinguishing between the contribution to the 'Christianization' of the topography of Rome made by emperors and that effected by bishops. Sometimes the two contributions coincided but this was uncommon.

According to the *Liber Pontificalis*, bishop Sylvester (31 Jan. 314–31 Dec. 335) founded a *titulus* on the site of some land owned by a friend (Equitius) near the baths of Domitian.[7] The same *vita* identified the Baths of Domitian as 'called those of Trajan' and indicated the great complex on the southern side of the Oppian Hill.[8] The testimony of the *Liber Pontificalis* has been called into question because of the apparent duplication of the notice of foundation at the beginning and the end of the *Vita Silvestri* but this need not present an insurmountable problem and Davis has suggested that the second reference in the *Vita Silvestri* may represent a late combination of earlier foundation accounts.[9] It has been accepted by Krautheimer and others that the church of Sylvester stood beneath the present church of San Martino ai Monti and it seemingly adapted existing structures on the site, perhaps a bazaar, a secular basilica, or a late antique *domus*.[10] Constantine, who gave land and gifts to the church, is not known to have taken an interest in the choice of site and the building was well within the walls of Aurelian, close to the Forum Esquilinum. The bishop, who, according to Piétri, was building a church 'pour la piété populaire', clearly did not employ the kind of massive architecture which the emperor was using to dominate certain roads leading into the city, and chose instead a more modest and appropriate layout.

Marcus, bishop from January 336 to October of the same year, is reported by the *Liber Pontificalis* to have built two basilicas. One was on the Via Ardeatina and the other was described as being 'iuxta Pallacinis'.[11]

According to Vielliard, the 'Pallacinae' was the area of the city which

[7] *LP*, i. 170. See Krautheimer, *Corpus*, iii. 87–124; Piétri, *RC*, i. 17–21.

[8] *LP*, i. 187.

[9] R. P. Davis, *The Book of Pontiffs (Liber Pontificalis)* (Liverpool: Liverpool University Press, 1989), p. xx.

[10] Ch. Piétri, 'Recherches sur les *domus ecclesiae*', *Revue des Études Augustiniennes*, 24 (1978), 3–21, at 11 (bazaar); Coarelli, *Guida*, 216–18 (secular basilica). *Domus* suggested by decorative details: F. Guidobaldi, 'L'inserimento delle chiese titolari di Roma nel tessuto urbano. Osservazioni ed implicazioni', in *Quaeritur inventus colitur: Miscellanea in onore di Padre U. M. Fasola* (Vatican City: Pontificio Istituto di archeologia cristiana, 1989), 386; id. 'Edilizia abitativa unifamiliare nella Roma tardoantica', in A. Giardina (ed.), *Società romana e impero tardoantico*, (Rome: Laterza, 1986), ii. 165–237, at 194–8.

[11] *LP*, i. 202. Constantinian gifts and endowments mentioned only at the Ardeatine site.

stretched from the Capitol to the Circus Flaminius and was characterized by dense but occasionally opulent housing.[12] Krautheimer accepted that the ancient foundation of Marcus was beneath the present church of S. Marco al Corso and the fourth-century church stood therefore beside the Via Lata and close to what may have been the Vicus Pallacinae.[13]

The church founded by Marcus within the walls is particularly significant. Constantine made no move to prevent the building of a Christian shrine so close to the 'pagan monumental heart' of the city. The truth is that neither emperor nor bishop perceived a problem. Constantine's interest in the centre was, as argued above, influenced by a number of considerations. But the bishop of the city, in providing for the growing Christian community, felt no inhibition in arranging for a new church to serve the populous zone of the Via Lata. The church itself was considerably humbler than the great Constantinian foundations and apparently made no attempt to adhere to the same architectural plan.

The *Liber Pontificalis* alleges that the site on the Via Ardeatina was commended to the emperor by Marcus and recent excavations have revealed a 'Constantinian' basilica in the area.[14] The presence of an 'ecclesia Marci' was noted by the *Notitia Ecclesiarum Romae* and the *De locis sanctis martyrum quae sunt foris civitatis Romae* in the seventh century. Piétri guessed that it was a humble funerary basilica.[15] The extent of Constantine's interest in the churches of Marcus was to see that they were provided for in the form of liturgical vessels, imperial rents, and properties for maintenance.

From two sources we possess a list of the building which Julius (6 Feb. 337–12 Apr. 352) carried out at Rome:

He constructed many buildings: a basilica on the Via Portesis at the third milestone; a basilica on the Via Flaminia at the second milestone which is called [the church] of Valentinus; the basilica Iulia which is in the seventh

---

[12] R. Vielliard, *Recherches sur les origines de la Rome chrétienne*, 2nd edn., (Rome: Storia e letteratura, 1959), 68; Platner and Ashby, *Topographical Dictionary*, 381–2. Tertullian *Adversus Valentinianos*, 7 commented on the 'insula Felicles'.

[13] For most recent views, see M. Cecchelli, 'S. Marco a Piazza Venezia: Una basilica romana del periodo costantiniano', in C. Bonamente and F. Fusco (eds.), *Costantino il Grande* (Macerata: Pubblicazioni della Facoltà di lettere e filosofia, 1992), 299–310. Also, Krautheimer, *Corpus*, ii. 216 ff. See now Guidobaldi, art. cit. (n. 10), 389 who thought that another *domus* might underlie the present church of S. Marco al Corso.

[14] Piétri *RC* i. 532 n. 6 described attempts to reconstruct the Via Appia–Ardeatina zone as 'un bilan de nos ignorances'. But see A. Nestori, *La basilica anonima della Via Ardeatina*, Studi di antichità cristiana, 42 (Vatican City: Pontificio Istituto di archeologia cristiana, 1990).

[15] Piétri *RC*, i. 72; Valentini and Zucchetti, ii. 89 (*Notitia*); 110 (*De locis*).

region near to the forum of the deified Trajan; a basilica across the Tiber in the fourteenth region next to Callistus; a basilica on the Via Aurelia at the third milestone at Callistus.[16]

He built two basilicas, one in Rome close to the Forum, the other across the Tiber; and three cemeteries, one on the Via Flaminia, one on the Via Aurelia and one on the Via Portuensis.[17]

The *Liberian Catalogue* comes from the diverse collection of documents dating to AD 354. It was certainly read and used by an early compiler of the *Liber Pontificalis*.[18] The two accounts therefore probably originated from the same source. It has been suggested by Verrando that the *Liberian Catalogue* has recorded the buildings in the *chronological* order of construction, but this seems to be impossible to verify.[19] The *Liberian Catalogue*, on the other hand, was certainly drawn up close to the papacy of Julius and is to be regarded as a trustworthy document.[20]

Taking the evidence for the basilicas within the walls of Aurelian first, we find that Julius built one 'regione vii iuxta forum divi Traiani' (*Liberian Catalogue*) or 'iuxta forum' (*Liber Pontificalis*).[21] As with the church of bishop Marcus, the preposition 'iuxta' in both documents need not imply physical adjacency and can be better understood as the crudest possible orientation with reference to a major nearby monument. Similarly, the use of the term 'basilica' does not indicate architectural grandeur or a particular design. Here, the importance of the building lies in its position within the city. Duchesne, in his great edition of the *Liber Pontificalis*, identified the Julian foundation with the modern church of the SS. Dodici Apostoli.[22] Duchesne, as the editor of the *Liber Pontificalis*, was aware of a notice in the *vita* of Pope Pelagius I, referring to the *foundation* of a basilica *c*.561.[23] This basilica was certainly once on the site of the modern Church of the Holy

[16] *MGH*, i. 76: 'Hic multas fabricas fecit: basilicam in via Portese miliario iii; basilicam in via Flaminia mil. ii, quae appellatur Valentini; basilicam Iuliam, quae est regione vii iuxta forum divi Traiani; basilicam trans Tiberim regione xiiii iuxta Callistum; basilicam in via Aurelia mil. iii ad Callistum.'

[17] *LP*, i. 205: 'Fecit basilicas ii: una in urbe Roma iuxta forum et altera trans Tiberim; et cymiteria iii: unum via Flaminia, alium via Aurelia et alium via Portuense.'

[18] Davis, op. cit. (n. 9), pp. xxvii–xxviii; see also Salzman, *On Roman Time*, 47–50 on the Liberian Catalogue.

[19] C. N. Verrando, 'L'Attività edilizia di papa Giulio I e la basilica al III miglio della via Aurelia ad Callistum', *MEFRA*, 97 (1985), 1023.

[20] Piétri considered it 'une source incontestable': *RC*, i. 22.

[21] For what follows, see *Lexicon*, i. 180–1 (G. De Spirito).

[22] *LP*, i. 205 n. 4. Also L. Duchesne, 'Notes sur la topographie de Rome du moyen âge', *Mélanges d'archéologie et d'histoire*, 7 (1887), 235. Krautheimer, *Corpus*, i. 79 rejects.   [23] *LP*, i. 306 n. 2.

Apostles.[24] More importantly, the site could certainly be said to be in proximity to ('iuxta') the Forum of Trajan. Unfortunately, there was in Duchesne's time and up to our own no archaeological evidence to support this idea that the Julian site had been used in the sixth century, and the recorded epigraphical dedications in the basilica founded in 561 made no reference to bishop Julius.[25] An inscription which first made an appearance in the fourteenth century contains a puzzling reference to the church being founded originally by Constantine, but made no mention of bishop Julius:

This venerable basilica in honour of the Twelve Apostles, founded first of all by Constantine, was afterwards destroyed by heretics.[26]

Verrando has drawn attention to another passage in the *Liber Pontificalis* which records the rededication of one of the *basilicae Julii* by Celestine I (10 Sept. 422–27 July 432).[27] The reference indicates that the original building had been damaged by fire at the time of the Gothic sack of the city. Although Duchesne thought that the basilica of Julius in Trastevere was meant, Verrando argues convincingly that a church in the vicinity of the present church of SS. Dodici Apostoli is much more likely. The Goths are traditionally understood to have entered Rome at the Porta Salaria and poured southwards into the city.[28] Verrando thinks it unlikely that the basilica of Julius in Trastevere was damaged.

Though no physical remains of a fourth-century basilica are known, the topographical details of the *Liberian Catalogue* cannot be dismissed. Even those scholars hostile to the theory that Julius' basilica underlies the modern church admit that the older structure stood nearby and was probably abandoned when the new basilica was erected in the sixth century to serve the same community.[29] The basilica of Julius therefore stood near to if not under the sixth-century Church of the Holy Apostles. Since the preposition 'iuxta' would make little sense if a major architectural site lay between the new basilica and the Forum of Trajan, the position of the basilica is to be understood as being within the area bounded by the monuments: Barracks of the First Cohort of Vigiles–Temple of Serapis–Baths of Constantine–Forum of Trajan.

The early Christians of Rome had probably established themselves in the area long before Constantine although the precise location of

---

[24] Krautheimer, *Corpus*, i. 79.   [25] Ibid.

[26] E. Zocca, *La basilica dei Santi Apostoli in Roma: Note storico-artistiche: Miscellanea Francescana*, 59 (1959), 353: 'Haec ven. basilica in honorem XII apostolorum | Primo a Constantino fundata | Postmodum ab haereticis fuit destructa. . .'

[27] *LP*, i. 230; Verrando, art. cit. (n. 19), 1027–8.

[28] P. Courcelle, *Histoire littéraire des grandes invasions germaniques* (Paris: Hachette, 1948), 45.   [29] Verrando, art. cit. (n. 19), 1033.

their earliest churches (*tituli*) remains highly speculative and controversial.[30] It must be emphasized that the evidence for the position of
these buildings is almost exclusively literary, from much later Christian sources which had a vested interest in promoting the ancient
foundation of a number of churches which were prominent in the
medieval era. The widely held belief current in the early years of the
twentieth century that archaeology would confirm the antiquity of
Rome's *tituli* has been laid to rest by Charles Piétri who demonstrated
the slender and ambiguous nature of the archaeological evidence in an
important article written in 1977.[31] It was perhaps wrong of students of
the *tituli* to think that physical remains of early foundations would be
found but at the same time so little is known about the layout of early
Christian churches that Piétri's failure to discover any significant
evidence of Christian occupation is neither surprising nor absolutely
conclusive. The position of pre-Constantinian *tituli* are not the subject
of this chapter but the tradition of their presence is an interesting
context in which to locate the post-Constantinian foundations.

Julius' new building, like the basilica of Marcus, was designed
specifically for Christian worship, but it was not a *titulus*. That is to
say, it did not possess its own clergy given a stipend from the
proceeds of lands donated to the church to serve and live permanently
on the site.[32] In Vielliard's words, basilicas like this functioned as
'salles de réunions interparoissiales', large enough to accommodate the
congregations of several local *tituli*.[33] If Vielliard's reconstruction of
the earliest *tituli* of Rome is examined, it can be seen that a Christian
presence in the area of Julius' basilica had already been established by
a *Titulus Marcelli* placed probably to the north of the Julian structure
and just off the Via Lata, and more recently by the basilica established
by pope Marcus 'iuxta pallacinis' in the vicinity of the Via Lata.[34]
Presumably, the clergy from the *Titulus Marcelli* would serve the new
church when required.[35] The new basilica lay east of the Via Lata and
did not constitute a penetration of the Campus Martius by fourth-
century Christian architecture. Moving north-east, along the Alta
Semita and up the Quirinal, the ancient *tituli* of Gaius and Cyriacus
stood 300 m apart, the former being described in the *passio* of Saint
Susanna as 'ante forum Salustii'.[36] The fifth-century Hieronymian

[30] See above, 40 n. 249 and G. F. Snyder, *Ante Pacem: Archeological Evidence of
Church Life Before Constantine* (Macon, Ga.: Mercer, 1985), chap. 1.

[31] See n. 10.

[32] The *LP* has no record of any Constantinian endowments. Vielliard, *Recherches*, 29.

[33] Ibid. 69.

[34] Ibid. 35. Krautheimer, *Corpus*, ii. 205 ff.; M. Cecchelli, art. cit. (n. 13).

[35] Vielliard, *Recherches*, 69.

[36] *Passio* of Susanna: *AASS* August vol. 2, *Acta*, 6 (p. 632).

Martyrology recorded 14 April as the feast day of Cyriacus 'Romae in titulo iuxta [Thermas] Diocletianas Cyriaci'.[37] These *tituli* formed part of a band of Christian meeting places scattered on the eastern hills of the city. On the Esquiline were the *tituli* of Pudentia (S. Pudenziana), Praxedes (S. Prassede) and Equitius/Silvester (S. Martino ai Monti). Further south, on the slopes of the Caelian, stood the *tituli* of Clemens (S. Clemente) and Nicomedius (SS. Pietro e Marcellino).[38]

The significance attached by Julius to the Esquiline area may also be suggested by an examination of the site of the Roman council of 340 or 341, which cleared Athanasius of the accusations made against him at Tyre in 335.[39] According to Athanasius himself, the meeting was held 'in the house of the presbyter Vitus' and over fifty bishops came.[40] Verrando used the choice of site in 340 or 341 to argue that the urban basilicas of Julius had not yet been built.[41] This, however, is not a compelling view as the Lateran was certainly available at the time and had been used before, in 313, for a meeting to decide the Donatist problem.[42] The *episcopium* was a former imperial house and could certainly have held more prelates than it actually did in 313. It seems therefore, that Julius' choice was based upon his own *preference* for a particular site. In fact, Vitus has been identified with one of the two representatives of the Roman church who attended the Council at Nicaea and it could therefore be that Julius was deliberately invoking the authority of the decisions of that council in a particularly direct way as he aligned his community behind Athanasius.[43]

Where was the 'house of the presbyter Vitus'? Coarelli has claimed that there exist unidentified fourth-century remains under the little church of Saint Vito on the Esquiline.[44] We know from the *Liber Pontificalis* that a deaconry existed on the spot in the eighth century,[45] and the same building made an appearance in the ninth-century

---

[37] For 14 April in Hieronymian Martyrology see *AASS*, November vol. 2.2, p. 190.

[38] See Vielliard, *Recherches*, 41 ff.

[39] See T. D. Barnes, *Athanasius and Constantius*, (Cambridge, Mass./London: Harvard University Press, 1993), 47–55.

[40] Athanasius, *Historia Arianorum*, 15; *Apologia contra Arianos*, 20 (= *PG* 25, 281).

[41] Verrando, art. cit. (n. 19), 1023–4 with n. 4.

[42] Optatus Milevitanus 1, 23 (*CSEL* 26, 26). See p. 93 above.

[43] Although Vitus and Vincentius played little part in the debate, they followed bishop Ossius and were therefore second on the list of signatories to the canons of Nicaea. Vitus had also been bishop Silvester's representative at the council of Arles. See Piétri *RC*, i. 174 f. with n. 3 on p. 174 and id. 'Appendice prosopographique à la *Roma Christiana*', *MEFRA*, 89 (1977), 374.

[44] Coarelli, *Guida*, 220. See also V. Santa Maria Scrinari, 'Brevi note sugli scavi sotto la chiesa di S. Vito', *Archeologia Laziale*, 2 (1979), 58–62.

[45] *LP*, ii. 12. See Vielliard, *Recherches*, 130.

Einsiedeln Itinerary.[46] It acquired the topographical epithets 'in macello' and 'iuxta macellum Liviae' in the Dark Ages.[47] Naturally, the present church may not necessarily occupy the *precise* site of the ancient house, but from other Christian topographical examples (especially that of the so-called 'Liberian Basilica') we can be certain that it was not far away. For these reasons, the account of Athanasius can be taken to refer to a meeting of bishops which took place in a house on the Esquiline, probably close to the *Porta Esquilina* and *Macellum Liviae*, probably at the site presently occupied by the present church of Saint Vito adjacent to the Arch of Gallienus on the Esquiline. The evidence is only circumstantial and in the literary tradition goes no further back than the eighth century. Still, it is likely that the council of 340 or 341 gave to the place where it was held a status above that of other private dwellings in the city. It was this enhanced status that eventually made the site's transformation into a church both possible and desirable. A further encouragement may have been the apparent concentration of Christians in the area of the central Esquiline and its spurs.

In Trastevere, Julius visited another site untouched by Constantine. There he built a basilica 'iuxta Callistum', according to the more detailed *Liberian Catalogue*.[48] The full extent of the Julian structure as well as the dimensions of any building which had preceded it are unknown. Excavations under and around S. Maria in Trastevere between 1865 and 1871 brought to light 'le fondazioni di manufatti chiesastici precedenti' and De Rossi postulated two phases of building, under the Roman bishops Julius I and later Gregory IV (Oct. 827–25 Jan. 844).[49] The archaeological work on the site has been too patchy to provide firm evidence, but Krautheimer was confident that the site presently occupied by the church of S. Maria in Trastevere was that of the fourth-century church.[50] By the middle of the fourth century, when the *Liberian Catalogue* was drawn up, the church had clear associations with a 'Callistus' known in Trastevere. According to the *Liber Pontificalis*, the third-century bishop Callistus (217–22) had constructed a 'basilica' 'trans Tiberim'.[51] Christian

---

[46] G. Walser (ed.), *Die Einsiedler Inschriftensammlung und der Pilgerführer durch Rom (Codex Einsiedlensis 326)*, Historia Einzelschriften, 53 (Stuttgart: Steiner Verlag Wiesbaden, 1987), 162, 178, 179.

[47] H. Jordan, *Topographie der Stadt Rom* (Berlin: Weidmannsche Buchhandlung, 1907), i, pt. 3, 344 with n. 4; ibid. (1871), ii. 128. Ch. Huelsen, *Le chiese di Roma nel medio evo* (Florence: L. S. Olschki, 1927), 499–500 for the 'chiesa antichissima'.

[48] Quoted above p. 120.

[49] Full references in Verrando, art. cit. (n. 19), 1034–5.

[50] Krautheimer, *Corpus*, iii. 68.

[51] *LP*, i. 141. Duchesne believed the site to be that of S. Maria in Trastevere, ibid. 141 n. 5.

tradition located three ancient *tituli* here, those of Cecilia, Chryso-gonus, and Callistus.[52] Julius' basilica probably stood adjacent or close to the site associated with Callistus. The choice is not surprising. Though three *domus ecclesiae* are reputed to have stood in Trastevere, bishop Callistus was the most famous Christian patron in the area. He was the earliest non-apostolic martyr in the *Depositio Martyrum* or *Feriale Ecclesiae Romanae*, making him the foremost of the non-apostolic martyrs of the city.[53] The site of the new basilica thus put Julius into contact with a Christian bishop and martyr of particularly high status.

Outside the walls of the city, Julius patronized three points in the countryside around Rome (fig. 21). According to the *Liberian Catalogue* he constructed a basilica 'in via Portese [Portuensi] miliario iii'.[54] The building seems not to have been a martyrial cemetery and no martyr's name was attached to the fourth-century notice. No basilica has yet been found here and Verrando has suggested that we should visualize a simple edifice 'in un possesso personale del pontefice'.[55] There is no reason to think that the basilica was a particularly large building and of course, it was to be found in a zone which had not interested Constantine.

The Julian contribution on the Via Flaminia, however, is rather more controversial. The Christian cemetery, *memoria* to Saint Valentinus, and basilica developed beside a pagan necropolis.[56] Krautheimer postulated at least three stages in the growth of the Christian zone. At some stage the *memoria* was placed in the Christian cemetery. Then a basilica was constructed. At a later date, under bishop Honorius I (27 Oct. 625–12 Oct. 638), according to the seventh-century *Notitia Ecclesiarum Urbis Romae*, repairs and 'magnificent decoration' were carried out at the site.[57] Finally, the *Liber Pontificalis* alleged a rebuilding of the basilica 'from the ground' under bishop Theodore I (24 Nov. 642–14 May 649).[58] Krautheimer concluded that Julius had

---

[52] Vielliard, *Recherches*, 49–52. This zone may well have been called the 'area Callisti': *ILCV*, 1904 (a slave or dog collar) 'revoca me ad domnu meu Viventium in area Callisti.'

[53] *MGH*, i. 72. K. Baus, *From the Apostolic Community to Constantine* (London: Burns & Oates, 1980), 274–5. See also A. Stuiber, 'Heidnische und christliche Gedächtniskalender', *JbAC*, 3 (1960), 30. No martyrs except apostles pre-date the third century. See the remarks of H. Delehaye, *Les origines du culte des martyrs*, Subsidia Hagiographica, 20, 2nd edn., (Brussels: Société des Bollandistes, 1933), 262 ff. For a study of the *passio Callisti* see G. N. Verrando, 'La *passio Callisti* e il santuario della via Aurelia', *MEFRA*, 96 (1984), 1039–83.

[54] See above p. 120.   [55] Verrando, (n. 19), 1036.

[56] Krautheimer, *Corpus* iv. 289–312. See L. De Santis and G. Biamonte, *Le catacombe di Roma* (Rome: Newton & Compton, 1997), 142 ff.

[57] *Itinerarium Salisburgense/Notitia Ecclesiarum* in Valentini and Zucchetti, ii. 73. Cf. *De locis*: ibid. 118.   [58] *LP*, i. 332–3.

built the basilica, while the *memoria* pre-dated him, and was possibly created during Maxentius' reign.[59] Verrando has suggested, however, by a redating of some of the critical sources, that the *memoria* was built by Julius (thus interpreting basilica in the *Liberian Catalogue* in a vague sense) and the basilica appeared later, under Theodore I.[60] Verrando's arguments for the redating of the documents rest on stylistic grounds which, considering the brevity of the texts, are less than convincing. It is more satisfactory to accept the interpretation of Krautheimer and his important remarks on the significance of the new basilica. It was the first of the Christian three-naved basilicas in Rome. It was also the first site to reveal the employment of the three-naved basilica in a funerary context. Finally, and perhaps most obviously, it showed an architectural innovation quite distinct from the great Constantinian U-shaped cemeterial basilicas.[61]

On the Via Aurelia, Julius was reported to have built 'basilicam . . . mil. iii ad Callistum'.[62] In addition to this, the *Liber Pontificalis* claims that Julius was buried in the same place:

He was buried on the Via Aurelia in the cemetery of Calepodius at the third mile ⟨from Rome⟩ on 12 April.[63]

and the seventh-century *Notitia Ecclesiarum Urbis Romae* noted of the area:

on the same road [the Via Aurelia] you will arrive at a church: there you will find Saint Callistus pope and martyr, and Saint Julius pope and martyr [is] in the second [place] in the farther *domus*.[64]

Archaeological work was carried out at the site by Stevenson, Josi, and Nestori.[65] Excavations have revealed a catacomb complex which developed in several stages. Two points provided *foci* for the network. One has been identified by Nestori as the gallery where bishop

[59] Krautheimer, *Corpus* iv (1970), 308–11.

[60] Verrando, art. cit. (n. 19), 1037 ff.

[61] For dating of documents see ibid. with n. 63. I reproduce Krautheimer's conclusions, *Corpus*, iv. 311.

[62] See above p. 120. Verrando, art. cit. (n. 19). Also A. Nestori, 'La catacomba di Calepodio al iii miglio dell' Aurelia vetus e i sepolcri dei papi Callisto I e Giulio I (1 parte)', *RAC*, 47 (1971), 169–278. *Tavole* i and ii are indispensable. Also id. 'La catacomba di Calepodio al iii miglio dell' Aurelia vetus e i sepolcri dei papi Callisto I e Giulio I (2 parte)', *RAC*, 48 (1972), 193–233.

[63] *LP*, i. 205: 'qui etiam sepultus est in via Aurelia, in cymiterio Calepodi, miliario III, prid. id. april.'

[64] Valentini and Zucchetti, ii. 93–4: 'eadem via [Aurelia] pervenies ad ecclesiam: ibi invenies sanctum Cal[l]istum papam et martirem, et in altero [loco] in superiori domo sanctus Iulius papa et martir.'

[65] For references to earlier archaeological work see Verrando, art. cit. (n. 19), 1041–2.

Callistus was interred in the third century.[66] The other is the remains of what Nestori termed a 'basilica semipogea' in the shape of a Greek cross (fig. 22).[67] This has been understood to be the basilica constructed by Julius.[68] As for the spot where Julius himself was buried, the sources are unclear. The *Depositio Episcoporum* gave the location as 'in via Aurelia miliario iii in Callisti' but the *Notitia* gives the more precise 'in superiori domo'. Verrando accepted the testimony of the latter, concluding that the fourth-century bishop's grave was in the building 'sopratterra assimilabile tipologicamente ad una casa'.[69]

The *Notitia* was no model of topographical rigour, but the resting places of the Roman bishops Callistus and Julius were barely 50 m apart. It seems difficult to believe that the gallery where Callistus lay was construed by the author of the *Notitia* as an 'ecclesia'. He may even not have seen the site himself and assumed that it was. Clearly, the new basilica enjoyed no typological similarities to the Constantinian basilicas, except perhaps that it had some kind of funerary function; the pavement had had *formae* laid into it.[70]

The *Liberian Catalogue*, it is to be remembered, linked the basilica directly to the resting place of Callistus and the conclusion is unavoidable that bishop Julius deliberately attached himself to two important sites, one urban and the other rural, of particular significance to Callistus.

Julius and his immediate predecessors demonstrated the freedom of the bishops of Rome to choose sites for their churches independently of the emperor Constantine. Significantly, Marcus and Julius both built structures close to the so-called 'pagan monumental centre' of the city. They made no attempt, however, to outdo the emperor with regard to the scale of these churches.

Julius' choices of site were significant. If there is any value in the *tituli* tradition, it would suggest that Julius' basilica close to the centre of the city was a further contribution to a significant monumental Christian presence in the eastern sector of the city, dominated by the Quirinal, Viminal, Cispian, Oppian, and Esquiline Hills. On the western side of the city, Julius seems to have expressed an affinity for the presence of the traces of Saint Callistus, the third-century pope. Taken with the new churches of his recent predecessors, one has the impression of a steady extension of the Christian topography of Rome. The years after Julius' death, however, witnessed the emergence of a schismatic threat to this emerging topographical unity.

[66] Gallery A1 at the foot of the main entrance-staircase. Nestori, art. cit. (n. 62) 184–218 (plan II).   [67] Art. cit. (n. 62) [1972] plan on p. 196.
[68] Art. cit. (n. 62) [1972] 194; 204–6. Also G. N. Verrando, art. cit. (n. 19), 1054.
[69] Ibid. 1046.   [70] Analysed by Nestori, art. cit. (n. 62).

2. THE *BASILICA-MAUSOLEUM* COMPLEX ON THE VIA NOMENTANA

All of Julius' building projects were dwarfed by the appearance, sometime after the death of Constantine, of a large funerary basilica near the tomb of Saint Agnes on the Via Nomentana.[71] Though the *Liber Pontificalis* alleged that Constantine had built it 'ex rogatu filiae suae', Piétri has argued strongly that the structure belongs to the period after his death.[72] In the apse of the basilica the daughter of the emperor placed an inscription which claimed all the credit:

I, Constantina, venerating God and dedicated to Christ,
having provided all the expenses with devoted mind
at divine bidding and with the great help of Christ,
consecrated this *templum* of Agnes, victorious virgin,
because she has prevailed over the temples and all earthly works,
[Here] where the loftiest roof gleams with gold.[73]

As at the other major Constantinian sites, the bishops of the city had no part in the provision of this huge complex. The project was carried out in the name of the ruling dynasty. This link between the site and the family of Constantine was emphasized by the addition, after the death of Constantina, of a circular mausoleum housing her remains to the flank of the basilica.[74] Significantly, despite the extensive gifts of riches and land revenues recorded in the *Liber Pontificalis*, the site of the complex remained in the property of the imperial family.[75] When Helena, the Christian wife of Julian, died in 360, Julian sent her body back to Rome to be interred:

on his property near the city on the road to Nomentum, where her sister Constantina, once the wife of Gallus, was also buried.[76]

---

[71] See W. N. Schumacher in J. G. Deckers, H. R. Seeliger, and G. Mietke, *Die Katakombe "Santi Marcellino e Pietro" Repertorium der Malereien*, Roma Sotteranea, 6 (Vatican City: Pontificio Istituto di archeologia cristiana, 1987), 136–9; A. Frutaz, *Il complesso monumentale di sant'Agnese e di Santa Costanza*, 2nd edn. (Rome: Tipografia poliglotta vaticana, 1969), 27–34 with good plan. Coarelli, *Dintorni*, 196–9. Particularly good for mosaics is H. Stern, 'Les mosaïques de l'église Ste-Constance', *DOP*, 12 (1958), 157–218, esp. 160–6.

[72] Piétri *RC*, i. 47–50. See Coarelli, *Dintorni*, 196–7.

[73] Diehl *ILCV* 1768, ll. 1–6: 'Constantina dm [deum] venerans Xpoque dicata|Omnibus impensis devota mente paratis|Numine divino multum Xpoque iuvante|Sacravi templum victricis virginis Agnes,|Templorum quod vincit opus terrenaque cuncta,|Aurea quae rutilant summi fastigia tecti.'

[74] Ammianus 14, 1, 2. See also Ferrua, *Epigrammata*, no. 71, pp. 246 ff. For Constantina herself see *PLRE* I, 222 'Constantina 2'.

[75] Gifts and endowments: *LP*, i. 180f.   [76] Ammianus 21, 1, 5.

Episcopal interventions at the site tended to focus on the tomb of Agnes and will be examined in due course. For the moment it is enough to acknowledge the very special and predominantly non-episcopal nature of this large-scale imperial building work after Constantine.

3. LIBERIUS AND FELIX[77]

For the dispute between the bishop Liberius (17 May 352–24 Sept. 366) and the antipope Felix II (355–22 Dec. 365) there is little first-hand evidence. To make matters worse, the episode was extremely controversial not only in the fourth century but in later centuries as well, combining as it did the issues of Arianism and papal credibility. The available evidence may be divided into three categories. First, there is the *Liber Pontificalis*, whose account of the lives of the two antagonists was drawn up at least a century and a half after the events.[78] The problems in dealing with this text are many and best treated individually when they are particularly relevant to the theme of this chapter. It is worth noting, however, that unlike the majority of other sources for the dispute, the *Liber Pontificalis*, in its life of Felix, draws a decidedly favourable picture of the anti-pope.[79] Second is the preface to a work written in the later years of the fourth century and known as the *Libellus Precum*, a letter to the emperors Valentinian II, Theodosius I, and Arcadius, composed by partisans of one faction in the conflict which developed out of the events to be treated in this section.[80] Though suffering from the familiar tendency to distort the motivation of their enemies, the authors of this document nevertheless included some topographical details in their account of the origins of the dispute which affected them. Given the chronological proximity of this letter to the events it describes, these strictly topographical details are unlikely to have been fabricated, and in any event, the hostile *interpretation* put on the actual events themselves was what the authors hoped would impress the emperors. Third comes a host of Christian apologists and historians writing in the fourth and later centuries, often

---

[77] General bibliography: G. N. Verrando, 'Liberio-Felice: osservazione e rettifiche di carattere storico-agiografico', *Rivista di storia della chiesa in Italia*, 35 (1981), 97–104. S. L. Greenslade, *Schism in the Early Church*, 2nd edn. (London: SCM, 1964), 49–50. Piétri, *RC*, i. 237–68. Also H. Leclercq's two articles in *DACL*, 9/1 (1930), s.v. 'Liber Pontificalis' and 'Liberius'. Louis Duchesne's comments crucial at *LP*, i. pp. cxx–cxxv. Most recently, Maier, art. cit. (n. 1), 232–49, at 243 ff.

[78] *LP*, i, p. cxxiii. Also Davis, op. cit. (n. 9), pp. ii–iv and pp. xxxvii–xxxviii.

[79] For examples of later pro-Felician propaganda see W. Smith and H. Wace (eds), *Dictionary of Christian Biography* (London: Murray, 1911), s.v. 'Felix II'.

[80] *Collectio Avellana* I (*CSEL* 35, no.1).

with a vested interest in one side or the other and unfortunately only rarely capable of providing topographical information.[81]

As suggested above, the episcopate of Julius had seen the gradual extension of the Christian topography through the siting of two basilicas inside the city and three outside it. One of the features of the rivalry between Liberius and Felix, which engulfed the Roman church after Julius' death, was the association of particular areas of the city with one or other of the disputants. It will be argued here that this schismatic 'fracture' of the Christian topography of the city was to influence the monumental Christianization of the city, within the period of this study, until well into the papacy of Damasus.

Liberius succeeded Julius on 17 May 352.[82] There were two major issues in the Christian world at this time. One was that the emperor Constantius II, recently forced to become the sole legitimate holder of the purple, was a fervent Arian. He became the temporal master of bishops in the west who strongly resisted eastern Christological doctrine. The other issue was a new development in the long-running controversy between Athanasius, bishop of Alexandria, and the imperial power. Athanasius had been restored to his see in 346 after patching up his differences with Constantius. But during the brief reign of Magnentius in the western empire it was alleged that Athanasius had received an emissary from the usurper.[83] The old imperial distrust of the cleric resurfaced. At ecclesiastical councils in Arles (353) and Milan (355) the emperor attempted to force the western bishops to condemn Athanasius.

These councils occupied the early years of Liberius' papacy. Topographically, the most important development in this period in the city of Rome was the completion of the Constantinian basilica on the Vatican. Liberius himself is the first bishop of the city known to have celebrated the liturgy there.[84] Despite the presence of the bishop, however, the project was identified strongly with the imperial family.[85] Significantly, the *depositio martyrium* or *feriale ecclesiae Romanae* from 354 still recorded the site of the celebration of Rome's two apostolic martyrs (III kal. Iul.) as 'in catacumbas'.[86] The prestige of this festival would seem to have remained largely unaffected by the

---

[81] Athanasius, *Historia Arianorum* 35–41; Jerome, *Chronicon* MCCCLX (Helm, 237); Rufinus *HE* 10, 22; Socrates *HE* 2, 37; Sozomen *HE* 4, 8; Theodoret *HE* 2, 14.

[82] *MGH*, i. 76.

[83] See Barnes, op. cit. (n. 39), 101–8; Piétri *RC*, i. 195 on Athanasius *Apologia* 6.

[84] Ambrose, *de virginitate* 3, 1–3.

[85] See pp. 109–14 above and pp. 290–1 below.

[86] *MGH*, i. 71. See Piétri, *RC*, i. 57; M. Guarducci, 'Il 29 Giugno: Festa degli Apostoli Pietro e Paolo', *Atti della Pontificia Accademia Romana di Archeologia*, Serie 3, Rendiconti, 57 (1985–6), 115–27.

natalis of Peter 'de cathedra' on the Vatican earlier in the year (vii kal. Martias).[87]

We have seen, however, that alongside the imperial contribution to the Christian topography in this period rose that of the bishops themselves. Liberius too built a basilica but the date of the foundation is unknown precisely. The chronographer of 354, in a document listing the popes and their main achievements up until that date, did not mention the basilica as one might certainly have expected, if it had existed at that time.[88] It would seem more likely that the basilica of Liberius was constructed at some time in the period after 354 and before his death (September 366). Liberius was exiled in 355 by Constantius and the exile may have interrupted work then going on at the site. Alternatively, and more likely, the basilica was started and finished *after* the return of the popular pope from exile.

That exile came about in 355 because the bishop of Rome refused to acquiesce in the condemnation of Athanasius.[89] As a result of his opposition, Liberius was exiled to Thrace. According to the near contemporary first letter of the *Collectio Avellana*, on the same day that Liberius set out for exile the whole church in Rome swore that it would receive no new *pontifex* while Liberius lived.[90] But when Constantius II chose Liberius' arch-deacon Felix as his replacement, some clerics accepted the appointment. A division now occurred in the church at Rome with 'the entire Christian community' (universus populus) having nothing to do with Felix, according to the authors of the preface to the *Libellus Precum*.[91]

Of Felix himself we now know little. His memory revived in the Middle Ages when it was thought that he had stood against an expedient Liberius, but part of our most substantial source closest to these events, the *Liber Pontificalis*, is much more hostile. Louis Duchesne, the most important editor of the work, thought that the *vita* of Felix was a late interpolation, not least because the *vita* of Liberius included details of Felix which did not match those of the *vita*

---

[87] For discussions of this festival and the Caristia (on the same day) see Ch. Piétri, 'Concordia Apostolorum et Renovatio Urbis', *MEFRA*, 73 (1961), 275–322, at 275–6; id., *RC*, i. 381–9; Salzman, *On Roman Time*, 47; V. Saxer, 'Damase et le calendrier des fêtes de martyrs de l'église Romaine', in *Saecularia Damasiana*, Studi di antichità cristiana, 39 (Vatican City: Pontificio istituto di archeologia cristiana, 1986), 65 ff. See also M. Guarducci, 'Feste pagane e feste cristiane a Roma', *Atti della Pontificia Accademia Romana di Archeologia*, Serie 3, Rendiconti, 59 (1986–7), 119–25.

[88] *MGH*, i. 76.

[89] Ammianus Marcellinus 15, 7, 6–10. At 10: Liberius was spirited away but only with the greatest difficulty and in the middle of the night, for fear of the populace, who were devotedly attached to him. See Barnes, op. cit. (n. 39), 118.

[90] *Collectio Avellana* 1, 2.   [91] Ibid.

of Felix himself in important respects. He showed convincingly that *certain* elements of the life had untrustworthy origins.[92] Nevertheless, the testimony of the *Liber Pontificalis* provides some interesting topographical details which as we shall see are plausible and can be corroborated with other known evidence.

Felix was certainly less popular than Liberius. The former's election as bishop took place, according to Athanasius, at Rome in the imperial palace with court eunuchs 'representing' the people, and the consecration was performed by three villainous prelates.[93] Perhaps this was simply a slander against the enemy of a close friend of Athanasius based on the clear support which the Arian emperor had offered. Whether the accusation is true or not, Athanasius' disapproving account demonstrates the principle that bishops of Rome were at this date to be consecrated only at some Christian holy site in the city.[94]

The *Liber Pontificalis* records in the *vita* of Felix that at some stage during his irregular episcopate:

He built a basilica on the Via Aurelia while he still discharged the office of the priesthood, and at the same church he purchased the land around the place which he presented to the church he built ⟨at the second mile from Rome⟩.[95]

No basilica of Felix has ever been found here. The same work, in the *vita* of Felix I (268–73), said that this bishop too had constructed a basilica on the Via Aurelia.[96] Duchesne argued that the compiler of the *Liber Pontificalis* confused a *martyr* Felix with one or two later bishops of the same name.[97] The *Liber Pontificalis* further records that both bishops were buried in cemeteries on the Via Aurelia, a claim that is certainly not true in the case of Felix I who was interred in San Callisto.[98] But as we saw above, both Julius and the early bishop and martyr Callistus I were interred on the Via Aurelia. Without any firm archaeological evidence, it would be wrong to suggest that Felix II was associating himself with two of his most eminent predecessors but the author of the *Liber Pontificalis* clearly associated Felix II with the west of the city.

Duchesne demonstrated that the details of the death of Felix II as

---

[92] *LP*, i. pp. cxx–cxxv.

[93] Athanasius, *Historia Arianorum* 75. This account was dramatized to make Felix look like a court puppet, cf. Socrates *HE* 2, 37. Piétri *RC*, i. 249 rejects the accusation that Felix was a creature of a court theological faction. See Barnes, op. cit. (n. 39), 118.

[94] Cf. *Gesta Liberii*, 1 = *PL* 8, 1388 for the alleged ordination of Liberius as deacon by bishop Marcus in 327 in the 'basilica Constantiniana'. See also the discussion of Damasus and Ursinus below 139.

[95] *LP*, i. 211: 'Hic fecit basilicam Via Aurelia cum presbiterii honore fungeretur et in eadem ecclesia emit agrum circa locum quod obtulit ecclesiae quam fecit.'

[96] *LP*, i. 158 with n. 3.   [97] Ibid. pp. cxxiii f.   [98] *MGH*, i. 70.

reported in his *vita* in the *Liber Pontificalis* were in fact the 'debris' of an account of the death of a martyr Felix. But the account in the *vita* of Liberius was different. After the return of Liberius, according to the *Liber Pontificalis*:

Deprived of the bishopric, Felix lived on his small estate on the Via Portuensis, where he died peacefully on 29 July.[99]

The relationship between Felix and Liberius as recorded in the *Liber Pontificalis* is a strange one. We are surprised to find part of the text favourable to Felix and hostile to Liberius. Duchesne thought that this could only have come about through the confusion of Felix with 'un grand saint'. There were a number of martyrs named Felix associated with Rome but the most popular site was on the Via Portuensis where a sixth century *index* of cemeteries in Rome made mention of only one 'sanctus Felix'.[100] This is a theory with much to commend it: the extraordinary inversion of Felix and Liberius and the clear confusion over the date and manner of the demise of Felix. But I should like to suggest, perhaps obviously, that the reason why the identities of bishop and martyr were so effectively confused was because Felix had actually *spent* time in this quarter of the city.[101] It is not to be forgotten that Julius' basilica was constructed at the third milestone on the Via Portuensis, a site which became the focus of a Felix II cult in the fifteenth century.[102] The question of how exactly the confusion had come into existence is one that Duchesne did not fully explore. The truth is surely that Felix II's topographical association with this area made the confusion all the easier. Therefore the topographical details in the *Liber Pontificalis* account are credible: at some time during his episcopate he founded a basilica on the Via Aurelia and after his deposition from the bishopric of Rome he retired to the south-west of the city, to an estate on the Via Portuensis. Is the evidence of the *Liber Pontificalis* enough?

We may appeal to the near-contemporary *Collectio Avellana*:

in the third year [after his exile from Rome] Liberius returned . . . Felix was condemned by the senate and he was driven out of the city by the people. But after a short space of time at the urging of his priests, who had bound

---

[99] *LP*, i. 207: 'Qui depositus Felix de episcopatum habitavit in praediolo suo via Portuense, ubi et requievit in pace IIII kal. Aug.' Cf. *Gesta Eusebii* cited by G. N. Verrando, 'Il santuario di S. Felice sulla via Portuense', *MEFRA*, 100 (1988), 331–66, at 353.

[100] *LP*, i. cxxiii. Valentini and Zucchetti, ii. 66 with n. 2. For the date, ibid. 58: 'noi non crediamo di poter scendere col documento ad una età posteriore al secolo vii.'

[101] See Verrando, art. cit. (n. 99), 353.   [102] Verrando, (n. 19), 1036.

themselves falsely by oath, he burst into the city and he took it upon himself to hold a *statio* in [the basilica] of Julius across the Tiber.[103]

The *Collectio Avellana* document was much closer to the events themselves than the *Liber Pontificalis* but between them the two sources offer us the opportunity to see the topographical dimension to the struggle between Liberius and his rival. The fragments preserved in the *Liber Pontificalis* are based upon the decision of Felix to retreat to the south-west of Rome. After a time, according to the *Collectio*, the antipope decided to seize a major urban site for himself, in fact the nearest one to him, the basilica built by Julius in Trastevere.[104] He was clearly living outside the city, as the use of '*inrumpere*' testifies. From this point he was forcefully ejected a short time later.[105] The threat, however, would seem to have remained as the *Collectio Avellana* explains that eight years after his return, upon hearing the news of Felix's death, Liberius was anxious to be reconciled with the Felicians:

Liberius showed mercy to the priests who had sworn themselves falsely, and he received them in their own places.[106]

Up until the death of Felix, sectaries were holding holy sites of their own as *loca propria*. These places probably included some close to Rome and the western sector of the *campagna* would seem to be the prime location. Little wonder, then, that Liberius was so anxious to come to terms, since the followers of Felix had seized a major church in the city before and might attempt to do so again.

For the reasons stated above, the *Liber Pontificalis* is less helpful on the activities of Liberius than it is for his rival.[107] It can certainly be said, using the evidence of the *Collectio Avellana* material, that he was a popular bishop to whom, for example, an oath of loyalty had been taken by a considerable portion of Christians in Rome.[108] Constantius II, on his visit to the city in 357, had been pestered by noble ladies trying to bring about the recall of the bishop and Theodoret records the attempt of the emperor to bring about a compromise in the most democratic way: by announcing his decision in the Circus Maximus,

---

[103] *Collectio Avellana* 1, 3: 'tertio anno [after his exile from Rome] redit Liberius . . . Felix notatus est a senatu vel populo de urbe propellitur. et post parum temporis impulsu clericorum, qui peiuraverant, inrumpit in urbem et stationem in [basilica] Juli trans Tiberim dare praesumit.' See Verrando, art. cit. (n. 99), 348 ff.

[104] *Collectio Avellana* 1, 3 above. Reekmans in art. cit. (n. 1), 183 calls Felix II 'Jules II'. I know of no other indication that Felix may have been exploiting the name of his predecessor. [105] *Collectio Avellana* 1, 3.

[106] Ibid. 4: 'Liberius misericordiam fecit in clericos qui peiuraverant, eosque locis propriis suscepit.' [107] See above pp. 131–2. [108] *Collectio Avellana* 1, 2.

only to find his attempt wailed down by the pro-Liberian Christians attending the shows.[109] The sources friendly to Liberius do not record the fact that the bishop compromised his own Christological position in the winter of 357–8 at a council in Sirmium and thereby was able to convince Constantius that he was no longer a strong supporter of Athanasius.[110] In any event, Liberius was allowed to return to Rome, perhaps in August 358.[111]

He did not, however, enter Rome immediately. Felix was still in possession of the see and had to be expelled from the city. The threat of serious civil disorder would certainly have attended the entry of Liberius if Felix had remained. The *Liber Pontificalis* records:

On his return from exile Liberius lived at the cemetery of Saint Agnes with the emperor's sister.[112]

Duchesne pointed out the problems with this account.[113] There was no living sister of Constantius at this time. Constantina had been buried here in 354. The epigraphical record of her building activities led the compiler of the *Liber Pontificalis* to think that she had been alive and living here when Liberius came back to Rome. Ultimately, we cannot be sure when exactly Liberius had stayed at the site but he seems certainly to have been there at some stage. The *Liber Pontificalis* further records:

Liberius decorated the tomb of the martyr Saint Agnes with marble tablets.[114]

Duchesne thought that the physical remains of Liberius' interest in the spot played a part in convincing the author of his *vita* that he had stayed there.[115] The indications are certainly that Saint Agnes had a special significance for Liberius. It may be significant that the bishop chose to be buried in the north-east sector of the *campagna* in the catacomb of Saint Priscilla on the Via Salaria Nova.[116] The *Liber Pontificalis* is the only pre-seventh-century source to offer this information and Leclercq thought that later Christian topographers

---

[109] Theodoret, *HE* 2, 14. See Chapter 6 below.

[110] Piétri, *RC*, i. 258–63. Barnes, op. cit. (n. 39), 138. *Collectio Avellana* 1, 3 on his return: 'cui obviam cum gaudio populus Romanus exivit.' More than a passing similarity to an imperial *adventus*!

[111] Date from *LP*, i. 208: 2 August 358. Accepted by Seeck, *Regesten*, 205. Ultimately unverifiable.

[112] *LP*, i. 207: 'Rediens autem Liberius de exilio, habitavit in cymiterio sanctae Agnae apud germanam Constanti Augusti.'   [113] *LP*, i. 208 n. 10.

[114] Ibid. 208: 'Hic Liberius ornavit de platomis marmoreis sepulchrum sanctae Agnae martyris.'

[115] 'C'est sans doute ce souvenir qui a porté le légendaire à le faire s'arrêter en cet endroit avant sa rentrée à Rome': *LP*, i. 208 n. 10.   [116] Ibid.

omitted him from their lists as a result of effective pro-Felician propaganda.[117]

We have seen evidence of Liberius' popularity above and it is interesting to note that the examples all come from the period *after* his departure for exile. This great surge of support for the popular bishop encouraged Liberius in his decision to construct a new basilica after his return from exile:[118]

He built the basilica with his name close to the market of Livia.[119]

The only topographical indications which we have from literary sources are that it lay in proximity to the *macellum Liviae* (*Liber Pontificalis*) and that Liberius had constructed an 'apse' in the fifth region of the city (*Gesta Liberii*).[120] These meagre clues indicate no area other than the east of the city and the Esquiline. The question, in archaeological terms, has therefore come to be whether the present basilica of S. Maria Maggiore lies on top of the Liberian structure or close by. Excavations carried out by the Pontifical Institute in Rome between 1966 and 1971 revealed remains of a colonnaded courtyard 6 m beneath the pavement of S. Maria Maggiore but there was no indication that this building was a *macellum*.[121] It is possible, taking the usually untrustworthy *Gesta Liberii* at face value, that the building under the basilica was part of a larger complex which had included a secular basilica to which Liberius had added an apse.[122] Alternatively, the *macellum Liviae* lay nearby, and the building under S. Maria Maggiore was destroyed later, when the basilica was constructed by Sixtus III.[123] For our purposes, the importance of Liberius' basilica was that it was certainly located on the Esquiline, near the market of Livia.

The reasons why Liberius chose to build here cannot be established for certain but the evidence linking Julius to this area of the city should

---

[117] *DACL* IX pt. 1, 518. We have a seventh-century copy of his epitaph: *ICUR* 9, 24832. For French translation of the text see *DACL*, loc. cit., 520–1.

[118] See discussion above p. 131.

[119] *LP*, i. 208: 'Hic fecit basilicam nomini suo iuxta macellum Libiae.'

[120] Considerable controversy over the *basilica* of Liberius. See *Lexicon*, i. 181 'Basilica Liberii' ; 188 'Basilica Sicinini' (G. De Spirito); Geertman, art. cit. (n. 1), 69–70; Piétri, *RC*, i. 25 discusses the state of research at that time (1976); P. Künzl, 'Zur basilica Liberiana: basilica Sicinini = basilica Liberii', *Römische Quartalschrift*, 56 (1961), 1–61, 129–66. Krautheimer, *Corpus*, iii. 5, 53–60 for a useful discussion of the early source material.

[121] F. Magi, 'Il Calendrio dipinto sotto Santa Maria Maggiore', *APARA*, Serie 3, Memorie 11 (1972), 59–68. See too F. Coarelli, *Roma Sepolta* (Rome: Curcio, 1984), 181–9.   [122] *Gesta Liberii* in *PL* 8, 1397. Coarelli, op. cit. (n. 121), 189.

[123] *LP*, i. 232 with n. 2. Coarelli, op. cit. (n. 121), 188.

not be forgotten.[124] It seems likely that the Esquiline was the area where Liberius' Christian support was strongest. The new site lay directly across the city from the area which had sustained Felix who may, up until his death, still have had followers there. In any event, the status of the basilica of Liberius was assured as events following Liberius' death were to show.

The Liberius–Felix schism had topographical implications which contrasted sharply with the building activities of Julius and his predecessors. Sites in Trastevere and the western *campagna* passed out of the control of the legitimate bishop. It is not without significance that bishop Julius had patronized points in the same area. Liberius made his own contribution to the urban landscape by constructing a basilica in another region favoured by Julius. The danger of violence over Christian sites persisted under Liberius up until the death of Felix II in November 365 but any chance of swiftly mending the dislocation disappeared with the outbreak of another episcopal dispute barely a year later.

4. DAMASUS AND URSINUS[125]

With Damasus and Ursinus, we may view the continued association of particular zones of the city with different factions prepared to compete violently with each other to possess holy places, particularly those linked to the memory of the popular Liberius.

Before analysing the topographical significance of the events which ensued, it will be instructive to recall the undenied pro-Ursinian biases of the most important source document: the preface (*Collectio Avellana* I) to the *Libellus Precum* (*Collectio Avellana* II). It is clear that in its reporting of the chronology of the crucial first weeks of the dispute and of the violence which characterized the episode the authors of the document attempted to paint Damasus and his following in the blackest way possible. Having acknowledged this, however, one may observe that the topographical details have both plausibility and coherence against the background of the Liberius-Felix II dispute.

When Liberius returned to Rome in 358, he attempted a policy of

---

[124] See pp. 122–4 above. Vielliard, *Recherches*, 41–3. The *tituli Praxedis*, *Equitii* and *Pudentis*, on 'frontière du quartier surpeuplé'.

[125] For what follows see Ch. Piétri, 'Damasus Évêque de Rome', in *Saecularia Damasiana*, Studi di Antichità Cristiana, 39 (Vatican City: Pontificio Istituto di archeologia cristiana, 1986), 29 ff. Id., *RC*, i. 405–15. A. Lippold, 'Damasus und Ursinus', *Historia*, 14 (1965), 105–28. Id., *PW* Supplementum 10 (1965), 1141–8; Maier, art. cit. (n. 1), 244 ff.; J. N. D. Kelly, *Oxford Dictionary of Popes* (Oxford: Oxford University Press, 1985), s.v. 'Damasus', 'Ursinus'.

reconciliation and at this time probably received back into his community the deacon Damasus who had set out from Rome with him into exile in 355 but had later turned back.[126] The Ursinian preface to the *Libellus Precum* alleges that Damasus in 355 threw his lot in with Liberius' rival Felix, but this is probably a slander on the bishop who had once found the prospect of exile in Thrace too unpleasant to stomach.[127] In any event, the Felicians had been invited back into full communion with the bishop Liberius.[128] On Liberius' death, however, the shadow of Felix fell across the Christian community again and the succession was disputed.

Damasus, the successor who had been recommended by Liberius himself, was perceived by a small but vociferous Christian faction as a crypto-Felician. They were led by another deacon of Liberius, Ursinus. Ursinus was supported by three of the seven deacons of the Christian city but it seems clear enough that the overwhelming majority of the city's presbyters and lay Christians were behind Damasus.[129]

The *praefatio* states that immediately after the death of Liberius (24 Sept. 366) the Ursinians:

began to appear in the basilica of Julius and they called for Ursinus the deacon to be appointed bishop for themselves in place of Liberius.[130]

Künzle thought the *basilica Iuli* might be that just outside the Campus Martius on the slopes of the Quirinal.[131] Lippold refuted his ideas in detail but did not suggest what is most obvious; that if the *basilica Iuli* mentioned in the *praefatio* is that near the Quirinal, then the *praefatio* itself is unnecessarily obscure since barely ten lines before it had given an account of the activities of Felix at the *basilica Iuli in Trastevere*.[132] The author of the document for whom onomastic details were important would surely have given his reader (in this case the emperor) more precise information if he had now begun to mention events at a *different basilica Iuli*.

The choice of the site in Trastevere is interesting. The Ursinians were not pro-Felician but the availability of the building may have had something to do with Liberius' rival bishop. Liberius had not con-

---

[126] *Collectio Avellana* 1, 2; 4. A slander?   [127] Ibid.   [128] See p. 134 above.

[129] *Collectio Avellana* 1, 5 with Lippold, art. cit. (n. 125), 111.

[130] *Collectio Avellana* 1, 5: 'coeperunt in basilica Iuli procedere et sibi Ursinum diaconum pontificem in loco Liberii ordinari deposcunt.'

[131] Künzle, art. cit. (n. 120), 38 ff., 59 f., followed by Geertman, art. cit. (n. 1), 77–8.

[132] Lippold, art. cit. (n. 125), 112. *Collectio Avellana* 1, 3 for Felix in the 'basilica Juli'. Geertman, art. cit. (n. 1), 77–8 sceptical, arguing instead that basilica Juli in east of the city meant. See also *Lexicon*, i. 180 'Basilica Julii iuxta Forum Traiani' (G. De Spirito).

structed any Christian buildings in the region across the Tiber and is not known to have made any monumental attempt to consolidate his authority there. Like Felix, the Ursinians felt that they would be assured credibility by the possession of a Christian holy site for themselves.

Damasus was chosen (expostulant) by his followers as bishop 'in Lucinis' according to the *praefatio*, probably a reference to a *titulus* located near the Via Flaminia north of the Campus Martius (now San Lorenzo in Lucina) but was not *consecrated* as bishop in the Lateran basilica until one week after Liberius' death.[133] The prize in the dispute of autumn 366 was the *episcopium* itself on the Lateran but the actual *choice* of Damasus and Ursinus took place elsewhere. Neither faction was sufficiently prepared, at the moment of Liberius' death, to seize and hold a site as large as the Lateran. But it is important to recognize the significance of small parish churches for establishing the claim of the rival bishops quickly. When sufficient supporters had been mobilized, the Damasians succeeded in occupying the Lateran. As under Liberius, however, a popular pope found himself confronted by a recalcitrant faction based across the Tiber.

The timing of the two elections was of the utmost importance to the claims to legitimacy of the contenders and the Ursinians strove in the document that survives to suggest that the election of their man took place first.[134] It is impossible now to recover the chronology of the events, but within a fortnight of Liberius' death two rival bishops had become ensconced in separate areas of Rome. The initial exile of Liberius and the subsequent expulsion of Felix twice after the former's return had prevented the situation where Christian Rome possessed two bishops firmly entrenched at holy sites in the city. Damasus was determined that this should not happen now. When he heard that Ursinus had been consecrated by bishop Paul of Tibur, he and his followers stormed the basilica in Trastevere and after three days of fighting and much bloodshed repossessed the building.[135] A week later, on the first available Sunday,[136] the victorious party were in the Lateran, where Damasus was consecrated as the bishop of Rome.[137]

---

[133] For election of Damasus: *Collectio Avellana* 1, 5. For San Lorenzo, see Vielliard, *Recherches*, 52. Consecration of Damasus: *Collectio Avellana* 1, 6 with Piétri *RC*, i. 409.

[134] See ibid. 411–12. *LP* and Hieronymian Martyrology record Damasus' death on 11 Nov. 384. Fifth-century series of papal portraits from San Paolo claimed Damasus was bishop for 18 years, 2 months, and 10 days. Piétri calculates his date of elevation as 1 Oct. 366 and *after* Ursinus. Significantly, Jerome, in his *Chronicle*, did not refute the *Collectio Avellana* 1. See n. 141 below.   [135] *Collectio Avellana* 1, 5.

[136] See Piétri's comments on Sunday consecrations *RC*, i. 681–2 with n. 7: 'La vérification est possible pour Damase, Sirice peut-être, Boniface et Célestine.'

[137] *Collectio Avellana* 1, 6.

Between them, the *Praefectus Urbi* and the *Praefectus Annonae* expelled
Ursinus and two of his deacons from the city.[138]

But even without their leader, the Ursinians remained a determined
opposition. The dispute was over the legacy of Liberius and the
Ursinians made a bold move: the *praefatio* records that late in October
366 they secured the release of seven presbyters who were being
detained by the civic authorities and they occupied the 'basilica
Liberii'.[139] We have seen from our discussion earlier, that Liberius
built only a single basilica in Rome.[140] This church was somewhere on
the Esquiline. But the issue of the conflict under bishop Damasus is
complicated by the fact that Ammianus and Jerome do not give to the
site of the battle the appellation 'the basilica of Liberius' but 'basilica
Sicinini' and 'Sicininum' respectively.[141]

From the almost contemporary *praefatio*, which is by far the most
detailed of all our sources, it is clear that there were two major
incidents between the followers of Damasus and Ursinus. These
occurred at the basilica of Julius in Trastevere and the other at the
basilica of Liberius. It has been suggested by Ferrua and others that
the Sicininan basilica was in fact that of Julius in Trastevere.[142] The
archaeological and topographical arguments are inconclusive but the
texts available for the dispute show that this suggestion makes little
sense. The *praefatio*, Ammianus and Jerome all had the same reason
for recording the bloodshed. They were all aware that what had
occurred had been the worst outbreak of Christian violence to date
in Rome. If Ferrua is right, then Ammianus and Jerome, who had
both lived through the whole struggle, recorded only the events in
Trastevere and not those later which, according to the *praefatio*, had
been the more serious and had claimed more than one hundred
lives.[143]

A document sent by the emperors to the Prefect Praetextatus in the
year following the violence on the Esquiline ordered the return of the
last remaining church in Rome to be held by the Ursinians.[144] This
letter is known through the *Collectio Avellana* where it has received the

---

[138] *Collectio Avellana* 1, 6. Chastagnol, *La Préfecture*, 151–6 is important.

[139] *Collectio Avellana* 1, 6.   [140] See above p. 136.

[141] Ammianus 27, 3, 12 ff. For Jerome see Helm, 244–5: 'Romanae ecclesiae XXXV
ordinatur episcopus Damasus et post non multum temporis intervallum Ursinus a
quibusdam episcopus constitutus Sicininum cum suis invadit, quo Damasianae partis
populo confluente crudelissimae interfectiones diversi sexus perpetratae.'

[142] A. Ferrua, in *La civiltà cattolica* 89/3 (1938), 53 ff.; Lippold, art. cit. (n. 125),
122–6. See *Lexicon*, i. 181–2 (G. De Spirito).

[143] 160 dead according to *Collectio Avellana* 1, 7; cf. Ammianus' figure of 137: 27, 3, 13.

[144] *Collectio Avellana* 6 = Coleman-Norton, i, no. 138. Also Lippold, *PW* Suppl. 10,
1146. For the date of Praetextatus' Prefecture: Chastagnol, *Fastes*, 171–8.

title: 'Where the basilica of Sicininus is returned'.[145] But we know from various sources, most famously Ammianus Marcellinus, that the battle for the 'basilica Sicinini' was fought and won in October 366.[146] The letter in the *Collectio Avellana* gives no precise topographical details and says only that the remaining church occupied by the Ursinians is to be handed over to Damasus. The clear probability is that the Ursinians had actually laid hands on a *number* of sites in the city and were not all ejected at the same time. A later editor of the collection knew his Ammianus but was not rigorous about the chronology of the dispute. The basilica mentioned in the *Collectio Avellana* was therefore mistaken for the basilica Sicinini. But even if the Ursinians had seized more than one holy site in the city, it is clear enough that the basilica on the Esquiline was the point which Damasus was most anxious to recover. Its association with the previous legitimate bishop made it important.

The policy adopted by the civic administration was, unfortunately for Damasus, moderate, and by October 367 Ursinus had been recalled to the city.[147] Disorder broke out again and he was forced into exile little more than a month after his return.[148] As before, however, the supporters of the renegade bishop were undeterred. They made a bid for the other site in Rome which had connections with Liberius: the tomb of Saint Agnes on the Via Nomentana.[149] Chastagnol calculated the date of this, the last significant incident of the conflict, to September 368, although there is no way of fixing the date precisely.[150] The *praefatio* of the *Collectio Avellana* says that the followers of Ursinus gathered 'per coemeteria martyrum . . . sine clericis', but the measures taken by the Damasians against them were strongest at the tomb of Saint Agnes. Here, according to the *praefatio*, Damasus 'killed many through the savagery of his devastation'.[151] This last outbreak of violence was the final straw for the emperors. In 368 Valentinian I, Valens and Gratian dispatched a rescript to Aginatius, *Vicarius Romae*:[152]

Desiring to remove every reason for these discords, which, as your Prudence has written, confuse the most hallowed city by the people of the Christians being driven hither and thither, we command by this letter that no meeting

---

[145] Collectio Avellana 6: 'Ubi redditur basilica Sicinini.'

[146] Ammianus 27, 3, 12 ff. Precise chronology reconstructed from *Collectio Avellana*.

[147] Ibid. 1, 10.   [148] Ibid. 1, 11.

[149] Ibid. 1, 13. For these meetings as *stationes*, see Maier, art. cit. (n. 1), 245.

[150] Chastagnol, *Fastes*, 182.

[151] *Collectio Avellana* 1, 12: 'plurimos vastationis suae strage deiecit.'

[152] *CSEL* 35, no. 9 = *Collectio Avellana* 9. For Aginatius, see *PLRE* I, 29–30.

may be held within the twentieth milestone by those persons whom factious disunion delights, most dear and agreeable Aginatius.[153]

The dispute between Damasus and Ursinus had led to the most serious outbreak of Christian violence at Rome since the persecutions. The legacy of Liberius included the readiness to use violent means to possess Christian sites. Significantly, the sites for which Damasus and Ursinus competed most vigorously were those which had been similarly important to Liberius. These conflicts revealed the vulnerability of the suburban cemeteries to sectarian occupation. Damasus' appetite for the episcopal chair was followed, however, by a strong sense of the need for Christian unity. His lasting contribution to the Christian topography is evidence of a tenacious and embracing vision which was to set him apart from emperors as one of the most important Roman Christians of the fourth century.

5. THE ROMAN CHURCHES OF DAMASUS (FIG. 23)

Damasus' early years were marked by doctrinal disputes which had been fracturing the topographical development of Christianity in Rome since the death of Julius. In neither the urban area nor the *suburbium* did Damasus achieve a full 'Christianization' if by 'Christianization' we mean the complete replacement of non-Christian religious sites by Christian. Nevertheless, along with Constantine, his is the most significant contribution to the Christianization in the sense of the attentions paid to points on the topography of the city in the fourth century.

It is not possible to establish the chronological order of Damasus' church-building inside the city and it is also most uncertain that the full catalogue of his works can be known. Nevertheless, the impression of what *is* known shows the role played by Damasus in extending or drawing attention to the Christian topography of Rome.

Arguably the most significant of the building projects inside the city with which he was associated was the foundation of the church of Saint Anastasia at the western corner of the Palatine (fig. 24).[154] A fifth-century inscription, set up by the bishop Hilarius (461–7), honoured Damasus and included the lines:

[153] *Collectio Avellana* 9, 1 = Coleman-Norton, i. no.143: 'Omnem his dissensionibus causam, quae, ut prudentia ⟨tua⟩ scripsit, sacratissimam urbem Christianorum populo fluctuante confundunt, auferre cupientes iubemus his litteris, ut ab his, quos iuvat turbulenta seiunctio, nullus intra vicesimum lapidem conventus habeatur.'

[154] P. B. Whitehead, 'The Church of S. Anastasia in Rome', *AJA*, 2nd series, 31 (1927), 405–20. Krautheimer, *Corpus*, i. 43–63. Piétri, *RC*, i. 462 ff. with further bibliography 462 n. 3.

Damasus the priest adorned with the honour of a picture the ceiling to which [this] beautiful mosaic now gives ornament.[155]

Damasus had originally decorated the apse of the fifth-century church with pictures which were now replaced by mosaics. Whitehead, in his important study published in 1927 claimed that it was significant that the Hilarian inscription did not claim that Damasus had *founded* the basilica,[156] and the *Liber Pontificalis* made no mention of a basilica here being founded by Damasus. Some have found this objection powerful but it need not be so. There is no evidence to suggest that the collection of buildings on which the church of Saint Anastasia was built were arranged specifically for Christian use before the middle of the fourth century when structural changes were made with the addition of an apse.[157] One might therefore excuse the sources of *Liber Pontificalis* for failing to mention, what, compared to the foundation of a new *titulus*, appeared to be only a rearrangement. In addition to this, it is to be remembered that Hilarius' inscription was designed to make known his *own* work in the church and his text may, according to Piétri, have replaced the dedication originally placed on the spot by his predecessor.[158]

Archaeological research has revealed traces of a three-naved building erected here on a specially created platform in the second half of the fourth century.[159] The importance of the church for this study lies chiefly in its positioning. If there had been a Christian place of worship on the site earlier, then, as we have pointed out, it was probably within the *insula*. But whether there was a site there or not, the building of Damasus was a distinctive Christian temple, within 150 m of the complex of imperial palaces and extremely close to the great shrines located on the Palatine: the Lupercal, and the temples to Magna Mater and Apollo. S. Anastasia was therefore the first Christian church to be

[155] Diehl *ILCV*, 1782: 'Antistes Damasus picturae ornarat honore|Tecta quibus nunc dant pulchra metalla decus.'

[156] Whitehead, (n. 154), 412.

[157] Krautheimer, *Corpus*, i. 62 (though note that he mistakenly thought the fourth-century church was cruciform in plan). Piétri, *RC*, i. 462. He detected no traces of Christian settlement before Damasus. Compare Vielliard, *Recherches*, 76 and Whitehead on the possibility of an imperial princess from the family of Constantine as foundress: art. cit. (n. 154), 411 ff. Most recently, J. F. Matthews has argued on the strength of *CIL* VI, 1712 (now lost), that Clodius Celsinus Adelphius, *PUR* in 351, dedicated a column 'ad altare maius S. Anastasiae': J. F. Matthews, 'The Poetess Proba and Fourth-Century Rome: Questions of Interpretation', in M. Christol, S. Demougin, Y. Duval, C. Lepelley, and L. Piétri (eds.), *Institutions, société et vie politique dans l'empire romain au IVe siècle ap. J.-C.*, Collections de l'École française de Rome, 159 (1992), 277–304. [158] Piétri, *RC*, i. 462.

[159] Whitehead, art. cit., (n. 154), 410. The platform incorporated the first floor of an *insula*: Coarelli, *Guida*, 370; Guidobaldi, art. cit. (n. 10), 386.

situated in the monumental sacred Palatine–Forum area, although only just in that zone, resting at the western extremity of the Palatine Hill, the siting of the church was undoubtedly a symbolic statement: Christianity had entered the pagan heart of Rome with its own specially designed temple.

Penetration into new areas was also signalled by the foundation of the new *titulus* church of Saint Laurence ('in Damaso') in the Campus Martius, 'iuxta theatrum' according to the *Liber Pontificalis*[160] and close to the stable of the Green racing faction.[161] The *Liber Pontificalis* gives details of the resources put by Damasus himself at the disposal of the new church for its maintenance and clergy.[162] The new *titulus* lay more than half a kilometre from the nearest recorded Christian holy place, the *titulus Marci*.[163] It therefore marked a significant extension of the physical Christian presence in the Campus Martius.

The Campus Martius did not intimidate Damasus, indeed, the new church may have been the site of his paternal home[164] and Damasus had been elected to the papacy in a church 'in Lucinis', presumably the *titulus Lucinae* adjoining the Via Lata on the edge of the Campus Martius.[165] In the new foundation, Damasus placed a dedicatory inscription:

I confess that for these archives I wished to provide a new building and to add besides columns on the right and on the left.[166]

The reading 'archivis' is controversial and suggested modifications have included 'arcis hic' and 'arcubus'.[167] Reproduced here is the version published by Ferrua.[168] It has been suggested that Damasus installed a *papal* archive in his new church, moving it from the *episcopium* on the Caelian hill.[169] Piétri rightly points out, however,

---

[160] *LP*, i. 212. The Theatre of Pompey is meant.

[161] Ibid. 213 n. 7. Hence the medieval appellation 'in prasino'. See Krautheimer, *Corpus*, ii. 145–51.

[162] *LP*, i. 212–13.   [163] See pp. 118–19.

[164] As argued by Ferrua, *Epigrammata*, no. 57. See Guidobaldi, art. cit. (n. 10), 388.

[165] *Collectio Avellana* 1, 5. See Vielliard, *Recherches*, 52. At p. 72 Vielliard observes that for the first time the cult of a particular martyr was indicated by a relic physically removed from the place of interment. See Guidobaldi, art. cit. (n. 10), 389.

[166] Ferrua, *Epigrammata*, no. 57: 'Archivis fateor volui nova condere tecta|addere praeterea dextra laevaque columnas.'

[167] V. Peri, 'Gli inconsistenti archivi pontefici di S. Lorenzo in Damaso', *APARA*, Rendiconti, 41 (1968), 192–204. He wants: 'hic arcis.' G. Scalia, 'Gli "archiva" di papa Damaso e le biblioteche di papa Ilaro', *Studi Medievali*, 18 (1977), 49 thought 'arcibus' a mistake. He wanted 'arcib(us) his'. Other alternatives include 'arcubus'. See Piétri *RC*, i. 464 n. 5.   [168] Ferrua, *Epigrammata*, no. 57.

[169] Kelly, op. cit. (n. 125), 82–3. For the archive where Jerome worked: Jerome *Ep.* 48, 3.

that the 'archive' mentioned need only be for the sacred books kept in the *titulus*.[170] Arrangements at the new church are therefore no sure indication that the significance of the Lateran site had declined for Damasus.

The *Liber Pontificalis* referred to the new building as a *basilica*. It seems, from the inscription, that we are being given a description of a basilical design with three naves or a nave and two aisles, an architectural form that was beginning to emerge consistently among the Christian buildings of the west.[171]

These two examples of Damasian building may be securely dated to his papacy. A third innovation, the 'titulus Fasciolae' may or may not be his responsibility. An inscription from 377 has a reference to a certain 'Cinnamius . . . amicus pauperum' as 'lector tituli Fasciolae'.[172] We have no evidence of this church prior to this the eleventh year of Damasus' term. Modern scholarship assigns the site of this *titulus* to a point near the eastern side of the Baths of Caracalla, some associate it directly with the present church of SS. Nereo ed Achilleo.[173] In the eighth century, Leo III reconstructed a church on this site which was occupied by ruins at the time.[174] If Damasus *did* build this church then it shows his attention to the requirements of the southern sector of the city inside the walls, which was, according to Vielliard, the site of a number of very ancient Christian meeting places already.[175]

The evidence is far from conclusive, but by 384 there was also some kind of Christian structure in the region of the modern Santa Pudenziana to which a 'Leopardus' was appointed *lector* and which Piétri considered Damasian.[176] The significance of another Christian site on the Esquiline should be clear, if unsurprising.

In contrast to the previous legitimate pope, Damasus' building in the

---

[170] *RC*, i. 668.

[171] R. Krautheimer, *Early Christian Architecture*, 4th edn. (Harmondsworth: Penguin, 1986), 64.

[172] *ICUR* NS, 2,4815. See Krautheimer, *Corpus*, iii. 135–52 esp. 148. Piétri is in favour of Damasian intervention: *RC*, i. 466. A. Nestori, 'L'Attività edilizia in Roma di papa Damaso' in *Saecularia Damasiana*, Studi di Antichità Cristiana, 39 (Vatican City: Pontificio Istituto di archeologia cristiana, 1986), 166 is sceptical. Guidobaldi, art. cit. (n. 10), 388 says there is no evidence.

[173] Based on the fifth-century list of churches in *MGH* XII, 413. By AD 595 the name had apparently changed to SS. Nereus et Achilleus. See Piétri *RC*, i. 466 and Duchesne, art. cit. (n. 22).

[174] *LP*, ii. 33. But no traces of an older building under the present church of SS. Nereo e Achilleo: Krautheimer, *Corpus*, ii. 148; Guidobaldi, art. cit. (n. 10), 388.

[175] Vielliard, *Recherches*, 47–8.

[176] *ILCV*, 1270. Krautheimer, *Corpus*, iii. 277–302, at 279. Piétri *RC*, i. 468. 'Una grande aula termale privata' of second-century date according to Guidobaldi, art. cit. (n. 10), 390.

city did not seek merely to consolidate areas already associated with the Christian community. He provided, according to Piétri, three new churches (Sant' Anastasia, S. Laurentius 'in Damaso', and the 'titulus Fasciolae') and may have begun work on two more (S. Pudentiana and S. Clemente) in his eighteen years as bishop.[177] The church built or substantially reshaped at the western corner of the Palatine and the new foundation in the middle of the Campus Martius show how completely Damasus overcame his rival (Ursinus) and proceeded to the physical extension of the Christian topography. But although this work was innovatory, there is no question of a comprehensive programme to flood Rome with Christian places of worship. Beyond the Walls of Aurelian, however, the work of Damasus displays an altogether broader scope.

Here, Damasus carried out three main types of work: first, he made improvements to existing Christian basilicas; second, he carried out structural improvements to some of the resting places of the dead (catacombs). Third, he sought out and identified holy places associated with the saints and martyrs, places insufficiently well known or marked.

The extent of Damasus' work was remarkable. In his eighteen-year pontificate he was able to investigate a ring of holy sites around the city on a scale which was quite without precedent. The endeavours of the pope helped physically unite the sites beyond the walls into an almost unitary Christian hinterland of Rome.

The zone to the immediate south of the city dominated Damasus' efforts. Here, on the Via Ostiensis, in the last years of his papacy, were laid down the foundations of a massive new five-naved basilica designed to engulf the modest Constantinian structure which itself had replaced an earlier memorial to the apostle Paul. At an early stage in the planning, the Prefect of the City Sallustius had been ordered to contact the bishop and his congregation so that the Christian community might have some say in what was essentially an act of imperial devotion.[178] It is unclear exactly *when* the basilica was finished,[179] but the project envisaged the new building transforming the area. The apostle Paul now received a structure as grand as that dedicated to Peter. The new structure also constituted a substantial monumental presence on the Via

---

[177] Piétri, *RC*, i. 461 ff. Only Siricius can be securely linked with San Clemente: ibid. 470 ff. Guidobaldi, art. cit. (n. 10), 387 corrects the view that the site occupied an insula. He opts for a *domus*.

[178] *Collectio Avellana* 3, 2 = Coleman-Norton, no. 211. Symmachus *Relationes* 24 and 25. *PLRE* I, 797 'Sallustius 4' suggests the date of 387 for the letter but see Chastagnol, *Fastes*, 216–17. Accepted by Krautheimer, *Corpus*, v. 98. In general, see A. Chastagnol, 'Sur quelques documents relatifs à la basilique de Sainte-Paul-hors-les-murs', in *Mélanges Piganiol* (Paris: S. E. V. P. E. N., 1966), 421–37. [179] See n. 178 above.

Ostiensis, until now the site of modest catacombs and a small *memoria* to Paul. It confirmed the elevation in importance of the area guaranteed by the large number of pilgrims visiting the place.

Damasus had only a limited part to play in the construction of Saint Paul's basilica, but other building projects were completed by him. On the Via Labicana adjoining the *basilica-mausoleum* built by Constantine, Damasus built the little L-shaped chapel of Saints Marcellinus and Peter, in honour of the saints who were buried in the nearby catacomb.[180] Fragments of an epistyle bearing letters of a Philocalian character seem to indicate that Damasus was also responsible for Rome's first underground basilica, in the cemetery of Hermes, beside the Via Salaria Vetus.[181] His presence is attested by fragments of an inscription written in distinctive Philocalian script from the *basilica* of Julius at the cemetery of Saint Valentinus.[182] Similarly, at the cemetery of Generosa on the Via Portuensis, some fragments of another epistyle mention the names of Saints Faustinus and Viatrix.[183] Josi identified structural remains belonging to the middle years of the fourth century and suggested a Damasian date.[184] Finally, the *Liber Pontificalis* claimed that a second basilica was built by Damasus 'via Ardeatina ubi requiescit'.[185] This is supported by the testimony of the seventh-century *De Locis Sanctis Martyrum quae sunt foris Civitatis Romae* and the *Notitia Ecclesiarum Urbis Romae*.[186] Recent archaeological finds have been controversially identified as the remains of the Damasian *basilica* and tomb.[187]

Damasus displayed an interest in Christian monuments beyond the walls in the same spirit with which he had patronized new foundations within the walls: the desire to provide more and better facilities for the burgeoning Christian population of Rome. But, in contrast to his work in the city, the bishop undertook to give the cult of the martyrs beyond the walls a new impetus which was to change the topography of the city forever.

[180] Ferrua, *Epigrammata*, no. 29 for fragments of a monumental arch from the tomb of SS. Marcellinus and Petrus. J. Guyon, 'L'Œuvre de Damase dans le cimitière sur la vie Labicana', in *Saecularia Damasiana*, Studi di Antichità Cristiana, 39 (Vatican City: Pontificio Istituto di archeologia cristiana, 1986), 227–58, esp. 228 ff.

[181] Ferrua, *Epigrammata*, no. 49 (1) and (2). Ferrua himself was unsure whether Damasus or his successor Siricius was responsible. Krautheimer's attribution to Damasus reads: 'L'Iscrizione damasiana che fu trovata sopra la basilica e l'epigramma damasiano rendono verosimile l'ipotesi secondo la quale il fondatore sembrerebbe stato papa Damaso': *Corpus*, i. 207.

[182] Ferrua, *Epigrammata*, no. 48 (1). [183] Ibid., no. 6.

[184] E. Josi, 'Cimeterio di Generosa', *RAC*, 16 (1939), 325. [185] *LP*, i. 212.

[186] Valentini-Zuchetti, ii. 110; 89 with n. 1. See also the account of William of Malmesbury, ibid. 149.

[187] For the alleged site of the tomb see Nestori, art. cit. (n. 172), 170 ff.

6. THE *EPIGRAMMATA* OF DAMASUS (FIG. 26)

The *epigrammata* of Damasus were verse-inscriptions composed by the bishop and incised by Philocalus, one of the foremost artist-craftsmen of the day.[188] They were beautifully and expensively produced and their editor, Antonio Ferrua, estimated that originally almost sixty individual inscriptions existed.[189] The great Duchesne magisterially dismissed the medieval vogue for copying the *epigrammata*:

Never have worse verses been translated so exquisitely . . . they are empty of history, they are obscure, and contain scarcely anything but commonplaces. Thus they bear witness that the local tradition with regard to the martyrs was almost obliterated at the time when the pious pontiff sought to preserve it.[190]

But this is a harsh judgement. In a literary context, the verse inscriptions of the bishop are decidedly short on merit. But as documents illustrating Damasus' vision of the Christian city of Rome, they are invaluable. In particular, they can be used to assess the contribution to the Christian topography of the city made by Damasus, 'poète maladroit, mais pontife cultivé'.[191]

According to Jerome, Damasus 'elegans in versibus componendis ingenium habuit'.[192] A glance at the distribution of the *epigrammata* of Damasus shows that the pope marked sites on most of the main roads into Rome. The extent of this interest in the suburban sites of the martyrs was entirely without precedent. An examination of the inscriptions set up by him around Rome shows him to have been much more than an amateur poet. They reveal that he envisaged a unified Christian hinterland around the city. Up until his pontificate, the Christianization of the topography of the city had proceeded by means of a piecemeal monumentalization of selected holy or significant points. Damasus' labours introduced a new element as he drew popular attention to the saints and martyrs of Rome *en masse* beyond the walls of Aurelian.

The *Liber Pontificalis* says of Damasus:

He searched for and discovered the bodies of many saints and also celebrated them in verses.[193]

---

[188] For the identity of Philocalus, see Salzman, *On Roman Time*, 26; Ferrua, *Epigrammata*, 21–35.

[189] For the distribution of the *epigrammata* see Ferrua, *Epigrammata*, pp. xii–xv. Also the excellent article by H. Leclercq in *DACL* 4/1 (1920), 145–97. Distribution map in J. Guyon, art. cit. (n. 180), 250.

[190] L. Duchesne, *The Early History of the Christian Church* (London: Murray, 1910), ii. 483.   [191] Piétri, art. cit. (n. 87), 327.   [192] Jerome, *De Viris Illustribus*, 103.

[193] *LP*, i. 212: 'Hic multa corpora sanctorum requisivit et invenit quorum etiam versibus declaravit.'

The epigrams provide proof of Damasus' determination to bring more martyrs to the attention of the Christian community.[194] An unidentified group, for example, from the cemetery of Thrason on the Via Salaria Nova were honoured even though

Time was not able to preserve their names or their number.[195]

By way of contrast, where the identity of the martyrs might be known, as at the tombs of Saints Protus and Hyacinthus in the cemetery of Basilla off the Via Salaria Vetus, the bishop emphasized his own diligence and hinted at the danger of investigation:

The tomb was hidden under the hill's furthest mound: this Damasus reveals, because he preserves the bodies of the pious.[196]

One of the clearest statements of Damasus' claim to have revealed the importance of particular sites was given at the grave of Saint Eutychius on the Via Appia:

The hiding place which holds the bones of the innocent is exposed. He was sought, found, he is honoured, he offers his favour [and] grants everything.[197]

More commonly, the identity and location of the graves of martyrs were already known. In these cases, biographical or martyrological details of the individuals commemorated were inscribed in verse at the site and were more often accompanied by exhortations to the faithful to venerate the saints' memories. Damasus' father had been a Christian official at the time of the Diocletianic persecutions and Saxer has shown that the bishop had access to specifically Roman versions of the *depositiones martyrum* and *episcoporum*.[198]

Some of the most vivid Damasian sketches were attached to the holy men and women closest to Damasus' own time. The *elogium* of Saint

[194] For the small number of non-martyrial epigrams, composed apparently towards the end of the bishop's life, see J. Guyon, 'Cunctis solacia fletus ou le testament-épigraphie du pape Damase', in *Quaeritur inventus colitur: Miscellanea in honore di Padre U. M. Fasola* (Vatican City: Pontificio Istituto di archeologia cristiana, 1989), 423–37.

[195] Ferrua, *Epigrammata*, no. 42: 'nomina nec numerum potuit retinere vetustas.'

[196] Ibid., no. 47: 'Extremo tumulus latuit sub aggere montis|Hunc Damasus monstrat servat quod membra piorum.'

[197] Ibid., no. 21: 'Ostendit latebra insontis quae membra teneret,|Quaeritur, inventus colitur, fovet, omnia praestat.'

[198] V. Saxer, 'Damase et le calendrier des fêtes de martyrs de l'église romaine', in *Saecularia Damasiana*, Studi di Antichità Cristiana, 39 (Vatican City: Pontificio Istituto di archeologia cristiana, 1986), 67. It is important to note that Damasus' work included tombs of martyrs not mentioned in the *depositiones*. Delehaye, op. cit. (n. 53), 260 thought the *depositio martyrum* incomplete: 'il constate l'usage officiel et qu'il marque une date, mais qui paraît n'être qu'un extrait dont le text n'est même pas intact.' See also Guarducci, art. cit. (n. 87), 119, though perhaps dated too early.

Eutychius from the Via Appia, for example, made compelling reading.[199] From it the reader learned of Eutychius' torture, his dungeon strewn with sharp fragments of pottery, his twelve days without food and finally his death in a pit into which he had been thrown. The text ended with a direct appeal to the reader:

Damasus articulated [the martyr's] merit: venerate the tomb.[200]

The earlier martyrs Achilleus and Nereus, remembered at the cemetery of Domitilla on the Via Ardeatina, were reported by Damasus to have been serving soldiers, compelled by fear to obey the orders of the 'tyrant'.[201] They made a sudden and dramatic conversion to the Christian faith before casting away their weapons forever. Again, the reader was addressed by Damasus:

Believe through Damasus what the Glory of Christ is capable of.[202]

At the point on the Via Tiburtina associated with the third-century priest Hippolytus, reference was made to his schism with Novatus, his faithfulness to the 'catholica fides' before the people and finally his martyr's death. Damasus concluded his text with the statement:

Damasus passes on these things as reported. Christ approves them all.[203]

Such exhortations lead on to another important feature of the *epigrammata*, as documents which reveal what Damasus believed the bishop of Rome had become. Duchesne, in the passage with which this section opened, criticized the *epigrammata* for their banality but Duchesne also accused the bishop of 'blotting out' the local martyrial traditions of Rome. In this he was certainly correct as the views and personality of Damasus swamped the sites of the tombs. Through his unprecedentedly extensive patronage of the Christian holy sites, Damasus promoted his own claim to the position of intermediary between the *plebs Dei* and the saints and martyrs. He himself had contact with the authorized versions of their martyrdoms:

Your executioner relayed [this version] to me, Damasus, when I was a boy.[204]

[199] Ferrua, *Epigrammata*, no. 21.

[200] Ibid. 'Expressit Damasus meritum venerare sepulchrum.'

[201] Ibid., no. 8. 'Tyrant' is to be understood as a reference to a magistrate, governor, or the emperor himself. See D. H. Farmer, *Oxford Dictionary of Saints* (Oxford: Oxford University Press, 1987), 313–14.

[202] Ferrua, *Epigrammata*, no. 8: 'Credite per Damasum possit quid gloria Christi.'

[203] Ibid. no. 35: 'Haec audita refert Damasus probat omnia XPS [Christus].' Cf. the exhortation at the tomb of bishop Marcellus on the Via Salaria Nova: 'Haec breviter Damasus voluit comperta referre | Marcelli ut populus meritum cognoscere possit' . (Ferrua, *Epigrammata*, no. 40).

[204] Ibid., no. 28: 'Percussor retulit Damaso mihi cum puer essem.'

The position claimed by Damasus was somewhere between the devout visitors to the tombs and the saints and martyrs. In an inscription honouring those buried 'ad papas' on the Via Appia, he explained that he had once thought of having himself interred in the same place:

I confess that I, Damasus, wished to lay my bones here but I was afraid to disturb the holy ashes of the pious.[205]

But to Saint Agnes, on the Via Nomentana, Damasus was confident enough to make a direct and public appeal:

I entreat you, famous martyr, look with favour on the prayers of Damasus.[206]

And the bishop depicted himself as witness to even the hidden torments of the martyrs:

In the sleep-bring night [Eutychius' wounds] disturb the mind with insomnia [But] the hiding place of the innocent [now] shows the bones which it holds.[207]

It is impossible to read some of the *elogia* without recalling Damasus' own recent experiences. His succession had been disputed and controversy had dogged his tenure of the episcopal throne. This was the context in which Damasus chose to honour his recent predecessor Eusebius, bishop of Rome in the latter part of Maxentius' reign:[208]

Damasus made this [inscription].
Heraclius forbade the lapsed to repent of their sins,
Eusebius taught the unfortunate to weep for their crimes.
The people with blazing anger split themselves into parties.
Sedition, slaughter, violence, discord, quarrels;
Straightaway both were expelled by the savagery of the tyrant
When the rector was guarding intact the agreements of peace.
Rejoicing that the Lord was his judge he endured exile
He left this life and the world on the Trinacrian shore.
To Eusebius, bishop and martyr.[209]

---

[205] Ibid., no. 16: 'Hic fateor Damasus volui mea condere membra|Sed cineres timui sanctos vexare piorum.'

[206] Ferrua, *Epigrammata*, no. 37: 'Damasi precibus faveas precor inclyta martyr.' Identical phrase ibid., no. 8 (to S. Hermes).

[207] Ibid., no. 21: 'Nocte soporifera turbant insomnia mentem,|ostendit latebra insontis quae membra teneret . . .'

[208] See p. 65 above and Kelly, *Oxford Dictionary of Popes*, 26.

[209] Ferrua, *Epigrammata*, no. 18: 'Damasus episcopus fecit.|Heraclius vetuit labsos peccata dolere.|Eusebius miseros docuit sua crimina flere.|Scinditur in partes populus gliscente furore.|Seditio caedes bellum discordia lites|Extemplo pariter pulsi feritate tyranni|Integra cum rector servaret foedera pacis.|Pertulit exilium domino sub iudice laetus|Litore Trinacrio mundum vitamq. reliquit.|Eusebio episcopo et martyri.'

Damasus was calling upon a hagiographical tradition to vindicate and legitimize his own actions. The same motivation certainly lay behind the impulse given to the *concordia apostolorum*.

The brotherhood of the apostles Peter and Paul assumed its greatest importance from about 360 onwards according to Huskinson.[210] After this date even the most everyday Christian artefacts are to be found bearing images of the two apostles in fraternal embrace. Piétri has argued that the context of the *concordia apostolorum* is best understood as the great expansion in the Christian community in the middle years of the century. But expansion brought with it attendant difficulties. The pro-Ursinian tract, the *Libellus Precum*, accused Damasus of indiscreet association with aristocratic society in Rome.[211] It railed against rich clergy and the use of money to gain power. The bishop was said to have been ambitious and anxious to have powerful friends. Certain Christian groups in the city thought him indiscriminate in his admissions to the Christian community.[212] It would be wrong, however, to overlook the significance of Damasus' own perspective on the troubles examined in this chapter. Damasus' contribution to the concept of the *concordia apostolorum* was to compose one of the most remarkable Christian documents yet written:

Here, you ought to know, first lived the saints,
Whoever seeks the names of Peter and also of Paul.
Disciples, the East sent them, that we freely confess.
But by the merit of their blood they followed Christ through the Heavens
And sought the aethereal shores, the kingdom of the pious.
Rome deserved better to watch over her own citizens.
Let Damasus relate this as your praise, new stars.[213]

The fundamental elements of the Damasian vision of Rome are revealed in this inscription. The figure of Damasus was central. He was responsible for the composition and the presentation of the text. He gave an authoritative statement on the apostles in Rome as he had

---

[210] J. Huskinson, *Concordia Apostolorum: Christian Propaganda at Rome in the Fourth and Fifth Centuries*, BAR International Series, 148 (Oxford: BAR, 1982). Piétri *RC*, ii. 1590–6; id., art. cit. (n. 87), 275–322.

[211] *Collectio Avellana* 1, 10–11. Piétri, *RC*, i. 412 ff. Huskinson, op. cit. (n 210), 1. See 280–98 below.

[212] Piétri, *RC*, i. 414.

[213] Ferrua, *Epigrammata*, no. 20: 'Hic habitasse prius sanctos cognoscere debes|Nomina quisque Petri pariter Paulique requiris|Discipulos Oriens misit quod sponte fatemur|Sanguinis ob meritum Christumque per astra secuti|Aetherios petiere sinus regnaque piorum.|Roma suos potius meruit defendere cives|Haec Damasus vestras referat nova sidera laudes.' See J. Ruysschaert, 'Pierre et Paul à Rome: Textes et contextes d'une inscription damasienne', *Rendiconti della Pontificia Accademia Romana d'Archeologia*, 42 (1969), 201–8.

done for the other martyrs of the city. He was also on hand to deliver up the prayers of the faithful to the apostles. The latter's *concordia* was prominently advocated. The concord between Peter and Paul was a peace between rivals for the position of the founder of Christian Rome. In promoting the idea of unity between the competing claims of the apostles, Damasus was appealing for an end to the kind of divisions which had tarnished his own and Liberius' episcopates. But in making this appeal, he made an extraordinary claim for the apostles: their martyrdom had won for them not only a place by Christ in Heaven but citizenship of earthly Rome. The special Christian dead of the city were now members of the Roman community, symbols of the unity which Damasus was anxious to promote.[214] The significance of the apostles' elevation was not lost on Damasus' critics. Maximinus complained to Ambrose that Peter's memory belonged to the whole church and not just to the bishop of Rome.[215] Although the *Romanitas* of the martyrs was most powerfully advocated through Peter and Paul, they were by no means unique. Saturninus, for example, a martyr from Carthage, had had his status redefined by martyrdom:

A dweller now in Christ [Saturninus], was previously of Carthage.
During the time when the sword tore the sacred vitals of the mother [church]
Through his blood he changed his *patria*, his name and his people.
His descent made him Roman, a citizen of the community of saints.[216]

Hermes had undergone the same transformation:

Long ago, as tradition tells, Greece sent you;
Through your blood you changed *patria*: and love of the law [of Christ] made you a citizen and a brother.[217]

Damasus thus staged a massive *Roman* Christianization of the zone immediately beyond the walls of the city. The project was orchestrated

[214] According to Piétri, art. cit. (n. 87), 305 n. 4, Damasus was criticized by Arian opponents for appropriating Peter and Paul who properly belonged to the whole community. See F. Kaufmann, *Aus der Schule des Wulfilas* (Strasbourg, 1899), 90. For the status of Peter and Paul in the fifth century, see Gaudentius of Brescia, *Sermo*, 20 (*PL* 20, 995A): Ambo nobiles, ambo insignes: duo vero mundi lumina, columnae fidei . . .'; Ps. Aug., *Sermo*, 381 (*PL* 39, 1684): 'Habet ergo Roma caput gentium, duo lumina gentium . . .' See now M. Maccarrone, 'La concezione di Roma città di Pietro e di Paolo: da Damaso a Leone I', in *Roma Costantinopoli Mosca: Da Roma alla terza Roma*, Documenti e studi, 1 (Naples: Edizioni Scientifiche Italiane, 1983), 63–85, at 66 ff.

[215] *Maximini contra Ambrosium dissertatio* (*PLS* 1, 722).

[216] Ferrua, *Epigrammata*, no. 46: 'Incola nunc Christi, fuerat Carthaginis ante,| Tempore quo gladius secuit pia viscera matris,|sanguine mutavit patriam nomenque genusque;|Romanum civem sanctorum fecit origo.'

[217] Ibid., no. 48: 'Iam dudum, quod fama refert, te Graecia misit;|Sanguine mutasti patriam: civemque fratremque|Fecit amor legis.'

by the bishop who provided the Christian inhabitants of Rome with a *suburbium* populated by the city's own saints and martyrs. The newly affirmed civic identity of the saintly dead was an appeal for solidarity to the living. The concept was to prove enduringly popular to other Christians. Ambrose was to 'discover', miraculously, the relics of the saintly patrons of Milan; Paulinus was to elevate Saint Felix to the position of protector of Nola; and Prudentius was to enshrine the idea in some of the finest poetry of the early Christian era.[218] The idea of the extra-urban *admissio* was to prove popular with Christian writers:

> The love of their religion masses Latins and strangers together in one body . . . The majestic city disgorges her Romans in a stream; with equal ardour patricians and the plebeian host are jumbled together, shoulder to shoulder, for the faith banishes distinctions of birth.[219]

Peter Brown saw the cult of the martyrs as the key to a change in the landscape of Rome.[220] Writing from Palestine in 403 Jerome remarked:

> The city is stirred to its depths and the people pour past the half-ruined shrines to visit the tombs of the martyrs.[221]

Brown saw in this passage evidence that the ancient city of Rome had been turned inside out by the dramatic increase in the extent and importance of the cult of the martyrs. In addition to this, the attendance of the Christian faithful at the tombs of the martyrs brought about a dissolution of the wordly social barriers so important inside the city. In contrast to the highly ceremonial and hierarchical urban liturgies, the gatherings at the saintly tombs witnessed the levelling of such distinctions. As Brown is aware, the worldly status of aristocratic Christians did not disappear, but the revelation of such a large number of heavenly *patroni* did tend to put the earthly social hierarchy into a new context.[222]

As for the theory that the city was turned inside out, it would be

---

[218] See P. Brown, *The Cult of the Saints* (Chicago: University of Chicago, 1981), 50 ff.; N. B. McLynn, *Ambrose of Milan* (Berkeley: University of California Press, 1994), 209 ff.; for Prudentius, see A. M. Palmer, *Prudentius on the Martyrs* (Oxford: Oxford University Press, 1989).

[219] Prudentius, *Peristephanon*, 11, 191–2, 199–202 (trans. Croke and Harries): 'Conglobat in cuneum Latios simul ac peregrinos|permixtim populos religionis amor. . .|Urbs augusta suos vomit effunditque Quirites,|una et patricios ambitione pari|confundit plebeia phalanx umbonibus aequis|discrimen procerum praecipitante fide.'

[220] P. Brown, 'Dalla "Plebs Romana" alla "Plebs Dei": Aspetti della Cristianizzazione di Roma', in P. Brown, L. Cracco Ruggini, and M. Mazza (eds.), *Governanti e intellettuali: popolo di Dio I–IV secolo*, Passatopresente (Turin: Giappichelli, 1982), ii. 130 ff.

[221] Jerome, *Ep.* 107, 1 (*CSEL* 55, 291). [222] See 311–19 below.

quite wrong to suggest that the work of Damasus brought the *suburbium* to life since, as Reekmans and Purcell have made clear, the ancient urban phenomenon was a complex which embraced both city and surrounding countryside.[223] Damasus' labours show a distinct awareness of this the traditional understanding of the city. He achieved what Piétri called 'a conquest of urban space' within the city and it is perverse to deny that his achievement was sprung from a vision which united the city with the *suburbium*.[224] It is to be noted, however, that the classical Roman 'street of tombs' never convincingly integrated with the city. The pagan cemeteries

never wholly succeeded in 'sanitising' the world of the dead . . . The world of the dead, carefully excluded from the city, never became thoroughly safe and acceptable in the suburb. It remained a place of fear and ill-omen, the more so when changing a demographic régime reversed the process of increasing density of land use.[225]

The perceived distinction in the classical city between the living and the dead was profoundly changed by the Christians and in the fourth century by Damasus in particular. By providing a number of 'new' saints and martyrs for Rome and by improving access to the burial places of those already known, Damasus deliberately drew attention to the presence of Christian Rome's heavenly intercessors. This in turn fostered a development which would have been unthinkable in classical Rome: the appearance of communities of the living among the dead. By the end of the fourth century the tombs of the martyrs were drawing to themselves permanent settlements of the devoted, either as monastic communities or as staff for the maintenance of the little oratories.[226]

The drawing of attention to these 'very special dead' under Damasus provided Rome with the kind of saintly patrons that characterized the medieval city:

autour de l'*urbs sancta*, se dresse une 'couronne de temples consacrés aux nouveaux héros de la ville'. Ces *cives Romani*, adoptés par Damase, font de Rome une capitale, lorsque s'établit une nouvelle hiérarchie des villes, fondée sur la piété.[227]

---

[223] Reekmans, art. cit. (n. 1), 173–4; N. Purcell, 'Tomb and Suburb', in *Römische Gräberstrassen: Bayerische Akademie der Wissenschaften*, Philosophisch-Historische Klasse Abhandlungen, 96 (1987), 25–41.

[224] Piétri, art. cit. (n. 125), 47.

[225] Purcell, art. cit. (n. 223), 41.

[226] See 298–311 below.

[227] Piétri, art. cit. (n. 87), 304.

CONCLUSION

Robert Markus has observed that one of the distinguishing features of the Christians of antiquity was that they believed their history to have been fundamentally different from that of any other people. Their geography was the projection of this identity.[228] But if the personal geography of the Christians showed their uniqueness it also showed the tensions within that community.

The imperial patronage of sites in the landscape of Rome continued after 337. Like almost all the foundations of Constantine, these sites were to be found exclusively outside the city and often on imperial property. The bishops of the city were frequent builders themselves, although they did not mobilize the same resources for their own building projects. In contrast to the emperors, however, they raised churches inside the city. Some of these churches, most notably the basilicas of Marcus and Julius and Saint Anastasia, demonstrate the absence of inhibition concerning the city centre. Certain areas of the city acted as poles around which Christian sites clustered. The hills on the eastern side of the city, for example, seem to have been important to Julius and his successors and the reconstructed map of early *tituli* illustrates a popularity of early origin. Bishop Julius also favoured the Trastevere region and there is sufficient evidence to suggest that the bishop's interest in the west of Rome was prompted by a devotion to Callistus, his martyred predecessor.

The period after Julius' death witnessed serious disruption both in the Christian community and its network of holy sites and we may glimpse a fascinating topographical dimension to these episcopal battles. The context of episcopal violence is crucial for understanding the building activities of Damasus. Inside the city of Rome Damasus significantly extended the monumental Christian presence in Rome by creating a new church in the Campus Martius and by placing a basilica at the south-western corner of the Palatine hill, a particularly striking demonstration of the increasing importance of Christianity in the city. Beyond the walls, however, Damasus came into his own as a purveyor and propagator of Christian myths. Here, the *epigrammata* reveal an impressive vision of Christian Rome. Damasus used the martyrs of the city as a means of unifying the Christians of Rome and fostering a spirit of reconciliation. The extent of his intervention at the tombs of the martyrs shows that he visualized the special Christian dead as a community of *Roman* martyrs. Through the promotion of this idea, Damasus managed to resolve one of the great tensions of ancient

---

[228] R. Markus, *End*, 139.

Roman life: that between the city and its dead. This sense of a community of saintly dead pointed the way to the early medieval world of civic and patron saints. At the same time, however, Damasus was the most worldly of patrons himself: he emphasized his own role at every turn in the drawing up of authoritative statements on the lives of the saints and martyrs and he continually offered himself as a channel for the devotion of the pilgrims. The vision of Rome which Damasus possessed was more complete and more Roman than that of Constantine.

PART TWO

Society

5

The Legal Standing of the
Ancient Cults of Rome

INTRODUCTION

The starting point for this study of Roman society in the fourth century is the legal standing of the ancient cults of the city. The study of late Roman law is reviving in newly sophisticated ways, allowing the historian of the empire to consider fresh perspectives on the processes of decision-making, legal composition, and publication.[1] The surviving texts on the ancient cults have often been discussed, but rarely in a systematic or sustained way. It is, in fact, impossible to form any reasonable assessment of the history of the decline of the non-Christian cults of the fourth century without taking a broad survey of the available material. Accordingly, what follows is a reign-by-reign survey and analysis of the most significant texts. These texts offer unique insights into the problems of the lawmakers and their expressed intentions in dealing with the ancient cults of the city. They suggest that the Christian aspirations of late antique emperors, like the laws themselves, were complex, inconsistent, and occasionally paradoxical. In these circumstances, the society which the laws addressed was little different.

I . WORKING WITH THE *THEODOSIAN CODE*

Historians no longer approach the legal texts of late antiquity with the confidence of Edward Gibbon who expressed his debt to the Theodosian Code as a 'full and capacious repository' of historical information on the political condition of the declining empire.[2] The *Codex Theodosianus* is not the *Code Napoléon*. The fifth-century compilation, like Roman law itself, is far from being a consistent and homogeneous unit. Thus the function of the Code must be understood before any evidence gained from it can be fully appreciated. The extraordinary

[1] See now in general the important works of S. Corcoran, *The Empire of the Tetrarchs* (Oxford: Oxford University Press, 1996) and J. Harries and I. Wood (eds.), *The Theodosian Code* (London: Duckworth, 1993).

[2] Quoted by J. Matthews in Harries and Wood (eds.), op. cit. (n. 1), 26.

undertaking of historical and legal research which culminated in the publication of the Code in late 438 was completed in two stages.[3] Theodosius II's law of 26 March 429 initiated the first. A carefully selected commission of nine men were charged with the collection of

all the constitutions that were issued by the renowned Constantine, by the sainted emperors after him, and by Us and which rest upon the force of edicts or sacred imperial law of general force.[4]

The commission's editorial powers were also established. *Tituli* would be formulated, under which the texts, or relevant fragments of texts, would be listed in chronological order.[5] Validity was to be assured to the most recent law on a given subject, but the code did not omit the redundant texts:

let us recognize that this code and the previous ones were composed for more diligent men, to whose scholarly efforts it is granted to know even those laws which have been consigned to silence and have passed into desuetude, since they were destined to be valid for the cases of their own time only.[6]

Most importantly, this statement illustrates the anticipated readership of this intermediate collection: scholars and specialists. The *Codex Theodosianus* as we possess it was never designed to be a legal handbook used in the everyday judicial process of the empire and its compilers were very well aware of its inconsistencies.[7]

Stringent efforts were made to preserve

the very words themselves of the constitutions, in so far as they pertain to the essential matter.[8]

What the commission actually did in the years 429–35 was merely to authenticate and accumulate material. The law of 429 stated that

---

[3] See A. Honoré, 'The Making of the Theodosian Code', *Zeitschrift der Savigny-Stiftung für Rechtsgeschichte*, 103 (1986), 133 ff.; J. Matthews, 'The Making of the Text', and B. Sirks, 'The Sources of the Code', in Harries and Wood (eds.), op. cit. (n. 1), 19–44, 45–67.

[4] *CT* 1, 1, 5: 'cunctas colligi constitutiones decernimus, quas Constantinus inclitus et post eum divi principes nosque tulimus, edictorum viribus aut sacra generalitate subnixas.' For a discussion of *leges generales*, see J. Harries, 'Introduction: The Background to the Code', in Harries and Wood (eds.), op. cit. (n. 1), 1–16, at 5–6.

[5] Honoré, art. cit. (n. 3), 192–3 estimates that 30 per cent of the texts require redating. For disputed dates, I have relied upon Seeck, *Regesten*; *PLRE* and Chastagnol, *Fastes*. For a critique of Seeck, see Sirks, art. cit. (n. 3), 45 ff.

[6] *CT* 1, 1, 5: 'hunc quidem codicem et priores diligentioribus conpositos cognoscamus, quorum scholasticae intentioni tribuitur nosse etiam illa, quae mandata silentio in desuetudinem abierunt, pro sui tantum temporis negotiis valitura.'

[7] Though cf. W. Turpin, 'The Purpose of the Roman Law Codes', *ZRG*, 104 (1987), 620–30.

[8] *CT* 1, 1, 5: 'constitutionum ipsa etiam verba, quae ad rem pertinet, reserventur.'

ultimately the aim of Theodosius was to draw up a further code which would be completely free of inaccuracies and inconsistencies. This project was never realized and the commission of 429 compiled a *corpus* of texts which contains a number of incongruities and contradictions.[9]

A second imperial letter, dating from 20 December 435, marked the opening of a new phase of the project.[10] The commission was expanded, receiving eight new members. The original editorial parameters were renewed, but further clarifications were added. The commission was now, in the interests of brevity and clarity, to get to the legal point before the original text had done. Superfluities were to be removed, clarification added, ambiguities and incongruities ironed out. It is clear, however, that these prima facie extensive editorial powers were sparingly used in practice. Honoré's studies demonstrate, through their attempts to identify individual fourth-century *quaestores sacri palatii* by stylistic analysis of the texts, that those working after 435 still sought to preserve, where possible, the words originally used.[11] For our purposes, the survival of the *Codex Theodosianus* as we know it is certainly fortunate and we may be thankful that the scheme begun in 429 did not reach its original conclusion. The legal weaknesses of the Code are its historical strengths. The respect paid to invalid or contradictory texts has furnished us with an admirable body of material on different ideas concerning religion in the fourth and early fifth centuries. As Honoré has stated, the ideology of the Code was the rule of law; it was not committed to any particular doctrinal point of view.[12]

A difficulty lies, however, in the state of the texts as the commission encountered them. Had they been edited or paraphrased? This is certainly an important question and one that answered positively might seem to undermine the validity of the *Codex Theodosianus* in an enquiry of this nature. Unfortunately, it is a question that evades a confident answer. Some idea of the practices and competence of the commission may be gained by comparing the collection of apparently complete constitutions discovered by Jacobus Sirmondus with traceable fragments in the Theodosian Code. Mommsen was in no doubt

---

[9] See the cautionary remarks of Corcoran, *Empire*, 12: 'Care is therefore needed in remembering that what survives [of imperial pronouncements], both within and without the codes, is neither full nor necessarily representative.'

[10] *CT* 1, 1, 6. For a discussion of the possible change of editorial direction, see Matthews, art. cit. (n. 2), 24 ff. and Sirks, art. cit. (n. 3), 56 ff.

[11] Honoré, art. cit. (n. 3); and his 'Some Quaestors of the Reign of Theodosius II', in Harries and Wood (eds.), op. cit. (n. 1), 68–94. For some cautionary comments on this kind of enquiry, however, see J. Harries, 'The Roman Imperial Quaestor from Constantine to Theodosius II', *JRS*, 78 (1988), 148–72, at 150.

[12] Honoré, art. cit. (n. 3), 182.

that the *sylloge* of Sirmondian constitutions antedated the publication of the Code.[13] Ten of the sixteen Sirmondian Constitutions were quoted or condensed in the Code.[14] When the texts are matched up, it can be seen that the chosen editorial method was *verbatim* quotation of selected passages from imperial constitutions of full length.[15] The passages selected by the compilers of the Code were invariably the legal core of the law itself or one of its important subsections.[16] With our shortened texts in the Code the best approach is therefore to trust the commission and the traditional civic practice of publishing the text of an imperial letter verbatim in a public place. The commissioners knew their brief and also the importance of authenticity. It is likely that their efforts were no less rigorous than those of modern scholarship—and they were better informed.

Accepting, in principle, the historical validity of the texts in the Code, a new series of questions arises. Who *made* the law and what was being said? In detail, these questions can only be answered in dealing with the texts themselves. It will be enough here to outline the main sources of initiative in the making of laws in the later Roman Empire.

The reconstruction of the legislative procedure in the later Roman Empire is a hazardous task. A law from October 446 outlining some fifth-century changes has prompted some recent attempts.[17] According to Honoré's analysis, elements in the finished text could derive from the emperor himself; any administrative official who originally submitted a *suggestio* on some legal deficiency; the imperial *consistorium* and the drafter himself, the *quaestor sacri palatii*.[18] According to Jill Harries, the emperors of the fourth century were much more mobile than their predecessors and they made law on an ad hoc basis as they moved about the empire. Long stays in imperial capitals allowed a more complicated system to develop, so that by 446 the workings of a more systematic legislative machine could be seen. In the law of this date much discussion of the drafting of laws took place both inside and outside the *consistorium*. Senators, court ministers, the quaestor, and

[13] Th. Mommsen and P. M. Meyer (eds.), *Theodosiani Libri XVI cum Constitutionibus Sirmondianis et Leges Novellae ad Theodosianum Pertinentes*, (Berlin: 1905), i. p. ccclxxviii.

[14] They are: 2, 4, 6, 9, 10, 11, 12, 14, 15, 16.

[15] For verbatim quotations, compare, e.g.: *Sirm.* 2 with *CT* 16, 2, 35; *Sirm.* 6 with *CT* 16, 2, 47 and 16, 5, 64; *Sirm.* 9 with *CT* 16, 2, 39, etc.

[16] See *Sirm.* 4 with *CT* 16, 9, 1 and 16, 8, 5; *Sirm.* 12 with *CT* 16, 10, 19; *Sirm.* 16 with *CT* 5, 7, 2.

[17] *CJ* 1, 14, 8 (17 Nov. 446). The most important recent discussions are Corcoran, *Empire*, 13 ff., for editing in general; Honoré, art. cit. (n. 3), 136–42 and Harries, art. cit. (n. 11), 164–9. They disagree on the extent of discussion within and outside the imperial *consistorium*.

[18] For the role of the governor, see Corcoran, *Empire*, 234 ff.

the emperor himself were all involved, although it is clear that circumstances might require the presence of other experts and advisers.

Many modern scholars have looked at the language used in the Theodosian Code and decided that it is long-winded, tedious, obscure, repetitive, and confused. In a survey of late Roman bureaucratese, MacMullen quoted George Orwell in support of his view that the difficult language of official documents concealed the sinister manœuvrings of an autocracy.[19] MacMullen himself concluded:

the very object of language—to be understood—was forgotten. One kind of proof is the great difficulty experienced by modern readers in making out just what an ancient writer was trying to say.[20]

In reality, the difficulties experienced by modern readers of the Code prove only that the thought world of the era in which the Code was compiled was markedly different from that of modern times, or, for that matter, preceding centuries. The fact that texts included in the Code employed a language different from earlier periods in Roman legal history is illustrative of change but this was not necessarily a movement which left men and women of the time baffled and frightened into docility.[21]

The theory that late Roman law is in any sense a 'vulgarization' of early classical paradigms has also come under attack. W. E. Voss examined the laws relating to buying and transference of property in the post-classical period.[22] Voss revealed that while the language of the general constitutions of later emperors was less technical than that of classical jurists, the classical principles of law remained intact.[23] The stylized rhetoric of the later texts was thus no proof that a vulgarization of law had taken place, either through increased despotism or a falling-off of standards of legal education on the part of the drafters.

We must therefore reject the view that the language of the Code represents a decline in the standards of law or education. It cannot be

[19] R. MacMullen, 'Roman Bureaucratese in the Fourth Century', *Traditio*, 18 (1962), 364–78. Orwell cited at p. 369: 'political speech and writing are largely the defence of the indefensible . . . political language has to consist largely of euphemism, question-begging and sheer cloudy vagueness.'

[20] MacMullen, art. cit. (n. 19), 377.

[21] Ibid.: 'People in the fourth century must often have laboured through contracts, laws and so forth, not quite certain what they were reading or writing; and the fog grew thicker as one moved up to the more important levels of government . . . By the time one reached the emperor, it was insulting to be explicit.'

[22] W. E. Voss, *Recht und Rhetorik in den Kaisergesetzen der Spätantike*, Forschungen zur Byzantinischen Rechtsgeschichte, 9 (Frankfurt: Löwenklau, 1982). See also Corcoran, *Empire*, 3.

denied, however, that much of the language in which the texts were written is strident, haughty, and violent. How can we account for this? A detailed and satisfactory examination of the language of the Code has yet to be made, but some recent and suggestive ideas on the subject have a bearing on how best some of the texts may be approached.[24]

In 1977, P. Wormald looked at the role of written law (*lex scripta*) in the Germanic kingdoms from Euric to Cnut.[25] The notorious obscurities and discrepancies in the surviving barbarian law codes had been interpreted by the nineteenth-century *Rechtsschule* as evidence that an inferior barbarian mind had struggled feebly to emulate the Roman legal genius. Wormald argued, however, that the requirements of justice and government did not account for much of the legislation and he focused his attention instead on 'the ideological aspirations of Germanic kingship'.[26] The barbarians had no tradition of written law and their *codices* seemed to be neither attempts to codify existing law nor programmes to revise the whole body of law. Much barbarian legislation seemed instead to be concerned with producing what *looked* like written law codes. The use of Latin, the division of some Codes into twelve books and the addition of numerous titles were all designed to give a thoroughly Roman impression. Wormald cautioned against conceiving of these documents in terms of court-room application.[27] They were, he concluded, designed to enhance the regal status of certain Germanic kings who were aware that written law-making had been one of the most impressive characteristics of Roman emperors. At the same time, educated Latin-speaking Romans, like Cassiodorus, were prepared to offer their legal advice believing that by doing so they might convince themselves that the legal aspects of *Romanitas* lived on.

The avenues of enquiry opened by an awareness of the ideological implications of barbarian law-making seem to apply just as much to the language employed in late Roman laws.[28] In a significant phrase, Honoré described the function of the imperial *quaestor sacri palatii* as combining 'the roles of a Minister of Justice and of Propaganda'.[29]

---

[23] See e.g. Voss, op. cit. (n. 22), 249 on Cassiodorus' continued use of Cicero's theory of *interpretationes*.

[24] G. Vidén, *The Roman Chancery Tradition: Studies in the Language of the Codex Theodosianus and Cassiodorus' Variae*, Studia Graeca et Latina Gothoburgensa, 46 (Gothenburg: Acta Universitatis Gothoburgensis, 1984) is excessively syntactical.

[25] P. Wormald, '*Lex scripta* and *verbum regis*: Legislation and Germanic Kingship from Euric to Cnut', in P. H. Sawyer and I. N. Wood (eds.), *Early Medieval Kingship* (Leeds: 1977), 105–38.

[26] Ibid. 106.   [27] Ibid. 119.   [28] See Corcoran, *Empire*, 75 ff.

[29] Honoré, art. cit. (n. 3), 139. See also his study of Ausonius, whose technical legal knowledge was thin: T. Honoré, 'Ausonius and Vulgar Law', *Iura* 35 (1984), 75–85. For a more detailed assessment of these views, see Corcoran, *Empire*, 75 ff., 92 ff.

Harries has also made an important contribution to the understanding of the language of the Code by looking closely at the *quaestores* from Constantine I to Theodosius II.[30] The emergence of the *quaestor* as an official with special responsibility for the framing of *edicta* and *epistulae* was due to an increased centralization in the law-making process during the fourth century:

The point was not that the emperor had never issued general laws before, but that he (as an institution) had become more consciously and more explicitly the source of general law for the empire.[31]

The same awareness was to lead ultimately to the compilation of the *Codex Theodosianus* itself. Harries outlined the different areas of responsibility of imperial *quaestores*, from ambassadorial missions to 'leges dictandae' and she also explored the relationship between late emperors and their *quaestores*.[32] The imperial *quaestor*[33] was the most important palatine official involved in framing the style of imperial edicts and letters.[34] He was expected to be highly trained in rhetoric but was only rarely so in law.[35] His rhetorical background enabled him to range through the Latin language constructing an imperial style suitable for both the emperor and the matter in hand. Emperors themselves, however, continued to subscribe laws personally precisely because the texts, when promulgated, would communicate to listeners the personality of the emperor himself:

The language of the constitutions was therefore expected to be, at the very least, correct and to conform to the literary criteria employed by the rhetors of late antiquity; thus the language of the law was influenced by considerations which were not strictly legal but which derived from the nature of imperial rule.[36]

The emperor was what he said and wrote.[37]

[30] Harries, art. cit. (n. 11).

[31] Ibid. 149. See Millar, *ERW*, 257 where he observes that general imperial edicts, absent from the record since the Flavians, make a reappearance under the Tetrarchs. He suggests that this development might indicate 'a real change in the nature and ambitions of imperial government'. [32] Ibid. 152 ff.

[33] Not, strictly speaking, *known* as the *quaestor sacri palatii* until 429. See Harries, art. cit. (n. 11), 154.

[34] I accept Harries's reconstruction which shows that impressive *suggestiones* from provincial governors, prefects, or palatine officials might emerge as *leges generales* without the intervention of the *quaestor*. I also accept that the *magistri* probably had the authority to make slight alterations of the texts of the *quaestor*: Harries, art. cit. (n. 11), 161–2. In any case, all officials had the same end in mind when composing: to portray the emperor himself in the best possible light. [35] Ibid. 158.

[36] J. Harries in Harries and Wood (eds.), op. cit. (n. 1), 7.

[37] Harries cites Millar, *ERW*, 206: 'that not all emperors approached the distinction of Julius Caesar, and that some received assistance in composition is less important than

Fortunately, we have access to the reflections of an accomplished drafter of late antique laws. R. MacPherson's monograph on the world of Cassiodorus opens with an interesting survey of the 'language of Roman authority':[38]

The two chief characteristics of the language of many governmental communiqués of the Tetrarchy and the fourth century are perhaps prolixity and sheer elemental power, affected by the most uninhibited exploitation of the emotive resources of the Latin language, and inadequately explained in terms of the organic development from the official latinity of previous centuries.[39]

It is from Cassiodorus that we have received the most important insights into the function of the imperial *quaestores* as the composers of legislation. Serving the Ostrogothic kings as *quaestor*, Cassiodorus explained the importance of the rhetorical requirement for the task. Revealing the king's *persona* required, on different occasions, conciliatory, violent, or contemptuous language; and depending on the circumstances, the repetition of previous legislation virtually word for word.[40]

In the preface to his *Variae*, Cassiodorus recalled the ancient theory which had established three modes of speech:

it is a fine rule of our ancestors, that you should speak with such fitness as to sway the hopes your hearers have already conceived. For it was not in vain that the wisdom of the ancients defined three modes of oratory: the humble, that seems to creep along in true lowliness; the middle, which is neither swollen with magnificence, nor thin and impoverished, but is placed between the two, enriched with its own beauty, and contained in its own bounds; and the third, which is raised to the highest peak of argument by choice conceits.[41]

As a speaker, and certainly also as a legal drafter, Cassiodorus was aware of his different audiences:

the expectation itself'. For evidence that fourth-century emperors continued to feel it important to associate themselves closely with pronouncements issued in their name, Harries usefully provides the following examples: (Constantine) Eusebius *VC* 4, 8; 29; 32; 2, 27; (Constantius II) Ammianus 15, 1, 3.

[38] R. MacPherson, *Cassiodorus. Politics in Involution* (Poznan: 1988), ch. 1.

[39] Ibid. 20.

[40] In less bureaucratic times the emperor had been able to reveal his *persona* himself. Fronto, *Ep. ad Verum Imperatorem Invicem* 2, 1, 8: 'the imperial office (*imperium*) is a term not merely of power but also of oratory, in view of the fact that the force of commanding (*vis imperandi*) is exercised through orders and prohibitions. Were he not to praise good deeds and denounce bad ones, encourage to virtue, deter from vice, he would be called emperor for nothing.'

[41] Cassiodorus, *Praefatio Variorum* 16 (*CCL* 96, 6): 'Humile, quod communione ipsa serpere videatur. Medium, quod nec magnitudine tumescit, nec parvitate tenuatur; sed inter utrumque positum, propria venustate ditatum, suis finibus continetur. Tertium genus, quod ad summum apicem disputationis exquisitis sensibus elevatur.' (Trans. S. J. B. Barnish.)

Clearly, different persons may thus enjoy the eloquence which suits them; and, though it may flow from a single breast, it does so in separate streams.[42]

There is no reason to think that the Roman *quaestor sacrii palatii* acted in a significantly different way.

The dismissal of the language of many of the laws in the Code as 'mere rhetoric' is therefore unhelpful. The vividness of the language was a further technique for impressing upon the listener, reader, or enforcer the personality of the emperor himself. Far from acting as a smokescreen, this kind of language could communicate directly the immanence of the emperor. In many of the texts which are discussed below, the rhetorico-psychological element was just as important as the legal substance of the law.

2. CONSTANTINE[43]

When he entered Rome in 312, Constantine can hardly have been ignorant of the religious dimension of the *adventus* and in particular, of the act of thanksgiving which his predecessors had customarily made at the temple of Juppiter on the Capitol.[44] There is no record in the surviving sources that Constantine made such a visit in 312. Some have suggested a deliberate refusal to sacrifice on account of the emperor's recent conversion to Christianity, a course which may have attracted criticism.[45] It should be noted, however, that such sacrifices were merely customary; the procession was not a formal triumph.[46] Slight evidence also precludes too rigid an understanding of the importance of the Capitol.[47] A busy emperor with much on his mind need not have

[42] Ibid.: 'ut varietas personarum congruum sortiretur eloquium, et licet ab uno pectore proflueret, diversis tamen alveis emanaret.'

[43] A version of this section has appeared as 'Constantine and the Ancient Cults of Rome: The Legal Evidence', *Greece and Rome*, 43 (1996), 68–80 and I am grateful to the Clarendon Press for permission to reproduce much of that article here.

[44] Two panegyrics delivered before him had made explicit reference to the importance of the gods as part of the *adventus*: *Pan. Lat.* 7 (6), 8, 7–9 (AD 307): 'Te primo ingressu tuo tanta laetitia, tanta freqentia populus Romanus excepit ut, cum te ad Capitolini Iovis gremium vel oculis ferre gestiret, stipatione sui vix ad portas urbis admitteret.' Cf. 5 (8), 8, 4 (AD 311/312). See S. MacCormack, *Art and Ceremony in Late Antiquity* (Berkeley: University of California Press, 1981), 22–33. See my discussion above, 71–5.

[45] J. Straub, 'Konstantins Verzicht auf den Gang zum Kapitol', *Historia*, 4 (1955), 297 ff.

[46] See the discussion of A. Fraschetti, 'Costantino e l'abbandono del Campidoglio', in A. Giardina (ed.), *Società romana e impero tardoantico* (Rome: Laterza, 1981), ii. 74–80 with n. 51 for further references.

[47] Josephus *BJ* 7, 4, 1 (68–74) shows that Vespasian went straight to the Palatine and offered his thanks there to the *lares*, not Juppiter. Cf. the admittedly dubious *SHA*

hesitated to proceed straight to rest and preparation for business. It is even possible, though undocumented, that Constantine did offer sacrifice.[48] Constantine's activities in Rome in 312 are of greater significance for his personal inclinations than for the legal standing of the old cults in the city. Within months, however, he had formulated a policy on his non-Christian subjects.

Early in January 313 Constantine was in Milan, offering his sister in marriage to his imperial colleague Licinius.[49] The two emperors also took the opportunity to draw up a letter which was to be circulated among the governors of the eastern empire which ordered the immediate restitution of Christian properties to the recently legitimized sect, thereby bringing the law in the eastern empire into line with that operating in Constantine's dominions.[50] The significance of this letter for the Christian community is well known, but the same letter also declared unequivocally that the co-authors of the regulations wanted no action to be taken against the non-Christian cults. At two points in the document this expression of toleration was forcefully made:

among all the other things that we saw would benefit the majority of men . . . were those which ensured reverence for the Divinity (divinitas), so that we might grant both to Christians and to all men freedom to follow whatever *religio* each one wished, in order that whatever divinity there is in the seat of heaven may be appeased and made propitious towards us and towards all who have been set under our power.[51]

The *pax deorum* was thus best served by the inclusion of Constantine's new god alongside those of the state. After giving detailed instructions

Heliogabalus 15, 7 for a refusal by the emperor to attend ceremonies on the capitol. The duties were performed by the Urban Praetor. See L. Cracco Ruggini, 'Elagabalo, Costantino e i culti "Siriaci" nella *Historia Augusta*', *Historia Augusta Colloquium MCMXC* (1991), 123–46.

[48] See A. Alföldi, *Constantine and the Conversion of Pagan Rome*, 2nd edn. (Oxford: Clarendon Press, 1948), 61–2. Also F. Paschoud, *Cinq Études sur Zosime* (Paris: Belles lettres, 1975), 24–62.

[49] Lactantius *DMP* 45, 1.

[50] Ibid. 48, 2–12, the so-called 'Edict of Milan'. Cf. Eusebius *HE* 10, 5, 2–14. See Corcoran, *Empire*, 158–60; 189; T. Christiensen, 'The So-called Edict of Milan', *Classica et Medievalia*, 35 (1984), 129–75; Millar, *ERW*, 582–4; Lane Fox, *Pagans and Christians* (1986), 621 denies Constantine's role in the choice of words. See also S. Mitchell, 'Maximinus and the Christians in AD 312', *JRS*, 78 (1988), 105–24, at 116.

[51] Lactantius *DMP* 48, 2 (*CSEL* 27, 228–9): 'haec inter cetera quae videbamus pluribus hominibus profutura . . . quibus divinitatis reverentia continebatur, ut daremus et Christianis et omnibus liberam potestatem sequendi religionem quam quisque voluisset, quo quicquid est divinitatis in sede caelesti, nobis atque omnibus qui sub potestate nostra sunt constituti, placatum ac propitium possit existere.' (Trans. J. L. Creed.) Cf. for a similar expression of God-fearing, letter of Constantine to Aelafius, *Vicarius Africae* in 314: *CSEL* 26, 204–6.

to the governor regarding the restoration of Christian property, the emperors warned him to make sure that no Christian backlash occurred:

your Devotedness understands that others too have been granted a similarly open and free permission to follow their own *religio* and worship as befits the peacefulness of our times, so that each man may have a free opportunity to engage in whatever worship he has chosen. This we have done to ensure that no cult or religion may seem to have been impaired by us.[52]

The so-called 'Edict of Milan' left the legal standing of the old cults intact. A pantheon of officially sanctioned deities would continue to receive cult on behalf of the state. That cult required the provision of a large number of priestly intermediaries between people and gods, and the emperors, as Pontifices Maximi, continued to be the most important of them. Temples to these deities were to continue to be the setting for cult sacrifices and the estates and revenues held by the temples for this purpose were to remain unmolested. The highly visible and public ceremonies connected with these cults would continue.

On 25 July 315 Constantine held his *decennalia* celebrations in Rome.[53] Eusebius of Caesarea is the only source to provide any details of Constantine's actions at the thanksgiving:

On this occasion he ordered the celebration of festivals for the whole populace, and he offered prayers of thanksgiving to God, the King of all, as sacrifices without flame or smoke.[54]

It is not safe to conclude that the character of the *decennalia/vicennalia* celebrations was diminished by the emperor's actions.[55] Eusebius drew a contrast between the festivals attended by the whole city and what Constantine *himself* had done. It was irregular, but not unknown, for emperors to loathe blood sacrifices.[56] Nothing, however,

---

[52] Lactantius *DMP* 48, 6 (*CSEL* 27, 230–1): 'intellegit dicatio tua etiam aliis religionis suae vel observantiae potestatem similiter apertam et liberam pro quiete temporis nostri esse concessam, ut in colendo quod quisque delegerit, habeat liberam facultatem. Quod a nobis factum est, ut neque cuiquam honori neque cuiquam religioni detractum aliquid a nobis videatur.' Cf. guarantees of toleration in the edict of April 311 published by Galerius, Constantine, and Licinius: Lactantius *DMP* 33, 11–35, 1; Eusebius *HE* 8, 17, 3–10. See Mitchell, art. cit. (n. 50), 112–13.

[53] Seeck, *Regesten*, 163.

[54] Eusebius *VC* 1, 48: Οὕτω δ' ἔχοντι δεκαέτης αὐτῷ τῆς βασιλείας ἠνύετο χρόνος. ἐφ' ᾧ δὴ πανδήμους ἐκτελῶν ἑορτὰς τῷ πάντων βασιλεῖ θεῷ εὐχαρίστους εὐχὰς ὥσπερ τινὰς ἀπύρους καὶ ἀκάπνους θυσίας ἀνεπέμπετο.

[55] J. Geffcken, *The Last Days of Graeco-Roman Paganism*, rev. and trans. by S. MacCormack, (Amsterdam-Oxford: North Holland, 1978), 119 thought that the passage quoted in the text above showed the prohibition of sacrifices at Rome during the official games.

[56] *VC* 4, 10. See also 3, 15 (*Vicennalia*) and Eusebius *Laus Constantini* 2, 5–6. Philip

inhibited the customary sacrifices which most of the population of Rome saw as an integral part of the celebrations.

Constantine was notably more traditional, however, on the subject of harmful magic. In a letter addressed to the Prefect of Rome, Septimius Bassus, dated 23 May 318, the emperor attacked those who used the *scientia* of practitioners of *magicae artes*. Certain activities were specified: the use of the 'magic arts' in plotting against men's lives; and the perversion of modest minds to lust. But if the *scientia* was used for more positive purposes, like the curing of other men or the protection of crops, then it was to be permitted:

by such devices no person's safety or reputation is injured, but by their action they bring it about that divine gifts and the labours of men are not destroyed.[57]

The distinction between good and harmful magic, enshrined in the Twelve Tables, was reinforced by Constantine.[58]

On 15 May the following year, the emperor addressed 'the People'. His letter concerned the activities of *haruspices* and *sacerdotes*. Henceforth, *haruspices*, *sacerdotes*, and those who carried out the kind of rites associated with these men were no longer allowed to enter private homes, nor, on the pretext of friendship, were they to cross another's threshold. But the *public* exercise of their skills was permitted, at the 'aras publicas adque delubra' for those who thought that this kind of thing was of use to them :

we do not prohibit the rites of a past superseded practice from being celebrated openly.[59]

The important phrase 'praeterita usurpatio' is difficult to translate. Pharr's translation of the two words as 'a bygone perversion' is too

'the Arab' had also abhorred sacrifice: Orosius 7, 20, 3. For Christian attitudes towards blood sacrifice, see S. Bradbury, 'Constantine and the Problem of Anti-Pagan Legislation in the Fourth Century', *Classical Philology*, 89 (1994), 120–39, at 129 ff., although he does not make the connection with magic and divination.

[57] *CT* 9, 16, 3: 'quibus non cuiusque salus aut existimatio laederetur, sed quorum proficerent actus, ne divina munera et labores hominum sternerentur.' (Trans. C. Pharr.)

[58] See J. Gaudemet, 'La Législation anti-païenne de Constantin à Justinien', *Cr. St.*, 11 (1990), 449–68, at 452 f. Also J. Maurice, 'La terreur de la magie au IVème siècle', *Revue historique de droit français et étranger*, 4ème série, 6 (1927), 108–20, at 109; Chastagnol, *La Préfecture*, 144 calls the legislation a 'tentative d'épuration' and points out the lack of evidence for a specifically Christian policy at work. See A. Barb, 'The Survival of the Magic Arts', in Momigliano, *Conflict*, 102–3. Also J. H. W. G. Liebeschuetz, *Continuity and Change in Roman Religion* (Oxford: Clarendon Press, 1979), 127 with references and R. MacMullen, *Enemies of the Roman Order* (London: Routledge, 1966), ch. 3 'Magicians'.

[59] *CT* 9, 16, 2: 'nec enim prohibemus praeteritae usurpationis officia libera luce tractari.' (Trans. Croke and Harries.) See Corcoran, *Empire*, 193–4.

pejorative; Croke and Harries have preferred the similarly rhetorical but milder 'a past superseded practice'. This law therefore ordered a ban on private divination. This attitude, again, was far from new. Emperors throughout the Principate had treated reports of illicit divination with the utmost seriousness.[60] Constantine therefore upheld the fundamental distinction between legal and illegal divination like that which existed for 'magic'.

In February 320, the Prefect of Rome received more precise instructions.[61] The core of this law was essentially the same as that of 15 May 319 (*CT* 9, 16, 2). No *haruspex* was to enter the house of another person for any reason, not even if there existed a long-standing friendship between the two. Punishments were specified: the *haruspex* was to be burned alive and the consultor was to have his property confiscated before being exiled to an island.[62] As before, an imperial statement was made making it clear that the practice could remain if performed in the open:

those persons who wish to serve their own *superstitio* will be able to perform their own ceremonies publicly.[63]

Constantine's use of 'superstitio' in this context was an expression of his distaste for the work of *haruspices*. But the term was being used traditionally and derogatively as a means of identifying those who pursued their religion with excessive zeal.[64] The last lines of the law established that information forthcoming on secret haruspicy would

[60] Dio 56, 25, 5 (AD 11): 'the seers were forbidden to prophesy to anyone alone or to prophesy regarding death even if others should be present.' Suetonius *Tiberius* 63: 'he lived a life of extreme fear and was even exposed to insult. He forbade anyone to consult soothsayers secretly and without witnesses.' See F. Cramer, *Astrology in Roman Politics and Law* (Philadelphia: American Philosophical Society, 1954), pt. 2; also Liebeschuetz, op. cit. (n. 58), 120 ff., with the apposite quotation from Ulpian *De Officio Proconsulis* 7: 'those who consult about the health of the emperor are punishable by death or some still heavier punishment; and about their own or relative's affairs by a lighter sentence.' Also: *Sent. Paul.* 5, 21, 3 condemned consultations 'de salute principis vel summae rei publicae'. See R. MacMullen, op. cit. (n. 58), 129 f.

[61] *CT* 9, 16, 1. Date from Seeck, *Regesten*, 169. For the Prefect Valerius Maximus Basilius, see *PLRE* I, 590.

[62] See R. MacMullen, 'Judicial Savagery in the Roman Empire', *Chiron*, 16 (1986), 147–66, at 155.

[63] *CT* 9, 16, 1: 'superstitioni enim suae servire cupientes poterunt publice ritum proprium exercere.'

[64] On the fluidity of the term in the fourth century, see M. R. Salzman, '*Superstitio* in the *Codex Theodosianus* and the Persecution of Pagans', *Vigiliae Christianae*, 41 (1987), 172–88; ead. *On Roman Time*, 205 ff. On superstitio, see D. Grodzynski, '*Superstitio*', *REA*, 76 (1974), 36–60; R. L. Wilken, *The Christians as the Romans Saw Them* (New Haven: Yale University Press, 1984), ch. 3, 'The Piety of the Persecutors'.

not mark the informant as a *delator*; an obvious indication of the seriousness of the emperor's intention to suppress such activity.

Constantine himself benefited from the public haruspicy which he had carefully legitimized. On 8 March 321, following an incident at Rome, Constantine sent a letter to the Prefect of the City, Valerius Maximus Basilius. Constantine stated that the (public?) consultation of haruspices was fully legal and necessary when state buildings had been struck by lightning. The Prefect was commended for dispatching a full report to the emperor's *magister officiorum*. But a clause was included maintaining the hostility towards private divination:

Permission shall be granted to all other persons also to appropriate this custom to themselves, provided only that they abstain from domestic sacrifices, which are specifically prohibited.[65]

Significantly, the practice of *haruspicina* was not here called a 'superstition' but a 'custom' (*observantia*).

The elevation of the Christian cult to a privileged position within Roman life was not achieved without friction. In May or December 323, Constantine sent a letter to Helpidius, Vicarius Romae. Some 'ecclesiastics' and Catholic Christians had been compelled 'by men of different *religiones*' to celebrate the 'lustrorum sacrificia'. Those devoted to the 'sanctissima lex' were not to be forced 'ad ritum alienae superstitionis'. A public beating awaited offenders of vulgar status, while members of the social élite could expect a heavy fine. In this law, Constantine used the term *superstitio* to apply to the activities of the followers of Rome's ancient cults generally; a much broader definition than had been used previously.[66] Alföldi was wholly mistaken, however, to think that this measure banned the lustral sacrifices.[67] There is no suggestion that the non-Christan population of the city lost anything as a result of the letter. In fact, Christians had clearly been on hand at these ceremonies and Fraschetti has suggested that they might have participated but stopped short of sacrificing, as Constantine himself had at his *decennalia* in 315.[68] The stridency of the emperor's language may reflect concern that in the east Licinius was invoking the old gods against his own.[69] Constantine therefore became more sensitive to non-Christian activities at Rome since they might now

---

[65] *CT* 16, 10, 1: 'ceteris etiam usurpandae huius consuetudinis licentia tribuenda, dummodo sacrificiis domesticis abstineant, quae specialiter prohibita sunt.'

[66] See Salzman, art. cit. (n. 64), 177.

[67] Alföldi, op. cit. (n. 48), 85–6.

[68] See Fraschetti, art. cit. (n. 46), 85.

[69] Cf. e.g. Eusebius *HE* 10, 8, 10; 16; *VC* 1, 52; 54; 56. Nöthlichs, *Massnahmen*, 25–6, 30.

be imbued with treasonable significance. Certainly the measure is insufficient ground for positing a general attack on the legal status of the old cults at Rome.

Late the following year, however, Constantine achieved a complete military victory over the man with whom he had divided the empire in 312. The defeat and death of Valerius Licinianus Licinius demonstrated to Constantine more clearly the favour of Heaven for his earthly enterprises and his success brought into his power the eastern provinces of the empire with their sophisticated Christian infrastructure. The effect on his personality and policies was so marked that a later hostile pagan tradition dated his *conversion* to Christianity to these years.[70]

Shortly after the victory, Constantine enacted a number of important measures in the empire, communicated through unsolicited letters.[71] Accompanying a flood of governors for the newly captured provinces was a 'law' which forbade senior officers of the administration, including Praetorian Prefects, offering sacrifice:[72]

If they were Christians [writes Eusebius], they were free to act consistently with their profession; if otherwise, the law required them to abstain from idolatrous sacrifices.[73]

Also among the letters was a law

which was intended to restrain the idolatrous abominations which in time past had been practised in every city and country and it provided that no one should dare to erect images or practice divination and other false and foolish arts or indeed offer sacrifice in any way.[74]

Barnes thought these enactments to be crucial for Constantine's establishment of Christianity as the 'official religion of the Roman Empire'.[75] But in the case of the ban applying to office-holders, there are a number of points to note. In the first place, Eusebius himself admits that not all of the governors sent out to the east were Christians, some were clearly non-Christians.[76] There is also an obvious paralleling

---

[70] Zos. 2, 29, 2–3. See D. F. Buck, *Eunapius of Sardis*, D. Phil. thesis, Oxford (1977), 306 f.; Paschoud, *Zosime*, i. 219–24.

[71] For what follows, see Bradbury, art. cit. (n. 56) and the items in nn. 76 and 77 below.   [72] *VC* 2, 44.

[73] Ibid. ἢ γὰρ Χριστιανοῖς οὖσιν ἐμπρέπειν ἐδίδου τῇ προσηγορίᾳ, ἢ διακειμένοις ἑτέρως τὸ μὴ εἰδωλολατρεῖν παρήγγειλεν.

[74] Ibid. 2, 45: ὁ μὲν εἴργων τὰ μυσαρὰ τῆς κατὰ πόλεις καὶ χώρας τὸ παλαιὸν συντελουμένης εἰδωλολατρίας, ὡς μήτ᾽ ἐγέρσεις ξοάνων ποιεῖσθαι τολμᾶν, μήτε μαντείαις καὶ ταῖς ἄλλαις περιεργίαις ἐπιχειρεῖν, μήτε μὴν θύειν καθόλου μηδένα . . . Cf. Socrates *HE* 1, 3.

[75] Barnes, *CE*, 97, 224, 269.

[76] The phrase was 'mostly such as were devoted to the saving faith': τῇ σωτηρίῳ πίστει καθωσιωμένους τοὺς πλείους.

of the preparations made by Licinius before hostilities and the actions of Constantine after victory. At *VC* 1, 52–4 Eusebius offered details of how Licinius had excluded Christians from his camp because their religious beliefs made them untrustworthy. Indeed, the impression Eusebius gives overall is that there was a marked religious dimension to the conflict. This need not be doubted, but there is also no need to see in Constantine's actions a policy different from that ascribed to Licinius. Politically motivated, he asked for a gesture from those he chose to govern the new regions under his power.

But Barnes has also argued, using the evidence of Eusebius, that Constantine did indeed issue a law banning sacrifice shortly after his victory over Licinius.[77] Barnes conceded that Eusebius did not *quote* the law which initiated the ban but believed that this showed only that Eusebius did not have a copy to hand when he was writing his *Vita Constantini*.[78] But Libanius of Antioch, in an oration written *c*.386[79], flatly contradicted Eusebius in declaring to Theodosius I that:

he [Constantine] made absolutely no alteration in the traditional forms of worship, but, although poverty reigned in the temples, one could see that all the rest of the ritual was fulfilled.[80]

Eusebius himself, several chapters after his reference to the law banning sacrifice, quoted at length a letter which Constantine sent to the provinces just liberated from Licinius and which closed with the words:

let no one use that to the detriment of another which he may himself have received on conviction of its truth . . . For it is one thing voluntarily to undertake the conflict for immortality, another to compel others to do so from

[77] Barnes, *CE*, 210 and n. 11. Restated in his article, 'Constantine's Prohibition of Pagan Sacrifice', *AJPh*, 105 (1984), 69–72. His riposte was to the important review by H. A. Drake in *AJPh*, 103 (1982), 462–6. See also the review by Averil Cameron in *JRS*, 73 (1983), 189.

[78] Barnes, *CE*, 269. Also art. cit. (n. 77), 72. *Contra*, see H. A. Drake, *In Praise of Constantine: A Historical Study and New Translation of Eusebius' Tricennial Oration* (Berkeley: University of California Press, 1976), 150 n. 17.

[79] For a discussion of the date see A. F. Norman, *Libanius Selected Works*, (Cambridge, Mass.: Loeb, 1977), ii. 96–7 following the article of P. Petit, 'Sur la Date du "Pro Templis"', *Byzantion*, 21 (1951), 293 ff. N. Q. King, *The Emperor Theodosius and the Establishment of Christianity* (London: SCM, 1961), Appendix C argued for 388.

[80] *Oratio* 30, 6: τοῖς ἱεροῖς ἐχρήσατο χρήμασι, τῆς κατὰ νόμους δὲ θεραπείας ἐκίνησεν οὐδὲ ἕν, ἀλλ' ἦν μὲν ἐν τοῖς ἱεροῖς πενία, παρῆν δὲ ὁρᾶν ἅπαντα τἆλλα πληρούμενα. Cf. here Libanius *Oratio* 30, 37: Constantine was punished for being a desecrator 'leaving aside the fact that he did not proceed against the sacrifices'. Bradbury, art. cit. (n. 56), 128 makes well-judged remarks on Libanius' capacity for protreptic rhetoric, but I interpret the circumstantial evidence differently.

fear of punishment . . . These are our words . . . since we understand that there are some who say that the rites of the heathen temples, and the power of darkness have been entirely removed.[81]

Dörries understood this paragraph to be an expression of toleration issued in the wake of Constantine's conquest of the east.[82] Barnes, however, having accepted the existence of a general Constantinian ban on sacrifice, perceived the absence of reference to sacrifices in the letter to the eastern provinces as 'pointed' and concluded that the latter document supported the existence of the general ban.[83] But while the general trend of the letter is to praise and flatter the Christians, it is also clearly an attempt to prevent the persecution of those who are not Christians.

Errington has argued that there was a ban on sacrifice but that the letter to the eastern provinces 'quietly superseded' it, when the law caused an outcry among pagans.[84] Eusebius of Caesarea did not, of course, broadcast the fact openly as he was seeking to portray Constantine in the most enthusiastically Christian fashion possible.[85] But if Constantine was reversing a policy, why should he fail to say so clearly? All the persecution-revoking edicts of the age, from Galerius' 'palinode' of 311 to the so-called 'Edict of Milan' and Constantine's own suspension of the persecution of Donatists (5 February 330), unequivocally declared that a change of direction was taking place.[86] In fact, as Barnes observed, the fundamental question concerns the trustworthiness of Eusebius as against Libanius on the question of

---

[81] VC 2, 60: Πλὴν ἕκαστος ὅπερ πείσας ἑαυτὸν ἀναδέδεκται, τούτῳ τὸν ἕτερον μὴ καταβλαπτέτω. ὅπερ θάτερος εἶδέν τε καὶ ἐνόησεν, τούτῳ τὸν πλησίον εἰ μὲν γενέσθαι δυνατὸν ὠφελείτω, εἰ δ' ἀδύνατον παραπεμπέσθω. ἄλλο γάρ ἐστι τὸν ὑπὲρ ἀθανασίας ἆθλον ἑκουσίως ἐπαναιρεῖσθαι, ἄλλο τὸ μετὰ τιμωρίας ἐπαναγκάζειν. ταῦτα εἶπον, ταῦτα διεξῆλθον μακρότερον ἢ ὁ τῆς ἐμῆς ἐπιεικείας ἀπαιτεῖ σκοπός· ἐπειδὴ τὴν τῆς ἀληθείας ἀποκρύψασθαι πίστιν οὐκ ἐβουλόμην, μάλισθ' ὅτι τινὲς ὡς ἀκούω φασὶ τῶν ναῶν περιῃρῆσθαι τὰ ἔθη καὶ τοῦ σκότους τὴν ἐξουσίαν. ὅπερ συνεβούλευσα ἂν πᾶσιν ἀνθρώποις, εἰ μὴ τῆς μοχθηρᾶς πλάνης ἡ βίαιος ἐπανάστασις ἐπὶ βλάβῃ τῆς κοινῆς σωτηρίας ἀμέτρως ταῖς ἐνίων ψυχαῖς ἐμπεπήγει.

[82] H. Dörries, Das Selbstzeugnis Kaiser Konstantins, Abhandlungen der Akademie der Wissenschaften in Göttingen, Philologisch-historische Klasse, 34 (Göttingen: Vandenhoeck & Ruprecht, 1954), 51–4.

[83] Barnes, CE, 210: 'An emperor with these convictions could not be expected to tolerate pagan practices which all Christians found morally offensive.'

[84] R. M. Errington, 'Constantine and the Pagans', GRBS, 29 (1988), 309–18, at 315.

[85] Ibid.: 'knowingly creating a false impression of his [Constantine's] actual practice and long-term policy in the central field of the suppression of paganism.'

[86] Galerius: Eusebius HE 8, 17, 1 and Lactantius DMP 34. Edict of Milan: see n. 50 above. Donatists: Optatus De Schismate Donatistarum App. 9 (CSEL 26, 212–13). Gallienus' edict of toleration: Eusebius HE 7, 13. Bradbury, art. cit. (n. 56), 125–6 is also sceptical of the 'quiet supersession' but I differ in the interpretation of Libanius and CT 16, 10, 2. See below 183 and 212.

the alleged law.[87] But the controversial passage in Eusebius' *Vita* referring to the law banning sacrifices is not a quotation. Barnes was mistaken to suggest that Eusebius' failure to quote was insignificant.

The *Vita Constantini* reflected the circumstances of the time when it was composed.[88] It was the last and the latest of Eusebius' works. It arose out of a panegyric delivered to an emperor whose Christian enthusiasms had increased perceptibly as his life progressed.[89] Eusebius promised moral improvement to those who read his catalogue of Constantine's good deeds.[90] As Lane Fox points out:

> It was not a biography or a straightforward work of history. It was a stylized work of praise and its general remarks about the emperor and his habits have to be read with this purpose in mind.[91]

In the year before Constantine's death, Eusebius felt confident in drawing a picture of the emperor as implacably opposed to the folly and error of idolatry. Constantine, for his part, may have been content to be so portrayed before his Christian court. Eusebius therefore reported *events* from earlier in the emperor's reign, but he misrepresented their scope and significance. As we shall see, Constantine's successors were quickly preoccupied with political affairs and unable or unwilling to quibble with details in the elderly bishop's biography.

The victory in the east had enlarged the dominions and enhanced the stature of Constantine. Among the immediate results of his success, Constantine decided to build a vast new Christian city from which he could rule the eastern empire. This new eastern orientation of Constantine's world-view made a notable impact on him and on some of his chroniclers, not all of them favourable. In 326 he visited Rome to celebrate a version of his *vicennalia* there.[92] Zosimus has preserved an unflattering tradition from Eunapius of Sardis which records that as a result of Constantine's refusal to ascend the Capitol at a state festival, an acrimonious breach occurred between the emperor and the city.[93] It may be that Constantine's aversion to sacrifice manifested itself more strongly in 326 than it had in 315; he may have refused to participate in the ceremonies in the way he had at his *decennalia*. Less inclined to respect the protocols of Rome, he gave offence. Constantine never returned to the city and the work on Constantinople proceeded apace.[94]

---

[87] Barnes, art. cit. (n. 77), 72.   [88] Barnes, *CE* 265–71, at 267.
[89] Ibid. 266.   [90] *VC* 1, 3, 4.   [91] Lane Fox, (n. 50), 627.
[92] Seeck, *Regesten*, 177. He entered the city on 18 July and the main festival was celebrated on 25 July. He had held a celebration the previous year at Nicomedia: Helm, 231.
[93] Zosimus *HN* 2, 29, 1–5.
[94] For a full discussion of the incident, see Paschoud, op. cit. (n. 48), 24–62.

Constantine returned east and within four years the new Rome was completed. The *Chronicle* of Eusebius, rendered into Latin by Jerome, placed the event in 330 and noted the wider effect of the emergence of the new city:

Dedicatur Constantinopolis omnium paene urbium nuditate.[95]

A year later, according to the same source, an edict of the emperor 'ruined' the temples:

Edicto Constantini gentilium templa subversa sunt.[96]

Did Constantine order a general destruction of temples at the beginning of the 330s? In his *Vita Constantini*, Eusebius certainly recorded the transportation of certain sacred objects from the pagan temples to the new capital.[97] This is supported by a statement of Libanius:

he employed the sacred treasures on the building of the city upon which his heart was set.[98]

Both the *Vita Constantini* and Eusebius' oration at the *tricennalia* record that a small number of the emperor's associates travelled to shrines and carefully removed what was precious from them. Before Constantine himself, Eusebius recalled

the melting of their [the pagan gods'] inanimate images in the flames and their conversion from worthless forms into necessary uses.[99]

Though Eusebius was happy to see in the activities of this small force of the emperor's 'friends' a desire to ridicule the old cults, and Constantine was doubtless flattered to have such an interpretation placed on his actions, it is clear that a particular need was served by the mission. This was either the acquisition of precious materials to adorn Constantinople, or it was a response to some financial crisis.[100] Though Eusebius emphasizes the apparent informality of the policy, saying that it was achieved without force, by 'friends' ('comites'?) and on the 'nod' of the emperor, it is not impossible that some imperial communication accompanied the visits of these officials. Thus the

---

[95] Helm, 232.   [96] Ibid. 233.

[97] Eusebius *VC* 3, 54. Cf. *De Rebus Bellicis* 2, 1.

[98] *Oratio* 30, 6: εἰς μὲν τὴν τῆς πόλεως περὶ ἣν ἐσπούδασε ποίησιν τοῖς ἱεροῖς ἐχρήσατο χρήμασι . . .

[99] *Laus Constantini* 9, 6: τὴν δὲ διὰ πυρὸς χωνείαν καὶ τὴν ἐξ ἀχρήστου ἰδέας εἰς ἀναγκαίας χρήσεις τῶν ἀψύχων μεταβολὴν τίς πώποτε ἡρώων διεστείλατο; . . . (Trans. H. A. Drake.) For my views on the religious ambivalence of statues, see J. Curran, 'Moving Statues in Late Antique Rome: Problems of Perspective', *Art History*, 17 (1994), 46–58.

[100] Probably the shortage of coins: A. Piganiol, *L'Empereur Constantin* (Paris: Rieder, 1932), 183–6; id. *L'Empire*, 57–8; R. MacMullen, *Constantine* (New York: Dial Press, 1969), 201. Cf. Ammianus 22, 4, 3.

edictum of 331, in connection with some pragmatic end, became the agent of the 'ruin' of an unknown number of temples, most probably in the eastern portions of the empire, a ruin gladly exaggerated by Eusebius and accepted by his translator. As Nöthlichs points out, the confiscations had some kind of religious background.[101] After all, no Christian churches were treated in this way, but it is more significant that no general closure or destruction of temples was ordered, despite the rubric added by a later editor to Eusebius *Vita Constantini* 3, 54: 'Destruction of Idol Temples and Images Everywhere'.

Constantine's horror of sacrifices affected his attitudes towards his own imperial cult. An inscription from Hispellum, less than 160 km. north of Rome and just off the Via Flaminia, records the arrangements which the emperor made for the cult there.[102] Between 25 December 333 and 18 September 335 Constantine responded to a request from the Umbrian town to build a temple to the Gens Flavia.[103] The erection of a temple in honour of members of the imperial family, alive and dead, was allowed. Theatrical and gladiatorial games were instituted, despite an earlier ban on them.[104] The city even received a new name in recognition of its outstanding loyalty: 'Flavia Constans'. Attached to the cult here and in Rome was a newly created priesthood: the Pontifices Gentis Flaviae.[105] But these priests were apparently to have a role only in the administration of the festivities attached to the cult, because Constantine stated:

a temple dedicated to Our name may not be defiled by the evils of any contagious *superstitio*.[106]

Some kind of practice was forbidden. *Contagio* was a term used widely for heresy, Judaism, or paganism, and Firmicus Maternus isolated the most distasteful practices of non-Christians by it.[107] But it is 'super-

---

[101] Nöthlichs, *Massnahmen*, 31.

[102] *ILS* 705. See Gaudemet, art. cit. (n. 58), 453–4; I. Karayannopulos, 'Konstantin der Grosse und der Kaiserkult', *Historia*, 5 (1956), 341–57, at 345 ff.; J. Gascou, 'Le Rescrit d'Hispellum', *MEFRA*, 79 (1967), 609–59; Nöthlichs, *Massnahmen*, 29–30; S. R. F. Price, 'Between Man and God: Sacrifice in the Roman Imperial Cult', *JRS*, 70 (1980), 40; G. L. Bowersock, 'The Imperial Cult: Perceptions and Persistence', in B. F. Meyer and E. P. Sanders (eds.), *Jewish and Christian Self-Definition* (London: SCM, 1982), iii. 76 ff.

[103] For the date see the discussion of Gascou, art. cit. (n. 102), 618–23.

[104] *CT* 15, 12, 1 (October 325).

[105] C. Matrinius Aurelius is a local example: *CIL* 11, 5283. At Rome, see L. Aradius Valerius Proculus: *CIL* 6, 1690, 1691.

[106] *ILS* 705, ll. 45–47 'ne aedis nostro nomini dedicata cuiusquam contagiose superstitionis fraudibus polluatur.' (Trans. Lewis and Reinhold.)

[107] A. Androtti, 'Contributo alla discussione del rescritto Costantiniano di Hispellum', *Atti del I Convegno di Studi Umbri* (1964), 278 ff. Firmicus Maternus *De Errore* 12, 1; 20, 7; 26, 2.

stitio' which must provide the meaning of the inscription. We have seen that Constantine used it to denote what he considered to be the abhorrent rituals (especially animal sacrifice) associated with the old cults. It would seem that this form of sacrifice was the *contagio* and, as one of the most objectionable acts which the pagans practised, Constantine could not sanction it in connection with the imperial cult. There is no reason to think, however, that the letter from Hispellum referred to anything other than the imperial cult.

The early years of Constantine had witnessed imperial legislation against divination and *artes magicae*. His confidence had been massively boosted by the demonstrations of the Christian God's favour in the contest with Licinius and his acquisition of the east had been accompanied by attacks upon individual shrines for traditional moral and financial reasons. His contempt for the ancient cults was openly voiced and he cut animal sacrifice out of the ceremony of the imperial cult. But he did not proscribe paganism by banning all sacrifice nor did he order the closure of the temples.[108]

3. THE HOUSE OF CONSTANTINE

Unlike his brother Constantius, Constans was an orthodox Christian.[109] There are indications that his regime was fanatically so. He was the only one of Constantine the Great's sons to have been baptized in the full bloom of life and he was reported by Athanasius to have threatened his brother Constantius with war if the bishop were not returned to his rightful see of Alexandria.[110] In addition to the emperor's own convictions, opinions of other enthusiastic Christians circulated freely in the west. Firmicus Maternus, an erstwhile pagan senator, was moved to write *De Errore Profanarum Religionum* and present it to Constans and Constantius II sometime between June 343 and 18 January 350.[111] This book was an exhortation to the emperors to wage war on the ancient pagan cults and was 'a veritable handbook of intolerance':[112]

---

[108] See below, 185 for the alleged 'law' of Constantine.

[109] O. Seeck, 'Constans', *PW* 4, coll. 948–52; J. Moreau, 'Nachträge zum Reallexicon für Antike und Christentum', *JbAC*, 2 (1959), 179–84; Piganiol, *L'Empire*, 87–90.

[110] Socrates *HE* 2, 22; Sozomen *HE* 3, 20; Athanasius *Apologia contra Arianos* 51. See T. D. Barnes, *Athanasius and Constantius* (Cambridge, Mass.: Harvard University Press, 1993), 63.

[111] For a biographical sketch see R. Turcan, *Firmicus Maternus: L'Erreur des religions païennes* (Paris: Belles lettres, 1982), 7–28. For the question of the date of composition see p. 24.

[112] C. N. Cochrane, *Christianity and Classical Culture* (Oxford: Clarendon Press, 1940), 254.

Only a little is lacking that the devil should be utterly overthrown and laid low by your laws, and that the horrid contagion (*contagio*) of idolatry should die out and become extinct . . . For your hands the benevolent Godhead of Christ has reserved the extermination of idolatry and the overthrow of the pagan temples (*profanarum aedium*).[113]

Concerning Constantius II, we have the vivid testimony of Ammianus Marcellinus and Julian.[114] Both writers had good reason to mistrust Constantius. Julian had spent his early youth as a virtual prisoner at Macellum in Cappadocia while Ammianus had been embroiled with his friend and commanding officer Ursicinus in some perilous investigations of Caesar Gallus in 354.[115] Despite the evidence of Constantius' mistreatment of both men, however, there seems to be no reason to think that either exaggerated in describing Constantius II as a profoundly suspicious emperor. In his summing-up on Constantius, Ammianus adds that the emperor was devoted to chastity and had a strong sense of moral rectitude.[116] But Constantius was also over-zealous when it came to religious belief:

The plain and simple religion (*religio*) of the Christians he obscured by a dotard's superstition (*superstitio*).[117]

And Ammianus gave details of some of the most notorious treason trials of the era as illustrations of the emperor's obsession with conspiracy. In his account of the events of 356–7, when Marcellus had failed to turn Constantius against his nephew Julian, the historian commented on the connection, in the emperor's mind, between risks to his own person and magic.[118] There is no doubt that Ammianus' treatment of Constantius is highly coloured, not least because the memory of the emperor's successor, Julian, was so dear to the soldier-historian. Nevertheless, there is a consistency between the pious, suspicious, and insecure character sketched by Ammianus and

---

[113] *De Errore Profanarum Religionum* 20, 7 (*CSEL* 2, 109): 'modicum tantum superest ut legibus vestris funditus prostratus diabolus iaceat, ut extinctae idololatriae pereat funesta contagio . . . idololatriae excidium et profanarum aedium ruinam propitius Christus populo vestris manibus reservavit.' (Trans. C. A. Forbes.) Cf. id. 16, 4; 29, 3–4.

[114] For an excellent discussion of the sources, see Ch. Piétri, 'La Politique de Constance II: Un première "Césaropapisme" ou l'*imitatio Constantini?*', in *L'Église et l'empire au IV siècle*, Entretiens sur l'Antiquité classique, 34 (Geneva: Fondation Hardt, 1987), 113–78.

[115] See J. F. Matthews, *Ammianus*, 34 ff.

[116] 21, 16, 6. Cf. Vict. *De Caes.* 42, 23: 'omnis libidinis atque omnium cupidinum victor. . .'

[117] Ammianus 21, 16, 18: 'Christianam religionem absolutam et simplicem anili superstitione confudens.' (Trans. J. C. Rolfe). Cf. Cicero *De Natura Deorum* 2, 21; 3, 92. [118] 16, 8, 2. Cf. 14, 5, 4.

the spirit which clearly motivated imperial measures against the ancient cults in the reign of Constantius.

Some time in 341, Madalianus, the Vicarius Italiae, received a letter, probably issued in the names of both Augusti but now showing only that of Constantius:

Superstition shall cease; the madness of the sacrifices shall be abolished. For if any man, in violation of the law of the Divine Emperor, Our Father, should dare to perform sacrifices, he shall suffer the infliction of a suitable punishment and the effect of an immediate sentence.[119]

On the face of it, this blunt declaration could not have been more straightforward; the ancient religion of the state had been banned. But some notable scholars disagree. Nöthlichs argued against any general ban.[120] He employed the suspect argument that Magnentius, who later restored nocturnal sacrifices in Rome, would surely have reversed any existing general ban as a means of attracting the support of the city's non-Christians. Elsewhere, however, Nöthlichs himself acknowledges the apparently Christian beliefs of Magnentius.[121] The evidence of Magnentius' actions is inconclusive. It is clearly possible that Magnentius had made a concession to non-Christian opinion in Rome but was prevented by his Christian scruples or *Realpolitik* from doing anything more.

On the other hand, a different and ingenious argument has been proposed by Martroye, who studied the use of the word *superstitio* in the Theodosian Code and concluded that it had never applied to the ancient religion of the state in the period before the reign of Theodosius.[122] *Superstitio* as used in the law of 341 therefore applied to 'pratiques superstitieuses au sens vulgaire': the constitution was a restatement of Constantine's measures against magic.[123] Martroye assumed that the Theodosian Code was a consistent document, using legal terms of fixed definition. He made no allowance for the fluid interpretation of terms in the fourth century which had been widely accepted in earlier periods. He was therefore unable to deal with clear

---

[119] *CT* 16, 10, 2: 'Cesset superstitio, sacrificiorum aboleatur insania. Nam quicumque contra legem divi principis parentis nostri et hanc nostrae mansuetudinis iussionem ausus fuerit sacrificia celebrare, conpetens in eum vindicta et praesens sententia exeratur.'

[120] Nöthlichs, *Massnahmen*, 54 and n. 325.

[121] Ibid. 57.

[122] F. Martroye, 'La repression de la magie et le culte des gentils au IVe siècle', *Revue historique de droit français et étranger*, 9 (1930), 669–701, at 672–3.

[123] Ibid. 672. See also Maurice, art. cit. (n. 58), 112 ff. Chastagnol, *La Préfecture*, 147 offered the controversial interpretation that the texts of *CT* 16, 10, 2, and 3 may have been doctored at a later date.

evidence of substantial innovation in the religious policy of the
Christian emperors.

M. R. Salzman has demonstrated that different parties employed the
term *superstitio* in significantly different ways during the fourth century.[124] Christian polemicists even before Constantine had used the
term to denote the beliefs of non-Christians generally.[125] By the end of
the fourth century this Christian definition had become widespread but
in the middle years of the century the whole gamut of the word's
meaning was employed as circumstances suited.

Lucius Caecilius Firmianus Lactantius, as a writer and thinker close
to the courts of Constantine the Great and his sons, can be taken to
illustrate the fluidity of the terms circulating in court circles at this
time.[126] Educated Christians were abandoning the ancient understanding of *superstitio* and *religio*.[127] Lactantius, writing in his *Institutiones
Divinae*, reviewed the Ciceronian distinction between *religio* (correct
worship) and *superstitio* (excessive religiosity).[128] Lactantius himself
was acutely conscious of a long Christian tradition which freely used
the term *superstitio* for the official cults of Rome. For him, the object of
worship was the key to the issue. *Religio* became the worship of what
was true, while *superstitio* was the worship of what was false. Other
western Christian writers of the fourth century, from Ambrosiaster in
Rome to Ambrose in Milan, concurred.[129] Naturally enough, the
changing meaning of terms such as these not universally accepted
and Ammianus described Christian heresies, ambiguously, as *superstitiones*.[130] Nevertheless, the significance of the ideas of Lactantius is
that they demonstrate how unwise it is to assume, with Martroye, a
well-defined meaning for *superstitio*. As Tomlin has put it:

The word's [*superstitio*] elusiveness—it was more pejorative than precise—was
an advantage in legislation whose propagandistic element was as strong as the
purely coercive.[131]

---

[124] Salzman, art. cit. (n. 64), 172–88. I differ from Salzman in reading the fluidity as a
manifestation of the way in which late Roman law was made, as opposed to viewing it as
a *deliberate* ambivalence.

[125] See e.g. Tertullianus *Adversus Marcionem* 1, 9, 2; *Scorpiace* 10, 6.

[126] See the excellent discussion of C. N. Cochrane, op. cit. (n. 112), 191 ff.

[127] This point has been made most succinctly by R. S. O. Tomlin, *Valentinian the
First*, D. Phil. thesis, Oxford (1973), 447–8. What follows is chiefly drawn from Tomlin.

[128] Lactantius, *Divinae Institutiones* 4, 28; See Cicero *De Natura Deorum* 2, 28, 72.
See R. R. Ross, 'Superstitio', *Classical Journal*, 64 (1969), 354.

[129] Ambrosiaster *Quaestiones veteris et novi Testamenti*, CSEL 50, no. 114, '*Adversus
Paganos*' 1. See also Ambrose *Ep.* 17, 6 where 'superstitio' is contrasted with 'vera fides'.

[130] 15, 13, 2. Ambiguous because it is unclear whether heretics' excessive and
misguided religiosity is the fault or the beliefs of the orthodox Christians.

[131] Tomlin, op. cit. (n. 127), 448.

Given what we know of the characters of Constans and Constantius II and the opinions of influential Christian writers close to the imperial court, it is clear that *superstitio* as used in the letter to Madalianus referred to the ancient cults of the Roman state. The first line of the letter of 341 was clearly general: *sacrificia* were vital to the survival of *superstitio* and since the latter must stop, the former were to be abolished. In Libanius' memory, all sacrifices had been banned.[132] But what of the reference to a 'law' of the emperor Constantine?

It has been suggested that the phrase in the measure of 341 referred to a Constantinian constitution ordering a general ban on sacrifice late in his reign. A misunderstanding or distortion of the earlier emperor's legislation on *haruspices* has also been proposed.[133] It is difficult to believe that Constantius II was so poorly informed on his father's legislation that he could construe measures against *haruspicina* to be a general attack on the old cults. In fact, Constantius was well aware of the legislation of his father and especially of the special relationship which Constantine had claimed to enjoy with the will of the Christian God.[134] In his letter to the Vicar of the City, Helpidius, in 323, Constantine had demanded that those devoted to the 'sanctissima lex' (of Christianity) be left unmolested at the lustral sacrifices.[135] Applied to the law of 341, the idea that *sacrificia* were a violation of the 'most sacred law' of the emperor Constantine thus means only that Constantine considered them to be incompatible with the will of God, an idea which Constantine held but did not enforce with a general ban. This Constantius II now did in a measure which attacked the whole structure of traditional Roman religion.

The significance of the decree of 341 cannot have been lost on the population at Rome. It is almost impossible, however, to detect any clues to the measure's effectiveness in the city. Officially, servants of the emperor were asked to enforce the edict vigorously but it is not possible to know how many did so. The assumption that the ban was not enforced is often advanced as evidence that Rome's conservative aristocracy retained enough influence to defy an emperor whose Christian fanaticism was manifest. But given the highly sensitive attitude of Constantius to disloyalty and intrigue, such an action would have been extremely dangerous. It seems likely, therefore, that an attempt *was* made to enforce the ban on sacrifice at Rome. It soon became clear however, that there

---

[132] *Oratio* 18, 23.   [133] See above, 172–4.

[134] For Constantine's exhortation to his sons to preserve the faith see Eusebius *VC* 4, 52, 1–2; also Vict. *De Caes.* 42, 23: 'cultu genitoris, satis pius suique nimis custos.' Constantius II organized Constantine's funeral on account of his being his father's favourite son. See Eusebius *VC* 4, 67–9; Julian *Oratio* 1, 16.

[135] *CT* 16, 2, 5. For other instances of '(Sanctissima) lex' as Christianity: Ambrose, *De Officiis* 2, 151; *Carmen ad senatorem ex Christiana religione ad idolorum servitutem conversum* 43–4; Symmachus *Relatio* 21, 1; *Collectio Avellana* 6, 2.

were significant difficulties with the enforcement of the law and refinements and clarifications became necessary.

On 1 November the following year (342), Catullinus, Prefect of the City, received a letter referring to some of the temples of Rome:

> Although all superstition must be completely eradicated, nevertheless, it is Our will that the buildings of the temples situated outside the walls shall remain untouched and uninjured. For since certain plays or spectacles of the circus or contests derive their origins from some of these temples, such structures shall not be torn down, since from them is provided the regular performance of long established amusements for the Roman people.[136]

It might reasonably be suggested that temples outside the city had been specified because the emperors had the maintenance of some particular ceremonies in mind. Unfortunately, the nature of the festivals with which these temples were associated has not been preserved.[137] The text of the measure as we have it is, after all, only a fragment of a longer letter. Gaudemet suspected that only those temples outside the walls were mentioned because, as a result of the legislation of the previous year, secret meetings were being convened here in defiance of that law and attracting fanatical Christian countermeasures.[138] But the religious convictions of the malefactors is not stated and they need not have been exclusively Christian. Other laws indicate that a veritable traffic in building materials was being carried on in the zone beyond the walls and it could be that the legislation of 341 was being interpreted generally to mean that the temples were redundant. Pilfering of the kind that resulted was, of course, illegal, but understandably the protection of the sites outside the walls was more difficult than those *intra*. This law constituted a warning to those engaged in the destruction of some of the shrines and confirmed their continued importance.[139]

---

[136] *CT* 16, 10, 3: 'Quamquam omnis superstitio penitus eruenda sit, tamen volumus, ut aedes templorum, quae extra muros sunt positae, intactae incorruptaeque consistant. Nam cum ex nonnullis vel ludorum vel circensium vel agonum origo fuerit exorta, non convenit ea convelli, ex quibus populo Romano praebeatur priscarum sollemnitas voluptatum.'

[137] See Wissowa, *RK*, 465 for the Capitoline Agon. Archaeology seems to show the abandonment of the *balneum* of the *Arvales* near the shrine of Dea Dia at around this period: H. Broise and J. Scheid, *Recherches archéologiques à la Magliana: le balneum des frères arvales*, Roma antica, 1 (Rome: École française de Rome/Soprintendenza archeologica di Roma, 1987), 275–7.

[138] J. Gaudemet, *L'Église dans l'empire romain* (Paris: Sirey, 1958), 648 n. 1. T. D. Barnes assumes the same in 'Christians and Pagans in the Reign of Constantius', *L'Église et l'empire au IVᵉ Siècle*, Entretiens sur l'Antiquité classique, 34 (Geneva: Fondation Hardt, 1987), 331.

[139] There is no reason to think, with Nöthlichs, *Massnahmen*, 55 that the toleration of festivals was also the toleration of sacrifices.

Some have suspected the apparently general scope of Constantius' legislation by pointing out that he retained the title of Pontifex Maximus and cannot have outlawed the practices of which he was officially the head. In fact, it is claimed, Constantius was regulating only divination and irregular practices in accordance with his position as the chief pontiff.[140] But Constantius' measures need not have convinced him that his tenure of the traditional title of Pontifex Maximus was inconsistent. The administrative structures associated with the ancient cults survived the ban of 341. In March 349, for example, the City Prefect Ulpius Limenius was contacted by the emperor.[141] The law addressed the subject of the destruction of tombs in the city after AD 333 (16 years before the issuance of the letter). Stiff fines were laid down for those stealing or selling such material:

for if it is contrary to divine law for anything to be touched, it cannot be purchased without pollution.[142]

This statement, made in the names of both emperors, seems to show a distinct awareness of ancient pontifical law.[143] A further letter of 356 to the Prefect Memmius Vitrasius Orfitus called for the punishment of tomb destroyers 'prescribed by the ancient statutes' ('priscis legibus') and may also be a reference to the procedures of pontifical law.[144] In the law of 349, the important role of the *pontifices* in securing tombs was acknowledged by the statement:

But if by petitions duly presented, they should impetrate from the pontiffs permission to take down falling monuments for the purpose of repairing them . . . they shall be exempted from the payment of the fine.[145]

The same law stated that the City Prefect, with the *pontifices*, was to inspect to see which monuments were likely to require repair.[146]

---

[140] Martroye, art. cit. (n. 122), 673.

[141] *CT* 9, 17, 2. Limenius was PPO and PUR simultaneously. See *PLRE* I, 510 and Chastagnol, *Fastes*, 128–30.

[142] *CT* 9, 17, 2: 'quidquid enim attingi nefas est, non sine piaculo comparatur.'

[143] See Firmicus Maternus *De Errore* 16, 2 for the continuation of the *lex pontificalis*. Other examples of pontifical responsibility (from the Principate) collected by K. Latte, *Römische Religionsgeschichte* (Munich: Beck, 1960), 102 n. 3.

[144] *CT* 9, 17, 3 (13 June 356). For Memmius Vitrasius Orfitus see *PLRE* I, 65. Cf. *CT* 9, 17, 4 (13 June 356: Seeck, *Regesten*, 202) also *ad populum*: 'quae poena priscae severitati accedit.'

[145] *CT* 9, 17, 2: 'Qui vero libellis datis a pontificibus impetrarunt, ut reparationis gratia labentia sepulchra deponerent, si vera docuerunt, ab inlatione multae separentur; at si in usum alium depositis abusi sunt, teneantur poena praescribta.'

[146] *CT* 9, 17, 2, 1.

The possession of the function and title of Pontifex Maximus was therefore not an anomaly for the Christian emperors. It is important to realize that in the instructions issued to fellow *pontifices* the emperors were performing important administrative functions and co-operating with representatives of the senatorial class.

The appearance of Magnentius, in January 350, led to the death of Constans in the same year.[147] Magnentius' death, late in 353, was followed by a letter of Constantius to Naeratius Cerealis, then Prefect of Rome.[148] Rome had briefly passed under the sway of the usurper and he had permitted 'sacrificia nocturna'. It is unclear exactly why Magnentius had allowed night-time sacrifices to take place. Perhaps he was urged to exempt them from the ban of 341 to please certain parties at his court or influential groups in Rome. It is also conceivable that he himself was induced to accept the efficacy of such sacrifices for his own regime.[149] A more cynical possibility might be that Magnentius had provided a convenient scapegoat for Constantius and was held responsible for 'permitting' sacrifices which, in fact, had never ceased at Rome. In any event, Constantius unambiguously banned them again.[150] There seems to be little doubt that the sacrifices in question were connected in some way to divination.[151]

Constantius' most significant act determining the legal status of the ancient cults up until 356 had been the general ban of 341. In February 356 another general edict, issued at Milan, reinforced that ban with the notable innovation of a clear statement that the penalty for infringing the law was to be severe:

If any persons should be proved to devote their attention to sacrifices or to worship images, We command that they shall be subjected to capital punishment.[152]

Simulacra and the offensiveness of their worship also made a first appearance in the Christian legislation. The views of Martroye

[147] Helm, 237. Zosimus *HN* 2, 42, 5. *Epitome de Caes.* 41, 23. *PLRE* I, 220 'Flavius Constans' has other primary sources. For Magnentius, see Barnes, op. cit. (n. 110), 101–8; W. Ensslin, 'Magnentius', *PW*, 14 (1928), 445–52 esp. 448 on Magnentius' religious disposition. Finally Nöthlichs, *Massnahmen*, 57 ff.

[148] *CT* 16, 10, 5. For Cerealis see *PLRE* I, 197–9.

[149] Nöthlichs, *Massnahmen*, 62. Previous views on nocturnal sacrifices: Cicero *De Legibus* 2, 9, 21.

[150] For evidence that Constantius built this war up into a clash of religions, see story of angels announcing Constantius' victory at Sulpicius Severus *Chronicon* 2, 38, 5–6. Coins with legend 'Hoc signo victor eris' in *RIC* 8, 368–9, 386, 416.

[151] For nocturnal sacrifice and divination see Firmicus Maternus *Mathesis* 2, 30, 10: 'Numquam nocturnis sacrificiis intersis, sive illa publica, sive privata dicantur.' Cf. *CT* 9, 16, 2 where divination is allowed 'libera luce'. See pp. 172–3 above.

[152] *CT* 16, 10, 6: 'Poena capitis subiugari praecipimus eos, quos operam sacrificiis dare vel colere simulacra constiterit.' The law was issued jointly with Julian.

notwithstanding, it seems clear that devotion to sacrifices and images delineated Roman religion generally, not magical practices alone.[153]

Later the same year, the Praetorian Prefect of Italy received *CT* 16, 10, 4.[154] The letter responded to further difficulties encountered in the enforcement of the previous laws. The means of preventing the forbidden *sacrificia* was to be the closure of the temples 'in all places and in all cities' and Flavius Taurus was to see to the matter in his region.[155] Most probably, the Prefect of the City received similar instructions since the emperors made it clear that they demanded general application of the measure.[156]

As with the ban on sacrifice ordered in 341, it is almost impossible to determine this measure's effectiveness. Chastagnol was unjustifiably 'certain' that it was not carried out.[157] Our only information comes from the eastern Empire and, though suggestive, cannot be interpreted as authoritative when used of the Roman situation.[158]

Libanius, in his lament for Julian, spoke glowingly of the promise which the young man had shown shortly before his elevation to the rank of Caesar (in 355). The orator dismissed the suggestion that Julian had sought office from any desire for power or luxury. Rather, he wished to see the ancient worship restored after its recent trials:

he saw their temples in ruins, their ritual banned, their altars overturned, their sacrifices suppressed, and their property divided up between a crew of rascals.[159]

This grim account of the attack on the old religion under Constantius accurately encapsulated the aims of the imperial edicts of the time but

---

[153] Martroye, art. cit. (n. 122), 675–6; Maurice, art. cit. (n. 58), 112–13. Nöthlichs, *Massnahmen*, 64 with n. 399 argued that *CT* 16, 10, 4 was earlier than *CT* 16, 10, 6 and that the latter was not an extension of the policy announced in the former. A. Barb, 'The Survival of the Magic Arts', in Momigliano, *Conflict*, 100 ff. thought Ammianus 19, 10, 4 showed that Constantius had made a distinction between magic and the ancient religion. See my comments below p. 194.

[154] The dating is disputed. I follow Seeck, *Regesten*, 203 who suggests 1 December 356. Nöthlichs, *Massnahmen*, 273 with n. 389 doubts. See *PLRE* I, 880.

[155] Not, therefore, a measure against sacrifice only, as argued by Nöthlichs, *Massnahmen*, 63.

[156] 'volumus etiam cunctos sacrificiis abstinere.'

[157] Chastagnol, *La Préfecture*, 148. Barnes, art. cit. (n. 138), 330 points out that neoplatonists will have argued that sacrifice was not necessary and hindered higher forms of devotion. Cf. Turcan, op. cit. (n. 111), 214.

[158] See G. Fowden, 'Bishops and Temples in the Eastern Roman Empire AD 320–435', *JTS*, 29 (1978), 53–78.

[159] *Oration* 18, 23: ᾧ δὴ καὶ διαφερόντως τὴν καρδίαν ἐπλήττετο νεώς τε ὁρῶν κειμένους καὶ τελετὰς πεπαυμένας καὶ βωμοὺς ἀνατετραμμένους καὶ θυσίας ἀνῃρημένας καὶ ἱερεῖς ἐλαυνομένους καὶ τὸν τῶν ἱερῶν πλοῦτον εἰς τοὺς ἀσελγεστάτους μεμερισμένον. . .

elsewhere in his speeches Libanius gives details that suggest inconsistent enforcement. In his autobiography, Libanius told a story of a fellow student at Athens in the middle of the fourth century. Libanius' family estates were reported to be up for auction and he felt that he ought to return home. His career might have taken a very different path had it not been for the intervention of a fellow student, Crispinus, who asked the young Libanius to accompany him home to Heraclea. Crispinus had been summoned home by his uncle. The latter was, according to Libanius, an impressive and pious man:

for he consorted more with gods than with men on earth; despite the law which banned it and the death penalty inflicted on any who dared to do so, he yet went through his life in the company of gods, and he laughed to scorn that evil law and its sacrilegious enactor.[160]

But the unprecedentedly wide-ranging bans of Constantius did not have the effect of crudely conflating *sacrificia* (associated with the ancient cults) with magic and divination, the consistent objects of imperial legislation in the fourth century. Four days after Taurus received his instructions, an imperial letter was issued *ad populum*.[161] The law, written at Milan, focused on areas not covered by the general bans. Many, it was claimed, still dared to practise 'artes magicae'. In doing so they were endangering 'the lives of innocents', through the summoning of *manes*. Such people were 'foreign to nature' ('naturae peregrini sunt') and a 'deadly plague' would annihilate them.

A second law *ad populum* in January 357 attacked divination.[162] No one was to consult a *haruspex*, *mathematicus*, or *hariolus*. The 'prava confessio' of *vates* and *augures* was to cease. *Chaldeii* and *magi*, whom the people called *maleficii* were not to attempt 'ad hanc partem aliquid', that is, any divinatory activity. The edict closed with a general statement of the imperial will:

the inquisitiveness of all men for divination shall cease for ever.[163]

---

[160] *Oration* 1, 27: οὗτος οἴκαδε καλούμενος ὑπὸ τοῦ θείου, θείου τινὸς ὡς ἀληθῶς ἀνθρώπου καὶ πλείω γε θεοῖς ἢ ἀνθρώποις ὁμιλήσαντος ἐν γῇ, καίτοι νόμος γε εἶργε καὶ ἦν ἡ δίκη τῷ τολμῶντι θάνατος, ἀλλ' ὅμως σὺν αὐτοῖς ἐκείνοις πορευόμενος τὸν βίον νόμου τε πονηροῦ καὶ νομοθέτου δυσσεβοῦς κατεγέλα... (Trans A. F. Norman.) Barnes, art. cit. (n. 138), 330 f. thinks that the law mentioned by Libanius was Constantinian. See also Bradbury, art. cit. (n. 56), 129 f. whose argument is unconvincing. *Contra*, A. F. Norman's commentary and Petit's observations in the Budé edition, p. 215.

[161] *CT* 9, 16, 5. The date from Seeck, *Regesten*, 203.

[162] *CT* 9, 16, 4. E. Massoneau, *La magie dans l'antiquité romain* (Paris: Sirey, 1934), 20 argued that it abolished the distinction between divination and magic. Nöthlichs, *Massnahmen*, 66–7 gives information on earlier legislation against *mathematici*.

[163] *CT* 9, 16, 4: 'sileat omnibus perpetuo divinandi curiositas.'

The impressive roll-call of practitioners of illicit practices is a measure of Constantius' determination to destroy divination. The distinction between public haruspicy and *maleficium* observed by Constantine had been abolished.

By early 357, with Magnentius, Silvanus, and their supporters firmly suppressed, Constantius was ready to stage a highly ceremonial entry into the ancient capital of the west. Above all, the *adventus* was to publicize the return of the west to his control and Constantius took the opportunity to emphasize the continuity of the Constantinian dynasty.[164] Accordingly, the military connotations of the ceremonies were made explicit and Ammianus disapproved, claiming that the victory over fellow-citizens was nothing to celebrate.[165] The visit also offered the senate and people the opportunity to demonstrate their loyalty to Constantius; they had, only a few years previously, been under the control of the usurper Magnentius.

As the author of general bans on sacrifice, the emperor deemed it inappropriate to speak in the senate house where sacrifices at the altar of Victory had been a focus of religious activity for three and a half centuries.[166] Ambrose explained why the altar was removed:

Constantius of august memory, when not yet baptized into the sacred mystery, thought that he was polluted were he to set eyes on that altar. He ordered its removal, he did not order its restoration.[167]

Whether the sacrifices had stopped in compliance with Constantius' earlier legislation or continued undisturbed is unknown. The decision to remove the altar was apparently taken before Constantius entered the city and was clearly connected with the visit. Symmachus claimed that the removal had been unpopular.[168] Constantius' orders were based upon a perception of his relationship with the citizens of a city which he had never seen. But Constantius was greatly surprised by what he found at Rome.

[164] The twentieth anniversary of the death of Constantine the Great occurred during the visit (22 May) i.e. the twentieth anniversary of Constantius' accession to power. The consular *fasti* of Constantinople record that Constantius 'celebrated his *vicennalia* there [Rome]'. See Matthews, *Ammianus*, 233; MacCormack, op. cit. (n. 44), 41–3.

[165] Ammianus 16, 10, 1.

[166] I disagree with Barnes, who argues, from Ambrose (*Ep.* 17, 10), that Constantius removed the Altar of Victory in order to prevent Christian senators being forced to sacrifice: art. cit. (n. 138), 332. In fact, Ambrose refers to the opinion of Christian senators mediated through Damasus that they did not wish to see the altar restored.

[167] Ambrose *Ep.* 18, 32 (*CSEL* 82, 51): 'Constantius augustae memoriae nondum sacris initiatus mysteriis contaminari se putavit, si aram illam videret. iussit auferri, non iussit reponi.' (Trans. Croke and Harries.)

[168] *Relatio* 3, 6 but no open grumbling according to D. Vera, *Commento storico alle Relationes di Quinto Aurelio Simmaco* (Pisa: Giardini, 1981), 13.

He arrived in the city on 28 April 357 and stayed until 29 May.[169] He was warmly received in the western capital. The populace crowded out to meet him and Constantius experienced the cosmopolitanism of the city for the first time.[170] He spoke before the senate and filled the vacancies in all the priestly boards.[171] The great shrines of Rome and the grandeur of the city amazed him; he gladly attended the circus and established a rapport with the racegoers.[172] After deliberating what would be an appropriate gift for the city, he set up an obelisk in the Circus Maximus.[173] The experience of the visit impressed him greatly and he realized that the city was something of a special case. From the end of the visit until Gratian's measures, a generation later, Rome appears to have enjoyed a special status with regard to general sacrifices unconnected to divination. Vera remarks that the period witnessed 'una reviviscenza della religiosità tradizionale a Roma negli anni successivi alla visita imperiale'.[174] Though Constantius did not explicitly order it, he did not prevent the return of the Altar of Victory shortly after his departure.[175] Libanius, thirty years later, was aware of the anomaly that ensued:

> those who appear to have been the chief opponents in this particular have honoured the gods even against their will. And who might these be? Why those who have not dared to rob Rome of its sacrifices.[176]

Ambrose, in his letter of 384, claimed that pagans in Rome sacrificed at altars in temples all over the city; proof that at that time both the general bans of Constantius were widely ignored.[177] Constantius is not

---

[169] Dates from Seeck, *Regesten*, 204. For the visit: Matthews, *Ammianus*, 231–5; MacCormack, op. cit. (n. 44), 40–3; Vera, op. cit. (n. 168), 35–6; R. Klein, 'Der Rombesuch des Kaisers Konstantius II im Jahre 357', *Athenaeum*, 57 (1979), 98–115; R. O. Edbrooke, 'The Visit of Constantius II to Rome in 357 and its Effects on the Pagan Senatorial Aristocracy', *AJPh*, 97 (1976), 40–61; Y. M. Duval, 'La venue à Rome de l'empereur Constance II en 357 d'après Ammien Marcellin', *Caesarodunum*, 2 (1970), 299–304. See also N. H. Baynes, *JRS*, 25 (1935), 87.

[170] Ammianus 16, 10, 5–6.

[171] Speech to the senate: ibid. 13. The priestly boards: Symmachus *Relatio* 3, 7.

[172] Ammianus 16, 10, 13. For Constantius' good relations with the *vulgus* see Julian *Oratio* 2, 77; Vict. *De Caes.* 42, 23; *Epitome* 42, 18; see Piétri, art. cit. (n. 114), 117.

[173] Ammianus 16, 10, 13–17.

[174] Vera, op. cit. (n. 168), 36. Chastagnol, *La Préfecture*, 148 wrote of a 'renaissance païenne'. J. Moreau, art. cit. (n. 109), 169 and Piganiol, *L'Empire*, 108–10 both posit a change of policy.

[175] Ambrose *Ep.* 18, 32: 'non iussit reponi.' Symmachus *Relatio* 3, 4: 'Merito divi Constantii factum diu non stetit. omnia vobis exempla vitanda sunt quae mox remota didicistis.'

[176] *Oratio* 30, 33: οἱ μάλιστα τοῦτο τὸ μέρος ἀτιμάσαι δοκοῦντες καὶ ἄκοντες τετιμήκασι. τίνες οὗτοι; οἱ τὴν Ῥώμην τοῦ θύειν οὐ τολμήσαντες ἀφελέσθαι. (Trans. A. F. Norman.)

[177] Ambrose *Ep.* 18, 31. See below, pp. 206–8.

known to have issued any statement on the illegality of general sacrifice again.[178]

But the antipathy towards divination did not subside. On his journey away from Rome, the emperor issued the most comprehensive law yet made on the subject.[179] Taurus, the Praetorian Prefect of Italy and Africa, received a copy. *Magi*, regardless of their social rank, were to be considered 'humani generis inimici'. Those in the imperial retinue violated the imperial person.[180] A list of those 'magicis contaminibus adsuetus' followed. It comprised *maleficii, haruspices, harioli* ('aut certe') *augures, mathematii*, 'or one who conceals some art of divination by interpreting dreams' ('aut narrandis somnis occultans artem aliquam divinandi'). Those detected in the imperial retinue would not escape as a result of their high rank. The recent *rapprochement* between senate and emperor was not to lead to a relaxation of the imperial stance on divination.

The legislation during the first decade of the administration of the sons of Constantine contrasted sharply with the pragmatism of their father. A clumsy ban was placed on paganism and the sacrifices which were seen to be its very lifeblood. Temple buildings were not closed, however, and were not to be destroyed. In Rome, the administrative tasks of the priestly boards remained. Briefly, in the early 350s nocturnal sacrifices made a return to the city of Rome but were banned again as soon as Constantius gained control. With the empire in the hands of Constantius and Gallus alone, more extensive legislation resulted. Death was decreed for those who devoted themselves to images and the closure of temples throughout the empire was ordered. Magic and divination were the objects of stringent measures which moved beyond the careful distinction drawn up by Constantine. In 357, the arrival of the emperor Constantius at Rome was preceded by the removal of the ancient Augustan Altar of Victory. But the impression made by the tradition of the city on Constantius was so favourable that he took no action when the altar was returned; a direct contradiction of his previous instructions. Rome proceeded to enjoy de facto special status with regard to the ancient cults of the city.

---

[178] Edbrooke, art. cit. (n. 169), 59–60 has argued that the apparent absence of hostile laws from the time of Constantius' visit until his death can be explained by recalling how sweeping his earlier laws were; there was no need to repeat them. This objection is invalid since Constantius' views on divination, strongly set out before 357, were reiterated in the years after. See Piétri, art. cit. (n. 114), 151 who also doubts a change of policy.

[179] *CT* 9, 16, 6 (7 July 357). For the date see Seeck, *Regesten*, 204.

[180] See Maurice, art. cit. (n. 58), 113.

4. JULIAN AND JOVIAN

By the time Julian became sole Augustus, the legal status of the old state religion had become confused, especially at Rome. Constantius' specific arrangements for his visit to the city had been overturned; the general bans were not, apparently, rescinded, but no action was taken at Rome to enforce them. Thus, when adverse weather conditions threatened the corn supply to the city, the Prefect of Rome, Tertullus, sacrificed at the temple of Castor and Pollux at Ostia in an attempt to end the danger and Memmius Vitrasius Orfitus, as Prefect of the City a second time, was able to dedicate a shrine to Apollo a few metres from the Theatre of Marcellus.[181]

Julian manifested his attachment to the old cults only after the breakdown of relations with Constantius. Until that time he had been, superficially, a Christian *lector*.[182] The church historian Socrates recorded that the recall of exiled bishops and the restoration of their estates to them preceded his orders that temples should be officially reopened throughout the empire.[183] This latter order was certainly issued soon after the death of Constantius and both Ammianus and Libanius make it clear that sacrifices, formally banned by Constantius, also recommenced.[184] Christians, however, were given assurances that they would be treated justly.[185] Temples which had been damaged or demolished were to be rebuilt by those who had caused the destruction.[186]

Julian thus reversed the direction of Constantius' early legislation against temples and sacrifices. There can be little doubt that Julian's measures produced noticeable change in certain areas of the empire. At Alexandria, for example, the Patriarch George was lynched by a pagan

---

[181] Tertullus: Ammianus 19, 10, 4. For Tertullus see Chastagnol, *Fastes*, 151–3. Orfitus: *CIL* 6, 45 = *ILS* 3222. See G. Lugli, 'Recent Archaeological Discoveries in Rome and Italy', *JRS*, 36 (1946), 7. Orfitus held his second urban prefecture in 357–9: *PLRE* I, 651–3.

[182] Ammianus 22, 5; Julian *Ep.* 8 (Loeb edn.), 415 C-D; Socrates *HE* 3, 1, 39; Sozomen *HE* 5, 2, 2; Zosimus *HN* 3, 11, 1.

[183] Socrates *HE* 3, 1; Sozomen *HE* 5, 1–7, temples at 5, 3; Ammianus 22, 5, 2. Sozomen *HE* 5, 5, 9 alleged that the recalling of bishops was a deliberately disruptive tactic. *Contra* see S. M. C. Lieu, *The Emperor Julian: Panegyric and Polemic* (Liverpool: Liverpool University Press, 1986), 45 with references. See especially Julian *Ep.* 24 (Loeb edn.) where Athanasius was returned to Egypt but not to his former see in Alexandria because Julian feared serious disorder.

[184] Ammianus 22, 5, 2; Libanius *Oratio* 18, 126; *Oratio* 30, 7.

[185] Julian *Ep.* 37 (Loeb edn.), 376 C-D.

[186] Sozomen *HE* 5, 5, 1–5; Julian *Ep.* 37 (Loeb edn.); Libanius *Oratio* 18, 126; Ammianus 22, 4, 3.

mob for refusing to hand over a *mithraeum* on which a church was being built.[187]

Social life in Rome, however, remained very much disturbed by the persistent presence of magic and undesirable practices. According to Ammianus, the subject came to obsess the Prefect of the City, Lucius Turcius Apronianus who entered office in December 362.[188] Ammianus explains that Apronianus had lost an eye just after his appointment as governor of Syria by Julian and he was convinced that he had been hexed.[189] He made it his prime concern to arrest the practitioners of magic who were at that time proliferating in Rome.[190] Cases were examined individually and those revealed to have harmed others were punished with death after disclosing the names of their accomplices. He carried out investigations at the games and condemned Hilarinus the charioteer for sending his son to learn the black arts. Not even the sacred confines of a Christian shrine saved him from execution.[191]

Apronianus' actions show that the war on harmful magic did not cease under Julian. Though Ammianus' portrayal shows Apronianus to have been particularly enthusiastic in his crusade against harmful magical practices, he did not exceed the judicial parameters of his office in so doing.[192] Nevertheless, through the vividness of Ammianus' account, it is possible to understand how much an office-holder's personal enthusiasm for the job could affect the implementation of law.

Like Constantine, Julian believed in the efficacy of divination carried out by the *haruspices* of the state.[193] When he marched against Persia in summer 363, Julian had in his camp interpreters of omens and 'Etruscan haruspices'.[194] Although Ammianus was to conclude that Julian was excessively religious rather than decently devout, he did believe, like many others, that divination, if properly carried out, could be valid.[195]

---

[187] Ammianus 22, 11, 5–8; Socrates *HE* 3, 2, 1–10.

[188] Ammianus 26, 3. For Apronianus see *PLRE* I, 88.

[189] Ammianus 26, 3, 2.

[190] The Latin is either 'rariscebant' or 'crebrescebant'. Compare the Loeb translation (p.580) with that of the Penguin (p. 316).

[191] Ammianus 26, 3, 3. Those with higher social status or wealth might fare better. See Ammianus 26, 3, 4; cf. 28, 1, 29 (AD 368) and 28, 4, 25. 29, 3, 5 records the condemnation of a (Christian?) charioteer, Athanasius, for sorcery in 372. See now *CT* 9, 16, 11 for an example of legislation against charioteers.

[192] Chastagnol, *La Préfecture*, 149.   [193] See above, pp. 172–4.

[194] See J. H. W. G. Liebeschuetz, 'Ammianus, Julian and Divination', in M. Weissmann (ed.), *Roma Renascens. Beiträge zur Spätantike und Rezeptionsgeschichte* (Frankfurt: Lang, 1988), 193–213. For the Etruscans: Ammianus 23, 5, 10. For Etruscan *haruspices* at Rome early in the fifth century, see Zosimus *NH* 5, 41, 3 and p. 306 below.

[195] Judgement on Julian: 25, 4, 17. For allegations of Julian's night-time sacrifices and necromancy, see Theodoret *HE* 3, 21. On the validity of divination: Ammianus 23, 5, 11.

Enough is known of Julian's thought for us to be able to say that his empire would not have marked a wholesale return to the traditional religion that had preceded Constantine.[196] But the necessary prelude to his projected reconstruction was the renunciation of the hostile legislation of his predecessors. Temples were reopened and sacrifices were legalized. The building of new temples was encouraged. At Rome, the capacity of the urban administration to deal with suspected cases of magic was amply demonstrated by Apronianus.

It would be wrong, however, to see an absolute break between Julian and the Christian emperors who followed him. The excesses of Constantius had led to the promotion of legislation which was unpopular at best and impossible to enforce at worst. Julian saved later Christian emperors the trouble of having to reshape the Constantian system. He was not alone in abandoning that system; so did his successors until Theodosius.

The details of Jovian's eight-month reign are obscure. One of many controversies concerns his policy towards non-Christian cults. Elected as emperor the day after Julian's death (27 June 363), Jovian's first achievement was to extricate Julian's expeditionary force from Persian territory. He must certainly have been as aware as Ammianus of the activities of soothsayers in the force, anxiously searching for signs of a happy outcome of events.[197] It is likely that legislation on religious matters did not therefore appear at once. Both our major sources for Jovian, the ecclesiastical historians Socrates and Sozomen, assign sweeping measures to him. Socrates claimed that the temples were closed and blood sacrifices abolished while Sozomen recorded the complete restoration of privileges to the Christian communities and a circular sent to all provinces urging all citizens to become Christians.[198] But the contemporary testimony of Themistius, who delivered a panegyric to Jovian at Ancyra on 1 January 364, contradicts the Christian versions.[199] Themistius opened by celebrating the return of philosophy to the imperial court after the excesses of Julian. He praised Jovian for refusing to employ coercion of individual souls in divine matters. The second half of the oration was a strong endorsement of

---

[196] See O. Nicholson, 'The "Pagan Churches" of Maximinus Daia and Julian the Apostate', *JEH*, 45 (1994), 1–10. See also P. Athanassiadi-Fowden, *Julian and Hellenism* (Oxford: Clarendon Press, 1981), 161–91; G. W. Bowersock, *Julian the Apostate* (London: Duckworth, 1978), 79–93; R. Browning, *The Emperor Julian* (London: Weidenfeld & Nicolson, 1975), 159–86.

[197] Ammianus 25, 6, 1. See F. Heim, 'Les Auspices publics de Constantin à Theodose', *Ktema*, 13 (1988), 41–53, at 47.

[198] Socrates *HE* 3, 24; Sozomen *HE* 6, 3.   [199] Themistius *Oratio* 5.

Jovian's overwhelmingly tolerant policy towards the non-Christians. Jovian is reported to have legislated that all men should have their own rituals and understood that there was more than one route to the divinity, an argument fruitlessly deployed by Symmachus twenty years later. Temples remained open but 'unholy practices' were condemned. 'Lawful sacrifices' were allowed but there was no freedom to practise 'magic arts'.[200]

Reconciling the Christian and the non-Christian sources has proved problematic. Piganiol drew attention to Jovian's rebuke to the Macedonian heretics:

I abominate contentiousness; but I love and honour those who exert themselves to promote unanimity.[201]

and saw in Jovian the revival of Constantinian toleration.[202] He also pointed out that although the sources suggested a strong reaction to Julian in the form of a policy of general temple closure, no source claimed that this was enforced by a law. He concluded that the 'policy', like the temple-closing activities of Constantine, was a misinterpretation of some local actions.[203] As Fowden has shown, certain areas of the East witnessed a violent episcopally inspired orgy of destruction but Piganiol is certainly right to resist the idea that any general law ordered such action. We can accept, however, that blood sacrifices were banned, as Themistius and Libanius stated, almost certainly because of the danger of illicit divination.[204]

As for the temples, Caesarius, the Comes Rei Privatae, was informed that all parcels of land and estates in the possession of temples and which had been donated by various emperors ('diversi principes'), were to be reclaimed by the imperial fisc.[205] The measure was aimed chiefly, though not exclusively, at the rehabilitation of the temples attempted by Julian. We hear of some temples being closed, but there is no reason for believing that this was the result of a general order to do so.

Themistius had expected much worse. Julian had been dynamic in his attempt to reverse the progress of Christianity. It might have been expected that a Christian successor would be much more zealous than

---

[200] Ibid. 70 B.

[201] Socrates, *HE* 3, 25: Cf. Theodosius and heresy, *CT* 16, 5, 5 (20 August 379).

[202] Piganiol, *L'Empire*, 165–6.

[203] Ibid. 165 with n. 5.

[204] Themistius *Oratio* 5, 70 B; Libanius *Ep.* 1147. O. Seeck, *Geschichte des Untergangs der antiken Welt* (Stuttgart: Metzler, 1920–2), iv. 517 (n. referring to p. 367) thought that the latter confirmed that in the first few months of Jovian's reign sacrifice had been banned: ἔστι καὶ τῶν πολλὰ τεθυκότων, ἡνίχα ἐξῆν.

[205] *CT* 10, 1, 8. Nöthlichs, *Massnahmen*, 289 with n. 523 thought that the date was 4 December 364. See also Gaudemet, art. cit. (n. 58), 456 n. 32.

the moderate Jovian turned out to be. Against the memory of Constantius, Jovian and Valentinian both satisfied pagan writers that they were commendably moderate.

5. VALENTINIAN AND THE WEST

Maurice, in his 1927 article on magic in the fourth century, called Valentinian 'le véritable continuateur de Constantin le Grand'.[206] Like Jovian, Valentinian impressed non-Christians with his approach to religion:

His reign was distinguished by toleration in that he remained neutral in religious differences neither troubling anyone on that ground nor ordering him to reverence this or that. He did not bend the necks of his subjects to his own belief by threatening edicts but left matters undisturbed as he found them.[207]

Jovian had forbidden blood sacrifice and Valentinian upheld the policy. Libanius seems to suggest that Valentinian and his brother Valens, appointed emperor some weeks after Valentinian's elevation, brought about the subversion of all but incense sacrifice:

after his [Julian's] death in Persia, the performance of sacrifice lasted for some little time until, after some untoward incidents, it was banned by the two imperial brothers, an exception, however, being made in the case of offerings of incense.[208]

We do not possess the text of such a general ban.[209] What is certain is that specific kinds of sacrifice had been outlawed early in the reign of Valens and Valentininan by a document which bore the names of both emperors. *CT* 9, 16, 7, from September 364, was addressed to Secundus, Praetorian Prefect of the East.[210] It attacked specific

[206] Maurice, art. cit. (n. 58), 114. This view endorsed by Chastagnol, *La Préfecture*, 149.

[207] Ammianus 30, 9, 5: 'Postremo hoc moderamine principatus inclaruit, quod inter religionum diversitates medius stetit, nec quemquam inquietavit, neque ut hoc coleretur, imperavit aut illud: nec interdictis minacibus subiectorum cervicem ad id, quod ipse coluit, inclinabat, sed intemeratas reliquit has partes ut repperit.'

[208] Libanius, *Oratio* 30, 7: μένει μέν τινα τὸ θύειν ἱερεῖα χρόνον, νεωτέρων δέ τινων συμβάντων ἐκωλύθη παρὰ τοῖν ἀδελφοῖν, ἀλλ' οὐ τὸ λιβανωτόν. Confirmation that Jovian's measures against sacrifice had been so short-lived or ineffective. Libanius either did not know of their existence or did not think them worthy of mention.

[209] *Pace* n. e of A. F. Norman, *Libanius Selected Works*, (Loeb, 1977), ii. 106–7, neither *CT* 9, 16, 7 nor 9, 16, 8 is a candidate for a general ban on sacrifice. Nöthlichs, *Massnahmen*, 327 with n. 939 thinks the ban was temporary and local. Jones, *LRE*, 1098 n. 32 thought that the incident over Theodorus had led to the ban (see Ammianus 29, 1). This occurred, however, in 371–2 and could hardly be described as happening 'a short time' after Valentinian's accession in 364.

[210] For Secundus see *PLRE* I, 814–16. Nöthlichs, *Massnahmen*, 84 says Valens sent the law.

forms of nocturnal practice. No one was to engage in 'wicked prayers' ('nefarias preces'), 'magic preparations' ('magicos apparatus') or 'bloody sacrifices' ('sacrificia funesta'). Death was to be the penalty. In agreement with their predecessors Constantine and Constantius, Valens and Valentinian regarded all these activities as attempts to make contact with sinister powers, the reason why divination was banned. All blood sacrifices had fallen under suspicion of setting out to achieve this end and so only incense offerings were allowed to remain. As Paschoud has pointed out, the measure was not a blow against cultic worship generally but against magical practices.[211] There is evidence, however, that in the west, at least, Valentinian was prepared to overlook certain kinds of blood sacrifice. According to Zosimus, who referred to the law on sacrifice as emanating from Valentinian alone, Vettius Agorius Praetextatus, the proconsul of Achaea (362–4), interceded for the mystery religions of his province.[212] Valentinian

abandoned the proposal and allowed everything to be done according to original natural custom.[213]

This moderate attitude towards Greek mystery cults might well explain the situation of certain forms of blood sacrifice in Rome. As Bloch showed in his important prosopographical study of late pagan senators published in 1945, the cult of Cybele and Attis continued to attract senior senatorial figures in the closing years of the fourth century. In all, some twenty-two dedicatory inscriptions of fourth-century date have been found on the Vatican Hill, where a shrine to the oriental deities seems to have existed.[214] During Valentinian's reign, on 17 July 374, Q. Clodius Hermogenianus Caesarius underwent the ritual of *taurobolium*, in which a bull was sacrificed to Magna Mater, Hermes, and Attis in order to purify the sacrificant who was ritually drenched by the animal's blood.[215] At the time of the ceremony, Caesarius was Prefect of the City of Rome.[216]

The temples of Rome remained open. On 17 November 364, L. Aurelius Avianius Symmachus, the Prefect of the City, was

---

[211] Paschoud, *Zosime*, ii, pt. 2, 337 n. 111.   [212] Zosimus *NH* 4, 3, 2.

[213] Ibid. 3: ἐπέτρεψεν ἀργοῦντος τοῦ νόμου πράττεσθαι πάντα κατὰ τὰ ἐξ ἀρχῆς πάτρια (Trans. R. T. Ridley). For the so-called 'oriental' cults of Rome see Salzman, *On Roman Time*, 164–76.

[214] The so-called 'Phrygianum' see above, 111–12. Also H. Bloch, 'A New Document of the Last Pagan Revival in the West, 393–394 A.D.', *HTR*, 38 (1945), 199–241 and id. 'The Pagan Revival in the West at the End of the Fourth Century', in Momigliano, *Conflict*, 193–218.

[215] Vermaseren, *CCCA* iii, no. 228 = *CIL* 6, 499 = *ILS* 4147.

[216] For Caesarius, see Chastagnol, *Fastes*, 192, no. 75.

contacted by Valentinian.[217] Neither *iudices* nor *apparitores* could appoint Christians as custodians of temples ('ad custodiam templorum homines') indicating that the temples were being maintained. This is certainly the conclusion to be drawn from Ammianus' version of the Urban Prefecture of Vettius Agorius Praetextatus in 367–8.[218] According-ing to Ammianus, Praetextatus was scrupulous in removing buildings which had been placed against temple walls ('ab aedibus sacris').[219] During his prefecture, Praetextatus also restored the Porticus Deorum Consentium.[220] The picture which we have of Praetextatus from later documents as an enthusiastic pagan need not lead us to assume that he took more care over these matters than his predecessors, both Christian and non-Christian. There is no reason for thinking that Praetextatus' concern for the sacred buildings of the city was motivated by a desire to challenge the Christianity of the emperors. The upkeep of temple buildings had traditionally been the responsibility of the Prefect of Rome.

The general statement of Jovian on the fate of land originally belonging to the imperial house but now in the ownership of temples was superseded on 23 December 364 by instructions which we know Mamertinus, Praetorian Prefect of Italy, Illyricum, and Africa received.[221] The lands which Julian had given to the temples were to be retrieved. It cannot be denied that the measure was hostile to the old cults. Nöthlichs rightly pointed out, however, that there were probably good financial reasons for recovering ownership of these lands: Valen-tinian went off to his first frontier war in spring 365.[222] The actual discomfort which the measure caused to the temples is, unfortunately, unknown.

For all his public utterances of religious toleration, Valentinian, like all emperors of the period, greatly feared the application of magic by ambitious men and women. In the late 360s a spate of treason and adultery trials at Rome exposed the insecurity of the court.[223]

During the the urban prefecture of Q. Clodius Hermogenianus Olybrius, a leading senator and his wife accused an assortment of humble citizens of attempting to poison them.[224] Olybrius began an

---

[217] *CT* 16, 1, 1. For Symmachus, see *PLRE* I, 863–5. For the date, Seeck, *Regesten*, 218.

[218] 18 August 367 until 20 September 368 according to Chastagnol, *Fastes*, 171–8.

[219] Ammianus 27, 9, 10.   [220] *ILS* 4003.   [221] *CT* 5, 13, 3.

[222] Nöthlichs, *Massnahmen*, 87–88. Cf. *CT* 10, 1, 8 from 4 December 364.

[223] Ammianus 28, 1 ff. Matthews, *WA*, 56–61; id. *Ammianus*, 209 ff. A. Alföldi, *A Conflict of Ideas in the Later Roman Empire* (Oxford: Clarendon Press, 1952), 65 ff. makes a strong attack on the trustworthiness of Ammianus. Compare N. H. Baynes' review in *JRS*, 43 (1953), 169–70.

[224] Ammianus 28, 1, 8. For Olybrius' prefecture (October 368 to 21 August 370) see

investigation but was debilitated by illness shortly afterwards and the Praefectus Annonae, Maximinus, was ordered to take charge of the affair.[225] On the basis of what the earliest detainees revealed under torture, Maximinus compiled and dispatched an urgent report to the court of Valentinian I, stating that the affair was much more serious than had been thought.[226] For his initiative and in order to carry out a thorough investigation, Valentinian promoted Maximinus to the position of Vicarius Urbis Romae.[227] The emperor was determined not to underestimate the danger and gave Maximinus exceptional instructions:

[Valentinian] gave one general judicial sentence to cover cases of the kind, which he arbitrarily fused with the design of treason, and ruled that all those whom the justice of the ancient code and the edicts of the deified emperors had made exempt from inquisition by torture should, if circumstances demanded, be examined with torments.[228]

As Maximinus' enquiries progressed, a large number of individuals were charged with serious offences, including magic and illegal religious practices. Marinus, for example, a public advocate, was alleged to have attempted to gain a certain Hispanilla as his wife by the use of 'forbidden arts' ('artibus pravis').[229] A former Proconsul of Africa, Iulius Festus Hymetius, was revealed by his own correspondence to have employed the *haruspex* Amantius to perform criminal acts ('prava implenda') and a sacrifice so that the emperors would be more favourable to Hymetius.[230] The condemnation of such a senior official on these charges made Valentinian all the more anxious to get to the bottom of the affair:

When the emperor learned this from the report of the judges, who gave what had been done a harsh interpretation, he issued orders that the affair should be investigated with excessive strictness.[231]

Chastagnol, *Fastes*, 178–84. According to Ammianus (28, 1, 29), one member of this group was a *haruspex*, a profession condemned by Constantius II as being contaminated with magic. In accordance with Constantine's law on *haruspices* and private divination, the man was burned alive.

[225] For Maximinus, see *PLRE* I, 577–8.
[226] Ammianus 28, 1, 10.   [227] Ibid. 12.
[228] Ibid. 11: [Valentinian] 'uno proloquio, in huius modi causas, quas arroganter proposito maiestatis imminutae miscebat, omnes quos iuris prisci iustitia, divorumque arbitria, quaestionibus exemere cruentis, si postulasset negotium, statuit tormentis affligi.'
[229] Ibid. 14.
[230] Ibid. 19. Hymetius had good reason to worry. He had already fallen foul of Valentinian by selling to starving Carthaginians grain allocated for Rome: ibid. 17.
[231] Ibid. 21: 'Haec Valentinianus relatione iudicum doctus, asperius interpretantium facta, vigore nimio in negotium iussit inquiri.'

It is not difficult to imagine that the 'harsh interpretation' placed on the actions of Hymetius was an intimation to the emperor that his own security was threatened by the invocation of magical forces. Frontinus, *consiliarius* to Hymetius in Africa, was exiled for having drawn up a prayer to be used by Hymetius for his own purposes.[232]

In December 371, Valentinian sent a letter to the senate which may have been part of a formal reply to an earlier senatorial delegation:

I judge that *haruspicina* has no connection with cases of magic, and I do not consider this *religio* or any other that was allowed by our elders to be a crime. Of this opinion the laws given by me at the beginning of my reign are witness,[233] in which free opportunity was granted to everyone to cultivate that which he had conceived in his mind. We do not condemn divination, but we do forbid it to be practised harmfully.[234]

As Maurice long ago pointed out, this statement declared a return to the Constantinian position against harmful magic and divination.[235] Again, the context in which the law was drafted and delivered is significant for ascertaining the precise judicial meaning of some of the terms used. Senatorial Rome was seriously disturbed by the trials then in progress and Valentinian sought to prevent an open rupture between himself and the senate. Most importantly, Valentinian established that he thought *haruspicina* had no relation to magic, and only if practised harmfully was it illegal. The meaning of *religio* is problematic but the text appears to be calling *haruspicina* and all such actions *religiones*. The legal religious practices were therfore termed *religiones*: strictly speaking, orthodox Christianity was one, *haruspicina* another. Finally, Valentinian drew attention to the laws issued at the beginning of his reign to show that he was not attempting to destroy the freedom of men to think what they liked. It was an attempt to restore confidence in the emperor's intentions. The exceptional nature of the circumstances makes it impossible to judge whether the law was primarily an emergency diplomatic gesture or a statement designed for general circulation throughout the empire.

The vigour of the investigations, however, did not cease. Lollianus, the son of Lampadius, ex-Prefect of the City, was executed after an appeal to the court against his conviction for having written a book on

---

[232] Ammianus 28, 1, 21.   [233] No longer extant.

[234] *CT* 9, 16, 9: 'Haruspicinam ego nullum cum maleficiorum causis habere consortium iudicio neque ipsam aut aliquam praeterea concessam a maioribus religionem genus esse arbitror criminis. Testes sunt leges a me in exordio imperii mei datae, quibus unicuique, quod animo inbibisset, colendi libera facultas tributa est. Nec haruspicinam reprehendimus, sed nocenter exerceri vetamus.'

[235] Maurice, art. cit. (n. 58), 114 thought it redolent of the 'Edict of Milan'. See Martroye, art. cit. (n. 122), 678.

the black arts.[236] Four senators, including two of the Ceionii, were accused of showing too much interest in a common charioteer and being his accomplices in poisonings.[237] Ammianus gives special prominence to the fate of Aginatius who had been a long-standing enemy of Maximinus.[238] Although Aginatius had insulted Maximinus' closest friend, Victorinus, the charge that finally secured his execution was brought by Anepsia, Victorinus' widow. She claimed, when she was charged with adultery, that she had been worked upon by 'evil arts' ('nefariis artibus') and raped in the house of Aginatius.[239]

Valentinian's resolution to root out the magical practices was powerfully reaffirmed even after Maximinus had been promoted to Gaul and replaced by the new Prefect of the City, Ampelius.[240] The prefect was given responsibility for cases involving senators and the practice of magic. If trials occurred which could not, for whatever reason, be handled by the prefect, then they were to be dispatched with all those involved to the emperor's court.[241] The desire of Valentinian to see these cases dealt with promptly and rigorously is obvious.

On the question of Valentinian's treatment of the ancient cults, Ammianus was essentially correct; the emperor was moderate. Like all fourth-century emperors, however, he was deeply concerned by magic and divination. In his anxiety to investigate threats from these quarters to himself, Valentinian allowed the issue of wide-ranging instructions to officials who could not or would not interpret them responsibly.

6. GRATIAN, VALENTINIAN II, AND THE WEST

With the death of Valentinian I at Brigetio in 375, the empire became the charge of his brother Valens and his sons Valentinian II and Gratianus.

In 377, the Prefect of Rome, Furius Maecius Gracchus, was responsible for a violent action against non-Christian cult in the city.[242] Prudentius gave an account of the events in his highly polemical *Contra Symmachum*, written early in the fifth century:

---

[236] Ammianus 28, 1, 26.

[237] Ibid. 27. These four were acquitted and one (Bassus) went on to become PUR in 390. Compare the fates of the senators Paphius and Cornelius, who both confessed to poisoning: ibid. 29.

[238] Ibid. 30 ff. For Aginatius see *PLRE* I, 29–30.

[239] Ibid. 50. I interpret as a reference to rape the phrase 'vim in domo Aginati perpessam.'

[240] *PLRE* I, 56–7.   [241] *CT* 9, 16, 10 (6 December 371).

[242] For Gracchus see Chastagnol, *Fastes*, 198–200; Matthews, *WA*, 23.

The Gracchi, the friends of the people, supported by the right and official power, eminent among the highest in the senate, who ordered the images of the gods to be pulled down and, with their lictors, offered themselves humbly to Christ the Almighty to be ruled by him.[243]

This account has been enthusiastically taken up by recent scholars, notably Chastagnol, to support the view that a policy of general destruction of shrines was initiated by the authorities from 377 onwards.[244] A more accurate version of the affair, however, was written by Jerome to Laeta, a Roman noblewoman, in 403.[245] Gracchus was a relation of Laeta's and Jerome recalled for her the dramatic circumstances of his conversion to Christianity:

Did not your kinsman Gracchus whose name betokens his patrician origin, when a few years back he held the prefecture of the city, overthrow, break up and shake to pieces a grotto of Mithras and all the dreadful images therein? . . . Did he not, I repeat, destroy these and then, sending them before him as hostages, obtain for himself Christian baptism?[246]

Jerome's vivid account referred to a *single* incident. If there had been a general policy applied at Rome, then he would certainly have made more of it. In fact, Gracchus was exercising his initiative in relation to objectionable religious practices; a responsibility which had traditionally fallen to Prefects of the City.[247]

The catastrophe at Hadrianople in summer 378, however, did have important consequences for the religious policies of the remaining emperors. The death of Valens left the sixteen-year-old Gratian as the

---

[243] *Contra Symmachum* 1, 561–5 (*CCL* 126, 205): 'Iam quid plebicolas percurram carmine Gracchos, iure potestatis fultos et in arce senatus praecipuos, simulacra deum iussisse revelli cumque suis pariter lictoribus omnipotenti suppliciter Christo se consecrasse regendos?' (Trans. Croke and Harries.)

[244] Chastagnol, *La Préfecture*, 159: 'les autorités préferent dès 377 les [statues] retirer de temples et les consacrer dans un lieu public, en dehors de toute consideration religieuse, à l'embellissement de l'urbs.' I have serious doubts about the existence of such a policy. For my interpretation of statues in the landscape, see art. cit. (n. 99).

[245] Jerome *Ep.* 107.

[246] Ibid. 2 (*CSEL* 55, 292): 'Ante paucos annos propinquus vester Gracchus nobilitatem patriciam nomine sonans, cum praefecturam regeret urbanam, nonne specu Mithrae et omnia portentuosa simulacra . . . subvertit, fregit, excussit et his quasi obsidibus ante praemissis inpetravit baptismum Christi?'

[247] Chastagnol, *La Préfecture*, 157 observed that Gracchus was a neophyte but we should avoid concluding that his Christianity motivated him in this incident. Vera, op. cit. (n. 168), 153–4 agreed with Chastagnol although Piétri was more circumspect, *RC*, 429 with nn. 1 and 2: 'l'église romaine poursuit l'œuvre de conversion par la prédication, la polémique, mais sans utiliser directement les moyens d'une offensive brutale.' *Pace* Chastagnol, *La Préfecture*, *CIL* 6, 736 (c.AD 391) does not prove a reopening of *mithraea* closed generally in Rome.

senior *Augustus* and the child Valentinian II, aged five, as his partner. The tone of legislation on religion was set, in the west, by the unfettered influence which bishop Ambrose of Milan came to exercise on Gratian and Valentinian II.[248] Affairs in the East became the responsibility of the Christian general Theodosius whom Gratian recalled to service as *Augustus* 19 on January 379.[249]

In the autumn of 382 Gratian returned to Milan after a summer spent campaigning on the Danube. Ambrose made his way to the same city after attending a church council in Rome. The following winter (382/3) saw a significant change in the disposition of Gratian. The new tone of Gratian's religious outlook may be sensed in a law delivered to Hypatius, Praetorian Prefect of Italy and Illyricum, on 21 May 383.[250] The law concerned apostasy and the prescript struck an aggressive note: Christians who turned to the altars and temples were guilty of a 'criminal act' ('admissum') while Judaism was a set of 'contagions' ('contagiones') which 'polluted' the apostate. Special vitriol was reserved for Manichaeans and their 'wicked seclusion' ('scelerosi secessus'). *Iudices* were encouraged to implement heavy penalties on those perpetrating such wickedness.

Gratian had been, like the Christian emperors before him, Pontifex Maximus. He had accepted and used the title at the outset of his reign and was happy to be called *pontifex* by Ausonius.[251] But sometime between 379 and 382, on the occasion of the sending of a formal deputation of senatorial priests (*pontifices*) from Rome, he refused the title.[252] No Christian emperor ever used it again.

At about the same time Gratian took the momentous step of undermining the economic position of the cults at Rome.[253] Ambrose's brief reference to Gratian's actions makes it clear that they were announced in *rescripta*.[254] It would seem that some form of request relating to the problem was addressed to Gratian, possibly originating in the office of the Urban Prefect. According to Chastagnol's *Fastes*, Anicius Auchenius Bassus was Prefect of the City at this time and he was described by

---

[248] Cf. N. B. McLynn, *Ambrose of Milan* (Berkeley: University of California Press, 1994), 151 who argues instead for the influence of 'Christian careerists in Gratian's entourage'.

[249] *Chronica Minora* 1, 243.   [250] *CT* 16, 7, 3.

[251] *CIL* 6, 1175; Ausonius *Gratiarum actio ad Gratianum Imperatorem pro consulatu* 7.

[252] Zosimus *HN* 4, 36, 5; Symm., *Rel.* 3, 1. A considerable controversy over the date: F. Paschoud, *Zosime*, ii. 419 ff. with n. 174 and id. op. cit. (n. 48), 63–79. Matthews, *WA*, 203 ff.; Nöthlichs, *Massnahmen*, 198 ff.; A. Cameron, 'Gratian's Repudiation of the Pontifical Robe', *JRS*, 58 (1968), 96–102; Chastagnol, *La Préfecture*, 157; J. R. Palanque, 'L'empereur Gratian et le grand pontificat païenne', *Byzantion*, 8 (1933), 41 ff.; T. D. Barnes thinks that Gratian visited Rome in 376 or 377: 'Constans and Gratian in Rome', *HSClPh*, 79 (1975), 325–33.

[253] Ambrose *Ep.* 17, 5.   [254] Ibid.

the author of one of the important documents of the *Collectio Avellana* as 'olim catholicam fidem venerans'.[255] The text of Gratian's law does not survive, but in 415 Honorius and Theodosius III referred to it:

in accordance with the constitution of the divine Gratian . . . from the time when the public expenditure was prohibited to be furnished to the worst superstition, the fruits from such places shall be exacted from the unlawful possessors thereof.[256]

Despite the objections of Martroye, the measure of 415 clearly reissued some, at least, of the decisions of Gratian.[257] Probably as part of the same initiative, Gratian delivered a mortal blow to the senate's religious prestige by ordering the Altar of Victory to be removed. It seems likely that the impact of the removal of the altar was felt chiefly in the highest senatorial circles, since neither Jerome nor Augustine, who were present in Rome at the time, mentioned it. Soon after the announcement of the law, the senate sent a delegation to see Gratian but Ambrose undermined the embassy by claiming, on behalf of Damasus and the Christian senators of Rome, that the delegation was not supported by the whole senate. The Christians threatened to boycott the Curia and the deputation left Milan unheard.[258]

The snub to the senate was a great disappointment to those who had heard Gratian's friendly sentiments in a speech delivered in the senate on the first day of 376.[259] Ultimate responsibility for the measures of 382/3 would seem to lie with Ambrose, although the bishop later disingenuously denied that he had ordered the removal of the funds for sacrifices.[260]

The dismay in certain senatorial circles at this drastic redefinition can be appreciated from the impassioned and rhetorical *Relatio* which Symmachus, as Prefect of the City, addressed to Valentinian II late in 384. The details of the 'debate' on the Altar of Victory between Ambrose and Symmachus are too well known to require detailed retelling here.[261] In a letter sent to Valentinian II before the emperor

[255] *Collectio Avellana* 2, 85 (*CSEL* 35, 30).

[256] *CT* 16, 10, 20 (30 August 415): 'secundum divi Gratiani constituta nostrae rei iubemus sociari ita ut ex eo tempore, quo inhibitus est publicus sumptus superstitioni deterrimae exhiberi, fructus ab incubatoribus exigantur.'

[257] Martroye, art. cit. (n. 122), 681 thought that this law of 415 did not reproduce Gratian's text and that it dealt only with Africa.

[258] Ambrose *Ep*. 17, 10; Symmachus *Relatio* 3, 1; 20 with Vera, op. cit. (n. 168), 26.

[259] Symmachus *Ep*. 1, 13.

[260] Ambrose *Ep*. 57, 2 (to the usurper Eugenius in 392).

[261] See J. J. Sheridan, 'The Altar of Victory: Paganism's Last Battle', *L'Antiquité Classique*, 35 (1966), 186–206; McLynn, op. cit. (n. 248), 151–2; Matthews, *WA*, 203–10; Croke and Harries, *Conflict*, ch. 2.

had even seen Symmachus' *Relatio*, Ambrose smoothed over the untidy record of Christian emperors' relations with the old state cults.[262] Aware that Christians at court might even support the petition, he admitted that Rome had enjoyed an anomalous position with regard to laws which had attacked such practices elsewhere but he gave no hint that Constantius II had been responsible for a reversal of policy in 357 nor that the successors of Julian had not returned to the Constantian position. The bishop suggested coolly that Valentinian I, the emperor's father, had been unaware that the Altar of Victory stood in the Curia legitimizing the acts of the senate.

Symmachus could afford to be more forward. After expressing his consternation that such action had been taken against ancestral tradition,[263] Symmachus recalled the visit to Rome of Constantius II, the emperor most hostile to the state religion in his lifetime. Symmachus claimed that Constantius II had made the 'mistake' of removing the Altar of Victory in 357 but even he had not withdrawn the privileges of the *vestales*. In fact, Constantius II had shown a great appreciation of the antiquity and grandeur of the city's cults and had filled the vacancies on the priestly boards. He had certainly not refused their funds to the cults.[264]

It is important to emphasize that non-Christians continued to be free to perform cult acts at Rome. Ambrose appreciated the great damage inflicted upon the cults by the withdrawal of temple estates and subsidies but in his letter written to Valentinian after he had read Symmachus' *Relatio*, the bishop made it clear that the measures of Gratian did not leave the shrines without resources:

No one, however, has refused the shrines their gifts, or the augurs their legacies. They are only being deprived of their estates because, although they defend them on grounds of religion they do not make use of them in a religious fashion.[265]

As for incense sacrifice, Ambrose indicated that it was not banned but was freely practised by pagans throughout Rome, confirming that the Altar of Victory question was relevant chiefly to the senate:[266]

---

[262] Ambrose *Ep.* 17. See McLynn, op. cit. (n. 248), 166–7.

[263] Symmachus *Relatio* 3, 2. [264] Ibid. 6.

[265] Ambrose *Ep.* 18, 16 (*CSEL* 82, 43): 'Nemo tamen donaria delubris et legata haruspicibus denegavit; sola sublata sunt praedia, quia non religiose utebantur his quae religionis iure defenderent'. (Trans. Croke and Harries.)

[266] The private resources of some individuals clearly remained sufficient to repair some shrines. See *CIL* 6, 2158 = *ILS* 4944 where the *vestales* paid for the repair of the *mansiones* of the Salii on the Palatine. Also the *mithraeum* repaired by Tamesius Olympius Augentius, who made explicit reference to the fact that the state could not be expected to pay for the upkeep of that particular shrine: *CIL* 6, 754 = *ILS* 4269.

They seek to set up an altar of this Victory . . . there are altars in all the temples, there is also an altar in the Templa Victoriarum. Because they get pleasure out of numbers, they perform sacrifices all over the place . . . is it not enough for them that the baths, the porticoes, the public squares are crowded with images?[267]

Ambrose won the day and the appeal of Symmachus was rejected.

The cult buildings at Rome were not an object of imperial attack. In spring 384 Valentinian II received reports that temples in Italy were being plundered. He ordered Praetextatus, then Praetorian Prefect of Italy, to investigate.[268] Shortly after assuming the office of Prefect of the City, Symmachus found himself the subject of some unfounded allegations. In particular, he was accused of championing the cause of the temples and injuring Christians. The Prefect of the City was able to pass on to the court a letter from the bishop Damasus which denied any such charge.[269] The importance of the *Relatio* is twofold. First, the identity of the plunderers is not known and cannot certainly be assumed to be Christian. Indeed, Symmachus makes it clear that he had not even started his enquiry. Secondly, the episode illustrates again the distance between the urban prefecture and the court. We have seen above the degree of initiative enjoyed by Prefects of the City in religious matters. This slightly sinister affair shows well the vulnerablity of an administrator to accusations sent to the distant and sometimes suspicious imperial court.

What Gratian had carried out was nothing less than a fundamental redefinition of the legal position of the ancient cults of Rome. By confiscating their estates and revenues, Gratian withdrew the support of the state from the ancient ceremonies. Traditionally these cults had had the well-being of the emperors as their very focus. With Gratian's refusal of the pontifical robe and undoubtedly the title and position of Pontifex Maximus as well, the emperor removed himself from occupying the focal point between the Romans and their gods. The worship of these deities was not now banned but became merely the preference of a number of individuals rather than the genuine religious expressions of the state itself. Much of the official prestige of the *vestales* and *ministri* disappeared along with their material privileges.[270]

---

[267] Ambrose *Ep.* 18, 31 (*CSEL* 82, 50): 'Huius aram strui in urbis Romae curia petunt . . . omnibus in templis arae, ara etiam in templo victoriarum. Quoniam numero delectantur, sacrificia sua ubique concelebrant . . . non illis satis sunt lavacra, non porticus, non plateae occupatae simulacris?'

[268] Symmachus *Relatio* 21, 5 with Vera, op. cit. (n. 168), 153–5.

[269] Symmachus, *Relatio* 21, 5.

[270] Including receipt of free corn: Symmachus *Relatio* 3, 15; 17. Ambrose *Ep.* 17, 3 and 18, 13. See Prudentius *Contra Symmachum* 2, 910–13.

7. THEODOSIUS

The new emperor appointed in 379 was a committed Catholic Christian and a number of scholars believe him to have fostered the idea of a Catholic state from the time of his elevation.[271] It would be wrong, however, to regard Theodosius as inveterately hostile to the ancient cults from the moment of his accession. A large number of his officials and advisers were non-Christian.[272] The first significant statement made by Theodosius on ancient tradition was made in June 379 to Pancratius, Count of the Privy Purse.[273] The right of the supervisor of the games at Antioch to plant and cut down (sacred?) cypress trees was upheld and was accompanied by the phrase:

You shall know that we have acceded both to the ancient custom and to the constitutions of our forefathers.[274]

Nöthlichs followed Ensslin in believing that the reference to cypress trees had no bearing on the ancient cults.[275] The specificity of the law is, however, striking. Cumont suggested in 1928 that this text showed the Alytarch officiating at a ceremonial cutting-down of cypress trees at the shrine of Apollo at Daphne as part of a rite commemorating the rebirth of the sun.[276] Cumont was, however, unaware that the Alytarchs of Antioch were connected with the Olympic Games at Antioch which Downey suggested as a context for this incident.[277] It seems probable that the trees in question had some cultic significance and MacMullen has collected substantial evidence to suggest that sacred groves and trees were an important feature of many cult sites in East and West.[278]

[271] Based, in most cases on *CT* 16, 1, 2 = *CJ* 1, 1, 1 (28 February 380). Gaudemet, art. cit. (n. 58), 457 thought: 'l'empire de Théodose passe de la liberté de culte à la religion d'État'. See also Piganiol, *L'Empire*, 237. For the important traditional views on Theodosius, see Piganiol, *L'Empire*, 237–43, 279–99; Nöthlichs, *Massnahmen*, 166 ff.; N. Q. King, *The Emperor Theodosius and the Establishment of Christianity* (London: SCM, 1961), 71–96; A. A. Erhardt, 'The First Two Years of Emperor Theodosius I', *JEH*, 15 (1964), 1–17; W. Ensslin, *Die Religionspolitik des Kaisers Theodosius* (Munich: Bayerische Akademie der Wissenschaften, 1953); Martroye, art. cit. (n. 122), 669–701.

[272] e.g. Richomer was consul 384 with the pagan Clearchos; Themistius was PUC and tutor to Arcadius; Nicomachus Flavianus was *quaestor sacri palatini*. See Nöthlichs, *Massnahmen*, 326 with n. 935.   [273] *CT* 10, 1, 12.

[274] Ibid. 'Et mori veteri et constitutis nos maiorum accessisse cognoscas.'

[275] Nöthlichs, *Massnahmen*, 326 with n. 936; Ensslin, op. cit. (n. 271), 10 ff.

[276] F. Cumont, *Syria*, 9 (1928), 106–7. See King, op. cit. (n. 271), 72; Erhardt, art. cit. (n. 271), 5 f.

[277] G. Downey, 'The Olympic Games of Antioch in the Fourth Century A.D.', *TAPA*, 70 (1939), 437 n. 44.

[278] R. MacMullen, *Paganism in the Roman Empire* (New Haven: Yale University Press, 1981), 35, 36, 161 nn. 9–11 and 166 n.3; id. *Christianity and Paganism*, 64 ff.

Although Theodosius did not legislate decisively against the old state religion until twelve years after his accession, he made his own distaste for the ceremonies obvious long before then. In May 381 Eutropius, Praetorian Prefect (of Illyricum), received a letter which instructed him to deny Christians who had apostatized ('pagani facti sunt') the right to make wills.[279] A law given six months later to Florus, Praetorian Prefect, attacked the other bugbear of fourth-century emperors, divination:

If any madman or sacrilegious person, so to speak, should immerse himself in forbidden sacrifices by day or night, as a consultor of uncertain events, and if he should suppose that he should employ, or should think that he should approach a shrine or a temple for the commission of such a crime, he shall know that he shall be subjected to proscription, since we give warning by our just provision that God must be worshipped by chaste prayers and not be professed by dire incantations.[280]

The temples were still open. They were not, however, to be utilized for the purposes of divination. Even the hostile Zosimus conceded that Theodosius had not restricted access to the temples. After painting a depressing picture of the state under Theodosius, Zosimus stated:

they [those who lived in the empire's cities] prayed to God that they might find deliverance from such afflictions since they were still allowed to frequent the temples and worship the gods according to ancient custom.[281]

The 'ancient custom' mentioned is most probably the burning of incense to images which Libanius makes clear was still permitted.[282] But Theodosius' measure superseded Valentinian I's studied declaration to the senate as it now announced a general prohibition on divination.[283]

Although Theodosius is not known to have passed any measure outlawing the old cults in the east, his appointment of Maternus Cynegius as Praetorian Prefect of the East in 384 inflamed the passions of extreme Christians and non-Christian apologists. Cynegius, accord-

---

[279] *CT* 16, 7, 1.

[280] *CT* 16, 10, 7: 'Si qui vetitis sacrificiis diurnis nocturnisque velut vesanus ac sacrilegus incertorum consultorem se inmerserit fanumque sibi aut templum ad huiuscemodi sceleris executionem adsumendum crediderit vel putaverit adeundum, proscribtione se noverit subiugandum, cum nos iusta institutione moneamus castis deum precibis excolendum, non diris carminibus profanandum' (21 December 381).

[281] Zosimus *HN* 4, 29, 2: οἱ τὰς πόλεις οἰκοῦντες . . . ἱκετεύοντες τὸν θεὸν καὶ δεόμενοι τῶν τοσούτων αὐτοῖς ἀπαλλαγὴν εὑρασθαι συμφορῶν. ἔτι γὰρ ἦν αὐτοῖς ἄδεια τοῦ φοιτᾶν εἰς τὰ ἱερὰ καὶ τὰ θεῖα κατὰ τοὺς πατρίους θεσμοὺς ἐκμειλίττεσθαι.

[282] Libanius *Oratio* 30, 7. See p. 198 above and p. 212 below.

[283] Valentinian's letter: *CT* 9, 16, 9. See p. 202 above.

ing to Libanius, was placed in charge of curial recruitment, but exceeded his brief, persecuting and destroying shrines.[284] As Fowden suggests, Cynegius must have enjoyed at least the tacit support of Theodosius, but it is significant that the only law on religious matters which we know Cynegius received from Theodosius was a vivid denunciation of divination.[285] The most delicate part of Libanius' *Oratio* 30 suggested that Theodosius was being duped in the east by an unnamed governor (Cynegius) who, it was claimed, was contravening the will of Theodosius himself.[286] Libanius was also aware that the use of force by Christians to bring about conversion was technically illegal.[287] Though Theodosius was probably aware of Christian violence against temples, he did not consider closing them as Constantius had ordered.[288]

Theodosius addressed the issue of the old religion in what appear to be a pair of rescripts dated to 382 and 385. The first was addressed to Palladius, Dux of Osrhoene. Some special event or *suggestio* had brought a well-known temple in the area (presumably that of Edessa) to the emperor's attention. The emperors, unusually, replied that they had taken advice ('publici consilii auctoritate')[289] before decreeing that the temple was to remain open. This was an *aedes* in which *simulacra* had been set up. The images may have been one source of trouble, but the emperors ordered them retained: 'by the value of their art rather than by their divinity'.[290] And in a phrase redolent of the law issued to Madalianus at Rome in 342 the emperors declared the temple 'for the common use of the people' ('iam populo quoque communem'). The continued public utility of this structure, like those earlier at Rome, saved it. The *Dux* was to make sure that votive festivals continued to be held there:

---

[284] Libanius *Oratio* 49, 3. See Zosimus *HN* 4, 37, 3 who claims that Cynegius had specific instructions to stamp out the old cults. For Zosimus' views as an exaggeration, see Jones, *LRE*, 167 and Fowden, art. cit. (n. 158), 63.

[285] Fowden, art. cit. (n. 158), 63. *CT* 16, 10, 9: 'No mortal man shall assume the audacity of performing sacrifices so that by the inspection of the liver and the presage of the entrails of the sacrificial victim, he may obtain the hope of a vain promise, or, what is worse, he may learn the future by an accursed consultation. The torture of a very bitter punishment shall threaten those persons who, in violation of our prohibition, attempt to explore the truth ('veritas') of present or future events.'

[286] *Oratio* 30, 46.

[287] Ibid. 27–9. Cf. Eusebius *VC* 2, 60.

[288] *Pace* King, op. cit. (n. 271), 73 who thinks that *CT* 16, 10, 8 implies that temples were normally closed. See my interpretation below, pp. 212–13.

[289] For the alternatives of Consistory or Senate of Constantinople, see Nöthlichs, *Massnahmen*, n. 945.

[290] *CT* 16, 10, 8: 'simulacra feruntur posita artis pretio quam divinitate metienda.'

but in such a way that no one believes that the performance of forbidden sacrifices is allowed because of the opportunity of access to the temple.[291]

The forbidden sacrifices were those connected with divination and long banned.

The second of these apparent rescripts is certainly the most significant statement of Theodosius on the ancient cults at this time:

In obtaining the Archierosyna, that person shall be considered preferable who has performed the most services for his municipality and who has not, however, withdrawn from the cult of the temples by his observance of Christianity.[292]

Alongside the concept of civic duty, Theodosius upheld the clearly sectarian principle first enunciated by Valentinian that Christians and non-Christians ought only to adhere to the duties of their own ceremonies:[293]

Because it is unseemly . . . it is illicit, for the temples and the customary rites of the temples to belong to the care of those whose conscience is imbued with the true doctrine of divine religion, and who ought properly to flee such compulsory service.[294]

Libanius, in the middle of the 380s,[295] contrasted the official policy of Theodosius with the practice of eastern Christians:

You have neither ordered the closure of temples nor banned entrance to them. From the temples you have banished neither fire nor incense, nor the offering of other perfumes.[296]

At Rome, a crucial redefinition of the role of the ancient cults in Roman life had been effected by Gratian. But the temples, as we saw from the evidence of Ambrose, were not left without resources entirely

---

[291] *CT* 16, 10, 8: 'ne illic prohibitorum usus sacrificiorum huius occasione aditus permissus esse credatur.'

[292] *CT* 12, 1, 112: 'In consequenda archierosyne ille sit potior, qui patriae plura praestiterit nec tamen a templorum cultu observatione Christianitatis abscesserit.'

[293] See *CT* 16, 1, 1 and cf. *CT* 16, 2, 5.

[294] *CT* 12, 1, 112: 'Quippe indecorum est . . . inlicitum ad eorum curam templa et templorum sollemnia pertinere, quorum conscientiam vera ratio divinae religionis imbuerit et quos ipsos decebat tale munus, etiamsi non prohiberentur, effugere.'

[295] For the date see n. 79 above. I accept Bradbury's scepticism on the *Pro Templis* as a source (art. cit. (n. 56), 127–8) but through a different interpretation of other evidence, I accept Libanius here. See above, 171–81.

[296] *Oratio* 30, 8: σὺ μὲν οὖν οὔθ᾿ ἱερὰ κεκλεῖσθαι [ἐκέλευσας] οὔτε μηδένα προσιέναι οὔτε πῦρ οὔτε λιβανωτὸν οὔτε τὰς ἀπὸ τῶν ἄλλων θυμιαμάτων τιμὰς ἐξήλασας τῶν νεῶν οὐδὲ τῶν βωμῶν.

and incense sacrifice was to be seen all over the city. Libanius' evidence supports this view:

And the most crucial point of all—those who appear to have been our chief opponents in this particular have honoured the gods even against their will. And who might these be? Why those who have not dared to rob Rome of its sacrifices.[297]

In 387, Magnus Maximus, who had held Gaul as *Augustus* since his overthrow of Gratian in the summer of 383, descended upon Italy. The campaign which Theodosius mounted to defeat Maximus and restore Valentinian II brought him, for the first time in his reign, into sustained contact with the west.[298] The three years between his arrival in the west and the promulgation of legislation unequivocally hostile to the old state religion have been understood to witness the clash between two great men of destiny: Ambrose of Milan and Theodosius. The traditional interpretation of these years has emphasized a psychological conflict between the overbearing bishop and the devout and superstitious emperor, climaxing in the former's victory when, as a result of a massacre of Thessalonicans ordered by Theodosius in 390, the emperor was forced to lay aside his imperial regalia and do penance in the cathedral of Milan.[299] From that point onwards, it has commonly been argued, Theodosius was a changed man. Violently hostile legislation against non-Christian cults followed soon afterwards.

Recently, however, a sophisticated and compelling alternative to this view has been advocated by N. B. McLynn.[300] According to McLynn, the interpersonal and psychological interpretations have been overplayed. The scope for contact between the two men was limited by the fact that both belonged to large organizations, the western Christian church on the one hand and the imperial court on the other. He rejects the theory that a pious Theodosius passed immediately into the power of the bishop of Milan. Rather, the two men desired very different political ends. Ambrose looked forward to the restoration of Valentinian II over whom he had established his influence. Once this was achieved by Theodosius, Ambrose hoped that the eastern emperor would retire home. Theodosius, however, wished to restore Valentinian II in little more than name. The latter was technically senior *Augustus* but Theodosius was anxious to extend his own control of power into the west. With this end in mind, Theodosius sedulously

---

[297] *Oratio* 30, 33: Τὸ δὲ μέγιστον, οἱ μάλιστα τοῦτο τὸ μέρος ἀτιμάσαι δοκοῦντες καὶ ἄκοντες τετιμήκασι. τίνες οὗτοί; οἱ τὴν Ῥώμην τοῦ θύειν οὐ τολμήσαντες ἀφελέσθαι. (Trans. A. F. Norman.)

[298] Matthews, *WA*, 223–38.

[299] Ambrose, *De Obitu Theodosii* 30–4; cf. Theodoret, *HE* 5, 17.

made contact with the senate in Rome in 389.[301] He pardoned
Symmachus for the *faux pas* of delivering a panegyric to Maximus
and made a number of shrewd appointments from within the senatorial
order.[302] The visit was a wholesale propaganda exercise and the tone
was perfectly captured by a panegyric delivered on the occasion by
Pacatus.[303]

There was, however, an uncompromisingly Christian atmosphere to
the visit. On 7 August, Theodosius issued instructions to the Prefect of
the City, Albinus, that all days were to be considered *juridici dies*
except the two-month summer break; 1 January; the *natales* of Rome
and Constantinople; the seven days before and after Easter; the *dies
natales* of the emperors, and all Sundays.[304]

Nine days later, Theodosius addressed the question of magical
practice in Rome with characteristic vigour.[305] There is no evidence
to suggest, however, that Theodosius' Christianity made him any more
hostile towards magic than his predecessors had been. Albinus was
ordered to prosecute anyone found to be 'polluted with magic' but if a
charioteer was found to have killed a magician himself, suspicion would
fall upon him as an accomplice in magical practices.

It was in this atmosphere of friendship towards the senate but
restriction of the festivals and antipathy towards magic that the
senate sent a delegation to Theodosius asking him to look again into
the question of the restoration of some of the privileges of the ancient
cults.[306] The request was sent to Milan whither Theodosius had
returned after his stay in Rome. It was turned down but not, according
to McLynn, before Ambrose had been censured for interfering in
imperial affairs and banned from the court.[307] Thus far, the picture has
been drawn of the bishop and the emperor moving in different
directions, neither one under the sway of the other. The massacre at
Thessalonica, however, brought about a very different situation.

After the lynching at Thessalonica of the Gothic general Butheric,
Theodosius ordered the arrest and execution of certain citizens.[308] The

[300] McLynn, op. cit. (n. 248), ch. 7.   [301] Ibid. 310 ff.
[302] Matthews, *WA*, 225 ff.
[303] *Pan. Lat.* 2 (12) = Nixon and Rodgers, 437–516.
[304] *CT* 2, 8, 19.   [305] *CT* 9, 16, 11.
[306] Our only source is the vague reference in Ambrose, *Ep.* 57, 4. The precise nature
of the request is unknown. McLynn, op. cit. (n. 248), 313 doubts whether a full reversal
of Gratian's decision was demanded. The embassy may have been the occasion of
Symmachus' unceremonial expulsion to beyond the hundreth milestone from Milan:
Ps. Prosper, *De promissionibus et praedictionibus dei* 3, 38, 2.
[307] Ambrose, *Ep.* 51, 3 with McLynn, op. cit. (n. 248), 314.
[308] Sozomen *HE* 7, 25. Cf. Theodoret, *HE* 5, 17–18; Matthews, *WA*, 234–7;
McLynn, op. cit. (n. 248), 315 ff.

planned reprisal in summer 390[309] was badly mishandled and 7,000 people were killed in a bloodbath at the hippodrome in the city.[310] McLynn again offers a political interpretation of the relations which ensued between Ambrose and Theodosius. The bishop had offended the court in 389 and needed reaccommodation while the emperor had been responsible for a horrendous error. The vivid account of Sozomen of the confrontation between the two was a concoction which suited Ambrose. Eunapius, by contrast, who would certainly have made mileage out of any affair that damaged the credibility of Christianity, did not mention it at all. Neither Rufinus nor Augustine mention Ambrose in connection wth the affair. The truth is that 'excommunication' of Theodosius was a discreet matter. The letter which Ambrose sent was by no means designed to humiliate the emperor.[311] The *rapprochement* between Ambrose and Theodosius suited them both; the penance of the emperor enabled him to accept responsibility for the massacre without admitting to incompetence. Ambrose, for his assistance, gained access to the court again. There is no evidence, however, that the bishop of Milan exerted any more influence over Theodosius than he had before 390.

What is certain, on the other hand, is that the experience of penance made Theodosius dwell deeply on the anomaly of the persistence of non-Christian beliefs in his Christian empire. The readmittance of Theodosius to communion probably took place on Christmas Day 390; within weeks Theodosius and his advisers were drafting laws which would universally condemn the ancient state religion. On 24 February 391, the Prefect of the City of Rome, Ceionius Rufius Albinus, received the most comprehensive law ever composed against the ancient cults.[312] The text which we possess may not be complete but there can be no doubt about the intention of the law. It had two parts. The first was a general ban:

No one shall pollute himself with sacrificial animals; no person shall slaughter an innocent victim; no person shall approach the shrines, shall wander through the temples, or revere the images formed by mortal labour, lest he become guilty by divine and human laws.[313]

---

[309] The date is controversial. I follow McLynn, op. cit. (n. 248), 315. See Matthews, *WA*, 234–5.

[310] Theodoret, *HE* 5, 17, 3.   [311] Ambrose *Ep.* 51 (*CSEL* 82, 212–18).

[312] *CT* 16, 10, 10. See J. Gaudemet, 'La condamnation des pratiques païennes en 391', in *Epektasis: Mélanges offerts au Cardinal J. Daniélou* (Paris: Beauchesne, 1972), 597–602; McLynn, op. cit. (n. 248), 331–2 suggests plausibly that the law may actually have been a response to *delatio*.

[313] *CT* 16, 10, 10: 'Nemo se hostiis polluat, nemo insontem victimam caedat, nemo delubra adeat, templa perlustret et mortali opere formata simulacra suspiciat, ne divinis adque humanis sanctionibus reus fiat.'

These terms indicated a return to the sweeping prohibitions of Constantius,[314] but instead of violent and rhetorical threats of punishment, the second part of the law revealed a pragmatic determination to attack the problem of active non-Christians in the administration. A series of fines were stipulated for Suburbicarian officials who were found guilty of visiting temples 'either on a journey or in the city' for the purposes of worship: *iudices* were to be fined fifteen pounds of gold as were their staffs if the latter had not attempted to prevent them. Lower fines would be levied on *consulares* (6 Roman pounds), *correctores* and *praesides* (4 Roman pounds).[315] Theodosius set out a code of behaviour for his officials which was designed to deny them the opportunity of expressing their non-Christian beliefs while they were in an official capacity. The same regulations were set out in a version of the same law which found its way to Evagrius, Augustal Prefect of Egypt and Romanus, Count of Egypt, in June of the same year.[316]

Next to the conversion of Constantine himself, the law of February 391 was the most significant legal point in the history of fourth-century Rome. Many scholars have pointed out that the law did not *prevent* cult acts taking place at Rome and on these grounds have sought to play down the significance of the measure.[317] This is, however, to miss the point. Theodosius I defined the central public acts of the state religion as illegal and henceforth such acts could be construed as acts of rebellion against the court. Unlike Constantius II, who had ordered much the same measures to be taken half a century previously, the Theodosian dynasty did not compromise or backtrack but followed up the law of Theodosius with a series of persecutory edicts designed to extinguish the ancient beliefs. Theodosius differed from Constantius in another important respect. Absent from Theodosius' measures are the chilling threats of death, replaced instead by fines, proscription, and the loss of status. The apparent humaneness of the punishments should not obscure the fact that Theodosius' laws made possible the systematic persecution of the old cults; a phenomenon that belongs to the fifth, not the fourth century.[318]

---

[314] Thus much more than a specific attack on 'des enterprises contra salutem principum' as argued by Gaudemet, art.cit. (n. 58), 459–60.

[315] For these magistracies, see B. Ward-Perkins, *From Classical Antiquity to the Middle Ages* (Oxford: Oxford University Press, 1984), 20–6.

[316] *CT* 16, 10, 11.

[317] Most recently and usefully by MacMullen, *Christianity and Paganism*, 24 f. See also McLynn, op. cit. (n. 248), 332–3. See also Gaudemet, art. cit. (n. 58), 460 ff, 463 ff.; K. W. Harl, 'Sacrifice and Pagan Belief in Fifth and Sixth Century Byzantium', *Past and Present*, 128 (1990), 7–27.

[318] For financial penalties, see MacMullen, *Christianity and Paganism*, 175 n.78.

CONCLUSION

The cults of paganism took a long time to die. This much has been accepted for many years. Less frequently acknowledged is the fact that there was little consistency in the attitudes of the emperors of the fourth century to the ancient cults. The rhetoric of annihilation is an indication of only a *single* element in the thinking of lawmakers, and it is simplistic to press it into service as 'policy'. There was no 'policy on paganism' eroding the legal status of the ancient cults with the accession of each new (Christian) emperor. There were, in fact, some notable discontinuities: Constantine as a tolerator of the cults was followed by his sons, who imposed clumsy bans which they themselves were forced to modify or ignore. The decision of Julian to move away from this stance is understandable but it is significant that his Christian successors did not emulate the early zealousness of Constantius. Significant changes were brought about by Gratian. Events of his reign have rightly been described as the 'disestablishment' of the old state religion, since the removal of the Pontifex Maximus himself and the privileges of the other priests left the cults as the choice of individuals rather than the religion of the state. It was left to Theodosius, however, to lay the foundations of a legal disqualification which would see the law turned effectively into an instrument of persecution.[319]

Altogether more striking is the unity of purpose in the war against magic and harmful divination, which links all the emperors of the fourth century, non-Christian and Christian alike, to their predecessors of the Principate.

[319] The first evidence for the *enforcement* of these fines occurs only in the sixth century. See MacMullen, *Christianity and Paganism*, 31.

6

Paganism, Christianity and the Imperial Celebrations in the Circus Maximus During the Fourth Century

INTRODUCTION

When the death of Constantine was announced at Rome in 337, a *iustitium*, a suspension of all legal and public business, was observed.[1] Eusebius gave an account of the distress in the city:

On the arrival of the news of the emperor's death in the imperial city, the Roman Senate and People felt the announcement as the heaviest and most afflictive of all calamities, and gave themselves up to an excess of grief. The baths and the markets were closed, the public spectacles and all the other recreations in which men of leisure are accustomed to indulge, were interrupted.[2]

What Eusebius certainly knew but did not record was the fact that the impact of the *iustitium* of 337 was heightened by the knowledge that the loss of the emperor was also felt by the deities worshipped in the city. The persistent presence of these deities in the rhythms of Roman life during the fourth century is the subject of this chapter.

The integration of the venues of public entertainment into the web of religious connotations was a fundamental part of the topography of the classical city. Cicero had observed that it was a world 'common to gods and men'.[3] This tradition of the civic intercourse between gods and men had also been discussed by Varro who isolated three prominent themes in pagan theology: the 'mythical' nature of the great poets'

---

[1] As was usual at imperial funerals. See D. Cannadine and S. R. F. Price (eds.), *Rituals of Royalty* (Cambridge: Cambridge University Press, 1987), 63 n. 8. For a later example of *iustitium* see *Carmen Contra Paganos* ll. 30–5.

[2] Eusebius, *Vita Constantini* 4, 69: Οἱ δὲ τὴν βασιλίδα πόλιν οἰκοῦντες αὐτῇ συγκλήτῳ καὶ δήμῳ Ῥωμαίων, ὡς τὴν βασιλέως ἐπέγνωσαν τελευτήν, δεινὴν καὶ πάσης συμφορᾶς ἐπέκεινα τὴν ἀκοὴν θέμενοι πένθος ἄσχετον ἐποιοῦντο. λουτρὰ δὴ ἀπεκλείετο καὶ ἀγοραὶ πάνδημοί τε θέαι καὶ πάνθ' ὅσα ἐπὶ ῥαστώνῃ βίου τοῖς εὐθυμουμένοις πράττειν ἔθος ἦν. (Trans. E. C. Richardson.) According to Eusebius, ibid., the Roman populace begged to be allowed to bury Constantine in the western capital.

[3] Cicero, *De Legibus* 1, 23: 'iam universus hic mundus una civitas communis deorum atque hominum sit existimanda.' Cf. *De Finibus* 3, 64. See MacMullen, *Christianity and Paganism*, 32; Markus, *End*, 141.

understanding, the 'physical' interpretation of philosophers, and the 'civil' aspect dear to the general public.[4] Augustine, in his onslaught against the ancient cults of Rome, attacked the distinction:

the gods who are laughed at in the theatres are the same as those adored in the temples, and the deities to whom you offer sacrifices are identical with those for whom you put on games.[5]

The debate on the nature of the public entertainments of the city was a debate about a landscape. Unfortunately the broad extent of this sacred landscape has been ignored in the modern treatments of the fate of paganism in Rome and other cities of the later Roman Empire. The result has been the positing of a narrow, élite, temple-based paganism, remote from the ordinary citizen and largely unsupported by him during its 'last revival'.[6] The traditional cults have often been understood to have given way to a mish-mash of external religious ideas and, as Barb argued notoriously in 1963, the 'refuse-heap' of magical and occult practice.[7]

More recently, Robert Markus has posed a challenging question for students of late paganism:

how 'pagan' were the festivals which were still being celebrated by Christians? Could it not be that there is substance behind the plea recounted in sermon after sermon according to which lay people saw no harm in enjoying 'secular' festivities to which they attached no religious significance? That, in other words, they recognized an implicit distinction between 'sacred' and 'secular'? Such questions are not answered by merely listing festivals found surviving in Christian calendars and labelling them 'pagan survivals', as if such survival proved anything. What is needed is searching investigation of what exactly the celebration of such festivals involved, and what those—pagans as well as Christians—who took part in them thought they were doing, and what those who tried to prohibit participation in them accused them of doing.[8]

[4] Augustine, *De Civitate Dei* 6, 6.

[5] 'nec alii dii derideantur in theatris, quam qui adorantur in templis, nec aliis ludos exhibeatis, quam quibus victimas immolatis.' Ibid. (trans. H. Bettenson). For the development of Augustine's ideas on the entertainments see R. Markus, 'Die *spectacula* als religiöses Konfliktfeld städtischen Lebens in der Spätantike', *Freiburger Zeitschrift für Philosophie und Theologie*, 38 (1991), 253–71; id., *End*, 107 ff. For Greek parallels, MacMullen, *Christianity and Paganism*, 184 n. 37.

[6] See H. R. Bloch, 'The Pagan Revival in the West at the End of the Fourth Century', in Momigliano, *Conflict*, 193–218; J. J. O'Donnell, 'The Demise of Paganism', *Traditio*, 35 (1979), 43–88; Croke and Harries, *Conflict*, 52–72 with further references; N. B. McLynn, *Ambrose of Milan* (Berkeley: California University Press, 1993), 341–60; A. Cameron, 'Forschungen zum Thema der heidnischen Reaktion in der Literatur seit 1943', in A. and E. Alföldi, and C. L. Clay (eds.), *Die Kontorniat-Medallions*, (Berlin: De Gruyter, 1990), ii. 63–74.

[7] A. A. Barb, 'The Survival of the Magic Arts', in Momigliano, *Conflict*, 100–25, at 100. See the important review of the book by P. Brown, *JRS*, 54 (1964), 207.

[8] Markus, *End*, 110.

The present chapter attempts to make a contribution to the answer to Markus' question by assessing the frequently overlooked religious atmosphere of the most important type of popular entertainment in late antique Rome: the spectacles at the Circus Maximus.[9] The use of the latter by Christian emperors constitutes an area of key interest to this study, since it illustrates some of the techniques used to ensure the continuity of civic institutions of greatest political importance.

In his impressive monograph, Michael McCormick studied the imperial victory celebrations of the later Roman Empire.[10] He concluded that there was a close continuity between victory celebrations of the Principate and those of the later era, successfully demonstrating that victory celebrations did not disappear altogether, as had once been thought.[11] But beneath the continuity, there was also evidence of considerable change:

the 'new' empire witnessed an extraordinary resurgence in the frequency and import of imperial victory festivals . . . [there occurred a] relentless change in their number, nature and identity within the context of overall continuity.[12]

He also pointed out that the influence of Christianity on the celebrations was muted and late; Christian bishops are known to have played some part in the festivities associated with the Persian victory of Constantius II in 343 but are first attested as offering masses of thanksgiving only after Theodosius' victory over Eugenius at the battle of the River Frigidus in 394.[13]

McCormick then posited two phases in the 'Christianization' of the victory ceremonies. He believed that the pagan elements in the celebrations were 'neutralized', before being replaced by explicitly Christian practices.[14] The crucial rejection of the pagan character of the traditional commemorations was the refusal of Constantine to ascend the Capitol in either 312 or 315:[15]

---

[9] For other types of *ludi* in general, see Salzman, *On Roman Time*, 116 ff.; L. Polverini, 'Ludi', in *Diz. epigr. di antich. romane* 4.63 (Rome: Tipografia della R. Accademia dei Lincei, 1975), 2006–9. For the church and theatrical shows, W. Weismann, *Kirche und Schauspiele* (Würzburg: Augustinus-Verlag, 1972) is still fundamental. For attitudes towards gladiatorial games, see G. Ville, 'Les Jeux de gladiateurs dans l'empire chrétien', *Mélanges d'archéologie et d'histoire*, 72 (1960), 273–335.

[10] M. McCormick, *Eternal Victory* (Cambridge: Cambridge University Press, 1986).

[11] For example by J. Kollwitz, *Oströmische Plastik der theodosianischen Zeit*, Studien zur spätantiken Kunstgeschichte, 12 (Berlin: DeGruyter, 1941), 63–6.

[12] McCormick, op. cit. (n. 10), 35.

[13] Constantius: Athanasius, *Historia Arianorum* 16, 2; Theodosius: Ambrose, *Ep.* 61.

[14] McCormick, op. cit. (n. 10), 101 ff.

[15] See above pp. 72–5.

Thanks to Constantine's innovation and its observance by his successors, imperial victory celebrations at Rome appear strangely neutral in the midst of an empire whose ideology increasingly relied on its religious content.[16]

The reason why McCormick perceived the celebrations of victory under the Christian emperors at Rome as 'strangely neutral' was because he had defined the pagan elements of those ceremonies too narrowly. He conceded that non-religious elements did remain in the ceremonies at Rome but maintained that the pagan occupation of the Urban Prefecture during the important celebrations of 312, 357, and 389 explained this.[17] Such an interpretation of the Christian emperors passively disregarding the activities of the non-Christians in Rome has convinced many who have looked no further into the matter. But the archaeological and legal evidence already examined suggests rather more: that emperors were acutely aware of the importance of Rome and its rituals. Constantine demonstrated an understanding of the imperial cult in his response to Hispellum and in his impact on the city-centre he showed himself to be both a shrewd politician and, for the most part, a respecter of Roman traditions. Emperors were, in fact, less distant from the city than scholars such as McCormick think and through their use of the festival calendar in particular they maintained a close contact with the Roman community massed in the city's largest venue for entertainment.

I. THE FESTIVAL CALENDAR

A fascinating dossier of documents and illustrations attributed to 'the Chronographer of 354' has survived from the middle of the fourth century.[18] Included in the collection are documents of an explicitly Christian character, for example the so-called *Feriale Ecclesiae Romanae*, the *Liber Generationis*, and the so-called 'Liberian Catalogue'. On the other hand, the two Regionary Catalogues, the Consular *Fasti*, and especially the festival calendar show that the compiler did not restrict himself to Christian material. An elaborately illuminated dedication appears to have offered the work to a certain 'Valentinus', identified by

---

[16] McCormick, op. cit. (n. 10), 101–2. Cf. A. Macarone, 'L'allestimento dei giochi annuali a Roma nel IV secolo d. C.: aspetti economici e ideologici', *Annali della Scuola Normale Superiore di Pisa*, serie 3, 11.1 (1981), 105–22. At 106: 'cioè proprio quelle relative ai gruppi di giochi in cui l'aspetto religioso è puramente formale mentre rilievo decisivo ha quello politico.' [17] McCormick, op. cit. (n. 10), 103.

[18] The most up-to-date treatment is Salzman, *On Roman Time*; see also A. Degrassi, *Inscriptiones Italicae*, 13, pt. 2, (Rome: Istituto Poligrafico dello Stato, 1963), 237–62 with *commentarii diurni* at 388–546 (hereafter Degrassi, *II*). The entry for April translated in M. Beard, J. North, and S. R. F. Price, *Religions of Rome* (Cambridge: Cambridge University Press, 1998), ii. no. 3.3d with *feriale ecclesiae romanae* at no. 3.6. The full collection (minus the texts of some documents, notably the calendar) also *MGH* (AA) 9, 13–148 and Mommsen's edition of the calendar is in *CIL* 1 (2nd edn., 1893), 254–82.

Mommsen as the *Dux* of Illyricum in 359 and more recently by Michelle Salzman as Avianius Valentinus, brother of Q. Aurelius Symmachus.[19] Two facts, in addition to the tentative identification of Valentinus, lead to the conclusion that the date of the compilation is the early part of the reign of Constantius II.[20] First, the list of *Natales Caesarum* records:

D(omini) N(ostri) Constanti VII IDV AUG[21]

indicating that Constantius II (337–61) was the reigning emperor. Second, the festival calendar, which, as we shall see, studiously recorded events of significance in the reign of Constantius II, does not have any entry commemorating his *adventus* to the city of Rome in 357. The festival calendar would seem, therefore, to predate this event.

Something must be said, finally, of the scribe responsible for the original calligraphy. The *dedicatio* page includes the signature of the illustrator:

Furius Dionysius Filocalus titulavit.[22]

It is likely that this was the same Philocalus who worked so closely with bishop Damasus in this period neatly illustrating that the professional man of the fourth century could find himself dealing with highly placed clerics and lay noblemen.[23]

The Festival Calendar contained in the collection of the 'Chronographer' is a fourth-century version of the ancient record of the sacred festivals and holidays observed in the city of Rome. Early commentators on the text believed that the ancient ceremonies had become neutralized and were largely devoid of any religious significance.[24] But since the work of H. Stern (1953) and the important book by Michelle Salzman (1990), the religious elements evident in the calendar have been firmly re-established as fourth-century realities: 'the evidence is convincing that the text of the calendar of 354 reflects contemporary cult practice and the civic round of holidays still celebrated in the mid-fourth-century city.'[25] These great pagan festivals do not concern us directly here, but are crucially important as the ever-present *context* within which the imperial festivals occurred.[26]

The rationale behind the staging of the imperial festivals under the Christian emperors was the same as that of the preceding centuries.

[19] Degrassi, *II*, 237; Salzman, *On Roman Time*, Appendix V.
[20] See ibid.   [21] *CIL* i (2nd edn.), 255.
[22] See Salzman, *On Roman Time*, fig. 1.   [23] Ibid. 25 ff.; See p. 148 above.
[24] Chiefly Wissowa, Mommsen, and Ferrua. For a discussion of their ideas see H. Stern, *Le calendrier de 354: étude sur son texte et ses illustrations* (Paris: Guenther, 1953), 94 ff.; Salzman, *On Roman Time*, 11 ff.
[25] Ibid. 117 n. 3. Cf. Markus, *End*, 107 ff. See Stern, op. cit. (n. 24), 107.
[26] For a full discussion of these festivals see Salzman, *On Roman Time*, ch. 4.

The emperors wished to associate their names, achievements and fortune with the social groups served by the festivals themselves. A rare fragment of a third-century Roman calendar from Dura-Europus, for example, shows that the essential core of festivals were observed empire-wide and could be modified to suit a frontier garrison.[27] The same was certainly true for Rome, where the grandest venues for entertaining the *populus* were utilized.

In the calendar of 354, the imperial festivals celebrated demonstrated the traditional desire to promote the imperial *dynasty*. Constantius II sought to associate himself with his illustrious father and for that reason Constantine's special actions continued to be remembered under the reign of his son. The dynastic profile of the calendar is indicated also by what is not included among the festivals: any reference to the unfortunate brothers of the reigning *Augustus*, Fl. Iulius Crispus (d. 326), Constantine II (d. 340), and Constans (d. 350), who have disappeared from the record and were certainly once there.

Days celebrating previous emperors and their achievements as well as other events of outstanding importance in Roman history add up to twenty-three. Those marking the life and achievements of the family of Constantine the Great and Constantius II amount to seventy-one.[28] Though one ought not to compare the military calendar of Dura-Europus too closely with that of Philocalus, one can with some confidence discuss their treatment of dynastic festivals. Including the *vota publica* of 3 January, the days associated with the reigning dynasty commemorated in the substantial surviving portion of the third-century document number eight.[29] Those on which some festival associated with an earlier emperor is mentioned total seven; a suggestive ratio.[30] Degrassi, in his edition of the calendar of Philocalus, commented:

In the age of the emperor Constantine and his family, with the desire for spectacles and the flattery of emperors increasing, games increased *ad infinitum*; of this trend the most beautiful and faithful evidence we possess is the Filocalian calendar of AD 354.[31]

---

[27] R. O. Fink, A. S. Hoey, and W. F. Snyder, 'The Feriale Duranum', *YCS*, 7 (1940), 1–222, at 202 ff. At 173–4 and 203 they point out that the presence of festivals associated with the imperial cult (27 out of 41 entries) does not show particular importance of the emperor's relationship with the army, but rather the growth of such festivals at the expense of the traditional ceremonies. The possibility still exists, however, *pace* 173 n. 800, that the Dura calendar had a definite shape precisely because the settlement served as a military outpost. See Salzman, *On Roman Time*, 132.

[28] Stern, op. cit. (n. 24), 70. Salzman, *On Roman Time*, 120 says that ninety-eight days were devoted to the 'imperial cult'.

[29] 3, 11, 28 January; 4 February; 13, 14 March; 7 May; 26 June.

[30] 24 January; 6 March; 26 April; 24 May; 12 July; 1 August; 23 September.

[31] Degrassi, *II*, 373: 'Aetate imperatoris Constantini eiusque familiae, spectaculorum

That representation was comprehensive. The anniversaries of the birthdays of emperors was marked by the designation 'Dies Natalis'. Claudius Gothicus (10 May), Constantine's alleged imperial ancestor, Constantius Chlorus (31 March), Constantine himself (27 February) and Constantius II (7 August) were all indicated.[32] For three of these four (excluding Claudius Gothicus), the pattern of the celebrations was the same. The day itself was marked by *ludi circenses* (twenty-four races) and the following day by *ludi votivi*.[33] These votive games were offered to no other imperial family in the calendar. Their significance would seem to be explicitly pagan, that is, *ludi* offered to the traditional gods of the state in fulfilment of a vow decreed, presumably, by the senate.[34]

In the third-century calendar from Dura-Europos, no imperial festival lasted longer than one day with the possible exception of the anniversary of the acclamation of Severus Alexander as emperor which fell on 13–14 March.[35] In the Calendar of 354, the designation 'Dies Natalis' also marked the days upon which members of the Constantinian house had attained the imperial rank (as *Caesar* or *Augustus*), thus replacing the old 'Dies Imperii' or 'Principatus'.[36] Stern suggested that the late antique concept of such an accession as a 'natalis' owed something to the influence of ideas of rebirth prevalent in the great oriental cults of the era:

Le nouveau prince change de nature, il sort du monde humain et naît à celui des Augustes . . . Depuis 293, aucune fiction ne maintient plus l'idée que l'empereur est l'élu du sénat et de l'armée. Son élévation à la dignité de César est un fait religieux.[37]

The *natalis* of Constantine the Great (in 306) was marked (25 July) as was that of Constantius II (November 324, on 8 November).[38] It is noteworthy that once again, the day itself was the occasion of *circenses*, while the day following saw *ludi votivi*. It may be that the *natalis* combined some element of hope for the 'birth' of a new era, but it cannot be forgotten that in the same document precisely this designa-

cupiditate imperatorumque adulatione crescentibus, ludi in infinitum creverunt, cuius rei pulcherrimum fidissimumque testimonium habemus fastos Filocalianos a.354.'

[32] Claudius Gothicus: Degrassi, *II*, 247 and 455–6; Constantius Chlorus: ibid. 243 and 433; Constantine I: ibid. 241 and 417; Constantius II: ibid. 253 and 492.

[33] 'Ludi [votivi]' to be restored after 1 April: Stern, op. cit. (n. 24), 71–4.

[34] W. Eisenhut, 'Votum', in *PW*, Suppl., 14 (1974), 964–73. Cf. the 'votorum nuncupatio' of 3 January: Degrassi, *II*, 239. The *vota* were finally abolished in 692 at the council of Trullo: Degrassi, *II*, 391.

[35] See Fink, Hoey, and Snyder, art. cit. (n. 27), 43. Nor did celebrations usually outlast the dynasty which instituted them, see Salzman, *On Roman Time*, 138; 141.

[36] The *Feriale Duranum* had included the *natales imperii* of five dead emperors. See Salzman, *On Roman Time*, 139. [37] Stern, op. cit. (n. 24), 78–9.

[38] Constantine: Degrassi, *II*, 251; Constantius II: ibid. 259.

tion marked the *natales* of the temples of the great pagan gods such as Hercules (1 February), Mars (1 March), and particularly interesting is the 'Natalis Urbis [Romae]' on 21 April.[39] The festival calendar thus self-consciously used the same designations for its traditional gods, *divi*, and reigning Christian emperors.

A fascinating and distinctively late antique presence in the Festival Calendar of the city of Rome are the recorded arrivals (*adventus*) and departure (*profectio*) of Constantine the Great at the city during his reign.[40] Three arrivals and one 'setting out' were commemorated.[41] The manner in which the *adventus* is recorded is uniform:

Adventus D(ivi) [Constantini] C(ircenses) M(issus) XXIIII

And again, the *adventus* anniversary was followed by *ludi votivi* on the day following. These games had probably been vowed for the safe conduct of the emperor to the imperial city.

The *adventus* of 29 October celebrated the arrival of Constantine in the city after the Battle of the Milvian Bridge in 312.[42] The 28th has been marked with the explicitly political designation 'Evictio Tyranni' illustrating that the Constantinian demolition of Maxentius examined above found expression also in the festival calendar.[43] Salzman suggested that *ludi votivi* were not staged to commemorate victories over Maxentius and Licinius because the victories had been won over Roman citizens but we have seen with Constantine that such considerations did not dampen victory celebrations.[44]

The sole *profectio* entry comes on 27 September and is a reference to the departure of Constantine after his *decennalia* celebrations in 315.[45] The absence of *ludi votivi* after the day puzzled Stern, who restored them to the text.[46] It may be suggested that the city would deem it indiscreet to appear to beg the gods for the emperor's *departure* but the traditional *ludi circenses* were still staged on this day. A further problem is posed by the apparent absence of the other two *profectiones*, those

[39] Hercules: Degrassi, *II*, 241 and 405–6; Mars: ibid. 243 and 417–19; Urbs Roma: ibid. 245 and 443–5. For *natalis* as a generic term applied to any anniversary, see Salzman, *On Roman Time*, 119 with n. 12 and also pp. 126–7.

[40] For the ceremony of *adventus* see S. MacCormack, *Art and Ceremony in Late Antiquity* (Berkeley: University of California Press, 1981), 17–89.

[41] Constantine I: 18 July (in 315, on the occasion of his *decennalia*); 21 July (in 326, for his *vicennalia*). See Degrassi, *II*, 251 and 484–5. For 29 October see n. 42.

[42] Degrassi, *II*, 257 and 527.

[43] See my discussion of Constantine and the centre of Rome above, 76–90.

[44] Salzman, *On Roman Time*, 141 but see Ammianus 16, 10, 1–3 and Matthews, *Ammianus*, 233–4.

[45] Degrassi, *II*, 255 and 514–15. See also Seeck, *Regesten*, 164.

[46] Stern, op. cit. (n. 24), 73.

which must have occurred in 313 and 326. It is just possible that the departure of 326 may have occurred on the same day as the anniversary of the departure of 315, though a redating of some texts in the *Codex Theodosianus* would have to follow. Mommsen suggested that the departure in 326 took place some time after 8 September.[47] The most satisfactory solution to the problem would seem to be to restore the missing entries to the text.

Imperial journeys away from the city of Rome were commonly to some frontier campaign, and it is the record of success in these campaigns that constitutes the most substantial Constantinian contribution to the festival calendar. Eight separate military victories were commemorated. A familiar pattern structured the festivities: a number of days of *ludi* climaxed in a day of *ludi circenses* which marked the actual day of victory:[48]

Games (*Ludi*)	Anniversary date	Victor and date of victory
Gothici	4–9 February	Constantine over the Goths in 332
Maximati	4–9 May	Constantine
Persici	13–17 May	Constantius II
Francici	15, 16, 17, 19, 20 July*	Constantius II in 342
Triumphales	18, 20, 21, 22 September*	Constantine over Licinius in 324
Alamannici	5–10 October	Constantine who bears the title *Alamannicus* after 331 (*CIL* 3, 7000)
Sarmatici	25 November–1 December	Constantine in 332(?)
Lancionici	12, 13, 14, 16, 17, 18 December*	Constantine

* The imperial festivals could be interrupted by other festivities, according to the evidence of the calendar.

In the entire festival year, only the *Ludi Apollinares* (5–13 July) and the *Ludi Cerealici* (12–19 April) lasted longer than the longest of these imperial commemorations. In marked contrast, the remains of the calendar from Dura-Europos, specifically designed for military use, made reference to only one victory festival and not even of the reigning emperor:

[47] *CIL* 1 (2nd edn.), 322.

[48] Only two victory *ludi* predate the Constantinian house: 'Victorias Sarmaticas' (27 July) and 'Victorias Marcomannas' (30 July). They are marked by only a single day's festivities. See Salzman, *On Roman Time*, 138.

28 January: The Arabian, Adiabenic, and very great Parthian victories of the deified Severus, and the accession of the deified Trajan.[49]

One of the most interesting features of the imperial celebrations was the ease with which they could be coupled with other festivals, especially those of previous emperors, falling on the same day. For example, 18 September is marked by the entry:

N(atalis) Traiani. Triumphales. C(ircenses) M(issus) XLVIII[50]

a pattern that is repeated for 8 November, the *natalis* of both Nerva and Constantius.[51]

It is, of course, no accident that the Constantinian festivals found their way into the ritual calendar of the fourth century. This is because of the nature of the calendar itself. Feasts inaugurated by former emperors slipped out of the 'official' list, names of festivals changed and entirely new celebrations were introduced. Mary Beard has discussed some very important features of the ancient Roman religious calendar, ideas which point towards the efficacy of the calendar as a means for portraying the reigning imperial house.[52] She analysed the survival of ancient religious festivals into periods when the passage of time and changing circumstances had made comprehension of the *original* ritual difficult. Thus the relationship between one festival and any other in ancient Rome was much less direct than that between the important festivals celebrated, for example, in Christianity. In the Christian calendar, the elements derive a great deal of their intelligibility from their relationship to other feasts in the same cycle, a cycle which is based upon the annual evocation of the life of Christ, from birth through to his death and resurrection, a 'syntagmatic' relationship.

In contrast, Beard suggested that intelligibility in the Roman religious calendar derived from an awareness of one or many *associations* of 'opposition or similarity' prompted by any or all ritual elements in the festival being attended, a 'paradigmatic' relationship; that is to say, not through their position relative to any *sequence* of feasts in the calendar at any given time. Hence the ease with which festivals in the Roman ritual calendar could be piled one on top of the other, multiplying the possible associations which might provide 'meaning':

[49] *YCS* 7 (1940), 41, 43: 'v k[a]l(endas) [feb]rarias ob v[i]ctori[as arabicam et adiabenicam et parthica]m maxim[a]m divi seve[ri e]t ob [imperium divi traiani, victoriae part]hic[a]e.' (Trans. Lewis and Reinhold.)

[50] Degrassi, *II*, 255.

[51] Degrassi, *II*, 259.

[52] M. Beard, 'A Complex of Times: No More Sheep on Romulus' Birthday', *Proceedings of the Cambridge Philological Society*, NS 33 (1987), 1–16.

It was precisely the Roman calendar's reliance on building up associations and images on a paradigmatic model outside any determining narrative that gave the individual festival a fluid meaning in relation to the others in the sequence.[53]

'Natural' historical time could therefore be set aside in the ritual calendar, in favour of an appeal to 'a pageant of what it was to be "Roman"'.[54] The feasts at which we have looked show that Constantine had tapped into a reservoir of as much or as little Roman history and greatness as those participating in his festivals cared to evoke.

The portrayal of the emperor and his family in the calendar reveals an area of great interest to all emperors. The ancestry of the house of Constantine as well as its successful future were represented here. Above all, an emperor had to be seen to be fit to rule. The transition of power along smooth lines of merit did not suit the age. A blooming imperial family seemed to promise continuity and security, and this is precisely what was portrayed.

Another crucial aspect of imperial 'fitness' was the 'constitutional' legitimacy of the reigning emperor's claim to the throne, that is, the reasons other than his competence at waging war for his occupation of the seat of power. In the calendar we see Constantine address the question decisively. On one hand the presence of an imperial antecedent suggested that imperial rule ran in his blood. On the other, former emperors at Rome were depicted as being singularly *un*fit for power. Hence, 28 October was marked by the words 'evictio tyranni' and the 3rd July by 'fugato Licinio (C[ircenses] M[issus] XXIIII)'.

But the security of the empire had the most important bearing on the 'fitness' of any individual for the throne. Tradition had hardened the format of letters dispatched to the senate and people of Rome:

to the consuls, praetors, *tribuni plebis*, and their own senate, greeting. If you and your children are well, it is well. We and our armies are well.[55]

The presence of the military achievements of Constantine in the calendar told the people under Rome (and outside) just that: Constantine and his armies were well. The victories and the celebrations which marked those successes belonged, however, where they had always belonged: to the people who called themselves 'Roman'.

The importance, success, and popularity of the great festivals of the

[53] Beard, art. cit. 8. An interesting exception to this is the cycle of Isiac feasts in the calendar of 354. Here I am concerned only with the imperial festivals. For the Isiac festivals, see Salzman, *On Roman Time*, 164 ff.

[54] Ibid. (n. 52), 12.

[55] *AE* (1934), no. 158: 'consulibus praetoribus tribunis plebis senatui suo salutem dicunt si vos liberique vestri valetis bene est nos exercitusque nostri valemus.' A Constantinian letter. See Millar, *ERW*, 354–5.

calendar explains the notable reticence of the fourth-century Roman church to compete with them. As we saw, fourth-century Rome witnessed no Christian attempt to impinge architecturally upon the major venues of popular entertainment.[56] Apologists attempted to draw a contrast between the *locus* of Christian celebration at shrines of the martyrs and the life of the ancient city within the walls. Jerome, writing in 403, described the Christian throng visiting the catacombs as a transformation of the city itself: 'the city is moved from its foundations...'[57] A theme which Prudentius enhanced by concentrating on the dissolution of social barriers, so observable at the traditional entertainments, before the graves of the martyrs.[58] But only two significant dates in the fourth-century Christian calendar of Rome coincide with pagan festivals. On 22 February, a Christian feast was held 'Natale Petri de Cathedra', the same day as the Caristia/Cara Cognatio.[59] Piétri was in no doubt that the coincidence was deliberate:

Dans un calcul qui mêle le souci pastoral à la propagande, Rome aurait choisi l'anniversaire de la *cara cognatio* pour souligner les liens de filiation entre l'Église et son fondateur.[60]

The 25 December, the day of a large number of races at the Circus in honour of Sol, was recorded in the *depositio martyrum* with the phrase 'natus Christus in Betleem Iudeae'.[61] But these Christian festivals were exceptional. Most of the *natales martyrum* were concentrated between July and September but none occurred on the same day as any pagan celebrations. As Pietri put it:

L'Église ne s'occupait guère de christianiser des cérémonies condamnés, mais elle pouvait chercher par souci pastoral, à populariser plus particulièrement les anniversaires qui détournaient les fidèles du cirque et de ses pompes.[62]

---

[56] The only suggestion is the juxtaposition of the church of Sant'Anastasia with the Circus Maximus. For the former, see 142–4 above.

[57] Jerome *Ep.* 107, 1: 'movetur urbs sedibus suis.' See P. Brown, *The Cult of the Saints* (Chicago: University of Chicago Press, 1981), 8, 40–5.

[58] *Peristeph.* 2, 191–2; 199–202. See P. Brown, 'Dalla "Plebs Romana" alla "Plebs Dei": Aspetti della cristianizzazione di Roma', in P. Brown, P. Cracco Ruggini, and M. Mazza, *Governanti e intelletualli. Popolo di Dio I-IV secolo*, Passatopresente, 2 (Turin: Giappichelli, 1982), 123–45, at 131 f.; id., op. cit. (n. 57), 41 ff.

[59] See Piétri, *RC*, i, 381 ff. Th. Klauser thought that 'cathedra' in the Christian ceremony might have derived from the empty seat traditionally provided for absent friends at the Caristia: *Die Cathedra im Totenkult* (Münster: Aschendorff, 1971), 153–83. See Salzman, *On Roman Time*, 47.   [60] Piétri, *RC* i, 388.

[61] No place of celebration was indicated, although pope Liberius may have held the earliest recorded Christmas liturgy at Saint Peter's basilica: Ambrose, *De Virg.* 3, 1.

[62] Piétri, *RC*, i, 618. A view repeated in id., 'La Roma cristiana', in A. Schiavone (ed.), *Storia di Roma 3*: L'Età tardoantica 1: Crisi e trasformazione* (Turin: Einaudi, 1993), 697–721, at 705.

Some idea of the difficulty involved in carrying out the task may be gained from a closer investigation of the circus entertainments themselves.

2. THE IMPORTANCE OF THE CIRCUS GAMES

Degrassi points out that there were some 177 days of *ludi* annually.[63] These *ludi* were held in theatres, the city's amphitheatre, and, on sixty-six days a year (an average of five per month), in the Circus Maximus.[64] It is with the activities which took place in the Circus that we are concerned here. According to the calendar of 354, the average number of races staged on any one of the sixty-six days was twenty-four. Thus, the race-going public at Rome in the mid-fourth century had approximately 1,584 races staged for its entertainment annually. These were official *ludi aeterni* and could be supplemented, as we have seen, by more celebrations arising out of imperial *adventus*, victories, or accessions.

The circus races were the most popular and prestigious of all the popular entertainments.[65] When the emperors were present in the city of Rome, they made a point of presiding at the games in the circus held in their honour.[66] When the emperors were absent, the circus games marked the climax to both the imperial victory festivals which lasted for more than one day and also the ancient pagan celebrations associated with the most prominent deities.[67]

With the exception of the dubious relationship between the Christian emperors and gladiatorial shows,[68] legislation of the period shows the immense pressure on the civic administrations of the empire to produce games of all kinds and indicates their continuing importance. Under Constantine, for example, the age of eligible *quaestores*, who

[63] Degrassi, *II*, 373. Salzman, *On Roman Time*, 120 points out that of course attendance was not compulsory or universal and the courts of the city did not shut for 177 days annually.

[64] Naturally the *ludi* could take a number of forms: *venationes*, *munera*, and chariot races are all known to have been held in the Circus Maximus. See chapter 1 above.

[65] See Salzman, *On Roman Time*, 119–20.

[66] McCormick, op. cit. (n. 10), 35–46. For emperors presiding over circus games: *Panegyrici Latini* 12 (9), 19, 6 (Constantine); Ammianus 16, 10, 13–14 (Constantius II); Ammianus 21, 10, 1–2 (Julian at Antioch); Claudian, *De VI Consulatu Honorii* 611–39 (Honorius).

[67] See Salzman, *On Roman Time*, ch. 4.

[68] See Ville, art. cit. (n. 9); Macarone, art. cit. (n. 16), 109 ff; B. Ward-Perkins, *From Classical Antiquity to the Middle Ages: Urban Public Building in Northern and Central Italy AD 300–850* (Oxford: Oxford University Press, 1984), 95 for epigraphical evidence of the performance of gladiatorial games in the fourth century. For the imperial cult at Hispellum, see above, pp. 180–1.

gave games in December, was affirmed to Julianus, Prefect of the City, as not less than twenty years in March 327.[69] But almost exactly two years later, in a letter to the same man, the minimum age was reduced to sixteen years.[70]

As the century progressed, minimum and maximum expenses were stipulated for the games-sponsors (*editores*) of Rome and Constantinople.[71] Under Constantius II the Praetorian Prefect Mecilius Hilarianus was instructed that *nobilissimi* were to be *forced* to come to Rome in order to give their *ludi*.[72] Orfitus, Prefect of the City of Rome in March 354, was informed by the emperor that those who failed to present themselves at their games were to be fined 'in accordance with the sacred laws of Constantine *Divus*'.[73] And by 357, the members of the senate could be addressed directly and threatened with detection in Achaea, Macedonia, and Illyricum if they had not yet acted as *editores*.[74] In January 370, Q. Clodius Hermogenianus, Prefect of the City, received an extraordinary imperial constitution. Constantine had ruled that if an incumbent *praetor* died, leaving only female heirs, they were not obliged to undertake and fulfil his duties. The Constantinian decision was now altered:

according to the hereditary portion of each person, you shall provide that such women shall be compelled to undertake the duties that were assigned to their fathers.[75]

The duties in question were chiefly the production of games. In a letter to the Prefect of the City, Valerianus, written in February 381, the interference of private individuals with horses designated for the *ludi circenses* was addressed by the emperors:

If any horses for the customary contests are furnished by the liberality of Our Clemency or by the liberality of various magistrates of the Most August Order,

[69] *CT* 6, 4, 2. *PLRE* I, 474 for Anicius Julianus.

[70] *CT* 6, 4, 1. Seeck, *Regesten*, 179 for amended date.

[71] Minimum amounts at Constantinople: *CT* 6, 4, 5 (340); 6, 4, 13 (361); 6, 4, 33 (398 or 399). For careful arrangement of *editores* at Constantinople see *CT* 6, 4, 20 (372); 6, 4, 25 (384). Rome: *CT* 6, 4, 23 (June 373) could refer to games. Note the concern of Symmachus that he should not upstage Stilicho with his son's praetorian games in 401: *Ep*. 4, 8. See also Symmachus, *Relatio* 8, 1 for his attestation of an expenditure ceiling (384). See J. A. McGeachy, *Quintus Aurelius Symmachus and the Senatorial Aristocracy of the West*, Ph. D. diss. Chicago (1942), 104–5; Macarone, art. cit. (n. 16).

[72] *CT* 6, 4, 4. See the important note on Hilarianus at *PLRE* I, 433.

[73] See nn. 72, 69 and 70. Also *CT* 6, 4, 18 (June 365) for reference to a law fining *editores* for being absent while games for which they were responsible were being staged.   [74] *CT* 6, 4, 11.

[75] Ibid. 17: 'verum etiam feminas hereditario iure succedentes advenire.' (Trans. C. Pharr.)

Our Serenity decrees that they shall be provided in great number, so that if any horses are assembled that are glorious in the number of prizes or noble by the reason of victories celebrated on both sides, they shall rather serve the spectacles for the populace than be assigned to any advantage and gain.[76]

By Symmachus' day, a special board of senators, the *censuales*, were on hand to receive the cash and stage the shows of such reluctant provincials.[77]

Naturally enough, since most of the circus races were connected with state festivals, the treasury covered the costs. Nevertheless, the imperial family could intervene directly to ensure the smooth running of the entertainments. In January 371 the emperors dispatched a letter to P. Ampelius, then Prefect of the City, assuring him that state funds would be diverted to the upkeep of the finest racehorses.[78] In August 372 a constitution shows that something of a crisis had descended upon the city of Rome and its games. The senate had asked that two or three of the candidates for the quaestorship or praetorship, 'should be able to be associated with the *arca*'.[79] This request for financial assistance was apparently accepted in the interests of maintaining the games. An interesting note was added, however, that those who wished to continue to spend large sums on the games could of course do so.

The capacity of some of the wealthier members of the senatorial aristocracy to put on sumptuous shows even into the fifth century is well known. Olympiodorus claims that Symmachus lavished 2,000 pounds of gold on his son's praetorian games in 401.[80] In the letters of Symmachus one can catch a glimpse of the importance of the production of games for these wealthy Roman families. He mentions the competition between *editores* and refers to the *plebs* as a demanding audience.[81] Other literary material points to the immense popularity of the circus games. Ammianus, in his scathing attack on the life and manners of the fourth-century city, included a passage on the commons:

[76] *CT* 15, 7, 6: 'Equos, quos ad sollemne certamen vel mansuetudinis nostrae largitio subministrat vel diversorum ex amplissimo ordine magistratuum, hactenus ad copiam providendos serenitas nostra decrevit, ut, quidquid illud est, quod palmarum numero gloriosum et celebratis utrimque victoriis nobile congregatur, spectaculis potius urbanae plebis inserviat quam praedae adque compendio deputetur.'

[77] Symmachus, *Ep.* 4, 8, 3. See Jones, *LRE*, 538; 707.

[78] *CT* 15, 10, 1. Chastagnol, *Fastes*, no. 71; *PLRE* I, 56–7.

[79] *CT* 6, 4, 21: 'qui nominantur candidati arcae.'

[80] R. C. Blockley, *The Fragmentary Classicising Historians of the Later Roman Empire*, (Liverpool: Cairns, 1983), ii. 205–6. See also McGeachy, op. cit. (n. 71), 55–6 and Jones, *LRE*, 537–8.

[81] Symmachus *Ep.* 4, 63.

it is most remarkable to see an innumerable crowd of plebeians . . . hanging on the outcome of the chariot races. Their temple, their dwelling, their assembly, and the height of all their hopes is the Circus Maximus.[82]

The popular passion for the races is further exemplified by the tale told by a scandalized Ammianus of some notorious cases of magic at the circus or involving charioteers.[83] Apronianus, the one-eyed Prefect of the City (362–4), waged a personal war against magic:

more than once during the races in the amphitheatre, while throngs of people were crowding in, he investigated the greatest crimes.[84]

And Ammianus also records a near lynching of another Prefect, Leontius (355–6), following the arrest of the charioteer Philoromus in 355.[85]

The evidence for the attractions of the circus races is not, of course, confined to non-Christians. When Constantius II decided to recall the exiled bishop of Rome, Liberius, in 357, he made his announcement in the circus (Maximus), according to Theodoret.[86] One of the accusations made against the controversial successor to Liberius was that he was attended by a vicious band:

Then Damasus enticed with lies arena-attendants, charioteers, and catacomb-tunnellers and the whole clergy and with axes, swords, and cudgels he besieged the basilica.[87]

And in Jerome's fascinating story of the life of Saint Hilarion, he tells of the means by which many non-Christians living in the city of Gaza were converted, when the holy man intervened on the side of a racing team owned by a local Christian.[88]

We have seen that the imperial victory festivals climaxed in the

---

[82] Ammianus 14, 6, 26; 28, 4, 29: 'Et est admodum mirum videre plebem innumeram . . . e dimicationum curulium eventu pendentem. . .eisque templum et habitaculum et contio et cupitorum spes omnis circus est maximus.' (Trans. J. C. Rolfe.)

[83] Charioteers: Ammianus 15, 7, 2; 26, 3, 1–3 (Hilarinus); 28, 1, 27; 28, 4, 25; 29, 3, 5 (note Athanasius as the apparently Christian name of the charioteer). See also for example *CT* 9, 16, 11 among a number of constitutions on charioteers in *CT*. Finally, Barb, art. cit. (n. 7), 119–20.

[84] Ammianus 26, 3, 2: 'in amphitheatrali curriculo undatim coeunte aliquotiens plebe, causas dispiciens criminum maximorum.' Here the Circus Maximus is an 'amphitheatre', it is termed an 'arena' in Claudian, *De VI Consulatu Honorii* 615–25.

[85] Ammianus 15, 7, 2 ff. For a discussion of this incident, see J. F. Matthews, 'Peter Valvomeres, Re-arrested', in *Homo Viator: Essays for John Bramble* (Bristol: Bristol Classical Press, 1987), 277–84.   [86] Theodoret, *HE* 2, 14.

[87] *Collectio Avellana* 1, 7 (*CSEL* 35, 3): 'Tunc Damasus cum perfidis invitat arenarios quadrigarios et fossores omnemque clerum cum securibus gladiis et fustibus et obsedit basilicam [Liberiam].' See above, pp. 138–42.

[88] Jerome, *Life of Hilarion*, 20.

circus races. According to McCormick, the shattering defeat at the hands of the Gothic people in the summer of 378 at Hadrianople had a marked effect upon Roman morale and the incidence of victory celebrations.[89] Thereafter, we may notice an attempt to magnify even the smallest imperial success and the most important element in these celebrations remained the circus race.

One of the most famous constitutions in the Theodosian Code shows the anxiety of Constantius II and (probably) Constans to preserve the non-Christian religious sites of the city outside the walls in order that the popular entertainments might proceed.[90] One can say with confidence, moreover, that the Circus Maximus remained the premier venue in the city for the holding of circus races.

Leaving aside the evidence from the *Codex Theodosianus*, one may consider the considerable labour and expense which the Christian emperors ordered for the great arena. The attention paid to the venue by Constantine was literally conspicuous. According to Aurelius Victor[91] the whole building was 'excultus mirifice' and the work was an early priority, being finished by March 321 when the panegyricist Naziarius at Rome gave an account of the decoration:

Lofty porticoes and columns glowing red with gold have given such uncommon adornment to the Circus Maximus itself that people gather there no less eagerly for the sake of the place than for the pleasure of the spectacle.[92]

Humphrey provides evidence which suggests that Constantine added a tier of seats around the circus, thus *increasing* its seating capacity.[93] The regionary catalogues, compiled towards the mid-fourth century and listing various public buildings, put the capacity of the Circus Maximus at 485,000 people, although Humphrey estimates a much lower figure, between one and two hundred thousand.[94] According to Ammianus, Constantine's plans for the circus included the transportation of an obelisk from one of the foremost temples of ancient Egypt.[95]

After Constantine, the upkeep of the Circus Maximus remained an important praefectural duty and the venue continued to be an appropriate place in which to honour emperors and prominent senators. A statue base discovered inside the Circus Maximus near the Arch of

[89] McCormick, op.cit. (n. 10), 41 ff.   [90] See above, p. 186 and below, p. 254–5.

[91] Vict. *De Caes.* 40, 27.

[92] *Panegyrici Latini* 4 (10), 35, 5: 'Circo ipsi maximo sublimes porticus et rutilantes auro columnae tantum inusitati ornatus dederunt, ut illo non minus cupide conveniatur loci gratia quam spectaculi voluptate.' (Trans. Nixon and Rodgers.)

[93] Humphrey, *Roman Circuses*, 129 and n. 287.

[94] Humphrey, *Roman Circuses*, 126.   [95] See below, pp. 247–9.

Titus in 1935 recorded two interventions by Prefects of the City after Constantine. The text on one side of the stone reads:

> To the imitator of his unconquered father
> [Flavius Julius Constan]s
> Victor and triumphator
> Ever Augustus.
> Aurelius Celsinus, v.c., Prefect of the City
> Judge in the Sacred Court, devoted to his might and majesty.[96]

The Prefect mentioned held office in 341–2 and the names of Constans are understood to have been erased as part of a *damnatio memoriae* when the city fell under the control of Magnentius.[97] Under the Prefect of the City Turcius Apronianus, however, the same base was reused and the image of Constans was either restored or replaced by something else. There is no reason to believe that the statues in question stood anywhere but in the Circus Maximus.

Apart from the addition of statues to the building, it would seem that serious structural repair was undertaken, according to Ferrua, in the middle years of the fourth century. A fragment of a second inscription has been dated to this period and reads:

> . . . v.c., Prefect of the City repaired the work [and ornamentation of the right ha]nd side of the Circus from the doors as far as the [Public] Bathing pool [and. . .] . . . ia [?] collapsed overhanging section.[98]

Although the nature of structural improvements and the repair of the Circus Maximus after the middle years of the fourth century is unknown, the popular circus entertainments lasted at Rome until the Ostrogothic domination.[99]

The trouble taken to maintain the Circus Maximus and the performances staged in it indicate that the strongest links existed in the fourth century between the *plebs Romana*, the senatorial aristocracy, and the Christian emperors.[100] The popularity of the games was undiminished

---

[96] P. Ciancio Rossetto, 'Due epigrafi prefettizie dal circo massimo', *Tituli 4. Epigraphia e ordines senatorio 1*, (1982), 571–3 with plate viii: 'Imitatori Invicti patris | [Flavio Iulio Constant]i | victori ac triunfatori | semper Augusto | Aur(elius) Celsinus, v.c., praefectus urb(i) | iudex sacr. cogn. d(evotus) n(umini) m(aestati)q(ue) eius.' Aurelius Celsinus was *PUR* twice (341 and 351—under Magnentius): *PLRE* I, 192. [97] Ibid.

[98] A. Ferrua, 'Antiche iscrizioni inedite di Roma', *Epigraphica*, 32 (1970), 90–126, at no. 184 with fig. 11: '[salvo d.n. . . . triumphatore perp]etuo semper Au[gusto | . . . ille] v.c. praef. Vrb(i) fabricam [et ornamenta | dextrae pa]rtis Circi a ianuis usq(ue) ad Piscinam [Publicam et . . .]ia labsu(m) minantem | reparavit.'

[99] Ward-Perkins, op. cit. (n. 68), 93.

[100] Well noted by Brown, art. cit. (n. 58). See also C. Huecke, *Circus und Hippodrom als politischer Raum* (Hildesheim: Olms-Wiedmann, 1994).

and the number of circus races annually staged increased markedly during the century. The emperors of the fourth century exploited the Circus Maximus as the largest and most prestigious venue in the city of Rome, putting on circus races as the high point of their victory celebrations. It is to be recalled that McCormick considered these festivities 'strangely neutral' because of Constantine's refusal to sacrifice on the Capitol in 312. In her book on the calendar of 354, Salzman argues that these celebrations differed in length and 'nature' from those of the third century. For her, the refusal of Constantine to sanction sacrifice in connection with the imperial cult at Hispellum was crucial:

Constantius pursued the same policy, continuing imperial support for aspects of the imperial cult redefined in an increasingly secular and civic way while attempting to remove its pagan religious backbone.[101]

It is clear, however, that the Circus Maximus was not a temple of the imperial cult. We must therefore ask the question, how 'neutral' was the environment of the Circus Maximus in the fourth century?

3. THE ICONOGRAPHY OF THE CIRCUS MAXIMUS IN THE FOURTH CENTURY[102]

The circuses of the empire and especially the Circus Maximus were frequently depicted on coins of the Principate. Circus mosaics can be attested as early as the second century AD.[103] The similarities in iconographical detail between circus representations in different media separated by considerable periods of time has led to the suggestion that a certain stylization assisted the craftsman.[104] The artistic details could have their origins in general impressions of a number of circuses of which the craftsman had experience; the example of some local circus; or in some reference to the Circus Maximus at

[101] Salzman, *On Roman Time*, 142, cf. 144.

[102] For the cosmological, seasonal, and astrological symbolism of the circus and its entertainments see Tertullian, *De Spectaculis* 9; Cassiodorus, *Variae* 3, 51. Also P. Wuillemier, 'Cirque et astrologie', *MEFR*, 44 (1927), 184–209; G. Dagron, *Naissance d'une capitale: Constantinople et ses institutions de 330 à 451* (Paris: Presses universitaires de France, 1974), 330 ff.; A. Cameron, *Circus Factions* (Oxford: Clarendon Press, 1976), 231 ff.

[103] Humphrey, *Roman Circuses*, 208, cf. 59, mosaic pavements discussed at 208–54. K. M. D. Dunbabin, 'The Victorious Charioteer on Mosaics and Related Monuments', *AJA*, 86 (1982), 65–89, at 72–6.

[104] For the importance of north African workshops before and into the late antique period see K. M. D. Dunbabin, *The Mosaics of Roman North Africa: Studies in Iconography and Patronage* (Oxford: Clarendon Press, 1978). Also ead., art. cit. (n. 103), 65.

Rome. Exceptionally, however, the vivid detail in some depictions of the circus may be taken as evidence of the special interest paid to a particular place at a particular time. The great circus mosaic from the villa at Piazza Armerina in Sicily is such a depiction (fig. 27).

The vast literature concerned with the large house at Piazza Armerina has focused on three areas: when the villa was built; when the mosaics were laid down; and who owned the property. It is not possible here to enter fully into the debate on any of these questions, but they can be dealt with in so far as they touch directly on the view that the mosaic created at the site shows the Circus Maximus in the first quarter of the fourth century.

The site displays a continuity of settlement from the second century through to the Norman occupation.[105] Virtually the only secure date of any construction work at the site was provided by the discovery of a coin minted under the emperor Maximianus (*Augustus* 286–310) embedded in the mortar of the wall of the *frigidarium*,[106] but the appearance of a single coin is, of course, only the most limited assistance. The question of the date of the most important phase of settlement at the site and the owner of the property at that time has lent great significance to the impressive mosaics which remain *in situ*. Through the sophistication and the sumptuousness of the mosaics, the villa complex displays the great wealth of its owner. Not surprisingly, early analysis led some to conclude that the villa had been owned by an emperor. Gentili (the original excavator of the villa) suggested Maximianus Herculianus and Settis has advocated Maxentius as the imperial owner.[107] The attempt to identify some of the characters featured in the mosaics as these emperors lacks conviction, however, and the grandness of the property need not preclude an aristocratic owner.[108]

Contemporary scholarship has thus moved away from the theory of an imperial owner and a lively debate is in progress on the identity of likely aristocratic candidates for occupancy.[109] Among the early candidates

---

[105] E. De Miro, 'La villa del casale di Piazza Armerina: Nuove ricerche', in S. Garraffo (ed.), *La villa romana del casale di Piazza Armerina*, Atti della IV riunione scientifica della scuola di perfezionamento in archeologia classica dell'Università di Catania (Catania: Istituto di archeologia, 1988), 58–73.

[106] R. J. A. Wilson, *Piazza Armerina* (London: Granada, 1983), 36.

[107] G. V. Gentili, 'Le gare del circo nel mosaico di Piazza Armerina', *Bollettino d'Arte*, 42 (1957), 7 ff.; S. Settis, 'Per l'interpretazione di Piazza Armerina', *MEFRA*, 87 (1975), 873–994.

[108] For a study of the wealth of late antique Sicily see R. J. A. Wilson, 'Piazza Armerina and the Senatorial Aristocracy in Late Roman Sicily', in Garraffo, op. cit. (n. 105), 170–82.

[109] Well summarized and analysed by S. Calderone, 'Contesto storico, committenza e cronologia', in Garraffo, op. cit. (n. 105), 13–57.

was a friend of Symmachus, since it appeared that Nicomachus Flavianus had edited a section of Livy's *History of Rome* 'apud Hennam', that is, 'at Enna', near which the villa of Piazza Armerina stands.[110] Subsequent studies, however, have been sceptical about the lateness of the date which results from the idea that one of Flavianus' contacts owned the villa, since the iconographical details of the mosaic programme bear particularly strong resemblances to work being produced by North African workshops at the turn of the third/fourth century.[111] In an attempt to harmonize the iconographical style of the mosaics and at the same time refute the theory that the villa belonged to a Tetrarchic emperor, Carandini, Ricci, and de Vos argued for Proculus Populonius, *Praetor* at Rome sometime between 315–18, as the first owner of the main settlement which they suggest was constructed starting *c.*315.[112] They suggested that the surviving mosaics at the villa constituted a programme, designed to commemorate particularly magnificent games staged by the owner during his praetorship.[113] Pottery recovered by Carandini from the site has been tentatively confirmed as early fourth-century African ware.[114] At the present time, therefore, a date of 300–25 as the construction date of the settlement with the mosaics is acceptable.

The single most important feature of the villa for the purposes of this discussion is the impressive circus mosaic which decorates the floor of the biapsidal hall or *atrium* of the house.[115] It is the most vivid surviving depiction of the Circus Maximus at Rome. Certain iconographical features, such as the view from behind of the statue of Magna Mater seated on a lion on the barrier of the circus, demonstrate that the mosaic was deliberately designed to portray the Circus Maximus as seen from the Palatine Hill, where the chief imperial residence in the city of Rome was sited.[116] Speaking of the statue of Magna Mater (Cybele), Humphrey states: 'This and other details indicate that the mosaic is to be read virtually as a map by one standing on the slope of the Palatine in the vicinity of the imperial palace.'[117] What is mapped out on the floor of the biapsidal hall of the villa at Piazza Armerina is nothing less than the physical and symbolic context in which the circus celebrations of the early fourth century were played out. Like so many

[110] See Jones, *LRE*, 560.

[111] Dunbabin, op. cit. (n. 104), 196–212.

[112] A. Carandini, A. Ricci, and M. de Vos, *Filosofiana. The Villa of Piazza Armerina* (Palermo: S. F. Flaccovio, 1984), 28 ff., 43.

[113] Ibid. 32–4.   [114] Wilson, op. cit. (n. 106), 37.

[115] The best drawing in G. V. Gentili, *La villa erculia di Piazza Armerina: I mosaici figurata* (Rome: Edizioni mediterranee, 1959); the best plates in Carandini, op. cit. (n. 112).

[116] Settis, art. cit. (n. 107), 958.   [117] Humphrey, *Roman Circuses*, 230.

cultured individuals of the fourth century, the owner(s) of the villa felt no inhibitions when it came to expressing the symbols of non-Christian religious actions and beliefs.[118]

Tertullian, writing at the end of the second century or the beginning of the third, stated of the circus (and certainly with the Circus Maximus in mind):

In the very decoration of the place itself, how many idolatries do you recognize? The ornaments of the circus are in themselves so many temples.[119]

Tertullian had in mind both the pagan theological theory of the ancient origins of the entertainments and at the same time his own contemporary knowledge of what took place there. With time, there is little doubt that the theory and the practice underwent modification, so that the situation as Tertullian understood it changed. There seems to be no reason, however, to accept the dismissive remarks of K. Dunbabin on Tertullian as a source:

His [Tertullian's] account of the *Circus Maximus* is essentially antiquarian; the majority of the deities whom he connects with it can hardly have constituted a very present danger to the faith of his flock.[120]

As revealed by depictions at Piazza Armerina and elsewhere, the Circus Maximus was not a neutral environment, merely the locus of an exciting spectacle; it was a venue with a carefully constructed religious dimension.

In approaching the iconography of the arena we may make a distinction between statuary and structures. It is obvious that many of the statues portrayed on the mosaic and present in the Circus Maximus received no official cult act, that is, they do not appear to have had altars for that purpose near them. There is clearly evidence, however, that the presence of statues of gods was *appropriate* in the sense that an impression was created of divine as well as human participation in the entertainments. The *pompa circensis* for example, ended with the cult images of the gods being given the best seats in the arena.[121] Above the starting-gates (*carceres*) on the Piazza Armerina mosaic one can make out various statues; among them Gentili identified the deities Mercury and Fortuna.[122] On the *acroterion* of what

---

[118] G. Manganaro, 'Aspetti pagani dei mosaici di Piazza Armerina', *Archeologia Classica*, 11 (1959), 241–50. A familiar phenomenon, see Chapter 7, n. 161 below.

[119] Tertullian, *De Spectaculis* 8 (*CSEL* 20, 9): 'Quot igitur in habitu loci illius idololatrias recognoscis? Singula ornamenta circi singula templa sunt.' (Trans. T. R. Glover.) Cf. id., *De Spectaculis* 7; *De Idololatria* 18, 1. See below, section 4.

[120] Dunbabin, op. cit. (n. 104), 88–9.   [121] See section 4 below.

[122] Gentili, art. cit. (n. 107), 7. Humphrey, *Roman Circuses*, 226 thinks Genius or Fortuna.

appears to be the *editor*'s box stands a group identified as Cybele with
crenellated crown in a quadriga drawn by four lions.[123] On the *meta*
nearest the *carceres* an ox is depicted being led to sacrifice, while on the
barrier itself, among the statues of athletes and animals, the figures of
Victoria and Magna Mater on the lion are conspicuous.[124] As we have
seen, the upkeep of the Circus Maximus included the upkeep of these
statues of men and gods.

It would be perverse to claim that all statues of deities placed around
the city possessed an equal level of religious significance. At this period
the statue of the deity in his or her temple and receiving sacrifices of
animals and incense remained, to many Christians, the most offensive
symbol of the non-Christian cults.[125] As Eusebius of Caesarea so
tendentiously argued, statues which had received cult acts in the
provinces suffered a definite demotion when they were transferred to
the city of Constantinople and re-erected in extra-temple contexts.[126] It
is, however, equally perverse to dismiss the statues of the gods outside
of temples and not receiving sacrifices as merely 'works of art'. As long
ago as 1963, C. Mango pointed out in relation to the Constantinian
plundering of cities of the East for statues of deities which he wished to
erect in the new city bearing his name:

It would be a mistake, I think, to suggest—as some modern scholars have
done—that these statues were used simply for decoration. The answer is rather
to be sought in the ambiguity of the religious policy pursued by Constantine's
government.[127]

And more recently, Jas Elsner has drawn attention to the resonating
evocations of cult statuary all over the urban landscape:

The visual correlative of such religion, Roman religious art, is characterised by
a propensity to overdetermine what we would consider *secular* space (the
forum, markets, gardens, baths) with signs that evoke the sacred. The visual
environment of the Roman world in its civic and public aspect is notable for its
being mapped by a wide diffusion of 'thin' signifiers for the sacred, whose
meaning, because either not entirely clear or very complex in a culture full of
signs for the sacred, is very little different from their status as *sign*.[128]

---

[123] Humphrey, *Roman Circuses*, 226.   [124] See Settis, art. cit. (n. 107), fig. 55.
[125] See Minucius Felix, *Octavius* 27, 1; Firmicus Maternus, *De Errore* 13, 4 for the
cult of Serapis.
[126] Eusebius, *VC* 2, 45 and 4, 25. Cf. id., *Laus Constantini* 8, 3; 9, 6. For my views on
the tendentious character of these remarks see J. R. Curran, 'Moving Statues in Late
Antique Rome: Problems of Perspective', *Art History*, 17 (1994), 46–58. See above,
179–80.
[127] C. Mango, 'Antique Statuary and the Byzantine Beholder', *DOP*, 17 (1963), 56.
[128] J. Elsner, *Art and the Roman Viewer: The Transformation of Art from the Pagan
World to Christianity* (Cambridge: Cambridge University Press, 1995), 243 where 'thin
signifiers' of the Roman state religion are contrasted with the 'thick discourse of images

Evidence exists which supports the idea that the image of the deity in the late antique city played a more complex part in the web of religious symbolism than has often been accepted. The distinction between two categories of statues, 'cult' and 'works of art' in particular, places unwarranted limitations on the religious connotations which statuary evoked in a number of different urban contexts in this period. Tertullian, in his treatise on idolatry, stated the danger well for his third-century flock:

Most men simply regard idolatry as to be interpreted in these senses alone, viz: if one burns incense or immolates [a sacrificial victim], or gives a sacrificial banquet, or is bound to some sacred functions or priesthoods . . . if the head of unrighteousness is idolatry, the first point is that we be fore-armed against the abundance of idolatry, while we recognize it not only in its palpable manifestations.[129]

Those who have promoted the 'works of art' theory have avoided the question of statues which did not receive sacrifices but which recalled, imitated, or copied statues which did. Statues of deities which stood in public places in all periods of antiquity were only rarely labelled: their identities were well known as a result of the constant exposure of their attributes to the urban population.[130] Almost all the statues of deities which were to be found outside temple contexts belonged to this group. Richard Gordon identified and discussed the problems of meaning in regard to the images of the gods in classical antiquity.[131] He showed that the categories familiar to the connoisseur have been afforded more significance than 'vulgar' or 'popular' conceptions:

But the notion of 'importance' conceals more than it reveals. For it is in effect being suggested that the sheer familiarity of vulgar notions, as well as their 'non-intellectual quality', permits us to discount them.[132]

and initiations whose constant feature was an interpretative or exegetic mapping of the sacred in terms of highly complex myths, texts or astrologies'.

[129] *De Idololatria* 2 (*CSEL* 20, 31–2): 'plerique idololatrian simpliciter existimant his solis modis interpretandam, si quis aut incendat aut immolet aut polluceat aut sacris aliquibus aut sacerdotiis obligetur . . . quod si caput iniustitiae idololatria est, prius est, uti adversus abundantiam idololatriae praemuniamur, dum illam non solum in manifestis recognoscimus.' See Minucius Felix, *Octavius* 27, 3 where the writer is anxious to point out the dangers from seers located outside temples.

[130] Lane Fox, *Pagans and Christians*, 159.

[131] R. Gordon, 'The Real and the Imaginary: Production and Religion in the Graeco-Roman World', *Art History*, 2 (1979), 5–34, repr. in id., *Image and Value in the Roman World: Studies in Mithraism and Religious Art* (Aldershot: Variorum, 1996).

[132] Gordon, art. cit. (n. 131), 8. For the contrast between pagan images and the 'stereotypy' of Mithraic and Christian images, see now Elsner, op. cit. (n. 128), 190–245.

It is well known that some members of the educated pagan élite baulked at the idea that the statues of the gods were in any sense divine, but this view was not universal.[133] What Gordon advocated was a broader perspective, embracing non-élite notions of what images of the gods meant. Starting with the myth of Daedalus, Gordon illuminated the essential paradox of the ancient statue as something alive and at the same time not alive. According to Gordon, statues served as

the visible, noted entries, whether as 'headwords' or as 'derived senses', in the lexicon of religious meanings.[134]

Nor can the juxtaposition of statues which were the focus of sacrifices with statues which received no such act be explained by means of the 'works of art' theory. Price has shown that temples of the East during the early empire could often house cult images and statues of *other* gods.[135] It is not controversial to say that the same situation existed in the temples and shrines of the city of Rome in the fourth century. Doubtless, part of the impression created by the collection of images in this way was an impressive manifestation of human craftsmanship. But just as likely is the deliberate creation of the impression that the gods, like men, were sociable. Tertullian knew that when he termed the Capitol of Rome the 'curia deorum' and 'daemoniorum conventus', his listeners could see, represented in the crowding statuary of their own towns, precisely the point he was making.[136] The relationship between the images of the gods and those special images which received cult acts was exploited by the emperor Julian, according to Sozomen, who attempted to resuscitate the veneration of the gods, by situating images of the gods *alongside* his own in the hope that the respectful feelings shown by the beholder to his image above all might be diverted to them.[137]

Statues could also act as the *foci* of magical practices and pagan 'miracles' in the fourth century. A mosaic floor at El-Djem in North Africa dating to a period not earlier than the mid-fourth century depicts a figure of Dionysus in the amphitheatre. Dunbabin has noted the sculptural features of the figure and it is clearly based on a statue prototype.[138] Although the composition is heavily symbolic, some elements are particularly interesting, given the clear connection

---

[133] See MacMullen, *Christianity and Paganism*, 49; E. Bevan, *Holy Images* (London: Allen & Unwin, 1940), 21–9.

[134] Gordon, art. cit. (n. 131), 13.

[135] S. R. F. Price, *Rituals and Power* (Cambridge: Cambridge University Press, 1984), 146–7.

[136] Tertullian, *Apologeticus* 6, 8; *De Spectaculis* 7.   [137] Sozomen, *HE* 5, 17.

[138] Dunbabin, op. cit. (n. 104), 77.

of the statue with a major venue for public entertainment. The figure of Dionysus is nimbate and to his right hand is tied a gecko. This theme, examined by Merlin and Poinssot emerges as a symbol of the triumph of Dionysus over the evil incarnate in the gecko.[139] The mosaic may have portrayed an actual magical act, but the animation of the statue itself, filled with the prophylactic power of the god, is not in doubt and it is apparently achieved without the common forms of cult sacrifice.[140]

Zosimus alludes to the miraculous animation of two statues which stood outside the senate-house in Constantinople which was burned down in 404. When the rubble was being cleared, all expected the statues of Zeus and Athena to have been destroyed as well. But they had escaped destruction and the historian recorded:

This inspired the more cultured people to be optimistic that these deities would always take care of it [Constantinople].[141]

There were certainly no non-Christian cult acts taking place before the senate-house at Constantinople in the fifth century and this was the reason why the miracle was so welcome to the pagan historian.

The intervention of the gods could, however, be actively solicited by the theurgists of the period, whose skills in animating statues are claimed by Zosimus to have saved the city of Athens from barbarian attack.[142] A fourth-century Latin translation of the Hermetic dialogue *Asclepius* spoke of statues 'animatas sensu et spiritu plenas' which were manufactured, using special elements of an innately occult nature:

Thus is man a maker of gods.[143]

The Laurentian Fragment of the early fifth-century Hieronymian Martyrology records some details of the Roman martyrdom of the monk Almachius:

The *natalis* of Alamachus who, with Alypius administering [Rome] as the prefect of the city, said: 'Today, the eighth, [is] sacred to the Lord; desist from

---

[139] A. Merlin and H. Poinssot, 'Deux mosaïques de Tunisie à sujets prophylactiques', *Fondation Piot Monuments et Memoires*, 34 (1934), 129–78. For civic violence at Carthage on the occasion of the gilding of a beard on a statue of Hercules, see Augustine, *Sermo* 24 (AD 401).

[140] Precisely the same image was associated with the months of September in the Calendar of 354. See Salzman, *On Roman Time*, 103–6.

[141] Zosimus, *NH* 5, 24, 8: 'ὅπερ ἅπασι τοῖς χαριεστέροις ἀμείνους ἐπὶ τῇ πόλει δέδωκεν ἔχειν ἐλπίδας, ὡς δὴ τῶν θεῶν τούτων ἔχεσθαι τῆς ὑπὲρ αὐτῆς ἀεὶ βουλομένων προνοίας.' (Trans. R. T. Ridley.)

[142] Zosimus, *NH* 4, 8. See the late 'miracle' of the supernatural defenders of Thrace in Lane Fox, *Pagans and Christians*, 134 with n. 37. Note E. R. Dodds, 'Theurgy and its Relationship to Neoplatonism', *JRS*, 37 (1947), 63 with remarks on συμπάθεια.

[143] *Asclepius* 3, 38ᵃ: 'sic deorum fictor est homo.'

the *superstitiones* of idols and from the sacrifices polluted by gladiators.' On account of this he was killed.[144]

Ville upheld the claims of this version of the monk's death against a later and garbled account of the ecclesiastical historian Theodoret.[145] The latter dates the year of the holy man's death to 404, when Honorius finally banned gladiatorial shows as a result. In the account of the Hieronymian Martyrology, however, reference is made to the Prefect of the City, Alypius, who held office in the period just before the implementation of Theodosius' anti-pagan legislation.[146] Ville concludes that the monk may have been executed as a result of his disruptive activities at the public games. The importance here for the passage of the martyrology is the alleged intention of Almachius in a major venue for popular entertainment: he is alleged to have wanted to stop the 'superstition' attached to idolatry and the polluting sacrifices. It is by no means certain that the two separate charges actually refer to the same practice, namely sacrifice. It rather seems that the abomination of sacrifice was located firmly, in the late fourth century, where Tertullian had located it in the third: the general 'idolatry' of the circus. The energies of Almachius were thus directed against what he and many other Christians of the period saw as the continuing pagan connotations of the venues of popular entertainment.

The place occupied by statues in public life was thus much more complex and fluid, where divine presence and animation remained a possibility in statues which did not receive sacrifices just as it did in statues which had altars associated with them. On this analysis, the context of the statuary which stood in the late antique Circus Maximus cannot be confined merely to the category of 'works of art'. There is space here only to restate the important principle that statues could be many things to many men and the standards of the ancient (or modern) 'connoisseur' should not prevent the attempt to examine problematic alternatives.

Statues of deities, placed at various points in the circus building, were complemented by the presence of actual temple structures and altars in the arena itself. The most striking of those recorded on the Piazza Armerina mosaic are the three buildings placed behind the *carceres* with open doors and variously identified statues within. Over their presence there is a major controversy. They constitute a significant innovation in the known iconography of circus mosaics and must

---

[144] *AASS*, November, 2/1, p. [4]: 'A K(a)l(endas) . . . Nat(alis) Alamachi qui iubente Alypio urbis p(rae)fecto cu(m) diceret hodie octavas dominicae diei s. cessate a superstitionibus idoloru(m) et sacrificiis pollutis a gladiatorib(us). Hac de causa occisus est.'

[145] Ville, art. cit. (n. 9), 326 ff.   [146] See *PLRE* I, 47. See above, 215–16.

therefore be examined. Explanation has taken two broad forms. S. Settis may be taken to represent the first:

I tre templi (di Roma, di Giove, di Ercole) posti nella testata settentrionale del Circo non vogliono offrire una puntuale collocazione topografica, ma piuttosto evocare presenze familiari (come il Circo, come l'Anfiteatro) della lontana *Urbs*.[147]

On this view, the presence of the temples constituted a statement of tetrarchic propaganda in the idea that the emperors, like the gods to whom they were particularly attached, were 'present' at the games at Rome. The location of a temple to what appeared to be Juppiter Fulminator suggested further that the ancient gods of the Capitol were also present.[148] It is worth noting that the Gerona mosaic, of later fourth-century date, depicted non-topographical features in the same area of the composition (fig. 28).[149]

As will become clear however, there was no need to imply that the ancient gods were present at the games in the Circus Maximus; the mosaicist probably knew that they were. The second view of these temples is that they are references to actual structures standing in the Forum Boarium and included because of the loose topographical interpretation of this zone. Lugli believed that two were shrines to Hercules and they flanked the Ara Maxima.[150] This explanation is unsatisfactory, however, because the identification of two of the statues as Hercules cannot be demonstrated; one of the three figures is, in addition, almost certainly female.

Carandini has identified the central temple as that of Ceres, Liber, and Libera, which is reported as possessing the three *cellae*, a podium and a central staircase, all of which it appears to have on the mosaic.[151] This temple is also known to have stood in the immediate vicinity of the Circus Maximus.[152] One of the remaining two temples is dedicated

---

[147] Settis, art. cit. (n. 107), 956.

[148] For an expression of such a theme, see *Pan. Lat.* 10 (2), 13, 1–5.

[149] See Humphrey, *Roman Circuses*, 240–1.

[150] G. Lugli, 'Contributo alla storia edilizia della villa romana di Piazza Armerina', *Rivista dell'Istituto nazionale d'archeologia e storia dell'arte*, NS, 10–11 (1963), 28–82, at 67. Note his (unconvincing) identification of the *tribunal* as a shrine to Venus Murcia. For all these temples, see *Lexicon*, iii. 15 s.v. 'Hercules Invictus, aedes (Forum Boarium)' (F. Coarelli); iii. 15–17 s.v. 'Hercules Invictus, Ara Maxima' (F. Coarelli); Platner and Ashby, *Topographical Dictionary*, 254, 255–6.

[151] Carandini, op. cit. (n. 112), 342; see *Lexicon*, i. 260–1 s.v. 'Ceres, Liber, Liberaque, aedes; aedes Cereris' (F. Coarelli); Platner and Ashby, *Topographical Dictionary*, 109–10.

[152] Vitruvius, *De Architectura* 3, 3, 5; for these three *cellae* see 4, 7. Also Tacitus, *Ann.* 2, 49.

to Hercules and the third remains unidentified. Carandini suggested that the entertainments depicted in the mosaic were, in fact, the *ludi Cerealici* (12–19 April).[153]

Humphrey, in his monumental work on Roman circuses, points out the weakness in Carandini's position. The identity of the statue inside the so-called temple of Ceres is by no means certain.[154] Carandini also fails to explain the presence of what looks like a temple to Juppiter among the three. Humphrey concludes: 'I prefer to see the temples as a reference to the whole city, not simply to temples which happened to be located near the *carceres*.'[155] Ultimate certainty is unlikely. In Carandini's favour, his interpretation of one building as the temple of Ceres is attractive, if unproved. One may accept his theory that this temple is represented on the mosaic, but need not go as far as to identify the nature of the games taking place from it. At the same time, however, *elements* in the composition may suggest the symbolism of the whole city. Accordingly, one of the two remaining buildings shows the temple of Juppiter Fulminator, not 'transferred' from the Capitol, but a statement of the god's omnipresence. The third temple may be taken to be that of Hercules from the Forum Boarium. Thus the three constitute a fusion of the topographically 'accurate' details and symbolic statement, but the reason why the temples could be so effectively combined in the mosaic was because they joined a composition of an environment already replete with representations of the sacred.

Humphrey has shown convincingly, for example, that the finishing line in the Circus Maximus was approximately half-way down the Aventine side of the arena (figs. 29, 30, and 31).[156] On a third-century marble plan of the Circus Maximus a structure was located here built into the terraces.[157] At exactly the same point on the plan of the Circus Maxentii on the Via Appia, a similar building was linked to the arena by stairs.[158] Humphrey thinks that this structure was the Temple of the Sun, using as evidence the presence of a radiant Sun on the acroterion of a building shown on coins and other objects from the time of Trajan onwards at the same point in the terraces of the Circus Maximus on the Aventine side.[159] Since the Temple of the Sun is shown to have dominated the finishing line, Humphrey thus explains the much-discussed phrase in Tertullian's *De Spectaculis*:

the circus is dedicated chiefly to Sol.[160]

---

[153] Carandini, op. cit. (n. 112), 342.   [154] Humphrey, *Roman Circuses*, 232–3.
[155] Ibid.   [156] Ibid. 84–91.   [157] Ibid. 119, fig. 53.
[158] Ibid. 87–8.   [159] Ibid. fig. 37a.
[160] Tertullian, *De Spectaculis* 8, 1: 'circus Soli principaliter consecratur.' See also W. Quinn Schofield, 'Sol in the Circus Maximus', in *Hommages à Marcel Renard*, Collection Latomus, 102 (Brussels: Latomus, 1969), ii. 639–49.

Constantine's adherence to Sol was featured prominently on his arch in Rome, on his early coinage, and in panegyrics to him,[161] and the fourth-century *Expositio Totius Mundi* drew attention to the special devotion of the Romans to Sol and Juppiter.[162] The largest number of circus race-heats for a single festival in the mid-fourth century was thirty-six, on the twenty-second of October, the *Ludi Solis.*[163] The next largest number was thirty, which was to be found on the twenty-fifth of December.[164] At the point in the Piazza Armerina mosaic roughly in front of the Temple of the Sun (not represented), the victorious charioteer is visible with a herald.[165]

At the same point on the mosaic, a large obelisk rises from the barrier. An involved argument has been raging for a quarter of a century about the precise identity of this monument.[166] There are three theories worth considering. First, the view championed by Carandini, that the obelisk portrayed here is that brought by Augustus to the city.[167] Second, the idea that the obelisk seen on the mosaic apparently shifted from a central position is in fact the obelisk of Augustus after it had been moved from its original position on the barrier to make way for the obelisk brought by Constantius to the city in the late 350s.[168] Lastly, the theory of Ragona that the obelisk depicted is actually the one imported by Constantius II.[169]

The identification of the obelisk as Constantius II's fails to explain satisfactorily why the older monument (the obelisk of Augustus) is lacking in the Piazza Armerina mosaic; it was known to have remained in the arena. Ammianus claimed that a bronze replica of a flaming torch surmounted the obelisk erected *c*.358 and Ragona has identified this as the object that seems to top the obelisk on the mosaic. The object on the fourth-century mosaic *could* also be a spear, however, and spears

---

[161] G. Halsberghe, *The Cult of Sol Invictus*, Études préliminaires aux religions orientales dans l'empire romain, 23 (Leiden: Brill, 1972), 167 ff. See above, 75, n. 23.

[162] Valentini and Zucchetti, i. 265.

[163] Degrassi, *II*, 257. These games instituted by Aurelian? See Salzman, *On Roman Time*, 150.

[164] According to Salzman, *On Roman Time*, 150, 25 December could be the anniversary of the dedication of Aurelian's Templum Solis.

[165] Humphrey, *Roman Circuses*, 87. The victor never appears anywhere else. See Dunbabin, art. cit. (n. 103), 84 ff., who plays down the connection with Sol.

[166] See A. Ragona, 'I tre indubbi segni di riconoscimento dell'obelisco di Costanzo II nel mosaico del circo di Piazza Armerina', in Garraffo, op. cit. (n. 103), 125–30; S. Calderone, art. cit. (n. 109).

[167] Carandini, op. cit. (n.112), 340 ff. For this obelisk, see *Lexicon*, iii. 355–6 s.v. 'obeliscus Augusti: Circus Maximus' (J.-C. Grenier).

[168] E. Nash, *Pictorial*, ii. 137.

[169] See Ragona, art. cit. (n. 166). For this obelisk, see *Lexicon*, iii. 356–7 s.v. 'obeliscus Constantii: Circus Maximus' (J.-C. Grenier).

are known to have been placed on top of obelisks elsewhere in the city.[170] It is not, therefore, out of the question that the traditional bronze globe which adorned the Roman *obelisci* of the early empire had been replaced at a later date by something else.

Contra Nash, it may be pointed out that there is no evidence to suggest that the obelisk of Augustus was ever moved from its original position. The apparently off-centre position of this obelisk may be an attempt by the artist to portray the optical illusion caused by viewing the Circus Maximus from a particular point on the Palatine; it could also be the result of second and third-century extensions made to the length of the barrier.[171]

Thus, the most reasonable conclusion would seem to be that the obelisk in the mosaic is that of Augustus, which stood unaccompanied on the barrier until the arrival of a second massive obelisk *c.*358.

When Ammianus came to tell the impressive story of how Constantine and then his son Constantius II had first begun and then completed the task of bringing the largest obelisk in the known world to Rome, he said a few words on the meaning of *obelisci*:

An obelisk is a very hard stone in the shape of a turning-post in the circus; it rises to a great height, gradually tapering to resemble a sunbeam.[172]

He wrote of the decision of Constantine to tear the great stone from its foundations at the temple of Amon-Ra at Karnak with approval:

he [Constantine] rightly thought that he was committing no sacrilege if he took this marvel from one temple and consecrated it at Rome, that is to say, in the temple of the whole world.[173]

Ammianus' appreciation of the obelisk as a sacred object has led one recent analyst of religion in his work to describe it as 'the greatest religious symbol of the history'.[174] Constantius' successor Julian was also anxious to move an obelisk which the former had intended for

---

[170] For a bronze spear on the Campus Martius obelisk, see Pliny, *Natural History* 36, 15. Also Wilson, op. cit. (n. 106), 36.

[171] Humphrey, *Roman Circuses*, ch. 5 for the fluidity of the iconography of the barrier.

[172] Ammianus 17, 4, 7: 'Est autem obeliscus asperrimus lapis, in figuram metae cuiusdam sensim ad proceritatem consurgens excelsam, utque radium imitetur, gracilescens paulatim . . .'

[173] Ibid. 13: 'nihilque committere in religionem recte existimans, si ablatum uno templo miraculum Romae sacraret, id est in templo mundi totius.' See J.-C. Golvin in Ch. Landes (ed.), *Cirque et cours de chars Rome-Byzance: Catalogue de l'exposition* (Lattes: Editions Imago, 1990), 49.

[174] R. L. Rike, *Apex Omnium. Religion in the Res Gestae of Ammianus* (Berkeley: University of California Press, 1987), 29. Matthews, *Ammianus*, 449–50.

Constantinople but which had remained lying on the shore at Alexandria:

The news has reached me that there are certain persons who worship there and sleep at its very apex, and that convinces me that on account of these superstitious practices I ought to take it away. For men who see those persons sleeping there and so much filthy rubbish and careless and licentious behaviour in that place not only do not believe that it is sacred, but by the influence of the superstition of those who dwell there come to have less faith in the gods.[175]

And at the end of the account of the arrival of Constantius' obelisk at Rome, Ammianus gave his readers a translation in Greek of the hieroglyphics which covered the sides of the obelisk and which showed that it had been, like the obelisk of Augustus alongside which it stood, the gift of a great king to the Sun.[176] Constantius II, naturally, made no such claim on the dedication which he had inscribed on the plinth upon which the obelisk stood in the Circus Maximus, but it would be naïve to suppose that he expected the obelisk to be viewed simply as a symbol of imperial power and munificence; in fact, Constantius had made almost the most appropriate contribution imaginable to the non-Christian iconography of the Circus Maximus at Rome. When Cassiodorus, writing in the sixth century, came to describe the circus at Rome, he claimed that *both* obelisks in the arena were dedicated to deities: the smaller (that of Augustus) to the Moon and the larger (that of Constantius II) to the Sun.[177]

Thus far, this discussion has focused upon the primacy of the Sun in the context of the Circus Maximus. But the presence of temples and altars dedicated to the other gods amplified the religious symbolism of the building. In the track on the Aventine side of the Piazza Armerina mosaic stands a brick-faced temple which can be securely identified as the ancient shrine of Venus Murcia, given an unusual prominence in the composition.[178] Late antique literary sources, among them the

---

[175] Julian, *Ep.* 48: καὶ τὸ λεγόμενον δέ, ὡς τινές εἰσιν οἱ θεραπεύοντες καὶ προσκαθεύδοντες αὐτοῦ τῇ κορυφῇ, πάνυ με πείθει χρῆναι τῆς δεισιδαιμονίας ἕνεκα ταύτης ἀπάγειν αὐτόν. οἱ γὰρ θεώμενοι τοὺς καθεύδοντας ἐκεῖ, πολλοῦ μὲν ῥύπου, πολλῆς δὲ ἀσελγείας περὶ τὸν τόπον ὡς ἔτυχεν οὔσης, οὔτε πιστεύουσιν αὐτὸν θεῖον εἶναι, καὶ διὰ τὴν τῶν προσεχόντων αὐτῷ δεισιδαιμονίαν ἀπιστότεροι περὶ τοὺς θεοὺς καθίστανται. (Trans. W. C. Wright.) See n. 174.

[176] Amm. 17. 4. 18–23. Cf. *CIL* 6, 701. G. Fowden, 'Nicagoras of Athens and the Lateran Obelisk', *JHS*, 107 (1987), 51–7 argues that Ammianus' account was designed to discredit Constantius II by depicting his action as vainglorious. See, however, Matthews, *Ammianus*, 450.　　　　[177] Cassiodorus, *Variae* 3, 51, 8.

[178] Compare the treatment of the shrine on the Foligno relief: M. Lawrence, 'The Circus-relief at Foligno', *Atti del II convegno di studi Umbri* (Gubbio: Centro di studi Umbri, 1964), 119–35; Humphrey, *Roman Circuses*, 95–7; Platner and Ashby, *Topographical Dictionary*, 348.

grammarian Servius, actually called the valley the 'vallis Murcia'.[179] Near the *carceres* on the Palatine side of the track stands a *tempietto* with a winged Victory on the roof. Lugli suggested that the structure was a shrine to the Sun and Moon and others have identified it as a *heroon*, designed to house the images of the visiting gods.[180] Humphrey has drawn attention, however, to the similarities borne by this building to the *falae* of the arena at the time of the Republic.[181] It might well be that its use was unconnected with cult but the *Victoria* statue on its roof took its place in a matrix of statuary references to deities positioned all around the structure.

The barrier of the circus, as represented by the mosaicist at Piazza Armerina, demonstrates the survival of sacred objects in addition to the obelisk(s). Tertullian's *De Spectaculis* claimed that three altars stood on the barrier, dedicated to the triple gods 'Magni Potentes Valentes'. The altars stood in relation to three-columned statues of Seia, Messia, and Tutilina.[182] 'Probus', in his late-antique commentary on the Sixth Eclogue of Virgil, says the altars were inscribed

[This altar is dedicated] to the gods Potentes [and Valentes], the gods over earth and sky.[183]

and stood 'ad columnas in quibus stant signa'. The barrier of the Circus Maximus in the fourth century clearly had more than one altar on it. One of these altars is depicted on the Piazza Armerina mosaic. Viewing the scene from the Aventine, past the obelisk and down towards the Arch of Titus, there stands a block-shaped structure which appears to have a door. The mosaic from Barcelona has a very similar depiction at the same point but has added a flaming sacrifice on top of what is clearly an altar (fig. 32). Though the portrayal of the flaming altar is a common iconographical form on all manner of artistic representations in all periods of antiquity, there is, in fact, no reason to believe that the fourth-century Circus Maximus ceased to use its altars for sacrifice before the age of Theodosius.[184] On the Foligno relief, of third- or fourth-century date, two altars are shown on the barrier; one appears to be being used for sacrifice and the other is shown without any flame. Gentili argued that the two other structures on the barrier of the Piazza Armerina mosaic, shown with conical roofs and, apparently,

[179] Servius, *In Aeneidos* 8, 636; Symm., *Rel.* 9, 6; Claudian, *De Cons. Stil.* 2, 404; Cassiodorus, *Variae* 3, 51. Cf. Polemius Silvius' calendar: Degrassi, *II*, 545.

[180] Lugli, art. cit. (n. 150), 68.

[181] Humphrey, *Roman Circuses*, 266–7.

[182] Tertullian, *De Spectaculis*, 8.

[183] *Ecl.* 6, 31: 'Diis Potentibus, [Valentibus hoc est] Diis terrae et caelo.'

[184] i.e. incense sacrifice. See the remarks of Ambrose, 208 above.

two-tiered construction, were also connected to the gods as altars but there is no reason to believe this. They seem to be simply *phalae* for race officials or spectators.[185]

Among the statues standing in this part of the circus was the famous Magna Mater on a lion, facing away from the Palatine, where her temple stood. To the right of this statue, on the other side of the arena, stands another *Victoria*, this time on a column. Taking the record of the definitely fourth-century Barcelona mosaic with the possibly fourth-century Foligno relief, Humphrey concluded that the barrier of the fourth-century Circus Maximus had at least two statues of Victory.[186]

According to Jerome's *Life of Hilarion*, the holy man once helped a Christian owner of a racing stable whose rival had hired a magician to hex his horses and charioteer. After some initial reluctance, the holy man relented and gave Italicus, the stable owner, some holy water in a cup:

Italicus took it and sprinkled it over his stable and horses, his charioteers and his chariot, and the hinges of the starting gates.[187]

Italicus was instructed to deploy the holy water against the demons who were tormenting his stable. This he did, by sprinkling it wherever the concentration of malevolent power was likely to be strong. The starting gates marked the barrier through which the teams passed into an environment replete with images of and altars to a congregating mass of demons.

When the fourth-century evidence for the physical appearance and symbolism of the Circus Maximus is examined, it becomes impossible to perceive it as a 'neutral' environment. Not only were the Christian emperors aware of the atmosphere of the circus but Constantine planned and his son executed a grand gesture which was entirely consonant with the ancient pagan iconography. It would be quite wrong, however, to conclude that the obelisk installed in 357 was the only way in which the Christian emperors directly involved themselves in the life of the Circus Maximus. The great racecourse was both a static and a fluid religious environment. The temples and statues adorning the course were regularly supplemented by a procession of mobile images from the city's shrines. It is necessary, therefore, to examine the fate of the *pompa circensis* under the Christian empire.

---

[185] Carandini, op. cit. (n. 112), 339.
[186] Humphrey, *Roman Circuses*, 269.
[187] Jerome, *Life of Hilarion*, 20 (*PL* 23, 38): 'Quem cum accepisset Italicus et stabulum, et equos, et aurigas suos, rhedam, carcerumque repagula aspersit.'

4. THE *POMPA CIRCI* AND THE CHRISTIAN EMPEROR

McCormick's study of victory celebrations at the end of the Late Antique period demonstrated that one of the most startling innovations of the Christian empire was the transferral of certain aspects of the ancient ceremonial of triumph to the venues of urban popular entertainment, especially the circus or hippodrome. According to McCormick, the techniques employed may be seen developing early in the fourth century in the east of the empire, but in the west, until the time of Honorius, triumphal entries into the city better characterized the main focus of imperial victory ceremonial.[188] Naturally enough, the literary material which constitutes our main evidence for the four fourth-century visits of emperors to Rome chose to concentrate on the significance of their entrances to the ancient capital. Constantinople, in contrast to Rome, had not been the home of *Augusti* for centuries. It is a mistake, however, to ignore the ancient circus ritual of the western capital.

Featured prominently on the mosaic of the circus race in the villa at Piazza Armerina is an archway, with six *carceres* on either side, placed in the middle of the western end of the Circus Maximus, facing the Forum Boarium. Through this archway passed the ancient ritual procession of the gods and their *exuviae*, placed on special vehicles, which began at the temples on the Capitol and finished with the deposition of the images in the *pulvinar* in the Circus Maximus.[189] This *pompa circensis/circi* traditionally opened each day of the circus entertainments in the city. From at least the second century, Christian apologists were referring to this procession as the *pompa diaboli*:[190]

But rather more pompous is the outfit of the games in the circus, to which the name pomp properly belongs. The *pompa* comes first and shows in itself to whom it belongs, with the long line of images, the succession of statues, the cars, the chariots, carriages, the thrones, garlands, robes. What sacred rites,

---

[188] McCormick, op. cit. (n. 10), 59.

[189] An extensive bibliography: J. Marquardt, *Römische Staatsverwaltung* (1885), iii. 504–28; Wissowa, *RK*, 451 ff.; J. Regner, *PW*, Suppl. 7 (1940), 1627, 1629; F. Bömer, 'Pompa', *PW*, 21 (1952), 1974–94; H. Jurgens, *Pompa diaboli: Die lateinischen Kirchenväter und das antike Theater* (Stuttgart: W. Kohlhammer, 1972); E. Künzl, *Der römische Triumph* (Munich: C. H. Beck, 1988). See the comments of R. MacMullen, *Paganism in the Roman Empire* (New Haven: Yale University Press, 1981), 155 n. 47.

[190] J. H. Waszink, 'Pompa Diaboli', *VC*, 1 (1947), 13–41. Cf. Tertullian, *De Spectaculis* 7: 'The *pompa* of the circus, whatever its character, offends God. Even if the images are few in its procession, one image is idolatry; if but one chariot is drawn, it is yet Jove's car; any idolatry in any form, meanly equipped, moderately rich, splendid, is still reckoned idolatry in its guilt.' (Trans. T. R. Glover.)

what sacrifices come at the beginning, in the middle, at the end; what guilds, what priesthoods, what offices are astir—everybody knows in that city [Rome] where the demons sit in conclave.[191]

It is extremely difficult to establish the date at which the *pompa circensis* at Rome was transformed under the Christian emperors and its more prominent pagan features removed to make way for the high profile political iconography of the Christian emperor in his circus. J. Waszink, in an important article on the subject published in 1947, suggested that Constantine the Great had suppressed it because of its explicit pagan symbolism.[192] In fact, there is no evidence that such an act of suppression ever took place and Alföldi, Stern, and Salzman have all argued convincingly that the Festival Calendar of 354 shows the survival of a large number of non-Christian festivals of a particularly 'visible' nature so that it would seem curious that Constantine should ban the *pompa circi* and at the same time permit the *Lupercalia*, the *Saturnalia*, and the individual festivals connected to the cult of Magna Mater.[193]

Lactantius, writing as one of the most powerful spokesmen of the Constantinian Christian laity, in a passage criticizing the baseless worship of idols, commented:

How much more is the uninstructed crowd, which rejoices in empty displays and gazes at all things with childish minds, delighted with *pompae* and captivated by the appearance of *simulacra*.[194]

As mentioned above, the concept of the *pompa diaboli* entered the Christian consciousness at an early date. Although a major problem when dealing with the *pompa circi* is the large number of references to 'pompous' public acts which are manifestly not ritual processions, the Lactantius passage seems to make a connection between spectators, some form of procession and the appearance of images.

A relief panel from Foligno has been well known since the Renaissance.[195] An early study of the piece considered that its probable date

---

[191] Tertullian, *De Spectaculis* 7 (*CSEL* 20, 8–9): 'sed circensium paulo pompatior suggestus, quibus proprie hoc nomen. Pompa praecedens, quorum sit in semetipsa probans de simulacrorum serie, de imaginum agmine, de curribus, de tensis, de armamaxis, de sedibus, de coronis, de exuviis. Quanta praeterea sacra, quanta sacrificia praecedant, intercedant, succedant, quot collegia, sciunt homines illius urbis, in qua daemoniorum conventus sedit.'   [192] Waszink, art. cit. (n. 190), 33 n. 80.

[193] Stern, op. cit. (n. 24), 92. For a discussion of these festivals, see Salzman, *On Roman Time*, 164–74 and A. Alföldi, *A Festival of Isis in the Fourth Century* (Budapest: Pázmány University, 1937).

[194] *Divinae Institutiones* 2, 3, 7: 'quanto magis vulgus indoctum, quod pompis inanibus gaudet animisque puerilibus spectat omnia, oblectatur frivolis et specie simulacrorum capitur. . .' (Trans. M. F. McDonald.)

[195] See Lawrence, art. cit. (n. 178).

was the third quarter of the third century but Humphrey, in his monograph on the circuses of the empire, takes it in conjunction with the mosaic at Piazza Armerina as fourth-century evidence for the layout of the building.[196] There can be no resolution of the problem of dating, as it rests on stylistic grounds, but regardless of whether the panel is third or fourth century in date, there certainly appears to be a late reference to the *pompa circensis* in the form of a *tensa* or special vehicle employed in the transportation of the images of the gods depicted in the top right-hand corner of the panel. It might be countered that the *tensa* is merely a common stock-motif in the depictions of circuses were it not that both Ammianus and Prudentius explicitly mention a ceremony at Rome which employed a ritual carriage. The former, speaking about the ill-fated Persian campaign of Julian in 363, described the date of the halt at the town of Callinicum:

Here on 27 March, the day on which a procession [pompa] in honour of the Mother of the Gods is held annually at Rome and the carriage [carpentum] which conveys her image is washed, we are told, in the waters of the Almo, he celebrated her festival according to the ancient ritual.[197]

This Ammianus passage may explain the much-quoted constitution of the emperor Constantius II (and Constans?) addressed to the Prefect of the City in 342:

Although all superstition must be utterly rooted out, we nevertheless decree that temple buildings located outside the city walls should remain intact and unviolated. For since some plays, circus spectacles and athletic contests originate from these temples, it is not expedient to tear down places where the traditional amusements of the Roman people are celebrated.[198]

Origo in this text might thus refer to a point in space from which a ritual procession such as that mentioned by Ammianus in connection with the

---

[196] Humphrey, *Roman Circuses*, 246: 'The Foligno relief and the Maffei relief are both particularly detailed representations of the monuments of the circus and, together with the fourth-century mosaics, provide good evidence for the appearance of the *euripus* at that date.'

[197] Ammianus 23, 3, 7: 'ubi diem sextum kalendas apriles, quo Romae Matri deorum pompae celebrantur annuales, et carpentum, quo vehitur simulacrum, Almonis undis ablui perhibetur, sacrorum sollemnitate prisco more completa . . .' Cf. Prudentius, *Peristephanon* 10, 160. For a depiction of Cybele in a *fercula* from a mid-fourth century sarcophagus, see N. Himmelmann, *Typologische Untersuchungen an römische Sarkophagreliefs des 3. und 4. Jahrhunderts nach Christus* (Mainz: Zabern, 1973), plates 56 and 57.

[198] *CT* 16, 10, 3: 'nam cum ex nonnullis vel ludorum vel circensium vel agonum origo fuerit exorta, non convenit ea convelli, ex quibus populo Romano praebeatur priscarum sollemnitas voluptatum.' Cf. *CT* 15, 7, 3 (10 March 376) to Hesperius, Proconsul of Africa and *CT* 16, 10, 8. See 186 above.

cult of Magna Mater could begin. It is to be remembered that one of the longest festivals of the year, climaxing in a day's racing at the Circus Maximus, was the Megalensian Games, the *Ludi Megalesiaci*.[199] Processions and cult sites outside the walls for the cult of Cybele were almost certainly linked in the case of other deities' rites.[200] Strictly speaking, such a procession was not the *pompa circi*, which took a route from the Capitol to the Circus Maximus, but any procession associated with popular entertainments would certainly evoke the more famous *pompa*.

According to Stern, two 2-*solidi* pieces minted at Trier in 326 which show a frontal view of the emperors Constantine and his son Constantius II in chariots do not portray the *processus consularis* of 1 January which had never used chariots, but refer instead to the *pompa circi* which introduced the consular games held on 3 January each year as part of the celebrations in honour of the reigning emperors.[201] Though neither of the coins has any reference to the ancient pagan symbolism, this need not prove that such elements were lacking. It hardly needs stating that the die-cutter was working with a very limited space. But evidence from outside Rome suggests that Constantine was aware of the utility of the ancient tradition of the *pompa circi*.

Part of the elaborately staged celebrations which marked the completion of Constantine's new city on the Bosporus focused on the hippodrome there. The *Chronicon Paschale* recorded details of a ceremony that took place on 11 May 330:

He made for himself another gilded monument of wood, bearing in its right hand a Tyche of the same city, itself also gilded, and commanded that on the same day of the anniversary chariot races, the same monument of wood should enter, escorted by the troops in mantles and slippers, all holding white candles; the carriage should proceed around the further turning-point and come to the arena opposite the imperial box; and the emperor of the day should rise and do obeisance to the monument of the same emperor Constantine and this Tyche of the city.[202]

---

[199] 4, 5, 6, 9, 10 April. See Degrassi, *II*, 245.

[200] See the *Carmen contra Paganos* (trans. in Croke and Harries, 80–3); J. F. Matthews, 'The Historical Setting of the Carmen Contra Paganos', *Historia*, 20 (1970), 464–79.

[201] Stern, op. cit. (n. 24), 157–62. See also J. M. C. Toynbee, *Roman Medallions* (New York: American Numismatic Society, 1944), 89 with plate 3. The appearance of elephant *quadriga* on New Year coins began in 287: ibid. 51–2.

[202] *Chronicon Paschale* AD 330: ποιήσας ἑαυτῷ ἄλλην στήλην ἀπὸ ξοάνου κεχρυσωμένην βαστάζουσαν ἐν τῇ δεξιᾷ χειρὶ τύχην τῆς αὐτῆς πόλεως, καὶ αὐτὴν κεχρυσωμένην, κελεύσας κατὰ τὴν αὐτὴν ἡμέραν τοῦ γενεθλιακοῦ ἱππικοῦ εἰσιέναι τὴν αὐτὴν τοῦ ξοάνου στήλην διριγευομένην ὑπὸ τῶν στρατευμάτων μετὰ χλανιδίων καὶ καμπαγίων, πάντων κατεχόντων κηροὺς λευκούς, καὶ περιέρχεσθαι τὸ ὄχημα τὸν ἄνω καμπτόν, καὶ ἔρχεσθαι εἰς τὸ σκάμμα κατέναντι τοῦ βασιλικοῦ καθίσματος, καὶ ἐπεγείρεσθαι τὸν κατὰ καιρὸν βασιλέα καὶ προσκυνεῖν τὴν στήλην τοῦ αὐτοῦ βασιλέως Κωνσταντίνου καὶ αὐτῆς τῆς τύχης τῆς πόλεως. (Trans. M. and M. Whitby.)

On any understanding, what had taken place was a variation on the theme of the *pompa circi*. The focus of the procession was a mobile image before a vast crowd of several hundred thousand people. The main difference between this *pompa* and its more ancient predecessor was that the most important images carried were not of deities but of Constantine himself. The procession made its way around the great racecourse before depositing the image on the barrier of the circus, at a place of honour, facing the imperial box. There, in times to come, the incumbent emperor was to 'venerate' the image of the great city's founder. Like the Constantinian profile revealed in the Festival Calendar from 354, the ceremony which took place at Constantinople twenty years before that calendar was compiled was carefully designed to serve the political ends of the reigning dynasty. 'Les rituels servent à exprimer l'actualité politique.'[203] This ceremony was to take place annually and there can be little doubt that the displaying of imperial images in the circus did continue until well into the fifth century. In 425, the emperors wrote to Asclepiodotus, then Praetorian Prefect of Oriens, in an attempt to play down the status being given in the ceremonies to the imperial visage:

If at any time, whether on festal days, as is usual, or on ordinary days, statues or images of us are erected, the *iudex* shall be present without employing the vainglorious heights of adoration . . . Likewise if our images (*simulacra*) are shown at *ludi*, they shall demonstrate that our divinity and glory live only in the hearts and the secret places of the minds of those who attend.[204]

According to Franz Bömer who based his own views on an earlier article by Nilsson, the Late Antique New Year *pompa* did not begin until the fourth century and was a development of the *pompa circi*.[205] Up until its introduction, the first day of January witnessed no procession. The festival calendar of 354 has merely the entry 'Senatus Legitimus' on that date, when the senate made its own declaration of loyalty to the emperor.[206] The *public* announcement of prayers offered

---

[203] Dagron, op. cit. (n.102), 329.

[204] *CT* 15, 4, 1: 'Si quando nostrae statuae vel imagines eriguntur seu diebus, ut adsolet, festis sive communibus, adsit iudex sine adorationis ambitioso fastigio, ut ornamentum diei vel loco et nostrae recordationi sui probet accessisse praesentiam. Ludis quoque simulacra proposita tantum in animis concurrentum mentisque secretis nostrum numen et laudes vigere demonstrent; excedens cultura hominum dignitatem superno numini reservetur.' See my discussion of statues above, 240–4 and also *CT* 16, 10, 20, 3.

[205] Bömer, art. cit. (n. 189), 1989. The first reference in the sources comes from Lydus, *De Mensibus* 4, 3.

[206] See M. Meslin, *La fête des kalendes de janvier dans l'empire romain* (Brussels: Latomus, 1970), 55 ff.; MacMullen, *Christianity and Paganism*, 36 ff.; J. Scheid, *Romulus et ses frères: Le collège des frères arvales, modèle du culte public dans la Rome des empereurs* (Rome: École française de Rome, 1990).

to the ancient gods of the city for the safety of the emperors did not take place until 3 January and were the occasion of general celebrations and *ludi*.[207] The so-called *Feriale Campanum*, from Capua and dating to 387, has no entry for 1 January, but 'vota' for the 3 January.[208] Sometime after the Festival Calendar of 387 was made, a change occurred and many of the elements of the *pompa circi* were transferred to the new procession, or, more probably, the new procession never had more than semi-official status and did not therefore make an appearance in the later civic calendars. Several late Christian writers commented on the offensiveness of this ceremony. Peter Chrysologus, living near Ravenna in the fifth century, described it vividly:

The *kalends* of January comes along and behold, the entire *pompa* of demons appears; the whole workshop of the idols is produced, and the newness of the year is consecrated by an ancient sacrilege. They mould Saturn, they make Juppiter, they fashion Hercules, they show Diana with her *venationes*, they lead Vulcan around, breathing out his base acts in words and after this men are dressed as cattle, and they turn men into women, they laugh at respectability, they violate right-thinking, they ridicule public restraint.[209]

What exactly became of the *pompa circi* at Rome is unclear but, as we saw, it is only in the last quarter of the fourth century that the emperors began effectively to demolish the edifice of the ancient religion.[210] In August 389 the Prefect of Rome, Albinus, was instructed to make sure that all days were *iuridici dies* except for two months during the summer, 1 January, the *natales* of Rome and Constantinople, the Easter fortnight, and the *natales imperii*.[211] It was not until April 392 that circus races in Constantinople were stopped on Sundays, although exceptions were made for *natales imperii*.[212] In 395 Arcadius and Honorius wrote to the *corrector* of Paphlagonia:

---

[207] Meslin, op. cit. (n. 206).

[208] *CIL* 10, 3792 = Degrassi, *II*, 283.

[209] *Homilia de pythonibus et maleficiis* (*PG* 65, 27): 'Ecce Kalendae venient et tota daemonum pompa praecedit, tota idolorum producitur officina, et sacrilegio vetusto anni novitas consecratur. Figurant Saturnum, faciunt Jovem, formant Herculem, exponent cum venatibus Dianam suis, circumducunt Vulcanum verbis haletantem turpitudines suas praeterea vestiuntur homines in pecudes, et in feminas viros vertunt, honestatem rident, iudicia violant, censuram publicam rident.' See MacMullen, *Christianity*, 179 n. 13 for the attribution of the short *sermo* to Peter.

[210] See Chapter 5 above.

[211] *CT* 2, 8, 19 (7 August 389); cf. *CT* 2, 8, 23 (27 August 399). The former is the first surviving indication of imperial interference in the status of the ancient *feriae*. See Salzman, *On Roman Time*, 236. Piétri, *RC* i, 437 saw it as an attempt to neutralize the entertainments.

[212] *CT* 2, 8, 20.

We call to remembrance that We formerly commanded by law that the ceremonial days of pagan superstition should not be considered among the holidays.[213]

The law to which the emperors referred does not survive but it is significant that the precedent which they wished to invoke dated to their own reign.

The importance of the use of some kind of formal procession as part of the ceremonial of the *circus* did not disappear. A sixth-century circus programme from Oxyrhynchus may give some indication of the extent to which the ancient rituals of the circus had been absorbed into circus entertainment under the Christian empire. The text reads:

> For good Fortune.
> Victories. [?]
> 1st chariot race.
> Procession . . .[214]

The editor of the text suggested that the reference to 'victories' in the second line might be understood as an announcement of the bringing in of statues of victories, the symbols of imperial and charioteering success. The references to 'fortune' and 'victory' were picked up as they were the most desirable and transferable ideas from the entertainments of the non-Christian to the Christian city. Strikingly, the *pompa* remained. Although no longer in its ancient position at the opening of the games, and certainly no longer parading the revered images of the pagan gods, the *pompa* retained a place in the ceremonial of the entertainments which it had once infused with so much religious atmosphere.

CONCLUSION

Scholars have traditionally found no difficulty in identifying the 'monumental centre' of Rome as the *locus* of a tenacious paganism. There was undoubtedly a concentration of both temples and rituals in this area but it is important to realize just how completely the presence of the gods had been integrated into the life of the whole city.

The festival calendar was an ancient means of exposing very large numbers of spectators to the presence of the gods; the utility of the circus and its ceremonial made it an early platform for the promotion of the imperial cult. Under the Christian empire, the births, accessions, and especially military victories of the emperors shared the festival calendar with the gods. The use of the same language (*ludi votivi,*

---

[213] *CT* 2, 8, 22 (3 July 395): 'sollemnes pagano[r]um superstitionis dies inter feriatos non haberi.'

[214] *Oxyrhynchus Papyri*, 34 (1968), 91 no. 2707: "ἀγαθῇ τύχῃ|νὶκ[α]ι|μίccoc ἡνιόχων | πομπή. . . ."

natales) to denote imperial festivals is notable but it is in the sharing of the most important Roman venue that the ambiguity and ambivalence of the age become clear.

The Circus Maximus was not a 'secular' building. Although it would be inaccurate to suggest that the religiosity of the circus entertainments loomed large in the minds of all the spectators, it would be unjust to attribute the values of some members of the élite to the majority. The traditions, iconography, and rituals of the Circus Maximus were as ancient as the temples of the Forum and in these respects it is not accurate to draw a distinction between the two zones; the *pompa circi* demonstrated vividly how close the relationship between the Forum and the great circus was. The layout of the Circus Maximus in the fourth century, under the Christian emperors, expressed this relationship with undiminished coherence; functioning temples and altars were to be found located in their ancient positions within the walls of the circus and the gods could be seen crowding, like the spectators, to view the spectacles.

The Christian emperors and their functionaries sought to keep the Circus Maximus and its races intact. Through their exploitation of the festival calendar they increased the number and frequency of the entertainments which characterized the observance of feast days. They were thus able to continue effectively and to enhance what their pagan predecessors had sought through the promotion of the same institutions: the keeping of their names and achievements before the populace of Rome. But far from 'evidently taking the view that secular activities, rejoicing, shows, and banquets could be dissociated from their religious origins', the Christian emperors achieved this only by entering the festival life of the city fully, maintaining the Circus Maximus, and even contributing to its traditional iconography and turning its ritual to their own ends.[215] Moreover, there is no convincing evidence that the process was a self-conscious 'neutralization' of the games. As with the legislation on the ancient cults, Christian emperors of the fourth century felt themselves free to employ whatever they found at the circus and considered of use. Though they retained their own theological views, and on occasion permitted these views to influence their policy, they cannot have been blind to the religious sustenance which some of their non-Christian subjects derived from the same entertainments. Until Theodosius, the lack of enthusiasm shown by Christian emperors for the suppression of the games and traditions of the Circus Maximus bears eloquent testimony to the ambivalence which was so vital to the continuity of Roman life in the fourth century.

[215] Quotation from Markus, *End*, 109.

7

Jerome, Asceticism, and the Roman Aristocracy, AD 340–410

INTRODUCTION

Around the middle of the fourth century, Marius Victorinus, professor of rhetoric at Rome, became a Christian. He was a well respected academic and friend of the nobility whose sons he trained:

Eventually the time came for making his profession of faith. At Rome, those who are about to enter into Your grace usually make their profession in a set form of words which they learn by heart and recite from a raised platform in full view of the faithful, but Simplicianus said that the priests offered to allow Victorinus to make his profession in private, as they often did for people who seemed likely to find the ceremony embarrassing.[1]

The existence of such a special arrangement illustrates that there was a group of public figures in Rome for whom Christianity was a sincere vocation but one which was subordinated to the general network of responsibilities and obligations which attended social status.

In the proliferation of modern studies on asceticism, those characterized below as the 'moderate' Christians have been neglected because of the tendency to concentrate on ascetics individually or on them as part of a 'history of monasticism'. Here, an attempt is made to restore the ascetics of Rome to their broader social context. By doing so, one gains a fuller picture of upper-class Christianity in Rome; an understanding of the degree of interdependence between different groups and an appreciation of the many limitations in viewing the period as one of pagan–Christian conflict.

---

[1] Augustine, *Confessiones* 8, 2 (*CSEL* 33, 173–4): 'Denique ut ventum est ad horam profitendae fidei, quae verbis certis conceptis retentisque memoriter de loco eminentiore in conspectu populi fidelis Romae reddi solet ab eis, qui accessuri sunt ad gratiam tuam, oblatum esse dicebat Victorino a presbyteris, ut secretius redderet, sicut nonnullis, qui verecundia trepidaturi videbantur, offerri mos erat . . .' (Trans. R. S. Pine-Coffin.) For further information on Victorinus' conversion, see P. Hadot, *Marius Victorinus. Recherches sur sa vie et ses œuvres* (Paris: Études augustiniennes, 1971), 235–52.

I. THE ROMAN ARISTOCRACY REDEFINED

In 1898, Samuel Dill published his *Roman Society in the Last Century of the Western Empire* which included an impressive survey of aristocratic life and manners in the Late Antique period.[2] Dill drew attention to the cultural fluidity necessary for senators who considered themselves to be Christian:

> In truth, the line between Christian and pagan was long wavering and uncertain. We find adherents of the opposing creeds side by side, even in the same family at the end of the fourth century. Mixed marriages (*imparia matrimonia*) were evidently not uncommon.[3]

The theme was revived by Peter Brown in 1961, when he published his short but influential paper on the 'Christianisation of the Roman aristocracy'.[4] Although his study marked a return to the perception of the aristocracy as a hazy overlapping of religious groups, it went much beyond Dill's understanding of the order. Instead of focusing on the supposed division between the pagan and Christian 'camps', Brown emphasized the continuity of senatorial prestige through a period of profound religious change. This led him to consider the diffusion of Christianity within what he argued was a culturally homogeneous group. He put the famous religious flashpoints involving the senate firmly in the context of the world of mixed marriages and common ties of family and culture, suggesting of the Anicii, for example:

> For Christians and pagans to live together, and, eventually, to accept wholeheartedly the *tempora Christiana*, a common ground had to be found in the classical culture of the age.[5]

And the intervention of militant Christian emperors, far from encouraging the process of Christianization, actually retarded it by creating circumstances in which the vague interface between the Christian and the non-Christian aristocrat hardened, periodically but never fatally, into a real division between the religions. In the end, the practice of the emperors in accepting the senatorial order on its own terms allowed the members of the aristocracy to get on with the establishment of a *modus vivendi* between the religions which was a necessary preliminary to the gradual conversion of the whole class.

There was, however, a second kind of polarity which Dill had accepted

---

[2] S. Dill, *Roman Society in the Last Century of the Western Empire* (London: Macmillan & Co., 1898), especially ch. 1. Still useful, despite Dill's Christian moralizing.

[3] Ibid. 11.

[4] P. Brown, 'Aspects of the Christianisation of the Roman Aristocracy', *JRS*, 51 (1961), 1–11, repr. in P. Brown, *Religion and Society in the Age of Saint Augustine* (London: Faber & Faber, 1972), 161 ff.   [5] Ibid. 178.

wholeheartedly and which concerned an alleged subdivision of pagan senators. Embraced by Wissowa, Robinson, and Bloch, this theory suggested that the late pagan aristocracy, under pressure from the inexorable growth of Christianity, divided itself into two camps each committed to the survival of discrete forms of paganism:[6] around Quintus Aurelius Symmachus gathered those who wished for the preservation of the 'traditional' cults of the state which had sustained the city since the most ancient times. This form of paganism was alleged to have advocated the continuance of the traditional cults because they were the means by which the *Pax Deorum* could be maintained. The famous third *Relatio* of Symmachus was understood to be the manifesto of this group. On the other hand, Vettius Agorius Praetextatus became the focus for those who wanted to preserve the intensely personal and mystical cults which were manifestly popular among some senators and which appeared to have originated in the Near East.[7] This religious grouping was taken to represent a tenacious 'oriental' form of paganism.

In 1973, John Matthews subjected the documentary evidence upon which this distinction was based to close examination.[8] He argued that the surviving inscriptions and literary sources (especially the *Letters* and *Relationes* of Symmachus) were documents which were designed to perform specialized functions in particular circumstances.[9] Scholarly tradition had asserted that these texts, by their inclusion or exclusion of information about the two poles of the religious world, were unquestionable commentaries on religion in society. But Matthews showed that the absences, for example, of 'traditional' priesthoods on inscriptions referring to men who were known to have been devotees of 'oriental' mysteries did not mean that such men were exclusively followers of only the latter cults. He did not detect evidence for a clear delimiting of the allegedly 'public' religious acts of 'traditional' religion and the 'private' oriental cults. There was clear testimony that some senators recorded both initiations and other cult acts.[10] The

---

[6] Wissowa, *RK*, 95 ff.; D. N. Robinson, 'An Analysis of the Pagan Revival of the Late Fourth Century, with especial reference to Symmachus', *TAPA*, 46 (1915), 87–101; H. Bloch, 'The Pagan Revival in the West at the End of the Fourth Century', in Momigliano, *Conflict*, 193–218. See Lane Fox, *Pagans and Christians*, 31–2, 36–7 for a 'debunking' of the living oriental versus the moribund traditional cults for an earlier period.

[7] Clodius Hermogenianus Caesarius hailed Magna Mater and Attis as 'guardians of his mind and soul': *CIL* 6, 499. For ideas of rebirth, see *CIL* 6, 510; Praetextatus' role in initiating his wife: *CIL* 6, 1779; and below 267.

[8] J. F. Matthews, 'Symmachus and the Oriental Cults', *JRS*, 63 (1973), 175–95. Epigraphic material chiefly relates to Mithras and Magna Mater.   [9] Ibid. 191–4.

[10] e.g. *CIL* 6, 1675 (Alfenius Caeonius Iulianus Kamenius). See Matthews, art. cit. (n. 8), 184–6.

absence of references to the 'oriental' rites in the third *Relatio* was not, therefore, significant, as the brief given to Symmachus when composing the document was undoubtedly restricted.[11] Thus the other main interpretation of polarity among the late aristocracy also collapsed.

In 1977 Alan Cameron turned his attention to the literary activities of senators in the late fourth century.[12] The survival of great non-Christian literature had, until then, been widely interpreted as an aspect of the pagan revival carefully managed by the circle of Symmachus.[13] Thus the efforts of these men to preserve works such as the *Aeneid* or Apuleius' *Metamorphoses* was attributed to a militant desire to maintain the pagan literary tradition. Cameron argued that only a minority of the most prominent literary men of the age had any acquaintance with Symmachus and chief among these was Ausonius, a *Christian*. Claudian, the most famous of the later 'pagan' poets, was patronized by the Anicii, the most influential Christian family in Rome. Cameron went on to argue that learned Christian readers, including Jerome, Ambrose, and Augustine, had no scruples about reading such books. The non-Christians, he further argued, did not interest themselves at all in histories, which one might have expected of them, if their desire was genuinely to use literature as religious propaganda. Nicomachus Flavianus, who was to die at the River Frigidus under the banner of the ancient gods, even dedicated his *Annales* to the Christian emperor Theodosius I. Cameron effectively undermined confidence in Roman literary activity as a key to the religious questions of the later fourth century.

Recent studies have undermined two further orthodoxies central to older views of 'the Christianization of the Roman aristocracy'. Largely through the prosopographical studies of T. D. Barnes, the process of 'Christianization' has been shown to have been significant much earlier in the century than Brown and many after him assumed.[14] At the same time, moreover, it has become important to review the role of women in upper-class conversion, chiefly again through prosopographical investigation but also as a result of sophisticated reassessment of the

---

[11] See my discussion above, 206–8.

[12] A. Cameron, 'Paganism and Literature in Late Fourth Century Rome', in *Christianisme et formes littéraires de l'Antiquité tardive en Occident*, Entretiens sur l'antiquité classique, 23 (Geneva: Fondation Hardt, 1977), 1–30.

[13] In his important article, 'The Date and Identity of Macrobius', *JRS*, 56 (1966), 25–38, Cameron removed the *Saturnalia* of Macrobius from its mistaken position as a document written in the last years of the fourth century.

[14] T. D. Barnes, 'Statistics and the Conversion of the Roman Aristocracy', *JRS*, 85 (1995), 135–47, at 138 ff. A critique in particular of R. von Haehling, *Die Religionszugehörigkeit der hohen Amtsträger des römischen Reiches seit Constantins I. Alleinherrschaft bis zum Ende der Theodianischen Dynastie* (Bonn: Habelt, 1978).

rhetorical character and implicit strategies of the most important texts.[15] As Kate Cooper has put it:

The insinuations of womanly influence which abound in the late Roman sources should not necessarily be read as reflecting accurately the agency of women in Christianization. Rather, the appeal to the *topos* of womanly influence should be understood as an element of cultural continuity with the earlier Empire.[16]

Our understanding of the nature of the senatorial order has thus been undergoing significant revision in recent times. As old notions have passed away, so the common culture of wealth, status, and privileged social life has become more prominent.[17] New vistas have opened up to the social historian of Late Antiquity. As Alan Cameron has suggested:

The Roman aristocracy will continue to repay study. The great families continued to play a prominent role in the social, literary and religious life of Rome. But it is the rival *Christian* factions that increasingly dominate the scene, while the pagans fade more and more into the background, thrown momentarily into a dazzling but perhaps misleading prominence by the occasional spectacular confrontations.[18]

2. THE CONTEXT OF SENATORIAL ASCETICISM

Individuals who had renounced the values of their social class or the world around them were not new in Rome.[19] Among the ancient festivals of the city, that of Magna Mater featured her priests mutilating themselves during the 'Day of Blood' ceremony of 24 March which

[15] See M. R. Salzman, 'Aristocratic Women: Conductors of Christianity in the Fourth Century', *Helios*, 16 (1989), 207–20; K. Cooper, 'Insinuations of Womanly Influence: An Aspect of the Christianization of the Roman Aristocracy', *JRS*, 82 (1992), 150–64. For general treatments of women, see K. Cooper, *The Virgin and the Bride: Idealized Womanhood in Late Antiquity* (Cambridge, Mass.: Harvard University Press, 1996); A. Arjava, *Women and the Law in Late Antiquity* (Oxford: Clarendon Press, 1996); S. Elm, *'Virgins of God': The Making of Asceticism in Late Antiquity* (Oxford: Clarendon Press, 1994); G. Clark, *Women in Late Antiquity* (Oxford: Clarendon Press, 1993).

[16] Cooper, art. cit. (n. 15), 155.

[17] To a greater or lesser degree, depending upon whether individuals were themselves or were related to one of the great senatorial families. See Jones, *LRE*, 545–6.

[18] Cameron, art. cit. (n. 12), 30.

[19] For the earliest Christian context, see J. W. Drijvers, 'Virginity and Asceticism in Late Roman Western Elites', in J. Blok and P. Mason (eds.), *Sexual Asymmetry: Studies in Ancient Society* (Amsterdam: J. C. Gieben, 1987), 241–73, at 242 ff. See also J. A. Francis, *Subversive Virtue: Asceticism and Authority in the Second-Century Pagan World* (Univerity Park, Penn.: Pennsylvania State University Press, 1995); MacMullen, *Christianity and Paganism*, 85 f. discusses the shifting definition of 'philosophy'.

marked the anniversary of Attis' death.[20] The priests of Isis shaved their heads as a sign of ritual grief on the anniversary of the death of Osiris and the ecclesiastical historian Rufinus claimed that the priests of the Serapeum in Alexandria had taken a vow of celibacy.[21] Turcan has described the great Temple of Isis and Serapis on the Campus Martius as 'a kind of foreign entity in the town'.[22] Such temples had annexes attached for 'recluses' (*katochoi*) who had withdrawn from the world.[23]

Individual senators are known to have participated in cults which had certain ascetical features.[24] In the later third century, the philosopher Plotinus, whose disdain for the material world was legendary, established a school at Rome which attracted 'not a few members of the senate' and possibly their wives as well.[25] Plotinus himself lodged with the wealthy and the politically ambitious.[26] Spectacular aristocratic conversions could take place. One of Plotinus' friends was the senator Rogatianus, who:

advanced to such detachment from political ambition that he gave up all his property, dismissed all his slaves, renounced every dignity, and, on the point of taking up his praetorship, the lictors already at the door, refused to come out or have anything to do with the office. He even abandoned his own house, spending his time here and there at his friends' and acquaintances', sleeping and eating with them and taking, at that, only one meal every other day.[27]

Despite this fascinating story, the overwhelming impression is that such conversions were extremely rare.[28] Nevertheless, it would be wholly

---

[20] Turcan, *Cults*, 45 ff.

[21] Priests of Isis: see R. MacMullen, *Paganism in the Roman Empire* (New Haven: Yale University Press, 1981), 43; Rufinus, *HE* 2, 23, 294. For early examples of ritual purity see Tibullus 1. 3. 23–32 Apuleius, *Metamorphoses* 11, 22, 1; Juvenal, *Satires* 6, 538–40.

[22] Turcan, *Cults*, 107. On the design of temples for the cult, ibid. 104: 'instead of opening directly onto the street, forum, or any other public place, the Egyptian temple was generally isolated, separated from the profane world by an enclosing wall.' For third-century Isiac cult buildings in Rome, see above, 10–11.   [23] Turcan, *Cults*, 106.

[24] For the later period see n. 8 and the polemical tracts *Carmen contra Paganos* and *Carmen ad Senatorem ex Christiana religione ad idolorum servitutem conversum*, both translated in Croke and Harries, *Conflict*, docs. 50 and 51.

[25] Porphyry, *Vita Plotini* 7: Ἠκροῶντο δὲ αὐτοῦ καὶ τῶν ἀπὸ τῆς συγκλήτου οὐκ ὀλίγοι . . . He names 'Marcellus Orontius' and 'Sabellinus'. See ibid., 8 for his female followers.

[26] e.g. Zethos the doctor: ibid. 7.

[27] Ibid. (trans S. McKenna): ὃς εἰς τοσοῦτον ἀποστροφῆς τοῦ βίου τούτου προκεχωρήκει ὡς πάσης μὲν κτήσεως ἀποστῆναι, πάντα δὲ οἰκέτην ἀποπέμψασθαι, ἀποστῆναι δὲ καὶ τοῦ ἀξιώματος. καὶ πραίτωρ προιέναι μέλλων παρόντων τῶν ὑπηρετῶν μήτε προελθεῖν μήτε φροντίσαι τῆς λειτουργίας, ἀλλὰ μηδὲ οἰκίαν ἑαυτοῦ ἐλέσθαι κατοικεῖν, ἀλλὰ πρός τινας τῶν φίλων καὶ συνήθων φοιτῶντα ἐκεῖ τε δειπνεῖν κἀκεῖ καθεύδειν, σιτεῖσθαι δὲ παρὰ μίαν. Cf. ibid. 9 for the great man being entrusted with the care of children of the highest born.

[28] As seen by MacMullen, op. cit. (n. 21), 43. He has collected much of the available material: ibid. 146 n. 51, 147 n. 63, 166 n. 7; 191 n. 5. For sex and abstinence in an early Christian environment, see P. Brown, *The Body and Society* (London: Faber & Faber,

wrong to give general credence to the highly coloured account of the nobles of Rome in Ammianus, where the historian depicted a morally bankrupt class enfeebled by effeminate luxury.[29] In reality, there is much to suggest the existence of a more or less formalized senatorial 'code of conduct' which frequently had austere moral overtones. Jones stressed its most fundamental aspects: the importance of high birth, the possession of landed property, and moral rectitude.[30] But it is clear that this behavioural paradigm also influenced the religious activities of senators. In several letters, Symmachus reproached a number of his friends, including the arch-pagan of the day, Vettius Agorius Praetextatus, for not attending to their priestly functions.[31] Occasionally, Symmachus' traditionalism spilled over into sinister farce, as when he recommended the ancient punishment of live burial for an adulterous *vestalis*.[32]

One of the most noteworthy features of the later Roman aristocracy, however, is the presence alongside the traditional class virtues of an altogether different kind of quest for religious truth. A significant number of senators, both pagan and Christian, have left records of a search for purity in which the traditional offices and rewards of a senator's career played no part. Between the years 305 and 390 twenty-two inscriptions were set up at the Vatican shrine to Magna Mater.[33] These record the presence or participation of senators and sometimes their wives in the rituals carried out at the site. These rituals included mainly the *tauro-* and *criobolia* in which a bull or a ram was slaughtered directly over an initiate standing beneath a grill through which the purifying blood poured.[34] Some of the surviving inscriptions make explicit reference to the significance of the act; the initiates understood themselves to be being reborn (*renatus*).[35] One dramatic text illustrates the initiate's sense of release:

I bring in this sacrifice the words, thought, action, excellent life, and all the goodness of Ga[rgi?]lius' understanding. For he offered and brought to the

---

1989), 17 ff.; A. Rousselle, *Porneia: On Desire and the Body in Antiquity* (Oxford: Blackwell, 1988).

[29] See Amm. 14, 6; 28, 4.

[30] Jones, *LRE*, 523 ff. See also the classic discussion of senatorial *otium* in Matthews, *WA*, 1–31. For the 'rhetoric of conjugal unity in antiquity' see Cooper, art. cit. (n. 15), 151 ff.   [31] Symmachus, *Ep.* 1, 47; cf. 2, 34 (to Flavianus).

[32] Symmachus, *Ep.* 9, 147.

[33] See Vermaseren, *CCCA*, iii. 46–61, nos. 225–45a; Matthews, art. cit. (n. 8). For the so-called 'Phrygianum', see above, 111–12.

[34] See fig. 1 in Turcan, *Cults*, 50 and 51 ff. Also Prudentius, *Peristeph.* 11, 1007 ff.

[35] e.g., Vermaseren, *CCCA*, iii. no. 242 (from 376). Sextus Agesilaus Aedesius: 'tauribolio criobolioq[ue] in aeternum renatus'. Cf. *CCCA*, iv. nos. 271 and 272. Turcan, *Cults*, 52: 'The Latin *aeternus* indeed implies durability rather than transcendental eternity in the Christian sense.'

Mighty One, who rose again, the bull and ram that are the tokens of happiness. Yea, he scattered the night of eight-and-twenty idle years and kindled again the light. . .[36]

Vettius Agorius Praetextatus himself underwent the *taurobolium* and held priesthoods of the cults which administered it.[37] He introduced his wife, Fabia Aconia Paulina, to the same ritual and many little-known cults.[38] On the epitaph which she set up for him, Paulina claimed that the 'gate of heaven' lay open for 'the wise' whose works her husband had translated from Greek.[39] Through the mysteries in which he was an initiate, Praetextatus was alleged to have 'discovered' secrets, presumably pertaining to fate or the workings of the cosmos.[40] His earthly honours, which were impressive, were considered by him to be 'transient and trivial'.[41] Paulina viewed her own initiations as a deliverance from the 'lot of death'.[42] Because of her religious experiences, people proclaimed her 'holy and blessed'.[43] She expected to join him after her death in 'a shining white palace', a sentiment which Jerome dismissed with a contemptuous remark that she was likely to meet him not as a resplendent heavenly official but naked, in the darkness of hell.[44]

These ideas were strikingly paralleled in a document set up by a Christian wife for Sextus Petronius Probus, her Christian husband and an outstandingly successful Christian servant of the state. The long inscription was set up at the family mausoleum beside the Constantinian basilica on the Vatican.[45] Probus' earthly life was described as 'but a garment' and his soul now roamed the heavens. The 'gift of Christ' outweighed and outlasted his earthly honours. Now Probus was living closer to Christ in the company of saints. He was transformed, purified, glittering white, and 'a dweller in unaccustomed mansions'. Rome had been exchanged for the stars.[46]

---

[36] Vermaseren *CCCA*, iii. no. 239: Ἔργα, νόον, πρῆξιν, βίον ἔξοχον, ἐσθλὰ πρόπαντα Γα[ργι]λίου πραπίδων, τοῦτο φέρω τὸ θύμα. ὃς δὴ[.]ις παλίνορσον ἐπ' Εὐρυβίην πάλι ταῦρον ἤγαγε καὶ κρειόν, σύμβολον εὐτυχίης. ὀκτὼ γὰρ λυκάβαντας ἐπ' εἴκοσιν ἠρεμέοντας νύκτα διασκεδάσας, αὖθις ἔθηκε φάος. . . . ανιη κυ. . .ι νόος ἡμῶν." (Trans. H. J. Rose.)
[37] *CIL* 6, 1778. [38] *CIL* 6, 1779, 1780.
[39] *ILS* 1259 third section, l. 9: 'porta quis caeli patet.'
[40] Ibid.: 'tu pius m[y]stes sacris teletis reperta mentis arcano premis.'
[41] Ibid.: 'quae tu caduca ac parva semper autumans divum sacerdos infulis celsus clues?' Cf. Symmachus, *Relatio* 12, 2. [42] *ILS* 1259: 'sors mortis.'
[43] Ibid.: 'te propter omnis me beatam, me piam celebrant.'
[44] Jerome, *Ep.* 23, 3.
[45] *CIL* 6, 1756. For the importance of Saint Peter's to high-born Christians, see below 290–3.
[46] Cf. Damasus' *elogium* in honour of Peter and Paul above, 152 and the funeral of Bassus below, p. 268.

The undiminished importance of outstanding senators in public life is perhaps best illustrated by a dramatic account of the funeral of Junius Bassus who died while holding the prefecture of the city in 359.[47] His funeral was a highly public affair and a fragment of his epitaph records that the *populus* rather than his family carried the dead man's sarcophagus; grief was widespread and a huge crowd of citizens, from senators to the city's *matres*, turned out to pay their respects.[48] Bassus had died a recent convert to Christianity but it was the streets and buildings of Rome, over which he had had control, which significantly seemed to groan with grief.[49]

These men found the material world contextualized by a world beyond it. Praetextatus and Probus had been enthusiastic office-holders during their earthly lives but both felt bound to express a disdain for worldly office on their epitaphs. For other senators, immaterial reality could be achieved in other ways. Firmicus Maternus' *Mathesis* was dedicated to a Q. Flavius Maesius Egnatius Lollianus Mavortius. The *Mathesis* attributed the recent misfortunes of two anonymous senators explicitly to astrological causes.[50] One of the senators had been exiled for occult practices and the infamous trials recorded by Ammianus under Valentinian I show that some aristocrats were prepared to turn to the black arts in search of answers.[51]

Though it is difficult to resist impressions, it is not possible to state definitely that late Roman senators were any more interested in other-worldly answers than senators of any other period. It is clear, however, that Christian ascetical ideas did not enter a psychological vacuum. Senators had long been exposed to ideas which invited them to contemplate different levels of reality. Many resisted the invitation. Nevertheless, it is significant that the representatives of those who were sensitive to a higher order should have included some of the most successful and influential Christian and non-Christian senators of the period.[52]

---

[47] Ammianus 17, 11, 5; *AE* (1953), no. 239. For a generally excellent analysis of his sarcophagus, see E. S. Malbon, *The Iconography of the Sarcophagus of Iunius Bassus* (Princeton: Princeton University Press, 1990).

[48] Cf. the funeral of Blesilla below, pp. 278–9.

[49] Conversion: *ILS* 1286; funeral details: *AE* (1953), no. 239.

[50] See T. D. Barnes, 'Two Senators under Constantine', *JRS*, 65 (1975), 40–9. Cf. Augustine, *Confessiones* 5, 3 where he claims that he had read 'many' such books.

[51] See above, pp. 200–3.

[52] The recipient of the *Carmen contra Paganos* has been convincingly identified as Virius Nicomachus Flavianus by J. F. Matthews, 'The Historical Setting of the Carmen Contra Paganos', *Historia*, 20 (1970), 464–79.

3. CHRISTIAN ASCETICISM: POINTS OF CONFLICT

Extreme Christian asceticism provoked a strong reaction in Christians who considered it an illegitimate or excessive form of religious expression. The circle, chiefly of ladies, which surrounded Jerome was drawn from some of the noblest houses in the city. Their introduction to the circle was rarely achieved without some reluctance or even resistance on the part of their families. The old lifestyles and responsibilities of the initiates were supreme tests set for the men and women Jerome knew, and his eulogies on the spiritual strength of his followers also disclose the psychology and attempted resistance of Rome's moderate Christians.

Long before Jerome arrived in Rome as scholar, preacher, and friend of the pope in summer 382, a number of notable ladies of rank, aspiring to the ascetic state, had faced the hostility of an outraged Christian public. The impulse for the new movement was the example of the Egyptian monk Anthony, who had lived as an anchorite in the desert since 286 and who died, aged 106, in 356.[53] It was the news of this saint which Athanasius is reported to have brought to Rome on his visit there in 340. Shortly after his visit, the widow Marcella had decided to devote herself to a life of celibacy, seclusion, and good works in the capital. She was the first aristocratic lady to profess such a life.[54]

Marcella came from an exalted Roman family which numbered consuls and Praetorian Prefects among its ancestors.[55] But the process of renouncing the world was anything but straightforward. On two issues she found herself at odds with her widowed mother, Albina. Marcella's husband had died after only seven months of marriage and her mother was certain that a second marriage would follow. She had her daughter's security in mind as well as the desire to link her own family to another suitable house in Rome. The man chosen was the ageing Naeratius Cerealis, a man with connections at court. He was favoured by Constantius II, who had made him the first Prefect of the City in 352–3, after the usurpation of Magnentius. He went on to be Consul in 358 and his sister married into the imperial family and was

---

[53] For what follows, see D. Gordini, 'Origini e sviluppo del monachesimo a Roma', *Gregorianum*, 37 (1956), 220–60. For the fictitious Prefect of the City under Diocletian who is reported to have freed 1,400 slaves (*Acta S. Sebastiani* in *AASS* (20 January) vol. 2, 639) see Chastagnol, *La Préfecture*, 244, 451, 452 n. 2.

[54] Jerome, *Ep.* 127, 5.

[55] Ibid. 1; *PLRE* I, 543 'Marcella 2'. See M. T. W. Arnheim, *The Senatorial Aristocracy in the Later Roman Empire* (Oxford: Oxford University Press, 1972), 103–4. At p. 104 Arnheim states that her mother was a member of the Ceionii, 'one of the most important aristocratic families in the late empire.'

the mother of Gallus Caesar:[56] 'Her mother Albina went out of her way to secure for the widowed family so exalted a protector.'[57] Albina was anxious to marry off Marcella to her second husband because she was the family's only remaining unattached daughter.[58] Asella, who was almost certainly the sister of Marcella, had been dedicated as a Christian virgin when still a child. But Marcella scorned the old man, and other suitors were put off by her single-minded determination to take up the kind of life which her recent ecclesiastical guests had informed her was taking shape in Egypt.[59] The worldliness of the older woman was not completely dispelled, however, because when it came to the disposal of her own property, Albina wanted to keep it in her family, against the wishes of her daughter who had disposed of much of her own in aid of the poor and wanted her mother to do the same:

Albina was devoted to her own kinsfolk, and wished to leave all her property to her son's children, being without sons and grandsons: Marcella would have preferred to give it to the poor . . .[60]

If Albina's husband had made her his *heres* in his will, then she will already have received part of his property.[61] If he had died intestate, she was also bound to receive a portion, either as a legitimate *heres* (if she had been his wife *in manu*) or from his *heredes* if she had returned to the *potestas* of her own *paterfamilias* after the death of her husband.[62] She may also have received back part or all of her own dowry (*dos*) or retained her *donatio ante nuptias*, if it had been given.[63] Even part of the property, dowry or *donatio* from a wealthy senatorial marriage would have been considerable and Marcella came from a consular family.[64] What Albina attempted to do was to disinherit her own daughters so

[56] *PLRE* I, 197 'Naeratius Cerealis 2'. See Ps.-Jer., *Exhortatio ad Marcellam* 2 (*PL* 30, 53) for the one-time imperial ambitions of Marcella's family.

[57] Jerome, *Ep.* 127, 2 (*CSEL* 56, 146): 'Albinaque mater tam clarum praesidium viduitati domus ultro appeteret . . .'

[58] A. Yarbrough, 'Christianisation in the Fourth Century: The Example of Roman Women', *Church History*, 45 (1976), 149–64, at 155.

[59] Jerome, *Ep.* 127, 5.

[60] Ibid. 4 (*CSEL* 56, 148–9): 'Nam cum illa suum diligeret sanguinem, et absque filiis ac nepotibus, vellet in fratris liberos universa conferri: ista pauperes eligebat.'

[61] See J. F. Gardner, *Women in Roman Law and Society* (London: Routledge, 1986), 5 ff, 163–204; H. F. Jolowicz and B. Nicholas, *Historical Introduction to Roman Law*, 3rd edn. (Cambridge: Cambridge University Press, 1972), 123–4; B. Nicholas, *An Introduction to Roman Law* (Oxford: Clarendon Press, 1962), 237–9 for different types of *heredes*. This portion of the husband's estate could, of course, be very large: J. Harries, '"Treasure in Heaven": Property and Inheritance Among Senators of Late Rome', in E. M. Craik (ed.), *Marriage and Property* (Aberdeen: Aberdeen University Press, 1984), 54–70, at 55.

[62] Nicholas, op. cit. (n. 61), 250.   [63] Ibid. 88–9.   [64] Jerome, *Ep.* 127, 1.

that they could not become her *heredes*.[65] As her daughters, they would be entitled to a share of Albina's property from whoever was the appointed *heres*, but the fate of most of the possessions of Albina could be assured. The 'brother' mentioned here in the account of Jerome was, according to Rampolla and Chastagnol, none other than the great pagan C. Ceionius Rufius Volusianus *signo* Lampadius, Prefect of the City from April 365 to February 366, a fine illustration of how the concern for property cut across any religious boundaries.[66] Jerome skims over the outcome of the story, praising Marcella for her obedience to her mother in testing circumstances, but it is clear that Albina got her way: 'she [Marcella] made over her necklaces and other effects to persons already rich, content to throw away her money rather than to sadden her mother's heart.'[67]

Asella was a noble Christian virgin whom Jerome found living on the Aventine when he reached Rome. She may have been the sister of Marcella, as some scholars have deduced from a statement of Jerome.[68] Her development sheds interesting light on the Christianity of her parents, Albina and a member of the Claudii.[69] Asella was consecrated as a virgin of Christ when scarcely ten years old, but the future that she wanted for herself, when it quickly emerged, was in contradiction to the wishes of her elders.[70] Jerome tells of her early ascetic tendencies. She once sold a golden necklace which her parents had given her without consulting them. Jerome gloried in the child's renunciation of the kind of ostentation for which he was to vilify the 'sham' Christians of the city. But she made further demonstrations of her fervency when she resolved to put aside her expensive clothes and assume the dark dress of an ascetic 'such as her mother had never been willing that she should wear.'[71] She eventually embraced a rigorous ascetic regime of seclusion, fasting, vigils and prayer. Asella's parents were joined in their concern by other family members. Jerome claimed that her

[65] Jerome can be read as referring to grandchildren but the interpretation is problematic. Albina, as far as we know, had only two children: Marcella and Asella (?). Either Marcella had a child through her short-lived marriage or Albina had other children who themselves produced offspring.

[66] Chastagnol, *Fastes*, no. 67, pp. 164–9, at 164 with n. 37 where he accepts M. Rampolla, *Santa Melana Giuniore* (Rome: 1905), 140–2 but also acknowledges Rampolla's occasional confusion. See A. Chastagnol, 'Le sénateur Volusien et la conversion d'une famille de l'aristocratie romaine au Bas-Empire', *REA* 58 (1956), 241–53, at 250 n. 2; *PLRE* I, 978–80 'Volusianus 5'.

[67] Jerome, *Ep.* 127, 4 (*CSEL* 56, 149): 'divitibus peritura concedens, magisque volens pecuniam perdere, quam parentis animum contristare.'

[68] Jerome, *Ep.* 24, 4.

[69] See *PLRE* I, 32 'Albina 1'. She later became an ascetic herself: Jerome, *Ep.* 32, 2; 45, 7; 127, 2; 4. [70] Jerome, *Ep.* 24.

[71] Jerome, *Ep.* 24, 3 (*CSEL* 54, 215): 'quam a matre inpetrare non poterat.'

asceticism was too strong for her other relations who ceased attempting to deflect her: 'she thus showed her relatives that they need hope to wring no further concessions from one who, by her very dress, had condemned the world.'[72] It seems clear that the status of Christian virgin had been chosen for Asella but on terms that envisaged her continued integration in the family and excluded the kind of extremism to which she later turned. Anne Yarbrough states that Christian families which dedicated girls as Christian virgins released them completely and irrevocably into the power of the church.[73] But as we shall see, although some Christian families were content to allow their daughters to remain as Christian virgins for life, others could recall their daughters in time of need. Asella may have begun life as one of the 'sham' virgins of Jerome.[74]

These two early examples illustrate that the appearance of asceticism caused internal difficulties in aristocratic houses. These domestic problems focused on three areas. First, the fate of the share of family property possessed by or due to the converting party. Second, the perpetuation of the family line; and third, the common perception of the life of the ascetic. Jerome says of Marcella's experience: 'At that time no noble lady had professed the monastic life and called herself a nun, so strange and ignominious and degrading did it seem.'[75] Marcella's conversion from the world was, however, not followed by a general desire to imitate her. Jerome explains that only 'many years later' was her example followed by an unknown lady, Sophronia, 'and others'.[76]

In the late 360s and early 370s, before Jerome's arrival in the city, the widow of the Prefect of the City of Rome, Valerius Maximus, caused a sensation by her adoption of the ascetic life after his death.[77] This woman was Melania the Elder.[78] She was born and lived in Spain until the death of her husband and two children in the same year when she decided to come to Rome.[79] In Rome, according to Murphy, she

[72] Jerome, *Ep.* 24, 3 (*CSEL* 54, 216): 'ut intellegeret universa cognatio non posse ei aliud extorqueri, quae iam saeculum damnasset in vestibus.'

[73] Yarbrough, art. cit. (n. 58), 155 ff. Cf. Brown, op. cit. (n. 28), 260–2.

[74] See below, section 4.

[75] Jerome, *Ep.* 127, 5 (*CSEL* 56, 149): 'Nulla eo tempore nobilium feminarum noverat Romae propositum monachorum, nec audebat propter rei novitatem, ignominiosum, ut tunc putabatur.' [76] Ibid.

[77] For Valerius Maximus, *PUR* 361–2, see *PLRE* I, 582; Chastagnol, *Fastes*, no. 64.

[78] See *PLRE* I, 592 'Melania I (the elder)' and F. X. Murphy, 'Melania the Elder: A Biographical Note', *Traditio*, 5 (1947), 59–77; Clark, op. cit. (n. 15), 53.

[79] See Paulinus, *Ep.* 29, 8–9. The chronology is confused. Murphy, art. cit. (n. 78), suggested a marriage for Melania in 356 or 357 (when she was 14 or 15) and the death of her husband c.364 (when she was 22). He placed her arrival in Rome in 365 and departure to the east in 372.

made contact with an ascetic group and Palladius, in his collection of
lives of famous ascetics, records that she took a secret vow of celibacy:
'for she would have been stopped at that time.'[80] She was twenty-two
and, as with Marcella, a second marriage seemed the natural course of
action.[81] She was the granddaughter of Marcellinus, the consul of 341
who was a member of either the *gens Anicia* or *Antonia*.[82] She herself
had married into the Valerii Maximi. Through her own family and that
of her husband, she had sizeable estates distributed in Italy and the
provinces. Paulinus noted that although she had a crowd of relatives at
Rome, she decided not to give her remaining son, Valerius Publicola,
to their care when she finally decided on an ascetic life.[83] Instead he
was left with the Prefect of the City and she promptly resolved not to
see him: 'for she thought it a sin of distrust to give her own attention to
one whom she had entrusted to Christ.'[84] Presently she announced her
intention to travel east to the Holy Land. Paulinus was in no doubt
about the reaction of her family to this development: '[The devil]
attempted, through the utmost pressure of her noble relatives, whom
he equipped to detain her, to block her design and prevent her from
going.'[85] Jerome did not attempt to play down the judgement of 'the
world' on Melania. She had not remarried and instead had begun to
treat her property in a bizarre fashion, selling off some and donating
the revenues from other parts to the Christian Church. She had
physically removed herself from the world, first by the adoption of
simple dress and subsequently by removing herself to the holy places of
the east.

By 377 the progress made by asceticism into the families of the high-
born led Ambrose of Milan to compose a work designed to encourage
and guide those contemplating conversion.[86] This tract, the *De
Virginibus*, was addressed to his sister, Marcellina, who, like Ambrose,
had lived most of her early years at Rome. It was full of advice for
Christian virgins and contained observations drawn from Ambrose's

[80] Palladius, *Historia Lausiaca* 46, 1: ἐκωλύετο γὰρ—ἐν τοῖς καιροῖς . . . (Trans. R. T.
Meyer.)

[81] Ibid.

[82] See Murphy's discussion, art. cit. (n. 78), 61–2 and Arnheim, op. cit. (n. 55), 70.

[83] Paulinus, *Ep.* 29, 8; Palladius, *Historia Lausiaca* 46. For Publicola see *PLRE* I, 753
'Publicola 1'.

[84] Paulinus, *Ep.* 29, 9 (*CSEL* 29, 256): 'diffidentiae peccatum iudicans, si quem
Christo commiserat ipsa curasset.'

[85] Ibid. 10 (*CSEL* 29, 257): 'sed tota nobilium propinquorum potentia ad retinen-
dum armata propositum inpedire et eunti obstare conatus est.'

[86] See N. B. McLynn, *Ambrose of Milan* (California: University of California Press,
1994), 60–3. For a general discussion of the rise of ascetical literature, see R. Lizzi, 'Una
società esortata all'ascetismo: Misure legislative e motivazioni economiche nel IV–V
secolo d.C.', *Studi storici*, 30 (1989), 129–53.

and Marcellina's own experiences there. A significant portion of the work was given over to detailing the kind of opposition which a Christian girl was likely to encounter as she laid aside her worldly life:

You are being exercised, virgin, whilst you are being urged [to accept 'exquisite allurements']. And the anxious entreaties of your parents are your first battles. Conquer your affection first, girl. If you conquer your family, you conquer the world.[87]

It was a good thing for parents to encourage their children to become Christian virgins but more glorious if the decision was spontaneous.[88] Not surprisingly, the objections which Ambrose outlined would appear again in the letters which Jerome wrote to members of the same social class. The men in the lives of Ambrose's virgins would want to become fathers and grandfathers and these women would be put under great pressure to marry.[89] The bishop explained that in their desire to protect family property the parents of virgins might refuse to hand over the dowry which had been set aside, arguing that if such women would not marry earthly husbands, then there was no reason why Christ should have their dowries.[90]

Converting noble virgins could, however, expect special treatment from the Church. Marcellina had accepted the veil symbolizing Christian virginity from the hand of Bishop Liberius himself, in the Basilica of Saint Peter, on Christmas Day 353.[91] The ceremony had been impressive and made less controversial by the goodwill of Marcellina's close relations. Other virgins, however, experienced hostility even at the altar. Ambrose told the recent story of a woman who had attended an episcopal liturgy in one of the basilicas of Rome during which she had dashed to the altar to plead with the bishop to be accepted into the Church as a Christian virgin.[92] There was uproar in the basilica as one of her relatives shouted out: 'Do you think that if your father was alive, he would have allowed you to remain unmarried?'[93] But the woman replied: 'Maybe he died so that no one should stand in my way!'[94] Ambrose explained that the relative who had objected died soon afterwards and warned parents to take careful

---

[87] Ambrose, *De Virginibus* 1, 11, 63 (*PL* 16, 206): 'Exerceris, virgo, dum cogeris. Et haec tibi prima certamina anxia parentum vota proponunt. Vince prius, puella, pietatem: si vincis domum, vincis et saeculum'; Cf. Jerome, *Ep.* 54, 3; 22, 1; 39, 6.

[88] Ambrose, *De Virginibus* 1, 11, 62.

[89] Ibid. 1, 7, 33.   [90] Ibid. 1, 11, 62.   [91] Ibid. 3, 1–3.

[92] Ibid. 1, 11, 65–6. See Brown, op. cit. (n. 28), 343–4.

[93] Ambrose, *De Virginibus* 1, 11, 66 (*PL* 16, 207): 'Quid si—inquit pater tuus viveret, innuptam te manere pateretur?'

[94] Ibid. (*PL* 16, 208): 'Et ideo fortasse defecit, ne quis impedimentum posset adferre.'

note of 'the example of transgression'.[95] There is no reason for thinking, however, that such hostile relatives regarded themselves as bad Christians. Ambrose himself lamented the fact that many of the virgins who had been prevented from adopting the ascetic life were, like Asella, the daughters of respectable Christian widows.[96]

In the period after the first dramatic conversions from 'the world', the same points of conflict arose between the enthusiastic ascetics and the 'respectable' Christians of the capital. Jerome suggests that a second impulse to the development of the ascetic life at Rome was provided by the visit of Athanasius' successor at Alexandria to the city in *c*.373.[97] Ascetic literature had begun appearing in the period between the retirement of Marcella from the world and the visit of Peter. An important biography of Saint Anthony, written by Athanasius in Greek in 357, was translated into Latin not long afterwards and Jerome also wrote a biography of Saint Anthony's famous disciple Paul, in Latin, early in the 370s.[98] Jerome, after his arrival at Rome, became deeply involved with a circle of aristocratic ladies living on the Aventine Hill.[99] His letters to these women and his *encomia* on them are our most substantial source for the relationship between them and their fellow noble Romans.

It will be useful to treat separately Jerome's evidence as it concerns two groups: Christian virgins, and Christian widows.[100]

Jerome considered the status of holy virgin to be the most sanctified human state saying: 'I praise wedlock, I praise marriage, but it is because they give me virgins.'[101]

Iulia Eustochium was the most famous virgin in Jerome's circle.[102] She was the daughter of Paula, who, according to Jerome, was descended on her mother's side from 'the Gracchi and the Scipiones'. Like Paula, Eustochium became an extreme ascetic, eventually retiring with Paula from the city of Rome in 385/6 to go east and join Jerome.[103]

---

[95] Ibid. 1, 11, 66. A familiar theme in Christian literature on 'holy men'. See MacMullen, *Christianity and Paganism*, 168 n. 32.

[96] Ambrose, *De Virginibus* 1, 10, 58: 'I have known many virgins who had the desire, but were prevented from going forward by their mothers, and, which is more serious, mothers who were [Christian] widows.'

[97] Jerome, *Ep.* 127, 5. Jerome does not make the interval between Athanasius and Peter clear. See Gordini, art. cit. (n. 53), 227.

[98] Ibid., 226–9; J. N. D. Kelly, *Jerome: His Life, Writings and Controversies* (London: Duckworth, 1975), 60–1.

[99] Ibid., chs. 9–11; see also P. Rousseau, *Ascetics, Authority, and the Church in the Age of Jerome and Cassian* (Oxford: Oxford University Press, 1978), pt. 3, ch. 1.

[100] See Drijvers, art. cit. (n. 19), 248 ff.

[101] Jerome, *Ep.* 22, 20 (*CSEL* 54, 170): 'Laudo nuptias, laudo coniugium, sed quia mihi virgines generant.'

[102] *PLRE* I, 312.

[103] Jerome, *Ep.* 108, 6.

In the spring of 384 Jerome addressed a long letter to her in praise of virginity and full of advice on how the virgin state was best preserved.[104] Her (pagan) uncle Hymetius and his wife Praetextata had attempted to cut short her ascetic career in the early 380s:[105]

[Praetextata] under instructions from her husband Hymetius, altered the virgin's dress and appearance and arranged her neglected hair in a styled wave, desiring to overcome the resolution of the virgin herself and the expressed wishes of her mother.[106]

The early 380s were years of tension over the future of the great pagan cults of the city, when, on Brown's thesis, the ideological divisions between the two kinds of religious belief became heightened. But of course, the mere religious affiliation of Hymetius and his wife do not constitute proof that he acted from anti-Christian motives. The incident had taken place very shortly before or after Jerome's visit to Rome, and it is even possible that he may have been in the city at the time. According to Ammianus, Hymetius was an office-holder and a man of outstanding ability.[107] He had had statues erected in his name in the city and must therefore have been known to Jerome. His paganism must also have been known. Yet in the account of the episode, Jerome nowhere mentions that he was pagan. Elsewhere in his letters he exults over the misfortunes of high-born pagans, notably Vettius Agorius Praetextatus, who died at the same time as a friend of Jerome, late in 384.[108] But the letter in which he recorded the Eustochium episode was written in 403, to Laeta at Rome, from Bethlehem, where Jerome was living near both Eustochium herself and Paula. In fact, the intervention of Hymetius around the year 384, was on strictly *family* grounds and relations between him and his sister-in-law Paula were not bad. Hymetius knew well the kind of life upon which Eustochium was embarking, and Paula's asceticism was cutting her off from her own children.[109] The reconstructed *stemma* of the family in *PLRE* suggests that Paula was an only child. If her parents and husband were both dead then her husband's brother (Hymetius) became the children's nearest male relative.[110] It is probable that Hymetius was fearful for Eustochium's health under such a regime, which was to contribute to

---

[104] Jerome, *Ep.* 22.
[105] Iulius Festus Hymetius: *PLRE* I, 447 and Von Haehling, op. cit. (n. 14), 425. For Praetextata see *PLRE* I, 721. For them both see Arnheim, op. cit. (n. 55), 178–80. Praetexta related to Vettius Agorius Praetextatus?
[106] Jerome, *Ep.* 107, 5 (*CSEL* 55, 296): 'iubente viro Hymetio . . . habitum eius cultumque mutavit et neglectum crinem undanti gradu texuit vincere cupiens et virginis propositum et matris desiderium.'
[107] Ammianus 28, 1, 17.
[108] Jerome, *Ep.* 23, 3.
[109] Jerome, *Ep.* 108, 5.
[110] *PLRE* I, 1143, *stemma* 23.

the death of her sister Blesilla in 384–5. Jerome, exploiting the same rhetorical techniques as Ambrose, related how Praetextata had met a swift death after her actions but added carefully:

I have related this story here not from any desire to exult over the misfortunes of the unhappy, but to warn you that you must with much fear and carefulness keep the vow which you have made to God.[111]

Whatever the reason for Hymetius' actions, there is certainly evidence from Jerome to suggest that Roman *Christians* disapproved of the strong emphasis placed on Christian virginity. One of the strongest objections raised against Christian virgins led Jerome to devote a significant portion of *Letter* 22 to rebutting it. This was the pressure upon Eustochium to marry. According to Yarbrough, Paula, like Albina, was content to dedicate *one* daughter as a Christian virgin when her other daughters lived in the world.[112] But even this arrangement was not well received by other nobles. The pressure on women to marry and produce children was considerable and on girls like Eustochium this pressure was all the stronger because of the necessity of maintaining the great senatorial houses of the city.[113] There were, of course, benefits. A wealthy successful husband could guarantee a comfortable life and the respect of one's peers.[114] Jerome reminded Eustochium of the fleeting pleasures of marriage which her recently widowed sister Blesilla had lost.[115]

Widowhood was 'the second rank of chastity' for Jerome.[116] He was strongly against second marriage, and considered it the duty of widows to remain such.[117] This view brought both Jerome and other ascetics directly into conflict with the moderate Christians of the city.

Paula was a noble lady who had married Iulius Toxotius 'in whose veins ran the noble blood of Aeneas and the Julii'.[118] Jerome claimed

---

[111] Jerome, *Ep.* 107, 5 (*CSEL* 54, 296): 'et hoc retuli, non quod insultare velim calamitatibus infelicium, sed ut te moneam, cum quanto metu et cautione servare debeas, quod domino spopondisti.' Cf. Ambrose, *De Virginibus* 1, 11, 66. See above, 274–5.

[112] See Jerome, *Ep.* 66, 13 (397) to Pammachius: 'I myself was not at Rome but in the desert . . . at the time when your father-in-law Toxotius [Pammachius had married Paula's daughter Paulina] was still alive and his daughters were still given up to the world.'

[113] For marriage as 'a reassuring microcosm of the social order' see Brown, op. cit. (n. 28), 17.

[114] See below, section 4.   [115] Jerome, *Ep.* 22, 15.   [116] Ibid.

[117] Jerome, *Ep.* 38, 3 (to Marcella, on Blesilla). Cf. Fabiola's error of second marriage: Jerome, *Ep.* 77, 3 (399).

[118] See *PLRE* I, 674 'Paula (St.)'. For Toxotius, the phrase is Jerome's, *Ep.* 108, 4: '[Paula] iunctaque viro Toxotio, qui Aeneae et Iuliorum altissimum sanguinem trahit.' See *PLRE* I, 921 'Toxotius 2'.

that before his death Paula had had a desire to take up a vow of celibacy but that she had felt obliged as a wife to provide him with a male heir.[119] Nevertheless, there was a deep affection between them and his death greatly saddened her.[120] After his death, *c.*380, she began her charity work in earnest but ran into the opposition of her family, horrified at the dissipation of the house's wealth: 'She robbed her children; and, when her relatives remonstrated with her for doing so, she declared that she was leaving to them a better inheritance in the mercy of Christ.'[121] For a time, Paula had to endure what had become the alien world of the moderate Christians: 'Nor was she long able to endure the visits and crowded receptions which her high position in the world and her exalted family entailed upon her.'[122] By spring 384, the situation, as her relatives saw it, was worsening. Her daughter Eustochium had taken a vow of perpetual virginity and was under ascetic instruction. Then, at the turn of the year, the husband of another daughter, Blesilla, died.[123] She fell ill a short time afterwards and underwent some kind of conversion experience, emerging from the sickness a devoted ascetic.[124] Jerome asked rhetorically, what the new Blesilla had to do with those who had attended her and who were now appalled at her change of course: 'The Christian must rejoice that it is so, and he that is vexed must admit that he has no claim to be called a Christian.'[125] Jerome of course advised her to remain a widow.[126] But within four months she was dead and bad feeling against Jerome reached a bitter climax. Responsibility for her funeral passed to those who thought it appropriate to hold it in proper aristocratic style. Jerome accepted their actions although he insidiously invoked the spirit of Blesilla to condemn them:

Her obsequies were celebrated with customary splendour. People of rank headed the procession, a pall made of cloth of gold covered her bier. But I seemed to hear a voice from Heaven saying: 'I do not recognize these trappings; such is not the garb I used to wear; this magnificence is strange to me.'[127]

---

[119] Jerome, *Ep.* 108, 4.   [120] Ibid.

[121] Ibid. 5 (*CSEL* 55, 310): 'expoliabat filios et inter obiurgantes propinquos maiorem se eis hereditatem Christi misericordiam dimittere loquebatur.'

[122] Ibid. 6 (*CSEL* 55, 310): 'Nec diu potuit excelsi apud saeculum generis et nobilissimae familiae visitationes et frequentiam sustinere.'

[123] Jerome, *Ep.* 39, 4. Kelly, op. cit. (n. 98), 98–9.

[124] Jerome, *Ep.* 38, 2.

[125] Ibid. (*CSEL* 54, 290): 'Qui Christianus est, gaudeat; qui irascitur, non esse se indicat Christianum.'

[126] Ibid. 3.

[127] Jerome, *Ep.* 39, 1 (*CSEL* 54, 295): 'ex more parantur exsequiae et nobilium ordine praeeunte aureum feretro velamen obtenditur. Videbatur mihi tunc clamare de caelo "Non agnosco vestem; amictus iste non meus, hic ornatus alienus est."'

Whether the family had overruled the wishes of Paula or she herself had assented to the ceremony in this form is unclear, but she was certainly present at the funeral and, overcome with grief, she fainted. Jerome wrote to reproach her. She had encouraged the whisperings of the crowd and the accusations of those present, the mourners at an aristocratic funeral ceremony. They complained that the ascetic life had killed the young woman and urged that those who promoted it ought to be ejected from the city. It was claimed also that Paula herself had wished Blesilla to remarry, 'that she might have grandchildren'. Yarbrough has made the interesting suggestion, on the strength of Jerome's account of Blesilla's funeral, that Paula herself may have objected to Blesilla's conversion.[128] Since Eustochium was a consecrated virgin and Paula's other daughter, Paulina, was living continently with her husband the hope of the transfer of family property lay with Blesilla.[129] As we shall see, there is evidence that Paula's disposal of property was as careful as that of Melania the Elder, but it is more likely that Jerome was trying to show Paula that her grief had been so indiscreet that their common enemies were wilfully misinterpreting what had happened; worse, the objectors were suggesting that Paula herself was being duped in some way by Jerome.[130] He was thus trying to shock her by summoning up allegations made by the mourners that his influence over her left her incapable of thinking clearly. It was up to her to demonstrate that this was not true.

Paula herself soon decided that her future lay with Jerome, as an ascetic, in the east. But her relations fought to the last to convince her otherwise: 'she went down to Portus accompanied by her brother, her kinsfolk and above all her children.'[131]

In a letter written in 394, ten years after his departure from Rome, Jerome addressed himself to Furia, the daughter-in-law of Sextus Petronius Probus, on how she could best preserve her widowhood.[132] Since 392, the writings of a certain Jovinianus had been circulating in the city. He had once been a strict ascetic himself but now advocated a less extreme course and in particular he asserted that sexual relations did not make certain kinds of Christians inferior to others.[133] In

[128] Yarbrough, art. cit. (n. 58), 155.

[129] *PLRE* I, 675 'Paulina 3'.

[130] Jerome, *Ep.* 39, 6.

[131] Jerome, *Ep.* 108, 6 (*CSEL* 55, 311): 'Descendit ad portum fratre, cognatis, affinibus et—quod his maius est—liberis prosequentibus.'

[132] Jerome, *Ep.* 54.

[133] For Jovinianus, see D. G. Hunter, 'Resistance to the Virginal Ideal in Fourth-Century Rome: The Case of Jovinian', *Theological Studies*, 48 (1987), 45–64; Kelly, op. cit. (n. 98), 180–7. Condemned and fled to Milan in 392. See Gordini, art. cit. (n. 53), 253.

addition, Rome itself was undergoing something of a pagan revival at the same time.[134] There had been apostasy.[135] Against this background, Furia had writen to Jerome. He well understood the dilemma of the young Christian widow, though he had no sympathy for those who succumbed to second marriages:

> Young widows . . . in heat generally make excuses such as these: 'My little patrimony is daily decreasing, the property which I have inherited is being squandered, a servant has spoken insultingly to me, a maid has neglected my orders. Who will appear for me before the authorities? Who will be responsible for the rents of my estates? Who will see to the education of my children and to the bringing-up of my slaves?' Thus, shameful to say, they put that forward as a reason for marrying again, which alone should deter them from so doing.[136]

Jerome laid before Furia the manifesto of the moderate Christians against whom she would have to struggle if she really desired to dedicate herself to Christ as a widow. The foundation of the moderate position was the acceptance of the value of property, family ties, and the responsibilities of status.

4. JEROME AND THE 'SHAM' CHRISTIANS OF ROME[137]

Tell me, what is that community or sect of monks and why are they the object of hatred even among Christians?[138]

The aristocratic opponents of extreme asceticism resisted above all else the wholesale, and to their minds indiscriminate, disposal of property which often accompanied a conversion. Jerome's letters give the impression that his Christian friends inhabited a world teeming with

[134] For bibliography see above 219, n. 6.

[135] Siricius, *Ep.* 7, 2 (*PL* 13, 1168–71); Augustine, *De Peccatorum Meritis et Remissione* 3, 7, 13 (*PL* 44, 193). See Gordini, art. cit. (n. 53), 252–3.

[136] Jerome, *Ep.* 54, 15 (*CSEL* 54, 481–2): 'Solent adulescentulae viduae . . . subantes dicere: "Patrimoniolum meum cottidie perit, maiorum hereditas dissipatur, servus contumeliose locutus est, imperium ancilla neglexit. Quis procedet ad publicum? Quis respondebit pro agrorum tributis? Parvulos meos quis erudiet? Vernulas quis educabit?" et hanc—pro nefas!—causam opponunt matrimonii, quae vel sola debuit nuptias inpedire.' Cf. Jerome, *Contra Helvidium* 20 (*PL* 23, 214); Chrysost., *De Virgin.* 56, 1.

[137] A version of this section has appeared as J. Curran, 'Jerome and the Sham Christians of Rome', *JEH*, 48 (1997), 1–17. I am grateful to Cambridge University Press for permission to reproduce some of the material. See the useful article by H. O. Maier, 'The Topography of Heresy and Dissent in Late-Fourth-Century Rome', *Historia*, 44 (1995), 232–49.

[138] *Consultationum Zacchaei Christiani et Apollonii Philosophi* 3, 3 (*PL* 20, 1151): 'Quae nunc igitur monachorum congregatio vel secta sit, vel quam ob causam etiam nostrorum odiis digni habeantur, exprome.'

'sham' Christians on every side.[139] He affirmed that his ascetic followers were wholly superior and removed from the worldly life of the 'sham' Christians but it is clear that many of his friends emerged from just such a world and some experienced difficulties in leaving it behind.

The question of Saint Jerome's general credibility as a source for the social history of this period has rarely been asked, let alone satisfactorily answered.[140] Too frequently ferociously vitriolic passages are dismissed as 'satire' or 'exaggeration' without any consideration of the difficult question of their historical validity. Jerome was a passionate and often impulsive man and his letters, which constitute the chief source material used in this chapter, vary greatly in tone and content. No general assessment would be applicable to them all. For that reason, it is best to consider the difficulties raised by individual letters in the main discussion. Here, it is necessary only to make some general remarks about his use of satire and why many satirical passages in his letters ought still to be regarded as an indispensable source for the lives and attitudes of senatorial Christians. Samuel Dill wrote of Jerome:

Saint Jerome is not only a monk but an artist in words; and his horror of evil, his vivid imagination, and his passion for literary effect occasionally carry him beyond the region of sober fact. There was much to amend in the morals of the Roman world. But we must not take the leader of a great moral reformation as a cool and dispassionate observer.[141]

Dill was certainly correct; Jerome exaggerated and embellished for effect. The question therefore arises: what can the historian believe? We must seek to understand what exactly it was that Jerome wrote and why he did so. Wiesen, though disappointing in other aspects of his study of Jerome, made an important contribution to our understanding of Jerome's familiarity with the traditional techniques of great Latin satire. As to the question of what Jerome believed he was writing,

---

[139] Jerome, *Ep.* 22, 3. Cf. Ambrose, *De Virginibus* 1, 11, 63. For a critique of modern work on demi-, half-, or paganized Christians, see Markus, *End*, 33. 'Sham' here derives from Jerome's own judgement.

[140] D. S. Wiesen, *Saint Jerome as a Satirist* (Ithaca, NY: Cornell University Press, 1964) is very unsympathetic to Jerome. See e.g. p. 259 for a belief in Jerome's 'uncontrollable penchant for malice'. Cf. A. Cameron, 'Virginity as Metaphor: Women and the Rhetoric of Early Christianity', in Averil Cameron (ed.), *History as Text* (London: Duckworth, 1989), 181–205. See Cooper, art. cit. (n. 15) for a thoughtful analysis of the rhetorical strategies of Jerome, Chrysostom, and Augustine.

[141] Dill, op. cit. (n. 2), 131. Cf. Harries, art. cit. (n. 61), 55–6: 'Like all propagandists, he enhanced aspects of his saintly protégées most favourable to his message, while playing down or discarding facts which showed them to be more mindful of traditional obligations than he would care to admit.'

Wiesen stated: 'satire is to his mind a clear mirror of life wherein human behaviour is so accurately reflected that its ludicrous inconsistencies are mercilessly exposed.'[142] Antin, Wiesen's reviewer, believed that Wiesen was too much influenced by classical notions of satire.[143] Wiesen thought that Jerome concentrated on the 'ludicrousness' of those he satirized but this is a misunderstanding of Jerome's *Christian* satire. Christianity had become, among other things, an interlocking system of ethical prescriptions. Interpretations of the sayings of Christ or the Fathers were, of course, frequent, but all Christians were under greater or lesser pressure to conduct themselves in conformity with a set of ethical guidelines. Jerome focused on the serious moral discrepancy between the standards and behaviour of his satirical targets and his own well-defined views on the Christian life and how it ought to be conducted. It is this clearly defined Christian form of behaviour that distinguished Jerome's satire from that of his classical forerunners. Wiesen pointed out that Jerome, like the classical satirists, had a reforming purpose. But in a fundamental sense, Jerome and his Christian enemies were attempting to move in the same ethical direction. It was the fact that they and Jerome had so much in common that made their inadequacy so painful to him. He wrote to Eustochium in 384: 'My purpose is to show you that you are fleeing from Sodom and should take warning by Lot's wife.'[144]

If Wiesen underestimated what was at stake in Jerome's view of proper Christian conduct, he was surely right in pointing out the importance to Jerome of the painting of vivid pictures. But one reason why Jerome became such a controversial figure in the city was because his satirical writings struck their targets so accurately.[145]

The world of the 'sham' Christians of Rome was manifestly sociable. In 385, Jerome, still smarting from the criticism which had been levelled at his letter to Eustochium of the year before, wrote to Marcella, who had become the spiritual adviser to Blesilla.[146] Blesilla's adoption of a simple dress and diet was upsetting her contemporaries. Jerome wrote that the women who *ought* to scandalize the Christian community were those who painted their eyes and lips, whitened their skin with chalk, and donned wigs: 'A Christian woman should blush to do violence to nature or to stimulate desire by bestowing care upon the

[142] Wiesen, op. cit. (n. 140), 249.

[143] Review in *Latomus*, 23 (1964), 856–8. At 856: 'on a longtemps l'impression que Wiesen, avec Grützmacher, cherche à dénigrer Jérôme.'

[144] Jerome, *Ep.* 22, 2 (*CSEL* 54, 146): 'sed ut intellegeres tibi exeunti de Sodoma timendum esse Loth uxoris exemplum.' See *Genesis* 19, 26.

[145] Brown, op. cit. (n. 28), 367 on Jerome, *Ep.* 22: 'It was an album of caricatures in which too many clergymen and upperclass Christians recognised themselves.'

[146] Jerome, *Ep.* 38; cf. 54, 3.

flesh.'[147] These careful preparations were made before going out into the world of the city. The Christians whom Jerome had in mind enjoyed visiting each other's houses in Rome or meeting up at the tombs of the martyrs. In the long and controversial *Letter* 22 which was written in 384, Jerome instructed Eustochium to shun 'widows of necessity and not choice' whose houses were 'filled with flatterers and guests'.[148] His remark denoted women who called themselves Christian widows, but were so far from living the kind of Christian life which Jerome had prescribed that their status could be put down to their undesirability as wives for any man.

The houses of married Christian women were also depicted as dangerous distractions for Eustochium. The social status of these households is indicated by Jerome's remarks on the women there, preening themselves because their husbands were 'judges and dignified by some high rank'.[149] Many Christian senators continued to take an active part in public life, only becoming catechumens, rarely attending Christian services, or even refusing baptism altogether.[150] Fittingly, it was Faltonia Betitia Proba, the aunt of the worldly-wise Sextus Petronius Probus, who was to produce one of the fullest statements of moderate Roman Christianity from the female point of view.[151] Betitia Proba was married to Clodius Celsinus Adelphius who had been governor, proconsul and finally Prefect of Rome in 351.[152] Proba wrote the second of her *centones*, *De Laudibus Christi*, around 362.[153] Its subject ranged from creation to the life of Christ and its underlying

---

[147] Ibid. 3 (*CSEL* 54, 291): 'erubescat mulier Christiana, si naturae cogit decorem, si carnis curam facit ad concupiscentiam . . .'

[148] Jerome, *Ep.* 22, 16.

[149] Ibid.: 'de iudicibus viris et in aliqua positis dignitate . . .' Cf. 8 where Jerome argues that if *his* temptation in the desert was great, then how much greater must it be for Eustochium who is surrounded by 'luxury and ease'.

[150] See Brown, op. cit. (n. 28), 342 with an apposite quotation from Augustine, *Ep.* 2*, 4, 1–7 and 7, 4 to an African Christian (Firmus): 'you men who all fear the burdens imposed by baptism. You are easily beaten by your women . . . it is their presence in great number that causes the church to grow.'

[151] *PLRE* I, 732 'Proba 2' with *stemma* 24 for probable family link. See also J. F. Matthews, 'The Poetess Proba and Fourth-Century Rome: Questions of Interpretation', in M. Christol, S. Demougin, Y. Duval, C. Lepelley, and L. Piétri (eds.), *Institutions, société et vie politique dans l'empire romain au IVe siècle a. J.-C.*, Collections de l'École française de Rome, 159 (1992), 277–304. For Probus: *PLRE* I, 736–40. Ammianus 27, 11. See D. M. Novak, '*Anicianae domus culmen, nobilitatis culmen*', *Klio*, 62 (1980), 473–93.

[152] *PLRE* I, 192–3 'Clodius Celsinus *signo* Adelphius 6.'

[153] The date is reconstructed by E. A. Clark, 'Faltonia Betitia Proba and her Vergilian Poem: The Christian Matron as Artist', in E. A. Clark (ed.), *Ascetic Piety and Women's Faith*, Studies in Women and Religion, 20 (Lewiston: Edwin Mellon Press, 1986), 124–52, at 129.

social assumptions have been impressively studied by Elizabeth Clark.[154] Clark noticed that Proba exalted the maternal virtues of Mary who, for example, is solely responsible for saving the child Jesus during the Massacre of the Innocents.[155] Even more revealing, however, is the interpretation of the responsibilites of wealthy Christians. They were encouraged by Proba to share their goods with *kin* but the poor were never mentioned. There were in fact no references to the renunciation of riches in the whole *cento*.[156] As Clark puts it:

Proba has Jesus rather subtly sanction class distinction when she puts these words into his mouth, 'whatever wealth exists/For each', men should joyously call upon their common God.[157]

The Sermon on the Mount was recast by Proba so that Christ speaks of the necessity of being even-handed with one's *clientes*.[158] The rich young man of the New Testament made an appearance but was not asked to sell all that he had but was encouraged, ambiguously, to 'learn . . . contempt for wealth'.[159] In general, Proba's *cento* reflects the deep desire for social stability founded upon the virtues of respect for parents and kin, the sanctity of the home and marital chastity.[160]

In the houses of worldly and successful Christians Eustochium would find temptations from the world which she had renounced. These Christians entertained their friends in royal fashion. Their houses were the scene of what Jerome calls 'Christian banquets' and their tableware unashamedly portrayed images of the most abhorred pagan deities.[161] One of the recurring themes in Jerome's advice to his Christian ladies concerned the iniquities stimulated by excessive eating and drinking.[162] His careful advice to Eustochium to cut herself off completely from this social round was not misplaced. It clearly took some time for her to understand exactly what disturbed Jerome most. On Saint Peter's Day (29 June) 384 she earned a mild rebuke from her spiritual director for sending him some cooked doves, a basket of

---

[154] Clark (ed.), *Ascetic Piety and Women's Faith.*

[155] ll. 369–79; Clark, art. cit. (n. 153), 141–2.

[156] ll. 475–81; Clark, art. cit. (n. 153), 139.

[157] *Cento* ll. 470–1. Clark, art. cit. (n. 153), 139.

[158] l. 477.   [159] Clark, art. cit. (n. 153), 140.   [160] Ibid. 143.

[161] Jerome, *Ep.* 27, 2 (to Marcella, AD 385): 'Have I ever embellished my dinner plates with engravings of idols? Have I ever, at a Christian banquet, set before the eyes of virgins the polluting spectacle of satyrs embracing bacchanals?' See K. J. Shelton, *The Esquiline Treasure* (London: British Museum Publications, 1981); ead., 'The Esquiline Treasure', *AJA*, 89 (1985), 145–55; cf. A. Cameron, 'The Date and Owners of the Esquiline Treasure', *AJA*, 89 (1985), 135–45; K. J. Shelton, 'Roman Aristocrats, Christian Commissions: The Carrand Diptych', *JbAC*, 27–8 (1984–5), 166–80.

[162] See e.g. Jerome, *Ep.* 22, 8, 16, 17. Also *Ep.* 52, 11 (to Nepotianus); *Ep.* 54, 9–10 (to Furia).

cherries, and some bracelets: 'we must be careful to celebrate our holy day not so much with abundance of food as with exultation of spirit.'[163]

The 'sham' Christians of Jerome played host to an assortment of Christian guests. These were mainly male clerics and ascetics but occasionally also women. Jerome summoned up the picture of the forecourts of the houses of wealthy Christian ladies thronging with kissing clergy.[164] In 384, before she had decided to follow an ascetic life in the east, Jerome warned Eustochium to beware of ascetic frauds.[165] False ascetics could be seen in the city, barefoot, long-haired, dishevelled, and sometimes loaded with chains of self-mortification. He named the recent cases of two otherwise unknown men, Antimus and Sophronius, who had gained access to noble houses and had lodged there for some time. He hinted darkly that once inside, such men indulged in secret feasts and other unspeakable acts, an accusation that they enjoyed sexual relations with their female hosts.[166] Other men, monks like Jerome himself, were anxious to secure a place among the clergy of the city, believing that as deacons or presbyters they would enjoy easier access to the houses of the wealthy.[167] These men were visibly less ascetic in appearance than Jerome, who maliciously called them 'bridegrooms' rather than clerics:[168] 'Certain persons have devoted the whole of their life and energies to the single subject of knowing the names, houses and characters of married ladies.'[169] Jerome described one notorious character, whose name he suppressed, who extorted household items from pious Christian women.[170] Marcella herself was approached by Montanists and Jerome's *Letter* 41 was dispatched by him across the city to inform her fully of the errors of their teaching.[171]

The problem of clerical confidence tricksters had surfaced before, in 370, when Bishop Damasus himself received a letter from Valentinian I, Valens, and Gratian.[172] This was not, as has sometimes been supposed, an attempt to ban absolutely all contact between clerics and wealthy households.[173] The law stated that ecclesiastics, *ex-ecclesiasticis*, and 'those who wish to be called by the name of continents' would be denied access to the houses of widows and female wards: 'if hereafter the

---

[163] Jerome, *Ep.* 31, 3 (*CSEL* 54, 251): 'Unde nobis sollicitius providendum, ut sollemnem diem non tam ciborum abundantia quam spiritus exultatione celebremus . . .' See Kelly, op. cit. (n. 98), 100.

[164] Jerome, *Ep.* 22, 16.

[165] Ibid. 28.   [166] Ibid.   [167] Ibid.   [168] Ibid.

[169] Ibid. (*CSEL* 54, 185): 'Quidam in hoc omne studium vitamque posuerunt, ut matronarum nomina, domos moresque cognoscant.'   [170] Ibid.

[171] Written at Rome during AD 385. See Jerome, *Ep.* 42, also to Marcella, which attacked Novatianism. For this 'heterodox topography', see Maier, art. cit. (n. 137), and my remarks above, 129–42.

[172] *CT* 16, 2, 20.   [173] Piétri, *RC*, i. 419.

kinsmen, by blood or marriage, of the aforesaid women should suppose that such men ought to be reported to the authorities.'[174] Clearly, from the account of Jerome, not all Christians found the attention of clerics unwelcome. Indeed, elsewhere in his own letters, he is capable of adopting quite a different tone on the subject: '[Marcella] went nowhere without her mother, and would never see without witnesses such monks and clergy as the needs of a large house required her to interview.'[175] But contact between holy men and lay Christians had been sanctioned at the highest levels of society. The emperor Constantius II himself had been approached by a number of high-born Roman *matronae* on the occasion of his visit to Rome in 357, requesting the return of bishop Liberius.[176] The influence of such ladies could provoke the enemies of a bishop of Rome. The pro-Ursinian *Praefatio* to the *Collectio Avellana* bitterly attacked bishop Damasus as the 'auriscalpius matronarum' and alleged that his election had been secured with the use of bribes.[177] Piétri has interpreted the document as a reactionary statement from a Christian group hostile to what it saw as the watering down of the values of the 'Eglise persécutée'.[178]

A further indication that the great houses of Rome were the location of controversial contacts between the high-born and 'holy' men can be seen in a pair of significant laws from the eastern empire dating to 390. Prompted, allegedly, by a domestic scandal in Constantinople, the emperors Valentinian II, Theodosius and Arcadius put their names to a letter dispatched to Fl. Eutolmius Tatianus, a pagan holder of the Oriental Prefecture.[179] The emperors expressed concern at the manner in which certain women were disposing of their property in the name of Christianity. A rare citation of Scripture in the preamble led on to a stern regulation:

no woman shall be transferred to the society of deaconesses until she is sixty years of age and has the desired offspring at home.[180]

---

[174] *CT* 16, 2, 20: 'si posthac eos adfines earum vel propinqui putaverint deferendos.' (Trans. C. Pharr.)

[175] Jerome, *Ep.* 127, 3 (*CSEL* 56, 148) (where mother is Albina): 'Nusquam sine matre: nullum clericorum et monachorum (quod amplae domus interdum exigebat) vidit absque arbitris.'   [176] Theodoret, *HE* 2, 14.

[177] *Collectio Avellana* 1, 9; see 1, 5–6 for bribery allegations. See above, 137–42.

[178] Piétri, *RC*, i. 412 ff., at 414: 'Dans le lutte obscure des clans ecclésiastiques, l'élection d'Ursinus cristallise l'opposition d'une minorité romaine hostile à l'évolution de la Rome chrétienne.'

[179] The law: *CT* 16, 2, 27 (21 June 390). The scandal, possibly involving Olympias: Sozomen *HE* 7, 16.

[180] *CT* 16, 2, 27: 'Nulla nisi emensis sexaginta annis, cui votiva domi proles sit, secundum praeceptum apostoli ad diaconissarum consortium transferatur.' The preamble refers to 1 Tim. 5: 9.

Even then, such a woman's property was to be handed over to suitable persons 'to be managed diligently and conscientiously'. Only income from landed estates could remain in the control of the deaconess. A further clause stipulated:

she shall expend none of her jewels and ornaments, none of her gold and silver and other embellishments of a sumptuous home, under the pretext of religion.[181]

These goods were to be signed over, in writing, 'to her children or next of kin or any other persons whatsoever' according to the judgement of her own free will. Nothing, however, could be left to church, cleric, or pauper in a will:

nothing shall be bestowed on clerics to the fraud of Our venerable sanction, by secret trust, through cunning artifice or the disgraceful connivance of any person. Rather, they shall be deprived of all the goods which they had coveted.[182]

Remarkably, the law even went as far as to prescribe that:

Women who cut off their hair, contrary to divine and human laws, at the instigation and persuasion of some professed belief, shall be kept away from the doors of the churches.[183]

But within two months, presumably because of the support which the beneficiaries of upper-class patronage were able to mobilize, the law was completely repealed.[184]

In 394, Jerome wrote to Nepotianus, a nephew of Heliodorus and a former imperial official.[185] Heliodorus had become bishop of Altinum and had ordained Nepotianus, to whom Jerome offered advice on the clerical life. This letter forms a neat parallel with that addressed to Eustochium ten years earlier. Where Eustochium had been encouraged to modify her own behaviour, Nepotianus was warned about what he could expect to encounter in the priestly life. Jerome made it clear that Nepotianus would be expected to minister to the sick, including the well-born: 'It is your duty to visit the sick, to know the homes and children of ladies who are married, and to guard the secrets of noblemen.'[186] The letter gave details of the kind of treatment which

---

[181] *CT* 16, 2, 27: 'Nihil de monilibus et superlectili, nihil de auro argento ceterisque clarae domus insignibus sub religionis defensione consumat . . .'

[182] Ibid. 'nec tacito fideicommisso aliquid clericis in fraudem venerabilis sanctionis callida arte aut probosa cuiuspiam coniventia deferatur; extorres sint ab omnibus quibus inhiaverant bonis.'

[183] Ibid. 1: 'Feminae, quae crinem suum contra divinas humanasque leges instinctu persuasae professionis absciderint, ab ecclesiae foribus arceantur.'

[184] Ibid. 28 (23 August 390).

[185] Jerome, *Ep.* 52. See Kelly, op. cit. (n. 98), 190–1.

[186] Jerome, *Ep.* 52, 15 (*CSEL* 54, 438): 'Officii tui est visitare languentes, nosse domos, matronas ac liberos earum et nobilium virorum non ignorare secreta.'

Nepotianus could expect to receive from wealthy and worldly Christians. Jerome warned Nepotianus that his celibacy would be tested, as would his renunciation of property. Mentioning the law of Valentinian I which placed restrictions upon clerics and monks inheriting property, Jerome explained that there were cunning ways around it which were known to certain churchmen: 'By a fiction of trusteeship we set the statute at defiance.'[187] He drew a contrast between the riches of the churches and the truly pious life and commented on the carelessness of the choice of Christ's priests.[188] Jerome was well aware that the influence of wealthy Christians was increasing and he warned Nepotianus that it was likely that he would be approached by powerful Christians:

Avoid entertaining men of the world, especially those whose honours make them swell up with pride . . . it is a disgrace to you if the consul's lictors or soldiers keep watch before your door, and if the *iudex* of the province has a better dinner with you than in his own palace.[189]

In his earlier letter to Eustochium, Jerome also made reference to female ascetics whom, he suggested, feigned fasting, worldly withdrawal, dressed sombrely in hooded garments, and shaved their heads.[190] He further mentioned a class of women whom he called, satirically, *agapetae* and who lodged with the city's clergy, ostensibly for instruction but in reality for sex.[191]

Jerome urged Eustochium to attract to herself only respectable Christian virgins, not the type of women who called on married or high-born ladies.[192] He described the 'virgins who daily fall' who were likely to be a distraction for her. They were women who called themselves Christian virgins and some were clearly noble. Some of these virgins were prominent figures in the city's streets. Jerome alleges that crowds attended them when they left their houses, a statement which can be taken as much as a reference to their social status as to any Christian virtue. The same interpretation is possible for Jerome's comment that 'troops' of young men (suitors?) often formed the core of an attending crowd.[193] Jerome makes it clear that one of his suggestions to Eustochium which had caused particular distress to his Christian opponents was that Christian virgins ought to live more in

---

[187] Jerome, *Ep.* 52, 6 (*CSEL* 54, 425): 'per fideicommissa legibus inludimus.' Cf. Ambrose, *Ep.* 18, 16.

[188] Jerome, *Ep.* 52, 10.

[189] Ibid. 11 (*CSEL* 54, 433): 'Convivia tibi vitanda sunt saecularium et maxime eorum, qui honoribus tument. Turpe est ante fores . . . lictores consulum et milites excubare iudicemque provinciae melius apud te prandere quam in palatio.'

[190] Ibid. 27. Cf. the description of Melania the Elder (who had not washed anything but her fingertips in 60 years): Palladius, *Historia Lausiaca* 55; Paulinus, *Ep.* 29, 12.

[191] Jerome, *Ep.* 22, 14.   [192] Ibid. 16.   [193] Ibid. 13.

the company of women than men.[194] Marriage was always an option for these Christian virgins. Augustine reproached a Christian lady who had originally dedicated her daughter as a virgin but reclaimed her for the world when she was left without an heir.[195] Jerome alleged that some who claimed to be virgins indulged in secret sex and were forced to conceal pregnancies or have abortions.[196] The Christians about whom Jerome was writing knew and quoted scripture in defence of their transgressions: 'Yet it is these who say: "Unto the pure all things are pure".'[197] There is no reason to think that Jerome's citation of the New Testament was purely for satirical purposes. The Christians about whom he was talking certainly knew scripture. Ambrose too, encountered élite Christians who had acquainted themselves with relevant texts. In 396 the bishop of Milan was approached by Aemilius Florus Paternus who hoped that Ambrose would intercede for him with emperor Theodosius because he was anxious to marry off his son to a niece in violation of imperial marriage legislation. The bishop found Paternus prepared to cite scripture in the first instance, and confident enough to carry on without episcopal assurance when Ambrose refused to accede.[198]

These Christians also had a consciousness of charitable works. Jerome claimed that their Christian gatherings could more appropriately be announced by criers throughout the city, so sumptuous were they.[199] Similarly, their alms-giving was attributed by Jerome to a desire for attention.[200] There is, however, no reason to doubt that such charitable behaviour did take place. Like all Roman Christians, the aristocracy were becoming increasingly aware of the significance of the new topography of the city, made up of the great basilicas, martyr shrines, and small urban churches.[201] All these points were held in

---

[194] Jerome, *Ep.* 27, 2.

[195] See Brown, op. cit. (n. 28), 260 ff. The dedications were sometimes made in order to avoid paying dowries. See Jerome, *Ep.* 130, 6 (AD 414, to Demetrias): '[they] give their daughters sums scarcely sufficient for their maintenance, and bestow the bulk of their property upon sons and daughters living in the world . . . would that such instances were rare, but unfortunately they are not.'

[196] Jerome, *Ep.* 22, 13. See the case of Indicia, a Roman virgin associated with Marcellina (sister of Ambrose) who was accused of having a secret abortion: Ambr., *Ep.* 5–6 = *CSEL* 82. 10, nos. 56–7.

[197] *Ep.* 22, 13 (Quoting Saint Paul's letter, Titus 1: 15) (*CSEL* 54, 160–1).

[198] Ambrose, *Ep.* 60 = *CSEL* 82. 10, no. 58. For the legislation: *CT* 3, 12, 3 (396); Aug., *CD* 15, 16, 2. See J. F. Matthews, 'A Pious Supporter of Theodosius I: Maternus Cynegius and his Family', *JTS*, 18 (1967), 438–46. For the possible involvement of Paulinus of Nola, see Lizzi, art. cit. (n. 86), 133.

[199] Jerome, *Ep.* 22, 32.   [200] Ibid.

[201] See Ch. Piétri, 'Evergétisme et richesses ecclésiastiques dans l'Italie du IVe à la fin du Ve siècle: l'exemple romain', *Ktema*, 3 (1978), 317–37.

common by the community. Early examples of Marcella's devotion had found her hastening to the tombs of the martyrs with her mother, unnoticed.[202] Yet for Eustochium, exposure in public at these sites was not recommended: 'Rarely go abroad, and if you wish to seek the aid of the martyrs, seek it in your own chamber.'[203]

By the middle of the century, the two great suburban basilicas, those of Peter and the old Lateran Estate, were significant points for both ascetics and others. The great church which rose on the site of the apostle's grave was the most significant of all the Constantinian foundations. Liberius is known to have held a liturgical meeting in the basilica on Christmas Day sometime during his episcopate.[204] Other evidence for clerical interest in the site is scarce, but the basilica was not unvisited. In fact, from the middle of the fourth century, there is a body of evidence which suggests that the development of this Christian site and its continued Christian associations owed a great deal to a section of the Christian well-off.

We have already noted the report of Liberius' presence at the basilica sometime during his episcopate. The evidence comes from a letter written by Saint Ambrose to his virgin sister Marcellina in the last third of the fourth century.[205] At the Christmas liturgy celebrated by Liberius, she had been given the symbolic veil of Christian virgin. The ceremony was packed out. Certainly the committed Christianity of those attending is not in doubt, but the status of Marcellina, the daughter of a Praetorian Prefect, cannot be discounted as an additional attraction.[206]

At around the same time, an ambitious pagan nobleman, C. Ceionius Rufius Volusianus Lampadius, later to be Prefect of the City (365–6), staged his praetorian games. They were, according to Ammianus, notorious for an incident in which the *editor* had insulted the games-goers. They had been less than satisfied with the entertainment and complained loudly in the arena: 'in order to show his generosity and contempt of the mob, he summoned some beggars from the Vatican and presented them with valuable gifts.'[207] Lampadius found a ready supply of beggars at the Vatican. Peter Brown has suggested that Lampadius' action actually constitutes a highly symbolic gesture and: 'the shrine of S. Peter on the Vatican Hill had achieved a symbolic

---

[202] Jerome, *Ep.* 127, 4. For a first-rate discussion of Christian and pagan burial customs, see MacMullen, *Christianity and Paganism*, 109 ff.

[203] Jerome, *Ep.* 22, 17 (*CSEL* 54, 165): 'Rarus sit egressus in publicum: martyres tibi quaerantur in cubiculo tuo.'

[204] Ambrose, *De Virginibus* 3, 1–3.   [205] Ibid.

[206] *PLRE* I, 544 'Marcellina 1'. For her father see *PLRE* I, 51 'Ambrosius 1'.

[207] Ammianus 27, 3, 6: 'ut et liberalem se et multitudinis ostenderet contemptorem, accitos a Vaticano quosdam egentes, opibus ditaverat magnis.'

significance, as an antithesis to the Circus Maximus and the Colosseum.'[208] This is to conclude too much from what is, as far as we know, an *isolated* incident. As already noted, Lampadius knew where he could find a significant number of beggars. By his action, Lampadius was demonstrating his *own* patronage and there is no suggestion that his action embarrassed himself or his pagan practices. Clearly he did not lose face in the affair precisely because many of his *Christian* colleagues patronized the Vatican, demonstrating *their* status, in this way. He had simply switched the recipients of his own patronage temporarily to punish the *populus*. The insult was so well aimed and understood precisely because the *populus* knew what went on at the Vatican.

We can also gain some idea of that kind of patronage from what may admittedly be a satirical sketch drawn by Jerome during his stay in the city in the last quarter of the century. In his attack on Christians who had a part-time commitment to the faith, he mentioned an incident which he himself had witnessed:

I lately saw the noblest lady in Rome—I suppress her name for I am no satirist—with a band of eunuchs before her in the basilica of the blessed Peter. She was giving money to the poor, a coin apiece; and with her own hand, that she might be counted the more religious. Hereupon, a by no means uncommon incident occurred. An old woman 'full of years and rags', ran forward to get a second coin, but when her turn came she received not a penny but a blow hard enough to draw blood from her veins.[209]

From the account it is clear that the satirical problem focuses on whether Jerome was giving an account of *the* noblest lady in the city or *a* noblewoman. The location of the scene, however, accords well with the gesture of Lampadius as reported in Ammianus. Indeed, the association of Christian aristocrats with the great churches of Rome continued beyond Jerome's stay in the city; at the end of the century the Christian senator Pammachius had the *basilica* decked out for a banquet on the anniversary of his wife's death.[210]

There is therefore good reason for concluding that Christian charity, as exercised by the aristocracy at Rome, perceived the *basilica* on the Vatican as a particularly appropriate place at which to carry out this kind of activity. It is not surprising then, that traditional patterns in

---

[208] P. Brown, *The Cult of the Saints* (Chicago: University of Chicago Press, 1981), 46.

[209] Jerome, *Ep.* 22, 32 (*CSEL* 54, 193–4): 'Vidi nuper—nomina taceo, ne saturam putes—nobilissimam mulierum Romanarum in basilica beati Petri semiviris antecedentibus propria manu, quo religiosior putaretur, singulos nummos dispertire pauperibus. Interea—ut usu nosse perfacile est—anus quaedam annis pannisque obsita praecurrit, ut alterum nummum acciperet; ad quam cum ordine pervenisset, pugnus porrigitur pro denario et tanti criminis reus sanguis effunditur.'

[210] Paulinus of Nola, *Ep.* 13, 11–15.

monumental patronage should also find particular expression in this area of the city. By *c.*380, for example, the Porticus Maximae had been completed. It ran from the theatre of Balbus in the densely populated Campus Martius to the Pons Aelius, the only remaining bridge across the Tiber in the area, directly in front of the mausoleum of Hadrian.[211] There it terminated with the great arch of Gratian, Valentinian, and Theodosius (379–83) which bore an inscription that testifies to the traditional themes of imperial and aristocratic patronage:

Our Lords the emperors Gratian Valentinian and Theodosius Dutiful and Fortunate, ever Augusti ordered this arch [and] the entire work of the Porticus Maximae of everlasting name to be constructed and decorated to conclusion from their own personal resources.[212]

On the far side of the river, at the tomb of Hadrian, a second *porticus* may have been erected at this time.[213] It was certainly in place by the sixth century and the likelihood is that it is of earlier date.[214] This structure ran from the Pons Aelius to the steps of Old St. Peter's.

The practice of burial *ad corpus* was widespread in the city at this time, but it is no accident that many of the most eminent of the Christian dead chose the shrine of Peter as their final resting place. They were drawn partly by Christian devotion but also by the irresistible attraction of grand, imperially sponsored architecture. The famous sarcophagus of Junius Bassus (d. 359) was recovered where it had been placed in 359: on the floor in the apse behind Constantine's 'confessio' of Peter.[215] The widow of Sextus Petronius Probus set up an impressive epitaph for her husband in an abutting

[211] *CIL* 6, 1184 and 1184a. L. Reekmans, 'Le développement topographique de la région du Vatican à la fin de l'antiquité et au début du moyen âge (300–850)', in *Mélanges d'archéologie et d'histoire de l'art offerts au Professeur Jacques Lavalleye* (Louvain: University of Louvain, 1970), 202. For the Vatican region generally, F. Castagnoli, *Il Vaticano nell'antichità classica*, Studi e documenti per la storia del Palazzo apostolico vaticano, 6 (Vatican City: Biblioteca Apostolica Vaticana, 1992).

[212] *CIL* 6, 1184: 'Imperatores Caesares DDD NNN Gratianus Valentinianus|et Theodosius Pii Felices semper Auggg|Arcum ad concludendum opus omne porticuum maximarum aeterni|nominis sui pecunia propria fieri ornariq. iusserunt.'

[213] Reekmans, art. cit. (n. 211), 206 with n. 22. 'Le porticus n'aurait pas été un vrai portique indépendant mais une suite de maisons pourvues de portiques le long de la rue.'

[214] B. Ward-Perkins, *From Classical Antiquity to the Middle Ages: Urban Public Building in Northern and Central Italy* AD 300–850 (Oxford: Oxford University Press, 1984), 64.

[215] J. M. Huskinson, *Concordia Apostolorum: Christian Propaganda at Rome in the Fourth and Fifth Centuries: A Study of Early Christian Iconography and Iconology*, BAR, 148 (Oxford: BAR, 1982), 24. For the sarcophagus, see E. S. Malbon, op. cit. (n. 47); F. W. Deichmann, *Repertorium der christlich-antiken Sarkophage 1: Rom und Ostia* (Wiesbaden: Franz Steiner, 1967), no. 680.

mausoleum on the site sometime between 390 and 410.[216] Most significant, however, was the appearance, *c.*400, of a new imperial mausoleum for the Honorian dynasty.[217] By the end of the century, the social hierarchy of the Christian dead, from apostle to beggar, could clearly be seen. The physical grandeur of the site was due to the efforts of a section of the city's traditional monumental patrons for whom the Vatican Hill had come to have special significance.

On the other side of the city, the Lateran had been the site of notable acts of renunciation in the second half of the century. The case of Fabiola, scion of the house of the Fabii, was altogether more dramatic. After the death of her second husband she had made a public renunciation in the Lateran:

> It was then that in the presence of all Rome . . . she stood up in the ranks of the penitents and exposed before bishop, presbyters and people—all of whom wept when they saw her weep—her dishevelled hair, pale features, soiled hands, and unwashed neck.[218]

It is clear that Fabiola's actions were unusual and like a true ascetic she set aside her former life. One possible interpretation is that the Lateran site had been *deliberately* chosen as appropriate by Fabiola because it conveniently provided the perfect witnesses to her renunciation: the 'respectable' Christians of her own order.

The Christians who upset Jerome were not embarrassed by their worldly status. To Eustochium Jerome cautioned: 'I do not think it necessary to warn *you* against boasting of your riches, or against priding yourself on your birth, or against setting yourself up as superior to others.'[219] Jerome went on to draw a mordant sketch of noble Christian virgins who ostentatiously adopted a narrow purple stripe on their clothing, thus envisaging their symbolic renunciation of the world in terms of the social gradations of Roman urban life.[220]

Beneath the satire of Jerome, it is clear that all the 'good' Christian virtues of his friends, renunciation, biblical study, and charity were being practised, but to a much lower pitch by other noble Christians in Rome. We have seen above that on the questions of the disposal of property and the continuation of family lines these moderate Christians

---

[216] *ILCV* no. 63.

[217] Krautheimer, *Corpus*, v. 180. H. Koethe, 'Zum Mausoleum der weströmischen Dynastie bei Alt-Sankt-Peter', *MDAI*, 46 (1931), 9 ff.

[218] Jerome, *Ep.* 77, 4 (*CSEL* 55, 40): 'et tota urbe spectante Romana . . . staret in ordine paenitentum, episcopo et presbyteris et omni populo conlacrimanti sparsum crinem, ora lurida, squalidas manus, sordida colla submitteret.'

[219] Jerome, *Ep.* 22, 27 (*CSEL* 54, 183): 'Neque vero moneo, ne de divitiis glorieris, ne de generis nobilitate te iactes, ne te ceteris praeferas . . .'

[220] Jerome, *Ep.* 22, 13.

and their non-Christian colleagues found common ground, in the shape of their ancient senatorial values, on which to reject extreme asceticism. In theological controversy they also had their champions.

Very shortly after Jerome's arrival in Rome some individuals began making attacks on the extreme ascetic community. We are dependent upon Jerome himself for details of the ideas of his adversaries in this and subsequent theological controversies. In strictly theological terms, this might be a difficulty, but my interest here is to observe the groups which espoused the anti-ascetic ideas, and Jerome gives significant information on this matter. In 383 Helvidius suggested that the virginity of Mary could not be upheld and he thus undermined one of the theological foundations of Christian continence. He also advocated marriage as not inferior to virginity in the eyes of God.[221] Jerome responded to Helvidius' teaching with the *Contra Helvidium*, written *c*.383. This treatise was a clever attempt to refute Helvidius using a combination of sophistry, theological insight, and polemic. In his defence of virginity, Jerome went out of his way to assure his readers that he did not consider marriage to be without value. Nevertheless, he was convinced that a woman could not maintain the highest devotion to Christ in marriage:

She that is unmarried is careful for the things of the Lord, that she may be holy both in body and in spirit. But she that is married is careful for the things of the world, how she may please her husband.[222]

To illustrate the point, Jerome set out the kind of distractions and disappointments which married life could bring to young women.[223] In fact, the lifestyle which he summarized was unquestionably that of the élite bride. She was to be found in her house surrounded by the burdens of domestic administration. These included seeing to slaves, cooks, and weavers. Her children would receive an education which she would want to oversee. Her husband would want to entertain his friends at home and she would be forced not only to provide for them but also, perhaps, to put up with the indignity of having half-naked dancing girls in the house.[224] Like a great number of Jerome's letters, the *Contra Helvidium* was written for a readership which included the very well-off.

---

[221] Jerome, *Contra Helvidium* 1, 20. The text is to be found at *PL* 23, 193–216.

[222] Jerome, *Contra Helvidium* 20 (*PL* 23, 213): 'et virgo, quae non est nupta, cogitat quae sunt Dei, ut sit sancta corpore et spiritu. Nam quae nupta est, cogitat, quae sunt mundi, quomodo placeat viro. . .' Cf. Saint Paul, 1 Cor. 7: 34.

[223] The theme much used by ascetical authors but Jerome uniquely vivid. See Lizzi, art. cit. (n. 86). See also the article by Consolino, n. 366 below.

[224] Jerome, *Contra Helvidium* 22. Cf. p. 280 above.

The attacks on Jerome did not cease with the publication of the *Contra Helvidium*. In 385 he wrote to Marcella about another of his opponents, Onasus of Segesta.[225] The details of Onasus' attack cannot be known, since Jerome's letter was taken up chiefly with personal insults. He was, however, clearly a well-educated and capable speaker. There may be a reference to high-born friends on Onasus' side:

I say that certain persons [Onasus himself] have by crime, perjury, and false pretences, attained to this or that high position. How does it hurt you who know that the charge does not touch you?[226]

The suggestion here was that Onasus was from a poor or provincial background and had found elevation through the favour of his social superiors. Jerome plucked an appropriate gibe from Persius: 'May you be a catch for my lord and lady's daughter.'[227]

The personal hostility towards Jerome himself culminated, after the death of Damasus (late 384), in his leaving Rome altogether.[228] Within the space of a few months he had been followed by Eustochium and Paula.[229] Some notable and committed ascetics remained, however, and various documents exist which attest the widespread distrust of extreme asceticism among Rome's civic élite. Jovinianus had once been a Christian ascetic but had renounced his old enthusiasm for mortification in favour of a more moderate line.[230] He may well have been active during Jerome's sojourn in Rome but after the former's departure to the east Jovinianus' public profile was significantly raised. In the early 390s his writings were circulating in the city and Jerome's friend, the senator Pammachius, drew the attention of bishop Siricius to some of the disturbing tracts.[231] Jovinianus was condemned by church councils which sat in Rome and Milan sometime between 390 and 393. Jerome was approached, however, to compose a detailed refutation of Jovinianus and did so in his *Contra Jovinianum*, written *c*.393. As with the *Contra Helvidium*, the tract was aimed at a literate upper-class Christian public.

Among Jovinianus' teachings had been the suggestion that although widows and virgins would do well to adopt the ascetic life, they could

---

[225] Jerome, *Ep.* 40.

[226] Ibid. 2 (*CSEL* 54, 310): 'Dico quosdam scelere, periurio, falsitate ad dignitatem nescio quam pervenisse: quid ad te, qui te intellegis innocentem?'

[227] Persius, *Satires* 2, 37–8.

[228] Jerome, *Ep.* 45. See Kelly, op. cit. (n. 98), 111 ff.

[229] Jerome, *Ep.* 45, 7. They were still in Rome. By *Ep.* 46 (written at Bethlehem 386) they were with him.

[230] Jerome, *Contra Jovinianum* 2, 21, hence Jerome's abusive name for him: 'the Christian Epicurus'. See Hunter, art. cit. (n. 133).

[231] Jerome, *Ep.* 48, 2.

certainly also marry with clear consciences. The position of Christian virgins was not superior to that of married women.[232] He had acknowledged that Christian women were married to non-Christian husbands and suggested that such unions ought not to be dissolved on religious grounds. Jerome replied: 'Yet at the present day many women, despising the Apostle's command, are joined to heathen husbands and prostitute the temples of Christ to idols.'[233] Although Jerome knew that 'crowds of *matronae*' would be furious with him, he stated that such women belonged to Belial, not Christ.

Jovinianus had argued that the status of Christian virgin or widow was nothing without good works.[234] Jerome's response was to tell the story of Jacob's dream at Bethel and ridicule Jovinianus' ideas: 'There are angels who descend from heaven; but Jovinianus is sure that they retain their inheritance.'[235] And in a bitter crescendo to the tract, Jerome attacked Jovininaus and his followers:

> You have, moreover, in your army many subalterns, you have your guardsmen and your skirmishers at the outposts, the round-bellied, the well-dressed, the exquisites, the noisy orators. . . The nobles make way for you, the wealthy print kisses on your face.[236]

When Pammachius received his copy of Jerome's text, he made a desperate attempt to stop it circulating. Not only was Jerome's defence of virginity widely interpreted as being an indictment of marriage, but the contemptuous references to Jovinianus' friends, followers, and supporters wounded a class of Roman citizens whom Pammachius knew only too well.[237]

Jerome's attack upon marriage provoked an outcry and he wrote another letter to Pammachius to clarify his position.[238] He made a reference to the traducers of his work: 'They are educated; in their own eyes no mean scholars; competent not merely to censure me but to instruct me.'[239] Those to whom he referred were the senior clergy and

---

[232] Jerome, *Contra Jovinianum* 1, 9.

[233] Ibid. 10 (*PL* 23, 234): 'At nunc pleraeque contemnentes Apostoli jussionem, junguntur gentilibus, et templa Christi idolis prostituunt . . .' For mixed marriages, see Brown, art. cit. (n. 4).

[234] Jerome, *Contra Jovinianum* book 1, paras. 11; 13.

[235] Ibid. 2, 27 (*PL* 23, 338): 'Angeli de caelis descendunt. Et Jovinianus de eorum possessione securus est.'

[236] Ibid. 37 (*PL* 23, 351–2): 'Habes praeterea in exercitu plures succenturiatos, habes scurras et velites, crassos, comptos, nitidos, clamatores . . . Tibi cedunt de via nobiles, tibi osculantur divites caput.' See Maier, art. cit. (n. 137), 241 n. 46 for further examples of Jerome's formidable satirical talents.

[237] Jerome, *Ep.* 48, 1–2.   [238] Jerome, *Ep.* 49.

[239] Jerome, *Ep.* 39, 3 (*CSEL* 54, 348): 'Norunt litteras, videntur sibi scioli: possunt me non reprehendere, sed docere.'

Christian laymen of Rome. Jerome recalled how bishop Damasus had not reproached him for his *Contra Helvidium* or his *Letter* 22 to Eustochium. He was disappointed that the clerics of Rome, who themselves were celibate, had not backed his ideas in support of Christian virginity: 'Thus, while I try to protect myself on one side, I am wounded on the other. To speak more plainly still, while I close with Jovinianus in hand-to-hand combat, Manichaeus stabs me in the back.'[240] It is clear that the *Contra Jovinianum* did not enjoy Siricius' support.[241] This galled Jerome because Siricius himself had come out in favour of celibacy for senior clergy as long ago as 384–5.[242] But the bishop was profoundly suspicious of ascetics whom he did not know in Rome and therefore refused to endorse Jerome's robust defence of general asceticism.[243] Even the blue-blooded Paulinus, a convert to Christian asceticsm, found himself unexpectedly refused access to the bishop of Rome in the summer of 395.[244]

In the middle of the last decade of the fourth century, a Roman priest, Pelagius, came into his own promoting a form of Christian virtue which did not require the rigours of Hieronymian asceticism but appealed instead to a natural tendency among late Roman aristocrats to form themselves into exclusive spiritual groups.[245] He can certainly be linked to an impressive circle of nobles in the years after the fall of Rome but there is precious little evidence of the actvities of Pelagius before this date. Pelagianism freed Christian asceticism from the shadow of Manichaeism and at the same time suggested that salvation could be achieved largely through the efforts of the individual Christian.[246]

---

[240] Jerome, *Ep.* 48, 2 (*CSEL* 54, 352): 'dum unum latus protego, in altero vulneratus sum atque, ut manifestius loquar, dum contra Iovinianum presso gradu pugno, a Manicheo mea terga confossa sunt.' Cf. Jerome, *Ep.* 48, 3: 'Jovinian is the foe of all indiscriminately, but can I condemn as Manichaean heretics persons whose prayers I need and whose assistance I entreat to help me in my work?' For a convincing interpretation of the *Contra Jovinianum* as an anti-Manichaean work, see Hunter, art. cit. (n. 133).   [241] Jerome, *Ep.* 48, 18.

[242] Siricius, *Ep.* 1, 7, 10 (*PL* 13, 1139A); Piétri, *RC*, ii. 888 ff.; Brown, op. cit. (n. 28), 358–9.

[243] The important passages in Siricius, *Ep.* 6, 2, 4 (*PL* 13, 1165); 1, 6, 7 (*PL* 13, 1137); 1, 13, 17 (*PL* 13, 1144). Cf. *LP*, i. 216 which alleges that Siricius used monasteries as prisons for ascetics. See Piétri, *RC*, i. 642 f.

[244] Paulinus, *Ep.* 5, 13–14 with P. G. Walsh, *Letters of Saint Paulinus of Nola*, Ancient Christian Writers, 35 (Westminster, Md.: Newman Press, 1967), 221 n. 46.

[245] See P. Brown, 'Pelagius and his Supporters: Aims and Environment', in id., *Religion and Society in the Age of Saint Augustine* (London: Faber & Faber, 1972), 183–207. For more sceptical views on Roman activities of Pelagius, see Markus, *End*, 40, with refs.

[246] See Kelly, op. cit. (n. 98), 309 ff.; Maier, art. cit. (n. 137), 235–6, who also points out that Augustine lodged in Rome with a Manichaean Hearer: *Conf.* 5, 10. Also R. F. Evans, *Pelagius: Enquiries and Reappraisals* (New York: Seabury Press, 1968), ch. 6.

Jerome is the only source to give any indication of the support which Pelagius enjoyed at Rome in the last years of the fourth and early years of the fifth century. In a letter written to Domnio during 394, Jerome made reference to a preacher who has been identified confidently as the young Pelagius:[247]

> He likes, I am told, to visit the cells of widows and virgins, and to lecture to them with his brows knit on sacred literature. He is a young man, a monk, and in his own eyes an eloquent one . . . I am surprised, therefore, that he can without a blush frequent noblemen's houses, pay constant visits to married ladies, make of our *religio* a subject of contention.[248]

It is fairly clear that even at this early stage in his career, Pelagius enjoyed contact both with ascetic Christians living in isolation at Rome and the more worldly married ladies about whom Jerome had warned Eustochium.

The surviving evidence of Jerome's theological disputes with other churchmen prominent in Rome reveals that the contests took place in full view of a stratum of society that was upper class, literate, and self-consciously Roman in its Christianity. The courtyards and salons of wealthy households were the battleground which the polemicists show themselves so anxious to conquer. In his own terms, Jerome's success was limited, but the generation after his expulsion from the city was to cast up a dramatic new challenge that would give the cantankerous old man of the desert his long-awaited satisfaction.

5. MELANIA THE YOUNGER, VALERIUS PINIANUS AND THE FALL OF ROME

The fate of family property as a point of conflict between the ascetic Christian aristocrats and the moderates has been discussed above, but in the last years of the century a controversy caused by the wishes of two young Christian nobles to adopt an extreme form of self-denial threw all the contentious issues into high relief. The case of Melania the Younger and Pinianus was the largest and most damaging act of renunciation of senatorial property in the name of Christian asceticism. As Harries has pointed out, the young couple were the only noble

---

[247] See Kelly, op. cit. (n. 98), 187–8, although see Maier, art. cit. (n. 137), 237 with nn.27, 28 for Y.-M. Duval's rhetorical interpretation.

[248] Jerome, *Ep.* 50, 3 (*CSEL* 54, 390–1): 'Audio praeterea eum libenter virginum et viduarum cellulas circumire et adducto supercilio de sacris inter eas litteris philosophari . . . non erubescere iuvenem et monachum et, ut sibi videtur, disertum . . . lustrare nobilium domos, haerere salutationibus matronarum, religionem nostram pugnam facere . . .'

Roman ascetics of the period to take to heart the exhortation of Christ: 'If you will be perfect, go and sell all that you have and give to the poor and you shall have treasure in Heaven':[249]

In so doing, they ignored, or perhaps were not aware of, the ways in which their own relation's enthusiasm [Melania the Elder] for the renunciation of worldly ties had been quietly modified by conventional and practical difficulties.[250]

They fought and won a fierce battle with other senatorial landowners and were victorious only because they invoked the power of the court. The intervention of Serena and Honorius was a blow delivered by the imperial court itself to the ancient *mores* of the senatorial aristocracy. This attack on the role of senators as property owners was followed almost at once by the graver and more physical assaults of Alaric. In this section, the significance of the events which unfolded around Melania and Pinianus during their time at Rome will be examined and an outline given of the process which led to a collapse of senatorial confidence in traditional property-holding at Rome among the upper class.

Melania the Younger was born between 383 and 385 to the son of Melania the Elder, Valerius Publicola.[251] He had been well educated and had 'participated in the honours of the world'.[252] He had made a good marriage, linking himself to the house of the Ceionii through his wife Albina.[253]

At an early stage in her life, Melania the Younger developed a desire to become an ascetic like her grandmother.[254] Publicola, the beneficiary of a worldly upbringing arranged by his ascetic mother, wanted to ensure the continuation of his family:[255]

Her parents, because they were illustrious members of the Roman senate and expected that through her they would have a succession of the family line, very forcibly united her in marriage to . . . Pinianus.[256]

---

[249] Harries, art. cit. (n. 61), 56; *Matthew* 19: 21; *Luke* 18: 22. See Section 6 below.

[250] Harries, art. cit. (n. 61), 56, see also 65 ff. Also A. Giardina, 'Carità Eversiva: Le donazioni di Melania La Giovane e gli equilibri della società tardoromana', *Studi storici*, 29 (1988), 127–42, at 130 ff.

[251] For Publicola see *PLRE* I, 753 'Publicola 1'. Brown, op. cit. (n. 28), 279: an amiable and utterly conventional senator. For the date of birth, see E. A. Clark, 'Piety, Propaganda and Politics in the Life of Melania the Younger', in Clark, op. cit. (n. 153), 61.

[252] Palladius, *Historia Lausiaca* 54, 3.

[253] *PLRE* I, 33 'Albina 2'. See Chastagnol, art. cit. (n. 66) [1956].

[254] *Vita Melaniae* (Gr.), 1; Palladius, *Historia Lausiaca* 61, 1.

[255] Cf. fifth-century *Vita Theclae* where Thecla's fiancée defends marriage. Discussed in Brown, op. cit. (n. 28), 5.

[256] D. Gorce, *Vie de Sainte Mélanie*, Sources chrétiennes, 90 (Paris: Editions du Cerf, 1962), 1: Οἱ δε γονεῖς αὐτῆς, ἅτε περιφανεῖς τῆς συγκλήτου Ῥωμαίων ὑπάρχοντες καὶ ἐξ αὐτῆς τὴν διαδοχὴν τοῦ γένους ἔχειν ἐλπίζοντες, μετὰ πολλῆς βίας συνάπτουσιν αὐτὴν πρὸς γάμον τῷ μακαρίῳ αὐτῆς . . . Πινιανῷ. (Trans. E. A. Clark.)

Sometime around the year 396, Melania was married at the age of 13 to a distant relative, Valerius Pinianus, then aged 17.[257] Publicola, like the moderate Christians whom Jerome attacked, was anxious to retain his standing in senatorial society in Rome. His daughter was thus forced unwillingly into the public life of a young senatorial lady; sent to the baths (*balnea*), she used to pretend that she had bathed and paid her attendants not to inform others.[258]

Pinianus initially shared the same aspirations as his father-in-law. He was unwilling to face the future without heirs and he insisted that their marriage should provide children. According to the Latin *Vita* he proposed: 'wait so that we can have two children because of the inheritance of our properties, and then by the will of God we will renounce the world at the same time.'[259] Pinianus displayed a typical aristocratic desire for male children, but good Christian that he also was, his first-born child, a daughter, was consecrated at once as a virgin.[260] He strongly resisted Melania's invitation to abstain from marital relations until her third pregnancy (her second child, a boy, had died at birth) when she became seriously ill.[261] The *Vitae* record his earnest prayers that his wife might be saved at any cost to himself.[262] Upon recovery, she herself explained that the cost was to be his renunciation of the world.[263] Pinianus accepted, but the announcement dumbfounded Publicola, with whom the couple were living on the Caelian:[264] 'how will we be able to bear the insults of wicked men?'[265] This was a natural fear on the part of a man who had carefully and deliberately united himself with another respectable Christian family in the city. The opprobrium which Publicola expected would come from members of his order, pagan and Christian.

This opposition was sufficiently strong to warrant the intervention of a controversial figure from the generation preceding Publicola. His own mother, Melania the Elder, the grandmother of Melania the

---

[257] *Vita Melaniae* (Gr.), 1; Palladius, *Historia Lausiaca* 60, 1. For Pinianus, see *PLRE* I, 702 'Valerius Pinianus 2'. Arnheim, op. cit. (n. 55), 191–2. See also the full discussion in Rampolla, op. cit. (n. 66), n. vi on pp. 122–5.

[258] *Vita Melaniae* (Gr.), 2.

[259] Rampolla, *Vita Latina* 1: 'sustine ut habeamus duos natos propter substantiarum nostrarum hereditatem, et tunc Dei voluntate pariter mundo abrenuntiabimus.'

[260] *Vita Melaniae* (Gr.), 1.

[261] Ibid. 5.

[262] He prayed at S. Lorenzo according to the *Vita Melaniae* (Gr.), 5.

[263] Ibid. 6.

[264] See Gorce, op. cit. (n. 256), 155 n. 7; Rampolla, op. cit. (n. 66), 166–75. Diehl *ILCV*, 1592.

[265] Rampolla, *Vita Latina* 6: 'quomodo poterimus pessimorum hominum ferre vituperationes?'

Younger, decided to come to the aid of the young couple.[266] In 399 or 400 she made her way from the Holy Land to Italy:

She strengthened her granddaughter Melania along with the latter's husband Pinianus and taught her daughter-in-law Albina, her son's wife. She got them ready to sell publicly their possessions, led them out from Rome, and brought them into the calm and holy harbour of life. In doing so, she fought with beasts in the shape of all the senators and their wives who tried to prevent her, in view of [similar] renunciations of the world on the part of the other houses.[267]

The hostility of her peers and the breach with her father led Melania the Younger, under the care of her grandmother, to retire to a family villa outside Rome where Palladius visited her in 405.[268] From here, Melania kept in contact with other noble Christian ascetics in Italy, notably Paulinus of Nola whom she visited in 406.[269]

It later emerged that Publicola, who had funded charitable work but was not prepared to permit a wholesale renunciation, had considered transferring his patrimony away from his daughter and her husband to other relatives.[270] But he delayed and never carried out the plan, a course of events which the accounts of Melania's life attributed to a dramatic deathbed apology made by the enlightened Publicola to his daughter and son-in-law.[271] Harries has argued that Publicola may

---

[266] Palladius, *Historia Lausiaca* 54, 3–5. If Palladius is to be believed, the difficulties of the couple brought Melania back but Paulinus of Nola, who witnessed the return, seems to show a harmonious family and makes no reference to their problems: *Ep.* 29, 12 ff. For the date see Murphy, art. cit. (n. 78), 73–4. For the possibility that the return may have been to prevent the couple falling under the influence of Hieronymian asceticism, see Clark, art. cit. (n. 251), 73 ff.

[267] Palladius, *Historia Lausiaca* 54, 4–5: Στερεώσασα δὲ καὶ τὴν ἰδίαν ἐγγόνην Μελάνιαν σὺν τῷ ταύτης ἀνδρὶ Πινιανῷ, καὶ κατηχήσασα Ἀλβίναν τὴν ἑαυτῆς νύμφην, γυναῖκα δὲ τοῦ υἱοῦ αὐτῆς, καὶ παρασκευάσασα πάντας τούτους διαπωλῆσαι τὰ ὑπάρχοντα αὐτοῖς, τῆς Ῥώμης ἐξήγαγε, καὶ ἐπὶ τὸν σεμνὸν καὶ γαληνιῶντα λιμένα τοῦ βίου ἤγαγε. [5] καὶ οὕτως πρὸς πάντας ἐθηριομάχησε τοὺς συγκλητικοὺς καὶ τὰς ἐλευθέρας κωλύοντας αὐτὴν ἐπὶ τῇ ἀποταξίᾳ τῶν λοιπῶν οἴκων.

[268] Palladius, *Historia Lausiaca* 61, 7.

[269] Paulinus of Nola, *Carmen* 21.

[270] *Vita Melaniae* (Gr.), 12 with Gorce, op. cit. (n. 256), 150 n. 3. Publicola was a convinced Christian: Palladius, *Historia Lausiaca* 54, 2 recounts how Publicola and other members of his [wife's] family provided Melania with funds to help her make 'donations to churches, monasteries, guests and prisons'. In other words, Publicola supported Melania's alms-giving. Clark, art. cit. (n. 251), 82–3 suggests that the hostile treatment of Publicola in the *Vitae* may be because the author of the lives (Gerontius) felt Publicola to be tainted by his mother's [Melania the Elder] heresy. Harries, art. cit. (n. 61), 66 says that Publicola had no other children and, strictly speaking, had powers only over *Melania's* property. The threat to disinherit was clear enough.

[271] Harries, art. cit. (n. 61), 66 suggests a date of *c.*407. Clark, art. cit. (n. 251), 85 n. 2 explains that a late date for Publicola's death must result from a revised chronology of the letters of Paulinus and Augustine. A. Demandt and G. Brummer, 'Der Prozess

have been dissuaded by certain practical difficulties in carrying out this threat, notably the disgrace which would fall upon his family if a father had to disinherit his daughter.[272] As we have seen, however, this was a threat which had been made to several other noble ascetics.[273] It was a bluff intended to prevent the adoption of an extreme ascetic regime but, as Ambrose pointed out to the readers of one of his treatises on the subject of virginity, no one had yet heard of an aristocrat carrying out such a threat.[274]

The property in question was vast. The Greek version of the *Vita* mentions an annual income of 120,000 *solidi*.[275] The house on the Caelian was so expensively priced that when the couple came to sell it, it was on the market for several years until it was damaged by the Goths in 410.[276] It is known too that they possessed an estate in the *suburbium* of Rome to which they retired permanently from the city after the death of Publicola. Other estates were to be found in Campania, Apulia, and Sicily as well as in Africa, Mauretania, Numidia, Spain, and Britain.[277]

After the declaration of *abrenuntatio* and the death of Publicola, all these properties were certain to fall into the hands of the Church or be broken up and sold separately to fund the couple's good works.[278] But this highly untraditional use of property was tantamount to a rejection of the responsibilities and burdens which the whole senatorial order shared.[279] Several thousand slaves working their *fundus* near Rome threatened to revolt, though both the Greek and Latin versions of the *Vita* allege that Severus, Pinianus' brother, made secret approaches to them to agitate against the sale.[280] Giardina studied the episode of

gegen Serena im Jahre 408 nach Christus', *Historia*, 26 (1977), 489–90 contend that only two dates are possible since the court of Honorius, which became embroiled in the affair, was at Rome only twice during the period: between the end of 403 and the start of 405 or the end of 405 and May 408 [dates from Seeck]. Rampolla opted for the earlier, placing the death of Publicola late in 403 and the interview with Serena in summer 404.

[272] Harries, art. cit. (n. 61), 66. Publicola himself had no siblings and his wife's family had no claim on his property.

[273] See above, section 3.   [274] Ambrose, *De Virginibus* 1, 11, 63.

[275] *Vita Melaniae* (Gr.), 15. This was independent of Pinianus, see Clark, art. cit. (n. 251), 67 ff.

[276] *Vita Melaniae* (Gr.), 14. See Giardina, art. cit. (n. 250), 128–9 who remarks that Serena's refusal to accept the property for less than a 'just price' is evidence of 'l'etica aristocratica'.

[277] *Vita Melaniae* (L.), 10; 21. The Latin version says that her African holdings, near Thageste, were bigger than the town, had two bishops, one for Catholics and one for Donatists, a bath and were inhabited by numerous craftsmen. See *Vita Melaniae* (Gr.), 7, 11, 18, 19, 20.

[278] Ibid. 9; Palladius, *Historia Lausiaca* 61, 4

[279] Demandt and Brummer, art. cit. (n. 271), 487.

[280] *Vita Melaniae* (Gr.), 10. See Demandt and Brummer, art. cit. (n. 271), 485–6. Melania freed 8,000 slaves before selling the rest to 'her brother' (probably Severus)

Melania the Younger and Pinianus and was drawn to the plight of Melania's slaves.[281] He rightly pointed out that great senatorial estates were part of a fundamental link between land and labour in the Late Antique period. He suggests that the social upheaval which threatened the slaves of Melania would naturally have affected the other communities living on their lands and the dangers were easily perceived by the couple's fellow landowners. There existed also the additional danger of *latrones* in central Italy whose bands might have been swelled by the dispersal of the landed communities.[282] Vera has looked carefully at the agricultural responsibilities revealed by another senatorial landowner (Symmachus) in his letters.[283] Though a senator of only average wealth, Symmachus' holdings were extensive and widely distributed in the Italy–Sicily–Africa zone. Vera argues strongly that Symmachus' estates played a significant role in agricultural production.[284] The social and economic stability of the couple's *fundi* was thus profoundly threatened by the ascetics' actions. It is highly significant that those opposed to the breakup of the properties should have belonged to social groups as disparate as slaves and senators.

The couple's relatives raised legal objections. On the death of Publicola, Pinianus was only 24 and Melania 20, both were still minors and technically unable to gain full legal power over the inherited properties until the age of 25.[285] Constantinian legislation had conceded that in certain circumstances a young man of senatorial rank could prove himself sufficiently 'of the age of stability' (*firmatae aetatis*) even if he had just reached his twenties.[286] But the tone of the Constantinian law was clear enough; this was not an occurrence which the emperor expected to be common and an abundance of legislation still existed which checked the capacity of the young or the infirm to dispose of property.[287]

It is not known whether Melania and Pinianus ever approached the Prefect of the City who presumably had jurisdiction over the legal

---

for 'three pieces of money': Palladius, *Historia Lausiaca* 61, 5. Harries, art. cit. (n. 61), 66 explains that Severus was Pinianus' next-of-kin in circumstances of intestate succession.

[281] Giardina, art. cit. (n. 250).   [282] Ibid. 139 ff.

[283] D. Vera, 'Simmaco e le sue proprietà: struttura e funzionamento di un patrimonio aristocratico del quarto secolo d.C.', in F. Paschoud (ed.), *Colloque genevois sur Symmaque* (Paris: Belles lettres, 1986), 231–75.   [284] Ibid. 234 ff.

[285] *Vita Melaniae* (Gr.), 8. The Latin version says 21. For their legal position see Gorce, op. cit. (n. 256), 138 n. 1. See E. A. Clark, art. cit. (n. 251), 69; also Demandt and Brummer, art. cit. (n. 271), 488 with n. 35.

[286] *CT* 2, 17, 1 (given at Rome 1 June 324). Cf. *CJ* 2, 45, 1 (321).

[287] See n. 286 and Digest 27, 10, 1; 3; see Clark, art. cit. (n. 251), 69 and Gorce, op. cit. (n. 256), 138 n. 1.

competence of the couple, but in the early years of the fifth century
their plight came to the attention of Serena, wife of the *magister
utriusque militiae* Stilicho.[288] The imperial court had made one of its
infrequent visits to Rome and Melania approached Serena. Bringing
rich gifts for the empress herself and the palace eunuchs, the couple
secured an interview late in 407 or early in 408.[289] Serena heard the
couple's difficulties and agreed to intercede with the emperor on their
behalf. She used her influence with Honorius to secure an imperial
directive to all the provincial officials concerned, ordering that Melania
and Pinianus' properties should be sold under supervision and the
proceeds sent directly to the vendors.[290] The conditions of the law of
Constantine had been set aside with unprecedented haste.[291] The
objections of the law and the self-preserving instincts of the senatorial
aristocracy had been overridden.

Before their final departure from the city, the couple spent at least a
year in their suburban villa, which had been turned into a religious
community.[292] By the early 400s, however, a house in the *suburbium* of
Rome was no longer as tranquil a retreat as it had once been. Barbarian
incursions into northern Italy had recently brought the danger much
closer to the population of the city.[293] In spring 408 Alaric contacted
Stilicho and demanded compensation for the inconvenience of the
delay which had forced himself and his men to loiter in one of the least
hospitable areas of the Balkans.[294] Honorius' court had moved briefly
to Rome and Stilicho put the request to the emperor there.[295] The
passage in which Zosimus records the meeting of the senate is
confused.[296] The appearance of a civilized discussion is conveyed:
'Everyone . . . thought that Stilicho spoke reasonably and the Senate
voted that 4,000 pounds of gold should be paid to Alaric.'[297] Ridley

---

[288] *Vita Melaniae* (Gr.), 11–13 with Paschoud, *Zosime*, iii. pt. 1, 258–66; Demandt
and Brummer, art. cit. (n. 271), 488. For Serena, see *PLRE* I, 824.

[289] *Vita Melaniae* (Gr.), 11. See previous note for chronology.

[290] Ibid. 13.   [291] *CT* 2, 17, 1.

[292] *Vita Melaniae* (Gr.), 7. See Palladius, *Historia Lausiaca* 61, 6; Rampolla, op. cit.
(n. 66), 10 ff.; 168; 176 f. thought that this *fundus* was 10–11 km. along the Via
Ardeatina.

[293] AD 401: siege of Milan and defeats for Alaric at Pollentia and Verona: Claudian,
De Bello Getico 50–60, 205 ff., 230–2, 450 ff.; id., *De VI Consulatu Honorii.* (405/6)
defeat of Radagaesus: Zosimus, *NH* 5, 26, 3 ff.

[294] Ibid. 29. For the date see Paschoud, op. cit. (n. 288), 281 n. 96 and also 217 n. 65
where he thinks that Zosimus is mistaken. Alaric was not claiming compensation but
putting pressure on Stilicho directly.

[295] The court was there from at least 15 Nov. 407 until the beginning of May 408. See
Seeck, *Regesten*, 312, 314.   [296] Zosimus, *NH* 5, 29, 5.

[297] Ibid. 9: πᾶσι τοίνυν δόξαντος δίκαια λέγειν Στελίχωνος, ἐδόκει τῇ γερουσίᾳ χρυσίου
τετρακισχιλίας ὑπὲρ τῆς εἰρήνης Ἀλλαρίχῳ δίδοσθαι λίτρας . . . Olympiodorus concurs. See

thought that other sources, particularly the poems of Claudian, confirmed that relations between the Senate and Stilicho were good.[298] Paschoud argues, however, that Claudian was voicing a propagandist's optimism and that the account of Zosimus itself contained traces, admittedly faint, of the real situation.[299] The Senate was convened in the imperial palace (the Palatine?), not the Curia. Honorius advocated compliance with Alaric's demand but this was opposed by truculent senators who were in favour of war but, faced with the obvious ascendancy of Stilicho, they abandoned their resistance and began to support the payment of the bribe: 'most voted that way not from preference but out of fear of Stilicho.'[300] The sum was small but the payment was a serious blow to Roman prestige. Olympiodorus, on whom Zosimus depended for much of his account of the period, recorded the simmering discontent among some senators.[301] Lampadius, 'a man of high birth and reputation',[302] denounced the payment: 'this is not peace but a contract of servitude.'[303] It was clear enough from what source the court relied for the cash: the senators of Rome.[304] As we have seen, the visit of Honorius to Rome in this year also witnessed the climax to the crisis between Melania the Younger and the upholders of senatorial responsibilities. The issues of the demand of Alaric and those of Melania prompted a presumptuous response from the court. On the one hand, the dignity of the order was offended by the cynical attitude that senators of Rome could be used as an easy supply of ready cash. On the other, the imperial decision to aid Melania and Pinianus rudely curtailed discussion of the rights of senators to exert influence on members of their own order.

After their successful interview with Serena, Melania and Pinianus

R. C. Blockley, *The Fragmentary Classicising Historians of the Later Roman Empire* (Liverpool: Cairns, 1983), Olympiodorus *Fragment* 7, 2 with n. 10.

[298] R. T. Ridley, *Zosimus: New History* (Canberra: Australian Association for Byzantine Studies, 1982), 217 n. 102. The texts are: *CT* 7, 13, 14; Claudian, *De Consulatu Stilichonis I* 325–32; id. *De Consulatu Stilichonis II* 297; id. *De Consulatu Stilichonis III* 85–6; id. *De VI Consulatu Honorii* 548–51, 587–91.

[299] Paschoud, op. cit. (n. 288), 218 n. 65.

[300] Zosimus *NH* 5, 29, 9: τῶν πλειόνων οὐ κατὰ προαίρεσιν ἀλλὰ τῷ Στελίχωνος φόβῳ τοῦτο ψηφισαμένων . . .

[301] J. F. Matthews, 'Olympiodorus of Thebes and the History of the West', *JRS*, 60 (1970), 79–97.

[302] Ridley, op. cit. (n. 298), 217 n. 104 thinks he may have been *PUR* early in 398 on the strength of Symmachus, *Ep.* 6, 64; 8, 63; 65; *CJ* 4, 61, 11. See Chastagnol, *Fastes*, no. 102 with cautionary n. 32.

[303] Zosimus *NH* 5, 29, 9: 'non est ista pax sed pactio servitutis.' As Ridley points out, Zosimus/Olympiodorus voiced the dissent in a phrase already used by Appius Claudius, opposing peace with Pyrrhus: Appian, *Sam.* 10, 2.

[304] See Matthews, *WA*, 275–6.

left Rome for good and the Greek version of the *Vita* records that the sale of their Roman, Italian, Spanish, and Gallic properties had just been made when Alaric arrived before the city late in 408.[305] His siege began in the last two months of the year. The city held out, confidently expecting an expeditionary force to be despatched from Ravenna.[306] No such force appeared and Alaric set up an impenetrable cordon around the city, preventing the movement of supplies and people into or out of Rome. A senatorial embassy to Alaric was informed that he wanted 'all the gold and silver in the city, as well as all movable property and the barbarian slaves'.[307] The confirmation that it was Alaric himself and not some other Gothic chieftain who was besieging the city caused widespread panic in Rome.[308] The Prefect of the City, Gabinius Barbarus Pompeianus,[309] even attempted to consult some soothsayers present in the city and obtained the authorization of bishop Innocentius to do so:

The priests declared . . . the customary rites had to be performed publicly by the Senate on the Capitol and in the Forum, but no one dared to participate in the ancestral worship, so they dismissed the men from Tuscany [the *haruspices*] and turned to flattering the barbarian as best they could.[310]

Pompeianus realized that Alaric would have to be paid again. Zosimus explains that the burden of finding the money again fell on the senators of Rome since the city had no real public funds.[311] But the cost of buying Alaric off this second time looked likely to cripple many aristocrats:[312]

Palladius was empowered to compute how much was to be paid from each estate, but was unable to collect the whole sum, either because the owners

[305] *Vita Melaniae* (Gr.), 19.   [306] Zosimus, *NH* 5, 39, 1.
[307] Ibid. 40, 3. See Matthews, *WA*, 288. The delegation included Basilius (*PUR*) and Johannes, a former client of Alaric.
[308] Zosimus, *NH* 5, 40, 4.   [309] *PLRE* II, 897–8.
[310] Zosimus *NH* 5, 41, 3: ἐπεὶ δὲ οὐκ ἄλλως ἔφασαν τῇ πόλει τὰ γενόμενα συντελέσειν, εἰ μὴ δημοσίᾳ τὰ νομιζόμενα πραχθείη, τῆς γερουσίας εἰς τὸ Καπιτώλιον ἀναβαινούσης, αὐτόθι τε καὶ ἐν ταῖς τῆς πόλεως ἀγοραῖς ὅσα προσήκει πραττούσης, οὐκ ἐθάρρησεν οὐδεὶς τῆς κατὰ τὸ πάτριον μετασχεῖν ἁγιστείας, ἀλλὰ τοὺς μὲν ἀπὸ τῆς Τουσκίας παρῆκαν, ἐτράπησαν δὲ εἰς τὸ θεραπεῦσαι τὸν βάρβαρον καθ' ὅσον ἂν οἷοί τε γίνωνται. Cf. Sozomen, *HE* 9, 6, 3. See F. Heim, 'Les auspices publics de Constantin à Théodose', *Ktema*, 13 (1988), 41–53, at 47–8. Also, A. Fraschetti, 'Spazi del sacro e spazi della politica', in A. Schiavone (ed.), *Storia di Roma 3*: 1. L'Età tardoantica. Crisi e trasformazioni* (Turin: Einaudi, 1993), 675–96.
[311] Zosimus, *NH* 5, 41, 4. See Paschoud, op. cit. (n. 288), 282 n. 96 where he points out that the *PUR* did have 'd'un budget alimenté par divers impôts'.
[312] Zosimus, *NH* 5, 41, 4: Alaric's earlier demand for all the gold and silver had been modified to 5,000 Roman pounds of gold, 30,000 Roman pounds of silver, 4,000 silk tunics, 3,000 scarlet skins, and 3,000 Roman pounds of pepper. Matthews, *WA*, 288 thinks the more moderate sum was the result of a second delegation to Alaric.

concealed part of their property or because the city had been reduced to poverty through the emperor's continual greed.[313]

The sacrosanctity of the senatorial estates was doubly violated. Alaric had ravaged Italy and physically encamped himself in areas belonging to senators.[314] In addition to this, however, the senators of Rome were being asked, for the second time in a year, to put their financial resources at the disposal of the state for the meeting of extraordinary payments. The reluctance of the ancient aristocratic families to sacrifice their own properties led Pompeianus to consider some desperate measures. Zosimus tells how the authorities of the city laid hands on the ancient statues of the gods in precious metals.[315] The *Vita* of Melania reports that Pompeianus with the backing of the Senate seized the opportunity to lay claim to the lands recently sold by the ascetic couple.[316] It is not clear exactly what the intention of Pompeianus was. He may have been intending to take possession of the land in order to put it to use providing emergency supplies or as a means of generating revenue.[317] In any event, he was unable to carry through the enterprise since he was murdered by a starving mob.[318] The *Vita* gleefully records the distracting detail that Pompeianus was 'an ardent pagan' but it is clear that his attempt to recover the lands sold up by Melania and Pinianus was motivated by the economic circumstances of Rome in late 408 and early 409.[319] The money was paid in December 408 or January 409 when a senatorial delegation was also sent by Alaric to Honorius demanding aristocratic hostages as a guarantee of good faith.[320] The hostages did not materialize, however.

Alaric had stayed close to Rome, anxious not to repeat the mistake he had made of trusting Ravenna and lifting the siege of spring 408. Now,

---

[313] Zosimus *NH* 5, 41, 5: ἐπιτραπεὶς δὲ Παλλάδιος τῇ δυνάμει τῆς ἑκάστου περιουσίας τὸ δοθησόμενον συμμετρῆσαι, καὶ ἀδυνατήσας εἰς ὁλόκληρον ἅπαντα συναθροῖσαι, ἢ τῶν κεκτημένων μέρος τι τῶν ὄντων ἀποκρυψάντων ἢ καὶ ἄλλως πως εἰς πενίαν τῆς πόλεως ἐλθούσης διὰ τὰς ἐπαλλήλους τῶν κρατούντων πλεονεξίας . . . Ridley, op. cit. (n. 298), 222 n. 154 identifies 'Palladius' as Fl. Iunius Quartus Palladius who was proconsul of Africa in 410. See *PW* 18.3, 220.

[314] Alaric occupied the lands being sold by Melania and Pinianus just after they left Rome: *Vita Melaniae* (Gr.), 19.

[315] Zosimus, *NH* 5, 41, 6–7. [316] *Vita Melaniae* (Gr.), 19.

[317] For senatorial estates as the providers of foodstuffs, see Vera, art. cit. (n. 283).

[318] *Vita Melaniae* (Gr.), 19.

[319] Ibid. See Matthews, *WA*, 290 and n. 5 where he suggests the following sequence of events: (1) siege of Alaric and first embassy to him; (2) pagan revival (consultation of haruspices); (3) second embassy which secured more moderate terms from Alaric; (4) exactions of Palladius; (5) proposal of Pompeianus and latter's death.

[320] Matthews, *WA*, 291–2: Caecilianus was made *PPO* of Italy (keeping him at Ravenna), Priscus Attalus made *Comes Sacrarum Largitionum*.

he prevented the passage of citizens to and from Rome again.[321] The
bishop of Rome joined a deputation from the Senate to Ravenna with a
view to securing the handover of hostages to Alaric.[322]

Encouraged by a change of personnel around the emperor, the entire
court had sworn to wage war on Alaric and his new terms were ignored.
Alaric set his course for Rome a third time.[323] No improvement had
been made to the city's defences. Alaric seized the supplies which had
been stockpiled at Portus and demanded that the citizens of Rome join
him against Honorius.[324] The Senate was forced by means of a short
blockade to realize that the situation was hopeless and agreed to
Alaric's terms. Alaric was invited into the city late in 409 where he
made Priscus Attalus emperor.[325] Alaric himself at last became *magister
utriusque militiae*.[326] The Senate had had no alternative but to throw its
weight behind Alaric's emperor. The appointments of the new regime
came as a pleasant surprise since Attalus carefully selected respected
senators, good administrators, and pagans.[327] A sufficient number were
convinced that the Senate could play a significant role in public affairs.
The tone of the regime was conservative and traditionalist.[328] On the
day after his elevation, Attalus had made an optimistic speech to the
Senate expressing his hope that Rome would again become a powerful
city with nations under her direct control.[329] This was a feeling,
however, that not all aristocrats echoed:

Only the family of the Anicii was grieved by what everyone else thought
beneficial: they were discontented with the universal prosperity because they
controlled virtually all the city's wealth.[330]

Ammianus had already criticized the acquisitive tendencies of Sextus
Petronius Probus, the most famous and successful of the Petronii who
had married into the Anicii in the 360s or 370s.[331] The orthodox
interpretation of the passage is that the new regime's pagan character

---

[321] Zosimus, *NH* 5, 45, 4.   [322] Ibid. 5.   [323] Ibid. 6, 1, 1.

[324] Ibid. 6, 1–2; see Matthews, *WA*, 294 ff.

[325] Zosimus, *NH* 6, 6, 3–7, 4. *PLRE* II, 180–2.   [326] Zosimus, *NH* 6, 7, 2.

[327] Ibid. 1–4; Matthews, *WA*, 295 f. von Haehling, op. cit. (n. 14), 403–4. Lampadius
(*PPO*), Marcionus (*PUR*), and Tertullus (*cos.*) were all pagans.

[328] See Zosimus, *NH* 6, 7; Sozomen, *HE* 9, 8; 9. Orosius, *Historiarum libri septem* 7,
42, 8 reports the desire for a pagan pontificate. For reports of the hopes of pagans and
Arians dashed by his death, see Sozomen, *HE* 9, 9, 1.

[329] Zosimus, *NH* 6, 7, 3.

[330] Zosimus *NH* 6, 7, 4: μόνον δὲ τὸν τῶν λεγομένων Ἀνικίων οἶκον ἐλύπει τὰ κοινῇ
δοκοῦντα πᾶσι λυσιτελεῖν, ἐπειδὴ μόνοι τὸν πάντων ὡς εἰπεῖν ἔχοντες πλοῦτον ἐπὶ ταῖς κοιναῖς
ἐδυσχέραινον εὐπραγίαις.

[331] Ammianus 27, 11. Cf. 16, 8, 13. See *PLRE* I, 736–40. The marriage produced
highly successful children.

fostered hostility towards the most prominent Christian family in Rome. The Anicii and Proba in particular were further accused by Procopius, writing in the sixth century, of admitting Alaric into the city in summer 410.[332] Matthews thought that Olympiodorus and subsequently Zosimus had heard the same allegation and on this basis maintained a bitter hatred for the family.[333]

There are problems, however, with this interpretation of the passage. Probus himself had been dead since *c*.388 and there is no specific indication that the activities of his surviving relatives aroused similar misgivings. It seems odd, too, that the ardently pagan Zosimus, if he had in mind the Christianity of the Anicii, should have been so vague about the grievance. However, while the passage may be vague on the Anicii themselves, it is specific about *property*. Zosimus has drawn a contrast between ἡ εὐπραγία welcomed by his pro-senatorial source and ὁ πλοῦτος of the Anicii which played no part in what Zosimus understood to be the short-lived revival of the city. In fact, at least one member of the Anicii had adopted a profoundly *un*traditional attitude towards senatorial property holding. Proba, wife of the great office-holder himself, had established a community of Christian virgins in her house.[334] She was, in the words of Matthews, 'since his [Probus'] death the exemplar of the piety of the most Christian senatorial family'.[335] Furia, Sextus Petronius Probus' daughter-in-law, had refused second marriage and received one of Jerome's strongest letters in support of her decision to embrace the ascetic life in 394.[336] The family may even have patronized Pelagius, the most important Christian heretic of the age, at the outset of his controversial career.[337] Chiefly through the matriarchal Proba's asceticism, the Anicii represented the most visible example of the irregular attitudes of Christian nobles to property at a time of economic distress. Under Attalus, when a belief in a renewed Senate was gaining currency, the attitude of Proba to her estate was particularly noticed and interpreted as 'unsenatorial'. The allegation that she had conspired against Rome with Alaric in 410 is therefore malicious. Nevertheless, Procopius may have preserved an echo of Proba's high Christian profile during the

---

[332] Procopius, *Vandalic War* 1, 2, 27. Paschoud, op. cit. (n. 288) pt. 2 (1989), 46 n. 126.

[333] See Matthews, art. cit. (n. 301), 93 with n. 144 where he notes that a direct link between Olympiodorus and Procopius has not been established.

[334] Jerome, *Ep.* 130, 7; Gennadius, *De Viris Illustribus* 17 (Rufinus of Aquileia) records that Proba received 'many epistles exhorting to fear God'. See Gordini, art. cit. (n. 53), 246.

[335] Matthews, *WA*, 374.   [336] See above, 279–80.

[337] Brown, art. cit. (n. 245), 185. His letter to Demetrias may have been his first communication with the family.

siege. He claimed that she had admitted Alaric because she thought that the inhabitants of the city had suffered enough.[338]

Attalus was not a success. He was overconfident and Alaric's deference to the ancient aristocracy of Rome which appears to have allowed Attalus a remarkably free hand led the new emperor to make certain strategic military blunders.[339] Honorius, isolated and terrified in Ravenna, perceived Attalus as a real threat and when the latter marched with Alaric on the northern capital, drew up plans to share the western empire with him.[340] The fortuitous appearance at Ravenna of six cohorts of good quality troops from the east transformed the attitude at the court. The city now prepared for a siege.[341] Treachery had entered the camp of Alaric, however, and intrigues were being woven around Attalus and his court. The new emperor's incompetence exasperated Alaric who eventually lost patience with him in July 410 and deposed him at Ariminum, hoping that the deposition would be interpreted at Ravenna as a conciliatory gesture.[342] But the chance arrival of the Goth Sarus, an inveterate enemy of Alaric's brother, led to the termination of the negotiations. Alaric, thoroughly frustrated, marched for the last time to Rome.

In the sack of the city Proba's community was entered and a number of her virgins were abducted.[343] Proba herself decided to dispose of her property at once, a turn of events which particularly impressed Jerome, who was unable to suppress either his amazement at Proba's change of heart or his distaste for the grasping clergy of Rome:

> Who would believe it? That Proba, who of all persons of high rank and birth in the Roman world bears the most illustrious name . . . that Proba, I say, now that Rome has been taken and its contents burned or carried off, is said to be selling what property she has and to be making for herself friends of the mammon of unrighteousness that these may receive her into everlasting habitations.[344]

The example of Proba shows that the hostility of the regime of Attalus was directed against the Anicii on account of their asceticism and not necessarily their Christianity *per se*. Her reaction to the fall of the city was an example which was followed by a number of noble Roman ascetics.

Ironically, the disaster touched these ascetic groups as much as

---

[338] Procopius, *Vandalic War* 1, 2, 27.   [339] Zosimus, *NH* 6, 7, 5.
[340] Ibid. 8, 1.   [341] Ibid. 2–3.   [342] Ibid. 12, 2.
[343] Jerome, *Ep.* 130, 7.
[344] Ibid. (*CSEL* 56, 182–3): 'Quis hoc credat? Proba illa omnium dignitatum, et cunctae nobilitatis in orbe Romano nomen illustrius . . . cum incensis direptisque omnibus in urbe captivitas sit, nunc habitas venundare dicitur possessiones, et facere sibi amicos de iniquo mamona, qui se recipiant in aeterna tabernacula . . .'

anyone. Those who had renounced the world but not Rome were exposed to the raiders in August 410. Pammachius died in the siege, according to Jerome.[345] The large familial house of Marcella on the Aventine, among the other houses of Rome's aristocracy, attracted a mob of Goths looking for gold. Marcella was beaten badly and died a few days later at the basilica of Paul on the Via Ostiensis.[346]

Violence of this nature against the Roman community had not been experienced in over 750 years. The catastrophe threw Jerome into the deepest despair. In one sense, the disaster was a traumatic demonstration of the temporality of the world, an idea which Jerome had promoted passionately. The remarkable aftermath of the fall of the city, however, was the re-emergence of the same social gradations which had existed previously; the senatorial order did not disintegrate and its services to the Church continued with unprecedented industry. The seeds for this recovery lay, paradoxically, with the ascetics themselves.

6. STATUS IN AN ASCETIC CONTEXT

Like a number of other Roman nobles, Melania the Younger, her mother Albina and Pinianus fled to Africa.[347] This little aristocratic group of refugees headed for their family estate in the province. The citizens of Hippo, however, knew at once who the visitors were and in an embarrassing and frightening incident tried to force Pinianus to become their priest.[348] Pinianus' continued wealth and visible status encouraged the Christian congregation to demand the installation of one of the foremost noble Christian ascetics as priest-*patronus*. This illuminating episode suggests that some noble ascetics never detached nor were able to detach themselves from their worldly status.

If what we have seen so far in this chapter has outlined the divisions which fragmented the Christian aristocracy, then the appearance of what we may call 'respectable Christian asceticism' represents the drawing together of strands which wove themselves into the confident Christian aristocracy of Rome in the fifth century.[349]

The extreme noble ascetics of Rome during the age of Saint Jerome

---

[345] *Comm. in Ezech.* 1, 1.

[346] Jerome, *Ep.* 127, 13. St. Peter's basilica was untouched out of respect for the apostle, according to Sozomen, *HE* 9, 9.

[347] See P. Brown, *Augustine of Hippo* (London: Faber & Faber, 1968), 300; P. Courcelle, *Histoire littéraire des grandes invasions germaniques* (Paris: Hachette, 1948), 40 ff.

[348] Augustine, *Ep.* 124; 126. See Brown, op. cit. (n. 347), 294.

[349] For what follows, see E. A. Clark, 'Ascetic Renunciation and Feminine Advancement: A Paradox of Late Ancient Christianity', in Clark, op. cit. (n. 153), 175–208.

demonstrated their renunciation of the world most dramatically by withdrawing from the city of Rome itself. Melania the Elder, Paula, and Eustochium were followed by Melania the Younger and Pinianus at the beginning of the fifth century. It is important to realize, however, that a significant number of noble ascetics renounced only the social round of Roman Christianity which was discussed above, retiring within their Roman palaces or to villas in the *suburbium*.[350] Some, like Paulinus of Nola, believed that a withdrawal from the world could be best achieved by rural peace and quiet.[351] Other leading ascetics, like Melania and Pinianus, seem to have been forced rather against their wishes to abandon the city.[352]

Of the Christian ascetics who stayed in Rome, some renounced the world more than others. Those who stayed used resources to found religious communities or institutions for the care of the poor.[353] The object of their charity, the urban poor of Rome, was no different from that of the alms-givers whom Jerome satirized and the increasingly important donations to the Church by wealthy senators constituted a further element in the physical growth of the Christian city.[354] We have already seen that Pammachius was in close contact with the Roman clergy and was aware of the sensitivity of certain moderate members of the Roman congregation,[355] so the extent to which ascetics at Rome had rejected the city can be exaggerated. Certainly their decision to adopt the ascetic life troubled their families and colleagues but this was because they feared renunciation on the pattern established by Melania the Elder or Paula. In a significant number of cases this was not what happened and there is no evidence that ascetics who stayed in Rome faced continual harrassment from members of their own class after it was perceived that their conversions would not mean leaving Rome. Yarbrough thought that the form of ascetic life adopted by these Roman Christians was influenced more by the western tradition of philosophical life than the eastern tradition of flight to the desert.[356] Often, however, the refusal to leave Rome had more to do with the desire to maintain limited family ties and a reluctance to face the hardships of the desert.

[350] e.g. Marcella. See Jerome, *Ep.* 45, 7 for a list of women living on the Aventine. Palladius' holy man Serapion visited her or Asella there: *Historia Lausiaca* 37, 12: a maiden living in seclusion who did not meet anyone. Also Paulinus, *Ep.* 5, 4; Aug., *De moribus ecclesiae Catholicae* 1, 33, 70 and Gordini, art. cit. (n. 53), 243ff.

[351] Paulinus, *Ep.* 24, 3 (to Severus): 'You are a host in your own house so that your home may be a hospice.' For Paulinus' concern about vintage wines in Narbo: *Ep.* 5, 22.

[352] For their retirement to their suburban villa, see above, 301.

[353] For Pammachius and Fabiola see Jerome, *Ep.* 77, 10.

[354] e.g. the *Titulus Vestinae*. See *LP*, i. 221–2 and above, 289–93.

[355] See above, p. 295–6.   [356] Yarbrough, art. cit. (n. 58), 157–8.

The Christian literary tradition sought to make the act of renunciation as dramatic as possible. The most tangible sign of the world which the noble ascetics of Rome renounced was property and conflict over the fate of property is an important part of the record of the struggle between Christian noble ascetics and their families examined in Section 3. If, however, the record is examined closely, it is possible to detect in the lives of these noble Christians what Harries appropriately described as 'the tenacious presence of property'.[357] With the exception of Melania and Pinianus, the actual *process* of renunciation frequently took many years and was almost invariably accompanied by the careful disposal of wealth.

The circle of ladies into which Jerome insinuated himself had its base in the houses of wealthy senators. Extreme asceticism convinced these men and women that their earthly property should be used in the service of the Church but until Melania and Pinianus the disposal of property was extremely carefully handled. In particular, the *gradual* liquidation of wealth and continued property-holding was a feature of these ascetic renunciations. There is evidence also that a desire or obligation to provide for non-ascetic family members governed the decisions of some of the most notable ascetics of the period. Melania the Elder, for example, invoked the wrath of her family by deciding to leave Rome and retire to the East.[358] As we saw above, she left her son, Valerius Publicola, in the care of the Prefect of the City, not her family. There is clear evidence that she wanted worldly success for him:

Thanks to her prayers, the young man attained a high standard of education and a good character and an illustrious marriage; and participated in the honours of the world.[359]

It was more than Melania's prayers which secured the young man's future. Jerome indicates that she left property to him.[360] With the Prefect of the City as his guardian and resources of his own, there can be little surprise that Publicola made such a satisfactory marriage which may have brought him a dowry. As Harries points out, this was a scrupulous arrangement designed to protect his share of Melania's family property.[361]

Melania's renunciation of the world, spectacular as it was, was not accompanied by the complete dispersal of her own family property. Palladius, in his *Historia Lausiaca*, recorded that she took with her to

---

[357] Harries, art. cit. (n. 61), 56.　　　　　　[358] See above, 272–3.

[359] Palladius, *Historia Lausiaca* 54, 3: ἀλλὰ ταῖς προσευχαῖς αὐτῆς ὁ νεώτερος εἰς ἄκρον παιδείας καὶ τρόπων ἤλασε καὶ γάμον τὸν ἐπίδοξον, καὶ ἐντὸς τῶν κοσμικῶν ἀξιωμάτων ἐγένετο.

[360] Jerome, *Ep.* 39, 5 (to Paula, AD 384).　　　　　　[361] Harries, art. cit. (n. 61), 58 ff.

Alexandria all her portable goods.[362] These possessions were exchanged for gold which she distributed among the Christian holy men and poor of the region.[363] Palladius also tells how her distinguished thirty-seven years of charitable service was funded from family resources.[364] When her granddaughter, Melania the Younger, was experiencing difficulties in following her ascetic path, the older woman returned to Italy *c.*399 to throw her considerable influence on the side of the young couple. On her return to Italy, Paulinus of Nola, to whom she was related, drew considerable satisfaction from witnessing the respect which Melania's wealthy and well-dressed family showed to their dirty and dishevelled relative.[365] But it is clear that Melania the Elder had never ceased being the possessor of a very large senatorial patrimony which she managed with great shrewdness. Despite Paulinus' interpretation, considerable worldly status still adhered to Melania precisely because she was known to be, still, a very wealthy woman.[366] Melania escorted Pinianus and Melania the Younger to Sicily where she decided to sell off estates which she had held there up until that time. The final liquidation of the property of Melania the Elder was achieved, according to Palladius, in only forty days but was effected over thirty years after her original departure from Rome.[367]

The case of Paula, the mother of Eustochium, may also serve to illustrate certain realities in the disposal of the property by senatorial ascetics. Jerome claimed that the renunciation had been achieved at a single stroke: 'Disregarding her house, her children, her property, and in a word, everything connected with the world, she was eager . . . to go to the desert made famous by its Pauls and its Antonies.'[368] But Jerome himself gives ample evidence that Paula retired only after carrying through a transfer of wealth to her children staying in Rome: 'Before setting out she gave them all that she had, disinheriting herself upon earth that she might find an inheritance in Heaven.'[369]

[362] Palladius, *Historia Lausiaca* 46, 1. Jerome, *Chronicon* [Helm, 247] implied mistakenly that she had sailed straight to Jerusalem.

[363] Palladius, *Historia Lausiaca* 46, 2.

[364] Ibid. 54, 2: Her own family and stewards provided the funds for this. See Brown, op. cit. (n. 4), 279–81.

[365] Paulinus, *Ep.* 29, 8 ff.

[366] F. E. Consolino, 'Modelli di comportamento e modi di santificazione per l'aristocrazia femminile d'occidente', in A. Giardina (ed.), *Società romana e impero tardoantico I. Istituzione, ceti, economie* (Rome: Laterza, 1986), 273–306, at 290.

[367] Palladius, *Historia Lausiaca* 54, 6.

[368] Jerome, *Ep.* 108, 6 (*CSEL* 55, 311): 'Non domus, non liberorum, non familiae, non possessionum, non alicuius rei, quae ad saeculum pertinet . . . ad heremum Antoniorum atque Paulorum pergere gestiebat.'

[369] Jerome, *Ep.* 108, 6 (*CSEL* 55, 312): 'antequam proficisceretur, cuncta largita est exheredans se in terra, ut hereditatem inveniret in caelo.'

Like Melania before her, Paula took funds with her from which she drew to finance her charitable activities and travels in the Holy Land.[370]

In the early 390s two senatorial men adopted the ascetic life. In both cases we can see that the continued holding of property played an important part in the Christian lives of each. To Paulinus of Nola Jerome wrote in 394 advising him to sell up his property if it was in his power and if not, to cast it from himself.[371] He was well aware that what was holding Paulinus back was a rather worldly appreciation of the value of property: 'You are all for delay, you wish to defer action: unless—so you argue—unless I sell my goods piecemeal and with caution, Christ will be at a loss to feed his poor.'[372] Pammachius, too, was careful to keep enough property to qualify as a senator and Palladius records that his Roman property was sold off only after his death.[373]

Significantly, the only noble ascetics to step out of line concerning property were quickly dissuaded from their course of action. When Melania and Pinianus arrived in Africa in 410–11 to announce the liquidation of their estates there, the senior Christian bishops intervened:

the most saintly and important bishops of Africa (I mean the blessed Augustine, his brother Alypius, and Aurelius of Carthage) advised them, saying, 'The money that you now furnish to monasteries will be used up in a short time. If you wish to have a memorial forever in heaven and earth, give both a house and an income to each monastery.'[374]

The African bishops thus recommended to the holy couple precisely the same economic arrangement adopted by Constantine and his imperial successors, Vestina and various extreme ascetics from Melania the Elder to Paula.[375] Paulinus of Nola had fifteen years earlier described the quiet sundering of his earthly body from its landed possessions:

---

[370] Ibid. 5, 2; 7, 3 (funds spent on Cyprus); 10, 1 (outlay at Bethlehem); 14, 4 (Egypt); 15, 5–7 (where her *loans* for charitable purposes are mentioned); 16, 1. See Lizzi, art. cit. (n. 86), 149; E. A. Clark, 'Authority and Humility: A Conflict of Values in Fourth-Century Monasticism', in ead. (ed.), *Ascetic Piety and Women's Faith: Essays on Late Antique Christianity* (Lewiston: Edwin Mellon Press, 1986), 213.

[371] Jerome, *Ep*. 53, 11.

[372] Jerome, *Ep*. 53, 11 (*CSEL* 54, 465): 'Scilicet, nisi tu semper recrastinans et diem de die trahens caute et pedetemptim tuas possessiunculas vendideris, non habet Christus, unde alat pauperes suos.' (Trans. P. G. Walsh.)

[373] Palladius, *Historia Lausiaca* 62; Paulinus, *Ep*. 13; Jerome, *Ep*. 66; 77; 118. See Arnheim, op. cit. (n. 55), 121.

[374] *Vita Melaniae* (Gr.) 20: Ἅπερ νῦν παρέχετε τοῖς μοναστηρίοις νομίσματα, εἰς ὀλίγον ἀναλίσκεται χρόνον. εἰ δὲ βούλεσθε ἄληστον ἔχειν μνήμην ἐν οὐρανῷ καὶ ἐπὶ γῆς, δωρήσασθε ἑκάστῳ μοναστηρίῳ καὶ οἰκίαν καὶ πρόσοδον.

[375] See Piétri, art. cit. (n. 201).

Finally, when I seemed to obtain rest from lying scandal and from wanderings, unbruised by public affairs and far from the din of the market place, I enjoyed the leisure of country life and my religious duties, surrounded by pleasant peace in my withdrawn household. So gradually my mind became disengaged from worldly troubles, adapting itself to the divine commands, so that I strove more easily towards contempt for the world and comradeship with Christ, since my way of life actually bordered on it.[376]

This idea of the contempt for wealth among the wealthy was what ultimately bolstered up the economic position of the Christian aristocracy. After the incident with Pinianus at Hippo, Augustine responded to the accusation that he and his grasping flock had seized an opportunity to capture a rich aristocrat for their church. Augustine wrote to Albina: 'what they [the mob] esteemed in you was your contempt of money.'[377] But Augustine was aware that what the Church needed was individuals *with* money before any contempt of it could be shown. What we have seen consistently is that almost all the noble ascetics of Rome who demonstrated such a contempt to the great distress of their peers, actually retained wealth on a scale that *supported* rather than undermined their economic status. It is surely ironic that when the foremost Latin theologian of the age was called upon to defend this use of property, he should only have been echoing the sentiments of a thoroughly respectable Roman matron and authoress of the cento, *De Laudibus Christi*.[378]

Theoretically, the adoption of an ascetic life by aristocratic men and women was the final humbling of their earthly identities in exchange for a heavenly reward. The renunciation of social status, wealth, and family ought to have left the ascetic as a solitary figure. What is noticeable about the exhortations to the ascetic life which churchmen like Jerome addressed to aristocratic converts and especially women, is that they emphasized a sense of community and status of a different kind. Consolino has made a detailed study of the modes of behaviour and role models recommended to aristocratic women in the west in late antiquity.[379] The ascetic life as portrayed by the Fathers in the period after 313 was 'un martirio incruento protatto per tutta la vita'.[380] As

---

[376] Paulinus, *Ep.* 5, 4 (*CSEL* 29, 27) written in summer 396 to Severus: 'postea denique ut a calumniis et peregrinationibus requiem capere visus sum, nec rebus publicis occupatus et a fori strepitu remotus ruris otium et ecclesiae cultum placita in secretis domesticis tranquillitate celebravi, ut paulatim subducto a saecularibus turbis animo praeceptisque caelestibus accommodato proclivius ad contemptum mundi comitatumque Christi iam quasi de finitima huic proposito via dimicaverim. See Walsh, op. cit. (n. 244), 218 n. 1.

[377] Augustine, *Ep.* 126, 7 (*CSEL* 44, 12): 'vestrum pecuniae contemptum dilexit in vobis.'

[378] See above, pp. 283-4.   [379] Consolino, art. cit. (n. 366).   [380] Ibid. 273.

living martyrs, however, such individuals could be guaranteed a holy status among ordinary pious Christians in the world.[381] We have seen above that the reaction of noble Christians to extreme ascetics was likely to be much more hostile. Faced with the resistance of many of their peers, the noble Christian ascetics sometimes required the strongest encouragement.

Although Jerome called upon a number of women to renounce the world, he explained the value of the ascetic life in terms which were familiar to them. He exhorted Iulia Eustochium to leave behind her married acquaintances, swollen with pride at their husbands' achievements, and then appealed to her own pride:

Why do you, then, wrong your husband? Why do you, God's bride, hasten to visit the wife of a mere man? Learn in this respect a holy pride (*superbia sancta*); know that you are better than they.[382]

The significance and status of noble birth was never submerged beneath the exhortations to renunciation. Eustochium was carefully reminded of her aristocratic rank:

I now bring all my speech to bear upon you who, as it is your lot to be the first virgin of noble birth in Rome, have to labour the more diligently not to lose good things to come as well as those present.[383]

And Furia was encouraged to preserve her widowhood by keeping before her the example of Marcella: 'who, while she is true to the claims of her birth and station, has set before us a life which is worthy of the gospel.'[384] In praising these individuals, Jerome was careful to note their high birth. This was because their indelible social status was still important to him, to them, and to the other readers of his letters.[385] Jerome was not alone in this attitude. Ambrose was proud to have Marcellina as a virgin sister while Paulinus of Nola upheld his family links with Melania the Elder.[386] When Paula died in Bethlehem in 404, Jerome did not hesitate to commemorate her with a tomb and two

---

[381] See Palladius, *Historia Lausiaca* 55.

[382] Jerome, *Ep.* 22, 16 (*CSEL* 54, 163): 'cur tu facias iniuriam viro tuo? Ad hominis coniugem dei sponsa quid properas? Disce in hac parte superbiam sanctam, scito te illis esse meliorem.'

[383] Ibid. 15 (*CSEL* 54, 162): 'nunc ad te mihi omnis dirigitur oratio, quae quanto prima Romanae urbis virgo nobilis esse coepisti, tanto tibi amplius laborandum est, ne et praesentibus bonis careas et futuris.'

[384] Jerome, *Ep.* 54, 18 (*CSEL* 54, 485): 'quae respondens generi suo aliquid nobis de evangelio retulit'. Cf. *Ep.* 123 (to Geruchia).

[385] For a later example see his *Ep.* 130 to Demetrias, especially 6: 'Had you become a man's bride but one province would have known you; while as a Christian virgin you are known to the whole world.'

[386] Marcellina: Ambrose, *De Virginibus* 3, 37. Melania: Paulinus, *Ep.* 29, 5.

epitaphs near the spot of Christ's birth. One of the epitaphs is a strong affirmation of her worldly position:

> Within this tomb a child of Scipio lies,
> A daughter of the far-famed Pauline house,
> A scion of the Gracchi, of the stock
> Of Agamemmnon's self, illustrious:
> Here rests the lady Paula, well-beloved
> Of both her parents, with Eustochium
> For daughter; she the first of Roman dames
> Who hardship chose and Bethlehem for Christ.[387]

The adoption of the ascetic life did not automatically mean a loss of autonomy and there are examples of noble Christain ascetics appealing to their worldly status when it was convenient. Melania the Elder, for example, found herself in conflict with the governor of Palestine.[388] And Melania the Younger happily used the *cursus publicus* for a trip to Constantinople where she helped arrange a family marriage.[389]

In presenting ascetic virtue to a class suffused with perceptions of rank, Jerome drew upon a hierarchy of biblical personalities with whom the ascetic convert might unblushingly associate herself.[390] Christ Himself might become a husband, as in the case of Eustochium discussed above.[391] On the other hand, Principia, who had asked for a biography of Marcella shortly after the latter's death, was informed that the great ascetic of the Aventine was a finer example of Christian virtue than the prophetess Anna.[392] Jerome wrote to Furia at Rome in 394 telling her that her 'sister' (probably Eustochium) was like Miriam, singing to the virgin choir after the drowning of Pharaoh:[393] 'Let Rome

[387] Jerome, *Ep.* 108, 34 (*CSEL* 55, 350); 'Scipio quam genuit, Pauli fudere parentes,|Gracchorum suboles, Agamemnonis inclita proles|Hoc iacet in tumulo, Paulam dixere priores.|Eustochiae genetrix, Romani prima senatus|Pauperiem Christi et Bethlemitica rura secuta est.' Cf. ibid. for another epitaph to Paula put on the entrance to the grotto of Christ's nativity. Compare Diehl, *ILCV* 1700 (in honour of the noble virgin Manlia Daedalia): 'Clara genus, censu pollens et mater egentum,|Virgo sacrata deo Manlia Daedalia,|Quae mortale nihil mortali in pectore volvens,|Quo peteret caelum semper amavit iter.'

[388] Palladius, *Historia Lausiaca*, 46, 4.   [389] See Brown, art. cit. (n. 4), 175.

[390] In a negative sense, figures from Roman history could be introduced to show the superior virtues of Christians: Jerome, *Ep.* 54, 4 (to Furia, AD 394) where the fecundity of Cornelia, mother of the Gracchi, had not saved her from heartbreak. See Consolino, art. cit. (n. 366), 285.

[391] As Consolino points out, ibid. 279 this attitude conflicted directly with Ambrose's emphasis on the *dignitas* of Christ: *De Virginibus* 1, 11, 60 ff. but was nevertheless held by Jerome and others.

[392] Jerome, *Ep.* 127, 2 discussing Marcella and Luke 2: 36. See Consolino, art. cit. (n. 366), 281–2 and cf. Jerome, *Ep.* 54 (to Furia, AD 394).

[393] Jerome, *Ep.* 54, 13. See Exodus 15: 21.

have [in you] what a humbler city than Rome, I mean Bethlehem, has [in her].'[394] Jerome was advocating what might be called a 'triangular' method of spiritual association. At the highest point was placed Christ himself or some saint[395] but at a different level, the recipients of Jerome's letters were frequently encouraged to emulate the great Christians of their own time and social class. In a letter written just after the death of Blesilla, Jerome recalled for Paula the grief of Naomi and Job before citing Melania the Elder as a great example from her own time.[396]

As in the case of aristocratic wealth, the 'lofty through lowliness' retained marks of high social distinction. In the monastery founded by Paula in Bethlehem the nuns were divided into groups based upon the social status of women who entered.[397] The former wealth and social position of aristocrats were constantly set before the eyes of a Christian public convinced that miraculous changes of heart were taking place all around them. But the persistent echoes of their worldly lives made the ascetic friends of Jerome formidable role models for the fifth-century aristocracy of Rome.

CONCLUSION

The traditional scholarly anxiety to assign Roman aristocrats to 'pagan' or 'Christian' camps has led to the neglect of a particularly vivid and important chapter in late Roman social relations.

If the establishment of a 'common ground in the classical culture of the age' was the necessary precursor to the creation of a Christianized aristocracy, then the extreme noble ascetics of fourth-century Rome played both a negative and a positive part in the process. They were a very small group; barely ten examples are known to us in any detail in the fourth century. The evidence of the opposition which they aroused, however, makes it quite clear that their impact was disproportionately great on senatorial life and attitudes towards property. In particular, noble Christian asceticism seemed often to embody bizarre uses of senatorial wealth, the rupturing of family ties, and the abandonment of the city of Rome. The vigorous resistance of moderate Christian nobles to extreme asceticism laid the foundation of a Christian nobility which took its urban Christian piety very seriously indeed. The Christians

---

[394] Jerome, *Ep.* 54, 13 (*CSEL* 54, 481): 'Habeat Roma, quod angustior urbe Romana possidet Bethleem.'

[395] See Jerome, *Ep.* 130 for Olympias and Saint Agnes. See Consolino, art. cit. (n. 366), 287 for the panegyrical qualities of the letter.

[396] Jerome, *Ep.* 39, 5.

[397] Jerome, *Ep.* 108, 20.

whom Jerome dismissed as frauds had, in fact, a coherent Christian view of their role as part of the social élite of Rome. They enjoyed significant contact with Christian holy men and women as well as offering support to some capable Christian polemicists and theologians. There is evidence to show that their relations with the city's clergy were close. They were influential enough to bring about the banishment from Rome of Jerome, the most enthusiastic promoter of upper-class asceticism.

But if Jerome had misjudged the strength of the moderate Christians, they themselves were for a long time blind to the part played by retained social status in the lives of ascetic nobles. The renunciation of Rome did not, paradoxically, deny noble ascetics worldly status. There is evidence that an aristocratic shrewdness accompanied some of the most notable ascetics to the east. The crisis of confidence in senatorial landholding occasioned first by the conversion of Melania the Younger and then Alaric's sack of the city created an atmosphere in which a broader spectrum of aristocratic involvement in the life of the Roman church could be developed. The regeneration of the city in the first half of the fifth century was achieved largely through a partnership of the bishop and a nobility confident in its Romanness and anxious to achieve a place in the next life.

Towards an understanding of 'Christianization' in Rome

Even the fragmentary picture of Rome in the third century available to the historian provides a valuable context for the tetrarchic and Constantinian age. The dynamics of power required emperors to express their civic sense, generosity, and, on occasion, their personal contribution to *religio* on the landscape of the city. But quite separately from the emperors, the topography was subject to change or threat from other forces as well. If the presence of Christians periodically caused disorder, including direct imperial intervention from the middle of the century, it was a minor matter compared to the abiding threat of violence between soldiers and civilians. Prudent emperors of the period, like those of the Principate, attempted to balance the competing expectations of different groups within Rome and even the skilful could, like Diocletian, end up pleasing no one. Maxentius, too, may be said to have tried in a short reign to have worked within the parameters of his predecessors, only to find that repeated military emergencies shifted his political balance fatally, leading to a precipitate campaign against the more accomplished Constantine.

In observing the impact of Constantine on Rome, we see many of the precepts of third-century government in high relief. A usurper of outstanding military energy, enthusiastically in personal contact with a great god, captured the symbolic heart of the Roman empire. Understandably, Constantine's churches have been considered to be the most important of his contributions to the life of Rome. The positioning of these sites relative to 'the pagan monumental centre' of the city, however, has given rise to colourful theories which unconvincingly visualize Constantine as a timid builder of these massive edifices, afraid of piquing the pagans of the centre. But when all the elements of his programme of construction are taken together, it is possible to see a familiar pattern: they were a sustained attempt to make the new emperor known to the citizens of the city and they were a means of erasing the memory of the old regime. While there can be no denying the strength of Constantine's religious motivation and the unprecedented scale of his Christian building, at the same time there is no concealing Constantine's tetrarchic pedigree with its taste for urban ceremonial, political propaganda, and the extensive use of imperial property.

Developments after the death of Constantine direct the historian away from emperors and towards the influential churchmen of the city. The architectural idiom in which these Christians expressed their claims was considerably humbler than that of the great Constantinian sites but the importance attached to the Christian topography was passionately demonstrated. The 'new geography' of Christian Rome was drawn only with difficulty. But the pagans of the city, often assigned the character of a determined opposition, played no part in impeding the development of the Christian landscape. Rather, the competing claims of aspirants to the episcopal seat of the city provided the fluctuating forces. The prestige of certain holy sites drew factions into different areas of Rome and the result was an urban territorial factionalism by no means uncommon in modern cities. The most successful of the disputants proved to be bishop Damasus who supplemented a ruthless appetite for episcopal power with an unprecedentedly extensive vision of Christian Rome. In seeking to lead the Christian community forward under firm episcopal guidance, he gave to the cult of the martyrs a powerful impulse which laid a more significant claim on specifically Roman time and space than the labours of Constantine.

The complex and surprising history of the Roman landscape prompts a revision of the most important themes of social history.

In legal terms, the idea of the pagans of Rome as an embattled group facing an endless succession of hostile imperial edicts is no longer helpful. The mere fact that almost all the emperors of the fourth century were Christian and Rome was the ancient centre of paganism is not sufficient to posit an unrelenting religious war. The evidence of the laws themselves, freed from certain modern legal preconceptions, shows that the attitudes of the emperors were not consistent with each other over time and could be inconsistent within a single reign. Until Theodosius I, the most consistent object of attack in the laws of the emperors was not paganism but harmful magic and divination. The pagans of fourth-century Rome, like the Christians of the third century, lived for the most part in peace, occasionally experiencing the uncomfortable attentions of a huge and unwieldy system of government as it attempted to enforce the often erratic wishes of emperors.

Much more consistent, however, was the enduring utility of civic patronage. In particular, the exploitation of Roman time by Christian emperors was the key to their search for universal appeal. It is also the aspect of Roman life which illustrates most clearly the eclectic nature of culture in the city at this period. Based upon the kind of preconceptions which have clouded our understanding of the import of the most important laws of the fourth century, scholars have suggested that the festival calendar of the city was either grudgingly tolerated by the Christian emperors or modified by them in an attempt to 'neutralize' the entertainments. This is true only of the last quarter of the century, when, as we saw, the laws of the emperors began to attack the temples and the beliefs of paganism on an unprecedentedly broad front. Until that time, however, the thriving ceremonial life was used by the Constantinian dynasty to promote its own interests in ancient fashion. The fluidity of the calendar and the rituals of the Circus Maximus enabled the Christian emperors to patronize the most lavish and important civic events. The overwhelmingly pagan associations of the venue and its rituals make it impossible to conceive of these entertainments as 'neutral'. Their pagan atmosphere, until the Theodosian age, highlights the capacity of Christian emperors to shape their own patronage to the rhythms of urban life.

The pleasures and values of that urban life came under attack from Christian ascetics from the middle years of the fourth century. Evidence of the turmoil which this new form of religious expression caused comes most clearly from the ranks of the Roman aristocracy. Difficult as this evidence may be, it nevertheless permits us to dismiss the idea that the division between pagan and Christian was the only or even the most significant division of the citizenry in late Rome. In reality, the situation was much more complicated. The emergence of a senatorial class loyal to the city of Rome and its bishop developed out of a conflict between *Christians* as much as the process of the conversion of non-Christians. The new asceticism threatened the traditional patterns of holding and using aristocratic property. Thrown initially into disarray by these attacks, however, the moderate Christians of the city produced a coherent response to the criticism that was both Christian and Roman. The tenacity of aristocratic status is illustrated by the refusal or inability of even the most extreme noble ascetics to abandon their earthly prominence *in toto*. The strength of the aristocratic response to extreme Christian asceticism enabled the senatorial order both to survive the sack of the city in the summer of 410 and to act as the vanguard of a brilliant flowering of Roman Christian culture in the fifth century.

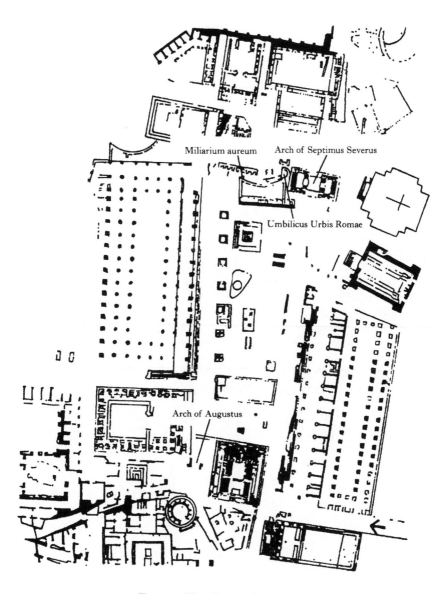

Fig. 1: The Forum Romanum
(after Coarelli).

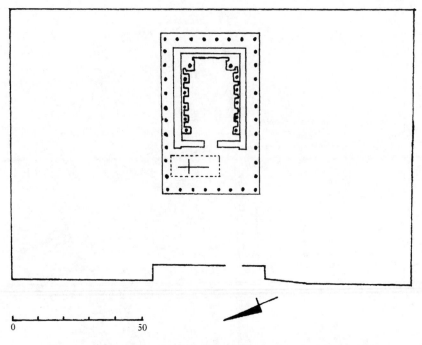

FIG. 2: The Temple of Heliogabalus at the *vigna Barberini*
(after Castagnoli).

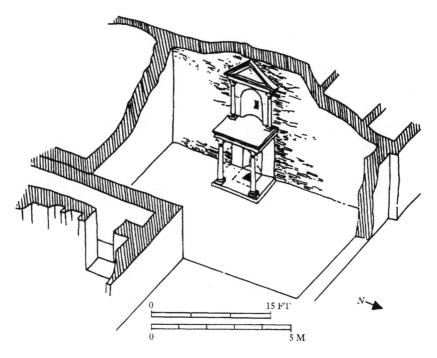

FIG. 3: The *tropaion* of Peter.

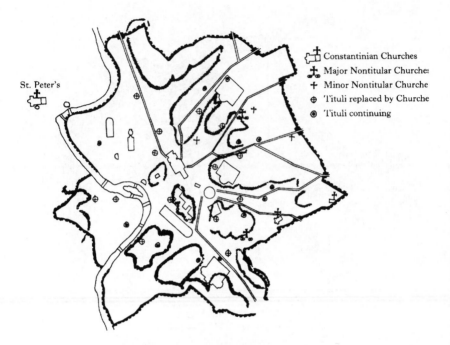

St. Peter's

Constantinian Churches
Major Nontitular Churches
Minor Nontitular Churche
Tituli replaced by Churche
Tituli continuing

FIG. 4: The churches of late antique Rome
(after Krautheimer).

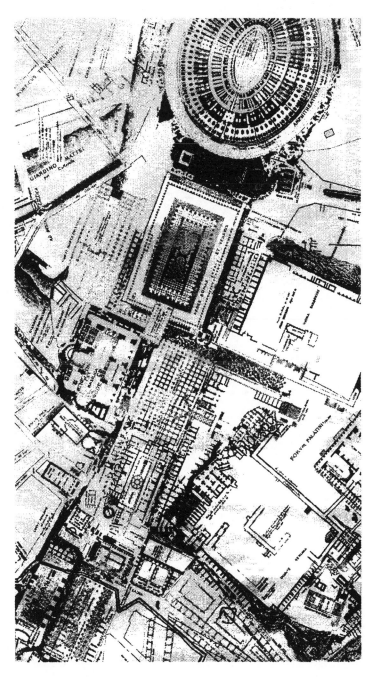

FIG. 5: The Velia in Lanciani's *Forma Urbis Romae*.

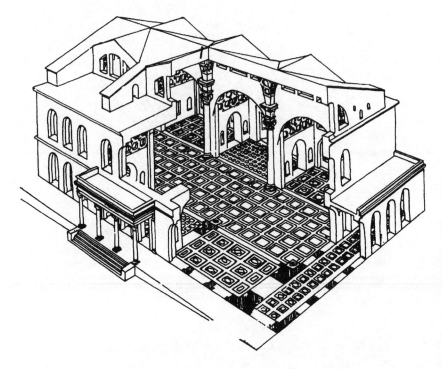

FIG. 6: The Basilica of Maxentius/Constantine, reconstruction.

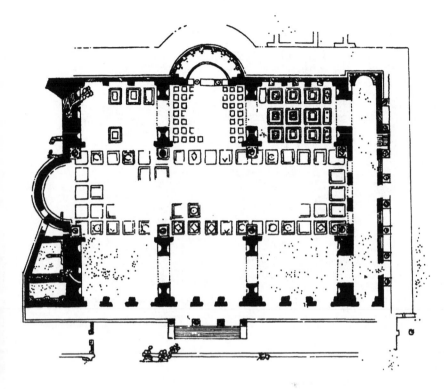

FIG. 7: The Basilica of Maxentius/Constantine, with traces of floor panelling.

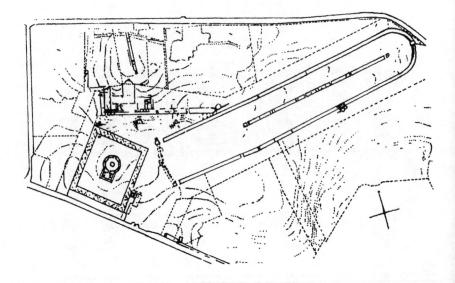

FIG. 8: The villa of Maxentius, plan of the complex.

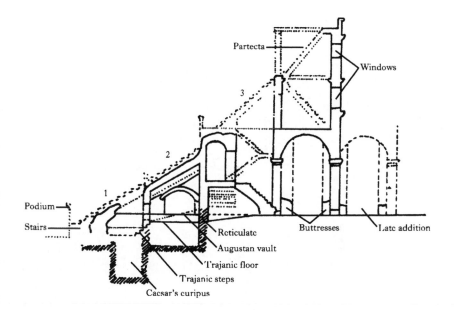

FIG. 9: Section of the seating at south-east end of the Circus Maximus
(after Ciancio Rossetto).

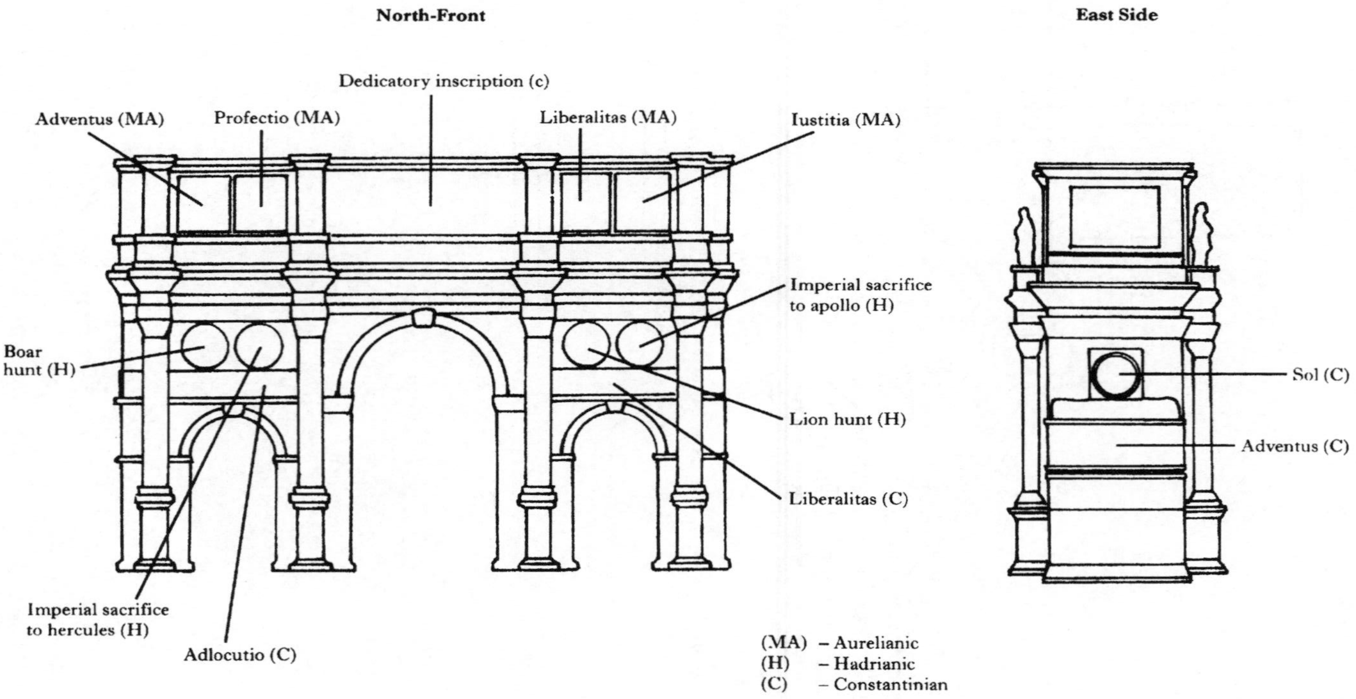

East Side

Sol (C)

Adventus (C)

North-Front

Iustitia (MA)

Liberalitas (MA)

Dedicatory inscription (c)

Profectio (MA)

Adventus (MA)

Imperial sacrifice to apollo (H)

Lion hunt (H)

Liberalitas (C)

Adlocutio (C)

Imperial sacrifice to hercules (H)

Boar hunt (H)

(MA) – Aurelianic
(H) – Hadrianic
(C) – Constantinian

Fig. 10: Arch of Constantine (north front and east side).

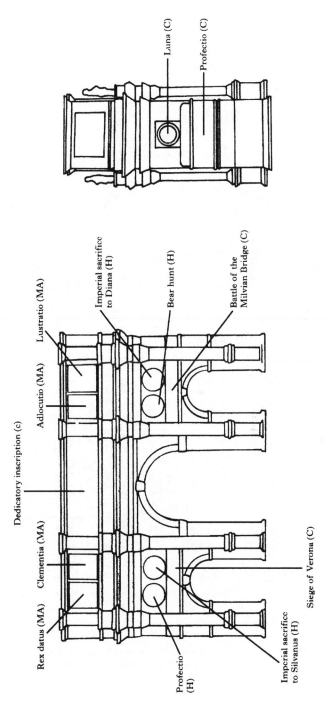

West Side

Luna (C)

Profectio (C)

South Front

Rex datus (MA)

Clementia (MA)

Dedicatory inscription (c)

Adlocutio (MA)

Lustratio (MA)

Imperial sacrifice to Diana (H)

Bear hunt (H)

Battle of the Milvian Bridge (C)

Siege of Verona (C)

Imperial sacrifice to Silvanus (H)

Profectio (H)

FIG. 11: Arch of Constantine (south front and west side).

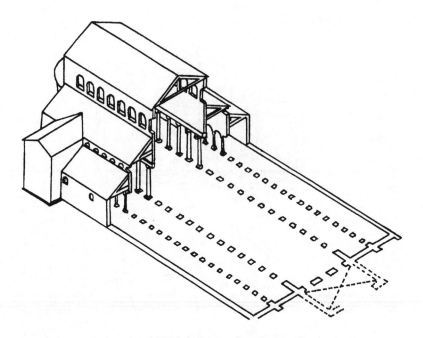

FIG. 12(a): Lateran basilica, reconstruction Waddy, revised Lloyd.

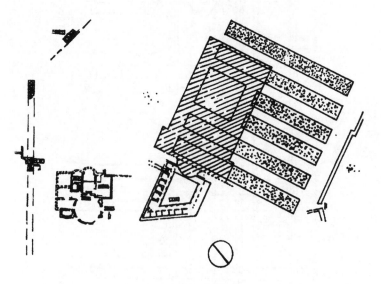

FIG. 12(b): The Lateran basilica overlying the camp of the
equites singulares

(after Pelliccioni).

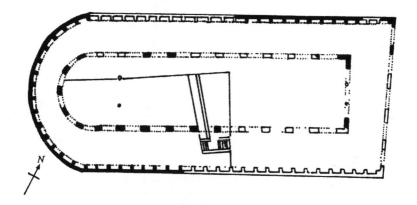

FIG. 13(a). The Basilica Apostolorum (San Sebastiano).
Reconstruction of the Constantinian church

(after Krautheimer).

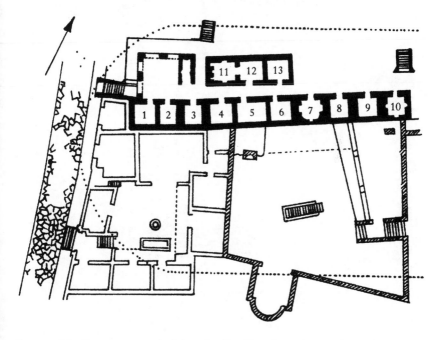

FIG. 13(b): Structures underlying the *Basilica Apostolorum* (San Sebastiano).

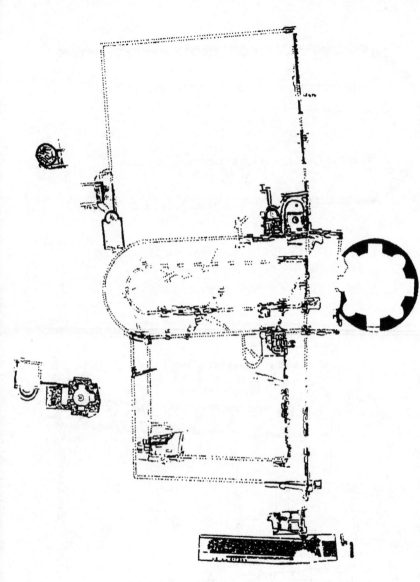

Fig. 14: SS. Marcellino e Pietro: general plan of structures revealed by excavation on the Via Labicana site between 1896 and 1984

(after Guyon)

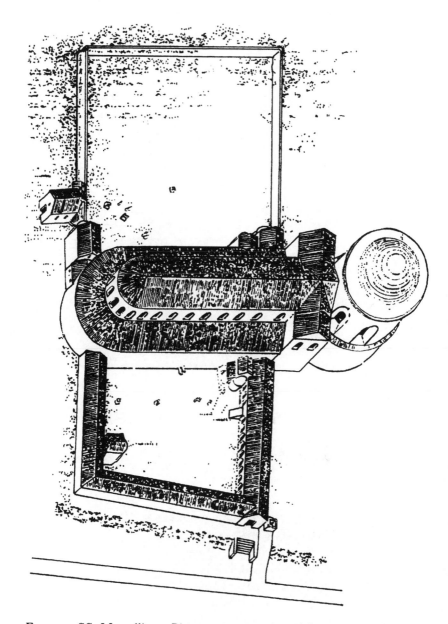

FIG. 15: SS. Marcellino e Pietro: reconstruction of Constantinian church
(after Colalelli).

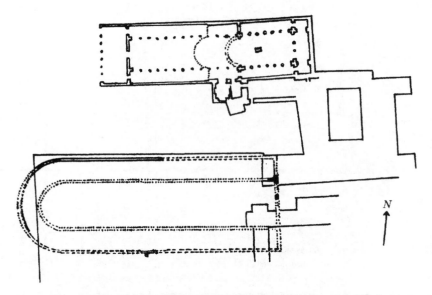

FIG. 16(a): Constantinian basilica adjacent to present church of S. Lorenzo fuori le mura

(after Frankl).

FIG. 16(b): Constantinian basilica in honour of Laurentius with *memoria* to north

(after Krautheimer).

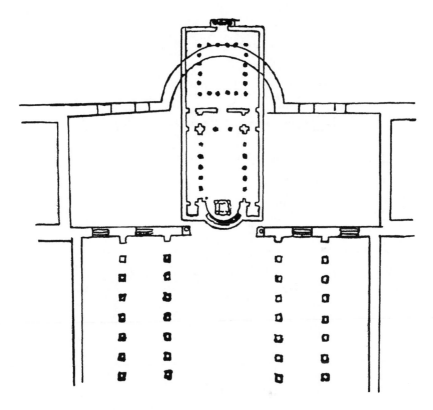

FIG. 17: Belloni's reconstruction of the early basilica of Saint Paul.

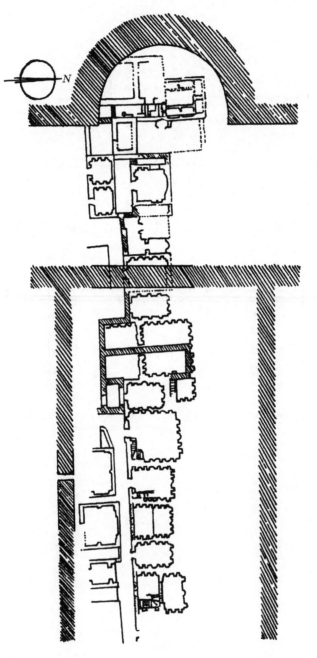

FIG. 18: Part of the Vatican necropolis
(after Toynbee and Ward-Perkins).

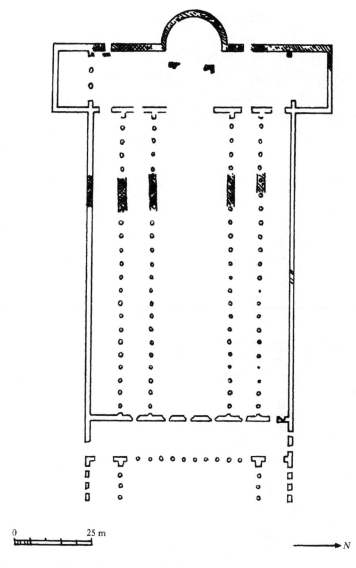

0   25 m

→ N

FIG. 19: Constantine's basilica for Saint Peter

(after *Esplorazioni*).

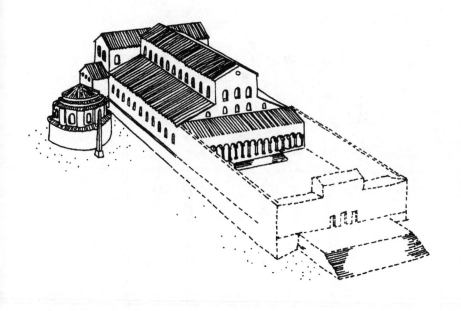

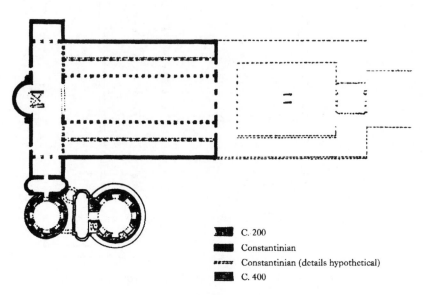

	C. 200
	Constantinian
	Constantinian (details hypothetical)
	C. 400

FIG. 20: Saint Peter's *circa* AD 400
(after Krautheimer).

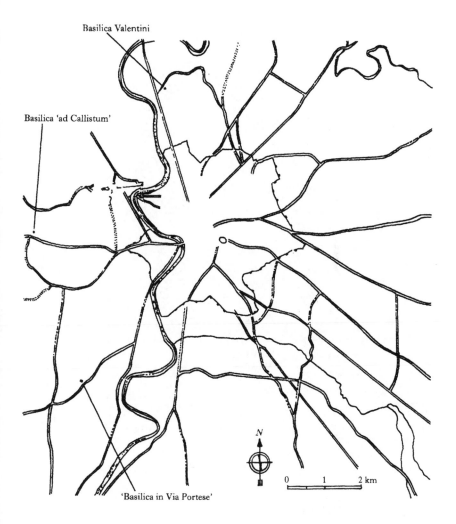

Basilica Valentini

Basilica 'ad Callistum'

'Basilica in Via Portese'

FIG. 21: Julius' intervention beyond the walls.

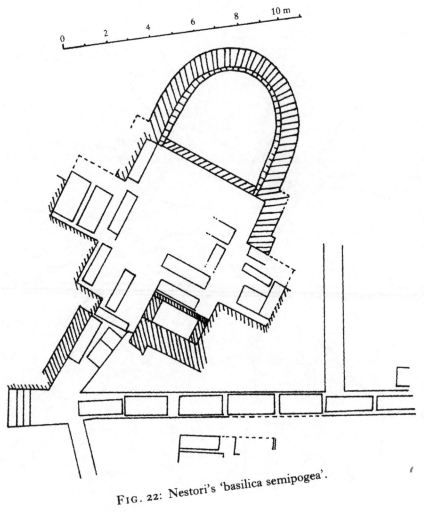

FIG. 22: Nestori's 'basilica semipogea'.

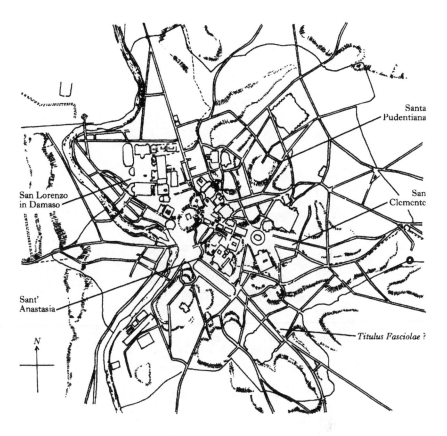

Santa
Pudentiana

San
Clemente

San Lorenzo
in Damaso

Sant'
Anastasia

Titulus Fasciolae ?

N

FIG. 23: Damasus' intervention at intramural sites.

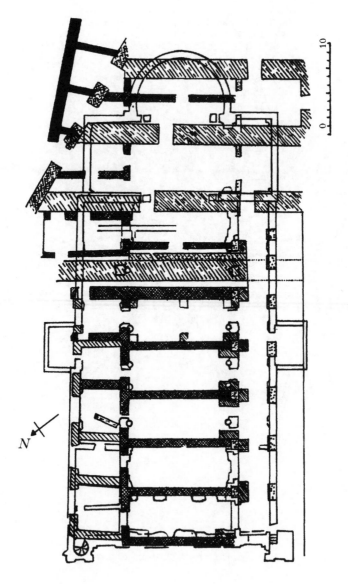

F IG . 24: Sant'Anastasia with substructures.

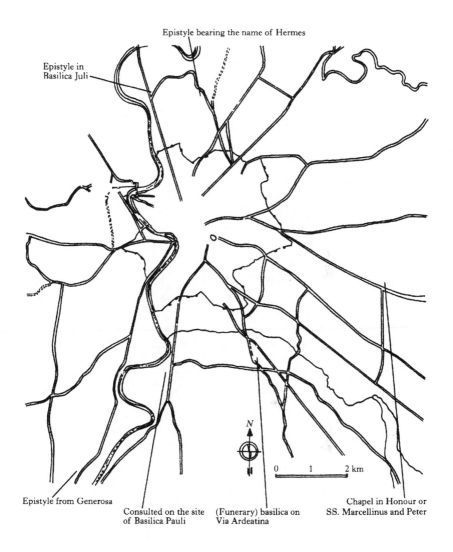

Epistyle bearing the name of Hermes

Epistyle in
Basilica Juli

Epistyle from Generosa

Consulted on the site
of Basilica Pauli

(Funerary) basilica on
Via Ardeatina

Chapel in Honour or
SS. Marcellinus and Peter

N

0   1   2 km

FIG. 25: Damasus' intervention at extramural sites.

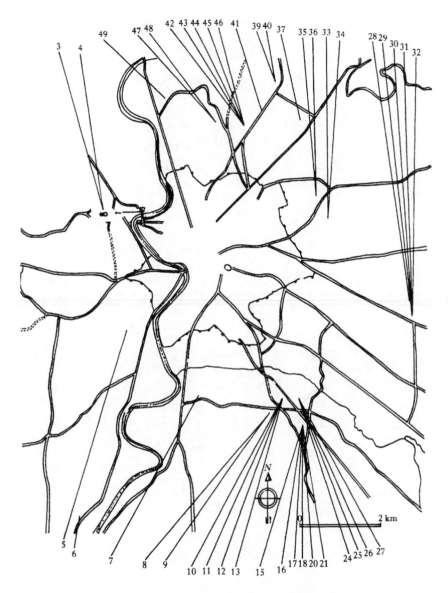

FIG. 26: The distribution of the *epigrammata* of Damasus
(using numbers from Ferrua's edition).

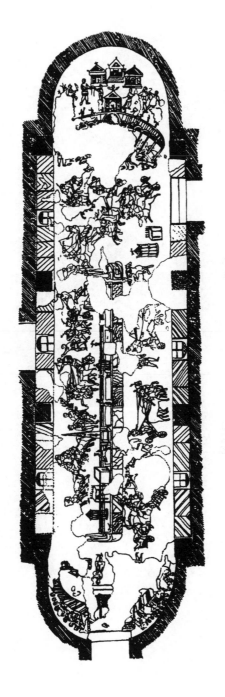

FIG. 27: The Piazza Armerina circus mosaic.

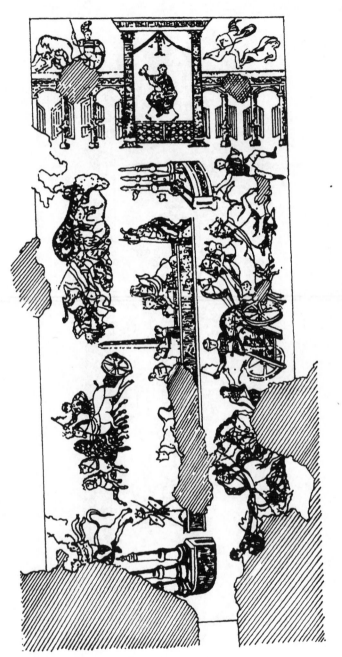

Fig. 28: Gerona circus mosaic.

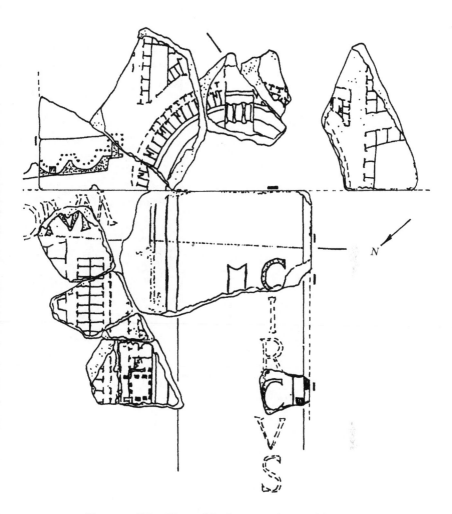

FIG. 29: The Circus Maximus on the marble plan.

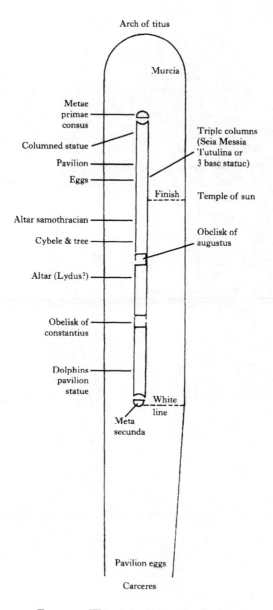

Arch of titus

Murcia

Metae primae consus

Columned statue

Pavilion

Eggs

Finish — Temple of sun

Triple columns (Seia Messia Tutulina or 3 base statue)

Altar samothracian

Cybele & tree

Obelisk of augustus

Altar (Lydus?)

Obelisk of constantius

Dolphins pavilion statue

White line

Meta secunda

Pavilion eggs

Carceres

FIG. 30: The monuments on the barrier
of the Circus Maximus

(after Humphrey).

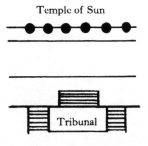

Temple of Sun

Tribunal

FIG. 31(a): Restoration of
box at the finishing line
in the Circus Maximus.

FIG. 31(b): Reconstruction of
the box at the finishing line
in the circus of Maxentius

(after Ioppolo).

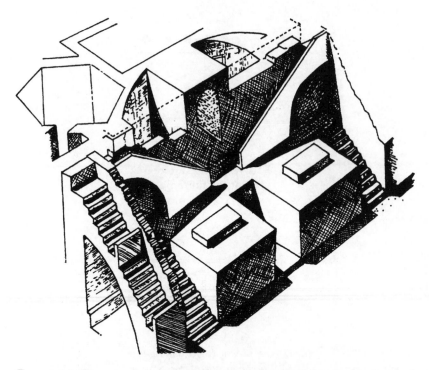

FIG. 31(c): Reconstruction of the box at the finishing line in the circus of
Maxentius

(after Ioppolo).

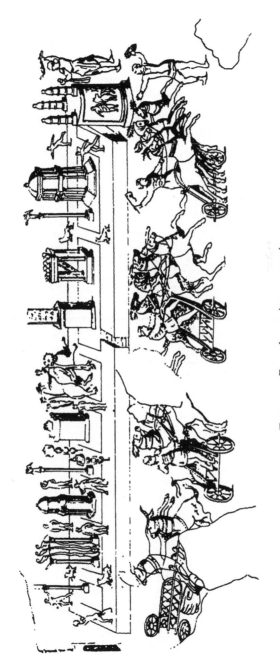

Fig. 32: Barcelona circus mosaic
(after Hübner)

Bibliography

Alexander, S. S., 'Studies in Constantinian Church Architecture' (pt. 1), *RAC*, 47 (1971), 281–330; (pt. 2), *RAC*, 49 (1973), 33–44.

Alföldi, A., *A Festival of Isis in the Fourth Century* (Budapest: Pázmány University, 1937).

—— *A Conflict of Ideas in the Later Roman Empire* (Oxford: Clarendon Press, 1952).

—— *The Conversion of Constantine and Pagan Rome*, 2nd edn. (Oxford: Clarendon Press, 1969).

Alföldi, M. R., 'Die Sol-Comes Münze vom Jahre 325: Neues zur Bekehrung Constantins', *Mullus: Festschrift Th. Klauser* (Münster: Aschendorff, 1964), 10–16.

Anderson, G., *Sage, Saint and Sophist: Holy Men and Their Associates in the Early Roman Empire* (London: Routledge, 1994).

Antin, P., 'La Ville chez S. Jérôme', *Latomus*, 20 (1961), 298–311.

Apollonj-Ghetti, B. M., 'Le basiliche cimiteriali degli apostoli a Roma', in *Saecularia Petri et Pauli*, Studi di antichità, 28 (Vatican City: Pontificio Istituto di archeologia cristiana, 1969), 9–34.

Arbeiter, A., *Alt-St. Peter in Geschichte und Wissenschaft: Abfolge der Bauten, Rekonstruktion, Architekturprogramm* (Berlin: Mann, 1988).

Arjava, A., *Women and the Law in Late Antiquity* (Oxford: Clarendon Press, 1996).

Arnheim, M. T. W., *The Senatorial Aristocracy in the Later Roman Empire* (Oxford: Oxford University Press, 1972).

Ashby, Th., 'The Classical Topography of the Roman Campagna II', *PBSR*, 3 (1906), 1–212.

—— and Lugli, G., 'La villa dei Flavi cristiani "ad duas lauros" e il suburbano imperiale ad oriente di Roma', *APARA*, Memorie, 2 (1928), 157–92.

Athanassiadi-Fowden, P., *Julian and Hellenism* (Oxford: Clarendon Press, 1981).

Baldovin, J. F., *The Urban Character of Christian Worship: The Origins, Development and Meaning of Stational Liturgy*, Orientalia Christiana Analecta, 228 (Rome: Pontificium Institutum Studiorum Orientalium, 1987).

Baldus, H. R., 'Zur Aufnahme des Sol Elagabalus-Kultes in Rom, 219 n. Chr.', *Chiron*, 21 (1991), 175–8.

Baratollo, A., 'Nuove ricerche sull'architettura del tempio di Venere e Roma in età adrianea', *RM*, 80 (1973), 240–69.

—— 'Il tempio di Venere e di Roma: Un tempio "greco" nell'urbe', *RM*, 85 (1978), 397–410.

Barb, A., 'The Survival of the Magic Arts', in A. Momigliano (ed.), *The Conflict Between Paganism and Christianity in the Fourth Century* (Oxford: Clarendon Press, 1963), 100–25.

Barceló, P., 'Die Religionspolitik Kaiser Constantins der Grossen vor der Schlacht an der Milvischen Brücke', *Hermes*, 116 (1988), 76–94.

—— 'Una nuova interpretazione dell'arco di Costantino', in G. Bonamente and F. Fusco, (eds.), *Costantino il Grande* (Macerata: Pubblicazioni della Facoltà di lettere e filosofia, 1992), 105–14.

Barnes, T. D., 'Legislation Against the Christians', *JRS*, 58 (1968), 32–50.

—— *Tertullian. A Historical and Literary Study* (Oxford: Clarendon Press, 1971).

—— 'Two Senators under Constantine', *JRS*, 65 (1975a), 40–9.

—— 'Constans and Gratian in Rome', *HSClPh*, 79 (1975b), 325–33.

—— *Constantine and Eusebius* (Cambridge, Mass.: Harvard University Press, 1981).

—— *The New Empire of Diocletian and Constantine* (Cambridge, Mass.: Harvard University Press, 1982).

—— 'Constantine's Prohibition of Pagan Sacrifice', *AJPh*, 105 (1984), 69–72.

—— 'The Conversion of Constantine', *Classical Views, Échos du Monde classique*, 4 (1985), 371–91.

—— 'Christians and Pagans in the Reign of Constantius', in *L'Église et l'empire au IVe Siècle*, Entretiens sur l'Antiquité classique, 34 (Geneva: Fondation Hardt, 1987), 301–43.

—— *Athanasius and Constantius*, (Cambridge, Mass./London: Harvard University Press, 1993).

—— 'Statistics and the Conversion of the Roman Aristocracy', *JRS*, 85 (1995), 135–47.

—— and Westall, R. W., 'The Conversion of the Roman Aristocracy in Prudentius' *Contra Symmachum*', *Phoenix*, 45 (1991), 50–61.

Baus, K., *From the Apostolic Community to Constantine* (London: Burns & Oates, 1980).

Baynes, N. H., *Constantine the Great and the Christian Church*, 2nd edn., Proceedings of the British Academy, 15 (London: Oxford University Press, 1972).

Beard, M., 'A Complex of Times: No More Sheep on Romulus' Birthday', *PCPhS*, NS 33 (1987), 1–16.

—— North, J., and Price, S. R. F. (eds.), *Religions of Rome*, 2 vols. (Cambridge: Cambridge University Press, 1998).

Belvederi, G., 'L'origine della basilica ostiense', *RAC*, 22 (1946), 103–38.

Benario, H. W., 'Rome of the Severi', *Latomus*, 17 (1958), 712–22.

Bernand, A., *Les Portes du désert* (Paris: Éditions du Centre national de la recherche scientifique, 1984).

Bevan, E., *Holy Images* (London: Allen & Unwin, 1940).

Birley, E., 'Septimius Severus and the Roman Army', *Epigraphische Studien*, 8 (1969), 63–82.

Bloch, H., 'A New Document of the Last Pagan Revival in the West, 393–394 AD', *HTR*, 38 (1945), 199–241.

—— 'The Pagan Revival in the West at the End of the Fourth Century', in A. Momigliano (ed.), *The Conflict Between Paganism and Christianity in the Fourth Century* (Oxford: Clarendon Press, 1963), 193–218.

Blockley, R. C., *The Fragmentary Classicising Historians of the Later Roman Empire*, 2 vols. (Liverpool: Cairns, 1981–3).

Bömer, F., 'Pompa', *PW*, 21 (1952), 1974–94.

Bovini, G., *Edifici cristiani di culto d'età costantiniana a Roma* (Bologna: R. Pàtron, 1968).

Bowersock, G. W., *Julian the Apostate* (London: Duckworth, 1978).

Bradbury, S., 'Constantine and the Problem of Anti-Pagan Legislation in the Fourth Century', *Classical Philology*, 89 (1994), 120–39.

Brandenburg, H., *Roms frühchristliche Basiliken des 4. Jhs* (Munich: Heyne, 1979).

—— 'Die konstantinischen Kirchen in Rom. Staatsragender Kult und Herrscherkult zwischen Tradition und Neuerung', in O. Brehm and K. Sascha, (eds.), Μουσικὸς ἀνήρ: Festschrift für Max Wegner zum 90. Geburtstag, Antiquitas R., 3, 32, (Bonn: Habelt, 1992), 27–58.

Brenk, B., 'Spolia from Constantine to Charlemagne', *DOP*, 41 (1987), 102–9.

Brilliant, R., *The Arch of Septimius Severus in the Roman Forum*, MAAR, 29 (1967).

Broise, H. and Scheid, J., *Recherches archéologiques à la Magliana: Le Balneum des frères arvales*, Roma antica, 1 (Rome: École française de Rome/Soprintendenza archeologica di Roma, 1987).

Brown, P., 'Aspects of the Christianisation of the Roman Aristocracy', *JRS*, 51 (1961), 1–11.

—— *Augustine of Hippo* (London: Faber & Faber, 1967).

—— *Religion and Society in the Age of Saint Augustine* (London: Faber & Faber, 1972).

—— 'Pelagius and his Supporters: Aims and Environment', in id., *Religion and Society in the Age of Saint Augustine* 183–207.

—— *The Cult of the Saints* (Chicago: University of Chicago Press, 1981).

—— 'Dalla "Plebs Romana" alla "Plebs Dei": Aspetti della Cristianizzazione di Roma', in P. Brown, L. Cracco Ruggini, M. Mazza, (eds.), *Governanti e intellettuali: popolo di Dio I–IV secolo*, Passatopresente, 2 (Turin: Giappichelli, 1982), 123–45.

—— *The Body and Society* (London: Faber & Faber, 1989).

—— *Authority and the Sacred: Aspects of the Christianisation of the Roman World* (Cambridge: Cambridge University Press, 1995).

Browning, R., *The Emperor Julian* (London: Weidenfeld & Nicolson, 1975).

Bruun, Ch., *The Water Supply of Ancient Rome: A Study of Roman Imperial Administration*, Commentationes Humanarum Litterarum, 93 (Helsinki: Societas Scientiarum Fennica, 1991).

Bruun, P., 'The Consecration Coins of Constantine the Great', *Arctos*, 1 (1954), 19–31.

—— 'The Church Triumphant *Intra Muros*', *Rivista ticinese di numismatica e antichità classiche*, 10 (1981), 353–74.

—— 'Una permanenza del "Sol Invictus" di Costantino nell'arte cristiana', in G. Bonamente and F. Fusco, (eds.), *Costantino il grande* (Macerata: Pubblicazioni della Facoltà di lettere e filosofia, 1992), i. 219–30.

Buck, D. F., *Eunapius of Sardis*, D. Phil. thesis (Oxford, 1977).

Buddensieg, H., 'Die Konstantinbasilika in einer Zeichnung Francescos di Giorgio und der Marmorkoloss Konstantins des Grossen', *Münchner Jahrb. d. bild. Kunst*, 13 (1962), 37–48.

Calderone, S., 'Teologia politica, successione dinastica e consecratio in età costantiniana', in *Le Culte des souverains dans l'empire romain*, Entretiens sur l'Antiquité classique, 19 (Geneva: Fondation Hardt, 1973), 215–61.

—— 'Contesto storico, committenza e cronologia', in S. Garraffo, (ed.), *La villa romana del casale di Piazza Armerina*, Atti della IV riunione scientifica della scuola di perfezionamento in archeologia classica dell'Università di Catania (Catania: Istituto di archeologia, 1988), 13–57.

Calza, R., 'Un problema di iconografia imperiale sull'arco di Costantino', *APARA*, Rendiconti, 32 (1960), 131–61.

Cameron, A., 'The Date and Identity of Macrobius', *JRS*, 56 (1966), 25–38.

—— 'Gratian's Repudiation of the Pontifical Robe', *JRS*, 58 (1968), 96–102.

—— *Circus Factions* (Oxford: Clarendon Press, 1976).

—— 'Paganism and Literature in Late Fourth Century Rome', in *Christianisme et formes littéraires de l'Antiquité tardive en Occident*, Entretiens sur l'Antiquité classique, 23 (Geneva: Fondation Hardt, 1977), 1–30.

—— 'The Date and Owners of the Esquiline Treasure', *AJA*, 89 (1985), 135–45.

—— 'Forschungen zum Thema der heidnischen Reaktion in der Literatur seit 1943', in A. and E. Alföldi and C. L. Clay (eds.), *Die Kontorniat-Medallions*, 2 (Berlin: De Gruyter, 1990), 63–74.

—— 'Observations on the Distribution and Ownership of Late Roman Silver plate', *JRA*, 5 (1992), 178–85.

Cameron, Averil, 'Constantinus Christianus', *JRS*, 73 (1983), 184–90.

—— 'Virginity as Metaphor: Women and the Rhetoric of Early Christianity', in Averil Cameron, (ed.), *History as Text* (London: Duckworth, 1989), 181–205.

Campbell, J. B., *The Emperor and the Roman Army 31 BC–AD 235* (Oxford: Clarendon Press, 1984).

Cannadine, D. and Price, S. R. F. (eds.), *Rituals of Royalty* (Cambridge: Cambridge University Press, 1987).

Carandini, A., Ricci, A., and de Vos, M., *Filosofiana: The Villa of Piazza Armerina* (Palermo: S. F. Flaccovio, 1984).

Carioli, C. F. and Verducchi, P., *L'Area centrale del Foro Romano* (Florence: Olschki, 1987).

Carletti, C., *Damaso e i martiri di Roma* (Vatican City: Pontificia commissione di archeologia sacra, 1985).

Carretoni, G., 'Terme di Severo e terme di Massenzio "in palatio" ', *Archeologia Classica*, 24 (1972), 96–104.

Carrie, J. M., 'Eserciti e strategie', in A. Schiavone, (ed.), *Storia di Roma 3*: L'Età tardoantica 1: Crisi e trasformazione* (Turin: Einaudi, 1993), 83–154.

Carson, R. A. G., 'Gold Medallions of the Reign of Maxentius', *Congresso internazionale di numismatica, Roma 11–16 settembre 1961*, Atti, 2 (1965a), 347–52.

—— 'The Reform of Aurelian', *RN*, 7 (1965b), 225–35.

Castagnoli, F., *Il Vaticano nell'antichità classica*, Studi e documenti per la storia del Palazzo apostolico vaticano, 6 (Vatican City: Biblioteca Apostolica Vaticana, 1992).

Cecchelli, M., 'S. Marco a Piazza Venezia: Una basilica romana del periodo costantiniano', in G. Bonamente and F. Fusco, (eds.), *Costantino il Grande* (Macerata: Pubblicazioni della Facoltà di lettere e filosofia, 1992), 299–310.

Chastagnol, A., 'Le Sénateur Volusien et la conversion d'une famille de l'aristocratie romaine au Bas-Empire', *REA*, 58 (1956), 241–53.

—— *La Préfecture urbaine à Rome sous le bas-empire* (Paris: Presses universitaires de France, 1960).

—— *Les fastes de la Préfecture de Rome au bas-empire* (Paris: Nouvelles Éditions Latines, 1962).

—— 'Sur quelques documents relatifs à la basilique de Saint-Paul-hors-les-murs', *Mélanges Piganiol* (Paris: S. E. V. P. E. N., 1966), 421–37.

—— 'Aspects concrets et cadre topographique des fêtes décennales des empereurs à Rome', in *L'Urbs: Espace urbain et histoire (1er siècle av. J.-C.–IIIe siècle ap. J. C.)*, Collection de l'École française de Rome, 98 (Rome: École française de Rome, 1987), 491–507.

Chausson, F., '*Vel Iovi vel Soli*: Quatre études autour de la Vigna Barberini (191–354)', *MEFRA*, 107 (1995), 661–795.

Christiensen, T., 'The So-called Edict of Milan', *Classica et Medievalia*, 35 (1984), 129–75.

Ciancio Rossetto, P., 'Due epigrafi prefettizie dal circo massimo', *Tituli 4: Epigraphia e ordines senatorio, 1* (1982), 571–3.

—— 'Circo massimo', in *Roma archeologia nel centro 1: L'area archeologica centrale*, Lavori e studi di archeologia, 6 (Rome: De Luca, 1986), 213–23.

Clark, E. A., 'Faltonia Betitia Proba and her Vergilian Poem: The Christian Matron as Artist', in E. A. Clark, (ed.), *Ascetic Piety and Women's Faith*, Studies in Women and Religion, 20 (Lewiston: Edwin Mellen Press, 1986), 124–52.

—— 'Ascetic Renunciation and Feminine Advancement: A Paradox of Late Ancient Christianity', in Clark, (ed.), *Ascetic Piety and Women's Faith*, 175–208.

—— 'Piety, Propaganda and Politics in the Life of Melania the Younger', in Clark, (ed.), *Ascetic Piety and Women's Faith*, 61–94.

Clark, G., *Women in Late Antiquity* (Oxford: Clarendon Press, 1993).

Clarke, G. W., *The Letters of St. Cyprian of Carthage*, Ancient Christian Writers, 43 (New York: Newman Press, 1984).

Coarelli, F., *Roma Sepolta* (Rome: Curcio, 1984).

—— 'L'Urbs e il suburbio', in A. Giardina, (ed.), *Società romana e impero tardoantico 1: Istituzioni, ceti, economie* (Rome: Laterza, 1986), 1–58.

—— 'La situazione edilizia di Roma sotto Severo Alessandro', in *L'Urbs: Espace urbain et histoire (1er siècle av. J.-C.-IIIe siècle ap. J. C.)*, Collection de l'École française de Rome, 98 (Rome: École française de Rome, 1987), 429–56.

—— *Dintorni di Roma*, 2nd edn., (Rome: Laterza, 1993).

—— *Guida archeologica di Roma*, 3rd edn., (Rome: Laterza, 1995).

Cochrane, C. N., *Christianity and Classical Culture* (London: Oxford University Press, 1940).

Cohen, H., *Description historique des monnaies frappées sous l'empire romain*, 2nd edn., 8 vols. (Paris: 1880–92).

Coleman-Norton, P. R., *Roman State and Christian Church*, 3 vols. (London: SPCK, 1966).

Colini, A. M., 'Storia e topografia del Celio nell'antichità', *Atti della Pontificia Accademia Romana di Archeologia*, Serie 3, Memorie, 7 (1944), 319–78.

—— 'Horti spei veteris, Palatium Sessorianum', *Atti della Pontificia Accademia Romana di Archeologia*, Serie 3, Memorie, 8 (1955), 137–77.

Colli, D., 'Il Palazzo Sessoriano nell'area archeologica di S. Croce in Gerusalemme: Ultima sede imperiale a Roma?', *MEFRA*, 108 (1996), 771–815.

Consolino, F. E., 'Modelli di comportamento e modi di santificazione per l'aristocrazia femminile d'occidente', in A. Giardina, (ed.), *Società romana e impero tardoantico 1: Istituzione, ceti, economie* (Rome: Laterza, 1986), 273–306.

Cooper, K., 'Insinuations of Womanly Influence: An Aspect of the Christianization of the Roman Aristocracy', *JRS*, 82 (1992), 150–64.

—— *The Virgin and the Bride: Idealized Womanhood in Late Antiquity* (Cambridge, Mass.: Harvard University Press, 1996).

Corby Finney, P., 'Early Christian Architecture: The Beginnings' (a review article), *HTR*, 81 (1988), 319–39.

Corcoran, S., *The Empire of the Tetrarchs* (Oxford: Clarendon Press, 1996).

Courcelle, P., *Histoire littéraire des grandes invasions germaniques* (Paris: Hachette, 1948).

Cracco-Ruggini, L., 'Elagabalo, Costantino e i culti "Siriaci" nella *Historia Augusta*', in G. Bonamente and N. Duval, (eds.), *Historiae Augustae Colloquium MCMXC* (1991), 123–46.

Cramer, F., *Astrology in Roman Politics and Law* (Philadelphia: American Philosophical Society, 1954).

Croke, B. and Harries, J. D. (eds.), *Religious Conflict in Fourth-Century Rome* (Sydney: University of Sydney Press, 1982).

Cullhed, M., *Conservator Urbis Suae: Studies in the Politics and Propaganda of the Emperor Maxentius* (Stockholm: P. Åström, 1994).

Curran, J., 'Moving Statues in Late Antique Rome: Problems of Perspective', *Art History*, 17 (1994), 46–58.

——'Constantine and the Ancient Cults of Rome: The Legal Evidence', *Greece and Rome*, 43 (1996), 68–80.

——'Jerome and the Sham Christians of Rome', *JEH*, 48 (1997), 1–17.

Dagron, G., *Naissance d'une capitale: Constantinople et ses institutions de 330 à 451* (Paris: Presses universitaires de France, 1974).

Davis, R. P., *The Book of Pontiffs (Liber Pontificalis)* (Liverpool: Liverpool University Press, 1989).

de Angelis Bertolotti, R., Ioppolo, G., and Pisani-Sartorio, G., *La Residenza imperiale di Massenzio. Villa, mausoleo e circo* (Rome: Fratelli Palombi, 1988).

DeDecker, D., 'La Politique religieuse de Maxence', *Byzantion*, 38 (1968), 472–562.

Degrassi, A. (ed.), *Inscriptiones Italiae*, 13.2 (Rome: Istituto Poligrafico dello Stato, 1963).

Deichmann, F. W., *Repertorium der Christlich-antiken Sarkophage 1: Rom und Ostia* (Wiesbaden: Franz Steiner, 1967).

——and Tschira, A., 'Das Mausoleum der Kaiserin Helena und die Basilika der Heiligen Marcellinus und Petrus an der Via Labicana vor Rom', *JDAI*, 72 (1957), 44–110.

Delehaye, H., *Les Origines du culte des martyrs*, 2nd edn., Subsidia Hagiographica, 20 (Brussels: Société des Bollandistes, 1933).

——*Étude sur le légendier romain, Subsidia Hagiographica, 23* (Brussels: Société des Bollandistes, 1936).

Demandt, A. and Brummer, G., 'Der Prozess gegen Serena im Jahre 408 nach Christus', *Historia*, 26 (1977), 479–502.

De Miro, E., 'La villa del casale di Piazza Armerina: Nuove ricerche', in S. Garraffo, (ed.), *La villa romana del casale di Piazza Armerina*, Atti della IV riunione scientifica della scuola di perfezionamento in archeologia classica dell'Università di Catania (Catania: Istituto di archeologia, 1988), 58–73.

De Santis, L. and Biamonte, G., *Le catacombe di Roma* (Rome: Newton & Compton, 1997).

Desnier, J.-L., *'Omnia et realia.* Naissance de *l'urbs sacra* sévérienne (193–204 ap. J.-C.)', *MEFRA*, 105 (1993), 547–620.

Dill, S., *Roman Society in the Last Century of the Western Empire*, 2nd edn., (London: Macmillan, 1899).

Dodds, E. R., 'Theurgy and its Relationship to Neoplatonism', *JRS*, 37 (1947), 55–69.

Dörries, H., *Das Selbstzeugnis Kaiser Konstantins*, Abhandlungen der Akademie der Wissenschaften in Göttingen, Philologisch-historische Klasse, 34 (Göttingen: Vandenhoeck & Ruprecht, 1954).

Downey, G., 'The Olympic Games of Antioch in the Fourth Century AD', *TAPA*, 70 (1939), 428–38.

Drake, H. A., *In Praise of Constantine: A Historical Study and New Translation of Eusebius' Tricennial Oration* (Berkeley: University of California Press, 1976).

—— 'Suggestions of Date in Constantine's *Oration to the Saints*', *AJPh*, 106 (1985), 335–49.

Drijvers, J. W., 'Virginity and Asceticism in Late Roman Western Elites', in J. Blok and P. Mason (eds.), *Sexual Asymmetry: Studies in Ancient Society* (Amsterdam: J. C. Gieben, 1987), 241–73.

—— 'Flavia Maxima Fausta', *Historia*, 41 (1992), 500–6.

Dubourdieu, A., *Les Origines et le développement du culte des Pénates à Rome*, Collection de L'École Française de Rome, 118 (Rome: École française de Rome, 1989).

Duchesne, L., 'Notes sur la topographie de Rome du moyen âge: Les Titres presbytéreaux et les diaconies', *Mélanges d'Archéologie et d'histoire*, 7 (1887), 17–36; 217–43.

—— *Early History of the Christian Church*, 3 vols. (London: John Murray, 1912–24).

—— 'Constantin et Maxence', *Nuovo Bullettino di archeologia cristiana*, 19 (1913), 29–35.

Dulière, C., *Lupa Romana. Recherches d'iconographie et essai d'interprétation* (Brussels/Rome: Institut historique Belge de Rome, 1979).

Dunbabin, K. M. D., *The Mosaics of Roman North Africa: Studies in Iconography and Patronage* (Oxford: Clarendon Press, 1978).

—— 'The Victorious Charioteer on Mosaics and Related Monuments', *AJA*, 86 (1982), 65–89.

Durry, M., *Les Cohortes prétoriennes* (Paris: De Boccard, 1938).

Duval, Y. M., 'La Venue à Rome de l'empereur Constance II en 357 d'après Ammien Marcellin', *Caesarodunum*, 2 (1970), 299–304.

Edbrooke, R. O., 'The Visit of Constantius II to Rome in 357 and its Effects on the Pagan Senatorial Aristocracy', *AJPh*, 97 (1976), 40–61.

Eisenhut, W., 'Votum', *PW* Suppl., 14 (1974), 964–73.

Elliot, T. G., 'Eusebian Frauds in the *Vita Constantini*', *Phoenix*, 45 (1991), 162–71.

Elm, S., *'Virgins of God': The Making of Asceticism in Late Antiquity* (Oxford: Clarendon Press, 1994).

Elsner, J., *Art and the Roman Viewer: The Transformation of Art from the Pagan World to Christianity* (Cambridge: Cambridge University Press, 1995).

—— 'Image and Ritual: Reflections on the Religious Appreciation of Classical Art', *CQ*, 46 (1996), 515–31.

Ensslin, W., *Die Religionspolitik des Kaisers Theodosius* (Munich: Bayerische Akademie der Wissenschaften, 1953).

—— 'Magnentius', *PW*, 14 (1928), 445–52.

Erhardt, A. A., 'The First Two Years of Emperor Theodosius I', *JEH*, 15 (1964), 1–17.

Errington, R. M., 'Constantine and the Pagans', *GRBS*, 29 (1988), 309–18.

Evans, R. F., *Pelagius: Enquiries and Reappraisals* (New York: Seabury Press, 1968).

Evers, C., 'Remarques sur l'iconographie de Constantin: à propos du remploi de portraits des "bons empereurs"', *MEFRA*, 103 (1991), 785–806.

Farmer, D. H., *The Oxford Dictionary of Saints* (Oxford: Oxford University Press, 1987).

Fasola, U. M., 'Le ricerche di archeologia cristiana a Roma fuori le mura', in *Actes du XIe Congrès internationale d'archéologie chrétienne*, Collection de l'École française de Rome, 123 (Rome: École française de Rome, 1989), 2149–76.

——and Testini, P., 'I cimiteri cristiani', *Atti del IX Congresso Internazionale di Archeologia Cristiana* (Vatican City: Pontificio Istituto di archeologia cristiana, 1978), 103–39.

Fears, J. R., *Princeps a diis Electus*, Papers and Monographs of the American Academy in Rome, 26 (Rome: American Academy, 1977).

Ferrua, A., *Epigrammata Damasiana*, Sussidi allo studio delle antichità cristiane, 2 (Vatican City: Pontificio Istituto di archeologia cristiana, 1942).

——'Nuove iscrizioni degli Equites Singulares', *Epigraphica*, 13 (1951), 96–141.

——'Antiche iscrizioni inedite di Roma', *Epigraphica*, 32 (1970), 90–126.

——*La basilica e la catacomba di S. Sebastiano* (Vatican City: Pontificia commissione di archeologia sacra, 1990).

Février, P.-A., 'Vie et mort dans les "epigrammata Damasiana"', in *Saecularia Damasiana*, Studi di Antichità Cristiana, 39 (Vatican City: Pontificio Istituto di archeologia cristiana, 1986), 91–111.

——'Quelques inscriptions damasiennes de la Via Salaria', *Quaeritur inventus colitur: Miscellanea in onore di Padre U. M. Fasola* (Vatican City: Pontificio Istituto di archeologia cristiana, 1989), 291–306.

Fink, R. O., Hoey, A. S., and Snyder, W. F., 'The Feriale Duranum', *YCS*, 7 (1940), 1–222.

Fishwick, D., 'Votive Offerings to the Emperor?', *ZPE*, 80 (1990), 121–30.

——*The Imperial Cult in the Latin West: Studies in the Ruler Cult of the Western Provinces of the Roman Empire*, 2 vols. (Leiden: Brill, 1987–92).

Fittschen, K. and Zanker, P., *Katalog der römischen Porträts in den Capitolischen Museen und den anderen kommunalen Sammlungen der Stadt Rom* (Mainz: Phillip von Zabern, 1985).

Fowden, G., 'Bishops and Temples in the Eastern Roman Empire AD 320–435', *JTS*, 29 (1978), 53–78.

——'Nicagoras of Athens and the Lateran Obelisk', *JHS*, 107 (1987), 51–7.

Franchi De' Cavalieri, P., 'I funerali ed il sepolcro di Costantino Magno', *Mélanges d'archéologie et d'histoire*, 36 (1916–17), 205–61.

Francis, R. A., *Subversive Virtue: Asceticism and Authority in the Second-Century Pagan World* (University Park, Penn.: Pennsylvania State University Press, 1995).

Fraschetti, A., 'Costantino e l'abbandono del Campidoglio', in A. Giardina, (ed.), *Società romana e impero tardoantico 2: Roma: politica, economia, paesaggio urbano* (Rome: Laterza, 1986), 59–98.

——'Spazi del sacro e spazi della politica', in A. Schiavone (ed.), *Storia di*

Roma 3*: *L'Età tardoantica 1: Crisi e trasformazione* (Turin: Einaudi, 1993), 675–96.

Frazer, A., 'The Iconography of the Emperor Maxentius' Buildings in Via Appia', *Art Bulletin*, 48 (1966), 385–92.

Frend, W. H. C., *Martyrdom and Persecution in the Early Church* (Oxford: Blackwell, 1965).

—— 'The Church in the Reign of Constantius II (337–361)', in *L'Église et l'empire au IVe Siècle*, Entretiens sur l'Antiquité classique, 34 (Geneva: Fondation Hardt, 1987), 73–112.

Frutaz, A., *Il complesso monumentale di Sant'Agnese e di Santa Costanza*, 2nd edn. (Rome: Tipografia poliglotta vaticana, 1969).

Gagé, J., 'Le "sollemne urbis" du 21 avril au 3e siècle ap. J.-C.: rites positifs et spéculations séculaires', in *Mélanges d'histoire des religions offerts à Henri-Charles Puech* (Paris: Presse universitaires de France, 1974), 239–41.

Gardner, J. F., *Women in Roman Law and Society* (London: Routledge, 1986).

Gascou, J., 'Le Rescrit d'Hispellum', *MEFRA*, 79 (1967), 609–59.

Gaudemet, J., *L'Église dans l'empire romain* (Paris: Sirey, 1958).

—— 'La Condamnation des pratiques païennes en 391', in *Epektasis. Mélanges offerts au Cardinal J. Daniélou* (Paris: Beauchesne, 1972), 597–602.

—— 'La Législation anti-païenne de Constantin à Justinien', *Cr. St.*, 11 (1990), 449–68.

Geertman, H., 'The Builders of the Basilica Maior in Rome', in *Festen aan A. N. Zadoks-Josephus Jitta bij haar Zeventigste verjaardag* (Groningen-Bussum: Tjeent Willink, 1976), 277–99.

—— 'Forze centrifughi e centripete nella Roma cristiana: Il Laterano, la basilica Iulia e la basilica Liberiana', *Rendiconti della pontificia accademia romana di archeologia*, 59 (1986–7), 63–91.

—— 'Nota sul "Liber Pontificalis" come fonte archeologica', in *Quaeritur inventus colitur: Miscellanea in onore di Padre U. M. Fasola* (Vatican City: Pontificio Istituto di archeologia cristiana, 1989), 347–61.

Geffcken, J., *The Last Days of Graeco-Roman Paganism*, rev. and trans. S. MacCormack (Amsterdam/Oxford: North Holland, 1978).

Gentili, G. V., 'Le gare del circo nel mosaico di Piazza Armerina', *Bollettino d'Arte*, 42 (1957), 7–27.

—— 'Aspetti pagani dei mosaici di Piazza Armerina', *Archeologia Classica*, 11 (1959), 241–50.

—— *La villa erculia di Piazza Armerina: I mosaici figurati* (Rome: Edizioni mediteranee, 1959).

Gibson, S. and Taylor, J. E., *Beneath the Church of the Holy Sepulchre, Jerusalem: The Archaeology and Early History of Traditional Golgotha* (London: Committee of the Palestine Exploration Fund, 1994).

Giardina, A., 'Carità Eversiva: Le donazioni di Melania La Giovane e gli equilibri della società tardoromana', *Studi storici*, 29 (1988), 127–42.

Giordani, R., 'Note sulla cronologia della costruzione della basilica vaticana', *Studi Romani*, 35 (1987), 346–58.

—— 'Postille in margine al complesso dei Santi Marcellino e Pietro al III miglio della via Labicana', *Latomus*, 55 (1996), 127–47.

Gnecchi, F., *I medaglioni Romani*, 3 vols. (Bologna: Forni Editore, 1912).

Gorce, D., *Vie de Sainte Mélanie*, Sources chrétiennes, 90 (Paris: Éditions du Cerf, 1962).

Gordini, D., 'Origine e sviluppo del monachesimo a Roma', *Gregorianum*, 37 (1956), 220–60.

Gordon, R., 'The Real and the Imaginary: Production and Religion in the Graeco-Roman World', *Art History*, 2 (1979), 5–34, repr. in R. Gordon, *Image and Value in the Roman World: Studies in Mithraism and Religious Art* (Aldershot: Variorum, 1996).

Greenslade, S. L., *Schism in the Early Church*, 2nd edn., (London: SCM, 1964).

Groag, E., 'Maxentius', *PW*, 14 (1930), 2417–84.

Grodzynski, D., '*Superstitio*', *REA*, 76 (1974), 36–60.

Gregoire, H., 'La Statue de Constantin et la signe de la croix', *L'Antiquité classique*, 1 (1932), 135–43.

Grünewald, Th., *Constantinus Maximus Augustus*, *Historia*, Einzelschriften, 64 (Stuttgart: Franz Steiner, 1990).

Guarducci, M., 'Il 29 Giugno: Festa degli Apostoli Pietro e Paolo', *Atti della Pontificia Accademia Romana di Archeologia*, Serie 3, Rendiconti, 57 (1985–6), 115–27.

—— 'Feste pagane e feste cristiane a Roma', *Atti della Pontificia Accademia Romana di Archeologia*, Serie 3, Rendiconti, 59 (1986–7), 119–25.

Guidobaldi, F., 'Edilizia abitativa unifamiliare nella Roma tardoantica', in A. Giardina, (ed.), *Società romana e Impero tardoantico* (Rome: Laterza, 1986), ii. 165–237.

—— 'Ricerche di archeologia cristiana a Roma (dentro le mura)', in *Actes du XIe Congrès International d'Archéologie Chrétienne 1986*, Collection de l'École Française de Rome, 123/Studi di Antichità Cristiana, 41, (Rome: École française de Rome, 1989a), 2127–48.

—— 'L'inserimento delle chiese titolari di Roma nel tessuto urbano preesistente: osservazioni ed implicazioni', in *Quaeritur inventus colitur: Miscellanea in onore di Padre U. M. Fasola* (Vatican City: Pontificio Istituto di archeologia cristiana, 1989b), 383–96.

Guignebert, C., 'Les Demi-chrétiens et leur place dans l'Église antique', *Revue de l'histoire des religions*, 83 (1923), 65–102.

Guyon, J., 'Dal praedium imperiale al santuario dei martiri. Il territorio "ad duas lauros"', in A. Giardina, (ed.), *Società romana e impero tardoantico* (Rome: Laterza, 1986a), ii. 299–332.

—— 'L'Oeuvre de Damase dans le cimetière sur la vie Labicana', in *Saecularia Damasiana*, Studi di Antichità Cristiana, 39 (Vatican City: Pontificio Istituto di archeologia cristiana, 1986b), 227–258.

—— *Le cimetière aux deux lauriers*, BEFAR, 264 (Rome: École française de Rome, 1987).

—— 'Cunctis solacia fletus ou le testament-épigraphie du pape Damase', in

Quaeritur inventus colitur. Miscellanea in honore di Padre U. M. Fasola (Vatican City: Pontificio Istituto di archeologia cristiana, 1989), 423–37.

—— 'Roma. Emerge la città cristiana', in Schiavone, A. (ed.), *Storia di Roma 3*. L'Età tardoantica 2: I luoghi e le culture* (Turin: Einaudi, 1993), 53–68.

——, Strüber, L., and Manacorda, D., 'Recherches autour de la basilique constantinienne des saints Pierre et Marcellin sur la via Labicana à Rome: le mausolée et l'enclos au nord de la basilique', *MEFRA*, 93 (1981), 991–1056.

Hadot, P., *Marius Victorinus: Recherches sur sa vie et ses œuvres* (Paris: Études augustiniennes,1971).

Halsberghe, G. H., *The Cult of Sol Invictus* (Leiden: Brill, 1972).

—— 'Le culte de Deus Sol Invictus à Rome au III siècle après J. C.', *ANRW*, 2. 17. 4 (1984*a*), 2181–201.

—— 'Le culte de Dea Caelestis', *ANRW*, 2.17.4 (1984*b*), 2203–23.

Harl, K. W., 'Sacrifice and Pagan Belief in Fifth- and Sixth-Century Byzantium', *Past and Present*, 128 (1990), 7–27.

Harries, J., '"Treasure in Heaven": Property and Inheritance Among Senators of Late Rome', in E. M. Craik, (ed.), *Marriage and Property* (Aberdeen: Aberdeen University Press, 1984), 54–70.

—— 'The Roman Imperial Quaestor from Constantine to Theodosius II', *JRS*, 78 (1988), 148–72.

—— 'Introduction: The Background to the Code', in J. Harries and I. Wood, (eds.), *The Theodosian Code* (London: Duckworth, 1993), 1–16.

—— and Wood, I. (eds.), *The Theodosian Code* (London: Duckworth, 1993).

Heim, F., 'Les auspices publics de Constantin à Théodose', *Ktema*, 13 (1988), 41–53.

—— *La théologie de la victoire de Constantin à Théodose*, Théologie historique, 89 (Paris: Beauchesne, 1992).

Heres, T. L., *Paries: A Proposal for a Dating System of Late Antique Masonry: Structures in Rome and Ostia*, Studies in Classical Antiquity, 5 (Amsterdam: Rodopi, 1982).

Herrmann, J. J., 'Observations on the Baths of Maxentius on the Palatine', *MDAI*, Römische Abteilung, 83 (1976), 403–24.

Hill, P. V., 'The Buildings and Monuments of Rome on the Coins of AD 217–294', *Riv. Ital. di Numis.*, 83 (1981), 47–74.

Himmelmann, N., *Typologische Untersuchungen römischen Sarkophag-reliefs an des 3. und 4. Jahrhunderts nach Christus* (Mainz: Zabern, 1973).

Honoré, A., 'Ausonius and Vulgar Law', *Iura*, 35 (1984), 75–85.

—— 'The Making of the Theodosian Code', *Zeitschrift der Savigny-Stiftung für Rechtsgeschichte*, 103 (1986), 133–222.

—— 'Some Quaestors of the Reign of Theodosius II', in J. Harries and I. Wood, (eds.), *The Theodosian Code* (London: Duckworth, 1993), 68–94.

Heucke, C., *Circus und Hippodrom als politischer Raum* (Hildesheim: Olms-Wiedmann, 1994).

Huelsen, Ch., *Das Septizonium des Septimius Severus* (Berlin: 1886, G. Reimer).

—— *Le chiese di Roma nel medio evo* (Florence: L. S. Olschki, 1927).

Humphrey, J., *Roman Circuses. Arenas for Chariot Racing* (London: Batsford, 1986).

Hunter, D. G., 'Resistance to the Virginal Ideal in Fourth-Century Rome: The Case of Jovinian', *Theological Studies*, 48 (1987), 45–64.

Huskinson, J. M., *Concordia Apostolorum: Christian Propaganda at Rome in the Fourth and Fifth Centuries: A Study of Early Christian Iconography and Iconology*, BAR, 148 (Oxford: BAR, 1982).

Jastrzebowska, E., *Untersuchungen zum christ. Totenmahl aufgrund der Monumente des 3. und 4. Jhs unter der Basilika des Hl. Sebastian in Rom* (Frankfurt: P. D. Lang, 1981).

Jolowicz, H. F. and Nicholas, B., *Historical Introduction to Roman Law*, 3rd edn., (Cambridge: Cambridge University Press, 1972).

Jones, A. H. M., *The Later Roman Empire, 284–602* (Oxford: Blackwell, 1964).

——, Martindale, J. R., and Morris, J., *The Prosopography of the Later Roman Empire 1: AD 260–395* (Cambridge: Cambridge University Press, 1971).

Jongkees, J. H., *Studies on Old St. Peter's*, Archeologica Traiectina, 8 (Groningen: J. B. Wolters, 1966).

Jordan, H., *Topographie der Stadt Rom in Alterthum*, (Berlin: Weidmannsche Buchhandlung, 1907), i., pt. 3.

Josi, E., 'Scoperte nella basilica costantiniana al Laterano', *RAC*, 11 (1934), 335–58.

—— 'Cimitero di Generosa', *RAC*, 16 (1939), 320–35.

Jurgens, H., *Pompa diaboli: Die lateinischen Kirchenväter und das antike Theater* (Stuttgart: W. Kohlhammer, 1972).

Kähler, H., 'Konstantin 313', *JDAI*, 67 (1952), 1–30.

Karayannopulos, I., 'Konstantin der Grosse und der Kaiserkult', *Historia*, 5 (1956), 341–57.

Kaufmann, F., *Aus der Schule des Wulfila* (Strasbourg, 1899).

Kelly, J. N. D., *Jerome: His Life, Writings and Controversies* (London: Duckworth, 1976).

—— *The Oxford Dictionary of Popes* (Oxford: Oxford University Press, 1986).

King, C. E., 'The Maxentian Mints', *NC*, 19 (1959), 47–78.

King, N. Q., *The Emperor Theodosius and the Establishment of Christianity* (London: SCM, 1961).

Kinch, K. F., *L'Arc de Triomphe de Salonique* (1890).

Kirsch, J. P., *Die römischen Titelkirchen im Altertum* (Paderborn: 1918).

Klauser, Th., *Die Cathedra im Totenkult der heidnischen und christlichen Antike*, 2nd edn. (Münster: Aschendorff, 1971).

Klein, R., 'Der Rombesuch des Kaisers Konstantius II. im Jahre 357', *Athenaeum*, 57 (1979), 98–115.

Koethe, H., 'Zum Mausoleum der weströmischen Dynastie bei Alt-Sankt-Peter', *MDAI*, 46 (1931), 9–26.

Kolb, F., *Diocletian und die Erste Tetrarchie: Improvisation oder Experiment in der Organization monarchischer Herrschaft?* (Berlin: De Gruyter, 1987).

—— 'L'ideologia tetrarchica e la politica religiosa di Diocleziano', in

G. Bonamente and A. Nestori, (eds.), *I Cristiani e l'impero nel IV secolo* (Macerata: Università degli studi di Macerata, 1988), 17–44.

Kollwitz, J., *Oströmische Plastik der theodosianischen Zeit*, Studien zur spätantiken Kunstgeschichte, 12 (Berlin: De Gruyter, 1941).

Krautheimer, R., *Corpus Basilicarum Christianarum Romae*, 5 vols., (Vatican City/New York: Pontificio Istituto di archeologia cristiana/Institute of Fine Arts, 1937–1977).

——'Mensa-Coemeterium-Martyrium', *Cahiers Archéologiques*, 11 (1960), 15–40.

——'Constantine's Church Foundations', in *Atti VII congresso internazionale di archeologia cristiana* (Vatican City: Pontificio Istituto di archeologia cristiana, 1965), 237–55.

——'The Constantinian Basilica', *DOP*, 21 (1967), 115–40.

——*Rome: Profile of a City, 312–1308* (Princeton: Princeton University Press, 1980).

——*Early Christian and Byzantine Architecture*, 4th edn. (Harmondsworth: Penguin, 1986).

——'A Note on the Inscription in the Apse of Old St. Peter's', *DOP*, 41 (1987), 317–20.

——and Striker, C. L., *Architectural Studies in memory of Richard Krautheimer* (Mainz: von Zabern, 1996).

Kriegbaum, B., 'Die Religionspolitik des Kaisers Maxentius', *Archivum Historiae Pontificae*, 30 (1992), 7–54.

Kuhoff, W., 'Ein Mythos in der römischen Geschichte: Der Sieg Konstantins des Grossen über Maxentius vor den Toren Roms am 28. Oktober 312 n. Chr.', *Chiron*, 21 (1991), 127–74.

Künzl, E., *Der römische Triumph* (Munich: C. H. Beck, 1988).

Künzl, P., 'Zur basilica Liberiana: basilica Sicinini = basilica Liberii', *Römische Quartalschrift*, 56 (1961), 1–61, 129–66.

Lanciani, R., *Ancient Rome in the Light of Recent Discoveries* (London: Macmillan, 1888).

——*Pagan and Christian Rome* (London: Macmillan, 1895).

——*The Ruins and Excavations of Ancient Rome* (London: Macmillan, 1897).

——*The Destruction of Ancient Rome* (London: Macmillan, 1899).

Landes, Ch. (ed.), *Cirque et cours de chars Rome-Byzance: Catalogue de l'exposition* (Lattes: Éditions Imago, 1990).

Lane Fox, R., *Pagans and Christians* (Harmondsworth: Viking, 1986).

LaPiana, G., 'The Roman Church at the End of the Second Century', *HTR*, 18 (1925), 210–77.

——'Foreign Groups in Rome', *HTR*, 20 (1927), 183–403.

Latte, K., *Römische Religionsgeschichte* (Munich: Beck, 1960).

Lawrence, M., 'The Circus-relief at Foligno', *Atti del II convegno di studi umbri* (Gubbio: Centro di studi umbri, 1965), 119–35.

LeGlay, M., 'Sur l'implantation des sanctuaires orientaux à Rome', in *L'Urbs: Espace urbain et histoire (1er siècle av. J.-C.–IIIe siècle ap. J. C.)*, Collection de l'École française de Rome, 98 (Rome: École française de Rome, 1987), 545–62.

Liebeschuetz, J. H. W. G., *Continuity and Change in Roman Religion* (Oxford: Clarendon Press, 1979).

——'Ammianus, Julian and Divination', in M. Weissmann (ed.), *Roma Renascens: Beiträge zur Spätantike und Rezeptionsgeschichte* (Frankfurt: Lang, 1988*a*), 193–213.

Lieu, S. M. C., *The Emperor Julian: Panegyric and Polemic* (Liverpool: Liverpool University Press, 1986).

Lippold, A., 'Damasus und Ursinus', *Historia*, 14 (1965), 105–28.

——'Ursinus', *PW*, Suppl., 10 (1965*b*), 1141–8.

Lizzi, R., 'Una società esortata all'ascetismo: Misure legislative e motivazioni economiche nel IV–V secolo d.C.', *Studi storici*, 30 (1989), 129–53.

—— and Consolino, F. E., 'Le religioni nell'impero tardoantico: persistenze e mutamenti', in A. Schiavone, (ed.), *Storia di Roma 3*: L'Età tardoantica 1: Crisi e trasformazione* (Turin: Einaudi, 1993), 895–974.

L'Orange, H. P. and von Gerkan, A., *Der spätantike Bildschmuck des Konstantinsbogens*, Studien zur spätantiken Kunstgeschichte, 10 (Berlin: De Gruyter, 1939).

Lugli, G., *I monumenti antichi di Roma e suburbio III: a traverso le regioni* (Rome: Bardi, 1938).

——*Roma Antica: Il centro monumentale* (Rome: Bardi, 1946*a*).

——'Recent Archaeological Discoveries in Rome and Italy', *JRS*, 36 (1946*b*), 1–17.

——'Contributo alla storia edilizia della villa romana di Piazza Armerina', *Rivista dell'Istituto nazionale di archeologia e storia dell'arte*, NS 10–11 (1963), 28–82.

Luschi, L., 'L'iconografia dell'edificio rotundo nella monetazione massenziana e il "tempio del divo Romolo"', *BC*, 89.1 (1984), 41–54.

—— and Ceccherelli, A., 'Mausoleo "dei Gordiani" e adiacente basilica', *BC*, 92 (1987–8), 421–7.

Macarone, A., 'L'allestimento dei giochi annuali a Roma nel IV secolo d. C.: Aspetti economici e ideologici', *Annali della Scuola Normale Superiore di Pisa*, Serie 3, 11.1 (1981), 105–22.

Maccarone, M., 'La concezione di Roma città di Pietro e di Paolo: da Damaso a Leone I' in *Roma Costantinopoli Mosca: Da Roma alla terza Roma (Documenti e studi 1)* (Naples: Edizioni Scientifiche Italiane, 1983), 63–85.

MacCormack, S., *Art and Ceremony in Late Antiquity* (Berkeley: University of California Press, 1981).

MacMullen, R., 'Roman Bureaucratese in the Fourth Century', *Traditio*, 18 (1962), 364–78.

——*Enemies of the Roman Order* (London: Routledge, 1966).

——*Constantine* (New York: Dial Press, 1969).

——*Paganism in the Roman Empire* (New Haven: Yale University Press, 1981).

——*Christianizing the Roman Empire* (New Haven: Yale University Press, 1984).

374 *Bibliography*

—— 'What Difference Did Christianity Make?', *Historia*, 35 (1986), 322–43.
—— 'Judicial Savagery in the Roman Empire', *Chiron*, 16 (1986), 147–66.
—— *Christianity and Paganism in the Fourth to Eighth Centuries* (New Haven: Yale University Press, 1997).
MacPherson, R., *Cassiodorus: Politics in Involution* (Poznan: 1989).
Magi, F., 'Il Calendrio dipinto sotto Santa Maria Maggiore', *APARA*, Serie 3, Memorie, 11 (1972), 59–68.
Maier, H. O., 'The Topography of Heresy and Dissent in Late Fourth-Century Rome', *Historia*, 44 (1995), 232–49.
Malbon, E. S., *The Iconography of the Sarcophagus of Iunius Bassus* (Princeton: Princeton University Press, 1990).
Manganaro, G., 'Aspetti pagani dei mosaici di Piazza Armerina', *Archeologia Classica*, 11 (1959), 241–50.
Mango, C., 'Antique Statuary and the Byzantine Beholder', *DOP*, 17 (1963), 53–75.
Marcone, A., 'La politica religiosa: dall'ultima persecuzione alla toleranza', in A. Schiavone, (ed.), *Storia di Roma 3*: L'Età tardoantica 1: Crisi e trasformazione* (Turin: Einaudi, 1993), 223–45.
Markus, R., 'Paganism, Christianity and the Latin Classics in the Fourth Century', in J. W. Binns, (ed.), *Latin Literature of the Fourth Century* (London: Routledge & Kegan Paul, 1974), 1–21.
—— *The End of Ancient Christianity* (Cambridge: Cambridge University Press, 1990).
—— 'Die *spectacula* als religiöses Konfliktfeld städtischen Lebens in der Spätantike', *Freiburger Zeitschrift für Philosophie und Theologie*, 38 (1991), 253–71.
Marquardt, J., *Römische Staatsverwaltung* (1885), iii.
Martroye, F., 'La répression de la magie et le culte des gentils au IVe siècle', *Revue historique de droit français et étranger*, 9 (1930), 669–701.
Massoneau, E., *La magie dans l'antiquité romaine* (Paris: Sirey, 1934).
Maurice, J., 'La terreur de la magie au IVème siècle', *Revue historique de droit français et étranger*, series 4, 6 (1927), 108–20.
Matthews, J. F., 'A Pious Supporter of Theodosius I: Maternus Cynegius and his Family', *JTS*, 18 (1967), 438–46.
—— 'The Historical Setting of the *Carmen Contra Paganos*', *Historia*, 20 (1970a), 464–79.
—— 'Olympiodorus of Thebes and the History of the West', *JRS*, 60 (1970b), 79–97.
—— 'Symmachus and the Oriental Cults', *JRS*, 63 (1973), 175–95.
—— 'The Letters of Symmachus', in J. W. Binns, (ed.), *Latin Literature of the Fourth Century* (London: Routledge & Kegan Paul, 1974), 58–99.
—— *Western Aristocracies and Imperial Court AD 364–425* (Oxford: Clarendon Press, 1975).
—— *The Roman Empire of Ammianus* (London: Duckworth, 1989).
—— 'Peter Valvomeres, Rearrested', in *Homo Viator: Essays for John Bramble* (Bristol: Bristol Classical Press, 1987), 277–84.

—— 'The Poetess Proba and Fourth-Century Rome: Questions of Interpretation', in M. Christol, S. Demougin, Y. Duval, C. Lepelley, and L. Piétri, (eds.), *Institutions, société et vie politique dans l'empire romain au IVe siècle ap J.-C.*, Collections de l'École française de Rome, 159 (1992), 277–304.

—— 'The Making of the Text', in J. Harries and I. Wood, (eds.), *The Theodosian Code* (London: Duckworth, 1993), 19–44.

Mattingly, H., *Coins of the Roman Empire in the British Museum*, 6 vols., (London: British Museum, 1923–62).

McCormick, M., *Eternal Victory* (Cambridge: Cambridge University Press, 1986).

McGeachy, J. A., *Quintus Aurelius Symmachus and the Senatorial Aristocracy of the West*, Ph.D. thesis, (Chicago: 1942).

McLynn, N. B., *Ambrose of Milan* (Berkeley: University of California Press, 1994).

Meeks, W., *The First Urban Christians* (New Haven: Yale University Press, 1983).

Merlin, A. and Poinssot, H., 'Deux mosaïques de Tunisie à sujets prophylactiques', *Fondation Piot Monuments et Memoires*, 34 (1934), 129–78.

Merriman, J. F., 'The Empress Helena and the Aqua Augustea', *Archeologia Classica*, 29 (1977), 436–46.

Meslin, M., *La fête des kalendes de janvier dans l'empire romain* (Brussels: Latomus, 1970).

Millar, F. G. B., *The Emperor in the Roman World* (London: Duckworth, 1977).

—— *The Roman Near East 31 B.C.–A.D. 337* (Cambridge, Mass.: Harvard University Press, 1993).

Minoprio, A., 'A Restoration of the Basilica of Constantine', *PBSR*, 12 (1932), 1–18.

Mitchell, S., 'Maximinus and the Christians in AD 312: A New Latin Inscription', *JRS*, 78 (1988), 105–124.

Mommsen, Th. and Meyer, P. M. (eds.), *Theodosiani Libri XVI cum Constitutionibus Sirmondianis et Leges Novellae ad Theodosianum Pertinentes*, (Berlin: 1905), i.

Moreau, J., *De la mort des persécuteurs*, Sources chrétiennes, 39 (Paris: Éditions du Cerf, 1954).

—— *La persécution du christianisme dans l'empire romain* (Paris: Presses universitaires de France, 1956).

—— 'Nachträge zum Reallexicon für Antike und Christentum', *JbAC*, 2 (1959), 179–84.

Murphy, F. X., 'Melania the Elder: A Biographical Note', *Traditio*, 5 (1947), 59–77.

Murray, A., 'Peter Brown and the Shadow of Constantine', *JRS*, 73 (1983), 191–203.

Nash, E., *Pictorial Dictionary of Ancient Rome* (London: Zwemmer, 1962).

—— 'Secretarium Senatus', in L. Bonfante and H. von Heintze (eds), *In Memoriam Otto J. Brendel* (Mainz: Zabern, 1976a), 192–5.

—— 'Convenerunt in domum Faustae in Laterano: S. Optatus Milevitani 1, 23', *Römische Quartalschrift*, 71 (1976*b*), 1–21.

Nestori, A., 'La catacomba di Calepodio al III miglio dell'Aurelia Vetus e i sepolcri dei papi Callisto I e Giulio I (1 parte)', *RAC*, 47 (1971), 169–278.

—— 'La catacomba di Calepodio al III miglio dell'Aurelia Vetus e i sepolcri dei papi Callisto I e Giulio I (2 parte)', *RAC*, 48 (1972*a*), 193–233.

—— 'La tomba di S. Callisto sull' Aurelia antica', in *Actas del viii Congresso Intern. de Arqueol. Cristiana (1969): Studi di Antichità Cristiana*, 30 (Vatican City: Pontificio Istituto di archeologia cristiana, 1972*b*), 367–72.

—— 'L'attività edilizia in Roma di papa Damaso', in *Saecularia Damasiana*, Studi di Antichità Cristiana, 39 (Vatican City: Pontificio Istituto di archeologia cristiana ,1986), 161–72.

—— *La basilica anonima della Via Ardeatina*, Studi di Antichità Cristiana, 42 (Vatican City: Pontificio Istituto di archeologia cristiana, 1990).

Nibby, A., *Roma nell'anno MDCCCXXXVIII* (Rome, 1838).

Nicholas, B., *An Introduction to Roman Law* (Oxford: Clarendon Press, 1962).

Nicholson, O., 'The "Pagan Churches" of Maximinus Daia and Julian the Apostate', *JEH*, 45 (1994), 1–10.

—— and Nicholson, C., 'Lactantus, Hermes Trismegistius, and Constantinian obelisks', *JHS*, 109 (1989), 198–200.

Nielsen, I., *Thermae et Balneae: The Architecture and Cultural History of Roman Public Baths*, 2nd edn., (Aarhus: Aarhus University Press, 1993).

Nixon, C. E. V., 'The Occasion and Date of Panegyric viii (v) and the Celebration of Constantine's Quinquennalia', *Antichthon*, 14 (1980), 157–69.

—— 'The Panegyric of 307 and Maximian's Visits to Rome', *Phoenix*, 35 (1981), 70–6.

—— and Rodgers, S. B., *In Praise of Later Roman Emperors* (Berkeley: University of California Press, 1994).

Nock, A. D., *Conversion: The Old and the New in Religion from Alexander the Great to Augustine of Hippo* (Oxford: Clarendon Press, 1933).

Nordh, A., *Libellus de Regionibus Vrbis Romae* (Lundae: Gleerup, 1949).

Nöthlichs, K.-L., 'Kirche, Rechte und Gesellschaft in der Jahrhundertmitte', in *L'Église et L'empire au IVe siècle*, Entretiens sur l'Antiquité classique, 34 (Geneva: Fondation Hardt, 1987), 251–99.

—— *Die gesetzgeberischen Massnahmen der christlichen Kaiser des vierten Jahrhunderts gegen Häretiker, Heiden und Juden*, Ph.D. diss. (Cologne: 1971).

Norman, A. F., *Libanius Selected Works*, 2 vols., (Cambridge, Mass.: Loeb, 1969–1977).

North, J. A., 'Conservatism and Change in Roman Religion', *PBSR*, 44 (1976), 1–12.

Novak, D. M., 'Constantine and the Senate: An Early Phase of the Christianisation of the Roman Aristocracy', *Ancient Society*, 10 (1979), 271–310.

—— 'Anicianae domus culmen, nobilitatis culmen', *Klio*, 62 (1980), 473–93.

O'Donnell, J. J., 'The Demise of Paganism', *Traditio*, 35 (1979), 43–88.

Pack, R., 'The Roman Digressions of Ammianus Marcellinus', *TAPA*, 84 (1953), 181–9.

Painter, K., 'Late Roman Silver-plate: A Reply to Alan Cameron', *JRA*, 6 (1993), 109–15.

Palanque, J. R., 'L'Empereur Gratian et le grand pontificat païenne', *Byzantion*, 8 (1933), 41–7.

Palladio, S., 'Le terme eleniane a Roma', *MEFRA*, 108 (1996), 855–74.

Palmer, A. M., *Prudentius on the Martyrs* (Oxford: Clarendon Press, 1989).

Paschoud, F., *Zosime: Histoire nouvelle*, 3 vols., (Paris: Belles Lettres, 1971–89).

—— 'Zosime 2, 29 et la version païenne de la conversion de Constantin', in F. Paschoud, *Cinq études sur Zosime* (Paris: Belles lettres, 1975), 24–62.

Passerini, A., *Le coorti pretorie* (Rome: Signorelli, 1939).

Paterna, C., 'Il circo Variano a Roma', *MEFRA*, 108 (1996), 817–53.

Pavis d'Esurac, H., 'Siècle et Jeux Séculaires', *Ktema*, 18 (1993), 79–89.

Pavolini, C., *et al.*, 'La topografia antica della sommità del Celio', *Röm. Mitt.*, 100 (1993), 443–505.

Peirce, P., 'The Arch of Constantine: Propaganda and Ideology in Late Roman Art', *Art History*, 12 (1989), 387–418.

Pergola, P., 'Le catacombe romane: Miti e realtà (a proposito del cimitero di Domitilla)', in A. Giardina, (ed.), *Società romana e impero tardoantico 2. Roma: Politica, economia, paesaggio urbano* (Rome: Laterza, 1986), 333–50.

Peri, V., 'Gli inconsistenti archivi pontefici di S. Lorenzo in Damaso', *APARA*, Rendiconti, 41 (1968), 192–204.

Petit, P., 'Sur la Date du "Pro Templis"', *Byzantion*, 21 (1951), 285–310.

Pezzella, S., 'Massenzio e la politica religiosa di costantino', *Studi e materiali di storia delle religioni*, 38 (1967), 434–50.

Piétri, Ch., 'Concordia Apostolorum et Renovatio Urbis', *MEFRA*, 73 (1961), 275–322.

—— *Roma Christiana: Recherches sur l'église de Rome, son organisation, sa politique, son idéologie de Miltiade à Sixte III (311–440)*, BEFAR, 224–5 (Rome: École française de Rome, 1976).

—— 'Appendice prosopographique à la *Roma Christiana*', *MEFRA*, 89 (1977), 371–415.

—— 'Recherches sur les *domus ecclesiae*', *Révue des Études Augustiniennes*, 24 (1978a), 3–21.

—— 'Evergétisme et richesses ecclésiastiques dans l'Italie du IVe à la fin du Ve siècle: L'Example romain', *Ktema*, 3 (1978b), 317–37.

—— 'Les Origines du culte des martyrs (d'après un ouvrage recent)', *RAC*, Serie 3, 4 (1984), 293–315.

—— 'Damasus Évêque de Rome', in *Saecularia Damasiana*, Studi di Antichità Cristiana, 39 (Vatican City: Pontificio Istituto di archeologia cristiana, 1986), 31–58.

—— 'La Politique de Constance II: Un première "Césaropapisme" ou l'*imitatio Constantini?*', in *L'Église et L'empire au IVe siècle*, Entretiens sur l'Antiquité classique, 34 (Geneva: Fondation Hardt, 1987), 113–78.

—— 'La Roma cristiana', in A. Schiavone (ed.), *Storia di Roma 3*: L'Età tardoantica 1: Crisi e trasformazione* (Turin: Einaudi, 1993), 697–721.

Piganiol, A., *L'Empereur Constantin* (Paris: Rieder, 1932).

—— *L'Empire chrétien*, 2nd edn., (Paris: Presses universitaires de France, 1972).

Pighi, G. B., *De ludis saecularibus populi Romani Quiritium* (Milan: Società editrice 'Vita e pensiero', 1941).

Pisani-Sartorio, G. and Calza, R., *La Villa di Massenzio sulla Via Appia. Il palazzo: le opere d'arte*, I monumenti Romani, 6 (Rome: Istituto di studi romani, 1976).

Platner, S. B. and Ashby, T., *Topographical Dictionary of Ancient Rome* (Oxford: Oxford University Press, 1929).

Quinn Schofield, W., 'Sol in the Circus Maximus', in *Hommages à Marcel Renard*, Collection Latomus, 102 (Brussels: Latomus, 1969), 639–49.

Polverini, L., 'Ludi', in *Diz. epigr. di antich. romane* 4.63 (1975), 2006–9.

Prandi, A., 'Il sepolcro di S. Pietro in Vaticano durante la costruzione della basilica', in *Atti del II Congresso Nazionale di archeologia cristiana 1969* (1971), 377–80.

Price, S. R. F., 'Between Man and God: Sacrifice in the Roman Imperial Cult', *JRS*, 70 (1980), 28–43.

—— *Rituals and Power* (Cambridge: Cambridge University Press, 1984).

—— and Cannadine, D. (eds.), *Rituals of Royalty* (Cambridge: Cambridge University Press, 1987).

Purcell, N., 'Tomb and Suburb', in *Römische Gräberstrassen*: Bayerische Akademie der Wissenschaften, Philosophisch-Historische Klasse Abhandlungen, 96 (1987), 25–41.

Ragona, A., 'I tre indubbi segni di riconoscimento dell'obelisco di Costanzo II nel mosaico del circo di Piazza Armerina', in S. Garraffo, (ed.), *La villa romana del casale di Piazza Armerina*, Atti della IV riunione scientifica della scuola di perfezionamento in archeologia classica dell'Università di Catania (Catania: Istituto di archeologia, 1988), 125–30.

Rampolla, Cardinal M., *Santa Melania Giuniore* (Rome: 1905).

Ramsay, H. G., 'A Third-Century Building Programme', *AC*, 4 (1935), 419–47.

Rasch, J. J., *Das Maxentius-Mausoleum an der Via Appia in Rom* (Mainz: Zabern, 1984).

—— *Das Mausoleum bei Tor de'Schiavi in Rom* (Mainz: Zabern, 1993).

Reekmans, L., 'L'Implantation monumentale chrétienne dans la zone suburbaine de Rome du IV au IX siècle', *RAC*, 44 (1968), 173–207.

—— 'Le Développement topographique de la région du Vatican à la fin de l'antiquité et au début du moyen âge (300–850)', in *Mélanges d'archéologie et d'histoire de l'art offerts au Professeur Jacques Lavalleye* (Louvain: University of Louvain, 1970).

—— 'L'Implantation monumentale chrétienne dans le paysage urbain de Rome de 300 à 850', in *Actes du IXe Congrès internationale d'archéologie chrétienne*, Collection de l'École française de Rome, 123/Studi di Antichità cristiana, 41 (Rome: École française de Rome, 1989), 861–915.

Richardson, L., 'The Date and Programme of the Arch of Constantine', *Archeologia Classica*, 27 (1975), 72–8.

Richmond, I. A., *The City Wall of Imperial Rome* (Oxford: Clarendon Press, 1930).

Rike, R. L., *Apex Omnium: Religion in the Res Gestae of Ammianus* (Berkeley: University of California Press, 1987).

Robert, L., 'Deux concours grecs à Rome', *CRAI* (1970), 18–27.

Robinson, D. N., 'An Analysis of the Pagan Revival of the Late Fourth Century, With Especial Reference to Symmachus', *TAPA*, 46 (1915), 87–101.

Rodgers, B. S., 'Divine Insinuation in the *Panegyrici Latini*', *Historia*, 35 (1986), 69–104.

—— 'The Metamorphosis of Constantine', *CQ*, 39 (1989), 233–46.

Roncaioli Lamberti, C., 'L'appellativo *sacrosanctus* su un nuovo miliario massenziano della Valeria', *Epigraphica*, 52 (1990), 77–84.

Ross, R. R., 'Superstitio', *Classical Journal*, 64 (1969), 354–8.

Rousseau, P., *Ascetics, Authority, and the Church in the Age of Jerome and Cassian* (Oxford: Oxford University Press, 1978).

Rousselle, A., *Porneia: On Desire and the Body in Antiquity* (Oxford: Blackwell, 1988).

Royo, M., 'Topographie ancienne et fouilles sur la Vigna Barberini (XIXe siècle–début XXe siècle)', *MEFRA*, 98 (1986), 707–66.

Ruysschaert, J., 'Essai d'interprétation synthétique de l'Arc de Constantin', *APARA*, Rendiconti, 35 (1962–3), 79–105.

—— 'L'Inscription absidale primitive de S.-Pierre: Texte et contexte', *APARA*, Rendiconti, 40 (1967–8), 171–90.

—— 'Pierre et Paul à Rome: Textes et contextes d'une inscription damasienne', *APARA*, Rendiconti, 42 (1969), 201–18.

Salzman, M. R., 'New Evidence for the Dating of the Calendar at Santa Maria Maggiore in Rome', *TAPA*, 111 (1981), 215–27.

—— '*Superstitio* in the *Codex Theodosianus* and the Persecution of Pagans', *Vigiliae Christianae*, 41 (1987), 172–88.

—— 'Reflections on Symmachus' Idea of Tradition', *Historia*, 38 (1989a), 348–64.

—— 'Aristocratic Women: Conductors of Christianity in the Fourth Century', *Helios*, 16 (1989), 207–20.

—— *On Roman Time: The Codex-Calendar of 354* (Berkeley: University of California Press, 1990).

—— 'How the West was Won: The Christianization of the Roman Aristocracy in the Years after Constantine', in C. Deroux, (ed.), *Studies in Latin Literature and Roman History*, Coll. Latomus, 217 (1992), 451–79.

—— 'The Evidence for the Conversion of the Roman Empire to Christianity in Book 16 of the Theodosian Code', *Historia*, 42 (1993), 362–78.

Santa Maria Scrinari, V., 'Per la storia e la topografia del Laterano', *BdA*, 50 (1965), 38–44.

—— 'Brevi note sugli scavi sotto la chiesa di S. Vito', *Archeologia Laziale*, 2 (1979), 58–62.

—— *Il Laterano imperiale 1: Dalle "aedes Laterani" alla "domus Faustae"*,

Monumenti di antichità cristiana, 11 (Vatican City: Pontificio Istituto di archeologia cristiana, 1991).

Santangeli Valenziani, R., '*ΝΕΩΣ ΥΠΕΡΜΕΓΕΘΗΣ*: Osservazioni sul tempio di piazza del Quirinale', *BC*, 94 (1991–2), 7–16.

Santangelo, M., 'Il Quirinale nell'antichità classica', *APARA*, Serie 3, Memorie 5 (1941), 203–10.

Saxer, V., 'Damase et le calendrier des fêtes de martyrs de l'église romaine', in *Saecularia Damasiana*, Studi di antichità cristiana, 39 (Vatican City: Pontificio istituto di archeologia cristiana, 1986), 61–88.

Scalia, G., 'Gli "archiva" di papa Damaso e le biblioteche di papa Ilaro', *Studi Medievali* 18 (1977), 40–50.

Scheid, J., *Romulus et ses frères: Le Collège des frères arvales, modèle du culte public dans la Rome des empereurs* (Rome: École française de Rome, 1990).

Schumacher, W. N., 'Die konstantinischen Exedra-Basiliken', in J. G. Deckers, H. R. Seeliger, and G. Mietke (eds.), *Die Katakombe "Santi Marcellino e Pietro": Repertorium der Malereien* (Vatican City: Pontificio istituto di archeologia cristiana, 1987), 132–86.

Schwarte, K.-H., 'Die Christengesetze Valerians', in W. Eck (ed.), *Religion und Gesellschaft in der römischen Kaiserzeit* (Cologne: Böhlau, 1989), 103–63.

Scullard, H. H., *Festivals and Ceremonies of the Roman Republic* (London: Thames and Hudson, 1981).

Seeck, O., 'Constans', *PW*, 4 (1900), 948–52.

—— *Regesten der Kaiser und Päpste für die Jahre 311 bis 476 n. Chr.* (Stuttgart: Metzler, 1919).

Seston, W., 'Hypothèse sur la date de la basilique constantinienne de Saint Pierre de Rome', *Cahiers archéologiques*, 2 (1947), 153–9.

Settis, S., 'Per l'interpretazione di Piazza Armerina', *MEFRA*, 87 (1975), 873–994.

Shelton, K. J., *The Esquiline Treasure* (London: British Museum Publications, 1981).

—— 'Roman Aristocrats, Christian Commissions: The Carrand Diptych', *JbAC*, 27–8 (1984–5), 166–80.

—— 'The Esquiline Treasure', *AJA*, 89 (1985), 145–55.

Sheridan, J. J., 'The Altar of Victory: Paganism's Last Battle', *L'Antiquité Classique*, 35 (1966), 186–206.

Silvestrini, M., 'Il potere imperiale da Severo Alessandro ad Aureliano', in A. Schiavone, (ed.), *Storia di Roma 3*: L'Età tardoantica 1: Crisi e trasformazione* (Turin: Einaudi, 1993), 155–91.

Sirks, A. J. B., 'From the Theodosian to the Justinian Code', *Atti dell'Accademia romanistica costantiniana (VI Convegno internazionale)* (1986), 265–302.

—— 'The Sources of the Code' in J. Harries and I. Wood (eds.), *The Theodosian Code* (London: Duckworth, 1993), 45–67.

Sivan, H., 'Anician Women, the Cento of Proba, and Aristocratic Conversion in the Fourth Century', *VC*, 47 (1993), 140–57.

Smith, W. and Wace, H. (eds.), *Dictionary of Christian Biography* (London: Murray, 1911).

Snyder, G. F., *Ante Pacem: Archeological Evidence of Church Life Before Constantine* (Macon, Ga.: Mercer, 1985).

Speidel, M. P., 'Maxentius and His Equites Singulares in the Battle of the Mulvian Bridge', *Classical Antiquity*, 5 (1986), 253–62.

——'Les prétoriens de Maxence: Les cohortes palatines romaines', *MEFRA*, 100 (1988), 183–6.

Steinby, M., 'L'industria laterizia di Roma nel tardo impero', in A. Giardina, (ed.), *Società romana e impero tardoantico 2. Roma: Politica, economia, paesaggio urbano* (Rome: Laterza, 1986), 99–164.

——(ed.), *Lexicon Topographicum Urbis Romae*, 5 vols. (Rome: Quasar, 1993–).

Stern, H., *Le calendrier de 354: étude sur son texte et ses illustrations* (Paris: Geuthner, 1953).

——'Les Mosaïques de l'église Ste-Constance', *DOP*, 12 (1958), 157–218.

Straub, J., 'Konstantins Verzicht auf den Gang zum Kapitol', *Historia*, 4 (1955), 297–313.

Stuart-Jones, H., *Catalogue of the Palazzo dei Conservatori* (1912).

Syme, R., *Emperors and Biography* (Oxford: Clarendon Press, 1971).

——'The Ancestry of Constantine', *Bonner-Historia-Augusta-Colloquium 1971*, Antiquitas Reihe 4. Beiträge zur Historia-Augusta-Forschung, 11 (1974), 237–53.

Testini, P., *Le catacombe e gli antichi cimiteri cristiani in Roma* (Bologna: Cappelli, 1966).

——, Cantino Wataghin, G., and Pani Ermini, L., 'La cattedrale in Italia', in *Actes du XIe Congrès International d'Archéologie Chrétienne 1986 (Collection de l'École française de Rome 123/Studi di Antichità cristiana XLI)* (Vatican City: Pontificio Istituto di archeologia cristiana, 1989), 5–17.

Tolotti, F., 'Le basiliche cimiteriali con deambulatorio del suburbio romano: Questione ancora aperta', *RM*, 89 (1982), 153–211.

——'Mausolei paleocristiani con vestibolo biapsidato', in *Quaeritur inventus colitur: Miscellanea in onore di Padre U. M. Fasola* (Vatican City: Pontificio Istituto di archeologia cristiana, 1989), 797–812.

Tomlin, R. S. O., *Valentinian the First*, D. Phil. thesis, (Oxford, 1973).

Toynbee, J. M. C., *Roman Medallions* (New York: American Numismatic Society, 1944).

——and Ward-Perkins, J. B., *The Shrine of Saint Peter* (London: Longmans, 1956).

Turcan, R., 'Le délit des monétaires rebellés contre Aurélien', *Latomus*, 28 (1969), 948–59.

——'Le culte impérial au III siècle', *ANRW*, 2.16.2 (1978), 996–1084.

——*Firmicus Maternus: L'Erreur des religions païennes* (Paris: Belles Lettres, 1982).

——*Héliogabale et le sacre du Soleil* (Paris: Michel, 1985).

——'Héliogabale précurseur de Constantin?', *Bull. De l'Ass. G. Budé*, 47 (1988), 38–52.

——'Les tondi d'Hadrien sur l'arc de Constantin', *CRAI* (1991), 53–80.

——*The Cults of the Roman Empire* (Oxford: Blackwell, 1996).

Turpin, W., 'The Purpose of the Roman Law Codes', *ZRG*, 104 (1987), 620–30.

Valentini, R. and Zucchetti, G., *Codice topografico della città di Roma*, 4 vols. (Rome: Tipografia del senato, 1940–53).

Vera, D., *Commento storico alle Relationes di Quinto Aurelio Simmaco* (Pisa: Giardini, 1981).

—— 'Simmaco e le sue proprietà: Struttura e funzionamento di un patrimonio aristocratico del quarto secolo d.C.', in F. Paschoud (ed.), *Colloque genevois sur Symmaque* (Paris: Belles Lettres, 1986), 231–75.

Vermaseren, M. J., *Corpus Cultus Cybelae Attidisque*, 7 vols. (Leiden: Brill, 1977–89).

Verrando, G. N., 'Liberio-Felice: Osservazioni e rettifiche di carattere storico-agiografico', *Rivista di storia della chiesa in Italia*, 35 (1981), 97–104.

—— 'La *passio Callisti* e il santuario della via Aurelia', *MEFRA*, 96 (1984), 1039–83.

—— 'L'attività edilizia di papa Giulio I e la basilica al III miglio della via Aurelia ad Callistum', *MEFRA*, 97 (1985), 1021–61.

—— 'Il santuario di S. Felice sulla via Portuense', *MEFRA*, 100 (1988), 331–66.

Viden, G., *The Roman Chancery Tradition: Studies in the Language of the Codex Theodosianus and Cassiodorus' Variae*, Studia Graeca et Latina Gothoburgiensia, 46 (Gothenburg: Acta Universitatis Gothoburgensis, 1984).

Vielliard, R., *Recherches sur les origines de la Rome chrétienne*, 2nd edn. (Rome: Storia e letteratura, 1959).

Ville, G., 'Les jeux de gladiateurs dans l'empire chrétien', *Mélanges d'archéologie et d'histoire*, 72 (1960), 273–325.

Vilucchi, S., 'Terme di Costantino', in *Roma archeologia nel centro I: L'area archeologica centrale*, Lavori e studi di archeologia, 6 (Rome: De Luca, 1985), 357–9.

Vittinghoff, F., 'Staat, Kirche und Dynastie beim Tode Konstantins', in *L'Église et l'empire au IVe Siècle*, Entretiens sur l'Antiquité classique, 34 (Geneva: Fondation Hardt, 1987), 1–34.

von Haehling, R., *Die Religionszugehörigkeit der hohen Amtsträger des römischen Reiches seit Constantins I. Alleinherrschaft bis zum Ende der Theodianischen Dynastie* (Bonn: Habelt, 1978).

von Schoenebeck, H., *Beiträge zur Religionspolitik des Maxentius und Konstantin*, Klio Beiheft, 43, 2nd edn., (Aalen: Scientia Verlag, 1962).

Voss, W. E., *Recht und Rhetorik in den Kaisergesetzen der Spätantike*, Forschungen zur Byzantinischen Rechtsgeschichte, 9 (Frankfurt: Löwenklau, 1982).

Walser, G. (ed.), *Die Einsiedler Inschriftensammlung und der Pilgerführer durch Rom (Codex Einsidlensis 326)*, Historia Einzelschriften, 53, (Stuttgart: Steiner Verlag Wiesbaden, 1987).

Walsh, P. G., *Letters of Saint Paulinus of Nola*, Ancient Christian Writers, 35 (Westminster, Md.: Newman Press, 1967).

Ward-Perkins, B., *From Classical Antiquity to the Middle Ages: Urban Public Building in Northern and Central Italy* AD 300–850 (Oxford: Oxford University Press, 1984).

Ward-Perkins, J. B., 'Constantine and the Origins of the Christian Basilica', *PBSR*, 22 (1954), 69–90.

—— 'Memoria, Martyr's Tomb and Martyr's Church', *JTS*, 17 (1966), 20–38.

Waszink, J. H., 'Pompa Diaboli', *VC*, 1 (1947), 13–41.

Weismann, W., *Kirche und Schauspiele* (Würzburg: Augustinus-Verlag, 1972).

Whitehead, P. B., 'The Church of S. Anastasia in Rome', *AJA*, 2nd series, 31 (1927*a*), 405–20.

—— 'The Church of SS. Cosma e Damiano in Rome', *AJA*, 31 (1927*b*), 1–18.

Whittaker, C. R., *Herodian*, 2 vols. (Cambridge, Mass.: Heinemann, 1969).

Wiesen, D. S., *Saint Jerome as a Satirist* (Ithaca, NY: Cornell University Press, 1964).

Wigg, D. G., 'Contorniates and the Pagan Revival', *JRA*, 8 (1995), 525–9.

Wilken, R. L., *The Christians as the Romans Saw Them* (New Haven: Yale University Press, 1984).

Williams, S., *Diocletian and the Roman Recovery* (London: Batsford, 1985).

Wilson, R. J. A., *Piazza Armerina* (London: Granada, 1983).

—— 'Piazza Armerina and the Senatorial Aristocracy in Late Roman Sicily', in S. Garraffo, (ed.), *La villa romana del casale di Piazza Armerina*, Atti della IV riunione scientifica della scuola di perfezionamento in archeologia classica dell'Università di Catania (Catania: Istituto di archeologia, 1988), 170–82.

Wiseman, T. P., 'The Circus Flaminius', *PBSR*, 42 (1974), 3–26.

Wirszubski, Ch., *Libertas as a Political Idea at Rome during the Late Republic and Early Principate* (Cambridge: Cambridge University Press, 1950).

Wissowa, G., *Religion und Kultus der Römer*, 2nd edn. (Munich: Beck, 1912).

Wormald, P., '*Lex scripta* and *verbum regis*: Legislation and Germanic Kingship from Euric to Cnut', in P. H. Sawyer and I. N. Wood, (eds.), *Early Medieval Kingship* (Leeds, 1977), 105–38.

Wrede, H., 'Der *genius populi Romani* und das Fünfsäulendenkmal der Tetrarchen', *Bonner Jahrbuch*, 181 (1981), 111–42.

Wuillemier, P., 'Cirque et astrologie', *MEFR*, 44 (1927), 184–209.

Wypustek, A., 'Magic, Montanism, Perpetua and the Severan Persecution', *VC*, 51 (1997), 276–97.

Yarbrough, A., 'Christianisation in the Fourth Century: The Example of Roman Women', *Church History*, 45 (1976), 149–64.

Zanker, P., *The Power of Images in the Age of Augustus* (Ann Arbor: University of Michigan, 1988).

Index